LORD BYRON

The Complete
Poetical Works

Stanzas for Music

There be none of Beauty's daughters
    With a magic like thee—
And like Music on the waters
    Is thy sweet voice to me—
When as if its sound were causing
The charmed Ocean's pausing—
The waves lie still & gleaming
And the lulled Winds seem dreaming—
And the midnight Moon is weaving
    Her bright chain on the Deep
Whose breast is gently heaving
    As an infant's asleep—

So the Spirit bows before thee
To listen and adore thee
With a full but soft emotion
Like the swell of Summer's Ocean.

No. 2
March 20. 1816

Byron's holograph of 'Stanzas for Music', poem no. 284

(Reproduced with permission, from the collection of John Murray Ltd.)

LORD BYRON

The Complete
Poetical Works

EDITED BY
JEROME J. McGANN

VOLUME III

OXFORD
AT THE CLARENDON PRESS
1981

Oxford University Press, Walton Street, Oxford OX2 6DP

OXFORD LONDON GLASGOW
NEW YORK TORONTO MELBOURNE WELLINGTON
KUALA LUMPUR SINGAPORE HONG KONG TOKYO
DELHI BOMBAY CALCUTTA MADRAS KARACHI
NAIROBI DAR ES SALAAM CAPE TOWN

*Published in the United States by
Oxford University Press, New York*

© *Oxford University Press 1981*

British Library Cataloguing in Publication Data

Byron, George Gordon, *Baron Byron*
  Lord Byron, the complete poetical works—(Oxford
  English texts)
  Vol. 3
  I. McGann, Jerome John—II. Series
  821'.7   PR4350   78-41111
  ISBN 0-19-812755-3
  ISBN 0-19-812765-0 Pbk

*Printed in Great Britain
at the University Press, Oxford
by Eric Buckley
Printer to the University*

PREFACE TO VOLUME III

THE poems in this volume, which spans Byron's 'Years of Fame', take the reader to the end of Byron's life in England (i.e. to April 1816). Thirty-two wholly new or previously uncollected pieces are printed, and their editorial problems are similar to those which had to be dealt with in Volume I. In addition, many of the shorter poems in this volume have important textual revisions, and so do some of the major works (for example the *Ode to Napoleon Buonaparte*).

The new poems here define more clearly the political character of Byron's poetical interests. The series of translations from Martial, here first printed, are not merely technical exercises; they constitute a special sort of satiric attack upon the life of the Regency, and they help to illuminate the political dimensions of all Byron's poetry (in this period especially), even works which may not seem, to a superficial view, concerned with social or political issues.

Once again, attention must be directed to the large corpus of primary material which the editor has had access to. This material, as in the previous two volumes, has allowed the editor to define, in much greater and more precise detail, the composition and publication histories of the poems, as well as the contexts which surround and penetrate them. The student will find, in the commentaries and notes to *The Giaour*, *The Bride of Abydos*, *The Siege of Corinth*, and *Parisina*, for example, important additions to what has been previously known to scholars about these works.

The editor wishes to express, once again, his thanks and appreciation to all those who have contributed so much to this editorial venture. I owe a special debt of gratitude to Ellen Mankoff, who helped me with the onerous task of proof-reading Volumes I–III.

CONTENTS

175   **[La Revanche]**

I.

There is no more for me to hope,
　　There is no more for thee to fear;
And, if I give my Sorrow scope,
　　That Sorrow thou shalt never hear.
Why did I hold thy love so dear?   5
Why shed for such a heart one tear?
Let deep and dreary silence be
My only memory of thee!

2.

When all are fled who flatter now,
　　Save thoughts which will not flatter then;   10
And thou recall'st the broken vow
　　To him who must not love again—
Each hour of now forgotten years
Thou, then, shalt number with thy tears;
And every drop of grief shall be   15
A vain remembrancer of me!

　　　　　　　　　　　　　　　　　　　[1812]

176   **On the Quotation**

'And my true faith can alter never
Though thou art gone perhaps forever'

[I.]

And thy true faith can alter never?—
Indeed it lasted for a—week!
I knew the length of Love's forever,
And just expected such a freak.

175. Copy text: *C*, collated with *MS. L*.

　4 Sorrow . . . never] ⟨grief . . . not⟩ *L*　　　7 ⟨Why rend thy soul on such a / that sweet face⟩ *L*　　10 ⟨An hour that / What comes / Save Thoughts remaining⟩ *L*　　11 the] thy *L*　　12 ⟨And more than I shall name again⟩ ⟨The broken⟩ *L*　　must not] ⟨neer can⟩ *L*　　13 hour] ⟨day⟩ *L*　　14 shalt] shall *L*　　15 grief shall] ⟨anguish⟩ *L*

176. Copy text: *C*, collated with *MS. M*, *MS. L*.

title　On ⟨receiving⟩ a quotation in a letter—And my true faith etc. *M*
　3 knew] know *C*

In peace we met, in peace we parted,   5
  In peace we vowed to meet again,
And though I find thee fickle-hearted
  No pang of mine shall make thee vain.

2.

One gone—'twas time to seek a second;
  In sooth 'twere hard to blame thy haste.   10
And whatsoe'er thy love be reckoned,
  At least thou hast improved in taste:
Though one was young, the next was younger,
  His love was new, mine too well known—
And what might make the charm still stronger,   15
  The youth was present, I was flown.

3.

Seven days and nights of single sorrow!
  Too much for human constancy!
A fortnight past, why then to-morrow,
  His turn is come to follow me: 20
And if each week you change a lover,
  And so have acted heretofore,
Before a year or two is over
  We'll form a very pretty *corps*.

4.

Adieu, fair thing! without upbraiding   25
  I fain would take a decent leave;
Thy beauty still survives unfading,
  And undeceived may long deceive.
With him unto thy bosom dearer
  Enjoy the moments as they flee;   30
I only wish his love sincerer
  Than thy young heart has been to *me*.

1812

9 a second] ⟨another⟩ *M*   10 'twere hard to] ⟨I cannot⟩ *M*   13 one] I *M*
the next] ⟨thy choice⟩ *M*   17 Seven days] ⟨A week⟩ *M*   20 ⟨Thou must have
changed⟩ *M*   follow] quit like *M*   25 upbraiding] ⟨reproaching⟩ *M*   27 ⟨I have
not known / seen thy beauty fading⟩ *M*   29 him unto] ⟨other to⟩ *M*
29–32   ⟨So make the most out of thy leisure
                   Whateer thy future lot may be
                 I only wish you all the pleasure
                   With others I have found in thee.⟩ *M*

177   [Again Deceived! Again Betrayed!]

I pull in resolution and begin
To doubt the equivocation of the fiend
That lies like truth.   Macbeth

[1.]

Again deceived! again betrayed!
In manhood as in youth,
The dupe of every smiling maid
That ever 'lied like truth'.—

2.

Well, dearly was the lesson bought   5
The present and the past,
What Love some twenty times has taught
We needs must learn at last.

3.

In turn deceiving or deceived
The wayward Passion roves,   10
Beguiled by her we most believed,
Or leaving her who loves.

4.

Oh thou! for whom my heart must bleed,
From whom this anguish springs,
Thy Love was genuine Love indeed,   15
And showed it in his wings.

5.

His pinions, had he deigned to stay,
I only meant to borrow.
I wish thy love remained today
To fly with mine tomorrow.   20

1812

177. Copy text: *MS. Y*, collated with *MS. L* and *Great Byron Adventure*
epigraph   *not in MS. L or Great Byron Adventure*
   1 deceived] beguiled *L, Great Byron Adventure*   3 dupe] slave *L, Great Byron*
Adventure
17–20   And wouldst thou not prolong thy stay
               Fair source of all my Sorrow,
               Oh had thy Love outlived today—
               My own had fled tomorrow. *L, Great Byron Adventure*

178   Stanzas

'Heu quanto minus est cum reliquis versari quam tui meminisse!'

1.

And thou art dead, as young and fair
 As aught of mortal birth;
And form so soft, and charms so rare,
 Too soon return'd to Earth!
Though Earth receiv'd them in her bed,   5
 And o'er the spot the crowd may tread
  In carelessness or mirth,
There is an eye which could not brook
A moment on that grave to look.

2.

I will not ask where thou liest low,   10
 Nor gaze upon the spot;
There flowers or weeds at will may grow,
 So I behold them not:
It is enough for me to prove
That what I lov'd and long must love   15
  Like common earth can rot;
To me there needs no stone to tell
'Tis Nothing that I lov'd so well.

3.

Yet did I love thee to the last
 As fervently as thou,
Who did'st not change through all the past,   20
 And can'st not alter now.

---

178. Copy text: *CHP(7)*, collated with *CHP(2)–CHP(6)* and *CHP(8)–CHP(10)*, the Huntington MS. and proof, the Clark printing
title   *not in the MS.; the title is the poem's first line in C, More*
epigraph   *not in the MS.*

 1 as] ⟨so / more⟩ *MS.*   4 ⟨Were never meant for Earth⟩ *MS.*   5 Though] ⟨Yet⟩ *MS.*   6 ⟨Unhonoured with the vulgar dead⟩ *MS.*   8 an eye] ⟨a heart⟩ *MS.* 10 liest low] ⟨art laid⟩ *MS.*   11 gaze . . . spot] ⟨look . . . scene⟩ *MS.*   12 ⟨It could but say that⟩ *MS.*   13 behold them] ⟨shall know it⟩ *MS.*   14 prove] ⟨feel / know / hear⟩ *MS.*   16 earth] ⟨dust⟩   can] must *MS.*   17–18 ⟨I would not wish to see or touch | The Nothing that I loved so much⟩ *MS.*   17 To . . . no] ⟨There hardly needs a⟩ *MS.*   20 As fervently] ⟨As well and warm⟩ *MS.*

The love where Death has set his seal,
Nor age can chill, nor rival steal,
   Nor falsehood disavow: 25
And, what were worse, thou can'st not see
Or wrong, or change, or fault in me.

4.

The better days of life were ours;
   The worst can be but mine:
The sun that cheers, the storm that lowers,   30
   Shall never more be thine.
The silence of that dreamless sleep
I envy now too much to weep;
   Nor need I to repine
That all those charms have pass'd away: 35
I might have watch'd through long decay.

5.

The flower in ripen'd bloom unmatch'd
   Must fall the earliest prey,
Though by no hand untimely snatch'd,
   The leaves must drop away: 40
And yet it were a greater grief
To watch it withering, leaf by leaf,
   Than see it pluck'd to-day;
Since earthly eye but ill can bear
To trace the change to foul from fair.   45

6.

I know not if I could have borne
   To see thy beauties fade;
The night that follow'd such a morn
   Had worn a deeper shade:

23–4 *transposed in MS., then cancelled*   25 falsehood] ⟨frailty⟩ MS.   26–7 ⟨Nor canst those, fair and faultless, see | Nor wrong or change or fault in thee⟩ MS.   30 cheers] shines MS.   32 ⟨If aught is blessed then thou art blessed⟩ / ⟨The silence of that sweetest sleep⟩ / ⟨The sweetness of that silent sleep⟩ MS.   37 ⟨The rose that some rude hand hath snatched / by some rude fingers snatched⟩ / ⟨The flower in loveliness unmatched⟩ / The flower in beauty's bloom unmatched MS.   38 ⟨Is earliest doomed to fall⟩ / Is still the earliest prey MS.   39 Though by no] ⟨By some rude⟩ MS.   43 ⟨Less lovely day by day⟩ MS.   44 eye] ⟨love⟩ MS.   45 ⟨Those cankered at the Summer's close⟩ MS.

Thy day without a cloud hath past,   50
And thou wert lovely to the last;
  Extinguish'd, not decay'd;
As stars that shoot along the sky
Shine brightest as they fall from high.

7.

As once I wept, if I could weep,   55
  My tears might well be shed,
To think I was not near to keep
  One vigil o'er thy bed;
To gaze, how fondly! on thy face,
To fold thee in a faint embrace,   60
  Uphold thy drooping head;
And show that love, however vain,
Nor thou nor I can feel again.

8.

Yet how much less it were to gain,
  Though thou hast left me free,   65
The loveliest things that still remain,
  Than thus remember thee!
The all of thine that cannot die
Through dark and dread Eternity
  Returns again to me,   70
And more thy buried love endears
Than aught, except its living years.

[1812]

179   From the Turkish

I.

The chain I gave was fair to view,
  The lute I added sweet in sound,
The heart that offered both was true,
  And ill deserved the fate it found.

58 bed;] bed, *all printings to CHP*(7), *corrected in Huntington proof*   59 gaze,] gaze—
all printings to CHP(7), *corrected in Huntington proof*

179. Copy text: *Corsair*(7), collated with MS., proofs, all editions of *Corsair* in which the
poem appeared
title   From a Turkish Song *MS.*, *Proof M*; The Chain I Gave. From the Turkish. *1832, C*

2.

These gifts were charmed by secret spell   5
   Thy truth in absence to divine;
And they have done their duty well,
   Alas! they could not teach thee thine.

3.

That chain was firm in every link,
   But not to bear a stranger's touch;   10
That lute was sweet—till thou could'st think
   In other hands its notes were such.

4.

Let him, who from thy neck unbound
   The chain which shivered in his grasp,
Who saw that lute refuse to sound,   15
   Restring the chords, renew the clasp.

5.

When thou wert changed, they altered too;
   The chain is broke, the music mute:
'Tis past—to them and thee adieu—
   False heart, frail chain, and silent lute.   20

[1812?]

180   To Time

Time!—on whose arbitrary wing
   The varying hours must flag or fly,
Whose tardy winter, fleeting spring,
   But drag or drive us on to die—
Hail thou!—who on my birth bestow'd   5
   Those boons—to all that know thee—known;
Yet better I sustain thy load,
   For now I bear the weight alone.

180. Copy text: *CHP*(7), collated with MS., proof, *CHP*(8)–*CHP*(10

I would not one fond heart should share
   The bitter moments thou hast given;   10
And pardon thee, since thou could'st spare
   All that I lov'd, to peace or heav'n;
To them be joy or rest—on me
   Thy future ills shall press in vain;
I nothing owe but years to thee,   15
   A debt already paid in pain.
Yet even that pain was some relief,
   It felt—but still forgot thy pow'r;
The active agony of grief
   Retards, but never counts the hour.   20
In joy I've sigh'd to think thy flight
   Would soon subside from swift to slow—
Thy cloud could overcast the light,
   But could not add a night to woe—
For then, however drear and dark,   25
   My soul was suited to thy sky;
One star alone shot forth a spark
   To prove thee—not Eternity.
That beam hath sunk—and now thou art
   A blank—a thing to count and curse   30
Through each dull tedious trifling part,
   Which all regret—yet all rehearse.
One scene even thou canst not deform—
   The limit of thy sloth or speed—
When future wanderers bear the storm   35
   Which we shall sleep too sound to heed;
And I can smile to think how weak
   Thine efforts shortly shall be shown,
When all the vengeance thou canst wreak
   Must fall upon—a nameless stone!   40

[1812–13]

18 ⟨And⟩ felt but ⟨not confessed⟩ thy power *MS*.   20 never counts] ⟨still forgets⟩
MS.   35 future . . . bear] ⟨other . . . leave⟩ *MS*.   *MS*.   37 weak] ⟨vain⟩ *MS*.

181   An Ode to the Framers of the Frame Bill

Oh well done Lord E[ldo]n! and better Lord R[yde]r!
Britannia must prosper with councils like yours;
HAWKESBURY, HARROWBY, help you to guide her,
Whose remedy only must *kill* ere it cures:
Those villains, the Weavers, are all grown refractory,   5
Asking some succour for Charity's sake—
So hang them in clusters round each Manufactory,
That will at once put an end to *mistake.*

The rascals, perhaps, may betake them to robbing,
The dogs to be sure have got nothing to eat—   10
So if we can hang them for breaking a bobbin,
'Twill save all the Government's money and meat:
Men are more easily made than machinery—
Stockings fetch better prices than lives—
Gibbets on Sherwood will *heighten* the scenery,   15
Showing how Commerce, *how* Liberty thrives!

Justice is now in pursuit of the wretches,
Grenadiers, Volunteers, Bow-street Police,
Twenty-two Regiments, a score of Jack Ketches,
Three of the Quorum and two of the Peace;   20
Some Lords, to be sure, would have summoned the Judges,
To take their opinion, but that they ne'er shall,
For LIVERPOOL such a concession begrudges,
So now they're condemned by *no Judges* at all.

Some folks for certain have thought it was shocking,   25
When Famine appeals, and when Poverty groans,
That life should be valued at less than a stocking,
And breaking of frames lead to breaking of bones.
If it should prove so, I trust, by this token,
(And who will refuse to partake in the hope?)   30
That the frames of the fools may be first to be *broken,*
Who, when asked for a *remedy,* sent down a *rope.*

[1812]

181.   Copy text: *Morning Chronicle*, collated with *Pearson, BLJ*

182   Lines to a Lady Weeping

Weep, daughter of a royal line,
    A Sire's disgrace, a realm's decay;
Ah, happy! if each tear of thine
    Could wash a father's fault away!

Weep—for thy tears are Virtue's tears—   5
    Auspicious to these suffering isles;
And be each drop in future years
    Repaid thee by thy people's smiles!

                                            [1812]

183   Stanzas

                              1.

If sometimes in the haunts of men,
    Thine image from my breast may fade,
The lonely hour presents again
    The semblance of thy gentle shade:
And now that sad and silent hour   5
    Thus much of thee can still restore,
And sorrow unobserv'd may pour
    The plaint she dare not speak before.

                              2.

Oh, pardon that in crowds awhile,
    I waste one thought I owe to thee,   10
And, self-condemned, appear to smile,
    Unfaithful to thy Memory!

182. Copy text: *Corsair*(7), collated with B's MS., Augusta's fair copy, Huntington proof, two Murray proofs, *Morning Chronicle*, *Corsair*(2), *Corsair*(4)–*Corsair*(6), *Corsair*(8)–*Corsair*(10)

title   Stanzas *B's MS.*; by Lord Byron *Augusta's copy*; Sympathetic Address to a Young Lady *Morning Chronicle*

    5 Virtue's] ⟨virtuous⟩ *Huntington proof*   8 thy] ⟨our⟩ *later correction in Augusta's fair copy*

183. Copy text: *CHP*(7), collated with *MS.*, proof, *CHP*(2)–*CHP*(6) and *CHP*(8)–*CHP*(10)

title   *untitled in MS.*; *title is the first line in C, More*

    2 from my breast] ⟨for a time⟩ *MS.*   3 presents] ⟨restores / gives back / resumes⟩ *MS.*   5 And] ⟨Tis⟩ *MS.*   8 she] ⟨she⟩ it *MS.*   10 ⟨I seem to lose?⟩ one thought of thee⟩ *MS.*   12 ⟨When all around is revelry⟩ *MS.*

Nor deem that memory less dear,
   That then I seem not to repine,
I would not fools should overhear   15
   One sigh that should be wholly *thine*.

3.

If not the Goblet pass unquaff'd,
   It is not drain'd to banish care,
The cup must hold a deadlier draught
   That brings a Lethe for despair;   20
And could Oblivion set my soul
   From all her troubled visions free,
I'd dash to earth the sweetest bowl
   That drown'd a single thought of thee.

4.

For wert thou vanish'd from my mind,   25
   Where could my vacant bosom turn?
And who would then remain behind
   To honour thine abandon'd Urn?
No, No—it is my sorrow's pride
   That last dear duty to fulfil;   30
Though all the world forget beside,
   'Tis meet that I remember still.

5.

For well I know, that such had been
   Thy gentle care for him who now
Unmourn'd shall quit this mortal scene,   35
   Where none regarded him, but thou:

13 ⟨So ? | To me thy memory is dear⟩ *MS.*   that] ⟨thy⟩ *MS.*   17 ⟨If not untouched the goblet pass⟩ *MS.*   18 drain'd to banish] ⟨quaffed to kill my⟩ *MS.*   19–20 ⟨A deadlier draught must fill the glass / cup | My Lethe must be found alas⟩ *MS.*   20 That brings a] ⟨There is no⟩ *MS.*   21–2 ⟨But / For⟩ could Oblivion ⟨give me back | My peace by⟩ *MS.*   21 set] ⟨to⟩ *MS.*   22 troubled visions] ⟨dreams of⟩ ⟨feverish / cherished⟩ visions *MS.*   23 ⟨I would not touch the sweetest cup⟩ *MS.*   24 drown'd] ⟨stole⟩ *MS.*   26 ⟨And if thou never hadst been true⟩ *MS.*   27 ⟨Few thoughts would then remain behind⟩ And ⟨then who would⟩ remain behind *MS.*   29 sorrow's] ⟨joy, my / soothing⟩ *MS.*   33–4 ⟨To ?, to wish⟩ For well I know ⟨that Forgetfulness | Of me and mine⟩ *MS.*   35 quit] ⟨sink⟩   mortal] earthly *MS.*   36 ⟨For who would weep for him⟩ but thou *MS.*

And, Oh! I feel in *that* was given,
   A blessing never meant for me;
Thou wert too like a dream of Heaven,
   For earthly Love to merit thee.   40

14 Mar. 1812

184   On a Cornelian Heart Which Was Broken

1.

Ill-fated heart! and can it be
   That thou shouldst thus be rent in twain!
Have years of care for thine and thee
   Alike been all employed in vain?

2.

Yet precious seems each shatter'd part,   5
   And every fragment dearer grown,
Since he who wears thee, feels thou art
   A fitter emblem of *his own*.

[1812]

185   [Epigram on Sir Humphry Davy]

Apreece with her Davy resolved an alliance,
A little for love and a good deal for Science,
And the *strength* of her *parts* has already been shewn,
For last night she found out the '*Philosopher's Stone*'.

1812

37–40
⟨Although thou couldst so soon⟩
⟨And couldst thou then so soon depart⟩
But thou and he who held that heart
Could never wish to covet more
Thou didst then resign my heart
⟨And dead departed as thou art⟩
For that is buried in thy grave *cancelled in MS.*

37 And . . . in] ⟨But thou and oh in⟩ *MS.*   38 ⟨Too much for one unworthy thee⟩
MS.   never meant] too too much *MS.*   39 ⟨Oh why wert thou like one of Heaven⟩
MS.   a dream] the things *MS.*

184. Copy text: *CHP(7)*, collated with proof, *CHP(2)–CHP(6)* and *CHP(8)–CHP(10)*

185. Copy text: *MS. W*

186 ## To Samuel Rogers, Esq.

Absent or present, still to thee,
   My friend, what magic spells belong!
As all can tell, who share, like me,
   In turn thy converse, and thy song.
But when the dreaded hour shall come,   5
   By Friendship ever deemed too nigh,
And 'MEMORY' o'er her Druid's tomb
   Shall weep that aught of thee can die,
How fondly will She then repay
   Thy homage offered at her shrine,   10
And blend, while Ages roll away,
   Her name immortally with *thine*!

                  19 Apr. 1812

187 ## [To Caroline Lamb]

Yet fain would I resist the spell
   That would my captive heart retain,
For tell me dearest, is this well?
   Ah Caro! do I need the chain?
Nor dare I struggle to be free,   5
   Since gifts returned but pain the giver,
And the soft band put on by thee,
   The slightest chain, will last for ever!

                  [1812]

188 ## Il Diavolo Inamorato

The Devil hath power to assume a pleasing shape.
                        Hamlet

I.

A Tale of early youth and olden time!
   Which seemeth now as it had never been;
Though what was pleasaunce then be now a crime,
   Yet such the jocund days that I have seen,

186. Copy text: *Poems1816*. All editions from *1832* print the poem in quatrains.
title   Written in a Blank Leaf of 'The Pleasures of Memory' *1831*; Lines 'Written . . . Memory' *1832*, *C*, *More*
187. Copy text: *MS. B*, collated with *Mirror of Lit.*
188. Copy text: *MS. L*

Though many a troublous year hath rolled between—   5
   Give me but back the pleasure with the pain,
Ah! might I but redeem a single scene!
   Withered, and woeful past life's very wane,
Such would I be for aye to live that spring again.

2.

All, all have loved, and some beloved in turn   10
   Have felt the life of life—but these be few.
To you, ye youthful, who have yet to learn,
   And teach that nought on earth can long be true,
Some portion of my tale may yet be new;—
   To you with hoary hair and wasted charms   15
I sing not—no—the Devil hath done with you,
   Nor aught prepares of happiness or harms,
And he, your earliest friend, his very *name* alarms.

3.

Light were the limbs and pure the freshening glow
   That marked the form and face of young Honóre,   20
Lord of himself;—his every joy and woe
   Were his own seeking as from shore to shore
He bent his course wherever fancy bore:
   All wealth could purchase, or that youth could win,
Were his ere yet his summers passed a score,   25
   And uncontrolled by Sire or aught akin,
What marvel such should be no foe to smiling Sin?

4.

'Twas nigh the Lenten time, or e'er began
   The penance which our holy rites prepare
To shrive the sinnings of ungodly Man   30
   By daily abstinence and nightly prayer;
But ere her sackcloth garb our City wear,
   Some days of Joyaunce are decreed for all
To take of pleasure each his secret share,
   In motley robe to daunce at masking ball   35
And join the mimic train of merry Carnival.

9 be . . . again] ⟨be to live that spring of love again⟩ *L*   18 And he] ⟨Some that⟩ *L*
33 of . . . share] ⟨such pleasure as may seem most⟩ *L*

5.

And whose more rife with merriment than thine,
   Ah Venice, once the Empress of the Main?
Though strangers rule thee now—thou still art mine,
   Dear native City whom I served in vain—   40
No more—thy wrongs are foreign to my strain;
   Gay were thy minstrels *then* for *free* thy throng,
All felt the common joy, or well could feign.
   Ne'er shall I see such sight or hear such song
As wooed the eye—or thrilled thy thousand streams along. 45

6.

Loud was the lightsome tumult of the shore,
   Oft Music changed but never ceased her tone,
And timely echoed back the measured oar,
   And rippled waters made a pleasing moan.
The Queen of tides on high consenting shone,   50
   And when a transient breeze swept o'er the wave,
'Twas as if darting from her heavenly throne
   A brighter glance her form reflected gave,
Till sparkling billows seemed to light the banks they lave.—

7.

Glanced the light Gondola along the foam,   55
   Danced on the shore the daughters of the land,
No thought had men or maids of rest—or home,
   While many a languid eye and thrilling hand
Exchanged the looks few bosoms may withstand,
   Or gently pressed, returned the pressure still.   60
Oh Love, young Love, bound in thy rosy band,
   (Let Sage or Cynic prattle as he will),
These hours are cheaply bought with future years of ill.

8.

But midst this throng in merry masquerade,
   Lurk there no hearts that throb to secret pain,   65
Even through the closest searment half betrayed?
   To such the gentle murmurs of the Main

Seem to re-echo all they mourn in vain,
  To such the Gladness of the giddy crowd
Is source of wayward thought and high disdain.   70
  How do they loathe the laughter idly loud—
How long to change the robe of Revel for the Shroud!

9.

Such seemed the Man, who mingled with the throng,
  Yet bent on none therein his glassy eye,
Nor answered aught, when those who glanced along   75
  With ribald question fain provoked reply.
Heedless—yet marked of many—stalked he by,
  For in his garb and gesture something strange
And wild seemed foreign to this Revelry.
  His front was veiled, all saw that eye, when change   80
Flashed as with long-desired—but still-deferred Revenge!

10.

His garb was that of godly Eremite,
  Such as on lonely Athos I have seen,
Watching at even on the giant height
  That looks o'er waves so blue, skies so serene,   85
That *he* who there at such an hour hath been,
  Will wistful linger on that hallowed spot,
Then slowly tear him from the witching scene,
  Sigh forth one wish that such had been his lot,
Then turn to hate a world he had almost forgot.   90

                                        1812

189   [To Lady Caroline Lamb]

1.

Go—triumph securely—the treacherous vow
Thou hast broken *I* keep but too faithfully now,
But never again shall thou be to my heart
What thou wert—what I fear for a moment thou *art*.

76 ribald] ⟨jocund⟩ *L*

189. Copy text: *MS. T*, collated with *MS. H*, *Brummell*, letter to Lady Melbourne.
title   To ——— *Brummell*; Unpublished Verses by Lord Byron Supposed to be Addressed
to Lady Frances Wedderburn Webster *H*; *untitled in T*
  3 shall] shalt *Brummell*; Yet never again wilt thou be to this heart *H*

2.

To see thee, to love thee! what breast could do more?   5
To love thee to lose thee 'twere vain to deplore;
Ashamed of my weakness however beguiled,
I shall bear like a Man what I feel like a Child.

3.

If a frown cloud my brow yet it lowers not on thee,
If my heart should seem heavy at least it is free;   10
But *Thou* in the pride of new conquest elate!
Alas! even Envy shall feel for thy Fate.

4.

For the first step of Error none e'er could recall,
And the woman once fallen forever must fall;
Pursue to the last the career she begun,   15
And be *false* unto *many* as *faithless* to *one*.

5.

And they who have loved thee will leave thee to mourne,
And they who have hated will laugh thee to scorn,
And he who adores thee yet weeps to foretell
The pangs that will punish thy falsehood too well.   20

[1812]

190 Address, Spoken at the Opening of Drury-lane
Theatre Saturday, October 10th, 1812

In one dread night our city saw, and sighed,
Bowed to the dust, the Drama's tower of pride;
In one short hour, beheld the blazing fane
Apollo sink, and Shakspeare cease to reign.

5 breast] heart *Brummell*, H   7 Not a sigh shall escape from my breast thus beguiled H
8 shall] will H   9 If] Though H   cloud] clouds H   lowers] lours *Brummell*
10 If . . . seem] Though my heart may be H   11 in . . . new] with . . . fresh H
13 For the] The *letter to Lady Melbourne*   15 she] thus H   17 will] shall H
18 will] shall H   19 who adores thee yet weeps] who adored thee now weeps H; who
adored thee—must weep *Brummell*   20 that] which *Brummell*

190. Copy text: *CHP*(7), collated with various MSS., the proof, *Morning Chronicle*. For
MSS., see commentary
  1 In . . . night] ⟨Bowed to the dust⟩ *BMa*

Ye who beheld, oh sight admired and mourned,   5
Whose radiance mocked the ruin it adorned!
Through clouds of fire, the massy fragments riven,
Like Israel's pillar, chase the night from heaven;
Saw the long column of revolving flames
Shake its red shadow o'er the startled Thames,   10
While thousands, thronged around the burning dome,
Shrank back appalled, and trembled for their home;
As glared the volumed blaze, and ghastly shone
The skies, with lightnings awful as their own;
Till blackening ashes and the lonely wall   15
Usurped the Muse's realm and marked her fall;
Say—shall this new nor less aspiring pile,
Reared, where once rose the mightiest in our isle,
Know the same favour which the former knew,
A shrine for Shakspeare—worthy him and *you*?   20

Yes—it shall be—the magic of that name
Defies the scythe of time, the torch of flame;
On the same spot still consecrates the scene,
And bids the Drama *be* where she hath *been*:

5–6   Ye who beheld—and those there are tonight
Who feared, admired and Ah! deplored the sight *BMa and b*
Ye who beheld—⟨and who forgets the sight⟩/
oh sight admired and mourned
⟨When burst the radiant Ruin into light?⟩
Whose radiance mocked the ruin it adorned *Rc*

7–8 Through sulphurous clouds the fiery fragments riven | Like Israel's pillars *BMa–d*, *cancelled and corrected in BMe*   10 Shake] Shake / Fling / Dart *BMa*   11 While crowds collected round the burning dome *BMa*   burning] glowing *BMc and d*   13 As ⟨flashed the⟩ glared each scorching flash, and ghastly shone *BMb*; As glared each rising flash and ghastly shone *BMc*; As ⟨burst⟩ flashed the volumed ⟨flames⟩ blaze and ⟨fear / glorious⟩ sadly / ghastly shone *Rb*   13–14 As flashing far the new Volcano shone | And swept the skies with meteors / Lightnings not their own *Rb first version*   15–16 Till all was whelmed beneath the livid wave | And blackening ashes marked the Muses grave *BMa and b* livid] glowing / burning / blazing / fiery / sulphurous *alternative possible readings sent in Ra* 16 Met the sad morn that gleamed oer Drury's fall *BMc and d, cor. in BMe*   17 new nor less] humbler yet *BMa–d, cor. in BMe*   22 Though thousand piles should sink in future flame *BMa*   thousand] other *BMb*   Defies] Which scorns *BMc*   23 still consecrates] shall consecrate *BMa, b, and c*   24 bids] bid *BMa, b, and c*

Though long in vain Melpomene deplore
And weep for her with whom she weeps no more
Yet Hope shall strive to banish Memory's fear
Till Time mature a second Siddons here
Though fled the Queen, our Monarchs still remain
Yes, here 'old Lear shall be King again'

This fabric's birth attests the potent spell—   25
Indulge our honest pride, and say, *How well!*

As soars this fane to emulate the last,
Oh! might we draw our omens from the past,
Some hour propitious to our prayers may boast
Names such as hallow still the dome we lost.   30
On Drury first your Siddons' thrilling art
O'erwhelm'd the gentlest, stormed the sternest heart.
On Drury, Garrick's latest laurels grew;
Here your last tears retiring Roscius drew,
Sighed his last thanks, and wept his last adieu: 35
But still for living wit the wreaths may bloom
That only waste their odours o'er the tomb.
Such Drury claimed and claims,—nor you refuse
One tribute to revive his slumbering muse;
With garlands deck your own Menander's head!   40
Nor hoard your honours idly for the dead!

> You who / whom no tyrants brook / rule but on the stage
> Will here endure Macbeth's and Richard's rage
> Here too when tragic tears forget to flow
> The voice of wit shall rise for / chase the sounds of woe
> And varied oft as varying taste allures
> Thalia's smile(s) be well repaid by yours. *inserted after 24 in BMa and b;*

the following are variants from BMa
You who / whom . . . rage] *not in BMb*   The voice . . . woe] Shall Congreve's wit succeed to
Otway's woe *Ra*   And . . . taste] And varying oft as varied taste *BMb*   25 This
. . . attests] These rising scenes confess *BMd, cor. in BMe*   27 Whateer our fate
—howeer our parts be cast *BMa–e*   29 Some future day should bid our Drury
boast *BMa, d, e*; Some happier day shall bid *BMb*; Some happier hour should bid *BMc*
30 Names . . . still] Such names as hallow still / hallowed once *BMa*   Names such] Such
names *BMb, c*   31 thrilling] searching *BMa, b* ⟨varied⟩ *BMc*   34 Here
Britain's Roscius your last teardrops drew *BMa, b*   retiring] retiring / departing *BMc*
36–7 And here could living Wit unenvied share | The praise which cannot make / fire the
Wits that were *BMa*   And here] Here too *BMd, e*   praise which] praise that *BMb*
38–41 *the two couplets are transposed in BMa–d*   38 Such] Him *BMa–d*   39 To
join her tribute to his matchless muse *BMa, b*

41   Far be from him that hour which asks in vain
                      Tears such as flow for Garrick in his Strain *BMd*
                      Far be from him that hour which asks in vain
                      Tears such as flow for Garrick in his Strain

                                   or

                      Far be that hour which vainly asks in turn
                      Such verse for him as crowned his Garrick's urn *BMe, Rg*
                      crowned his] crowned his / wept oer *Rg*

                      these couplets appear after 41 in the indicated MSS.

Dear are the days which made our annals bright,
Ere Garrick fled, or Brinsley ceased to write.—
Heirs to their labours, like all high-born heirs,
Vain of *our* ancestry as they of *theirs*;   45
While thus Remembrance borrows Banquo's glass
To claim the sceptred shadows as they pass,
And we the mirror hold, where imaged shine
Immortal names, emblazoned on our line—
Pause—ere their feebler offspring you condemn,   50
Reflect how hard the task to rival them!

Friends of the stage— to whom both Players and Plays
Must sue alike for pardon, or for praise—
Whose judging voice and eye alone direct
The boundless power to cherish or reject;   55
If e'er frivolity has led to fame,

42–3 Such ⟨were⟩ are the names that ⟨once⟩ here your plaudits sought | When Garrick acted and when Brinsley wrote *BMa, cancelled b*   42 Such were the names which made our / in Drury's annals bright *BMb*   Such . . . names] Such was the time / were the days *BMc*; Such were the days *BMd*; Those were the days *BMe*   43 fled] died *BMb* 44 labours] efforts *BMb*   48 While thus we boast the glories which enshrine *BMb–d*; And we the mirror hold / show where imaged / distant shine | And we that magic mirror show / hold where shine *alternatives in Rh*   49 Immortal names] ⟨The names emblazoned / The trophied names) Triumphant names *BMc*; The trophied names *BMd*; The Genius gifted Patriarchs of our line *BMb*   50 Oh should their Memory lead you to condemn / Oh do not by comparison condemn *BMa*   51 Those who succeed but dare not rival them *BMc*   52 to . . . Plays] for whom our voice we raise *BMa*; to whom *BMb*   53 Must sue alike] And sue in turn *BMa, b*; Must sue in turn *BMc, d, Ra*   54 Yours is the choice, as you decide direct *BMa, b, c*

55   The ample power to punish or protect *BMa, b*
           The same indulgence which your fathers gave
           For the same scenes is all your servants crave
           On the same spot we scarce can plead in vain
           That Sheridan and Shakespeare may resume / renew their
               reign / the Strain
           The Eye of Taste prophetically just
           Shall guard and guide us faithful to our trust
           The voice of Wit alike shall check or cheer
           The heartfelt efforts of our new career
           But know—our triumph this alone secures
           The judging voice and eye must first be yours
           Ours to obey your will or right or wrong
           To soar in Sentiment, or creep in song
           Nay lower still—the Drama yet deplores
           That late she deigned to crawl upon 'all fours'
           When Richard roars in Bosworth for a horse
           If you command—the *Steed* must come in course *inserted after 55 in BMa;
               the following are variants from subsequent MSS.*

The same indulgence . . . the Strain] *dropped in BMb; the entire insertion after 55 was dropped in BMc*

And made us blush that you forbore to blame—
If e'er the sinking stage could condescend
To soothe the sickly taste, it dare not mend—
All past reproach may present scenes refute,   60
And censure, wisely loud, be justly mute!—
Oh! since your fiat stamps the Drama's laws,
Forbear to mock us with misplac'd applause;
So pride shall doubly nerve the actor's powers,
And reason's voice be echo'd back by ours!—   65

This greeting o'er—the ancient rule obey'd,
The Drama's homage by her herald paid,
Receive *our* welcome too,—whose every tone
Springs from our hearts, and fain would win your own.
The curtain rises—may our stage unfold   70
Scenes not unworthy Drury's days of old!—
Britons our judges, nature for our guide,
Still may *we* please, long—long may *you* preside.

[1812]

58–61   ⟨If you demand—our intellectual feast
           Must furnish store alike for Man and Beast⟩
           ⟨As⟩ If you decree—the stage must condescend
           To soothe the sickly taste ⟨she⟩ we dare not mend
           Blush for such / Blame not our judgement—while / should
           we acquiesce
           And gratify you more by showing less *BMa*

Blush . . . acquiesce] Blame not their judgement, who must / could acquiesce *Rf*

58–63   Say—shall we soar again, or still descend
           To soothe the sickly taste we dare not mend
           Oh since your fiat stamps the drama's laws
           Forebear to mock us with misplaced applause
           All past reproach may present scenes refute
           Where whines no Baby, and cavorts no Brute. *BMc*

All past . . . Brute] The past reproach ⟨the present stage refutes⟩ let present scenes refute |
Nor ⟨sink⟩ shift from Man to Babe, from Babe to Brute *Rf*   Where . . . Brute] And censure
justly loud again be mute *BMd*   justly] ⟨justly / sternly⟩ wisely *BMe*

63   That public praise be never more disgraced
           From babes and brutes redeem a Nation's taste *BMa*
           That public praise be neer again disgraced
           From babes and brutes redeem / brutes to man recall a
           Nation's taste *BMb couplet after 63*

64 So] Then *BMa–d*; ⟨But⟩ Then *Rf*   65 When Reason's voice is echoed back by /
shall lend its strength to ours *BMa*   voice be] voice is *BMb, c, Rf*   66–8 This greet-
ing oer, this previous ⟨duty⟩ homage paid | The Drama's offering / Our virgin drama be no more
delayed ! | This humble welcome and this / told in faltering tone *BMa*   70 The] ⟨Our⟩
The *BMd*   71 When the Soul's Sovereign taught your tears to flow | Or Congreve's
wit relieved from Otway's woe *couplet added after 71 in BMd and e*   Soul's Sovereign]
⟨great Master⟩ *BMd*   72 Britons] ⟨You for⟩ *BMa*

191   Waltz:
        An Apostrophic Hymn
        By Horace Hornem, Esq.

*'Qualis in Eurotae ripis, aut per juga Cynthi
Exercet* DIANA *choros.'*—OVID.

TO THE PUBLISHER

SIR,
I AM a country gentleman of a midland county. I might have
been a Parliament-man for a certain borough, having had the offer
of as many votes as General T. at the last general election. But I
5 was all for domestic happiness; so fifteen years ago, on a visit to
London, I married a middle-aged Maid of Honour.—We lived
happily at Hornem Hall till last season, when my wife and I were
invited by the Countess of Waltzaway (a distant relation of my
spouse), to pass the winter in town. Thinking no harm, and our
10 girls being come to a marriageable (or, as they call it, *marketable*)
age, and having besides a Chancery suit inveterately entailed upon
the family estate, we came up in our old chariot, of which, by the
by, my wife grew so much ashamed, in less than a week, that I
was obliged to buy a second-hand barouche, of which I might
15 mount the box, Mrs. H. says, if I could drive, but never see the
inside—that place being reserved for the Honourable Augustus
Tiptoe, her partner general and Opera knight. Hearing great
praises of Mrs. H.'s dancing (she was famous for birth-night
minuets in the latter end of last century), I unbooted, and went to a

---

191. Copy text: *Waltz1813*, collated with *MS. B*, the Murray proofs, *Waltz1821*
title   Waltz] The Waltz *1831, 1832, C*
                epigraph   Such on Eurotas' banks, or Cynthia's height,
                                   Diana seems: and so she charms the sight,
                                   When in the dance the graceful goddess leads
                                   The quire of nymphs, and overtops their heads. *Dryden's Virgil.*

Added to the epigraph in *Waltz1821, 1831, 1832, C*. *Knight and Lacey* has no epigraphs;
C corrects *Cynthia's* to *Cynthus's.*

To the Publisher
     4 last general election] general election in 1812 *Waltz1821, 1831, 1832, C, More*
     5 so fifteen] as, fifteen *Waltz1821, 1831, 1832, C, More*   11–12 and having . . . estate,
added Proof 7   13 so much] so *C*

ball at the Countess's, expecting to see a country-dance, or, at most, 20
cotillions, reels, and all the old paces to the newest tunes. But
judge of my surprise, on arriving, to see poor dear Mrs. Hornem with
her arms half round the loins of a huge hussar-looking gentleman I
never set eyes on before, and his, to say truth, rather more than half
round her waist, turning round, and round, and round, to a d—d see- 25
saw up and down sort of tune, that reminded me of the 'Black
Joke', only more 'affettuoso', till it made me quite giddy with
wondering they were not so. By and by they stopped a bit, and
I thought they would sit or fall down:—but, no; with Mrs. H.'s
hand on his shoulder, '*quam familiariter*' (as Terence said when I 30
was at school), they walked about a minute, and then at it again,
like two cockchafers spitted on the same bodkin. I asked what all
this meaned, when, with a loud laugh, a child no older than our
Wilhelmina (a name I never heard but in the Vicar of Wakefield,
though her mother would call her after the Princess of Swappen- 35
bach), said, 'L—d, Mr. Hornem, can't you see they are valtzing?'
or waltzing (I forget which); and then up she got, and her mother
and sister, and away they went and roundabouted it till supper-
time. Now that I know what it is, I like it of all things, and so
does Mrs. H.; though I have broken my shins, and four times 40
overturned Mrs. Hornem's maid in practising the preliminary
steps in a morning. Indeed, so much do I like it, that having a turn
for rhyme, tastily displayed in some election ballads and songs,
in honour of all the victories (but till lately I have had little practice
in that way), I sate down, and with the aid of W. F. Esq. and a few 45
hints from Dr. B. (whose recitations I attend, and am monstrous
fond of Master B.'s manner of delivering his father's late success-
ful D. L. Address), I composed the following Hymn, wherewithal
to make my sentiments known to the Public, whom, nevertheless,
I heartily despise as well as the Critics. 50

I am, SIR, yours, &c. &c.
HORACE HORNEM.

25 round, and round, and round] round, and round *1856*, *C*   27 'affettuoso'] ex-
pressive *B*, *cor. in Proof 1*   29 would sit ⟨down⟩ or *B*   33 meaned] meant *all
other edns.*   35–6 Swappenbach] ⟨Swaffenbach⟩ *Proof 1*   36 they are] they're
1856, *C*   45 sate] sat *all other edns.*   W. F.] William Fitzgerald *1832*, *C*, *More*
46–7 B . . . B] Busby . . . Busby's *1832*, *C*, *More*   48 D. L.] Drury Lane *1832*, *C*,
More

Muse of the many-twinkling feet!—whose charms
Are now extended up from legs to arms;
Terpsichore!—too long misdeemed a maid—
Reproachful term—bestowed but to unbraid—
Henceforth in all the bronze of brightness shine,   5
The least a vestal of the virgin Nine.
Far be from thee and thine the name of Prude;
Mocked, yet triumphant, sneered at, unsubdued,
Thy legs must move to conquer as they fly,
If but thy coats are reasonably high;   10
Thy breast—if bare enough—requires no shield;
Dance forth—*sans armour* thou shalt take the field,
And own—impregnable to *most* assaults,
Thy not too lawfully begotten 'Waltz'.

Hail nimble nymph! to whom the young hussar,   15
The whiskered votary of Waltz and war—
His night devotes, despite of spur and boots,
A sight unmatched since Orpheus and his brutes:
Hail spirit-stirring Waltz!—beneath whose banners
A modern hero fought for modish manners;   20
On Hounslow's heath to rival Wellesley's fame,
Cocked—fired—and missed his man—but gained his aim.
Hail moving Muse! to whom the fair-one's breast
Gives all it can, and bids us take the rest.
Oh! for the flow of Busby, or of Fitz,   25
The latter's loyalty, the former's wits,
To 'energize the object I pursue',
And give both Belial and his dance their due!—

Imperial Waltz! imported from the Rhine,
(Famed for the growth of pedigrees and wine)   30
Long be thine import from all duty free,
And hock itself be less esteemed than thee;
In some few qualities alike—for hock
Improves our cellar—*thou* our living stock.

text

    5 Henceforth with due unblushing brightness shine *B, cor. in Proof 2*   9 must] but *B,
cor. in Proof 2*   11–12 *transposed, then cor., in B*   15–18, 23–8 *added in MS. in Proof 1*
19–22 *added in MS. in Proof 4*   21 heath to] ⟨plain the⟩ *Proof 4*   28 And weave a
couplet worthy them and you *Proof 1, cor. in Proof 2*   31 thine] thy *B, cor. in Proof 1*

The head to hock belongs—thy subtler art   35
Intoxicates alone the heedless heart;
Through the full veins thy gentler poison swims,
And wakes to wantonness the willing limbs.

O Germany! how much to thee we owe,
As heaven-born Pitt can testify below;   40
Ere curs'd Confederation made thee France's,
And only left us thy d—d debts and dances;
Of subsidies and Hanover bereft,
We bless thee still—for George the Third is left!
Of kings the best—and last, not least in worth,   45
For graciously begetting George the Fourth.
To Germany, and Highnesses serene,
Who owe us millions—don't we owe the Queen?
To Germany, what owe we not besides?
So oft bestowing Brunswickers and brides;   50
Who paid for vulgar with her royal blood,
Drawn from the stem of each Teutonic stud;
Who sent us —so be pardoned all her faults,
A dozen Dukes—some Kings—a Queen—and 'Waltz'.

But peace to her—her Emperor and Diet,   55
Though now transferred to Buonaparte's 'fiat';
Back to my theme—O Muse of motion say,
How first to Albion found thy Waltz her way?

Borne on the breath of Hyperborean gales,
From Hamburgh's port (while Hamburgh yet had *Mails*)   60
Ere yet unlucky Fame—compelled to creep
To snowy Gottenburgh—was chilled to sleep;
Or, starting from her slumbers, deigned arise,
Heligoland! to stock thy mart with lies;
While unburnt Moscow yet had news to send,   65
Nor owed her fiery exit to a friend,
She came—Waltz came—and with her certain sets
Of true dispatches, and as true Gazettes;
Then flamed of Austerlitz the blest dispatch,
Which Moniteur nor Morning Post can match;   70

36 heedless] giddy B, *cor. in Proof 3*   54 some] four B, *cor. in Proof 1*   62 chilled]
froze B, *cor. in Proof 2*   64 To make Heliogoland the mart for lies B, *cor. in Proof 2*
with lies] for lies *Proof 2, cor. in Proof 3*

And—almost crushed beneath the glorious news,
Ten plays—and forty tales of Kotzebue's;
One envoy's letters, six composers' airs,
And loads from Frankfort and from Leipsic fairs;
Meiner's four volumes upon womankind,   75
Like Lapland witches to ensure a wind;
Brunck's heaviest tome for ballast, and, to back it,
Of Heynē, such as should not sink the packet.

Fraught with this cargo—and her fairest freight,
Delightful Waltz, on tiptoe for a mate,   80
The welcome vessel reached the genial strand,
And round her flocked the daughters of the land.
Not decent David, when, before the ark,
His grand pas-suel excited some remark;
Not lovelorn Quixote—when his Sancho thought   85
The knight's fandango friskier than it ought;
Not soft Herodias, when, with winning tread,
Her nimble feet danced off another's head;
Not Cleopatra on her galley's deck,
Displayed so much of *leg*, or more of *neck*,   90
Than thou, ambrosial Waltz, when first the moon
Beheld thee twirling to a Saxon tune!

To you—ye husbands of ten years! whose brows
Ache with the annual tributes of a spouse;
To you, of nine years less—who only bear   95
The budding sprouts of those that you *shall* wear,
With added ornaments around them rolled,
Of native brass, or law-awarded gold;
To you—ye matrons, ever on the watch
To mar a son's, or make a daughter's match;   100
To you—ye children of —whom chance accords,
Always the ladies and *sometimes* their lords;
To you—ye single gentlemen! who seek
Torments for life, or pleasures for a week;
As Love or Hymen your endeavours guide,   105
To gain your own, or snatch another's bride:

77 tome] ⟨farce⟩ *Proof 1*   78 Of . . . as] As much of Heyne as *B, cor. in Proof 1*
94 ⟨Ben⟩ Ache *B*   95 nine] five *B, cor. in Proof 1*   98 awarded] accorded *B, cor.
in Proof 2*   101 children] daughters *B, cor. in Proof 2*

To one and all the lovely stranger came,
And every ball-room echoes with her name.

Endearing Waltz—to thy more melting tune
Bow Irish jig—and ancient rigadoon;   110
Scotch reels avaunt!—and country dance forego
Your future claims to each fantastic toe;
Waltz—Waltz—alone both arms and legs demands,
Liberal of feet—and lavish of her hands;
Hands which may freely range in public sight,   115
Where ne'er before—but—pray 'put out the light'.
Methinks the glare of yonder chandelier
Shines much too far—or I am much too near;
And true, though strange—Waltz whispers this remark,
'My slippery steps are safest in the dark.'   120
But here the Muse with due decorum halts,
And lends her longest petticoat to 'Waltz'.

Observant travellers! of every time,
Ye quartos! published upon every clime;
O say, shall dull Romaika's heavy round,   125
Fandango's wriggle, or Bolero's bound;
Can Egypts' Almas—tantalizing groupe—
Columbia's caperers to the warlike whoop—
Can aught from cold Kamschatka to Cape Horn,
With Waltz compare, or after Waltz be borne?   130
Ah no! from Morier's pages down to Galt's,
Each tourist pens a paragraph for 'Waltz'.

Shades of those belles, whose reign began of yore,
With George the Third's—and ended long before;
Though in your daughters' daughters yet you thrive,   135
Burst from your lead, and be yourselves alive!
Back to the ball-room speed your spectred host,
Fools' Paradise is dull to that you lost;

---

113 arms and legs] legs and arms *all other edns.*   120 My] ⟨Why⟩ *Proof 1*   123 *no
paragraph in Proof 1, cor. in Proof 2*   time] ⟨clime⟩ *B*   125 round] sound *Proof 1,
cor. in Proof 2*   129 cold] old *Proof 1, cor. in Proof 3*   130 borne] born *C*
134 Third's] Third *B, cor. in Proof 7*   135 Though . . . you thrive] Who . . . yet
survive *B, cor. in Proof 7*   136 Like Banquo's spirit, be yourselves alive *B, cor. in
Proof 7*   138 Elysium's ill exchanged for that you lost *B, cor. in Proof 7*

No treacherous powder bids Conjecture quake,
No stiff-starched stays make meddling fingers ache;   140
(Transferred to those ambiguous things that ape
Goats in their visage, women in their shape);
No damsel faints when rather closely pressed,
But more caressing seems when most caressed;
Superfluous hartshorn and reviving salts,   145
Both banished by the sovereign cordial 'Waltz'.

Seductive Waltz—though on thy native shore
E'en Werter's self proclaimed thee half a w—re;
Werter—to decent vice though much inclined,
Yet warm not wanton, dazzled but not blind;   150
Though gentle Genlis, in her strife with Stael,
Would e'en proscribe thee from a Paris ball;
Thee Fashion hails—from Countesses to queans,
And maids and valets waltz behind the scenes;
Wide and more wide thy witching circle spreads,   155
And turns—if nothing else—at least our *heads*;
With thee e'en clumsy cits attempt to bounce,
And cockneys practice what they can't pronounce.
Gods! how the glorious theme my strain exalts,
And rhyme finds partner rhyme in praise of 'Waltz'.   160

Blest was the time Waltz chose for her debût;
The Court, the R——t, like herself were new;
New face for friends, for foes some new rewards,
New ornaments for black—and royal guards;
New laws to hang the rogues that roared for bread;   165
New coins (most new) to follow those that fled;
New victories—nor can we prize them less,
Though Jenky wonders at his own success;
New wars, because the old succeed so well,
That most survivors envy those who fell;   170

139–40 *transposed in B, cor. in Proof 2*   139 treacherous] ⟨telltale⟩ B   140 meddling]
lovers' *B, cor. in Proof 2*   141–2 *added in MS. in Proof 2*   142 visage] ⟨whiskers⟩
Proof 2   148 E'en . . . w—re] Even . . . whore *1831, 1832, C, More*   152 e'en]
even *1831, 1832, C, More*   153 queans] ⟨Queens⟩ *Proof 1*; Queens *1831, 1832, C, More*
157 e'en] even *B, 1831, 1832, C, More*   162 R——t] Regent *1832, C, More*   were]
⟨was⟩ *Proof 1*   164 New caps and jackets for the royal guards *B, cor. in Proof 1*
170 most] all *B, cor. in Proof 4*

New mistresses—no—old—and yet 'tis true,
Though they be *old*, the *thing* is something new;
Each new, quite new—(except some ancient tricks)
New white-sticks, gold-sticks, broom-sticks, all new sticks!
With vests or ribbands decked alike in hue,   175
New troopers strut, new turncoats blush in blue;
So saith the Muse—my——, what say you?

Such was the time when Waltz might best maintain
Her new preferment in this novel reign;
Such was the time, nor ever yet was such,   180
Hoops are *no more*, and petticoats *not much*;
Morals and minuets, Virtue and her stays,
And tell-tale Powder—all have had their days.

The ball begins—the honours of the house
First duly done by daughter or by spouse,   185
Some potentate—or royal, or serene,
With K—t's gay grace, or sapient G—st—r's mien,
Leads forth the ready dame, whose rising flush
Might once have been mistaken for a blush.
From where the garb just leaves the bosom free,   190
That spot where hearts were once supposed to be;
Round all the confines of the yielded waist,
The strangest hand may wander undisplaced;
The lady's in return may grasp as much
As princely paunches offer to her touch.   195
Pleased round the chalky floor how well they trip,
One hand reposing on the royal hip;
The other to the shoulder no less royal
Ascending with affection truly loyal:
Thus front to front the partners move or stand,   200
The foot may rest, but none withdraw the hand;
And all in turn may follow in their rank,
The Earl of—Asterisk—and Lady—Blank;

175-7 *added in MS. in Proof 2*   177 my——] my M—ra *Proof 2, cor. in Proof 3*
178 best] well *B, cor. in Proof 2*; *verse paragraph here is missing in all other edns.*   179 pre-
ferment] preferments *all other edns.*   184 *verse paragraph missing in edns. after Waltz
1813*   187 K—t's] Kent's *1832, C, More*   sapient G—st—r's] ⟨G——r's booby⟩
silly Billy's *B*; silly Billy *Proof 1, 2*; ⟨gentle⟩ sapient G—st—r's *Proof 3*; sapient Gloster's
1832, C, More   198 The other ⟨with⟩ to *B*

Sir—Such a one—with those of Fashion's host,
For whose blest surnames—vide 'Morning Post';   205
(Or if for that impartial print too late,
Search Doctors' Commons six months from my date)—
Thus all and each, in movement swift or slow,
The genial contact gently undergo;
Till some might marvel, with the modest Turk,   210
If 'nothing follows all this palming work'?
True, honest Mirza—you may trust my rhyme,
Something does follow at a fitter time;
The breast thus publicly resigned to man,
In private may resist him—if it can.   215

   O ye! who loved our grandmothers of yore,
F—tz—t—k, Sh—r—d—n, and many more!
And thou, my Prince! whose sovereign taste and will
It is to love the lovely beldames still;
Thou ghost of Queensbury! whose judging sprite   220
Satan may spare to peep a single night,
Pronounce—if ever in your days of bliss—
Asmodeus struck so bright a stroke as this;
To teach the young ideas how to rise,
Flush in the cheek and languish in the eyes;   225
Rush to the heart, and lighten through the frame,
With half-told wish, and ill-dissembled flame;
For prurient nature still will storm the breast—
Who, tempted thus, can answer for the rest?

   But ye—who never felt a single thought   230
For what our morals are to be, or ought;
Who wisely wish the charms you view to reap,
Say—would you make those beauties quite so cheap?
Hot from the hands promiscuously applied,
Round the sight waist, or down the glowing side;   235
Where were the rapture then to clasp the form,
From this lewd grasp, and lawless contact warm?

204–9 Sir—Such a one—with Mrs.—Miss—So So, | The genial contact gently
undergo; B, cor. in Proof 2   207 my] ⟨this⟩ Proof 2   208 in] ⟨to⟩ Proof 2
217 F—tz—t—k, Sh—r—d—n] Fitzpatrick, Sheridan *1832*, C, *More*   218 sovereign
taste and] undisputed B, cor. in Proof 6   220 Queensbury] Queensberry Proof *1*, cor.
in Proof 6   221 peep] gaze B, cor. in Proof 2   237 From this abominable contact
warm? B, cor. in Proof 6

At once Love's most endearing thought resign,
To press the hand so pressed by none but thine;
To gaze upon that eye which never met   240
Another's ardent look without regret;
Approach the lip, which all, without restraint,
Come near enough—if not to touch—to taint;
If such thou lovest—love her then no more,
Or give—like her—caresses to a score;   245
Her mind with these is gone, and with it go
The little left behind it to bestow.

Voluptuous Waltz! and dare I thus blaspheme?
Thy bard forgot thy praises were his theme.
Terpsichore forgive!—at every ball,   250
My wife *now* waltzes—and my daughters *shall*;
My son (or stop—'tis needless to enquire—
These little accidents should ne'er transpire;
Some ages hence our genealogic tree
Will wear as green a bough for him as me)   255
Waltzing shall rear, to make our name amends,
Grandsons for me—in heirs to all his friends.

192   Hear My Prayer

The sacred song that on my ear
    Yet vibrates from that voice of thine,
I heard before from one so dear,
    'Tis strange it still appears divine.
But oh! so sweet that *look* and *tone*   5
    To her and thee alike is given,
It seemed as if for me alone
    That *both* had been recalled from Heaven!

255–6 ⟨Some generations hence our Pedigree | Will never look the worse for him, nor me⟩ *B*
256 Shall waltzing rear to make us all amends *B, cor. in Proof 1*   us all] his sire *correction
made, then removed, in Proof 6*

192. Copy text: *C*, collated with *MSS. T, LC, Foster*
title   To the Hon. Mrs. George Lamb *C, More*; Verses Addressed by Lord Byron in the
Year 1812 to the Honble. Mrs. George Lamb *LC*; Verses Addressed in 1812 by Lord Byron
to the Hon. Mrs. George Lamb *Foster*
  1 my] mine *C, More*

And though I never can redeem
The vision thus endeared to me,   10
I scarcely can regret my dream
When realised again by *thee*.

10 Oct. 1812

193   Parenthetical Address,
                by Dr. Plagiary,

Half stolen, with acknowledgements, to be spoken n an inarticu-
late voice, by Master——at the opening of the next new theatre.
(Stolen parts marked with the inverted commas of quotation,
thus, '——')

'When energizing objects men pursue',
Then Lord knows what—is writ by Lord knows who;
'A modest Monologue you here survey',
Hissed from the theatre the 'other day';
As if Sir FRETFUL wrote 'the slumberous' verse,   5
And gave his son 'the rubbish' to rehearse.
'Yet at the thing you'd never be amazed',
Knew you the rumpus which the Author raised,
'Nor even here your smiles would be represt',
Knew you these lines—the badness of the best,   10
'Flame! fire! and flame!!' (words borrowed from LUCRETIUS)
'Dread Metaphors which open wounds' like issues!
'And sleeping pangs awake—and—but away',
(Confound me if I know what next to say).
'Lo hope reviving re-expands her wings',   15
And Master G—— recites what Dr. B[us]by sings!—
'If mighty things with small we may compare',
(Translated from the Grammar for the fair!)
Dramatic 'Spirit' drives a conquering car',
And burned poor Moscow like a tub of 'tar'.   20

10 endeared] ⟨restored⟩ *T*

193. Copy text: *Morning Chronicle*, collated with *MS. M*

title   stolen, with] stolen, ⟨without⟩ *M*   Master ——ˌ Master P —— *M*

'This spirit WELLINGTON has shewn in Spain',
To furnish Melo-drames for Drury-lane;
'Another MARLBOROUGH points to Blenheim's story',
And GEORGE and I will dramatise it for ye.

'In Arts and Sciences our Isle hath shone',   25
(This deep discovery is mine alone).
'Oh! British Poesy, whose powers inspire'
My verse (or I'm a fool and Fame's a liar),
'These we invoke—your sister arts implore',
With 'smiles', and 'lyres', and 'pencils', and much more.   30
'These if we win, the Graces too we gain';
Disgraces too! 'inseparable train!'
'Three who have stolen their witching airs from Cupid',
(You all know what I mean unless you're stupid);
'Harmonious throng', that I have kept in petto,   35
Now to produce in a 'divine Sestetto!!'
'While Poesy', with these delightful doxies,
'Sustains her part' in all the 'upper' boxes!
'Thus lifted gloriously you'll soar along',
Borne in the vast balloon of B[us]by's song;   40
'Shine in your farce, masque, scenery and play',
(For this last line GEORGE had a holiday).
'Old Drury never, never soared so high',
So says the Manager, and so says I;
'But hold, you say, this self complacent boast',   45
Is this the Poem which the public lost?
'True, true, that lowers at once our mounting pride',
But lo! the Papers print what you deride.
''Tis ours to look on you—you hold the prize',
'Tis *twenty guineas*, as they advertize!   50
'A double blessing your rewards impart',
I wish I had them then with all my heart.
'Our *twofold* feeling *owns* its twofold cause',
My son and I both beg for your applause,
'When in your fostering beams you bid us live',   55
My next subscription list shall say how much you give!!

[1812]

32 too] ⟨who⟩ too M   44 says] say *1832*, C, *More*   50 advertize] ⟨rhymatize⟩ M
54 My] Why *1832*, C, *More*

194   From the Portuguese

In moments to delight devoted,
   'My life!' with tend'rest tone, you cry;
Dear words! on which my heart had doated,
   If youth could neither fade nor die.
To death even hours like these must roll,   5
   Ah! then repeat those accents never,
Or change 'my life!' into 'my soul!'
   Which, like my love, exists for ever.

                                     [1814]

(Another Version)

You call me still your *life*.—Oh! change the word—
   Life is as transient as the inconstant sigh:
Say rather I'm your soul; more just that name,
   For, like the soul, my love can never die.

                                     [1814?]

(A Third Version)

In moments to delight devoted
   'My life!' is still the name you give,
Dear words! on which my heart had doted
   Had man an endless term to live:
But, ah! so swift the seasons roll   5
   That name must be repeated never,
For 'Life' in future say 'My Soul',
   Which like my love exists for ever.

                                     [1812]

---

194. Copy text: *CHP(7)*, collated with *MS. M* and *CHP(8)*–*CHP(10)* (first version); *Life*,
collated with *1831, 1832* (second version); *Edgecumbe*, collated with *MS. T* (third version);
MS. L (fourth version).

title   *untitled in Life, L, Edgecumbe*

  4 (third version) term] race *T*; (fourth version) ⟨Had Man an endless term to live⟩ *L*

(A Fourth Version)

In moments to delight devoted
  'My Life' is still the name you give,
Dear words on which my heart had doated
  Could Man through endless ages live.
But ah so swift the moments roll   5
  That term to me no more apply!
For '*life*' in future say '*my Soul*'
  Which like *my Love* can never *die*.—

[1815?]

195   [Imitation of Martial, XI. 93]

Pierios vatis Theodori flamma penates
  abstulit. hoc Musis et tibi, Phoebe, placet?
o scelus, o magnum facinus crimenque deorum,
  non arsit pariter quod domus et dominus!

F[itzgeral]d's house hath been on fire—the Nine
All smiling saw that pleasant bonfire shine.
Yet—cruel Gods! Oh! ill-contrived disaster!
The house is burnt—the house—without the Master!—

[1812]

196   [Imitation of Martial, XI. 92]

Mentitur qui te vitiosum—Zoile, dicit.
Non vitiosus homo es, Zoile, sed Vitium.—

Who calls thee vicious, Jack, is rather nice;
Thou art no vicious mortal—but a Vice.—

[1812]

195. Copy text: *MS. L*, collated with *MS. M* and *Examiner*
title   Epigram *Examiner*
    1 F[itzgeral]d's] The Laureate's *Examiner*; Fitzgerald's *M*   3 But, cruel fate! O
damnable disaster! *Examiner*   ill-contrived] ⟨damnable / incomplete⟩ *L*   damnable *M*
4 The house—the house is burnt, and not the master. *Examiner*

196. Copy text: *MS. L*

197   [Imitation of Martial, ii. 88]

You don't recite, but would be deemed a poet;
You shall be Homer—so you do not show it.—

[1812]

198   [Imitation of Martial, iii. 26]

Dear friend, thou hast a deal of cash,
And wherewithal to cut a dash—
Of every kind in food and raiment,
Cooks, taylors praise thy punctual payment—
Thy wealth, thy wine, thy house thine own,   5
With none partaken, thine alone.—
Thy very heart and soul and wit
No partnership with man admit.—
All—all is thine—and were for life,
But that the Public share thy wife.   10

[1812]

199   [Imitation of Martial, xii. 12]

Omnia promittis cum tota nocte bibisti:
Mane nihil praestas: Postume, mane bibe.

You drink all night, and promise fairly;
But getting sober somewhat early,
Your promise is not worth a d——n:
For God's sake take a Morning dram!—

[1812]

197. Copy text: *MS. L*, collated with *Smith* text
title   *untitled in L, Smith*
     1 Would be deemed] still would *seem Smith*; would be ⟨thought⟩ *L*   2 ⟨Then be a⟩ /
⟨Be what you please—a bard—but never show it⟩ *L*   Homer] ⟨Homer⟩ Southey *Smith*

198. Copy text: *MS. L*
     1 deal of cash] ⟨world of wealth⟩ *L*   4 ⟨And short accounts and punctual payments⟩ *L*
5 house] ⟨dress⟩ *L*   6 ⟨Beheld by all and shared by none⟩ *L*   7 and wit] ⟨beside⟩ *L*
10 the Public share] ⟨the world / all men partake⟩ *L*

199. Copy text: *MS. L* (fair copy), collated with *MS. L* (rough draft)

200   # Imitation of Martial, II. 55

Vis te—Seste, coli: volebam amare.
Parendum est tibi; quod jubes, coleris:
Sed si te colo, Seste, non amabo.—

To love you well you bid me know you better,
And for that wish I rest your humble debtor;
But, if the simple truth I may express,
To love you better, I must know you less.—

[1812]

201   # Imitation of Martial, VI. 34

Give me thy kisses—ask me not to count
The sweet but never to be summed amount;
Or rather bid me number unto thee
Shells on the shore, or billows on the sea,
Or bees that wander with the busy wing   5
And hum in gladness through their wealthy spring;
Or every voice or clapping hand that hails
The face of every sovereign—but of W[a]les.
Even then the reckoning would be scarce begun—
But he who counts his kisses, merits none.   10

[1812]

202   # [Adaption of Martial, VI. 60]

I print sometimes—to judge of praise or blame—
Sam's face is my thermometer of fame.—
If he looks gay, the critic's was most fearful;
If sad, my publisher is wondrous cheerful.—

[1812]

200. Copy text: *MS. L* (fair copy), collated with *MS. L* (rough draft)
  1–2 ⟨You wish me Sir—to know you better | That I may like you well⟩ *L* (rough draft)

201. Copy text: *MS. Mo*, collated with *MS. L* (fair and rough copies)
  3 unto] ⟨Oceans⟩ *L* (rough draft)   5 wander] ⟨wanton⟩ *L* (rough draft)   8 ⟨The public second Titus⟩ Grateful and gratis—George the Prince of Wales *L* (rough draft); ⟨The red round royal face of portly Wales⟩ The red round face of unexpected Wales *L* (fair copy)   9–10 The climax is complete—the bard is done— | He who would number kisses—merits none. *L* (both copies)

202. Copy text: *MS. L*
  1 to judge of] ⟨and meet with⟩ *L*   2 Sam's face is] But thou art *L*, *alternate reading*
  3–4 ⟨If thou lookst lively—the world's begun to rail | If sad—I've six editions yet for sale.⟩
  L   3 ⟨If thou lookst friendly—the news is plaguey fearful / that omen is most fearful⟩ *L*

203   ## Translation from Martial [VI. 53]

Jack supped—and drank—and went to bed,
Morn breaks—and finds the sleeper dead.
What caused this healthy man's perdition?
Alas! he *dreamt* of his *Physician*.

[1812]

204   ## [Verses on W. J. Fitzgerald]

What's writ on me, cries Fitz, I never read.
What's writ by thee, dear Fitz, none will indeed.
The case stands simply thus then, honest Fitz—
Thou and thine enemies are fairly quits;
Or rather would be, if for time to come   5
They luckily were *deaf*, or *thou* wert dumb.
But to their *pens*, while scribblers add their tongues,
The Waiter only can escape their *lungs*!

[1812]

203. Copy text: *MS. TP*, collated with *MS. L*
title   *untitled in L*
  1 He laughed—he quaffed—supped—went to bed—*L*   2 Morn] Day *L*

204. Copy text: *MS. M*, collated with *MS. PM*, *Paris1822*, *C*

205   The Giaour,
A FRAGMENT OF A TURKISH TALE

'One fatal remembrance—one sorrow that throws
It's bleak shade alike o'er our joys and our woes—
To which Life nothing darker nor brighter can bring,
For which joy hath no balm—and affliction no sting.'
                                        MOORE

TO

SAMUEL ROGERS, ESQ.

AS A SLIGHT BUT MOST SINCERE TOKEN

OF ADMIRATION OF HIS GENIUS;

RESPECT FOR HIS CHARACTER,

AND GRATITUDE FOR HIS FRIENDSHIP;

THIS PRODUCTION IS INSCRIBED BY

HIS OBLIGED AND AFFECTIONATE SERVANT,

BYRON.

ADVERTISEMENT

THE tale which these disjointed fragments present, is founded
upon circumstances now less common in the East than formerly;
either because the ladies are more circumspect than in the 'olden
time'; or because the Christians have better fortune or less enter-
prise. The story, when entire, contained the adventures of a female 5
slave, who was thrown, in the Mussulman manner, into the sea for
infidelity, and avenged by a young Venetian, her lover, at the time

---

205. Copy text: *Giaour edn. 7*, collated with *MSS. L, M, LA, MA, OA*, all Proofs and
Revises, *editions 1–6* and *8–14, 1831, 1832, C, More*
title   The Giaour. Fragments of a Turkish Tale, Translated. *L* epigraph *not in L*   To
... bring] O'er . . . fling *edns. 2–6*

Advertisement
    4 fortune] luck *M and 1st edn.*   5–14 The story . . . of the faithful] *added in 2nd
edn.*

the Seven Islands were possessed by the Republic of Venice, and
soon after the Arnauts were beaten back from the Morea, which
10 they had ravaged for some time subsequent to the Russian invasion.
The desertion of the Mainotes, on being refused the plunder of
Misitra, led to the abandonment of that enterprise, and to the
desolation of the Morea, during which the cruelty exercised on all
sides was unparalleled even in the annals of the faithful.

No breath of air to break the wave
That rolls below the Athenian's grave,
That tomb which, gleaming o'er the cliff,
First greets the homeward-veering skiff,
High o'er the land he saved in vain—   5
When shall such hero live again?

★   ★   ★   ★   ★   ★   ★   ★

Fair clime! where every season smiles
Benignant o'er those blessed isles,
Which seen from far Colonna's height,
Make glad the heart that hails the sight,   10
And lend to loneliness delight.
There mildly dimpling—Ocean's cheek
Reflects the tints of many a peak
Caught by the laughing tides that lave
These Edens of the eastern wave;   15
And if at times a transient breeze
Break the blue chrystal of the seas,
Or sweep one blossom from the trees,
How welcome is each gentle air,
That wakes and wafts the odours there!   20
For there—the Rose o'er crag or vale,
Sultana of the Nightingale,
The maid for whom his melody—
His thousand songs are heard on high,

Text

3 That grave which ⟨neither⟩ white along the cliff *L*   4 veering] steering *L*
6 When shall] Ah! would *L*   7 Fair] ⟨Blest⟩ *MA2*   where . . . smiles] where
ceaseless summer smiles *MA2, 3* ⟨where endless summer smiles⟩ *Proof 9*   12–14 There
shine the bright abodes ye seek | Like dimples upon Ocean's cheek— | So smiling round the
waters lave *MA2*   12 ⟨There sparkle the abodes ye seek⟩ *MA3*   13 Deep sink
the ⟨shades⟩ steeps of many a peak *cancelled MA3*   14 Caught by] So smooth *MA3*
17 blue] smooth *MA2*   18 sweep] brush *MA2*   19 welcome] grateful *MA2,
3 and 2nd edn.; cor. Proof 11*   20 odours] fragrance *MA2, 3 and 2nd edn.; cor. Proof 13*
23–4 *MS. insertion Proof 11*

Blooms blushing to her lover's tale;   25
His queen, the garden queen, his Rose,
Unbent by winds, unchill'd by snows,
Far from the winters of the west
By every breeze and season blest,
Returns the sweets by nature given   30
In softest incense back to heaven;
And grateful yields that smiling sky
Her fairest hue and fragrant sigh.
And many a summer flower is there,
And many a shade that love might share,   35
And many a grotto, meant for rest,
That holds the pirate for a guest;
Whose bark in sheltering cove below
Lurks for the passing peaceful prow,
Till the gay mariner's guitar   40
Is heard, and seen the evening star;
Then stealing with the muffled oar,
Far shaded by the rocky shore,
Rush the night-prowlers on the prey,
And turn to groans his roundelay.   45
Strange—that where Nature lov'd to trace,
As if for Gods, a dwelling-place,
And every charm and grace hath mixed
Within the paradise she fixed—
There man, enamour'd of distress,   50
Should mar it into wilderness,
And trample, brute-like, o'er each flower
That tasks not one laborious hour;
Nor claims the culture of his hand
To bloom along the fairy land,   55
But springs as to preclude his care,
And sweetly woos him—but to spare!
Strange—that where all is peace beside
There passion riots in her pride,
And lust and rapine wildly reign,   60
To darken o'er the fair domain.
It is as though the fiends prevail'd

51 mar it into] wanton ⟨oer⟩ in a *MA2*   55 fairy] teeming *MA2*; ⟨willing⟩ *MA3*
59 riots] rages *MA2*   61 To darken] ⟨Deforming / And⟩ *MA3*

Against the seraphs they assail'd,
And fixed, on heavenly thrones, should dwell
The freed inheritors of hell—   65
So soft the scene, so form'd for joy,
So curst the tyrants that destroy!

He who hath bent him o'er the dead,
Ere the first day of death is fled;
The first dark day of nothingness,   70
The last of danger and distress;
(Before Decay's effacing fingers
Have swept the lines where beauty lingers)
And mark'd the mild angelic air—
The rapture of repose that's there—   75
The fixed yet tender traits that streak
The languor of the placid cheek,
And—but for that sad shrouded eye,
    That fires not—wins not—weeps not—now—
    And but for that chill changeless brow,   80
Where cold Obstruction's apathy
Appals the gazing mourner's heart,
As if to him it could impart
The doom he dreads, yet dwells upon—
Yes—but for these and these alone,   85
Some moments—aye—one treacherous hour,
He still might doubt the tyrant's power,
So fair—so calm—so softly seal'd
The first—last look—by death reveal'd!
Such is the aspect of this shore—   90
'Tis Greece—but living Greece no more!
  So coldly sweet, so deadly fair,
We start—for soul is wanting there.

65 inheritors] inhabitants *MA2*   71 danger and] doom and of *MA4*   72 Before
. . . effacing] Before Corruption's cankering *MA4*   73 swept the lines] tinged the hue
MA4   74 mild angelic] soft and settled *MA4*; almost dreaming *MA5*   75 That
dwells with all but Spirit there *MA4*; Which speaks the sweet repose that's there *MA5*
76 traits that streak] lines that speak *MA4*   77 The languor of] Of Peace along *MA4*
79 wins] pleads *MA4*   80 chill] ⟨cold⟩ *MA4*   chill changeless] pale chilling *MA4*
81 Whose touch tells of Mortality *MA4*; Whose touch thrills with mortality *MA5 and
2nd edn.*   82 And curdles to the gazer's heart *MA4, 5 and 2nd edn.*   84 dreads
. . . upon] only looks upon *MA4*   86 A moment—yet—a little hour *MA4*   87 He]
We *MA4, 5 and 2nd edn.*   92 sweet] ⟨soft⟩ *MA5*   93 We . . . soul] ⟨We
marvel soul⟩ *MA4*

Hers is the loveliness in death,
That parts not quite with parting breath;   95
But beauty with that fearful bloom,
That hue which haunts it to the tomb—
Expression's last receding ray,
A gilded halo hovering round decay,
The farewell beam of Feeling past away!   100
Spark of that flame—perchance of heavenly birth—
Which gleams—but warms no more its cherish'd earth!

Clime of the unforgotten brave!—
Whose land from plain to mountain-cave
Was Freedom's home or Glory's grave—   105
Shrine of the mighty! can it be,
That this is all remains of thee?
Approach thou craven crouching slave—
Say, is not this Thermopylae?
These waters blue that round you lave   110
Oh servile offspring of the free—
Pronounce what sea, what shore is this?
The gulf, the rock of Salamis!
These scenes—their story not unknown—
Arise, and make again your own;   115
Snatch from the ashes of your sires
The embers of their former fires,
And he who in the strife expires
Will add to theirs a name of fear,
That Tyranny shall quake to hear,   120
And leave his sons a hope, a fame,
They too will rather die than shame;
For Freedom's battle once begun,

98–9 Expression's bright departing ray— | A halo gilding round decay! *OA1*   102 gleams
. . . more] fain once more would warm *MA4, cancelled Proof 9*   103 Clime] ⟨Land⟩
MA6   104 ⟨Whose every plain and mount and cave⟩ *MA6*   106 Shrine . . .
mighty] ⟨Fountain of Wisdom⟩ *MA6*; ⟨Fountain / Temple of Wisdom⟩ *MA6*   108 ⟨Ye⟩
Oh the slave approaches *cancelled MA6*   109 Say] Why *MA6*   110 These]
⟨Does / You⟩ *MA6*   111 Oh] ⟨Ye⟩ *MA6*   Oh servile] ⟨Degenerate⟩ *MA6*
112 Pronounce . . . sea] How name ye then—*MA6*   113 gulf] wave *MA6*
114 ⟨Nor yet to you these⟩ *MA6*   These scenes] ⟨These tales⟩ *MA6*   115 again]
them all *MA6*   116 Snatch from] ⟨Search in⟩ *MA6*   118 strife] cause *MA6*
119 Will add a name of fate to them | Well worthy of his noble stem *MA6*   add to] ⟨add
unto⟩ *MA6*   121 hope] ⟨heritage⟩ *MA6*

Bequeathed by bleeding Sire to Son,
Though baffled oft is ever won.   125
Bear witness, Greece, thy living page,
Attest it many a deathless age!
While kings in dusty darkness hid,
Have left a nameless pyramid,
Thy heroes—though the general doom   130
Hath swept the column from their tomb,
A mightier monument command,
The mountains of their native land!
There points thy Muse to stranger's eye,
The graves of those that cannot die!   135
'Twere long to tell, and sad to trace,
Each step from splendour to disgrace,
Enough—no foreign foe could quell
Thy soul, till from itself it fell,
Yes! Self-abasement pav'd the way   140
To villain-bonds and despot-sway.

What can he tell who treads thy shore?
    No legend of thine olden time,
No theme on which the muse might soar,
High as thine own in days of yore,   145
    When man was worthy of thy clime.
The hearts within thy valleys bred,
The fiery souls that might have led
    Thy sons to deeds sublime;
Now crawl from cradle to the grave,   150
Slaves—nay, the bondsmen of a slave,
    And callous, save to crime;
Stain'd with each evil that pollutes
Mankind, where least above the brutes;
Without even savage virtue blest,   155
Without one free or valiant breast.

    124 ⟨Unlike the⟩ Commenced by Sire—renewed by Son MA6   125 Though baffled]
⟨Flags not till⟩ MA6   127 deathless] former MA6   128 dusty darkness] dark
oblivion MA6   130 Thy ... though] Thy sons although MA6   134 There let
the Muse direct thine eye MA6   136 'Twere] Though MA6   137 Each step
from] ⟨The course⟩ The fall from MA6   139 Thy] ⟨That⟩ MA6   140 Yes!]
And edns. 5–6, cor. in Proof 25; Yet! C; Till self-abasement ⟨paved⟩ smoothed the way MA6
141 despot] stranger's MA6   145 in days of yore] ⟨ethereal lore⟩ MA6   147 within
thy valleys] amid thy mountains MA6   150 crawl] ⟨form⟩ MA6   154 where]
⟨when⟩ MA6   155 even] ⟨the⟩ MA6   156 Without] ⟨Which⟩ MA6

Still to the neighbouring ports they waft
Proverbial wiles, and ancient craft,
In this the subtle Greek is found,
For this, and this alone, renown'd.   160
In vain might Liberty invoke
The spirit to its bondage broke,
Or raise the neck that courts the yoke:
No more her sorrows I bewail,
Yet this will be a mournful tale,   165
And they who listen may believe,
Who heard it first had cause to grieve.

   ★   ★   ★   ★   ★   ★   ★

   Far, dark, along the blue sea glancing,
The shadows of the rocks advancing,
Start on the fisher's eye like boat   170
Of island-pirate or Mainote;
And fearful for his light caique
He shuns the near but doubtful creek,
Though worn and weary with his toil,
And cumber'd with his scaly spoil,   175
Slowly, yet strongly, plies the oar,
Till Port Leone's safer shore
Receives him by the lovely light
That best becomes an Eastern night.

   ★   ★   ★   ★   ★   ★   ★   ★

   Who thundering comes on blackest steed?   180
With slacken'd bit and hoof of speed,
Beneath the clattering iron's sound
The cavern'd echoes wake around
In lash for lash, and bound for bound;
The foam that streaks the courser's side,   185
Seems gather'd from the ocean-tide:

157 Still . . . ports] Now to the neighboring shores *MA6*   158 Proverbial . . . ancient]
⟨Their ancient and proverbial⟩ *MA6*   160 For] In *MA6*   161 In . . . Liberty]
⟨Yet only with equal⟩ *MA6*   163 Or] ⟨Who⟩ *MA6*   168 Far, dark] High bright *L*
170 Start on] Seem to ⟨Look⟩ *L*; *cor. in Proof 4*   173 He silent shuns the doubtful
creek *M, L*   174 Though] ⟨And⟩ *M* ⟨till⟩ *L*   177 Port Leone's] ⟨Draco⟩ *L*
180 on . . . steed] ⟨along the shore⟩ *L*   181 slacken'd] ⟨bloody⟩ *L*   184 ⟨And
answer to the courser's bound⟩ *L*   185 that . . . side] that ⟨glistens on his⟩ streaks his
glistening side *L*   186 gather'd] ⟨borrowed / scattered⟩ *L*

Though weary waves are sunk to rest,
There's none within his rider's breast,
And though to-morrow's tempest lower,
'Tis calmer than thy heart, young Giaour!   190
I know thee not, I loathe thy race,
But in thy lineaments I trace
What time shall strengthen, not efface;
Though young and pale, that sallow front
Is scath'd by fiery passion's brunt,   195
Though bent on earth thine evil eye
As meteor-like thou glidest by,
Right well I view, and deem thee one
Whom Othman's sons should slay or shun.

On—on he hastened—and he drew   200
My gaze of wonder as he flew:
Though like a demon of the night
He passed and vanished from my sight;
His aspect and his air impressed
A troubled memory on my breast;   205
And long upon my startled ear
Rung his dark courser's hoofs of fear.
He spurs his steed—he nears the steep,
That jutting shadows o'er the deep—
He winds around—he hurries by—   210
The rock relieves him from mine eye—
For well I ween unwelcome he
Whose glance is fixed on those that flee;
And not a star but shines too bright
On him who takes such timeless flight.   215
He wound along—but ere he passed
One glance he snatched—as if his last—
A moment checked his wheeling steed—
A moment breathed him from his speed—

187 Though weary] But no—though L   188 his rider's] that horseman's M, L
189 though . . . tempest] when tomorrow's storm shall L   195 Is . . . by] Is ⟨marked⟩
scathed with L   196 Though . . . earth] Though scarcely marked M, L; cor. Proof 7
thine evil eye] thy gleaming eye L   200 and] ⟨yet / but⟩ MA7   201 With him
my ⟨roused and wondering view⟩ wonder as he flew MA7; cor. Proof 13   213 Whose
. . . flee] ⟨Whose ? gaze shall follow thee⟩ MA7; Whose ⟨visions / gazes⟩ glances shall follow
thee cancelled MA7   215 On . . . flight] For ⟨those who take so fast a flight⟩ MA7;
cor. Proof 13   217 glance] gaze MA7; cor. Proof 13

A moment on his stirrup stood—   220
Why looks he o'er the olive wood?—
The crescent glimmers on the hill,
The Mosque's high lamps are quivering still;
Though too remote for sound to wake
In echoes of the far tophaike,   225
The flashes of each joyous peal
Are seen to prove the Moslem's zeal.
To-night—set Rhamazani's sun—
To-night—the Bairam feast's begun—
To-night—but who and what art thou   230
Of foreign garb and fearful brow?
And what are these to thine or thee,
That thou should'st either pause or flee?
He stood—some dread was on his face—
Soon Hatred settled in its place—   235
It rose not with the reddening flush
Of transient Anger's hasty blush,
But pale as marble o'er the tomb,
Whose ghastly whiteness aids its gloom.
His brow was bent—his eye was glazed—   240
He raised his arm, and fiercely raised;
And sternly shook his hand on high,
As doubting to return or fly;—
Impatient of his flight delayed
Here loud his raven charger neighed—   245
Down glanced that hand, and grasped his blade—
That sound had burst his waking dream,
As Slumber starts at owlet's scream.—
The spur hath lanced his courser's sides—
Away—away—for life he rides—   250
Swift as the hurled on high jerreed,
Springs to the touch his startled steed,
The rock is doubled—and the shore

---

221 Why . . . o'er] And looked along *MA7*   236–7 It rose not with the reddening
flush | Of transient Anger's darkening blush *MA7, 1st–11th and 13th, 14th edns.; cor.*
Proof 28   reddening . . . hasty] hasty . . . darkening *12th edn., Text J J*   236 rose]
⟨fixed⟩ *MA7*   243 to return] if to stay *MA7; cor. Proof 13*   244–5 Impatient . . .
Here] Then turned it swiftly to his blade As *MA7; cor. Proof 13*   244 ⟨Too
firmly curbed—too long delayed⟩ *MS. insertion Proof 13*   246 *MS. insertion Proof 13*
247 That . . . burst] The sound dispelled *MA7; cor. Proof 13*   248 Slumber] sleeper
MA7; cancelled Proof 13   251 hurled on high] ⟨flight of hurled⟩ *Proof 22*

Shakes with the clattering tramp no more—
The crag is won—no more is seen   255
His Christian crest and haughty mien.—
'Twas but an instant—he restrained
That fiery barb so sternly reined—
'Twas but a moment that he stood,
Then sped as if by death pursued;   260
But in that instant, o'er his soul
Winters of Memory seemed to roll,
And gather in that drop of time
A life of pain, an age of crime.
O'er him who loves, or hates, or fears,   265
Such moment pours the grief of years—
What felt *he* then—at once opprest
By all that most distracts the breast?
That pause—which pondered o'er his fate,
Oh, who its dreary length shall date!   270
Though in Time's record nearly nought,
It was Eternity to Thought!
For infinite as boundless space
The thought that Conscience must embrace,
Which in itself can comprehend   275
Woe without name—or hope—or end.—

The hour is past, the Giaour is gone,
And did he fly or fall alone?
Woe to that hour he came or went,
The curse for Hassan's sin was sent   280
To turn a palace to a tomb;
He came, he went, like the Simoom,
That harbinger of fate and gloom,
Beneath whose widely-wasting breath
The very cypress droops to death—   285
Dark tree—still sad, when others' grief is fled,
The only constant mourner o'er the dead!

255 won] turned *MA7*; *cor. Proof 13*   257–8 he . . . reined] though so long When
thus dilated in my song *MA7*; *3rd–6th edns.*   259 a moment] an instant *MA7*; *3rd–6th
edns.*   266 pours the grief of] holds a thousand *MA7*   pours] ⟨proves⟩ *Proof 13*
276 Woe] ⟨Grief⟩ *MA8*   278 But neither fled nor fell alone *L, M; cor. Proof 13*
280 The curse for] ⟨A curse on⟩ *L*   for . . . sin] to . . . race *L*   281 *Written after
line 283 in L, M*   283 fate] ⟨death⟩ *M*

The steed is vanished from the stall,
No serf is seen in Hassan's hall;
The lonely Spider's thin grey pall   290
Waves slowly widening o'er the wall;
The Bat builds in his Haram bower;
And in the fortress of his power
The Owl usurps the beacon-tower;
The wild-dog howls o'er the fountain's brim,   295
With baffled thirst, and famine, grim,
For the stream has shrunk from its marble bed,
Where the weeds and the desolate dust are spread.
'Twas sweet of yore to see it play
And chase the sultriness of day—   300
As springing high the silver dew
In whirls fantastically flew,
And flung luxurious coolness round
The air, and verdure o'er the ground.—
'Twas sweet, when cloudless stars were bright,   305
To view the wave of watery light,
And hear its melody by night.—
And oft had Hassan's Childhood played
Around the verge of that cascade;
And oft upon his mother's breast   310
That sound had harmonized his rest;
And oft had Hassan's Youth along
Its bank been sooth'd by Beauty's song;
And softer seemed each melting tone
Of Music mingled with its own.—   315
But ne'er shall Hassan's Age repose

289 serf] ⟨slave⟩ *MA10a*   290 The lonely] And wide the *MA10a*   291 Is
curtain'd o'er the splendid wall *MA10ab and 4th edn.; cor. Proof 22*   292 Haram]
mother's *MA10ab; cor. Proof 15*   294 usurps the] hath fixed her *MA10ab; cor. Proof 16*
295 The . . . fountain's] ⟨The wild dogs steal in the court⟩ *MA10a*   295–6 The wild dog
howls oer the fountain's brink | But vainly lolls his tongue to drink *MA10ab; cor. Proof 15*
296 ⟨With thirst and famine doubly grim⟩ *MA10a*   298 Where . . . are] Where
Desolation's dust is *MA10a*   299 see] ⟨hear⟩ *MA10a*   301–2 The silver
dew of coldness sprinkling | In drops fantastically twinkling *MA10a*   301 As . . . high]
As from its spring *MA10b; cor. Proof 16*   303 flung] dashed *MA10ab*   304 the
ground] its bound *MA10ab*   305 when cloudless] ⟨of yore when the⟩ *MA10a*
306 the] ⟨its⟩ *MA10a*   307 And hear] ⟨While spread⟩ *MA10a*   308 ⟨While in
the / While spread⟩ *MA10a*   309 verge] ⟨bank⟩ *MA10a*   310 And oft upon] ⟨Or
sheltered on⟩ *MA10a*   311 That . . . his] ⟨Where sound hath harmonized to⟩ *MA10a*
314 softer . . . melting] ⟨sweeter . . . equal⟩ *MA10a*   each melting] its ⟨equal / charmed⟩
melting *MA10a*   melting] ⟨swelling⟩ *Proof 16*   316 ⟨But never now shall age recline⟩
MA10a

Along the brink at Twilight's close—
The stream that filled that font is fled—
The blood that warmed his heart is shed!—
And here no more shall human voice   320
Be heard to rage—regret—rejoice—
The last sad note that swelled the gale
Was woman's wildest funeral wail—
That quenched in silence—all is still,
But the lattice that flaps when the wind is shrill—   325
Though raves the gust, and floods the rain,
No hand shall close its clasp again.
On desert sands 'twere joy to scan
The rudest steps of fellow man,
So here the very voice of Grief   330
Might wake an Echo like relief—
At least 'twould say, 'all are not gone;
There lingers Life, though but in one'—
For many a gilded chamber's there,
Which Solitude might well forbear;   335
Within that dome as yet Decay
Hath slowly worked her cankering way—
But Gloom is gathered o'er the gate,
Nor there the Fakir's self will wait;
Nor there will wandering Dervise stay,   340
For Bounty cheers not his delay;
Nor there will weary stranger halt
To bless the sacred 'bread and salt'.

317 brink] ⟨font⟩ *Proof 15*   318–19 For thirsty fox and jackall gaunt | May vainly
for its waters pant *MA10ab*; *cor. Proof 15*   And ⟨vainly for its⟩ for its vanished waters
pant | The thirsty fox and jackall gaunt *MA10a*   318 The famished fox ⟨For ever the fox
and⟩—the wild dog gaunt *cancelled MA10a*   321 rage . . . rejoice] sadden or to rejoice
MA10a   322 The] ⟨But⟩ *MA10a*   swelled] filled *cor. Proof 15*   324 *That*] ⟨And⟩
MA10a   326–9 ⟨In desarts⟩ As in the desart cheers the sound | That leads where
life may yet be found *MA10a*   326–7 MS. insertion Proof 16   326 Though
raves] ⟨Blow on thou / Though chill⟩ *Proof 15*   328–9 MS. insertion Proof 15   330 So
here] And even *MA10ab, MA10b*   331 ⟨To⟩ Might ⟨yield to echo's care⟩ *MA10a*
Might wake] Might ⟨yield⟩ strike *MA10b*; ⟨To⟩ Might ⟨yield to echo's care⟩ strike *MA10b*
332–3   As in the desart cheers the sound |
                          That leads where life may yet be found *MA10a*
                          ⟨In desarts welcome were the sound |
                          That led where Man might still be found⟩ *Proof 15*
333 There . . . life] ⟨Here life is left⟩ *MA10a*   335 Unmeet for Solitude to share
MA10ab and 4th–6th edns., cor. in OA7   339 Nor . . . Fakir's] ⟨Nor hath the Der-
vish⟩ *MA10a*   340 stay] ⟨bless⟩ *MA10a*   343 To . . . sacred] To share the
master's *MA10ab and 4th–6th edns.; cor. in OA7*   share] ⟨taste⟩ *MA10a*

Alike must Wealth and Poverty
Pass heedless and unheeded by,   345
For Courtesy and Pity died
With Hassan on the mountain side.—
His roof—that refuge unto men—
Is Desolation's hungry den.—
The guest flies the hall, and the vassal from labour,   350
Since his turban was cleft by the infidel's sabre!

      ★   ★   ★   ★   ★   ★   ★   ★

I hear the sound of coming feet,
But not a voice mine ear to greet—
More near—each turban I can scan,
And silver-sheathed ataghan;   355
The foremost of the band is seen
An Emir by his garb of green:
    'Ho! who art thou!'—'this low salam
Replies of Moslem faith I am.'
'The burthen ye so gently bear,   360
Seems one that claims your utmost care,
And, doubtless, holds some precious freight,
My humble bark would gladly wait.'

'Thou speakest sooth, thy skiff unmoor,
And waft us from the silent shore;   365
Nay, leave the sail still furl'd, and ply
The nearest oar that's scatter'd by,
And midway to those rocks where sleep
The channel'd waters dark and deep.—
Rest from your task—so—bravely done,   370
Our course has been right swiftly run,

344 Alike] ⟨With him⟩ MA10a   345 unheeded] ⟨neglected⟩ MA10a   348 His
roof—that] That roof a MA10a   349 hungry] chosen MA10a   350 ⟨And cold
Hospitality shrinks from his labour / The slave fled his hall and the serf left his labour⟩
MA10a   Ah! who for the traveller's solace will labour MA10b; cancelled Proof 15   Ah!
there Hospitality light is thy labour MA10a   light is thy] ceased from her cor. in Proof
15, 4th edn.   350 Cor. to received version in Proof 21   358–9 'Ho . . . Replies]
Take ye and give ye that Salam | That says L, M   360 ye so gently] in those arms
ye L   363 ⟨That yonder barks at anchor wait⟩ L; ⟨That one of yonder barks may
wait⟩ M   364 sooth] ⟨well⟩ L   365 And ⟨bear us⟩ steer but gently from the
shore L   366–7 and ply . . . that's] ⟨and the oar that dangles nigh⟩ L   368 to
those] near the L   370 task] toil L

Yet 'tis the longest voyage, I trow,
That one of'—   ★   ★   ★   ★

★   ★   ★   ★   ★   ★   ★   ★

Sullen it plunged, and slowly sank,
The calm wave rippled to the bank;   375
I watch'd it as it sank, methought
Some motion from the current caught
Bestirr'd it more,—'twas but the beam
That chequer'd o'er the living stream—
I gaz'd, till vanishing from view,   380
Like lessening pebble it withdrew;
Still less and less, a speck of white
That gemm'd the tide, then mock'd the sight;
And all its hidden secrets sleep,
Known but to Genii of the deep,   385
Which, trembling in their coral caves,
They dare not whisper to the waves.

★   ★   ★   ★   ★   ★   ★   ★

As rising on its purple wing
The insect-queen of eastern spring,
O'er emerald meadows of Kashmeer   390
Invites the young pursuer near,
And leads him on from flower to flower
A weary chase and wasted hour,
Then leaves him, as it soars on high
With panting heart and tearful eye: 395
So Beauty lures the full-grown child
With hue as bright, and wing as wild;
A chase of idle hopes and fears,
Begun in folly, closed in tears.
If won, to equal ills betrayed,   400
Woe waits the insect and the maid,
A life of pain, the loss of peace,
From infant's play, or man's caprice:

373 of'—] ⟨of us shall ever go⟩ L; That one'— M, 1st–4th edns.   381 lessening] ⟨the
white⟩ L   383 tide] wave L   389 ⟨The fairest insect-child of spring⟩ L   390 ⟨The
Butterfly of soft Cashmeer⟩ L   391 young pursuer] ⟨playful infant⟩ L   392 And
leads him] ⟨Still following⟩ L   394 soars] mounts L   397 With] ⟨As⟩ L
400 won . . . ills] caught—to fate alike L, M   403 infant's] ⟨child's rude⟩ L; or edn.
7, cor. in Proof 25; and all other edns.

The lovely toy so fiercely sought
Has lost its charm by being caught,   405
For every touch that wooed its stay
Has brush'd the brightest hues away
Till charm, and hue, and beauty gone,
'Tis left to fly or fall alone.
With wounded wing, or bleeding breast,   410
Ah! where shall either victim rest?
Can this with faded pinion soar
From rose to tulip as before?
Or Beauty, blighted in an hour,
Find joy within her broken bower?   415
No: gayer insects fluttering by
Ne'er droop the wing o'er those that die,
And lovelier things have mercy shewn
To every failing but their own,
And every woe a tear can claim   420
Except an erring sister's shame.

★   ★   ★   ★   ★   ★   ★   ★

The Mind, that broods o'er guilty woes,
     Is like the Scorpion girt by fire,
In circle narrowing as it glows
The flames around their captive close,   425
Till inly search'd by thousand throes,
     And maddening in her ire,
One sad and sole relief she knows,
The sting she nourish'd for her foes,
Whose venom never yet was vain,   430
Gives but one pang, and cures all pain,
And darts into her desperate brain.—
So do the dark in soul expire,
Or live like Scorpion girt by fire;
So writhes the mind Remorse hath riven,   435
Unfit for earth, undoom'd for heaven,

404 lovely] living L   406 ⟨But ah the / A moment may its vivid hue⟩ L   407 the
edn. 7, cor. in Proof 25; its all other edns.   410 wounded] broken L   416 ⟨Ah
no / The insects⟩ L   fluttering by] ⟨soaring high⟩ L   418 lovelier] ⟨Woman⟩ L
419 failing but] ⟨sin except⟩ L   420 every] ⟨lovers⟩ L   a tear] ⟨can pity⟩ L   422 o'er
guilty] ⟨upon secret⟩ L   424 ⟨Now ? the flames enclose⟩ L   425 ⟨The gathering
flames around her close⟩ M   435 Remorse hath] by conscience L, M and 1st–2nd
edns.; cor. Proof 13

Darkness above, despair beneath,
Around it flame, within it death!—

★   ★   ★   ★   ★   ★   ★   ★

Black Hassan from the Haram flies,
Nor bends on woman's form his eyes,   440
The unwonted chase each hour employs,
Yet shares he not the hunter's joys.
Not thus was Hassan wont to fly
When Leila dwelt in his Serai.
Doth Leila there no longer dwell?   445
That tale can only Hassan tell:
Strange rumours in our city say
Upon that eve she fled away;
When Rhamazan's last sun was set,
And flashing from each minaret   450
Millions of lamps proclaim'd the feast
Of Bairam through the boundless East.
'Twas then she went as to the bath,
Which Hassan vainly search'd in wrath,
But she was flown her master's rage   455
In likeness of a Georgian page;
And far beyond the Moslem's power
Had wrong'd him with the faithless Giaour.
Somewhat of this had Hassan deem'd,
But still so fond, so fair she seem'd,   460
Too well he trusted to the slave
Whose treachery deserv'd a grave:
And on that eve had gone to mosque,
And thence to feast in his kiosk.
Such is the tale his Nubians tell,   465
Who did not watch their charge too well;
But others say, that on that night,
By pale Phingari's trembling light,
The Giaour upon his jet black steed
Was seen—but seen alone to speed   470

439 Black] ⟨Dark⟩ L   440 form] face 1st–6th edns.   443 Not . . . wont] Yet
Hassan was not wont L   448 eve] ⟨night⟩ L   450 And . . . each] And ⟨up⟩
flashing from the cancelled L   451 Millions of] ⟨A thousand⟩ L   455 her
master's] this Muslim's L   465 Such] ⟨This⟩ L

THE GIAOUR.

AS MIDST HER HANDMAIDS IN THE HALL

SHE STOOD SUPERIOR TO THEM ALL.

PUBLISHED BY JOHN MURRAY, ALBEMARLE STREET, DEC.R 1, 1814.

The Giaour lines 498–9

(Reproduced with the permission of the British Library)

With bloody spur along the shore,
Nor maid nor page behind him bore.

★　　★　　★　　★　　★　　★　　★

Her eye's dark charm 'twere vain to tell,
But gaze on that of the Gazelle,
It will assist thy fancy well,   475
As large, as languishingly dark,
But Soul beam'd forth in every spark
That darted from beneath the lid,
Bright as the jewel of Giamschid.
Yea, *Soul*, and should our prophet say   480
That form was nought but breathing clay,
By Alla! I would answer nay;
Though on Al-Sirat's arch I stood,
Which totters o'er the fiery flood,
With Paradise within my view,   485
And all his Houris beckoning through.
Oh! who young Leila's glance could read
And keep that portion of his creed
Which saith, that woman is but dust,
A soulless toy for tyrant's lust?   490
On her might Muftis gaze, and own
That through her eye the Immortal shone—
On her fair cheek's unfading hue,
The young pomegranate's blossoms strew
Their bloom in blushes ever new—   495
Her hair in hyacinthine flow
When left to roll its folds below,
As midst her handmaids in the hall
She stood superior to them all,
Hath swept the marble where her feet   500
Gleamed whiter than the mountain sleet

---

471 With bloody] ⟨Right swiftly / With fiery⟩ *L*   473 dark] ⟨soft⟩ *LA2*
474 gaze] ⟨look⟩ *LA2*   479 jewel] gem *LA2, 1st–4th edns.*; ruby *5th–6th edns.*
481 form] ⟨breast⟩ *LA2*   483 arch] ⟨rock⟩ *LA2* ⟨bridge⟩ *M*   484 Which]
⟨That⟩ *M*   487 Oh who that glance of hers could read *LA2*   494–5 strew . . .
new] ⟨view For there it blooms for ever new⟩ *LA2*   494 strew] ⟨grew⟩ *LA2*
496 ⟨Her waves of hyacinthine hair⟩ *LA2*   497 When . . . its] ⟨Which floating oer
her⟩ *LA2*   498 ⟨Had given / Would yield a month⟩ *LA2*   501 Gleamed . . . the]
Shone as if formed from *LA2*

Ere from the cloud that gave it birth,
It fell, and caught one stain of earth.
The cygnet nobly walks the water—
So moved on earth Circassia's daughter—   505
The loveliest bird of Franguestan!
As rears her crest the ruffled Swan,
  And spurns the wave with wings of pride,
When pass the steps of stranger man
  Along the banks that bound her tide;   510
Thus rose fair Leila's whiter neck:—
Thus armed with beauty would she check
Intrusion's glance, till Folly's gaze
Shrunk from the charms it meant to praise.
Thus high and graceful was her gait;   515
Her heart as tender to her mate—
Her mate—stern Hassan, who was he?
Alas! that name was not for thee!

    ★   ★   ★   ★   ★   ★   ★   ★

  Stern Hassan hath a journey ta'en
With twenty vassals in his train,   520
Each arm'd as best becomes a man
With arquebuss and ataghan;
The chief before, as deck'd for war,
Bears in his belt the scimitar
Stain'd with the best of Arnaut blood,   525
When in the pass the rebels stood,
And few return'd to tell the tale
Of what befell in Parne's vale.
The pistols which his girdle bore
Were those that once a pasha wore,   530
Which still, though gemm'd and boss'd with gold,
Even robbers tremble to behold.—
'Tis said he goes to woo a bride
More true than her who left his side;
The faithless slave that broke her bower,   535
And, worse than faithless, for a Giaour!—

    ★   ★   ★   ★   ★   ★   ★   ★

502 Ere from] ⟨Ere settling⟩ *LA2*   517 stern] dark *cor. Proof 13*   529 The
pistols in his belt he wore *L*   531 Which] ⟨And⟩ *L*   533 woo] gain *L*
535 ⟨Who left him at the midnight hour⟩ *L*

The sun's last rays are on the hill,
And sparkle in the fountain rill,
Whose welcome waters cool and clear,
Draw blessings from the mountaineer;   540
Here may the loitering merchant Greek
Find that repose 'twere vain to seek
In cities lodg'd too near his lord,
And trembling for his secret hoard—
Here may he rest where none can see,   545
In crowds a slave, in desarts free;
And with forbidden wine may stain
The bowl a Moslem must not drain.—

★   ★   ★   ★   ★   ★   ★   ★

The foremost Tartar's in the gap,
Conspicuous by his yellow cap,   550
The rest in lengthening line the while
Wind slowly through the long defile;
Above, the mountain rears a peak,
Where vultures whet the thirsty beak,
And theirs may be a feast to-night,   555
Shall tempt them down ere morrow's light.
Beneath, a river's wintry stream
Has shrunk before the summer beam,
And left a channel bleak and bare,
Save shrubs that spring to perish there.   560
Each side the midway path there lay
Small broken crags of granite gray,
By time or mountain lightning riven,
From summits clad in mists of heaven;
For where is he that hath beheld   565
The peak of Liakura unveil'd?

★   ★   ★   ★   ★   ★   ★   ★

540 mountaineer] ⟨traveller⟩ L   541 loitering] passing L   544 And] ⟨When⟩ L
545 rest . . . see] ⟨fill his cup with glee⟩ L   546 In . . . slave] ⟨And dream of
freedom⟩ L   547 And with] ⟨Or from the⟩ L   549 ⟨But if afar he hear the
sound⟩ L   554 thirsty] hungry L   561 ⟨The midway path around ?⟩ L
562 ⟨With shapeless crags of grey granite⟩ L   broken] ⟨shapeless⟩ L   563 lightning]
tempest L   564 clad in mists] clothed in ⟨clouds⟩ mists L   565 ⟨For who is he
that hath seen⟩ L   where . . . hath] ⟨who hath that peak⟩ L

They reach the grove of pine at last,
'Bismillah! now the peril's past;
For yonder view the opening plain,
And there we'll prick our steeds amain':   570
The Chiaus spake, and as he said,
A bullet whistled o'er his head;
The foremost Tartar bites the ground!
  Scarce had they time to check the rein
Swift from their steeds the riders bound,   575
  But three shall never mount again;
Unseen the foes that gave the wound,
  The dying ask revenge in vain.
With steel unsheath'd, and carbine bent,
Some o'er their courser's harness leant,   580
  Half shelter'd by the steed,
Some fly behind the nearest rock,
And there await the coming shock,
  Nor tamely stand to bleed
Beneath the shaft of foes unseen,   585
Who dare not quit their craggy screen.
Stern Hassan only from his horse
Disdains to light, and keeps his course,
Till fiery flashes in the van
Proclaim too sure the robber-clan   590
Have well secur'd the only way
Could now avail the promis'd prey;
Then curl'd his very beard with ire,
And glared his eye with fiercer fire.
'Though far and near the bullets hiss,   595
I've scaped a bloodier hour than this.'
And now the foe their covert quit,
And call his vassals to submit;
But Hassan's frown and furious word
Are dreaded more than hostile sword,   600
Nor of his little band a man

567 grove of pine] tufted grove L   568 Bismillah] Thank Allah L, M   573–4 Trans-
posed in L, M; cor. Proof 7   579 carbines M and 1st–6th edns.   580 o'er their
courser's] ⟨sheltered by their⟩ L   587 Stern] But L   592 ⟨That could⟩ L
Could . . . avail] Of rescue for L   594 glared] flamed L; ⟨flashed⟩ M   fiercer]
⟨native⟩ L   595 far and near] ⟨round⟩ L   598 his vassals] upon them L
599 frown] ⟨voice⟩ L

Resign'd carbine or ataghan—
Nor raised the craven cry, Amaun!
In fuller sight, more near and near,
The lately ambush'd foes appear,   605
And issuing from the grove advance,
Some who on battle charger prance.—
Who leads them on with foreign brand,
Far flashing in his red right hand?
' 'Tis he—'tis he—I know him now,   610
I know him by his pallid brow;
I know him by the evil eye
That aids his envious treachery;
I know him by his jet-black barb,
Though now array'd in Arnaut garb,   615
Apostate from his own vile faith,
It shall not save him from the death;
'Tis he, well met in any hour,
Lost Leila's love—accursed Giaour!'

As rolls the river into ocean,   620
In sable torrent wildly streaming;
  As the sea-tide's opposing motion
In azure column proudly gleaming,
Beats back the current many a rood,
In curling foam and mingling flood;   625
While eddying whirl, and breaking wave,
Roused by the blast of winter rave;
Through sparkling spray in thundering clash,
The lightnings of the waters flash
In awful whiteness o'er the shore,   630
That shines and shakes beneath the roar;
Thus—as the stream and ocean greet,
With waves that madden as they meet—
Thus join the bands whom mutual wrong,
And fate and fury drive along.   635
The bickering sabres' shivering jar;
  And pealing wide—or ringing near,

603 *MS. insertion Proof 9*   craven] coward *Proof 9; cor. Proof 10*   605 appear]
⟨draw near⟩ *L*   606–7 ⟨And some are issuing from the grove | As featly steeds are seen
to move⟩ *L*   619 Lost . . . accursed] ⟨My Leila's paramour⟩ *L*   626 breaking]
rushing *MA11*   630 awful] fearful *MA11*   634 join] ⟨must⟩ *MA11*

Its echoes on the throbbing ear,
The deathshot hissing from afar—
The shock—the shout—the groan of war—   640
 Reverberate along that vale,
 More suited to the shepherd's tale:
Though few the numbers—theirs the strife,
That neither spares nor speaks for life!
Ah! fondly youthful hearts can press,   645
To seize and share the dear caress;
But Love itself could never pant
For all that Beauty sighs to grant,
With half the fervour Hate bestows
Upon the last embrace of foes,   650
When grappling in the fight they fold
Those arms that ne'er shall lose their hold;
Friends meet to part—Love laughs at faith;—
True foes, once met, are joined till death!

★   ★   ★   ★   ★   ★   ★   ★

With sabre shiver'd to the hilt,   655
Yet dripping with the blood he spilt;
Yet strain'd within the sever'd hand
Which quivers round that faithless brand;
His turban far behind him roll'd,
And cleft in twain its firmest fold;   660
His flowing robe by falchion torn,
And crimson as those clouds of morn
That streak'd with dusky red, portend
The day shall have a stormy end;
A stain on every bush that bore   665
A fragment of his palampore,
His breast with wounds unnumber'd riven,
His back to earth, his face to heaven,
Fall'n Hassan lies—his unclos'd eye
Yet lowering on his enemy,   670

    641 Reverberate] ⟨Resound⟩ *MAii*   644 spares . . . speaks] gives . . . asks *MAii*;
cancelled Proof 9   645 hearts] ⟨Love⟩ *MAii*   661 by . . . torn] ⟨in fragments
rent⟩ *L*   662 crimson] ⟨purpled⟩ *L*   665 A . . . every] And stained was every *L*
667 breast] heart *1st edn.*   669 Fall'n] Dark *L*   670 lowering] ⟨threatening⟩ *L*

Painted by Tho.ˢ Stothard R.A.   Engraved by W.Finden.

GIAOUR.

HIS BACK TO EARTH, HIS FACE TO HEAVEN,
FALL'N HASSAN LIES. HIS UNCLOSED EYE
YET LOWERING ON HIS ENEMY.

PUBLISHED BY JOHN MURRAY, ALBEMARLE STREET, DEC.ᴿ 1.1814.

The Giaour lines 668–70

(*Reproduced with the permission of the British Library*)

As if the hour that seal'd his fate,
Surviving left his quenchless hate;
And o'er him bends that foe with brow
As dark as his that bled below.—

★　★　★　★　★　★　★　★

'Yes, Leila sleeps beneath the wave,　　　675
But his shall be a redder grave;
Her spirit pointed well the steel
Which taught that felon heart to feel.
He call'd the Prophet, but his power
Was vain against the vengeful Giaour:　　680
He call'd on Alla—but the word
Arose unheeded or unheard.
Thou Paynim fool!—could Leila's prayer
Be pass'd, and thine accorded there?
I watch'd my time, I leagu'd with these,　　685
The traitor in his turn to seize;
My wrath is wreak'd, the deed is done,
And now I go—but go alone.'

★　★　★　★　★　★　★
★　★　★　★　★　★　★

The browzing camels' bells are tinkling—
His Mother looked from her lattice high,　　690

672 Had vainly quenched his ⟨deepest⟩ living hate *L*　　676 his] ⟨thine⟩ *L*　　679 the
Prophet] ⟨on Mahmet⟩ *L*　　682 ⟨Too late resounded to be heard⟩ *L*　　683 could
. . . prayer] ⟨was Leila's grave⟩ *L*　　684 accorded] be granted *L*　　687 My . . .
wreak'd] I've crushed my wrath *L*

689–94　　　　　　　His mother looked from the lattice high
　　　　　　　　　⟨And watched each train that passed by⟩
　　　　　　　　　With ⟨beating⟩ throbbing heart and eager eye—
　　　　　　　　　The browzing Camels bells are tinkling
　　　　　　　　　And the last beam of twilight twinkling
　　　　　　　　　Tis eve—his train should now be nigh　*MA12b*
　　　　　　　　　The browzing Camels bells are tinkling
　　　　　　　　　And the first ⟨star of twilight / twilight planet⟩
　　　　　　　　　　　beam of Even twinkling
　　　　　　　　　His mother looked from the lattice high
　　　　　　　　　With throbbing breast and eager eye—
　　　　　　　　　Tis twilight—sure his train is nigh—　*MA12a*
　　　　　　　　　The browzing camel's bells are tinkling,
　　　　　　　　　The dews of Eve the pasture sprinkling,
　　　　　　　　　And rising planets faintly twinkling:
　　　　　　　　　His mother looked from her lattice high,
　　　　　　　　　With throbbing breast and eager eye—　*4th edn.; cor. Proof 21*

She saw the dews of eve besprinkling
The pasture green beneath her eye,
  She saw the planets faintly twinkling,
' 'Tis twilight—sure his train is nigh.'—
She could not rest in the garden-bower,   695
But gazed through the grate of his steepest tower—
'Why comes he not? his steeds are fleet,
Nor shrink they from the summer heat;
Why sends not the Bridegroom his promised gift,
Is his heart more cold, or his barb less swift?   700
Oh, false reproach! yon Tartar now
Has gained our nearest mountain's brow,
And warily the steep descends,
And now within the valley bends;
And he bears the gift at his saddle bow—   705
How could I deem his courser slow?
Right well my largess shall repay
His welcome speed, and weary way.'—
The Tartar lighted at the gate,
But scarce upheld his fainting weight;   710
His swarthy visage spake distress,
But this might be from weariness;
His garb with sanguine spots was dyed,
But these might be from his courser's side;—
He drew the token from his vest—   715
Angel of Death! 'tis Hassan's cloven crest!
His calpac rent—his caftan red—
'Lady, a fearful bride thy Son hath wed—
Me, not from mercy, did they spare,
But this empurpled pledge to bear.   720

---

  699 Why sends ⟨he not⟩ *MA12b*   700 barb] steeds *MA12b*; barbs *4th edn.*
701 yon] ⟨the⟩ *MA12b*   704 within . . . bends] his courser's pace amends *MA12b*
bends] wends *4th–6th edns.*   706 deem . . . slow] ⟨say my son was slow⟩ *MA12b*; ⟨deem
his steed so slow⟩ *MA12a*   708 His welcome] ⟨My faithful⟩ *MA12b*   709 The
Tartar sped ⟨and within⟩ beneath the gate *MA12b*   lighted at] sped beneath *MA12b*
710 ⟨His courser sunk beneath the weight⟩ *MA12b*; And flung to earth his fainting weight
MA12b   upheld] ⟨sustained⟩ *MA12a*   711 ⟨Ghastly his swarthy visage grew⟩ *MA12b*
713 sanguine] crimson *MA12ab*   spots] ⟨stains⟩ *MA12b*   715 the . . . from] the
gift from out *MA12b*   716 Angel of Death] ⟨Oh God / Angel of Allah⟩ *MA12b*
717 ⟨His turban's calpac rent and red⟩ *MA12b*   caftan] turban *MA12a and 4th edn.*
718 ⟨Is this the bride thy son hath wed / Thy son the grave hath for his bridal bed⟩ *MA12b*;
⟨The grave is Hassan's bridal bed⟩ *MA12b*   719 ⟨They spared me not for
mercy's sake⟩ *MA12b*   720 empurpled] ⟨dreadful⟩ accursed *MA12b*; detested
MA12a

Peace to the brave! whose blood is spilt—
Woe to the Giaour! for his the guilt.'

★   ★   ★   ★   ★   ★   ★

A turban carv'd in coarsest stone,
A pillar with rank weeds o'ergrown,
Whereon can now be scarcely read   725
The Koran verse that mourns the dead;
Point out the spot where Hassan fell
A victim in that lonely dell.
There sleeps as true an Osmanlie
As e'er at Mecca bent the knee;   730
As ever scorn'd forbidden wine,
Or pray'd with face towards the shrine,
In orisons resumed anew
At solemn sound of 'Alla Hu!'
Yet died he by a stranger's hand,   735
And stranger in his native land—
Yet died he as in arms he stood,
And unaveng'd, at least in blood.
But him the maids of Paradise
Impatient to their halls invite,   740
And the dark Heaven of Houri's eyes
On him shall glance for ever bright;
They come—their kerchiefs green they wave,
And welcome with a kiss the brave!
Who falls in battle 'gainst a Giaour,   745
Is worthiest an immortal bower.

★   ★   ★   ★   ★   ★   ★

But thou, false Infidel! shalt writhe
Beneath avenging Monkir's scythe;

721 brave] ⟨dead⟩ *MA12b*
723–6   Within a dark and ? ⟨isle⟩ coast
                             ⟨Hassan⟩ That ?
                             Who fought ? before
                             When ? *cancelled L*

724 with] ⟨half with⟩ *L*   rank] ⟨dark⟩ *M*   725 ⟨Whereon ye now / Ah now⟩ *L*
726 mourns] ⟨remem⟩ *L*   728 Within that dark and fearful dell *L*   729 true]
⟨proud⟩ *L*   731 scorn'd] ⟨loathed⟩ *L*   732 ⟨Or turned him eastward to the
shrine⟩ *L*   740 halls invite] ⟨bowers recall⟩ *LA1*   741 of Houri's] ⟨within their⟩
LA1   745 battle 'gainst] combat with *LA1*

And from its torment 'scape alone
To wander round lost Eblis' throne;   750
And fire unquench'd, unquenchable—
Around—within—thy heart shall dwell,
Nor ear can hear, nor tongue can tell
The tortures of that inward hell!—
But first, on earth as Vampire sent,   755
Thy corse shall from its tomb be rent;
Then ghastly haunt thy native place,
And suck the blood of all thy race,
There from thy daughter, sister, wife,
At midnight drain the stream of life;   760
Yet loathe the banquet which perforce
Must feed thy livid living corse;
Thy victims ere they yet expire
Shall know the daemon for their sire,
As cursing thee, thou cursing them,   765
Thy flowers are wither'd on the stem.
But one that for thy crime must fall—
The youngest—most belov'd of all,
Shall bless thee with a *father's* name—
That word shall wrap thy heart in flame!   770
Yet must thou end thy task, and mark
Her cheek's last tinge, her eye's last spark,
And the last glassy glance must view
Which freezes o'er its lifeless blue;
Then with unhallowed hand shalt tear   775
The tresses of her yellow hair,
Of which in life a lock when shorn,
Affection's fondest pledge was worn;
But now is borne away by thee,
Memorial of thine agony!   780
Wet with thine own best blood shall drip,
Thy gnashing tooth and haggard lip;

752 Around] Will⟩ *MA13*   753 ⟨And make that heart to⟩ *LA1*   755 But first]
⟨At times⟩ *LA1*   756 Thy . . . from] Thy body from *LA1*   757 Then . . . haunt]
⟨Then speed thee to⟩ *LA1*   ghastly haunt] ⟨speed through to⟩ *LA1*   763–4 ⟨Thy
victims see and know thee too | And in their Sire the Demon view⟩ *LA1*   769 bless]
⟨hail⟩ *LA1*   770 ⟨And scorch thy heart with fiercer flame⟩ *LA1*   771–2 mark
. . . spark] ⟨view Her fainting cheeks receding hue⟩ *LA1*   772 eye's] ⟨life's⟩ *LA1*
773 ⟨And glassy fixed her eye of blue⟩ *LA1*; its sightless blue *MA13*   781 thine . . .
drip] ⟨the blood of her and thine⟩ *LA1*   782 Thy . . . tooth] ⟨Thy lips shall⟩ *LA1*

Then stalking to thy sullen grave—
Go—and with Gouls and Afrits rave;
Till these in horror shrink away   785
From spectre more accursed than they!

★   ★   ★   ★   ★   ★   ★   ★

'How name ye yon lone Caloyer?
   His features I have scann'd before
In mine own land—'tis many a year,
   Since, dashing by the lonely shore,   790
I saw him urge as fleet a steed
As ever serv'd a horseman's need.
But once I saw that face—yet then
It was so mark'd with inward pain
I could not pass it by again;   795
It breathes the same dark spirit now,
As death were stamped upon his brow.'

' 'Tis twice three years at summer tide
   Since first among our freres he came;
And here it soothes him to abide   800
   For some dark deed he will not name.
But never at our vesper prayer,
Nor e'er before confession chair
Kneels he, nor recks he when arise
Incense or anthem to the skies,   805
But broods within his cell alone,
His faith and race alike unknown.
The sea from Paynim land he crost,
And here ascended from the coast,
Yet seems he not of Othman race,   810
But only Christian in his face:
I'd judge him some stray renegade,
Repentant of the change he made,
Save that he shuns our holy shrine,
Nor tastes the sacred bread and wine.   815
Great largess to these walls he brought,
And thus our abbot's favour bought;

788 His] ⟨Whose⟩ L   789 'tis many a] ⟨and in that⟩ L   790 Since] ⟨When⟩ L
by] past L   795 could . . . by] will remember it L   797 death . . . upon] time
were wasted on L, M; cor. Proof 2   802 But . . . at] ⟨Nor ever to⟩ L   805 Incense
or] ⟨The praising⟩ L

But were I Prior, not a day
Should brook such stranger's further stay,
Or pent within our penance cell   820
Should doom him there for aye to dwell.
Much in his visions mutters he
Of maiden 'whelmed beneath the sea;
Of sabres clashing—foemen flying,
Wrongs aveng'd—and Moslem dying.   825
On cliff he hath been known to stand,
And rave as to some bloody hand
Fresh sever'd from its parent limb,
Invisible to all but him,
Which beckons onward to his grave,   830
And lures to leap into the wave.'

  ⋆ ⋆ ⋆ ⋆ ⋆ ⋆ ⋆ ⋆

  ⋆ ⋆ ⋆ ⋆ ⋆ ⋆ ⋆ ⋆

Dark and unearthly is the scowl
That glares beneath his dusky cowl—
The flash of that dilating eye
Reveals too much of times gone by—   835
Though varying—indistinct its hue,
Oft will his glance the gazer rue—
For in it lurks that nameless spell
Which speaks—itself unspeakable—
A spirit yet unquelled and high   840
That claims and keeps ascendancy,
And like the bird whose pinions quake—
But cannot fly the gazing snake—
Will others quail beneath his look,
Nor 'scape the glance they scarce can brook.   845
From him the half-affrighted Friar
When met alone would fain retire—

---

819 brook . . . stranger's] see him urge his L 820 pent] safe L 823 Of foreign
maiden lost at sea L, M 826 cliff] ⟨crags⟩ L 830 Which beckons] Still leads
him L; Which leads him M; ⟨That beckoned⟩ L 832 unearthly] ⟨portentious / relent-
less⟩ MA14 834 ⟨And the hidden fire of his restless / faded / large eye⟩ OA2 The
flash of that] The fury of his OA2 835 too . . . times] a taste of woe OA2
836 Though varying] Though ⟨stern⟩ changing and OA2 838 that] ⟨some⟩ OA2
840 unquelled] unquenched OA2 841 That . . . keeps] A glance that claims OA2
844 others quail] ⟨lovelier souls⟩ OA2 847 would fain] ⟨must fast⟩ OA2

As if that eye and bitter smile
Transferred to others fear and guile—
Not oft to smile descendeth he,   850
And when he doth 'tis sad to see
That he but mocks at Misery.
How that pale lip will curl and quiver!
Then fix once more as if for ever—
As if his sorrow or disdain   855
Forbade him e'er to smile again.—
Well were it so—such ghastly mirth
From joyaunce ne'er deriv'd its birth.—
But sadder still it were to trace
What once were feelings in that face—   860
Time hath not yet the features fixed,
But brighter traits with evil mixed—
And there are hues not always faded,
Which speak a mind not all degraded
Even by the crimes through which it waded—   865
The common crowd but see the gloom
Of wayward deeds—and fitting doom—
The close observer can espy
A noble soul, and lineage high.—
Alas! though both bestowed in vain,   870
Which Grief could change—and Guilt could stain—
It was no vulgar tenement
To which such lofty gifts were lent,
And still with little less than dread
    On such the sight is riveted.—   875
The roofless cot decayed and rent,
    Will scarce delay the passer by—
The tower by war or tempest bent,
While yet may frown one battlement,
    Demands and daunts the stranger's eye—   880
Each ivied arch—and pillar lone,
Pleads haughtily for glories gone!

848 and bitter smile] and evil ⟨guile⟩ smile *OA2*   852 That . . . mocks] ⟨That quivering lip⟩ *OA2*   853 ⟨That lip would curl and quiver still⟩ *OA2*   pale] full *OA2* 854 once more] ⟨again⟩ *OA2*   858 From joyaunce] ⟨Bespoke dread⟩ From pleasure *OA2*   861 Time . . . yet] ⟨Age had not there⟩ *MA25*   yet] quite *MA25*   862 evil] bad were *MA25*   865 by] ⟨with⟩ *MA14*   867 ⟨Of evil days and worse to come⟩ *MA25*   868 can] might *MA25*   869 noble] nobler *MA25*   873 such lofty] ⟨a mind⟩ *MA24*   879 may frown] ⟨remains⟩ *MA14*

'His floating robe around him folding,
  Slow sweeps he through the columned aisle—
With dread beheld—with gloom beholding   885
  The rites that sanctify the pile.
But when the anthem shakes the choir,
And kneel the monks—his steps retire—
By yonder lone and wavering torch
His aspect glares within the porch;   890
There will he pause till all is done—
And hear the prayer—but utter none.
See—by the half-illumin'd wall
His hood fly back—his dark hair fall—
That pale brow wildly wreathing round,   895
As if the Gorgon there had bound
The sablest of the serpent-braid
That o'er her fearful forehead strayed.
For he declines the convent oath,
And leaves those locks unhallowed growth—   900
But wears our garb in all beside;
And—not from piety but pride
Gives wealth to walls that never heard
Of his one holy vow nor word.—
Lo!—mark ye—as the harmony   905
Peals louder praises to the sky—
That livid cheek—that stoney air
Of mixed defiance and despair!
Saint Francis! keep him from the shrine!
Else may we dread the wrath divine   910
Made manifest by awful sign.—
If ever evil angel bore
The form of mortal, such he wore—

884 through the columned] round the arching *OA2*   887 the anthem] ⟨an hymn⟩
OA2   889 lone and wavering] solitary *OA2*   890 aspect] figure *OA2*
893-4 ⟨His shadow lengthens on the wall | His raven locks around him fall⟩
See . . . back] Behold reflected oer the wall His cowl thrown back *MA26*, *OA4c*; Behold
as turns he from the wall His hood fly back *MA14*   894 ⟨His cowl flies back⟩ *MA26*
895-8 ⟨Along his forehead wreathing round | As though his brow with snakes was bound⟩
MA26   895 ⟨And oer his brow like serpents crawl⟩ *MA26*   pale brow wildly] pallid
aspect *OA4c*, *MA14*   898 strayed] played *OA4c*, *MA14*   899 oath] ⟨vow⟩
MA26   903 Enriched the ⟨walls where we abide⟩ shrine that neer hath heard *MA26*
905 ye] him *MA14*   907 That livid] His deadly *MA26*   909 Saint . . . from]
⟨Thank heaven—he stands without⟩ *MA14*   910 may] ⟨might⟩ *MA14*   912 bore]
⟨wore⟩ *MA27*   913 mortal] ⟨Mankind⟩ *MA27*

By all my hope of sins forgiven
Such looks are not of earth nor heaven!'   915

To love the softest hearts are prone,
But such can ne'er be all his own;
Too timid in his woes to share,
Too meek to meet, or brave despair;
And sterner hearts alone may feel   920
The wound that time can never heal.
The rugged metal of the mine
Must burn before its surface shine,
But plung'd within the furnace-flame,
It bends and melts—though still the same;   925
Then tempered to thy want, or will,
'Twill serve thee to defend or kill;
A breast-plate for thine hour of need,
Or blade to bid thy foeman bleed;
But if a dagger's form it bear,   930
Let those who shape its edge, beware!
Thus passion's fire, and woman's art,
Can turn and tame the sterner heart;
From these its form and tone are ta'en,
And what they make it, must remain,   935
But break—before it bend again.

★   ★   ★   ★   ★   ★   ★   ★

★   ★   ★   ★   ★   ★   ★   ★

916–17 To despair softest breasts are prone | But deem not love for these alone *LA7*
916 ⟨Tis not the smiling fool who / By nature turned to tender / The softest breasts to love
are prone⟩ *LA7*   918 timid] yielding *LA6b*   920 ⟨But sterner hearts alone can
feel⟩ *LA7*   And . . . alone] For only sterner hearts *LA7*   922–3 The rugged ore
within the mine | Seems hardly formed to smite or shine *LA7*; cor. *LA6a and Proof 3*
922 ⟨How cold and ⸮ is the rugged ore⟩ *LA7*   925 ⟨Behold how soon it burns and
bends⟩ *LA7*   It . . . melts] How burnt and bent *LA7*   926 Then mould it to what
⟨shape⟩ form you will *LA7*   927 Tis fitted to preserve or kill *LA7*   'Twill serve
thee] Tis fitted *LA7*   928 A shield to guard in hours of need *LA7*   930 But]
⟨And⟩ *LA7*   form it bear] shape it ⟨take⟩ wear *LA7*   931 ⟨It shows the maker's
fancy there⟩ *LA7*; Let those who made it thus beware *LA7*   934 are ta'en] ⟨it takes⟩
LA7

935–6   Where ⸮ through force can never bend
               Thus sterner ⟨hearts⟩ bosoms burn and bend
               And yielding to the circling flame
               To *cancelled LA7*

If solitude succeed to grief,
Release from pain is slight relief;
The vacant bosom's wilderness
Might thank the pang that made it less.   940
We loathe what none are left to share—
Even bliss—'twere woe alone to bear;
The heart once left thus desolate,
Must fly at last for ease—to hate.
It is as if the dead could feel   945
The icy worm around them steal,
And shudder, as the reptiles creep
To revel o'er their rotting sleep
Without the power to scare away
The cold consumers of their clay!   950
It is as if the desart-bird,
   Whose beak unlocks her bosom's stream
   To still her famish'd nestlings' scream,
Nor mourns a life to them transferr'd,
Should rend her rash devoted breast,   955
And find them flown her empty nest.
The keenest pangs the wretched find
   Are rapture to the dreary void—
   The leafless desart of the mind—
     The waste of feelings unemploy'd—   960
Who would be doom'd to gaze upon
A sky without a cloud or sun?
Less hideous far the tempest's roar,
Than ne'er to brave the billows more—
Thrown, when the war of winds is o'er,   965
A lonely wreck on fortune's shore,
'Mid sullen calm, and silent bay,
Unseen to drop by dull decay;—
Better to sink beneath the shock
Than moulder piecemeal on the rock!   970

---

937 ⟨Alone—it hath a dreary / The greatest grief I would not shun⟩ Were nothing left
to feel but grief *OA5*   938 ⟨To be secure⟩ Release from woe were no relief *OA5*   is]
⟨were⟩ *MA15*   942 'twere woe alone] ⟨must make it woe⟩ *MA15*   943 ⟨The
heart once thus⟩ And hearts once left thus *MA15*   944 ⟨Has nought to hope or fear
from hate⟩ *MA15*   948 rotting] seeming *MA15; cor. Proof 4*   957 pangs the]
⟨pangs that the⟩ *MA15*   964 ne'er . . . billows] feeling that we must feel no *MA15;*
feeling that we feel no *OA5*   967 ⟨To look upon the craggy beach⟩ *OA5*   silent]
⟨silent⟩ lonely *OA5*   968 Unseen—⟨unsought⟩ to drop *OA5*

*   *   *   *   *

'Father! thy days have pass'd in peace,
   'Mid counted beads, and countless prayer;
To bid the sins of others cease,
   Thyself without a crime or care,
Save transient ills that all must bear,   975
Has been thy lot, from youth to age,
And thou wilt bless thee from the rage
Of passions fierce and uncontroul'd,
Such as thy penitents unfold,
Whose secret sins and sorrows rest   980
Within thy pure and pitying breast.
My days, though few, have pass'd below
In much of joy, but more of woe;
Yet still in hours of love or strife,
I've scap'd the weariness of life;   985
Now leagu'd with friends, now girt by foes,
I loath'd the languor of repose;
Now nothing left to love or hate,
No more with hope or pride elate;
I'd rather be the thing that crawls   990
Most noxious o'er a dungeon's walls,
Than pass my dull, unvarying days,
Condemn'd to meditate and gaze—
Yet, lurks a wish within my breast
For rest—but not to feel 'tis rest—   995
Soon shall my fate that wish fulfil;
And I shall sleep without the dream
Of what I was, and would be still;
   Dark as to thee my deeds may seem—
My memory now is but the tomb   1000
Of joys long dead—my hope—their doom—
Though better to have died with those
Than bear a life of lingering woes—
My spirit shrunk not to sustain
The searching throes of ceaseless pain;   1005

972 ⟨Unbroken peace and fervent prayer⟩ *LA3*   countless] ⟨ceaseless⟩ *MA16*
975 transient ills] ⟨mortal pains⟩ *LA3*   977 And thou wilt] ⟨Well mayst thou⟩ *LA3*
991 Most noxious] Most loathsome *LA3* ⟨In dark⟩ *MA16*   996 ⟨And soon that wish
shall be fulfilled⟩ *LA3*,   999 Though Hope hath long withdrawn her beam *LA3*,
MA16, *1st and 2nd edns.*   1000 now is] is *MA11*

Nor sought the self-accorded grave
Of ancient fool, and modern knave:
Yet death I have not fear'd to meet,
And in the field it had been sweet
Had danger wooed me on to move   1010
The slave of glory, not of love.
I've brav'd it—not for honour's boast;
I smile at laurels won or lost.—
To such let others carve their way,
For high renown, or hireling pay;   1015
But place again before my eyes
Aught that I deem a worthy prize;—
The maid I love—the man I hate—
And I will hunt the steps of fate,
(To save or slay—as these require)   1020
Through rending steel, and rolling fire;
Nor need'st thou doubt this speech from one
Who would but do—what he *hath* done.
Death is but what the haughty brave—
The weak must bear—the wretch must crave—   1025
Then let Life go to him who gave:
I have not quailed to danger's brow—
When high and happy—need I *now*?

> ★   ★   ★   ★   ★   ★

'I lov'd her, friar! nay, adored—
    But these are words that all can use—   1030
I prov'd it more in deed than word—
There's blood upon that dinted sword—
    A stain its steel can never lose:
'Twas shed for her, who died for me,
    It warmed the heart of one abhorred: 1035
Nay, start not—no—nor bend thy knee,
    Nor midst my sins such act record,

1012 it] ⟨him⟩ *MA17*   1017 Aught] ⟨The man⟩ *MA17*
1020–3   ⟨Through ranks of steel and tracks of fire
                And all she threatens in her ire
                There are but wounds ?
                And these are but the words of one
                Who thus would do—who thus hath done⟩ *MA17*

1037 such] ⟨the⟩ *MA16*

Thou wilt absolve me from the deed,
For he was hostile to thy creed!
The very name of Nazarene   1040
Was wormwood to his Paynim spleen,
Ungrateful fool! since but for brands,
Well wielded in some hardy hands;
And wounds by Galileans given,
The surest pass to Turkish heav'n;   1045
For him his Houris still might wait
Impatient at the prophet's gate.
I lov'd her—love will find its way
Through paths where wolves would fear to prey,
And if it dares enough, 'twere hard   1050
If passion met not some reward—
No matter how—or where—or why,
I did not vainly seek—nor sigh:
Yet sometimes with remorse in vain
I wish she had not lov'd again.   1055
She died—I dare not tell thee how,
But look—'tis written on my brow!
There read of Cain the curse and crime,
In characters unworn by time:
Still, ere thou dost condemn me—pause—   1060
Not mine the act, though I the cause;
Yet did he but what I had done
Had she been false to more than one;
Faithless to him—he gave the blow,
But true to me—I laid him low;   1065
Howe'er deserv'd her doom might be,
Her treachery was truth to me;
To me she gave her heart, that all
Which tyranny can ne'er enthrall;
And I, alas! too late to save,   1070
Yet all I then could give—I gave—
'Twas some relief—our foe a grave.

1045 surest pass] swiftest path *LA3*   1051 But Passion meets its wished reward
LA3   1054 with remorse] ⟨in repentance⟩ *LA3*   in vain] ⟨and pain⟩ *MA16*
1055 I wish that I had ⟨sought⟩ loved in vain *LA3*   1056 dare not] cannot *LA3*,
MA16; *cor. Proof 3*   1059 unworn by time] ⟨Time cannot wear⟩ *LA3*   1061 ⟨The
act was his—though I the cause⟩ *LA3*   1066 her] ⟨such⟩ *MA19*   1067 Her]
⟨That⟩ *MA19*   1072 'Twas . . . our] ⟨My hope a tomb—my⟩ *MA19*

His death sits lightly; but her fate
Has made me—what thou well may'st hate.
His doom was seal'd—he knew it well,   1075
  Warn'd by the voice of stern Taheer,
  Deep in whose darkly boding ear
  The deathshot peal'd of murder near—
As filed the troop to where they fell!
He died too in the battle broil—   1080
A time that heeds nor pain nor toil—
One cry to Mahomet for aid,
One prayer to Alla—all he made:
He knew and crossed me in the fray—
I gazed upon him where he lay,   1085
And watched his spirit ebb away;
Though pierced like Pard by hunters' steel,
He felt not half that now I feel.
I search'd, but vainly search'd to find,
The workings of a wounded mind;   1090
Each feature of that sullen corse
Betrayed his rage, but no remorse.
Oh, what had Vengeance given to trace
Despair upon his dying face!
The late repentance of that hour,   1095
When Penitence hath lost her power
To tear one terror from the grave—
And will not soothe, and can not save!

★   ★   ★   ★   ★   ★

'The cold in clime are cold in blood,
  Their love can scarce deserve the name;   1100
But mine was like the lava flood
  That boils in Aetna's breast of flame.
I cannot prate in puling strain
Of ladye-love, and beauty's chain;

1073–4 ⟨His death sits lightly on my breast | But hers—oh would I were at rest⟩ *LA3*
1075 seal'd] fixed *OA8*   1076 From the true voice of stern Taheer *OA8; cor. MA18*
1077 ⟨Within whom⟩ *OA8*   1078 peal'd of] ⟨murmured⟩ *OA8*   1079 the troop
⟨with⟩ to *OA8*   1081 pain] ⟨wound⟩ *MA20*   1085 where] ⟨as⟩ *MA20*
1095 late] ⟨vain⟩ *MA20*   1097–8 Her power to soothe, her skill to save, | And doubly
darkens o'er the grave *MA20, 3rd edn.; cor. Proof 16*   1102 in . . . breast] ⟨within the
mount⟩ *LA4*   1103–4 ⟨I could prate of dart and chain | In pictures of ? swain⟩ *LA4*
1104 and beauty's chain] and dart—and chain *MA19* ⟨of a panting swain⟩ *LA4*

If changing cheek, and scorching vein—   1105
Lips taught to writhe, but not complain—
If bursting heart, and madd'ning brain—
And daring deed, and vengeful steel—
And all that I have felt—and feel—
Betoken love—that love was mine,   1110
And shewn by many a bitter sign.
'Tis true, I could not whine nor sigh,
I knew but to obtain or die.
I die—but first I have possest,
And come what may, I *have been* blest;   1115
Shall I the doom I sought upbraid?
No—reft of all—yet undismay'd
But for the thought of Leila slain,
Give me the pleasure with the pain,
So would I live and love again.   1120
I grieve, but not, my holy guide!
For him who dies, but her who died;
She sleeps beneath the wandering wave—
Ah! had she but an earthly grave,
This breaking heart and throbbing head   1125
Should seek and share her narrow bed.
She was a form of life and light—
That seen—became a part of sight,
And rose—where'er I turned mine eye—
The Morning-star of Memory!   1130

'Yes, Love indeed is light from heaven—
A spark of that immortal fire
With angels shar'd—by Alla given,
To lift from earth our low desire.

1105-7 If bursting heart and maddening brain, | And fire that raged in every vein *LA4,*
MA19; cor. Proof 3   1105 If] ⟨My⟩ *LA6c*   scorching] flushing *LA6c; cor. Proof 7*
1106 ⟨And tongue / preaching lips⟩ *LA6c*   1107 If] ⟨And⟩ *LA6c*   1108 And] ⟨If⟩
LA6c   1112 ⟨I would not⟩ *LA4*   whine] sing *MA19; cor. Proof 3*   1116-17 Even
now alone, yet undismay'd, | ⟨I know no friend, and ask no aid,⟩ *MA19, 1st-4th edns.; line*
1117 thus in LA4; cor. Proof 21   1116 Even now deserted—not dismayed *LA4*
1117 yet] ⟨and⟩ *MA19*   1118 But for the dead ⟨my rival⟩ her tyrant slain *cancelled*
LA4; ⟨My Leila dead—my rival slain⟩ *LA4*   1121 but] ⟨yet⟩ *LA4*   1123 beneath
the wandering] within the boundless *LA4*   1128 became . . . of] forever fixed the *OA4b*
1129 rose] ⟨shone⟩ *OA4b*   1131 ⟨If love indeed be born / descend from heaven⟩ *MA21a*
is light] ⟨doth spring⟩ *MA21b*   1132 immortal] ⟨celestial / eternal⟩ *MA21a*   1133 To
human hearts in mercy given *MA21a*

Devotion wafts the mind above,　　　　　　　1135
But Heaven itself descends in love—
A feeling from the Godhead caught,
To wean from self each sordid thought—
A Ray of him who form'd the whole—
A Glory circling round the soul!　　　　　　1140
I grant *my* love imperfect—all
That mortals by the name miscall—
Then deem it evil—what thou wilt—
But say, oh say, *hers* was not guilt!
She was my life's unerring light—　　　　　　1145
That quench'd—what beam shall break my night?
Oh! would it shone to lead me still,
Although to death or deadliest ill!—
Why marvel ye? if they who lose
　　This present joy, this future hope,　　　　1150
　　No more with sorrow meekly cope—
In phrenzy then their fate accuse—
In madness do those fearful deeds
　　That seem to add but guilt to woe.
Alas! the breast that inly bleeds　　　　　　1155
　　Hath nought to dread from outward blow—
Who falls from all he knows of bliss,
Cares little into what abyss.—
Fierce as the gloomy vulture's now
　　To thee, old man, my deeds appear—　　　1160
I read abhorrence on thy brow,
　　And this too was I born to bear!
'Tis true, that, like that bird of prey,
With havock have I mark'd my way—
But this was taught me by the dove—　　　　1165
To die—and know no second love.
　　This lesson yet hath man to learn,

1135 wafts] ⟨sends⟩ *MA21b*　　　1138 To] ⟨If to⟩ *MA21a*　　　1139 Ray of] ⟨glance from⟩ *MA21b*　　　1146 what . . . night] and I am lost in night *MA21c*; I wandered far in night *MA21b*　　　1151 Which taught them with all ill to cope *MA21a* 1152 phrenzy] madness *MA21a*　　　1153 fearful] ⟨desperate⟩ *MA21a*　　　1154 ⟨That seem but to augment their woe⟩ *MA21a*　　　1155 breast] heart *MA21c*　　1156 blow] foe *MA21a*　　　1158 Must plunge into a dark abyss *MA21a*; ⟨They must plunge⟩ *MA21a*　　1161 abhorrence] ⟨this horror⟩ *MA21a*　　　1163 ⟨Deemst thou my heart was over stern⟩ *MA21a*　　　1164 mark'd] tracked *MA21a*　　　1165 But . . . by] ⟨Yet know I learnt it of⟩ *MA21a*　　　1167 ⟨Though man the feeble lesson learns⟩ *MA21a*　　This . . . yet] ⟨This much at least⟩ *MA21a*

Taught by the thing he dares to spurn—
The bird that sings within the brake,
The swan that swims upon the lake,   1170
One mate, and one alone, will take.
And let the fool still prone to range,
And sneer on all who cannot change—
Partake his jest with boasting boys,
I envy not his varied joys—   1175
But deem such feeble, heartless man,
Less than yon solitary swan—
Far—far beneath the shallow maid
He left believing and betray'd.
Such shame at least was never mine—   1180
Leila—each thought was only thine!—
My good, my guilt, my weal, my woe,
My hope on high—my all below.
Earth holds no other like to thee,
Or if it doth, in vain for me—   1185
For worlds I dare not view the dame
Resembling thee, yet not the same.
The very crimes that mar my youth
This bed of death—attest my truth—
'Tis all too late—thou wert—thou art   1190
The cherished madness of my heart!

'And she was lost—and yet I breathed,
    But not the breath of human life—
A serpent round my heart was wreathed,
    And stung my every thought to strife.—   1195
Alike all time—abhorred all place,
Shuddering I shrunk from Nature's face,
Where every hue that charmed before
The blackness of my bosom wore:—

1172–3 And let the light inconstant fool | That sneers his coxcomb ridicule *MA21b*,
MA21c; cor. Proof 22   1172 And let the light and boasting fool *MA21a*
1174 Partake] Enjoy *MA21a*   1176 feeble, heartless] heartless, soulless *MA21a*
1178 Far . . . the] ⟨Less than the soft and⟩ *MA21b*; ⟨Less than the shallow weeping⟩ *MA21c*
1186 ⟨Nor care to view the brightest dame⟩ *MA21c*   I dare] ⟨I would dare⟩ *MA21b*
1188 mar] blast *MA21bc*   1190–1 Tis vain to strive—thou wert thou art | The joy—
the madness of my heart *MA21c*   1194 serpent] ⟨scorpion⟩ *MA28*   1196–7 All
all was changed—⟨to me the same⟩ on Nature's face | To me alike all time and place *MA28*;
cancelled *MA22a*   To me alike all time and place | Scarce could I gaze on Nature's face
MA22ab   1199 ⟨Thou knowest the rest⟩ *MA28*   wore] ⟨bore⟩ *MA22a*

The rest—thou dost already know,   1200
And all my sins and half my woe—
But talk no more of penitence,
Thou see'st I soon shall part from hence—
And if thy holy tale were true—
The deed that's done can'st *thou* undo?   1205
Think me not thankless—but this grief
Looks not to priesthood for relief.
My soul's estate in secret guess—
But would'st thou pity more—say less—
When thou can'st bid my Leila live,   1210
Then will I sue thee to forgive;
Then plead my cause in that high place
Where purchased masses proffer grace—
Go—when the hunter's hand hath wrung
From forest-cave her shrieking young,   1215
And calm the lonely lioness—
But soothe not—mock not *my* distress!

'In earlier days, and calmer hours,
    When heart with heart delights to blend,
Where bloom my native valley's bowers—   1220
    I had—Ah! have I now?—a friend!—
To him this pledge I charge thee send—
    Memorial of a youthful vow;
I would remind him of my end,—
    Though souls absorbed like mine allow   1225
Brief thought to distant friendship's claim,
Yet dear to him my blighted name.
'Tis strange—he prophesied my doom,
    And I have smil'd—(I then could smile—)

1202 ⟨But now I pray thee⟩ *MA28*   1203 part] ⟨pass⟩ *MA22b*   1206 this]
⟨my⟩ *MA22a*   1207 In sooth is not for thy relief *MA28*; ⟨Is not for man's and thy
relief⟩ *MA22a*   1208 My state thy thought can never guess *MA28, MA22a*; ⟨My
soul's estate thou canst not guess⟩ *MA22b*   1211 sue] ask *MA28*   1212–13 in . . .
grace] ⟨before the throne Where I shall go and she is gone⟩ *MA28*   1212 plead] ⟨will
plead⟩ *MA22b*   1213 Where thou it seems canst offer grace *MA28; cancelled MA22b*
1215–16 her . . . lioness] her ⟨first-born⟩ sleeping young | And ⟨rouse / soothe / view⟩ lull the
maddening lioness *MA29*   1217 ⟨Then of my anguish mightst thou guess⟩ *MA29*
1220 Where rise my native city's towers *MA23ab; cor. Proof 22*   1221 I . . . now] I
had— ⟨and though but one / and still may have⟩ *MA23a*   1223–4 I have no heart to
love him now | And tis but to declare my end *MA23ab*   1224 Tis but to tell him of
mine end *MA23a*   1225 ⟨A soul⟩ For souls *MA23a*   1226 Brief] ⟨Few⟩ *MA23a*
1229 then] once *MA23a*

When Prudence would his voice assume,   1230
  And warn—I reck'd not what—the while—
But now remembrance whispers o'er
Those accents scarcely mark'd before.
Say—that his bodings came to pass,
  And he will start to hear their truth,   1235
  And wish his words had not been sooth.
Tell him—unheeding as I was—
  Through many a busy bitter scene
  Of all our golden youth had been—
In pain, my faultering tongue had tried   1240
To bless his memory ere I died;
But heaven in wrath would turn away,
If Guilt should for the guiltless pray.
I do not ask him not to blame—
  Too gentle he to wound my name;   1245
  And what have I to do with fame?
I do not ask him not to mourn,
Such cold request might sound like scorn;
And what than friendship's manly tear
May better grace a brother's bier?   1250
But bear this ring—his own of old—
And tell him—what thou dost behold!
The wither'd frame, the ruined mind,
The wrack by passion left behind—
A shrivelled scroll, a scatter'd leaf,   1255
Sear'd by the autumn blast of grief!

     ★   ★   ★   ★   ★   ★

'Tell me no more of fancy's gleam,
No, father, no, 'twas not a dream;
Alas! the dreamer first must sleep,
I only watch'd, and wish'd to weep;   1260

1230 Prudence] ⟨Censure⟩ *MA23a*   1232 whispers] ⟨rushes⟩ murmurs *MA23a*
1233 scarcely mark'd] ⟨which I marked⟩ *MA23a*   1239 golden] early *MA23a*
1240 In pain I now had turned aside *MA23a*; ⟨In pain my thoughts / my feeble spirit tried⟩
MA23b   1242–3 If heaven to such a prayer would grant | ⟨The blessing this⟩ To him
cancelled MA23a   1242 in . . . away] ⟨would mock the vain essay⟩ *MA23ab*
1243 guiltless] ⟨guileless⟩ *cor. Proof 22*   1244 ⟨Tell him⟩ *MA23a*   1248 Such
cold] For such *MA23a*   1250 May better] So well can *MA23a*   1251 his own]
he gave *MA23a*   1254 The wrack by] The wreck that *MA23a*   1255 The
shrivelled and discoloured leaf *MA23a*   1260 ⟨And I could only watch and weep⟩ *LA5*

But could not, for my burning brow
Throbb'd to the very brain as now.
I wish'd but for a single tear,
As something welcome, new, and dear;
I wish'd it then—I wish it still,   1265
Despair is stronger than my will.
Waste not thine orison—despair
Is mightier than thy pious prayer;
I would not, if I might, be blest,
I want no paradise—but rest.   1270
'Twas then, I tell thee, father! then
I saw her—yes—she liv'd again;
And shining in her white symar,
As through yon pale grey cloud—the star
Which now I gaze on, as on her   1275
Who look'd and looks far lovelier;
Dimly I view its trembling spark—
To-morrow's night shall be more dark—
And I—before its rays appear,
That lifeless thing the living fear.   1280
I wander, father! for my soul
Is fleeting towards the final goal;
I saw her, friar! and I rose,
Forgetful of our former woes;
And rushing from my couch, I dart,   1285
And clasp her to my desperate heart;
I clasp—what is it that I clasp?
No breathing form within my grasp,
No heart that beats reply to mine,
Yet, Leila! yet the form is thine!   1290
And art thou, dearest, chang'd so much,
As meet my eye, yet mock my touch?

1262 ⟨Though throbbing was as firm as now⟩ *LA5*   1263 ⟨Twas then⟩ I slept not
cancelled LA5   I . . . but] ⟨I slept not⟩ *LA5*   1264 As something ⟨new⟩ welcome
and most dear *cancelled LA5*   1267 Nay—kneel not father!—rise—despair *MA19*,
LA5; *cor. Proof 3*   1268 mightier] stronger *LA5*   pious] friar's *cor. Proof 3*
1270 ⟨I ask not raptures—only rest⟩ *LA5*   1276 More lovely than Eve's harbinger
LA6d; *inserted and cancelled in Proof 3*   Who . . . far] Who living ⟨shone⟩ looked far *LA5*;
⟨Who breathing looked far⟩ *MA19*   1277 Dimly . . . its] Which now I view with *LA5*,
MA19; *cor. Proof 3*   its . . . spark] ⟨to view no more⟩ *LA5*   1278 ⟨Still she seems as
young and bright⟩ *LA5*; ⟨But ever vain for me to mark⟩ *LA5*   1279 ⟨But now again /
And I shall be ere it appear⟩ *LA5*   1288 breathing] trembling *LA5*; ⟨kindly⟩ trembling
LA5

Ah! were thy beauties e'er so cold,
I care not—so my arms enfold
The all they ever wish'd to hold.   1295
Alas! around a shadow prest,
They shrink upon my lonely breast;
Yet still—'tis there—in silence stands,
And beckons with beseeching hands!
With braided hair, and bright-black eye—   1300
I knew 'twas false—she could not die!
But he is dead—within the dell
I saw him buried where he fell;
He comes not—for he cannot break
From earth—why then art thou awake?   1305
They told me, wild waves roll'd above
The face I view, the form I love;
They told me—'twas a hideous tale!
I'd tell it—but my tongue would fail—
If true—and from thine ocean-cave   1310
Thou com'st to claim a calmer grave,
Oh! pass thy dewy fingers o'er
This brow that then will burn no more;
Or place them on my hopeless heart—
But, shape or shade!—whate'er thou art,   1315
In mercy, ne'er again depart—
Or farther with thee bear my soul,
Than winds can waft—or waters roll!—

    ✱   ✱   ✱   ✱   ✱   ✱

'Such is my name, and such my tale,
   Confessor—to thy secret ear,   1320
I breathe the sorrows I bewail,
   And thank thee for the generous tear
This glazing eye could never shed.

1296–7 ⟨Alas around thee vainly prest | They hold my own convulsive breast⟩ *LA5*
1299 beckons] ⟨woos me⟩ *LA5*   1300 ⟨Tis her⟩ *LA5*   1302 dead] ⟨fallen⟩ *LA5*
1306 They] He *cor. Proof 3*   wild waves] ⟨Ocean⟩ *LA5*   1307 face] ⟨form⟩
LA5   1309 tongue] heart *LA5; cor. Proof 3 and LA6e*   1310 thine ocean-
cave] ⟨thy watery cave⟩ *LA5*   1311 claim a calmer] ⟨find a holier⟩ *LA5*   1312 thy
dewy fingers] ⟨thine icy hand⟩ *LA5*   1314 ⟨But⟩ Or place ⟨them⟩ it on *LA5*   1316 In
mercy] ⟨Have pity⟩ *LA5*   1317–18 Winds shall not waft—nor waters roll | Thine
image from my ebbing soul *LA6g; cor. in MS. in Proof 3*

Then lay me with the humblest dead,
And save the cross above my head,   1325
Be neither name nor emblem spread
By prying stranger to be read,
Or stay the passing pilgrim's tread.'
He pass'd—nor of his name and race
Hath left a token or a trace,   1330
Save what the father must not say
Who shrived him on his dying day;
This broken tale was all we knew
Of her he lov'd, or him he slew.

206   [Love and Gold]

[1.]

I cannot talk of Love to thee,
   Though thou art young and free and fair!
There is a spell thou dost not see,
   That bids a genuine love forebear.

2.

And yet that spell invites each youth,   5
   For thee to sigh, or seem to sigh;
Makes falsehood wear the garb of truth,
   And Truth itself appear a lie.

3.

If ever Doubt a place possest
   In woman's heart, 'twere wise in thine: 10
Admit not Love into thy breast,
   Doubt others' love, nor trust in mine.

1324 humblest] nameless *L*   1326 spread] laid *L, M and 1st–4th edns.*   1333–4 This
. . . of] Nor whether most he mourned—none knew For *L, M; cor. Proof 2*

206. Copy text: *C*, collated with *MS. BM*
title   *untitled in BM*

   1 talk] ⟨speak⟩ *BM*   2 free] ⟨fair / gay⟩ *BM*   4 ⟨This dooms / genuine love⟩
BM   forebear] despair *C, More*   6 ⟨A spell that⟩ *BM*   7 ⟨That makes /
teaches / makes in / can⟩ Makes falsehood ⟨seem to be⟩ wear *BM*   10 thine] ⟨thee⟩
BM   11 Love]⟨there⟩ *BM*   12 ⟨Yet doubt thou all⟩ *BM*

4.

Perchance 'tis feigned, perchance sincere,
  But false or true thou couldst not tell;
So much hast thou from all to fear,
  In that unconquerable spell.   15

5.

Of all the herd that throng around,
  Thy simpering or thy sighing train,
Come tell me who to thee is bound
  By Love's or Plutus' heavier chain.   20

6.

In some 'tis Nature, some 'tis Art
  That bids them worship at thy shrine;
But thou deserv'st a better heart,
  Than they or I can give for thine.

7.

For thee, and such as thee, behold,   25
  Is Fortune painted truly—blind!
Who doomed thee to be bought or sold,
  Has proved too bounteous to be kind.

8.

Each day some tempter's crafty suit
  Would woo thee to a loveless bed:
I see thee to the altar's foot   30
  A decorated victim led.

---

14 couldst] canst *C*, *More*   17 that . . . around] ⟨which now / thee surround⟩ *BM*
19 ⟨Canst thou / Can thou pronounce / Pronounce⟩ *BM*   23 deserv'st] ⟨art worth⟩ *BM*
25–6 ⟨Wert thou but what thou shouldst have been | Ah how much happier both might be⟩
BM   25 For] ⟨In⟩ *BM*   26 ⟨Both Love and Fortune truly blind⟩ *BM*   27 ⟨If she
has⟩ *BM*   28 Has . . . too] ⟨And been less⟩ *BM*   29 ⟨Methinks even now I see /
read thy fate⟩ / ⟨Perchance even now / Within his⟩ *BM*

29–30   ⟨I see some ⁂ and foul brute
                        Has won thee to his loveless bed⟩
                        ⟨Even now⟩ some tempter's ⟨happier⟩ suit
                        ⟨May draw⟩ thee to a loveless bed *BM*

9.

Adieu, dear maid! I must not speak
  Whate'er my secret thoughts may be;
Though thou art all that man can reck   35
  I dare not talk of Love to *thee*.

[1812–13]

207   Remember Thee, Remember Thee!

Remember thee, remember thee!
  Till Lethe quench life's burning stream,
Remorse and shame shall cling to thee,
  And haunt thee like a feverish dream!

Remember thee! Ay, doubt it not;   5
  Thy husband too shall think of thee;
By neither shalt thou be forgot,
  Thou *false* to him, thou *fiend* to me!

[1813]

---

33 ⟨Oh had a humbler lot been thine / Had thou ? a humbler lot⟩ / ⟨Then go⟩ dear Maid !
⟨be / with many a prayer⟩ *BM*   34 ⟨And many a ? from me⟩ *BM*   36 talk]
⟨speak⟩ *BM*

207. Copy text: *Medwin*, collated with *Paris1828, 1837*

  8 *false . . . fiend*] *these two words first supplied in C alternate version*: To Bd., Feb. 22, 1813

            'Remember thee', nay—doubt it not—
              Thy Husband too may '*think*' of thee!
            By neither canst thou be forgot,
              Thou false to him—thou fiend to me!

            'Remember thee' ? Yes—yes—till Fate
              In Lethe quench the guilty dream.
            Yet then—ev'n then—Remorse and *Hate*
              Shall vainly quaff the vanquished stream.

208 [Genevieve]

Genevieve—Genevieve
　　Oh adieu,
The next you deceive
　　May be less true.
　　　But should he,　　　　　　　　　　　5
　　　Too, too like me,
Love in earnest enough to feel vext—
　　There's comfort still,
　　If he wait until
He sees how you'll deal by the next,　　　10
　　　　Genevieve—Genevieve—

Genevieve—Genevieve
　　One last kiss,
One more with your leave,
　　And only this.　　　　　　　　　　　15
　　Ah! you sigh,
　　And from that eye
I had wiped a less treacherous tear;
　　Though shed in vain
　　It shall not remain—　　　　　　　　20
Smiles become you much better, my dear
　　　　Genevieve—Genevieve—

[1813]

208. Copy text: *MS. L*

2 ⟨Fare thee well⟩ *L*　　　13 ⟨Part we in peace / as friends⟩ *L*　　18 ⟨I've once
wiped a truer tear⟩ *L*　　22 *B began seven lines of another stanza. It was cancelled and*
is indecipherable.

209 ## Windsor Poetics

Version A

Lines, composed on the occasion of
H.R.H. the P[rinc]e R[e]g[en]t being
seen standing betwixt the coffins of
Henry 8th and Charles 1st, in the Royal
vault at Windsor.

Famed for contemptuous breach of sacred ties,
By headless Charles, see heartless Henry lies;
Between them stands another Sceptered thing,
It moves, it reigns, in all but name—a King:
Charles to his People, Henry to his Wife,   5
—In him the double Tyrant starts to Life:
Justice and Death have mixed their dust in vain,
Each Royal Vampyre wakes to life again;
Ah! what can tombs avail—since these disgorge
The blood and dust of both——to mould a G[eor]ge.   10

[1813]

Version B

To the *discoverer* of the bodies of
Charles 1st. & Henry 8th.

Famed for their civil and domestic quarrels
See heartless Henry lies by headless Charles!
Between them stands another sceptred *thing*
It lives—it reigns 'aye every inch a king!'

209. *Version A.* Copy text: *Paris1818*, collated with Paris editions, *1831*, *1832*, *C*, and the Bodleian MS. copy
title   On opening the Vault at Windsor Castle containing the bones of Henry the Eighth and Charles the first. *Bodleian MS. copy*

   1 contemptuous] presumptuous *Bodleian MS. copy*   2 By . . . see] See . . . by
Bodleian MS. copy   4 moves . . . reigns] breathes . . . moves *Bodleian MS. copy*
8 The Royal Vampyres join and live again *Bodleian MS. copy*   9–10 What then
shall tombs avail since these disgorge | Their Blood and dust to mould a living, G——.
Bodleian MS. copy

Version B. Copy text: Murray MS., collated with Wildman MS. copy
title   Impromptu *Wildman MS. copy*

   1 quarrels] brawls *Wildman MS copy*   4 reigns 'aye] moves—yea *Wildman MS. copy*;
⟨breathes⟩ 'aye *Murray MS.*

Charles to his people—Henry to his wife   5
The double tyrant starts at once to life,
Justice and Death have mixed their dust in vain
Each royal vampire quits his vault again!
Curst be the tomb that could so soon disgorge
Two such to make a Janus or a George.   10

Version C

On a Royal Visit to the Vaults.
Famed for their civil and domestic quarrels,
See heartless Henry lies by headless Charles;
Between them stands another sceptred thing,
It lives, it reigns—'aye, every inch a king.'
Charles to his people, Henry to his wife,   5
In him the double tyrant starts to life:
Justice and Death have mix'd their dust in vain,
The royal Vampires join and rise again.
What now can tombs avail, since these disgorge
The blood and dirt of both to mould a George!   10

210

On Being Asked What Was the 'Origin of Love'?

The 'Origin of Love'!—Ah why
    That cruel question ask of me?
When thou may'st read in many an eye—
    He starts to life on seeing thee!
And should'st thou seek his *end* to know—   5
    My heart forebodes, my fears foresee,
He'll linger long in silent woe—
    But live—until I cease to be.

[1813]

6 at once] ⟨again⟩ *Murray MS.*   8 Each] ⟨The⟩ *Murray MS.*   quits his vault]
wakes to life *Wildman MS. copy*   9–10 What can new tombs avail, when these dis-
gorge | *Two such*, to make a Regent and a George? *Wildman MS. copy*

Version C. Copy text: Berg MS., collated with *C, More*
    8 rise] ⟨live / breathe⟩ *Berg MS.*

210. Copy text: *CHP*(7), collated with *MSS.* B and M, the proofs, *CHP*(8)–*CHP*(10)
title   To Ianthe On Being . . . Love *M*
    5 should'st] wouldst *B*

211   [To Thomas Moore.
Written the Evening Before his Visit to
Mr. Leigh Hunt in Cold Bath Fields Prison,
May 19, 1813]

Oh you, who in all names can tickle the town,
Anacreon, Tom Little, Tom Moore, or Tom Brown,—
For hang me if I know of which you may most brag,
Your Quarto two-pounds, or your Twopenny Post Bag;

        ★   ★   ★

But now to my letter—to yours 'tis an answer—   5
To-morrow be with me, as soon as you can, sir,
All ready and dress'd for proceeding to spunge on
(According to compact) the wit in the dungeon—
Pray Phoebus at length our political malice
May not get us lodgings within the same palace!   10
I suppose that to-night you're engaged with some codgers,
And for Sotheby's Blues have deserted Sam Rogers;
And I, though with cold I have nearly my death got,
Must put on my breeches, and wait for the Heathcote.
But to-morrow, at four, we will both play the *Scurra*,   15
And you'll be Catullus, the R[egen]t Mamurra.

                                    [1813]

212   [On Lord Thurlow's Poems]

I.

When T[hurlow] this damn'd nonsense sent,
(I hope I am not violent)
Nor men nor gods knew what he meant.

211. Copy text: *Life*
title *1832; untitled in Life*; Fragment of an Epistle to Thomas Moore *1831, C*; 'Oh You,
Who in All Names Can Tickle the Town' *More*

212. Copy text: *Life*
title *untitled in Life*

2.

And since not ev'n our Rogers' praise
To common sense his thoughts could raise—   5
Why *would* they let him print his lays?

3.

★ ★ ★ ★ ★ ★ ★ ★ ★ ★ ★ ★ ★ ★ ★

4.

★ ★ ★ ★ ★ ★ ★ ★ ★ ★ ★ ★ ★ ★ ★

5.

To me, divine Apollo, grant—O!
Hermilda's first and second canto,
I'm fitting up a new portmanteau;

6.

And thus to furnish decent lining,   10
My own and others' bays I'm twining—
So, gentle T[hurlow], throw me thine in.

[1813]

213   To [Lord Thurlow]

1.

'I lay my branch of laurel down.'

————

Thou 'lay thy branch of *laurel* down'!
    Why, what thou'st stole is not enow;
And, were it lawfully thine own,
    Does Rogers want it most, or thou?
    Keep to thyself thy wither'd bough,   5
Or send it back to Doctor Donne—
    Were justice done to both, I trow,
He'd have but little, and thou—none.

213. Copy text: *Life*
title   To —— *Life*

2.

'Then thus to form Apollo's crown.'

———

A crown! why, twist it how you will,
Thy chaplet must be foolscap still.   10
 When next you visit Delphi's town,
 Inquire among your fellow-lodgers,
They'll tell you Phoebus gave his crown,
Some years before your birth, to Rogers.

3.

'Let every other bring his own.'

———

When coals to Newcastle are carried,   15
 And owls sent to Athens, as wonders,
From his spouse when the Regent's unmarried,
 Or Liverpool weeps o'er his blunders;
When Tories and Whigs cease to quarrel,
 When Castlereagh's wife has an heir,   20
Then Rogers shall ask us for laurel,
 And thou shalt have plenty to spare.

[1813]

214   [On Southey's Laureateship]

Who gains the bays and annual Malmsey barrel—
Busby the bright—or Southey the sublime?
Southey with monarchs has made up his quarrel,
 Nor pities prisoned Martin's venial crime,
My Liege, (that same lopped off the head of [Charles]   5
 And Southey sang him once upon a [time.)]

17 Regent's] ——'s *Life*   20 Castlereagh's] ——'s *Life*

214. Copy text: *MS.*

 1 Who ... and annual Malmsey] ⟨Pronounce who ... and Malmsey⟩ *MS*   4 prisoned
Martin's] ⟨now the Regicide / Martin's punishment⟩ *MS.*

Bob now no more the sapphic patriot [warbles,]
And up to Pye's Parnassus he may climb—
George gives him what—God knows he wanted—laurels,
And spares him what—he never spared us—rhyme.   10

.   .   .

Blest day that shall a double joy insure—
For us his silence, him his sinecure.

.   .   .

'Tis wise, for Herculian were his task, my Guelph
To please his readers or to praise thyself.—

.   .   .

How like our Monarch and his Bard elect—   15
Prince of a party, poet of a sect.

.   .   .

Impartial Liege! whose equal judgement takes
Favourites from dirt—and minstrels from the Lakes—
Oh since so far thy tender mercy reaches,
With Southey's songs abolish Jenky's speeches.   20

[1813]

215   [Politics in 1813. To Lady Melbourne]

'Tis said *Indifference* marks the present time,
Then hear the reason—though 'tis told in rhyme—
A King who *can't*—a Prince of Wales who *don't*—
Patriots who *shan't*, and Ministers who *won't*—
What matters who are *in* or *out* of place   5
The *Mad*—the *Bad*—the *Useless*—or the *Base*?

[1813]

8 ⟨And George permits / And up thy ⟨steep⟩ terrace Windsor shall he climb⟩ *MS*.
11 a double joy] ⟨for us and thou⟩ *MS*.; ⟨Oh blest ? that taught us to endure⟩ *MS*.
12 ⟨Thy silence grant / Southey tis thine to teach us to endure⟩ *MS*.   13 Herculian
. . . Guelph] ⟨hard his task my gracious Guelph⟩ *MS*.   13–14 ⟨Tis wise that Anti-
jacobiner man | Hath sung no Prince before but ?⟩ *MS*.   17 Favourites] ⟨friends /
minstrels / poets⟩ *MS*.   19 ⟨Extend thy ?⟩ *MS*.   20 abolish] ⟨oh silence⟩ *MS*.

215. Copy text: *MS*., collated with *LBC*, *BLJ*

3–4 A King who *cannot*—and a Prince who don't—Patriots who *would not*—ministers
who won't—*alternate reading in MS*.

216   Impromptu, in Reply to a Friend

When from the heart where Sorrow sits
    Her dusky shadow mounts too high,
And o'er the changing aspect flits,
    And clouds the brow, or fills the eye;
Heed not that gloom, which soon shall sink: 5
    My thoughts their dungeon know too well;
Back to my breast the wanderers shrink,
    And droop within their silent cell.

[1813]

217   Remember Him, &c.

1.

Remember him, whom passion's power
    Severely, deeply, vainly proved—
Remember thou that dangerous hour
    When neither fell, though both were loved.

2.

That yielding breast, that melting eye,   5
    Too much invited to be blest—
That gentle prayer, that pleading sigh,
    The wilder wish reprov'd, repress'd.

---

216. Copy text: *CHP*(7), collated with *MS. M, MS. Ma*, the proof, *CHP*(8)–*CHP*(10)
title ⟨To ——⟩ *M*
    7 the wanderers] ⟨unuttered⟩ *M*   8 droop] bleed *M* and *Ma, cor. in proof*

217. Copy text: *CHP*(7), collated with *MS. Ma, MS. Mb*, all proofs, *CHP*(8)–*CHP*(10)
    2 Severely] Severely ⟨proved⟩ *Ma*   deeply] ⟨truly⟩   proved] tried *Ma*   3 that danger-
ous] the ⟨midnight⟩ *Ma*   4 ⟨When neither fell though both were loved⟩ | To him who
loves and her who loved *Ma*   5 yielding breast] ⟨trembling form⟩ *Ma*

3.

Oh! let me feel that all I lost,
   But saved thee all that conscience fears,   10
And blush for every pang it cost
   To spare the vain remorse of years!

4.

Yet think of this when many a tongue,
   Whose busy accents whisper blame,
Would do the heart that loved thee wrong,   15
   And brand a nearly blighted name.

5.

Think that—whate'er to others—thou
   Hast seen each selfish thought subdu'd;
I bless thy purer soul even now,
   Even now, in midnight solitude.   20

6.

Oh, God! that we had met in time—
   Our hearts as fond—thy hand more free;
When thou had'st lov'd without a crime,
   And I been less unworthy thee!

7.

Far may thy days as heretofore   25
   From this our gaudy world be pass'd!
And that too bitter moment o'er,
   Oh! may such trial be thy last!

9 ⟨Resigning thee—alas! I lost⟩ *Ma*   10 ⟨All that I had to dream of joy / Joys bought
too dear, if bright with tears / My Hope—but saved thy future fears⟩ *Ma*   11 ⟨And
blushed for all my / Yet neer regret the pangs it cost⟩ *Ma*   12 ⟨To spare what / To
save thy ? / I might deliver⟩ | ⟨To spare thy peril / all thine and my remorse⟩ | ⟨To spare the
vain / long remorse of years⟩ *Ma*   13 Yet] ⟨Then⟩ *Ma*   14 ⟨That / Whose accents
only⟩ whisper shame *Ma*   16 brand] crush *Ma*   19 ⟨Behold ? loving now⟩ *Ma*
20 ⟨My safety—and my solitude / And neer regret this solitude⟩ *Ma*   21 ⟨Would we
had met at that blest time / in earlier times⟩ *Ma*   22 ⟨When both / With hearts the
same but⟩ *Ma*   Our] ⟨With⟩ *Mb*   24 less] not *Ma*   25 Far be thy days *Ma*,
Mb, all proofs, *CHP*(7), *CHP*(8)   26 ⟨From this our world mayst thou⟩ *Ma*

8.

This heart, alas! perverted long,
    Itself destroyed might there destroy;   30
To meet thee in the glittering throng,
    Would wake Presumption's hope of joy.

9.

Then to the things whose bliss or woe
    Like mine is wild and worthless all—
That world resign—such scenes forego,   35
    Where those who feel must surely fall.

10.

Thy youth, thy charms, thy tenderness—
    Thy soul from long seclusion pure;
From what even here hath past may guess
    What there thy bosom must endure.   40

11.

Oh! pardon that imploring tear,
    Since not by Virtue shed in vain—
My frenzy drew from eyes so dear—
    For me they shall not weep again.

12.

Though long and mournful must it be,   45
    The thought that we no more may meet—
Yet I deserve the stern decree,
    And almost deem the sentence sweet.

13.

Still—had I lov'd thee less—my heart
    Had then less sacrificed to thine;   50
It felt not half so much to part,
    As if its guilt had made thee mine.   [1813]

29 ⟨From me be ever⟩ *Ma*   This] ⟨My⟩ *Ma*   30 ⟨Is fitter far ?⟩ *Ma*   32 Would]
⟨Might⟩ *Mb*   Presumption's hope of] my hope of guilty *Ma*   34 is] ⟨are⟩ *Mb*
35 That] The *Ma*   38 from] ⟨by⟩ *Ma*   40 must] ⟨might⟩ *Ma*   45 ⟨Bitter
and⟩ Though ⟨sad and bitter⟩ / long and ⟨sadder⟩ *Ma*   47 Yet] ⟨But⟩ *Ma*   48 the
sentence] ⟨denial⟩ *Ma*   50 Had less have sacrificed to thine *Ma, Mb, all proofs, CHP*(7),
CHP(8)

218   The Devil's Drive.—
a sequel to Porson's 'Devil's Walk'

[1.]
The Devil returned to Hell by two,
    And he stay'd at home till five,
When he dined on some homicides done in *Ragoût*,
With a rebel or so in an *Irish* stew—
And sausages made of a selfslain Jew,   5
And bethought himself what next to do—
    'And,' quoth he, 'I'll take a Drive.
I walked in the morning—I'll ride tonight;
In darkness my children take most delight,
    And I'll see how my favourites thrive.   10

2.

'And what shall I ride in,' quoth Lucifer then?
    'If I followed my taste indeed,
I should mount in a wagon of wounded men,
    And smile to see them bleed.
But these will be furnished again and again,   15
    And at present my purpose is speed.
To see of my Manor as much as I may,
And watch that no souls may be poached away.

3.

'I have a state-coach at Carlton House,
    A chariot in Seymour place;   20
But they're lent to two friends—who make me amends
    By driving my favourite pace;
And they handle the reins with such a grace
I have something for both at the end of their race.

218. Copy text: *C*, collated with *MSS. H, L*
title   The Devil's Drive *C, More*; The Devil's Drive—a continuation of 'The Devil's
Walk' *L, cor. in H*

3 homicides . . . *Ragoût*] ⟨? served up in a stew⟩ *L*   4–5 *transposed in L*
4   With] And *Life and all later texts*   14 ⟨And believe with ?⟩ *L*   19 Carlton]
C—l—n *L*; C—— *Life, 1831*   23 And ⟨both of them⟩ they *L*   24 I have]
I've *L*

4.

'So now for the earth—to take my chance'—   25
    Then up to Earth sprung he,
And making a jump from Moscow to France,
    He stepped across the Sea,
And rested his hoof on a Turnpike road—
No very great way from a Bishop's abode.   30

5.

But first as he flew, I forgot to say,
That he hovered a moment upon his way
    To look upon Leipsic plain;
And so sweet to his eye was its sulphury glare,
And so soft to his ear was the cry of despair,   35
    That he perched on a Mountain of Slain;
Then he gazed with delight from its growing height,
Nor seldom on earth had he seen such a sight,
    Nor his work done half so well:
For the field ran so red with the blood of the dead,   40
    That it blushed like the waves of Hell!
Then loudly and wildly and long laughed he:
'Methinks they have little need here of *Me*.'

6.

Long he looked down on the hosts of each clime,
    While the warriors hand to hand were—   45
Gaul—Austrian and Muscovite heroes sublime,
And—(Muse of Fitzgerald arise with a rhyme!)
    A quantity of *Landwehr!*
    Gladness was there,
For the men of all might and the monarchs of earth,   50
Were met for the wolf and the worm to make mirth,
    And a feast for the fowls of the Air!

25 the earth] earth *L*   26 Earth] the earth *L*, *Life and all later texts*   32 upon his
way] ⟨oer Leipsic plain⟩ *L*   33 To look] ⟨And looked⟩ *L*   34 its . . . glare] the
. . . ⟨air⟩ *L*   37 And he ⟨look⟩ gazed in joy from its growing height *L*, *cor. in H*
38 Nor seldom . . . had he seen] For seldom . . . he saw *L*; ⟨For⟩ Nor seldom . . . had he seen
H; Nor often . . . had he seen *Life* and *all later texts*   39 As ⟨tongue could never⟩ /
only his tongue could tell *L*, *cor. in H*   done half] ⟨performed⟩ *H*   41 That ⟨he
thought of the flames⟩ of Hell *L*   43 Methinks ⟨Man hath little need⟩ ⟨as earth do⟩
they have here little need of me. *L*   44 of each clime] ⟨that were there⟩ *L*   45 the
warriors] warriors *L*   46 Austrian . . . heroes] ⟨German⟩ . . . chieftains *L*   47 arise]
⟨descend⟩ rise up *L*   51 Were] There *C*, *More*   the wolf] the ⟨worm and⟩ wolf *L*

7.

But he turned aside and looked from the ridge
   Of hills along the river,
And the best thing he saw was a broken bridge,   55
   Which a Corporal chose to shiver;
Though an Emperor's taste was displeased with his haste,
   The Devil he thought it clever;
And he laughed again in a lighter strain,
   O'er the torrent swoln and rainy,   60
When he saw 'on a fiery horse' Prince Pon,
In taking care of Number *One*—
   Get drowned with a great *Many!*

8.

But the softest note that soothed his ear
   Was the sound of a widow's sighing;   65
And the sweetest sight was the icy tear,
   Which Horror froze in the blue eye clear
   Of a maid by her lover lying—
As round her fell her long fair hair,
And she looked to Heaven with that frenzied air   70
Which seemed to ask if a God were there!
And stretched by the wall of a ruined hut,
With its hollow cheek, and eyes half shut,
   A child of Famine dying:
And the carnage *begun,* when *resistance* is done,   75
   And the fall of the vainly flying!

9.

Then he gazed on a town by besiegers taken,
   Nor cared he who were winning;
But he saw an old maid, for years forsaken,
   Get up and leave her spinning;   80
And she looked in her glass, and to one that did pass,
   She said—'pray are the rapes beginning?'

54 along] ⟨up⟩ along *L*   58 he thought] thought *L*   60 torrent] ⟨floo⟩ *L*
61 on . . . horse] ⟨unfortunate⟩ *L*; on a fiery steed *C, More*   64 softest . . . soothed]
⟨sweetest⟩ sound that met *L*   65 widow's] widow *Life and all later texts*   66 was
. . . tear] ⟨that he saw here⟩ *L*   67 blue eye] ⟨eye so⟩ *L*   69–71 *not in L*
70 that frenzied] ⟨fearful⟩ *H*   71 Which seemed] ⟨As if⟩ *H*   76 fall] ⟨death⟩ *L*
77 Then he ⟨looked⟩ on a town ⟨that was taken by storm⟩ / assault had taken *L*   81 in
her] in ⟨the⟩ *H*   that] who *L*

10.

But the Devil has reached our cliffs so white,
   And what did he there, I pray?
If his eyes were good, he but saw by night   85
   What we see every day;
But he made a tour and kept a journal
Of all the wondrous sights nocturnal,
And he sold it in shares to the *Men* of the *Row*,
Who bid pretty well—but they *cheated* him, though!   90

11.

The Devil first saw, as he thought, the *Mail*,
   Its coachman and his coat;
So instead of a pistol he cocked his tail,
   And seized him by the throat;
'Aha!' quoth he, 'what have we here?   95
'T is a new barouche, and an ancient peer!'

12.

So he sat him on his box again,
   And bade him have no fear,
But be true to his club, and staunch to his rein,
   His brothel and his beer;   100
'Next to seeing a Lord at the Council board,
I would rather see him *here*.'

13.

Then Satan hired a horse and gig
   With promises of pay;
And he pawned his horns for a spruce new wig,   105
   To redeem as he came away:
And he whistled some tune, a waltz or a jig,
   And drove off at the close of day.

83 But the Devil ⟨is landed in fair England⟩ / has perched on our cliffs so white *L*
87 and kept] and he kept *L*   90 Who ⟨bought it as if it were Cowper's, I trow.⟩ *L*
91 ⟨The first thing he saw he took for⟩ *L*   first] he *L*   92 Its] With its *L*   95 Aha]
Heyday *L*   96 Tis ⟨my / a babe of mine own⟩ and an ⟨English⟩ peer *L*   97 Then he
set him on his seat again *L*   100 brothel] ⟨bottle / doxy⟩ *L*   102 I would] I'd *L*
103 ⟨Then the Devil he hired a horse and gig / But the Devil he got to fair England⟩ *L*
Then Satan hired] So the Devil he hired *L*; Satan hired *C, More*   104 of] to *C, More*
105 And he hid his horns in a borrowed wig *L*   106 To return when he came that way *L*

14.

The first place he stopped at—he heard the Psalm
  That rung from a Methodist Chapel: 110
' 'T is the best sound I've heard,' quoth he, 'since my palm
  Presented Eve her apple!
When *Faith* is all, 't is an excellent sign,
That the *Works* and Workmen both are mine.'

15.

He passed Tommy Tyrwhitt, that standing jest,   115
  To princely wit a Martyr:
But the last joke of all was by far the best,
  When he sailed away with 'the Garter'!
'And'—quoth Satan 'this Embassy's worthy my sight,
Should I see nothing else to amuse me tonight.   120
With no one to bear it, but Thomas à Tyrwhitt,
This ribband belongs to an "Order of Merit"!'

16.

He stopped at an Inn and stepped within
  The Bar and read the 'Times';
And never such a treat, as—the epistle of one 'Vetus',   125
  Had he found save in downright crimes:
'Though I doubt if this drivelling encomiast of War
Ever saw a field fought, or felt a scar,
Yet his fame shall go farther than he can guess,
For I'll keep him a place in my *hottest Press;*   130
And his works shall be bound in Morocco *d'Enfer,*
And lettered behind with his *Nom de Guerre.*'

109 Psalm] ⟨hymn⟩ L   113 ⟨Where faith is all / I'm fond of faith⟩ tis a certain
sign L   114 and] and ⟨good⟩ L   115 He ⟨met posthaste like one possesst⟩ L
116 To ⟨the⟩ Princely L   118 away] abroad L   119 ⟨And it made the⟩ L
121 Thomas à] poor Tommy L   122 an] ⟨no⟩ L   125 the ⟨lett⟩ epistle H
126 in . . . crimes] ⟨Fitzgerald's rhymes⟩ L   127–8 ⟨And yet he felt some loathing⟩ /
⟨For he prates extermination | To the present generation⟩ L   127 ⟨And saith he⟩ I
wonder if this same encomiast of war L   128 field fought] field L   129 Yet . . .
shall] ⟨But I'm equally obliged⟩ His fame will L   130 keep] save L   131 And
. . . bound] ⟨For⟩ his works shall be ⟨encumber⟩ bound L

17.

The Devil gat next to Westminster,
  And he turned to 'the room' of the Commons;
But he heard as he purposed to enter in there,   135
  That 'the Lords' had received a summons;
And he thought, as 'a *quondam* Aristocrat',
He might peep at the Peers, though to *hear* them were flat;
And he walked up the House so like one of his own,
That they say that he stood pretty near the throne.   140

18.

He saw the Lord Liverpool seemingly wise,
  The Lord Westmoreland certainly silly,
And Jockey of Norfolk—a man of some size—
  And Chatham, so like his friend Billy;
And he saw the tears in Lord Eldon's eyes,   145
  Because the Catholics would *not* rise,
    In spite of his prayers and his prophecies;
And he heard—which set Satan himself a staring—
A certain Chief Justice say something like *swearing*.
And the Devil was shocked—and quoth he, 'I must go,   150
For I find we have much better manners below.
If thus he harangues when he passes my border,
I shall hint to friend Moloch to call him to order.'

19.

Then the Devil went down to the humbler House,
  Where he readily found his way   155
As natural to him as its hole to a Mouse,
  He had been there many a day;
And many a vote and soul and job he
Had bid for and carried away in the Lobby:
But there now was a 'call' and accomplished debaters   160
Appeared in the glory of hats, boots and gaiters—
Some paid rather more—but *all* worse dressed than
    Waiters!

135 purposed] turned *L*   138 peep] ⟨look⟩ *L*   139 And] So *L, cor. in H*
his] our *Life and all later texts*   141 seemingly] ⟨looking most⟩ *L*   142 silly]
⟨foolish⟩ *L*   143 Jockey] Johnny *Life, 1831, 1832*   150 quoth he] he said *L*
153 hint to] ⟨order⟩ *L*   154 went down to] set off for *L*   156 its] ⟨a⟩ *L*
159 in] from *C, More*   160 and] and ⟨the⟩ *L*

20.

There was Canning for War, and Whitbread for peace,
    And others as suited their fancies;
But all were agreed that our debts should increase   165
    Excepting the Demagogue *Francis*.
That rogue! how could Westminster send him again
To leaven the virtue of these honest men!
But the Devil remained till the Break of Day
    Blushed upon Sleep and Lord Castlereagh: 170
Then up half the house got, and Satan got up
With the drowsy to snore—or the hungry to sup:—
But so torpid the power of some speakers, 't is said,
That they sent even him to his brimstone bed.

21.

He had seen George Rose—but George was grown   175
        dumb,
    And only lied in thought!
And the Devil has all the pleasure to come
    Of hearing him talk as he ought.
With the falsest of tongues, the sincerest of men—
    His veracity were but deceit—   180
And Nature must first have unmade him again,
Ere his breast or his face, or his tongue, or his pen,
Conceived—uttered—looked—or wrote down letters ten,
    Which Truth would acknowledge complete.

22.

Satan next took the army list in hand,   185
    Where he found a new 'Field Marshal';
And when he saw this high command
Conferred on his Highness of Cumberland,
    'Oh! were I prone to cavil—or were I not the Devil,
    I should say this was somewhat partial;   190

167 send] chuse *C, More*   168 To ⟨mix with a ? of such⟩ honest men *L*
173 torpid] ⟨powerful⟩ *L*   174 That they ⟨went not to⟩ sent *L*   177 has all the]
has got all that *L*   179 With] ⟨For⟩ *L*   180–1 In George Truth had him a
deceit | And Nature been forced to unmake him again *L, cor. in H*   184 By Truth
⟨put together⟩ / could acknowledge complete *L*   185 Satan] He *L*   188 Con-
ferred] Bestowed *L, cor. in H*   189 ⟨If⟩ Oh *L*

Since the only wounds that this Warrior gat,
    Were from God knows whom—and the Devil knows
        what!'

23.

He then popped his head in a royal Ball,
    And saw all the Haram so hoary;
And who there besides but Corinna de Staël!   195
    Turned Methodist and Tory!
'Aye—Aye'—quoth he—' 't is the way with them all,
    When Wits grow tired of Glory:
But thanks to the weakness, that thus could pervert her,
Since the dearest of prizes to me's a deserter: 200
Mem—whenever a sudden conversion I want,
To send to the school of Philosopher Kant;
And whenever I need a critic who can gloss over
All faults—to send Mackintosh to write up the Philosopher.'

24.

The Devil waxed faint at the sight of this Saint,   205
    And he thought himself of eating;
And began to cram from a plate of ham
    Wherewith a Page was retreating—
Having nothing else to do (for 'the friends' each so near
    Had sold all their souls long before),   210
As he swallowed down the bacon he wished himself a Jew
    For the sake of another crime more:
For Sinning itself is but half a recreation,
Unless it ensures most infallible Damnation.

25.

But he turned him about, for he heard a sound   215
    Which even his ear found faults in;
For whirling above—underneath—and around—
    Were his fairest Disciples Waltzing!

191 that this] this *L*   193 ⟨The Devil⟩ He *L*   194 ⟨Where he viewed a / a shower of its Glory⟩ And saw the Seraglio hoary *L, cor. in H*   195 And whom should he see there but Mme de Stael *L*   198 When wits ⟨turn rather hoary⟩ *L* 201–4 *not in L*   205 waxed] ⟨waxed⟩ grew *L*; ⟨grew⟩ waxed *H*   206 he thought] bethought *L*   209 each] ⟨all⟩ *L*   212 crime] ⟨sin⟩ *L*   214 Unless ⟨one is perfectly certain of⟩ / it be one that ensures damnation *L*   215 about] ⟨round⟩ *L* 216 Which ⟨he could find fair⟩ even himself found faults in *L, cor. in H*   217 ⟨And / Alas⟩ For whirling around and around and round *L*

And quoth he—'though this be—the *premier pas* to me,
  Against it I would warn all—   220
Should I introduce these revels among my younger devils,
  They would all turn perfectly carnal:
And though fond of the flesh—yet I never could bear it
Should quite in my kingdom get the upper hand of *Spirit*.'

26.

The Devil (but 't was over) had been vastly glad   225
  To see the new Drury Lane,
And yet he might have been rather mad
  To see it rebuilt in vain;
And had he beheld their 'Nourjahad',
  Would never have gone again: 230
For Satan had taken it much amiss,
They should fasten such a piece on a friend of his—
Though he knew that his works were somewhat sad,
He never had deemed them *quite* so bad:
For this was 'the book' which, of yore, Job, sorely smitten, 235
Said, 'Oh that *mine* enemy, *mine* enemy had written'!

27.

Then he found sixty scribblers in separate cells,
  And marvelled what they were doing,
For they looked like little fiends in their own little hells,
  Damnation for others brewing—   240
Though their paper seemed to shrink, from the heat of
    their ink,
  They were only *coolly* reviewing!
And as one of them wrote down the pronoun '*We*',
'That Phrase'—says Satan—'means *him* and *me*,

219 *premier pas* to] ⟨first step towards⟩ *L*   220 would] shall *L*   221 ⟨For⟩ Should *L*   222 perfectly] ⟨rather too⟩ / presently *L*   224 Should quite below get the better of Spirit. *L*   kingdom . . . upper hand⟩ ⟨realms . . . better⟩ *H*   225 The Devil ⟨had he too⟩ (but *L*   227 might] would *L*   228 ⟨To see the⟩ To see it built in vain *L*   229 he beheld] he but seen *L*   231 For] And *C, More* 233 that his] his *L*   234 deemed] dreamed *L*; found *C, More*   235–6 For this was 'the book' that Job in his fit | Said 'oh that mine enemy had writ.'— *L, cor. in H* 240 brewing] strewing *L*   241 *written as 2 lines in L*

244–6   Friend Lucifer whispered 'tis easy to see
                   By that plural he means himself and me
                   With the Editor added it just makes three
                   An Athanasian Trinity *L*

244 Phrase] Plural *C, More*

With the Editor added to make up the three   245
Of our Athanasian Trinity,
And render the believers in our "*Articles*" sensible,
How many must combine to make *one* Incomprehensible!'

                                                           [1813]

219   Sonnet. To Genevra

Thine eyes' blue tenderness, thy long fair hair,
    And the wan lustre of thy features—caught
    From contemplation—where serenely wrought,
Seems Sorrow's softness charm'd from its despair—
Have thrown such speaking sadness in thine air,   5
    That—but I know thy blessed bosom fraught
    With mines of unalloy'd and stainless thought—
I should have deem'd thee doom'd to earthly care.
With such an aspect by his colours blent,
    When from his beauty-breathing pencil born,   10
    (Except that *thou* hast nothing to repent)
    The Magdalen of Guido saw the morn—
Such seem'st thou—but how much more excellent!
    With nought Remorse can claim—nor Virtue scorn.

                                                           [1813]

220   Sonnet. To Genevra

Thy cheek is pale with thought, but not from woe,
    And yet so lovely, that if Mirth could flush
    Its rose of whiteness with the brightest blush,

246 our] an *C, More*   247 render . . . in our] make . . . in *L*   248 combine]
go *L* ⟨join⟩ *H*

219. Copy text: *Corsair*(2), collated with *MSS. L* and *M*, both proofs, all editions of
Corsair except *Corsair*(3)
title   To ⟨Her⟩ Genevra *MS. L*; To Genevra *MS. M, both proofs*

    1 tenderness] ⟨softness and⟩ *L*   2 features—caught] ⟨pensive face⟩ *L*   3 ⟨Have
lent / given to thee a mournful melting / a heart compelling grace⟩ *L*   From . . . where]
From pensive dreams for these *L, cor. in M*   4 softness . . . from] ⟨mildness shorn
of⟩ *L*   5 Have thrown such] ⟨And such the⟩ *L*   7 ⟨With all the / treasured /
drossless⟩ *L*   9 by his colours] ⟨to his canvas⟩ *L*   10 ⟨When underneath his⟩ *L*
beauty-breathing . . . born] ⟨life-bestowing pencil grew⟩ *L*   13 Such . . . but] ⟨Thee
had he seen⟩ *L*   14 nought Remorse] ⟨nothing Guilt⟩ *L*

220. Copy text: *Corsair*(2), with identical collation as in the previous sonnet.
title   To the Same *MS. L*; To Genevra *MS. M, both proofs*

    1 with . . . woe] Hope whispers not from woe *L, cor. in M*; ⟨I know not if from Sor-
row⟩ *L*   woe] ⟨Sadness / grief⟩ *L*   2 Mirth] joy *L, cor. in M*   3 rose of] ⟨pensive⟩ *L*
brightest] ⟨deeper⟩ *L*

My heart would wish away that ruder glow:—
And dazzle not thy deep-blue eyes—but oh!   5
   While gazing on them sterner eyes will gush,
   And into mine my mother's weakness rush,
Soft as the last drops round heaven's airy bow;
For, through thy long dark lashes low depending,
   The soul of melancholy Gentleness   10
Gleams like a seraph from the sky descending,
   Above all pain, yet pitying all distress;
At once such majesty with sweetness blending,
   I worship more, but cannot love thee less.

                                                  [1813]

221   A Song

1.

Thou art not false, but thou art fickle,
   To those thyself so fondly sought;
The tears that thou hast forc'd to trickle
   Are doubly bitter from that thought:
'Tis this which breaks the heart thou grievest,   5
Too well thou lov'st—too soon thou leavest.

2.

The wholly false the heart despises,
   And spurns deceiver and deceit;
But she who not a thought disguises,
   Whose love is as sincere as sweet,   10
When she can change who lov'd so truly,
It feels what mine has felt so newly.

---

4 ruder] ⟨foreign⟩ L   5 ⟨He who beheld would half regret that gladness⟩ L
6–7 ⟨Oft ? thine | That calls my mother's weakness into mine⟩ L   6 ⟨Their glance
can soften sterner eyes to gush⟩ L   8 last drops round] ⟨shower beneath⟩ L   9 low]
thence L; ⟨thence / meekly⟩ M   12 pain] ⟨suffering⟩ L   13 majesty] ⟨grandeur⟩ L

221. Copy text: CHP(7), collated with CHP(8)–CHP(10), MSS. M and BM, proofs
title   Stanzas ('Thou art not false') 1832

  2 And ⟨changest / lovest well but never long⟩ BM; ⟨And seekest often as thou art
sought⟩ M   5 ⟨For thus thou⟩ BM   8 spurns] ⟨loathes⟩ BM   9 she who] her
who ⟨m⟩ BM; her who Huntington proof, CHP(7), CHP(8); ⟨her⟩ / she who M; she who
Murray proof   11 When ⟨they can change who loved so truly / she whom we⟩ BM
12 It feels] ⟨We feel⟩ BM

3.

To dream of joy and wake to sorrow
　　Is doom'd to all who love or live;
And if, when conscious on the morrow,   15
　　We scarce our fancy can forgive,
That cheated us in slumber only,
To leave the waking soul more lonely,

4.

What must they feel whom no false vision,
　　But truest, tenderest passion warm'd?   20
Sincere, but swift in sad transition,
　　As if a dream alone had charm'd?
Ah! sure such grief is fancy's scheming,
And all thy change can be but dreaming!

　　　　　　　　　　　　　　　　　　　[1813]

222   Farewell! If Ever Fondest Prayer

Farewell! if ever fondest prayer
　　For other's weal availed on high,
Mine will not all be lost in air,
　　But waft thy name beyond the sky.
'Twere vain to speak, to weep, to sigh: 5
　　Oh! more than tears of blood can tell,
When wrung from guilt's expiring eye,
　　Are in that word—Farewell!—Farewell!

These lips are mute, these eyes are dry;
　　But in my breast, and in my brain,   10
Awake the pangs that pass not by,
　　The thought that ne'er shall sleep again.

14 ⟨Must⟩ Is *BM*   15 ⟨To love to day⟩ *BM*   on] of *BM*   17 slumber only] ⟨sleep so dearly⟩ / slumbers only *BM*   18 To . . . soul] ⟨What / And⟩ To make the waking heart *BM*   21 swift in sad] ⟨rapid in⟩ *BM*   23 ⟨It is indeed a dream—whence waking⟩ *BM*   such] this *BM*   24 ⟨Leaves⟩ Ah sure this ⟨Sorrow⟩ / Change can be but dreaming *BM*

222. Copy text: *Corsair*(7), collated with *MSS. M* and *ML*, proofs, all editions of *Corsair* in which the poem appears
　6 can] could *M, cor. in proofs*   7 When] Though *M, cor. in proofs*

My soul nor deigns nor dares complain,
  Though grief and passion there rebel;
I only know we loved in vain—   15
  I only feel—Farewell!—Farewell!

[1813]

223   The Bride of Abydos.
             A Turkish Tale

> Had we never loved so kindly,
> Had we never loved so blindly,
> Never met or never parted,
> We had ne'er been broken-hearted.
>   BURNS.

TO

THE RIGHT HONOURABLE

LORD HOLLAND,

THIS TALE

IS INSCRIBED, WITH

EVERY SENTIMENT OF REGARD

AND RESPECT,

BY HIS GRATEFULLY OBLIGED

AND SINCERE FRIEND,

BYRON.

CANTO I

I.

Know ye the land where the cypress and myrtle
  Are emblems of deeds that are done in their clime,
Where the rage of the vulture—the love of the turtle—
  Now melt into sorrow—now madden to crime?—

223. Copy text: *Bride* (ninth edn.), collated with *MSS. A, B, X, D, Proofs 1–11a*, and the first eleven edns. of *Bride*.

Dedication   THIS TALE (the following pages) *X* REGARD . . . OBLIGED] the most affectionate respect by his most gratefully obliged servt. *X, cor. in D2*

Canto 1

   1–19 *not in A*   1 where] ⟨of⟩ *X*   2 deeds that are] all that were *X, cor. in B*
   4 sorrow—now] ⟨sadness, or⟩ *X*

Know ye the land of the cedar and vine?   5
Where the flowers ever blossom, the beams ever shine,
Where the light wings of Zephyr, oppressed with perfume,
Wax faint o'er the gardens of Gúl in her bloom;
Where the citron and olive are fairest of fruit,
And the voice of the nightingale never is mute;   10
Where the tints of the earth, and the hues of the sky,
In colour though varied, in beauty may vie,
And the purple of Ocean is deepest in die;
Where the virgins are soft as the roses they twine,
And all, save the spirit of man, is divine—   15
'Tis the clime of the east—'tis the land of the Sun—
Can he smile on such deeds as his children have done?
Oh! wild as the accents of lovers' farewell
Are the hearts which they bear, and the tales which they tell.

2.

Begirt with many a gallant slave,   20
Apparelled as becomes the brave,
Awaiting each his Lord's behest
To guide his steps, or guard his rest,
Old Giaffir sate in his Divan,
    Deep thought was in his aged eye;   25
And though the face of Mussulman
    Not oft betrays to standers by
The mind within, well skill'd to hide
All but unconquerable pride,
His pensive cheek and pondering brow   30
Did more than he was wont avow.

3.

'Let the chamber be cleared'—the train disappeared—
    'Now call me the chief of the Haram guard—'
With Giaffir is none but his only son,
    And the Nubian awaiting the sire's award.   35

5 ye] you *X*   6 ever blossom, the beams] ⟨never fade⟩ and the ⟨skies⟩ *X*   9–10 *in
X, not in B; note in Proof 3 calls for their replacement*   9 fairest] finest *X, cor. in Proof 4*
11 hues] lines *X, Proof 1*   14 soft] ⟨bright⟩ *X*   18–19 *not in B, X, added in
Proof 7*   18 Oh! ... accents] ⟨For ... moments⟩ *Proof 7*   25 ⟨And now
approached his hour of prayer⟩ *A*   28 ⟨The secret workings of the soul⟩ *A*   30–1 ⟨The
day the working of his brow | Some change of feeling ? show⟩ *A*   30 His changing
cheek and knitting brow *A, cor. in B*   32 train] ⟨slaves⟩ *A*   33 call] send *A*
34 With Giaffir is] Remaineth *A*   35 awaiting] who waits for *A*

'Haroun—when all the crowd that wait
Are passed beyond the outer gate,
(Woe to the head whose eye beheld
My child Zuleika's face unveiled!)
Hence, lead my daughter from her tower—   40
Her fate is fixed this very hour;
Yet not to her repeat my thought—
By me alone be duty taught!'

'Pacha! to hear is to obey.—'
No more must slave to despot say—   45
Then to the tower had ta'en his way.
But here young Selim silence brake,
    First lowly rendering reverence meet;
And downcast looked, and gently spake,
    Still standing at the Pacha's feet.—   50
For son of Moslem must expire,
Ere dare to sit before his sire!
'Father!—for fear that thou should'st chide
My sister, or her sable guide—
Know—for the fault, if fault there be,   55
Was mine—then fall thy frowns on me!
So lovelily the morning shone,
    That—let the old and weary sleep—
I could not; and to view alone
    The fairest scenes of land and deep,   60
With none to listen and reply
To thoughts with which my heart beat high
Were irksome—for whate'er my mood,
In sooth I love not solitude:

37 beyond] ⟨without⟩ *A*

40–3   Hence—bid my daughter hither come
                            This hour decides her future doom—
                            Yet not to her these words express
                            But lead her from the tower's recess *A, B*

these words] this thought *B; Proofs 1–3 follow B text, Proof 4 as received*   44–6 *not
in A, B; added in Proof 4*   47 *placed before line 44 in Proof 4, cor. in Proof 5* But here
young] ⟨Then⟩ here young *A*; Here youthful *B, cor. in Proof 4*   48 ⟨As at⟩ First *A*
49 gently] slowly *A*   50 the Pacha's] his father's *A*   51 must] could *A*
56 then] ⟨and⟩ so *A, cor. in B*   57 shone] came *A*   58 ⟨That—breaking
on⟩ *A*   60 and] or *A*   63 Were] Is *A, B, cor. in Proof 4*

I on Zuleika's slumber broke,   65
   And, as thou knowest that for me
   Soon turns the Haram's grating key,
Before the guardian slaves awoke
We to the cypress groves had flown,
And made earth, main, and heaven our own!   70
There lingered we, beguiled too long
With Mejnoun's tale, or Sadi's song;
Till I, who heard the deep tambour
Beat thy Divan's approaching hour—
To thee and to my duty true,   75
Warn'd by the sound, to greet thee flew:
But there Zuleika wanders yet—
Nay, father, frown not—nor forget
That none can pierce that secret bower
But those who watch the women's tower.'   80

                         4.

'Son of a slave!'—the Pacha said—
'From unbelieving mother bred,
Vain were a father's hope to see
Aught that beseems a man in thee.
Thou, when thine arm should bend the bow,   85
   And hurl the dart, and curb the steed,
   Thou Greek in soul, if not in creed,
Must pore where babbling waters flow,
And watch unfolding roses blow.
Would that yon orb, whose matin glow   90
Thy listless eyes so much admire,
Would lend thee something of his fire!
Thou, who would'st see this battlement
By Christian cannon piecemeal rent—
Nay, tamely view old Stambol's wall   95
Before the dogs of Moscow fall—

65 broke] stole *A*   67 Soon] ⟨Slow⟩ *B*   grating] ⟨sullen?⟩ *A*   69 to the
⟨garden's arbor⟩ cypress *A*   72 With ⟨minstrel⟩ many a tale—and mutual song *A*
Mejnoun's] ⟨many a⟩ *B*   76 to ⟨the⟩ greet *A*   79 secret] lovely *A*
81 Pacha] ⟨father⟩ *A*   82 ⟨Son by a Christian⟩ mother bred *A*   83 a] thy *A*
87 soul] ⟨heart⟩ *A*   88 Must ⟨walk / sauntering⟩ pore *A*   89 ⟨And pore oer
every flower below⟩ *A*   91 Thy ⟨puling soul⟩ *A*   93 this] ⟨each⟩ *A*
95 tamely view] ⟨look upon⟩ *A*

Nor strike one stroke for life and death
Against the curs of Nazareth!
Go—let thy less than woman's hand
Assume the distaff—not the brand.　　　100
But, Haroun!—to my daughter speed—
And hark—of thine own head take heed—
If thus Zuleika oft takes wing—
Thou see'st yon bow—it hath a string!'

5.

No sound from Selim's lip was heard,　　　105
　At least that met old Giaffir's ear,
But every frown and every word
Pierced keener than a Christian's sword—
　'Son of a slave!—reproached with fear—
　Those gibes had cost another dear.　　　110
Son of a slave!—and *who* my sire?'
　Thus held his thoughts their dark career,
And glances even of more than ire
　Flash forth—then faintly disappear.
Old Giaffir gazed upon his son　　　115
　And started—for within his eye
He read how much his wrath had done,
He saw rebellion there begun—
　'Come hither, boy—what, no reply?
I mark thee—and I know thee too;　　　120
But there be deeds thou dar'st not do:
But if thy beard had manlier length,
And if thy hand had skill and strength,
I'd joy to see thee break a lance,
Albeit against my own perchance.'　　　125

As sneeringly these accents fell,
　On Selim's eye he fiercely gazed—
　　That eye returned him glance for glance,

97 stroke . . . and] blow . . . ⟨and⟩ or *A*, *B*, *Proof 1*　　　98 ⟨Upon the sons⟩ of *A*
99 ⟨Would⟩ Go *A*　　　105 sound . . . was heard] ⟨word . . . escaped⟩ *A*　　　sound]
⟨word⟩ *B*　　　106 old] stern *A*　　　108 Pierced] Sunk *A*, *B*, *cor. in Proofs 5, 6*
110 gibes] words *A*　　　113 For ⟨gentle looks and ? dire⟩ / looks of peace and hearts of
ire *A*, *cor. in B*　　hearts] ⟨breasts⟩ *B*　　　114 Are oft—too oft united here *A*, *cor. in B*
115 Old] ⟨And⟩ *A*　　　122–3 ⟨But when that hand hath skill and strength | And when
thy beard hath manly length⟩ *A*　　had . . . had] hath . . . hath *A*　　　124 ⟨Twould⟩
I'd joy to see thee ⟨wield⟩ a lance *A*　　　125 Albeit] ⟨Although⟩ *A*　　　126 As ⟨from
his⟩ sneeringly *A*　　　128 glance for] ⟨frown⟩ for *A*

And proudly to his sire's was raised,
   Till Giaffir's quailed and shrunk askance—   130
And why—he felt, but durst not tell.—
'Much I misdoubt this wayward boy
Will one day work me more annoy—
I never loved him from his birth,
And—but his arm is little worth,   135
And scarcely in the chace could cope
With timid fawn or antelope,
Far less would venture into strife
Where man contends for fame and life—
I would not trust that look or tone—   140
No—nor the blood so near my own—
That blood—he hath not heard—no more—
I'll watch him closer than before—
He is an Arab to my sight,
Or Christian crouching in the fight.—   145
But hark!—I hear Zuleika's voice,
   Like Houris' hymn it meets mine ear;
She is the offspring of my choice—
   Oh! more than even her mother dear,
With all to hope, and nought to fear,   150
My Peri! ever welcome here!
Sweet, as the desart-fountain's wave
To lips just cooled in time to save—
   Such to my longing sight art thou;
Nor can they waft to Mecca's shrine   155
More thanks for life, than I for thine
   Who blest thy birth, and bless thee now.'

6.

Fair—as the first that fell of womankind—
   When on that dread yet lovely serpent smiling,
Whose image then was stamped upon her mind—   160
   But once beguiled—and ever more beguiling;

129 proudly] ⟨boldly⟩ calmly *A* ⟨calmly⟩ *B*   131 durst] would *A*   132 I mis-
doubt] ⟨do I doubt⟩ *A*   133 Will ⟨many a future⟩ one *A*   more] much *A, cor. in B*
139 contends . . . and] ⟨with man contends for⟩ *A*   140 or] and *A*   141 so near]
I call *A*   142–3 *not in A*   142 he ⟨can⟩ hath *B*   145 crouching in] ⟨flying
from⟩ *A*   149 Oh . . . even] Nor much more was *A*   150 all] ⟨much⟩ *A*   151 My
Peri] ⟨Zuleika⟩ *A*   154 ⟨Oh ever to my⟩ Such *A*   155 can they ⟨thank the⟩ waft *A*
157 Who ⟨never was more blest than now⟩ *A*   159 on . . . yet] ⟨first upon that⟩ *A*
160 then . . . upon] ⟨ever since hath marked⟩ *A*   161 more] ⟨since⟩ *A*

Dazzling—as that, oh! too transcendant vision
  To Sorrow's phantom-peopled slumber given,
When heart meets heart again in dreams Elysian,
  And paints the lost on Earth revived in Heaven—   165
Soft—as the memory of buried love—
Pure—as the prayer which Childhood wafts above—
Was she—the daughter of that rude old Chief,
Who met the maid with tears—but not of grief.

Who hath not proved—how feebly words essay   170
To fix one spark of Beauty's heavenly ray?
Who doth not feel—until his failing sight
Faints into dimness with its own delight—
His changing cheek—his sinking heart confess
The might—the majesty of Loveliness?   175
Such was Zuleika—such around her shone
The nameless charms unmarked by her alone—
The light of love—the purity of grace—
The mind—the Music breathing from her face!
The heart whose softness harmonized the whole—   180
And, oh! that eye was in itself a Soul!

Her graceful arms in meekness bending
  Across her gently-budding breast—
At one kind word those arms extending
  To clasp the neck of him who blest   185
  His child caressing and carest,
Zuleika came—and Giaffir felt
His purpose half within him melt;
Not that against her fancied weal
His heart though stern could ever feel—   190
Affection chained her to that heart—
  Ambition tore the links apart.

162 ⟨Bright as a ?⟩ Dazzling as that oh too ⟨remembered dream⟩ / ⟨bewitching⟩ transcen-
dant vision A   163-4 ⟨To every / fainting Grief's first feverish slumber given | When
added charms / secret wants surround the heart again⟩ A   169 met the maid] ⟨gazed
on her⟩ A   170-81 not in A, B; note in Proof 7 calls for their insertion   172 Who
⟨hath not felt—till even his shrinking⟩ sight X   173 Faints ⟨with the languid dimness
of⟩ delight X   180 The] A X, cor. in D   181 that] her X   182 in meek-
ness] ⟨before her⟩ A   185 To clasp] Around A   186 His] ⟨That⟩ A   191 ⟨But
in his hope ?⟩ A   chained] ⟨chained / forged⟩ A; ⟨linked⟩ B

7.

'Zuleika—child of gentleness!
  How dear—this very day must tell,
When I forget my own distress   195
    In losing what I love so well
    To bid thee with another dwell,
  Another—and a braver man
  Was never seen in battle's van.
We Moslem reck not much of blood—   200
  But yet the line of Carasman
Unchanged—unchangeable hath stood,
First of the bold Timariot bands
That won and well can keep their lands.
Enough—that he who comes to woo   205
Is kinsman of the Bey Oglou—
His years need scarce a thought employ—
I would not have thee wed a boy—
And thou shalt have a noble dower:
And his and my united power   210
Will laugh to scorn the death-firman,
Which others tremble but to scan—
And teach the messenger what fate
The bearer of such boon may wait.
And now thou know'st thy father's will—   215
  All that thy sex hath need to know—
'Twas mine to teach obedience still,
  The way to love, thy lord may shew.'

8.

In silence bowed the virgin's head—
  And if her eye was filled with tears   220
That stifled feeling dare not shed,
  And changed her cheek from pale to red,
  And red to pale, as through her ears
  Those winged words like arrows sped—

202 ⟨First of the few⟩ A   203 bold . . . bands] ⟨few . . . chiefs⟩ A   204 Who
⟨hold of arms paternal fiefs⟩ / won of yon paternal lands A, cor. in B   205 Enough ⟨of
that—thy bridesman true⟩ A   206 Bey] ⟨great⟩ A   207 a thought] ⟨your⟩ / thy
thoughts A   210 my] mine A; mine / my B   213 what ⟨brings⟩ fate A
214 boon] ⟨gifts⟩ A   216 hath need] ⟨can wish⟩ A   219 the virgin's] her virgin A
220 ⟨And stifled feeling would not shed⟩ A   was] half A   223 as through] ⟨and
in⟩ A   224 winged words like] ⟨words like barbed⟩ A

What could such be but maiden fears?   225
So bright the tear in Beauty's eye
Love half regrets to kiss it dry—
So sweet the blush of Bashfulness,
Even Pity scarce can wish it less!

Whate'er it was the sire forgot—   230
Or if remembered, marked it not—
Thrice clapped his hands, and called his steed,
Resign'd his gem-adorn'd Chibouque,
And mounting featly for the mead,
With Maugrabee—and Mamaluke—   235
His way amid his Delis took,
To witness many an active deed
With sabre keen—or blunt jereed.
The Kislar only and his Moors
Watch well the Haram's massy doors.   240

9.

His head was leant upon his hand,
    His eye looked o'er the dark blue water,
That swiftly glides and gently swells
Between the winding Dardanelles;
But yet he saw nor sea nor strand,   245
Nor even his Pacha's turbaned band
    Mix in the game of mimic slaughter,
Careering cleave the folded felt
With sabre stroke right sharply dealt—
Nor marked the javelin-darting crowd,   250
Nor heard their Ollahs wild and loud—
    He thought but of old Giaffir's daughter.

226 ⟨Which⟩ / ⟨So sweet / clear / swimming⟩ A   tear] drops A   227 ⟨Scarce half
forgets⟩ to A   233 not in A, B; added in Proof 3   234 mounting] mounted A,
B, cor. in Proof 3   235 ⟨Where⟩ With Moslem there and Mamaluke A   236 amid]
⟨amidst⟩ B   his Delis] ⟨his band he⟩ A   237 an active] ⟨a vigorous⟩ A   238 or
blunt] and swift A, cor. in B   241 leant] leaned A   242 looked o'er] ⟨was on⟩ A
244 the ⟨near⟩ winding A   246 Nor ⟨marked⟩ even his father's A   247 game
of mimic] ⟨mimic game of⟩ A   248 ⟨The folded felt careering cleave⟩ A   249 With
⟨blows on⟩ sabre A   250 marked] ⟨saw⟩ A   251 wild] ⟨shrill⟩ A   252 old
Giaffir's] ⟨his father's / old Giaffir's⟩ the Pacha's A

10.

No word from Selim's bosom broke—
One sigh Zuleika's thought bespoke—
Still gazed he through the lattice grate,   255
Pale—mute—and mournfully sedate.—
To him Zuleika's eye was turned,
But little from his aspect learned;
Equal her grief—yet not the same,
Her heart confessed a gentler flame—   260
But yet that heart alarmed or weak,
She knew not why, forbade to speak—
Yet speak she must—but when essay?
'How strange he thus should turn away!
Not thus we e'er before have met,   265
Not thus shall be our parting yet.'—
Thrice paced she slowly through the room,
And watched his eye—it still was fixed:
She snatched the urn wherein was mixed
The Persian Atar-gul's perfume,   270
And sprinkled all its odours o'er
The pictured roof and marble floor—
The drops, that through his glittering vest
The playful girl's appeal addrest,
Unheeded o'er his bosom flew,   275
As if that breast were marble too—
'What sullen yet? it must not be—
Oh! gentle Selim, this from thee!'
She saw in curious order set
The fairest flowers of Eastern land—   280
'He loved them once—may touch them yet,
If offered by Zuleika's hand.'
The childish thought was hardly breathed
Before the Rose was pluck'd and wreathed—
The next fond moment saw her seat   285
Her fairy form at Selim's feet—

254 One] No *A*   258 little] ⟨nothing⟩ *A*   259 Equal] ⟨Alike⟩ *A*   260 a gentler
flame] no cause of shame *A, B, cor. in Proof 3*   263 when essay] ⟨how to say⟩ *A*
265 we ⟨ever met before⟩ *A*   271 odours ⟨round⟩ *A*   272–3 ⟨The drops that
flew upon his vest | Unheeded fell upon his / that breast | As those that idly ? to the
ground⟩ *A*   272 pictured] fretted *A*   273 through his glittering] ⟨scattered on
his⟩ *B*   274 ⟨Zuleika's⟩ *A*   277 yet? it] still—this *A*   281 touch]
⟨love / like⟩ *A*   283 The ⟨word scarce said⟩ ⟨girlish⟩ / childish *A*

Painted by Thos Stothard R.A.   Engraved by Chas Heath

BRIDE OF ABYDOS.

WHAT — NOT RECEIVE MY FOOLISH FLOWER?
NAY THEN I AM INDEED UNBLEST.

PUBLISHED BY JOHN MURRAY, ALBEMARLE STREET, DECR 1,1814.

The Bride of Abydos Canto I lines 295–6

(*Reproduced with the permission of the British Library*)

'This rose to calm my brother's cares
A message from the Bulbul bears;
It says to-night he will prolong,
For Selim's ear his sweetest song—   290
And though his note is somewhat sad,
He'll try for once a strain more glad,
With some faint hope his altered lay
May sing these gloomy thoughts away.

II.

'What—not receive my foolish flower?—   295
Nay then I am indeed unblest:
On me can thus thy forehead lower?
And know'st thou not who loves thee best?
Oh, Selim dear!—Oh, more than dearest!
Say, is it I thou hat'st or fearest?   300
Come, lay thy head upon my breast,
And I will kiss thee into rest,
Since words of mine—and songs must fail,
Even from my fabled nightingale.
I knew our sire at times was stern,   305
But this from thee had yet to learn—
Too well I know he loves thee not,
But is Zuleika's love forgot?
Ah! deem I right? the Pacha's plan—
This kinsman Bey of Carasman   310
Perhaps may prove some foe of thine—
If so—I swear by Mecca's shrine,
If shrines, that ne'er approach allow
To woman's step, admit her vow—
Without thy free consent, command—   315
The Sultan should not have my hand!
Think'st thou that I could bear to part
With thee—and learn to halve my heart?

290 ⟨Forsooth⟩ *A*   291 somewhat] often *A*; rather *B*, *cor. in Proof 3*   292 strain]
⟨note⟩ *A*   293 ⟨In fondest hope his offered⟩ lay *A*   294 sing] ⟨soothe⟩ *A*
296 Nay then ⟨there is a serpent there⟩ / ⟨I must have ? thy ?⟩ *A*   297 Would I had
never seen this hour *A*   298 And] What— *A*   300 I] me *Bride1, Bride10, 1815,*
1831, 1832, C, More   303 words . . . songs] ⟨promised melody⟩ *A*   305 knew]
know *A*   309 Ah—now I guess—that hasty plan *A*, *cor. in B*   hasty] ⟨sudden⟩ *B*
deem] dream *B*, *cor. in Proof 3*   312 I . . . Mecca's] by Mecca's ⟨curtained⟩ / hidden *A*
314 admit] ⟨will hear⟩ *A*

Ah! were I severed from thy side,
Where were thy friend—and who my guide?   320
Years have not seen—Time shall not see
The hour that tears my soul from thee—
Even Azrael from his deadly quiver
　　When flies that shaft—and fly it must—
That parts all else—shall doom for ever   325
　　Our hearts to undivided dust!'

　　　　　　　12.

He lived—he breathed—he moved—he felt—
He raised the maid from where she knelt—
His trance was gone—his keen eye shone
With thoughts that long in darkness dwelt—   330
With thoughts that burn—in rays that melt.—
As the stream late concealed
　　By the fringe of its willows—
When it rushes revealed
　　In the light of its billows,—   335
As the bolt bursts on high
　　From the black cloud that bound it—
Flash'd the soul of that eye
　　Through the long lashes round it.
A warhorse at the trumpet's sound,   340
A lion roused by heedless hound;
A tyrant waked to sudden strife
By graze of ill-directed knife,
Starts not to more convulsive life
Than he, who heard that vow, displayed,   345
And all, before repressed, betrayed.

'Now thou art mine, for ever mine,
　　With life to keep, and scarce with life resign;—

322 The day ⟨that divides / dividing thee from me⟩ / that teareth me from thee *A*
323 deadly] fatal *A*　　324 When ⟨comes that hour—and come⟩ it must *A*　　325 doom]
⟨join⟩ *A*　　　　326 Our] ⟨Two⟩ *A*　　　　329 keen] ⟨dark⟩ *A*　　　331 in] ⟨but⟩ *A*
332–9 *not in A, B; MS. insertion in Proof 6*　　332 late] ⟨half⟩ *Proof 6*　　　　336 bolt
bursts on] Moonbeam from *Proof 6*　　　337 From] Bursts *Proof 6*　　　338 soul] glance
Proof 6　　　342 sudden] ⟨Midnight⟩ *A*　　　343a-b Which thanks to terror and the
dark | Hath missed a trifle of its mark *A, B, removed in Proof 7*　　　346 repressed]
concealed *A, cor. in B*　　　347–50 *in A the sequence is 349, 350, 347, 348*　　　348 scarce]
not A

Now thou art mine, that sacred oath,
Though sworn by one, hath bound us both.   350
Yes, fondly, wisely hast thou done,
That vow hath saved more heads than one:—
But blench not thou—thy simplest tress
Claims more from me than tenderness;
I would not wrong the slenderest hair   355
That clusters round thy forehead fair,
For all the treasures buried far
Within the caves of Istakar.
This morning clouds upon me lowered,
Reproaches on my head were showered,   360
And Giaffir almost called me coward!
Now I have motive to be brave,
The son of his neglected slave:
Nay, start not—'twas the term he gave—
May shew, though little apt to vaunt,   365
A heart his words nor deeds can daunt.
His son, indeed!—yet, thanks to thee,
Perchance I am, at least shall be;
But let our plighted secret vow
Be only known to us as now.   370
I know the wretch who dares demand
From Giaffir thy reluctant hand;
More ill-got wealth, a meaner soul
Holds not a Musselim's control;
Was he not bred in Egripo?   375
A viler race let Israel show!
But let that pass—to none be told
Our oath—the rest shall time unfold;
To me and mine leave Osman Bey,
I've partizans for peril's day;   380
Think not I am what I appear,
I've arms, and friends, and vengeance near.'

350 Though] But *A*   351 Yes, fondly] Though kindly *A*; Though ⟨kindly⟩ *B, cor.
in Proof 3*   356 That strays along that heart so fair *A*   heart] neck *B*; *B var. in
Proof 1*   357 treasures buried] ⟨fabled treasures⟩ *A*   364 term] name *A*
366 A heart that Peril ⟨will⟩ / can not daunt *A*   367–8 *not in A*   368 Perchance]
Perhaps *B, Proof 1*   369 But ⟨still⟩ let *A*   371 dares] dared *A*   373 a] and *A*
374 a Musselim's] ⟨in Roumelie's⟩ *A*   375 Why—he was bred *A, B, Proof 1*
376 race] brood *A, B, cor. in Proof 5*   377 to . . . told] let none ⟨perceive⟩ / be told *A, B,
cor. in Proof 10*   380 peril's] danger's *A*   382 arms . . . friends] friends . . . arms *A*

13.

'Think not thou art what thou appearest!
My Selim, thou art sadly changed;
This morn I saw thee gentlest, dearest,   385
But now thou'rt from thyself estranged.
My love thou surely knew'st before,
It ne'er was less, nor can be more.
To see thee, hear thee, near thee stay,
And hate the night I know not why,   390
Save that we meet not but by day—
With thee to live, with thee to die,
I dare not to my hope deny:
Thy cheek, thine eyes, thy lips to kiss,
Like this—and this—no more then this,   395
For, Alla! sure thy lips are flame,
What fever in thy veins is flushing?
My own have nearly caught the same,
At least I feel my cheek too blushing.
To soothe thy sickness, watch thy health,   400
Partake, but never waste thy wealth,
Or stand with smiles unmurmuring by,
And lighten half thy poverty;
Do all but close thy dying eye,
For that I could not live to try;   405
To these alone my thoughts aspire—
More can I do? or thou require?
But, Selim, thou must answer why
We need so much of mystery?
The cause I cannot dream nor tell,   410
But be it, since thou say'st 'tis well;
Yet what thou mean'st by "arms" and "friends",
Beyond my weaker sense extends—

384 My] ⟨Dear⟩ A   385 I saw] I knew A, cor. in B   393 my hope] myself
A, cor. in B   394 ⟨To press / Thine eyes⟩ A   396 Oh! Allah! ⟨how⟩ thy lips
are ⟨burning⟩ A, cor. in B   397 thy ⟨cheek⟩ veins A   398 have nearly] hath
almost A; ⟨can never f⟩ hath nearly B, Bride1, 1a, 2, cor. in D1   399 too] is A
400 watch] ⟨cheer⟩ A   405 could not] scarce could A   407 But more must
do if thou require A, cor. in B   408 But Selim—why my heart's reply A, cor. in B
409 We] Should A, cor. in B   410 Is more than I can ⟨try to⟩ / grasp or tell A, cor.
in B   411 But ⟨since thou sayst tis so—⟩ tis well A   412 Yet] And A
413 weaker] duller A; humbler B, cor. in Proof 3

I meant that Giaffir should have heard
  The very vow I plighted thee;   415
His wrath would not revoke my word—
  But surely he would leave me free;
  Can this fond wish seem strange in me
To be what I have ever been?
What other hath Zuleika seen   420
From simple childhood's earliest hour?
  What other can she seek to see
Than thee, companion of her bower,
  The partner of her infancy?
These cherished thoughts with life begun,   425
  Say, why must I no more avow?
What change is wrought to make me shun
  The truth—my pride—and thine till now?
To meet the gaze of strangers' eyes
Our law, our creed, our God denies;   430
Nor shall one wandering thought of mine
At such, our Prophet's will, repine:
No—happier made by that decree,
He left me all in leaving thee.
Deep were my anguish, thus compelled   435
To wed with one I ne'er beheld—
This—wherefore should I not reveal?
Why wilt thou urge me to conceal?
I know the Pacha's haughty mood
To thee hath never boded good;   440
And he so often storms at nought,
Allah! forbid that e'er he ought!
And why I know not, but within
My heart concealment weighs like sin.
If then such secrecy be crime,   445
  And such it feels while lurking here;

414 should have ⟨known⟩ / heard *A*   416 His] ⟨And⟩ *A*   417 But yet I think
he'll leave me free *A*   418–38 *not in A, MS. insertion in B*   418 seem] ⟨be⟩ *B*
423 Than] But *B*   425 ⟨The fiend / Why must affection thus begun⟩ / ⟨Say can the
love⟩ with life begun *X*   426 ⟨Why should I fear to / Is this a time to disavow⟩ / Must
? not ? me to avow *X* ⟨Why in⟩ Say why *B*   428 ⟨What / A truth now hid ?⟩ / ⟨A /
The truth unmasked⟩ *X*   429 strangers'] ⟨other⟩ *B*   433 made] ⟨far⟩ *B*   434 left
. . . in] ⟨blest me more by⟩ *B*   435 Deep . . . anguish] ⟨Much should I suffer⟩ *B*
439 the Pacha's] his stern and *A, cor. in B*   441 at] ⟨for⟩ *A*   444 My ⟨consc⟩
heart is consciousness of sin *A, cor. in B*   445 But where—and ⟨what and⟩ / when
and what ⟨my⟩ / the crime *A, cor. in B*   446 I almost feel is lurking here *A, cor. in B*

Oh, Selim! tell me yet in time,
    Nor leave me thus to thoughts of fear.
Ah! yonder see the Tchocadar,
My father leaves the mimic war;   450
I tremble now to meet his eye—
Say, Selim, can'st thou tell me why?'

14.

'Zuleika—to thy tower's retreat
Betake thee—Giaffir I can greet;
And now with him I fain must prate   455
Of firmans, imposts, levies, state:
There's fearful news from Danube's banks,
Our Vizier nobly thins his ranks,
For which the Giaour may give him thanks!
Our Sultan hath a shorter way   460
Such costly triumph to repay.
But, mark me, when the twilight drum
    Hath warned the troops to food and sleep,
Unto thy cell will Selim come:
    Then softly from the Haram creep   465
    Where we may wander by the deep:
    Our garden-battlements are steep;
Nor these will rash intruder climb
To list our words, or stint our time;
And if he doth—I want not steel   470
Which some have felt, and more may feel.
Then shalt thou learn of Selim more
Than thou hast heard or thought before;
Trust me, Zuleika—fear not me!
Thou know'st I hold a Haram key.'   475

'Fear thee, my Selim! ne'er till now
Did word like this—'
                            'Delay not thou;

448 leave ⟨to me⟩ me thus A   452 Say] Oh A   454 ⟨Now hasten⟩ A
456 firmans] ⟨tidings⟩ A   459 Giaour ⟨claims⟩ may A   462 ⟨Zuleika⟩ A
463 sleep] ⟨rest⟩ A ; rest B, cor. in Proof 5   464 ⟨To thee⟩ Unto thy ⟨tower⟩ will A
Unto] ⟨Then to⟩ B   465 ⟨And we will wander⟩ A   from] ⟨through⟩ A   467 Our
. . . are] Our garden ⟨wall is tall and⟩ A   470 I ⟨have⟩ want A   472 of] from A
473 Than ⟨Giaffir knows—and thou⟩ thou hast A   476 my] ⟨dear⟩ A   477 Did
such a word— | Be silent thou A   Delay] ⟨Doubt⟩ B

I keep the key—and Haroun's guard
Have *some*, and hope, of *more* reward.
Tonight, Zuleika, thou shalt hear   480
My tale, my purpose, and my fear—
I am not, love! what I appear.'

CANTO II

1.

The winds are high on Helle's wave,
    As on that night of stormy water
When Love—who sent—forgot to save
The young, the beautiful, the brave,
    The lonely hope of Sestos' daughter.   5
Oh! when alone along the sky
Her turret-torch was blazing high,
Though rising gale, and breaking foam,
And shrieking sea-birds warn'd him home;
And clouds aloft, and tides below,   10
With signs and sounds forbade to go,
He could not see, he would not hear,
Or sound or sign foreboding fear;
    His eye but saw that light of love,
    The only star it hail'd above;   15
His ear but rang with Hero's song,
'Ye waves divide not lovers long!'
That tale is old, but love anew
May nerve young hearts to prove as true.

2.

The winds are high—and Helle's tide   20
    Rolls darkly heaving to the main;
And Night's descending shadows hide
    That field with blood bedew'd in vain;

478 keep] ⟨hold⟩ *A*   481 tale] ⟨hope⟩ *A*

Canto II

    2 night ⟨what blue / when⟩ of *A*   3 ⟨Became the daring lovers' grave⟩ *A*   who]
that *A*   5 ⟨Who now has ? to⟩ / ⟨The darling youth⟩ of Sestos' daughter *A*   6 Oh
when ⟨along in yon blackest⟩ sky *A*   8 breaking] ⟨whitening⟩ *A*   10 and ⟨skies⟩
tides *A*   12–13 *not in A*   16 rang with] ⟨dreamed of⟩ *A*   18 but
love ⟨is new⟩ *A*   19 ⟨And hearts may yet be found as true⟩ *A*   20 and] ⟨as⟩ *A*
23 field ⟨of slaughter⟩ with *A*

The desart of old Priam's pride—
 The tombs—sole relics of his reign—   25
All, save immortal dreams that could beguile
The blind old man of Scio's rocky isle!

3.

Oh! yet—for there my steps have been,
 These feet have press'd the sacred shore,
These limbs that buoyant wave hath borne—   30
Minstrel! with thee to muse, to mourn—
 To trace again those fields of yore—
Believing every hillock green
 Contains no fabled hero's ashes—
And that around the undoubted scene   35
 Thine own 'broad Hellespont' still dashes—
Be long my lot—and cold were he
Who there could gaze denying thee!

4.

The night hath closed on Helle's stream,
 Nor yet hath risen on Ida's hill   40
That moon, which shone on his high theme—
No warrior chides her peaceful beam,
 But conscious shepherds bless it still.
Their flocks are grazing on the mound
 Of him who felt the Dardan's arrow;—   45
That mighty heap of gather'd ground
Which Ammon's son ran proudly round,
By nations rais'd, by monarchs crown'd,
 Is now a lone and nameless barrow.
 Within—thy dwelling-place how narrow!   50

---

26 save ⟨the⟩ immortal *A*   30 These limbs ⟨that rapid water bore⟩ / ⟨those waves have buoyant borne⟩ *A* 31 ⟨With thee to melt—⟩ to muse—to mourne *A* 32 fields of yore] ⟨scenes once more⟩ *A* 35 And ⟨on the⟩ that *A* 37 long . . . were] ⟨still . . . is⟩ *A* 38 denying] ⟨and doubt in⟩ *A* 40 ⟨But Pindus / Nor yet oer Ida's hill hath risen⟩ *A* 41–3 That ⟨light⟩ moon whose everlasting beam | May bless the conscious shepherds still *A* 41 which . . . high] ⟨that⟩ which shone upon thy *B*, *Proof 1* 42 chides her peaceful] now can hail her *B*, *Proof 1* 44–56 *not in A* 44 grazing on the mound] ⟨feeding⟩ on the ⟨barrow⟩ *X* 46 ⟨Pride of all nations / song —theme of⟩ ⟨Alas! within that lonely mound⟩ *X* 47 Which nations raised and monarchs crowned *X* 48 And Ammon's son ran proudly round *X* 50 ⟨And in⟩ thy dwelling place is narrow *X*, *cor. in B*

Without—can only strangers breathe
The name of him that *was* beneath.
Dust long outlasts the storied stone—
But Thou—thy very dust is gone!

5.

Late, late tonight will Dian cheer   55
The swain, and chase the boatman's fear;
Till then—no beacon on the cliff
May shape the course of struggling skiff;
The scatter'd lights that skirt the bay,
All, one by one, have died away;   60
The only lamp of this lone hour
Is glimmering in Zuleika's tower.

Yes, there is light in that lone chamber,
     And o'er her silken Ottoman
Are thrown the fragrant beads of amber,   65
     O'er which her fairy fingers ran;
Near these, with emerald rays beset,
(How could she thus that gem forget?)
Her mother's sainted amulet,
Whereon engraved the Koorsee text,   70
Could smooth this life, and win the next;
And by her Comboloio lies
A Koran of illumin'd dyes;
And many a bright emblazon'd rhyme
By Persian scribes redeem'd from time;   75
And o'er those scrolls, not oft so mute,
Reclines her now neglected lute;
And round her lamp of fretted gold
Bloom flowers in urns of China's mould;

51 only strangers] strangers only *X*, *B*, *Proof 1*   52 ⟨Of whom the very dust must⟩ *X*
55 will Dian] that orb will *B*, *Proof 1*   56 ⟨And chase the struggling⟩ boatman's
fear *B*   57 ⟨Is yon a beacon on the cliff⟩ / No beacon on the shaggy cliff *A, cor. in B*
61 only] latest *A*   62 Is ⟨light⟩ beaming in *A*   64 her] the *A*   65 Are
⟨careless⟩ thrown the ⟨famed⟩ fragrant *A*   67–71 *not in A, B*   67 ⟨And there⟩
There too with emeralds beset *X5*; ⟨Near too with emeralds beset⟩ / ⟨Near these in emeralds—
sapphires set⟩ *X5a*   68 *no parentheses in first nine edns.*   68–9 ⟨Her mother's
sacred amulet | How could she thus that gem forget⟩ *X5*   71 Could . . . life] ⟨This
life could smooth⟩ *X5a*   72 her] that *A, B, cor. in Proof 6*   73 A] ⟨The⟩ Her
A, B, cor. in Proof 6   76 o'er] ⟨near⟩ *A*   77 neglected] forgotten *A, B, cor. in
Proof 3*   78 lamp of fretted] ⟨little lamp of⟩ *A*   79 ⟨Rays⟩ Bloom *A*

The richest work of Iran's loom,   80
And Sheeraz' tribute of perfume;
All that can eye or sense delight
    Are gather'd in that gorgeous room—
    But yet it hath an air of gloom.—
She, of this Peri cell the sprite,   85
What doth she hence, and on so rude a night?

6.

Wrapt in the darkest sable vest,
    Which none save noblest Moslem wear,
To guard from winds of heaven the breast
    As heaven itself to Selim dear;   90
With cautious steps the thicket threading,
    And starting oft, as through the glade
    The gust its hollow moanings made,
Till on the smoother pathway treading,
More free her timid bosom beat,   95
    The maid pursued her silent guide;
And though her terror urged retreat,
    How could she quit her Selim's side?
    How teach her tender lips to chide?

7.

They reach'd at length a grotto, hewn   100
    By nature, but enlarged by art,
Where oft her lute she wont to tune,
    And oft her Koran conned apart;
And oft in youthful reverie
    She dream'd what Paradise might be—   105
Where woman's parted soul shall go
Her Prophet had disdain'd to show;
But Selim's mansion was secure,

80 of Iran's] of ⟨Per⟩ Iran's *A*   82 ⟨And all that sense and sight⟩ *A*   86 ⟨For whom⟩ *A*   87 ⟨Slowly is raised the garden wicket⟩ Wrapt in ⟨this wicked robe of sable⟩ *A*
88 That ⟨Pacha's kinsmen well may wear⟩ / none save a Pacha's kinsman wear *A*; Which none save Pacha's ⟨kin may⟩ kinsmen wear *B*, *Proof 1*   noblest Moslem] Pacha's kin may *Proof 2*, *cor. in Proof 3*   90 More than that heaven to Selim dear *A*   92 And ⟨stumbling? when / starting oft the⟩ starting oft as through the ⟨cypress shade⟩ *A*
96 The maid ⟨and youth⟩ pursued *A*   100 ⟨How sweet how⟩ *A*   105 She ⟨there⟩ dreamed *A*   106 shall] ⟨might⟩ must *A*; might *B*, *cor. in Proof 10a*   107 had ... to] did not clearly *A*, *B*, *cor. in Proof 3*   108 mansion was] place was quite *A*, *B*, *cor. in Proof 3*

Nor deem'd she, could he long endure
His bower in other worlds of bliss,   110
Without *her* most beloved in this!
Oh! who so dear with him could dwell?
What Houri soothe him half so well?

8.

Since last she visited the spot
Some change seem'd wrought within the grot: 115
It might be only that the night
Disguis'd things seen by better light—
That brazen lamp but dimly threw
A ray of no celestial hue;
But in a nook within the cell   120
Her eye on stranger objects fell.
There arms were piled, not such as wield
The turban'd Delis in the field;
But brands of foreign blade and hilt,
And one was red—perchance with guilt—   125
Ah! how without can blood be spilt?
A cup too on the board was set
That did not seem to hold sherbet.
What may this mean—she turn'd to see
Her Selim—'Oh! can this be he?'   130

9.

His robe of pride was thrown aside,
   His brow no high-crown'd turban bore,
But in its stead a shawl of red,
   Wreath'd lightly round, his temples wore:—
That dagger, on whose hilt the gem   135
Were worthy of a diadem,
No longer glitter'd at his waist,
Where pistols unadorn'd were braced.

---

111 ⟨With the maid⟩ *A*   112–13 *not in A, B, added in MS. in Proof 4*   115 wrought]
worked *A*   117 Made strange things ⟨only⟩ seen by better light *A, cor. in B*
118 dimly ⟨falls⟩ threw *A*   119 A light of ⟨most unusual⟩ hue *A*   120 But
⟨where its rays⟩ *A*   121 stranger] curious *A*   122 piled] ranged *A*   123 Delis]
warriors *A*   125 And one seemed red with recent guilt *A, cor. in B*   126 *not
in A*   130 Oh . . . be] ⟨Allah is it⟩ *A*   131 His ⟨Pach⟩ robe of ⟨prince⟩ pride *A*
132 ⟨No high⟩ *A*

And from his belt a sabre swung,
And from his shoulder loosely hung   140
The cloak of white—the thin capote
That decks the wandering Candiote:
Beneath—his golden plated vest
Clung like a cuirass to his breast—
The greaves below his knee that wound   145
With silvery scales were sheathed and bound.
But were it not that high command
Spake in his eye—and tone and hand—
All that a careless eye could see
In him was some young Galiongée.   150

10.

'I said I was not what I seemed—
    And now thou seest my words were true;
I have a tale thou hast not dreamed,
    If sooth—its truth must others rue.
My story now 'twere vain to hide,   155
I must not see thee Osman's bride:
But had not thine own lips declared
How much of that young heart I shared,
I could not, must not, yet have shown
The darker secret of my own.—   160
In this I speak not now of love—
That—let time, truth, and peril prove;
But first—Oh! never wed another—
Zuleika! I am not thy brother!'

11.

'Oh! not my brother!—yet unsay—   165
    God! am I left alone on earth?—
To mourn—I dare not curse—the day
    That saw my solitary birth!

139 belt ⟨and at⟩ a *A*   140 loosely hung] ⟨loose along⟩ *A*   142 wandering]
⟨sea-bred⟩ *A*   145 below his knee] ⟨around his legs⟩ *A*   146 ⟨Behind with
silvery scales were bound⟩ *A*   148 tone] ⟨voice⟩ *A*   154 must others ⟨too⟩ *A*
155 ⟨Twere⟩ *A*   162 ⟨That Time and ripening deeds shall prove⟩ *A*   163 Oh
. . . wed] ⟨that truth must bring⟩ *A*   165 yet unsay] Selim say *A*   167 Why have
I lived to curse the day *A*; What! have . . . day *B, Proof 1, cor. in Proof 1a* ⟨To curse—if
I could curse—the day⟩ And mourne—I dare not curse—the day *MS. cor. in Proof 1a, cor.
again in Proof 3*

Oh! thou wilt love me now no more!
   My sinking heart foreboded ill;   170
But know *me* all I was before,
   Thy sister—friend—Zuleika still.
   Thou led'st me here perchance to kill;
If thou hast cause for vengeance—See!
   My breast is offered—take thy fill!   175
Far better with the dead to be
Than live thus nothing now to thee—
Perhaps far worse—for now I know
Why Giaffir always seemed thy foe;
And I, alas! am Giaffir's child,   180
For whom thou wert contemned—reviled—
If not thy sister—wouldst thou save
My life—Oh! bid me be thy slave!'

12.

'My slave, Zuleika!—nay, I'm thine:
   But, gentle love, this transport calm,   185
Thy lot shall yet be linked with mine;
I swear it by our Prophet's shrine,
   And be that thought thy sorrow's balm.
So may the Koran verse displayed
Upon its steel direct my blade,   190
In danger's hour to guard us both,
As I preserve that awful oath!
The name in which thy heart hath prided
   Must change—but, my Zuleika, know,
That tie is widened—not divided—   195
   Although thy Sire's my deadliest foe.
My father was to Giaffir all
   That Selim late was deemed to thee;
That brother wrought a brother's fall,
   But spared—at least, my infancy—   200
And lulled me with a vain deceit
That yet a like return may meet.

174 ⟨But⟩ *A*   175 My] ⟨My⟩ This *A*   177 Than live ⟨a nothing unto⟩ thee
A   live] ⟨thrive⟩ *B*   185 But . . . love] ⟨Thou shalt be more⟩ *A*   187 ⟨And let
this⟩ *A*   188 And ⟨let this⟩ be *A*   190 its] ⟨this⟩ *A*   191 ⟨To guard us both⟩
In *A*   192 preserve] regard *A*   193 in which ⟨Affection⟩ thy *A*   195 is]
⟨but⟩ *A* ⟨though⟩ *B*   197 to . . . all] ⟨in blood to him⟩ *A*   201 a] the *A*

He reared me—not with tender help—
　　But like the nephew of a Cain,
He watched me like a lion's whelp,　　　　　　　　　205
　　That gnaws and yet may break his chain.
My father's blood in every vein
Is boiling—but for thy dear sake
No present vengeance will I take—
　　Though here I must no more remain.　　　　　　210
But first—beloved Zuleika!—hear
How Giaffir wrought this deed of fear.

13.

'How first their strife to rancour grew—
　　If love or envy made them foes—
It matters little if I knew;　　　　　　　　　　　215
In fiery spirits, slights though few
　　And thoughtless will disturb repose:
In war Abdallah's arm was strong,
Remembered yet in Bosniac song,
And Paswan's rebel hordes attest　　　　　　　　220
How little love they bore such guest.
His death is all I need relate,
The stern effect of Giaffir's hate;
And how my birth disclosed to me,
Whate'er beside it makes—hath made me—free.　　　225

14.

'When Paswan, after years of strife,
At last for power—but first for life—
In Widin's walls too proudly sate—
Our Pachas rallied round the state;
Nor last nor least in high command　　　　　　　230
Each brother led a separate band;
They gave their horsetails to the wind,
　　And mustering in Sophia's plain
Their tents were pitched—their post assigned—
　　To one, alas! assigned in vain!—　　　　　　235

205 like] ⟨like⟩ as *A*　　　210 Though . . . must] ⟨But⟩ . . . can *A*　　　217 thought-
less will] ⟨light will soon⟩ *A*　　　219 Bosniac] Arnaut *A*　　　223 stern] vile *A*
224 my . . . to] ⟨that death made known⟩ to *A*　　　225 Whateer beside—hath made me
free. *A*　　　227 but] ⟨at⟩ *A*　　　231 ⟨The⟩ Each *A*　　　232–3 *transposed, then cor., in A*

What need of words?—the deadly bowl,
  By Giaffir's order drugged and given,
With venom subtle as his soul,
  Dismissed Abdallah's hence to heaven.
Reclined and feverish in the bath,   240
  He, when the hunter's sport was up,
But little deemed a brother's wrath
  To quench his thirst had such a cup.
The bowl a bribed attendant bore,
He drank one draught—nor needed more!   245
If thou my tale, Zuleika, doubt—
Call Haroun—he can tell it out.

15.

'The deed once done—and Paswan's feud
In part suppressed—though ne'er subdued—
Abdallah's Pachalick was gained—   250
  (Thou know'st not what in our Divan
  Can wealth procure for worse than man):
Abdallah's honours were obtained
By him a brother's murder stained;
'Tis true—the purchase nearly drained   255
His ill got treasure—soon replaced—
Would'st question whence?—Survey the waste—
And ask the squalid peasant how
His gains repay his broiling brow!
Why me the stern usurper spared,   260
Why thus with me his palace shared,
I know not.—Shame—regret—remorse—
And little fear from infant's force—
Besides—adoption as a son
By him whom Heaven accorded none: 265
Or some unknown cabal—caprice—
Preserved me thus, but not in peace;

236 deadly] ⟨poisoned⟩ *A*   237 ⟨By Giaffir was dr⟩ *A*   238 With] In *A*, *B*,
cor. in Proof 10a   subtle as] ⟨blacker than⟩ *A*   240 Reclined . . . in] ⟨Administered
within⟩ / Reclined and ⟨thirsting⟩ in *A*   242 But] ⟨He⟩ *A*   243 To ⟨work⟩
quench *A*   247 can] will *A*   248 feud] ⟨bride⟩ *A*   250 was ⟨give⟩ gained *A*
256 treasure] wishes *A*   257 whence] him *A*; how *B*, *cor. in Proof 1a*   260 stern]
⟨sullen?⟩ vain *A*   261 thus . . . me] ⟨I have long⟩ *A*   264 adoption as] ⟨that
policy / scheme which made⟩ *A*   265 By] ⟨Of / For⟩ *A*

He cannot curb his haughty mood,
Nor I forgive a father's blood.

16.

'Within thy father's house are foes—   270
    Not all who break his bread are true;
To these should I my birth disclose,
    His days—his very hours were few:
They only want a heart to lead,
A hand to point them to the deed.   275
But Haroun only knows—or knew
    This tale—whose close is almost nigh—
He in Abdallah's palace grew,
    And held that post in his Serai
    Which holds he here—he saw him die: 280
But what could single slavery do?
Avenge his lord—alas! too late—
Or save his son from such a fate?
He chose the last—and when elate
    With foes subdued—or friends betrayed—   285
Proud Giaffir in high triumph sate,
He led me helpless to his gate,
    And not in vain it seems essayed
    To save the life for which he prayed.
The knowledge of my birth secured   290
    From all and each—but most from me;
Thus Giaffir's safety was ensured,
    Removed he too from Roumelie
To this our Asiatic side,
Far from our seats by Danube's tide—   295
    With none but Haroun, who retains
Such knowledge—and that Nubian feels
    A tyrant's secrets are but chains,
From which the captive gladly steals,
And this and more to me reveals.   300

268–9 not in A   274 heart] ⟨chief⟩ A   275 point] ⟨guide⟩ win A   277 This
tale ⟨that⟩ whose end ⟨is⟩ at length is nigh A   278 in ⟨my⟩ Abdallah's A
282 Avenge ⟨my⟩ his A   283 from ⟨Giaffir's⟩ such A   286 ⟨He humbly
entered Giaffir's gate⟩ A   290 secured] ⟨concealed⟩ A   292 Thus ⟨tyrant's⟩
Giaffir's A   296 Haroun ⟨in his⟩ who A   297 Such . . . and . . . feels] ⟨That . . .
soon . . . felt⟩ A

Such still to guilt just Alla sends
Slaves—tools—accomplices—no friends!

17.

'All this, Zuleika, harshly sounds,
  But harsher still my tale must be,
Howe'er my tongue thy softness wounds,   305
    Yet I must prove all truth to thee;
    I saw thee start this garb to see,
  Yet is it one I oft have worn,
    And long must wear—this Galiongée
To whom thy plighted vow is sworn,   310
    Is leader of those pirate hordes,
    Whose laws and lives are on their swords;
  To hear whose desolating tale
  Would make thy waning cheek more pale;
Those arms thou see'st my band have brought,   315
  The hands that wield are not remote;
  This cup too for the rugged knaves
    Is filled—once quaffed, they ne'er repine:
Our Prophet might forgive the slaves,
  They're only infidels in wine.   320

18.

'What could I be?—Proscribed at home,
And taunted to a wish to roam;
And listless left—for Giaffir's fear
Denied the courser and the spear;
Though oft—Oh, Mahomet! how oft   325
In full Divan the despot scoffed,
As if *my* weak unwilling hand
Refused the bridle or the brand:
He ever went to war alone,
And pent me here untried—unknown—   330

301 Such . . . just] ⟨Thus slaves⟩ to guilt ⟨great⟩ *A*   306 prove] be *A, cor. in B*
308 is it] it is *A, B, cor. in Proof 10a*   309 long] ⟨oft⟩ *A*   312 on] in *A*
315-20 *not in A, MS. insertion in B*   315 see'st] saw'st *X, B, cor. in Proof 10a*
317 This] That *X, cor. in B*   318 filled—once] ⟨poured and⟩ / filled—that *X, cor.
in B*   319-20 Nor need I steal it to the slaves | They're only Christian in their wine. *X*
324 Denied . . . and] ⟨Forbade my hand to wield⟩ *A*   330 pent] ⟨left⟩ pent *A*; left *B
cor. in Proof 11*

To Haroun's care with women left,
By hope unblest—of fame bereft.
While thou—whose softness long endeared,
Though it unmanned me, still had cheered—
To Brusa's walls for safety sent,   335
Awaited'st there the field's event;—
Haroun, who saw my spirit pining
    Beneath inaction's sluggish yoke,
His captive, though with dread resigning,
    My thraldom for a season broke;   340
On promise to return before
The day when Giaffir's charge was o'er.
'Tis vain—my tongue can not impart
My almost drunkenness of heart,
When first this liberated eye   345
Surveyed Earth—Ocean—Sun and Sky!
As if my spirit pierced them through,
And all their inmost wonders knew—
One word alone can paint to thee
That more than feeling—I was Free!   350
Ev'n for thy presence ceased to pine—
The World—nay—Heaven itself was mine!

                    19.

'The shallop of a trusty Moor
Conveyed me from this idle shore;
I longed to see the isles that gem   355
Old Ocean's purple diadem:
I sought by turns, and saw them all,
    But when and where I joined the crew,
With whom I'm pledged to rise or fall,
    When all that we design to do   360
Is done—'twill then be time more meet
To tell thee, when the tale's complete.

331 To . . . with women] ⟨In . . . in idlesse⟩ A   332 By . . . unblest] ⟨In spirit
bowed⟩ A   333 ⟨And thou whom night's too⟩ A   337 Haroun] That slave A
338 sluggish] heavy A, cor. in B   339 Compassionate his charge resigning A, cor. in B
341–2 not in A   343 ⟨Oh could my tongue to thee⟩ impart A   344 My . . . of]
That ⟨Liberation of my⟩ A, cor. in B   345 When . . . this] With which my A, cor.
in B   346 Sun and] mountain A, B, cor. in Proof 1a   349 paint] ⟨teach⟩ A
351 presence ceased] absence ⟨seemed⟩ A, cor. in B   354 from . . . idle] ⟨safely from
this⟩ A   355 see the] view those A   357 I ⟨saw—I⟩ sought A   359 pledged]
sworn A

20.

'   'Tis true—they are a lawless brood,
But rough in form, nor mild in mood;
And every creed, and every race,   365
With them hath found—may find a place;
But open speech, and ready hand,
Obedience to their chief's command;
A soul for every enterprize,
That never sees with terror's eyes;   370
Friendship for each, and faith to all,
And vengeance vow'd for those who fall;
Have made them fitting instruments
For more than even my own intents.
    And some—and I have studied all   375
        Distinguish'd from the vulgar rank,
    But chiefly to my council call
        The wisdom of the cautious Frank:—
    And some to higher thoughts aspire,
        The last of Lambro's patriots there   380
    Anticipated freedom share;
And oft around the cavern fire
On visionary schemes debate,
To snatch the Rayahs from their fate.—
So let them ease their hearts with prate   385
Of equal rights, which man ne'er knew,
I have a love for freedom too.
Ay! let me like the ocean-Patriarch roam,
Or only know on land the Tartar's home,
My tent on shore—my galley on the sea—   390
Are more than cities and Serais to me;
Borne by my steed, or wafted by my sail,
Across the desart, or before the gale,
Bound where thou wilt, my barb! or glide my prow,
But be the star that guides the wanderer—Thou!   395
Thou, my Zuleika, share and bless my bark—
The Dove of peace and promise to mine ark!

371 faith] ⟨truth⟩ A   374 my own] my A   378 cautious] ⟨wily⟩ A
381 Anticipated] ⟨Of visionary⟩ A   382 And ⟨while those⟩ oft A   383 On]
Of A   384 To free their country from her fate A   snatch] ⟨free⟩ B   388 ocean-]
⟨deluge⟩ A   389 Or . . . land] ⟨And . . . shore⟩ A   390 my ⟨bark at⟩ galley A
391 ⟨Are palaces more⟩ ⟨Are more that palaces for / to me) A; than ⟨Stamboul's⟩ cities A

Or since that hope denied in worlds of strife—
Be thou the rainbow to the storms of life!
The evening beam that smiles the clouds away,   400
And tints to-morrow with prophetic ray!
Blest—as the Muezzin's strain from Mecca's wall
To pilgrims pure and prostrate at his call;
Soft—as the melody of youthful days,
That steals the trembling tear of speechless praise;   405
Dear—as his native song to Exile's ears,
Shall sound each tone thy long-loved voice endears.
For thee in those bright isles is built a bower
Blooming as Aden in its earliest hour.
A thousand swords—with Selim's heart and hand—   410
Wait—wave—defend—destroy—at thy command!
Girt by my band—Zuleika at my side—
The spoil of nations shall bedeck my bride:—
The Haram's languid years of listless ease
Are well resign'd for cares—for joys like these: 415
Not blind to fate—I see where'er I rove
Unnumber'd perils—but one only love!

398–467 *not in A, B*   398–401 *MS. addition to Proof 1a*   398 in worlds] ⟨to men⟩ *X*   400 beam] ⟨calm⟩ *X*   401 prophetic] an airy / a fancied *X alternate readings*; a fancied *Proof 2, cor. in Proof 3*   And gilds / tints the hope of Morning with its ray / And gilds tomorrow's hope with heavenly ray *D2*   402–3 Soft—as the Mecca Muezzin's strains invite | Him who hath journeyed far to join the rite *X8a, cor. in X8b* Blest—as the call which from Medina's dome | ⟨Which welcomes faith to ?⟩ Invites devotion to the Prophet's tomb *X8b, D2*   402–7 *added in Bride3*   404 Dear—as the melody of ⟨better⟩ days *X8, X8a, D3a, MS. addition in Bride1a (Murray copy)*   405 That steals ⟨our⟩ a silent tear instead of praise *MS. addition in Bride1a (Murray copy)*   406 Dear] Sweet *X8, X8a, D3a, MS. addition in Bride1a (Murray copy)*   408 ⟨For in / For in each isle for thee⟩ *X9*   409 in . . . hour] guarded like a tower *X9*   410 with . . . hand] thy Selim's ⟨hand and heart⟩ *X9*; thy Selim's heart and hand *X9a, X10, X10a* 411 ⟨Shall soothe ?⟩ Wait on thy voice—and bow to thy command *X9a, X10*   bow to] worship *X10a*

412   No danger daunts the pair that love hath blest
     With ⟨feet long wandering⟩ steps still roving but with
        hearts at rest
     With thee all toils were sweet each clime hath charms
     ⟨And be our⟩ Earth sea alike our world within our arms
     How dear the thought in ⟨life such⟩ darkest hours of ill
     Should all be changed to find thee faithful still *X9a version*

With . . . charms] ⟨In thee my blade shall shine my hand shall toil⟩ *X9a*   band] horde *X10a, cor. in Proof 3*   413 bedeck] ⟨adorn⟩ *X10*   414 languid years] ⟨sluggish⟩ slumbering life *X9a*   415 Are . . . joys] Is well resigned for cares and joys *X9a*   416 ⟨Mine be the lot to see whereer I rove⟩ / ⟨A thousand pains / perils wait me where I rove⟩ / ⟨Though mine be the destined doom whereer I rove⟩ *X9a*   see] view *X9a*   417 Unnumber'd] A thousand *X9a, X10, X10a, cor. in Proof 8*

Yet well my toils shall that fond breast repay,
Though fortune frown, or falser friends betray.
How dear the dream! in darkest hours of ill,   420
Should all be changed, to find thee faithful still!
Be but thy soul, like Selim's, firmly shown—
To thee, be Selim's tender as thine own!
To soothe each sorrow—share in each delight—
Blend every thought—do all but disunite!   425
Once free—'tis mine our horde again to guide—
Friends to each other, foes to aught beside:—
Yet there we follow but the bent assign'd
By fatal Nature to man's warring kind,
Mark! where his carnage and his conquests cease—   430
He makes a solitude—and calls it—peace!
I like the rest must use my skill or strength,
But ask no land beyond my sabre's length;—
Power sways but by division—her resource
The blest alternative of fraud or force!   435
Ours be the last—in time deceit may come
When cities cage us in a social home:
There even thy soul might err—how oft the heart
Corruption shakes—which Peril could not part!—
And woman, more than man, when death or woe   440
Or even Disgrace would lay her lover low—

418 ⟨But⟩ well my cares shall *X9a*   419 When Fortune frowns or *X9a*   420 dream]
⟨thought⟩ *X10*   dream! in] dream in *Bride10, 1815, 1831, 1832, C, More*   422 ⟨Firm
as my own I deem thy tender heart⟩ *X9a*   423 ⟨Be mine as tender as⟩ *X9a*
424–5 Exchange or mingle every thought with his | And all our future days unite in this
X9a   Exchange or] Oh! turn and *X10, X10a*   in] on *X10, X10a*   426 ⟨Mankind
I / What though⟩ *X10*   426–7 Man I may lead but trust not—I may fall | By those
now friends to me yet foes to all *X9a, X10, cor. in X10a*   horde] band *X10a, cor. in Proof 3*
aught] all *X10a, cor. in Proof 8*   428 Yet . . . bent] ⟨But⟩ In this they follow but the
⟨doom⟩ / bent *X9a, X10, cor. in X10a*   429 fatal] ⟨savage⟩ *X9a*   man's] our *X9a,
X10, X10a, cor. in Proof 8*   430–3 *MS. addition in Proof 8*   430 Look round
our earth and lo where battles cease *Proof 8, cor. in Proof 10a to* Mark—even where Con-
quest's deeds of carnage cease   431 ⟨They raise⟩ / Behold a wilderness and call it peace!
Proof 8; Behold a Solitude—and call it peace *Proof 10 in MS.*; She leaves a Solitude and calls
it—peace! *Proof 10a in MS.; cor. to received text in D5*   432 I too must cleave my
way by skill or strength *Proof 8, cor. in Proof 10*   433 ask no land] ⟨need no lands⟩
Proof 8   434 Whose wisdom is distrust—whose sole resource *X10a, cor. in Proof 8
to* True wisdom is distrust, her sole resource [cor. to received text in Proof 11]   436 in
time deceit] the first in time *X10a, cor. in Proof 8*   437 cage] ⟨bind⟩ *X10a*   438 There
even thy ⟨heart might wander⟩ soul *X11*   439 Corruption . . . which] ⟨Example taints
which⟩ / Corruption poisons *X11, Proof 8, cor. in Proofs 10, 10a*   440 And
Woman ⟨found yet firm in⟩ more than man when death and ⟨disgrace⟩ *X11, Proof 8, cor. in
Proof 10*

Sunk in the lap of Luxury will shame—
Away suspicion!—*not* Zuleika's name!
But life is hazard at the best—and here
No more remains to win, and much to fear—   445
Yes, fear! the doubt, the dread of losing thee,
By Osman's power, and Giaffir's stern decree—
That dread shall vanish with the favouring gale,
Which Love tonight hath promised to my sail—
No danger daunts the pair his smile hath blest,   450
Their steps still roving, but their hearts at rest;
With thee all toils are sweet—each clime hath charms,
Earth—sea alike—our world within our arms!
Ay—let the loud winds whistle o'er the deck—
So that those arms cling closer round my neck—   455
The deepest murmur of this lip shall be
No sigh for safety, but a prayer for thee!
The war of elements no fears impart
To Love, whose deadliest bane is human Art:
There lie the only rocks our course can check,   460
Here moments menace—*there* are years of wreck!
But hence ye thoughts! that rise in Horror's shape—
This hour bestows—or ever bars escape—
Few words remain of mine my tale to close—
Of thine but *one* to waft us from our foes:—   465
Yea—foes—to me will Giaffir's hate decline?
And is not Osman—who would part us—thine?

444 But . . . hazard] Life is but peril *X10a, cor. in Proof 8*; ⟨But thou—oh far be every
thought of fear⟩ *X10*   445 ⟨Yet ? thou there as stranger bands unkind⟩ / ⟨Is nought but
thee⟩ to win and much to fear *X9a*   446 ⟨With thee that dread will vanish⟩ *X9a*
the doubt,] ⟨yet but⟩ *X9a*   447 power] force *X10*   448 shall] must *X9a*
449 promised to my] lent my swelling *X10*   450 ⟨What dread can a / Our feet may
rove / To roam with⟩ *X9*   his smile] that Love *X9*   451 Their] ⟨With⟩ *X10*   454 o'er
the] oer ⟨my⟩ *X11*   456–7 Then—if my lip once murmurs—it must be— | No sigh for
safety—but a prayer for thee! *D6, cor. in second D6 version, as errata slip in Bride1* [lines
added to text in *Bride1a*]   458 The ⟨storms by Nature⟩ war *X11*   460 only
rocks] rocks ⟨that⟩ alone *X11, cor. in Proof 10*   461 ⟨Where hope / years of⟩ Here
moments threat—but there are *X11, cor. in Proof 8*   462 ⟨Avaunt / Away all thoughts
that come in danger's shape⟩ But ware ye thoughts that ⟨show⟩ rise in terror's shape *X11*
463 This hour ⟨must seek a / must send or ? from all escape⟩ decides my doom or thy escape
X11   464 of mine my] ⟨my lingering⟩ *X10*   465 Of . . . one] ⟨And but thy will⟩
X10   466 Yea] ⟨Yes⟩ *X10*

21.

'His head and faith from doubt and death
  Returned in time my guard to save;
  Few heard—none told—that o'er the wave   470
From isle to isle I roved the while;
And since, though parted from my band
Too seldom now I leave the land,
No deed they've done—nor deed shall do,
Ere I have heard and doomed it too;   475
I form the plan, decree the spoil,
'Tis fit I oftener share the toil.
But now too long I've held thine ear,
Time presses—floats my bark—and here
We leave behind but hate and fear.   480
To-morrow Osman with his train
Arrives—to-night must break thy chain;
And would'st thou save that haughty Bey
  Perchance—*his* life who gave thee thine—
With me this hour away—away!   485
  But yet, though thou art plighted mine,
Would'st thou recal thy willing vow,
Appalled by truths imparted now—
Here rest I—not to see thee wed:
But be that peril on *my* head!'   490

22.

Zuleika—mute and motionless,
Stood like that statue of distress—
When, her last hope for ever gone,
The mother hardened into stone;
All in the maid that eye could see   495
Was but a younger Niobe!—
But ere her lip, or even her eye,
Essayed to speak, or look reply—

468–9 *transposed in A*   468 ⟨Poor Haroun's head and seeming faith⟩ / ⟨His faith
from doubt his head from danger⟩ *A*   469 Returned ⟨again in time to save⟩ *B*
471 ⟨Thy Selim had been long a ranger⟩ *A*   475 Ere . . . heard] Till I have known *A*
476 ⟨As I direct⟩ I form the plan—⟨I share⟩ decree *A*   477 the] their *A*   479 floats]
waits *A*, *B*, *cor. in Proof 3*   480 ⟨Is nothing left⟩ but *A*   481 Osman ⟨Bey⟩
with *A*   482 must] ⟨may⟩ *A*   484 Perchance] ⟨Nay more⟩ *A*   486 ⟨Remember⟩
thou art *A*   487 ⟨I'll tell thee all⟩ thy ⟨true⟩ willing vow *A*   488 truths im-
parted] ⟨all thou hearest⟩ *A*   493 hope] child *A*   495 ⟨And all in her⟩ *A*
498 look] ⟨glance⟩ *A*

Beneath the garden's wicket porch
Far flashed on high a blazing torch!   500
Another—and another—and another—
'Oh! fly—no more—yet now my more than brother!'
Far—wide through every thicket spread
The fearful lights are gleaming red;
Nor these alone—for each right hand   505
Is ready with a sheathless brand:—
They part, pursue, return, and wheel
With searching flambeau, shining steel;
And last of all his sabre waving,
Stern Giaffir in his fury raving: 510
And now almost they touch the cave—
Oh! must that grot be Selim's grave?

                    23.

Dauntless he stood—' 'Tis come—soon past—
One kiss, Zuleika—'tis my last;
    But yet my band not far from shore   515
May hear this signal—see the flash—
Yet now too few—the attempt were rash—
    No matter—yet one effort more.'
Forth to the cavern mouth he stept,
    His pistol's echo rang on high;   520
Zuleika started not, nor wept,
    Despair benumbed her breast and eye!
'They hear me not, or if they ply
Their oars, 'tis but to see me die;
That sound hath drawn my foes more nigh.   525
Then forth my father's scimitar,
Thou ne'er hast seen less equal war!
Farewell, Zuleika!—Sweet! retire—
    Yet stay within—here linger safe,
    At thee his rage will only chafe.—   530

    499 Beneath] ⟨Within⟩ A   502 ⟨Oh who shall save thee less yet more than
brother⟩ A   503 through] on A   505 Not lights alone— ⟨in⟩ / for each A
507 part] spread A   510 Stern] ⟨Old⟩ A   511 touch] near A   515 not
far] ⟨as near⟩ A   516 this signal] this sound—or A   517 Yet now] But all A,
B, cor. in Proof 1a   519 to] ⟨from⟩ A   523 or if] ⟨now even⟩ A   525 hath . . .
foes] but draws the foe A   528 Sweet! retire—] ⟨all is over⟩ A   529-32 not in A
529 linger] ⟨thou art⟩ B   530 thee] ⟨this⟩ Proof 1a

Stir not—lest even to thee perchance
Some erring blade or ball should glance:
Fear'st thou for him?—may I expire
If in this strife I seek thy sire!—
No—though by him that poison poured—   535
No—though again he call me coward!—
But tamely shall I meet their steel?
No—as each crest save *his* may feel!'

24.

One bound he made, and gained the sand—
    Already at his feet hath sunk   540
The foremost of the prying band—
    A gasping head, a quivering trunk;
Another falls—but round him close
A swarming circle of his foes:
From right to left his path he cleft,   545
    And almost met the meeting wave;—
His boat appears—not five oars' length—
His comrades strain with desperate strength—
    Oh! are they yet in time to save?
His feet the foremost breakers lave;   550
His band are plunging in the bay,
Their sabres glitter through the spray;
Wet—wild—unwearied to the strand
They struggle—now they touch the land!
They come—'tis but to add to slaughter—   555
His heart's best blood is on the water!

25.

Escaped from shot—unharmed by steel,
Or scarcely grazed its force to feel—
Had Selim won—betrayed—beset—
To where the strand and billows met—   560

531–2 *not in B, added in MS. in Proof 6*   533 ⟨At least ? like thy Sire⟩ *A*
536 No—though ⟨this morn he called⟩ again he name me coward *A*   537 shall I] I
⟨will not⟩ shall *A*   538 save *his* may] but his shall *A, cor. in B*   539 One . . .
made] He made one bound *A*   540 ⟨And those⟩ Already *A*   544 swarming]
clustering *A*   545 path] ⟨way⟩ *A*   546 ⟨And won his way toward the wave⟩ *A*
547 five] three *A*   551 are plunging in] have plunged into *A*   554 now] fast *A*
558 Or grazed by wounds he ⟨scarce would⟩ / scorned to feel *A*   its force] ⟨enough⟩ *B*
559 betrayed] though thus *A, B, cor. in Bride*4

There as his last step left the land,
And the last death-blow dealt his hand—
Ah! wherefore did he turn to look
    For her his eye but sought in vain?
That pause—that fatal gaze he took—   565
    Hath doomed his death—or fixed his chain—
Sad proof—in peril and in pain
How late will Lover's hope remain!—
His back was to the dashing spray—
    Behind but close—his comrades lay—   570
When at the instant, hissed the ball,
    'So may the foes of Giaffir fall!'
Whose voice is heard? whose carbine rang?
Whose bullet through the night-air sang?
Too nearly, deadly aimed to err—   575
    'Tis thine—Abdallah's Murderer!
The father slowly rued thy hate,
    The son hath found a quicker fate—
Fast from his breast the blood is bubbling,
    The whiteness of the sea-foam troubling;   580

562 dealt] ⟨left⟩ *A*   563 ⟨I know not why he turned⟩ to look *A*   564, 566–8 *not*
in A, B, added in Proof 6 [there are four early versions of 563–8]

    a. That glance he paused to send ⟨in vain⟩ again
        To her for whom he dies in vain *MS. addition in Proof 5 for*
        566–8

    b. Since fatal was the gaze he took—
        So far escaped from death or chain—
        To search for her and search in vain—
        ⟨How late will lover's hope remain⟩
        Sad proof in peril and in pain
        How hope may die but love remain.

    c. Thus far escaped from death or chain
        Ah wherefore did he turn to look
        For her his eye must seek in vain?
        Since fatal was the gaze he took
        Sad proof in peril and in pain
        How late will lover's hope remain.

    d. So far escaped from death or chain
        Since fatal was the gaze he took
        For her his eye ⟨would seek⟩ but sought in vain
        Sad proof in peril and in pain
        How late will lover's hope remain! *cancelled versions in X12*

565 That . . . that] ⟨Since that last⟩ *X12*   568 Lover's] Love's rash *X12 alternate*
reading   570 close] near *A, B, cor. in Proof 6*   571 hissed] sped *A*   575 Too
⟨deadly aimed⟩ nearly *A*   576 'Tis thine] ⟨Tis his⟩ / ⟨By⟩ thine *A*   579 Fast . . .
blood] ⟨His blood upon his breast⟩ *A*   580 sea-foam] waters *A*

BRIDE OF ABYDOS.

—————————— THE SURGES SWEEP
THEIR BURTHEN ROUND SIGŒUM'S STEEP.

PUBLISHED BY JOHN MURRAY, ALBEMARLE STREET, DECR 1,1814.

The Bride of Abydos Canto II lines 600–1

(*Reproduced with the permission of the British Library*)

If aught his lips essayed to groan
The rushing billows choaked the tone!—

26.

Morn slowly rolls the clouds away—
　Few trophies of the fight are there—
The shouts that shook the midnight-bay   585
Are silent—but some signs of fray
　That strand of strife may bear—
And fragments of each shivered brand—
Steps stamped—and dashed into the sand
The print of many a struggling hand   590
May there be marked—nor far remote
A broken torch—an oarless boat—
And tangled on the weeds that heap
The beach where shelving to the deep—
There lies a white Capote!   595
'Tis rent in twain—one dark-red stain
The wave yet ripples o'er in vain—
　But where is he who wore?
Ye! who would o'er his relics weep
Go—seek them where the surges sweep   600
Their burthen round Sigaeum's steep
　And cast on Lemnos' shore:
The sea-birds shriek above the prey,
O'er which their hungry beaks delay—
As shaken on his restless pillow,   605
His head heaves with the heaving billow—
That hand—whose motion is not life—
Yet feebly seems to menace strife—

582 billows] ⟨waters⟩ B   583–620 not in A, B   583 Morn ⟨breaking but⟩
slowly X13   584 ⟨The / There are / No⟩ Few relics of X13   586 Are silent
⟨and the⟩ but X13   588 And] ⟨Yet⟩ X13   589 Steps . . . dashed] Deep footsteps
dashed X13; ⟨Deep footprints⟩ dashed X14   590 not in X13   591 nor far remote]
and eye may note X13, cor. in X14, D7   592 ⟨A torch thrown⟩ X13   593 And
tangled on ⟨that / the heap of weeds⟩ X13   594 shelving] bending X13   596 rent]
⟨torn⟩ X13   one dark-red] ⟨its deep-red⟩ X14   597 yet . . . o'er] as yet hath
laved X13; yet ⟨breaks upon⟩ X14   600 surges sweep] rushing deep X13; currents
sweep X14, cor. in Proof 10   601 Their . . . bound] Hath borne them by X13
603 shriek above] ⟨shrieking oer⟩ X13   604 hungry beaks] ⟨sabres yet⟩ X13
605 shaken] ⟨turning⟩ X13   606 ⟨As heaving / raising with⟩ ⟨As raising now his⟩ X13
607–8 And that ⟨dead⟩ clenched hand whose only life | Is motion—seems to menace strife
X13, X14, cor. in Proof 1a

Flung by the tossing tide on high,
   Then levelled with the wave—   610
What recks it? though that corse shall lie
   Within a living grave?
The bird that tears that prostrate form
Hath only robbed the meaner worm!
The only heart— the only eye—   615
Had bled or wept to see him die,
Had seen those scattered limbs composed,
   And mourned above his turban-stone—
That heart hath burst— that eye was closed—
   Yea—closed before his own!   620

27.

By Helle's stream there is a voice of wail!
And woman's eye is wet—man's cheek is pale—
Zuleika! last of Giaffir's race,
   Thy destin'd lord is come too late—
He sees not—ne'er shall see thy face!—   625
   Can he not hear
The loud Wul-wulleh warn his distant ear?
   Thy handmaids weeping at the gate,
   The Koran-chaunters of the hymn of fate—
   The silent slaves with folded arms that wait,   630
Sighs in the hall—and shrieks upon the gale,
   Tell him thy tale!
Thou didst not view thy Selim fall!
   That fearful moment when he left the cave
   Thy heart grew chill—   635
He was thy hope—thy joy—thy love—thine all—
   And that last thought on him thou could'st not save
   Sufficed to kill—
Burst forth in one wild cry—and all was still.
   Peace to thy broken heart—and virgin grave!   640

611 that corse shall] the corse may *X13*   613 that] his *X13*   616 Had bled or] ⟨That would have⟩ *X13*   617 ⟨That would see his⟩ limbs composed *X13* 618 ⟨Within⟩ And gazed upon his *X13*   619 closed] is closed *X13*   621 By . . . stream] ⟨On . . . banks⟩ *A*   623 ⟨Woe to the last of Giaffir's line⟩ *A*   624 is . . . late] ⟨arriv / too late is come⟩ *A*   626–7 *not in A*   629 The Koran ⟨chapter chants thy⟩ fate *A*   630 arms] ⟨arm⟩ *Proof 1a*   633 ⟨On Helle's bank there is a voice of wail⟩ / Thou didst not ⟨live to see him⟩ fall *A*   634 ⟨Thou didst not / Nor for a fearful⟩ The moment that he left thy cave *A*

Ah! happy! but of life to lose the worst,
That grief—though deep—though fatal—was thy first!
Thrice happy! ne'er to feel nor fear the force
Of absence—shame—pride—hate—revenge—remorse!
And, oh! that pang where more than Madness lies—   645
The Worm that will not sleep—and never dies—
Thought of the gloomy day and ghastly night,
That dreads the darkness, and yet loathes the light—
That winds around, and tears the quiv'ring heart—
Ah! wherefore not consume it—and depart!   650

Woe to thee, rash and unrelenting chief!
    Vainly thou heap'st the dust upon thy head—
    Vainly the sackcloth o'er thy limbs dost spread:
    By that same hand Abdallah—Selim bled—
Now let it tear thy beard in idle grief—   655
Thy pride of heart—thy bride for Osman's bed—
She—whom thy sultan had but seen to wed—
        Thy Daughter's dead!
Hope of thine age—thy twilight's lonely beam—
    The Star hath set that shone on Helle's stream—   660
What quench'd its ray?—the blood that thou hast shed!
Hark—to the hurried question of Despair!
'Where is my child?'—an Echo answers—'Where?'

28.

Within the place of thousand tombs
    That shine beneath, while dark above   665
The sad but living cypress glooms
    And withers not, though branch and leaf

641–50 *not in A, B*   641 ⟨Ah⟩ Yet happy thou—but once to feel the worst *X14*
but . . . lose] ⟨then / thus of life to shun⟩ *X14a*   642 thy] the *X14a*   643 Happy
? and neer to feel the force *X14, cor. in X14a*   fear] ⟨share⟩ *X14a*   644 Of sick-
ness—absence—shame—regret—remorse *X14*; Of Absence—⟨Passion—shame—regret⟩—
remorse *X14a*   645 ⟨Each pang / The jealous pang⟩ And oh that pang—⟨that thought
where⟩ madness lies *X14a*   648 loathes] ⟨shuns⟩ *X14a*   649 winds . . . quiv'ring]
⟨tears⟩ . . . living *X14a, cor. in X14b*   651 chief] ⟨Sire⟩ *A*   652 dust upon]
⟨ashes on⟩ *A*   653 o'er . . . dost] ⟨round . . . shall⟩ *A*   656 ⟨Thy daughter's
dead!⟩ *A*   657 ⟨She whom the / a Sultan had been fain to wed⟩ *A*   658 *last line
in A, B*   659–61 *MS. addition in Proof 1a*   662–3 *added in Bride4*   664–86 *added
in Proof 1*   665 That] ⟨White oer ? / All white below⟩ Which *X16*   666 ⟨Where
tenderly the⟩ There the sad cypress ever glooms *X16*   667 though] ⟨but⟩ *X16a*

Are stamped with an eternal grief;
 Like early unrequited Love!
One spot exists—which ever blooms,   670
 Ev'n in that deadly grove.—
A single rose is shedding there
 Its lonely lustre, meek and pale:
It looks as planted by Despair—
 So white—so faint—the slightest gale   675
Might whirl the leaves on high;
 And yet, though storms and blight assail,
And hands more rude than wintry sky
 May wring it from the stem—in vain—
 To-morrow sees it bloom again!   680
The stalk some spirit gently rears,
And waters with celestial tears.
 For well may maids of Helle deem
That this can be no earthly flower,
Which mocks the tempest's withering hour 685
And buds unsheltered by a bower,
Nor droops—though spring refuse her shower,
 Nor woos the summer beam.—
To it the livelong night there sings
 A bird unseen—but not remote—   690
Invisible his airy wings,
But soft as harp that Houri strings
 His long entrancing note!
 It were the Bulbul—but his throat,
 Though mournful, pours not such a strain; 695
For they who listen cannot leave
The spot, but linger there and grieve
 As if they loved in vain!
And yet so sweet the tears they shed,
'Tis sorrow so unmixed with dread,   700
They scarce can bear the morn to break

671 Even in that still and dreary grove *X16*   deadly] deathly *X16a, cor. in Proof 1a*
675 ⟨Nor Summer's / Winter's blight⟩ *X16* 676 whirl the] strew its *X16, cor. in*
X16a 678 hands more rude] ⟨ruder hands⟩ *X16* 679 ⟨May pluck today / Today
may pluck⟩ *X16* 680 bloom] ⟨blow / shine⟩ *X16* 681 ⟨Some Spirit its⟩ *X16*
683 And well ⟨the virgins⟩ may *X16* 685 Which] That *X16* 686 buds] shines
X16 687 *MS. addition in Proof 3* refuse] ⟨withold⟩ deny *Proof 3, cor. in Proof 4*
688 woos] ⟨needs⟩ *X16* 690 A] Some *X16* 691 ⟨Though none his⟩ *X16*
699 sweet] ⟨soft⟩ *X16*

That melancholy spell,
And longer yet would weep and wake,
    He sings so wild and well!
But when the day-blush bursts from high—   705
Expires that magic melody.
And some have been who could believe,
(So fondly youthful dreams deceive,
    Yet harsh be they that blame)
That note so piercing and profound   710
Will shape and syllable its sound
    Into Zuleika's name.
'Tis from her cypress' summit heard,
That melts in air the liquid word—
'Tis from her lowly virgin earth   715
That white rose takes its tender birth.
There late was laid a marble stone,
Eve saw it placed—the Morrow gone!
It was no mortal arm that bore
That deep-fixed pillar to the shore;   720
For there, as Helle's legends tell,
Next morn 'twas found where Selim fell—
Lashed by the tumbling tide, whose wave
Denied his bones a holier grave:
And there by night, reclin'd, 'tis said,   725
Is seen a ghastly turban'd head—
And hence extended by the billow,
'Tis named the 'Pirate-phantom's pillow'!
Where first it lay—that mourning flower
Hath flourished—flourisheth this hour—   730
Alone—and dewy—coldly pure and pale—
As weeping Beauty's cheek at Sorrow's tale!

1813

703 yet] ⟨again⟩ *X16*   704 ⟨Lulled by that⟩ *X16*   705 But with ⟨the blush of
Morn / the first blush of the day⟩ / the day blush of the sky *X16*, *X16a, cor. in Proof 3*
707 have been] ⟨there be⟩ *X16*   708 (So fondly] ⟨But sure / Such the⟩ 'Tis that *X16*
709 be they that] are they who *X16*   710 so ⟨sweet⟩ piercing *X16*   711 its] the *X16*
713 from] on *X16, X16a, cor. in Proof 1a*   716 takes its tender] ⟨trembles into⟩ *X16*
717 late was laid] once there was *X16*   718 Morrow] ⟨Morning⟩ *X16*   723 Lashed]
Washed *X17, cor. in Proof 3*   725–8 *MS. addition in Proof 1a*   728 phantom's]
⟨Spectre's⟩ *Proof 1a*   729 Where . . . lay] And in its stead *X16, X16a, cor. in Proof 1a*
first] once *Proof 1a, cor. in Proofs 3, 4*   730 flourished ⟨from⟩ *X16*   731 dewy] ⟨chill⟩
X16   732 As the young cheek that saddens to the tale *X16, X16a*; ⟨As childhood's
cheek at Sorrow's saddest tale⟩ As weeping Childhood's cheek at Sorrow's tale *Proof 1a*

224 The Corsair;

A TALE

'—I suoi pensieri in lui dormir non ponno.'
TASSO, *Canto decimo, Gerusalemme Liberata*. [st. 78]

TO

THOMAS MOORE, ESQ.

MY DEAR MOORE,

I dedicate to you the last production with which I shall trespass on public patience, and your indulgence, for some years; and I own that I feel anxious to avail myself of this latest and only opportunity of adorning my pages with a name, consecrated by unshaken public
5 principle, and the most undoubted and various talents. While Ireland ranks you among the firmest of her patriots—while you stand alone the first of her bards in her estimation, and Britain repeats and ratifies the decree—permit one, whose only regret, since our first acquaintance, has been the years he had lost before
10 it commenced, to add the humble, but sincere suffrage of friendship, to the voice of more than one nation. It will at least prove to you, that I have neither forgotten the gratification derived from your society, nor abandoned the prospect of its renewal, whenever your leisure or inclination allows you to atone to your friends for too
15 long an absence. It is said among those friends, I trust truly, that you are engaged in the composition of a poem whose scene will be laid in the East; none can do those scenes so much justice. The wrongs of your own country, the magnificent and fiery spirit of her sons, the beauty and feeling of her daughters, may there be
20 found; and Collins, when he denominated his Oriental, his Irish Eclogues, was not aware how true, at least, was a part of his parallel. Your imagination will create a warmer sun, and less

---

224. Copy text: *Corsair9*, collated with *MSS. ML, M, MLa, Ma, L, Y, Y2, Proofs 1–8, Corsair1–Corsair8, Corsair10*
title ⟨The Renegade⟩ *ML*, Text *EM*
Dedication
   9 our first] ⟨the commencement of our⟩ *Ma*   22 create] ⟨supply⟩ *Ma*

clouded sky; but wildness, tenderness, and originality are part
of your national claim of oriental descent, to which you have
already thus far proved your title more clearly than the most   25
zealous of your country's antiquarians. May I add a few words on
a subject on which all men are supposed to be fluent, and none
agreeable?—Self. I have written much, and published more than
enough to demand a longer silence than I now meditate; but for
some years to come it is my intention to tempt no further the   30
award of 'Gods, men, nor columns'. In the present composition
I have attempted not the most difficult, but, perhaps, the best
adapted measure to our language, the good old and now neglected
heroic couplet:—the stanza of Spenser is perhaps too slow and
dignified for narrative; though, I confess, it is the measure most   35
after my own heart; and Scott alone, of the present generation,
has hitherto completely triumphed over the fatal facility of the
octo-syllabic verse; and this is not the least victory of his fertile
and mighty genius. In blank verse, Milton, Thomson, and our
dramatists, are the beacons that shine along the deep, but warn   40
us from the rough and barren rock on which they are kindled. The
heroic couplet is not the most popular measure certainly; but as
I did not deviate into the other from a wish to flatter what is called
public opinion, I shall quit it without further apology, and take my
chance once more with that versification, in which I have hitherto   45
published nothing but compositions whose former circulation is
part of my present and will be of my future regret.

  With regard to my story, and stories in general, I should have
been glad to have rendered my personages more perfect and amia-
ble, if possible, inasmuch as I have been sometimes criticised, and   50
considered no less responsible for their deeds and qualities than if
all had been personal. Be it so—if I have deviated into the gloomy
vanity of 'drawing from self', the pictures are probably like, since
they are unfavourable; and if not, those who know me are un-
deceived, and those who do not, I have little interest in undeceiving.   55
I have no particular desire that any but my acquaintance should
think the author better than the beings of his imagining; but I
cannot help a little surprise, and perhaps amusement, at some odd
critical exceptions in the present instance, when I see several bards

24 national . . . descent] ⟨nation's oriental inheritance⟩ Ma   32 attempted] ⟨adopted⟩
Ma   36 alone, of] alone (he will excuse the Mr. 'we do not say Mr. Caesar') Scott
alone of Ma   38 fertile] varied Ma   46–7 former ⟨success⟩ is part of my present
and future Ma   57 the author ⟨at all⟩ much better Ma

60 (far more deserving, I allow) in very reputable plight, and quite exempted from all participation in the faults of those heroes, who, nevertheless, might be found with little more morality than 'The Giaour', and perhaps—but no—I must admit Childe Harold to be a very repulsive personage; and as to his identity, those who like

65 it must give him whatever 'alias' they please.

If, however, it were worth while to remove the impression, it might be of some service to me, that the man who is alike the delight of his readers and his friends—the poet of all circles—and the idol of his own, permits me here and elsewhere to subscribe

70 myself,

most truly,
and affectionately,
his obedient servant,

BYRON.

January 2, 1814.

CANTO I

'————nessun maggior dolore,
Che ricordarsi del tempo felice
Nella miseria,————'
DANTE

I.

'O'er the glad waters of the dark blue sea,
Our thoughts as boundless, and our souls as free,
Far as the breeze can bear, the billows foam,
Survey our empire and behold our home!
These are our realms, no limits to their sway—   5
Our flag the sceptre all who meet obey.
Ours the wild life in tumult still to range
From toil to rest, and joy in every change.
Oh, who can tell? not thou, luxurious slave!
Whose soul would sicken o'er the heaving wave;   10

66–7 it were . . . it might] anything could remove the impression it may be *Ma, cor. in Proof* 7

Canto I

1 glad . . . dark blue] ⟨blue / dark . . . boundless / beauteous / dashing / glorious / mounting⟩ *ML*   2 Our . . . our] ⟨With hearts as strong and with⟩ *ML*   3 billows ⟨range⟩ *ML*   4 Survey] ⟨Behold⟩ *ML*   5 sway] ⟨range⟩ *ML*   6 Our . . . all] ⟨And ours the life / laws that all⟩ *ML*   7 life ⟨which every joy of change⟩ *ML*

Not thou, vain lord of wantonness and ease!
Whom slumber soothes not—pleasure cannot please—
Oh, who can tell, save he whose heart hath tried,
And danced in triumph o'er the waters wide,
The exulting sense—the pulse's maddening play,   15
That thrills the wanderer of that trackless way?
That for itself can woo the approaching fight,
And turn what some deem danger to delight;
That seeks what cravens shun with more than zeal,
And where the feebler faint—can only feel—   20
Feel—to the rising bosom's inmost core,
Its hope awaken and its spirit soar?
No dread of death—if with us die our foes—
Save that it seems even duller than repose:
Come when it will—we snatch the life of life—   25
When lost—what recks it—by disease or strife?
Let him who crawls enamoured of decay,
Cling to his couch, and sicken years away;
Heave his thick breath; and shake his palsied head;
Ours—the fresh turf, and not the feverish bed.   30
While gasp by gasp he faulters forth his soul,
Ours with one pang—one bound—escapes controul.
His corse may boast its urn and narrow cave,
And they who loathed his life may gild his grave:
Ours are the tears, though few, sincerely shed,   35
When Ocean shrouds and sepulchres our dead.
For us, even banquets fond regret supply
In the red cup that crowns our memory;
And the brief epitaph in danger's day,
When those who win at length divide the prey,   40
And cry, Remembrance saddening o'er each brow,
How had the brave who fell exulted *now!*'

11 vain] proud *ML*   12 Whom ... pleasure] ⟨Whose ... pleasures⟩ *ML*   15 ⟨The exulting rapture and the thrilling sense⟩ *ML*   16 ⟨That wants to feel the joy of turbulence⟩ *ML*   trackless] ⟨watery⟩ *ML*   19 ⟨Whose⟩ That seeks what others shun *ML* 23 ⟨The only dread of death that Spirit knows⟩ *ML*   24 even duller than] ⟨the dullness of⟩ *ML*   25 will] may *ML, cor. in M*   26 ⟨If⟩ lost *ML*   27 crawls] ⟨breathes⟩ *ML*   28 Protract to age his painful years away *ML, cor. in M*   years away] ⟨doting day⟩ *M*   31 ⟨Short be our pangs / are our sorrows⟩ ⟨Long may he pant and faulter forth his soul⟩ ⟨While drop by drop / sigh by sigh⟩ he faulters forth his soul *ML*   36 When ... and] ⟨And the wide Ocean⟩ *ML*; ⟨And the green coral pillows for⟩ *ML*   37 ⟨The future⟩ *ML*   38 red] ⟨full⟩ *ML*   39 in ⟨conquest's hour⟩ *ML*   41 Remembrance ... each] ⟨while Sadness ... the⟩ *ML*   o'er] ⟨on⟩ *Proofs 3, 4*

2.

Such were the notes that from the Pirate's isle,
Around the kindling watch-fire rang the while;
Such were the sounds that thrilled the rocks along,   45
And unto ears as rugged seemed a song!
In scattered groups upon the golden sand,
They game—carouse—converse—or whet the brand;
Select the arms—to each his blade assign,
And careless eye the blood that dims its shine: 50
Repair the boat, replace the helm or oar,
While others straggling muse along the shore;
For the wild bird the busy springes set,
Or spread beneath the sun the dripping net;
Gaze where some distant sail a speck supplies,   55
With all the thirsting eye of Enterprize;
Tell o'er the tales of many a night of toil,
And marvel where they next shall seize a spoil:
No matter where—their chief's allotment this;
Theirs, to believe no prey nor plan amiss.   60
But who that CHIEF? his name on every shore
Is famed and feared—they ask and know no more.
With these he mingles not but to command;
Few are his words, but keen his eye and hand.
Ne'er seasons he with mirth their jovial mess,   65
But they forgive his silence for success.
Ne'er for his lip the purpling cup they fill,
That goblet passes him untasted still—
And for his fare—the rudest of his crew
Would that, in turn, have passed untasted too;   70
Earth's coarsest bread, the garden's homeliest roots,
And scarce the summer luxury of fruits,
His short repast in humbleness supply
With all a hermit's board would scarce deny.

43 were the notes] ⟨was the song⟩ ML   45 thrilled . . . along] ⟨from a rugged voice⟩ /
that thrilled the ⟨rocky shore⟩ ML   46 ⟨Taught / Thrilled ears as rude⟩ ML   48 They
. . . converse] ⟨Some . . . discourse⟩ ML   49 blade] ⟨own⟩ M   52 straggling muse
along] singly straggle ⟨oer⟩ by ML, cor. in M   53 wild] ⟨sea⟩ ML   54 Or
⟨slowly coil the dank but ?⟩ net ML   55 Gaze ⟨for a distant sail with longing eyes⟩
ML   56 With . . . eye] ⟨And recount the gains⟩ / With all the ⟨eager hope⟩ M
57 many a ⟨toilsome night⟩ ML   58 seize] take ML   60 Theirs ⟨to obey⟩ ML
62 famed] ⟨known⟩ ML   67 Ne'er for his ⟨people⟩ lip the purpling ⟨goblet⟩ fill ML
68 That . . . passes] But even passes ML   74 a . . . scarce] ⟨that Nature cannot
well⟩ / ⟨spare Bigotry⟩ would scarce ML   board] ⟨vow⟩ M

But while he shuns the grosser joys of sense,   75
His mind seems nourished by that abstinence.
'Steer to that shore!'—they sail. 'Do this!'—'tis done.
'Now form and follow me!'—the spoil is won.
Thus prompt his accents and his actions still,
And all obey and few enquire his will;   80
To such, brief answer and contemptuous eye
Convey reproof, nor further deign reply.

3.

'A sail!—a sail!'—a promised prize to Hope!
Her nation—flag—how speaks the telescope?
No prize, alas!—but yet a welcome sail: 85
The blood-red signal glitters in the gale.
Yes—she is ours—a home returning bark—
Blow fair, thou breeze!—she anchors ere the dark.
Already doubled is the cape—our bay
Receives that prow which proudly spurns the spray.   90
How gloriously her gallant course she goes!
Her white wings flying—never from her foes—
She walks the waters like a thing of life,
And seems to dare the elements to strife.
Who would not brave the battle-fire—the wreck—   95
To move the monarch of her peopled deck?

4.

Hoarse o'er her side the rustling cable rings;
The sails are furled; and anchoring round she swings:
And gathering loiterers on the land discern
Her boat descending from the latticed stern.   100
'Tis manned—the oars keep concert to the strand,
Till grates her keel upon the shallow sand.

75 shuns . . . joys] thus abjures the joys *ML*   78 ⟨Now follow me⟩ *ML*   79 Thus prompt] Still such *ML, cor. in M*   80 few] ⟨scarce⟩ *ML*   82 ⟨At once convey reproof but little brook reply⟩ *ML*   nor . . . deign] but never made *ML*; ⟨but no⟩ further deign *M*   83–4 ⟨A sail—a sail—tis one of ours—a sail | The blood-red flag is flapping in the gale⟩ *ML*   84 speaks] tells *ML, M*; ⟨speaks⟩ tells *Proofs 1, 5*; ⟨tells⟩ speaks *Proof 6a*   86 signal glitters in] ⟨flag is flapping⟩ signal ⟨shines⟩ glitters in *ML*   87 Yes . . . is] ⟨Tis one of⟩ *ML*   89 our] the *ML, cor. in M*   90 that . . . spurns] ⟨her and she bravely breasts⟩ *ML*   92 ⟨In beauty / And⟩ *ML*   95 ⟨and⟩ wreck *ML*   98 round] ⟨now⟩ *ML*   100 ⟨The⟩ boat *M*   101 ⟨The Crowd is⟩ Tis manned— ⟨they pull in⟩ concert to the ⟨land⟩ *ML*   102 grates] creaks *ML, M*; ⟨grates⟩ creaks *Proof 1*; ⟨creaks⟩ grates *Proof 6a*

Hail to the welcome shout!—the friendly speech!
When hand grasps hand uniting on the beach;
The smile, the question, and the quick reply,   105
And the heart's promise of festivity!

5.

The tidings spread, and gathering grows the crowd:
The hum of voices, and the laughter loud,
And woman's gentler anxious tone is heard—
Friends'—husbands'—lovers' names in each dear word: 110
'Oh! are they safe? we ask not of success—
But shall we see them? will their accents bless?
From where the battle roars—the billows chafe—
They doubtless boldly did—but who are safe?
Here let them haste to gladden and surprize,   115
And kiss the doubt from these delighted eyes!'—

6.

'Where is our chief? for him we bear report—
And doubt that joy—which hails our coming—short;
Yet thus sincere—'tis cheering, though so brief;
But, Juan! instant guide us to our chief: 120
Our greeting paid, we'll feast on our return,
And all shall hear what each may wish to learn.'
Ascending slowly by the rock-hewn way,
To where his watch-tower beetles o'er the bay,
By bushy brake, and wild flowers blossoming,   125
And freshness breathing from each silver spring,
Whose scattered streams from granite basins burst,
Leap into life, and sparkling woo your thirst;
From crag to cliff they mount—Near yonder cave,
What lonely straggler looks along the wave?   130

---

103 the . . . speech] ⟨the arms that reach⟩ *ML*   104 ⟨The hands that grasp in springing for the beach⟩ *ML*   107 The ⟨news⟩ *ML*   109 tone is ⟨there⟩ *ML* 110 dear] fond *ML*   112 will] ⟨can⟩ *ML*   113 billows ⟨swell⟩ *M*   114 did] sped *ML*   who are] ⟨are they⟩ *M*   115 Here] ⟨Oh⟩ *ML*   118 which] that *ML* 119 Yet ⟨tho⟩ so sincere tis welcome though but brief *ML, cor. in M*   121 greeting] homage *ML*   122 each may] all must *ML, cor. in M*   125 and] the *ML* 126 each] ⟨the⟩ *ML*   127 ⟨That ? from rifted granite cells⟩ / That scattered there from granite basins burst *ML, M*   granite basins] ⟨cells of granite⟩ *ML*   128 ⟨And sparkling⟩ *ML*   130 lonely] pensive *ML, cor. in M*

In pensive posture leaning on the brand,
Not oft a resting-staff to that red hand?
"'Tis he—'tis Conrad—here—as wont—alone;
On—Juan! on—and make our purpose known.
The bark he views—and tell him we would greet   135
His ear with tidings he must quickly meet:
We dare not yet approach—thou know'st his mood,
When strange or uninvited steps intrude.'

                    7.

Him Juan sought, and told of their intent—
He spake not—but a sign expressed assent.   140
These Juan calls—they come—to their salute
He bends him slightly, but his lips are mute.
'These letters, Chief, are from the Greek—the spy,
Who still proclaims our spoil or peril nigh:
Whate'er his tidings, we can well report,   145
Much that'—'Peace, peace!'—He cuts their prating short.
Wondering they turn, abashed, while each to each
Conjecture whispers in his muttering speech:
They watch his glance with many a stealing look,
To gather how that eye the tidings took;   150
But, this as if he guessed, with head aside,
Perchance from some emotion, doubt, or pride,
He read the scroll—'My tablets, Juan, hark—
Where is Gonsalvo?'
                    'In the anchored bark.'
'There let him stay—to him this order bear.   155
Back to your duty—for my course prepare:
Myself this enterprize to-night will share.'

'To-night, Lord Conrad?'
                    'Ay! at set of sun:

The breeze will freshen when the day is done.
My corslet—cloak—one hour—and we are gone.   160
Sling on thy bugle—see that free from rust,
My carbine-lock springs worthy of my trust;
Be the edge sharpened of my boarding-brand,
And give its guard more room to fit my hand.
This let the Armourer with speed dispose;   165
Last time, it more fatigued my arm than foes:
Mark that the signal-gun be duly fired,
To tell us when the hour of stay's expired.'

8.

They make obeisance, and retire in haste,
Too soon to seek again the watery waste: 170
Yet they repine not—so that Conrad guides,
And who dare question aught that he decides?
That man of loneliness and mystery,
Scarce seen to smile, and seldom heard to sigh;
Whose name appals the fiercest of his crew,   175
And tints each swarthy cheek with sallower hue;
Still sways their souls with that commanding art
That dazzles, leads, yet chills the vulgar heart.
What is that spell, that thus his lawless train
Confess and envy, yet oppose in vain?   180
What should it be? that thus their faith can bind?
The power of Thought—the magic of the Mind!
Linked with success, assumed and kept with skill,
That moulds another's weakness to its will;
Wields with their hands, but, still to these unknown,   185
Makes even their mightiest deeds appear his own.
Such hath it been—shall be—beneath the sun
The many still must labour for the one!
'Tis Nature's doom—but let the wretch who toils
Accuse not, hate not *him* who wears the spoils.   190

159 will freshen] ⟨still freshens⟩ *ML*   162 springs] ⟨answers⟩ *ML*   167 ⟨With /
e / Oh⟩ Mark . . . guns were *ML*   168 ⟨Twill / And⟩ To tell us when our time of
ML   170 Too] ⟨So⟩ *M*   173 That ⟨lonely⟩ man *ML*   174 Scarce]
⟨Neer⟩ *ML*   176 And ⟨turns⟩ *ML*   177 Still] Yet *ML, cor. in M*   179 spell . . .
train] ⟨art⟩—that thus ⟨even⟩ lawless ⟨men⟩ *ML*   181 thus ⟨can bind⟩ their faith *ML*
182 power] ⟨tower / sway⟩ *ML*   184 moulds ⟨each⟩ another's *ML*   185 ⟨And
?—when Fortune far ?⟩ *ML*   187 ⟨And such in sooth they are—whose will is due⟩
ML   shall] must *ML, cor. in M*   188 The many ⟨are⟩ still ⟨must⟩ but labour *ML*
189 but] ⟨yet⟩ *ML*   190 Accuse . . . wears] ⟨Neer envy him who seems to wear⟩ *ML*

Oh! if he knew the weight of splendid chains,
How light the balance of his humbler pains!

9.

Unlike the heroes of each ancient race,
Demons in act, but Gods at least in face,
In Conrad's form seems little to admire,   195
Though his dark eye-brow shades a glance of fire;
Robust but not Herculean—to the sight
No giant frame sets forth his common height;
Yet, in the whole, who paused to look again,
Saw more than marks the crowd of vulgar men;   200
They gaze and marvel how—and still confess
That thus it is, but why they cannot guess.
Sun-burnt his cheek, his forehead high and pale
The sable curls in wild profusion veil;
And oft perforce his rising lip reveals   205
The haughtier thought it curbs, but scarce conceals.
Though smooth his voice, and calm his general mien,
Still seems there something he would not have seen:
His features' deepening lines and varying hue
At times attracted, yet perplexed the view,   210
As if within that murkiness of mind
Worked feelings fearful, and yet undefined;
Such might it be—that none could truly tell—
Too close enquiry his stern glance would quell.
There breathe but few whose aspect might defy   215
The full encounter of his searching eye;
He had the skill, when Cunning's gaze would seek
To probe his heart and watch his changing cheek,

---

191 weight] ⟨price⟩ ML   195 seems] ⟨was⟩ ML ⟨seemed⟩ M   196 eye . . . a]
⟨brow bends oer a⟩ ML   197 but] ⟨yet⟩ ML   198 frame sets forth] ⟨stature⟩ frame
set forth ML; frame ⟨exalts⟩ M   201 and still] ⟨but⟩ still M; but yet ML   203 high
and pale] ⟨pale and cold⟩ ML   205 And oft ⟨his⟩ ML   rising] ⟨rising⟩ ⟨haughty⟩ rising
Proof 2   206 it . . . scarce] his smile but ill ML; his bosom ill M, Proof 1, cor. in Proof 2
207 general] ⟨common⟩ ML   209 ⟨His varying features—could their hue / ranging
in their hue⟩ ML; features ⟨vary⟩ deepening M   210 At times ⟨? forth the gazers⟩
view ML   211 that . . . of] ⟨the workings of⟩ ML   212 Worked] ⟨Lurked⟩ ML
214 close enquiry] ⟨near a scrutiny⟩ ML   would] could ML, M, all proofs, Corsair 1–
Corsair 6   215 might] could ML, M, all proofs, Corsair 1–Corsair 6   216 encounter]
⟨observance⟩ ML   217 He had] ⟨He had⟩ His was Proof 6a; ⟨His was⟩ He had
Proof 6   Cunning's gaze] ⟨others gaze⟩ prying souls ML; prying souls M, Proofs 1–5,
cor. in Proof 6   218 To ⟨gather omens from his⟩ watch ⟨the meaning⟩ his words and
trace his pensive cheek ML; To watch his words and trace his pensive cheek M, Proofs 1–5

At once the observer's purpose to espy,
And on himself roll back his scrutiny,   220
Lest he to Conrad rather should betray
Some secret thought, than drag that chief's to day.
There was a laughing Devil in his sneer,
That raised emotions both of rage and fear;
And where his frown of hatred darkly fell,   225
Hope withering fled—and Mercy sighed farewell!

                                10.

Slight are the outward signs of evil thought,
Within—within—'twas there the spirit wrought!
Love shows all changes—Hate, Ambition, Guile,
Betray no further than the bitter smile;   230
The lip's least curl, the lightest paleness thrown
Along the governed aspect, speak alone
Of deeper passions; and to judge their mien,
He, who would see, must be himself unseen.
Then—with the hurried tread, the upward eye,   235
The clenched hand, the pause of agony,
That listens, starting, lest the step too near
Approach intrusive on that mood of fear:
Then—with each feature working from the heart,
With feelings loosed to strengthen—not depart;   240
That rise—convulse—contend—that freeze, or glow,
Flush in the cheek, or damp upon the brow;
Then—Stranger! if thou canst, and tremblest not,
Behold his soul—the rest that soothes his lot!
Mark—how that lone and blighted bosom sears   245
The scathing thought of execrated years!
Behold—but who hath seen, or e'er shall see,
Man as himself—the secret spirit free?

  219 observer's] ⟨enquirer's⟩ ML   220 on . . . roll back] ⟨to . . . repel⟩ ML
225 hatred] ⟨anger⟩ ML   227–48 added in Proof 7   229 shows] ⟨hath⟩ shows
Proof 7   235 with] when MLa ⟨when⟩ with Proof 7   tread] step MLa–Corsair6
241 ⟨Convulsive gather, varying,⟩ freeze or glow MLa; Released but to convulse—or freeze
or glow MLa, cor. in Proof 7   or . . . or] ⟨now . . . now⟩ MLa   contend] subside Proof 7–
Corsair6   242 Flush] Fire MLa, cor. in Proof 7   cheek] ⟨veins⟩ MLa   244 the . . .
lot] once seen not soon forgot MLa, cor. in Proof 7   245–6 All that there burns its hour
away—but sears | The scathed Remembrance of long-coming years. MLa, cor. in Proof 7
scathed] ⟨seeth'd⟩ Proof 7

II.

Yet was not Conrad thus by Nature sent
To lead the guilty—guilt's worst instrument—   250
His soul was changed, before his deeds had driven
Him forth to war with man and forfeit heaven.
Warped by the world in Disappointment's school,
In words too wise, in conduct *there* a fool;
Too firm to yield, and far too proud to stoop,   255
Doomed by his very virtues for a dupe,
He cursed those virtues as the cause of ill,
And not the traitors who betrayed him still;
Nor deemed that gifts bestowed on better men
Had left him joy, and means to give again.   260
Feared—shunned—belied—ere youth had lost her force,
He hated man too much to feel remorse,
And thought the voice of wrath a sacred call,
To pay the injuries of some on all.
He knew himself a villain—but he deemed   265
The rest no better than the thing he seemed;
And scorned the best as hypocrites who hid
Those deeds the bolder spirit plainly did.
He knew himself detested, but he knew
The hearts that loathed him, crouched and dreaded too.   270
Lone, wild, and strange, he stood alike exempt
From all affection and from all contempt:
His name could sadden, and his acts surprize;
But they that feared him dared not to despise:
Man spurns the worm, but pauses ere he wake   275
The slumbering venom of the folded snake:
The first may turn—but not avenge the blow;
The last expires—but leaves no living foe;
Fast to the doomed offender's form it clings,
And he may crush—not conquer—still it stings!   280

249 sent] ⟨meant⟩ *ML*   250 To . . . worst] ⟨The guiltless Leader—Guilt's own⟩ *ML*
252 with . . . forfeit] ⟨alike with man and⟩ *ML*   254 *there*] still *ML*   255 yield]
⟨shrink⟩ *ML, M*   259 Nor ⟨deemed⟩ recked that ⟨favours showered⟩ on better men
ML   260 means] ⟨power⟩ *ML*   261 All all was fled eer Youth had spent its
force *ML*; ⟨All—all—was fled⟩ ere Youth had lost its force *M*   her] his *Proof 1, cor. in
Proof 2*   263 And ⟨deemed the injuries⟩ *ML*   268 ⟨In clouds⟩ The deeds ⟨that⟩
the ⟨open⟩ bolder Sinner plainly did *ML*   plainly] ⟨barely⟩ *Proof 1*   269–80 *not in ML*
274 they . . . to] ⟨Man must cease to fear or to⟩ *M*   277–80 *added in Corsair7*
277 turn] ⟨writhe⟩ *Text JJ*   279 Fast] ⟨still⟩ *Text JJ, Y*   280 may] must *Text JJ*

12.

None are all evil—quickening round his heart,
One softer feeling would not yet depart;
Oft could he sneer at others as beguiled
By passions worthy of a fool or child;
Yet 'gainst that passion vainly still he strove,   285
And even in him it asks the name of Love!
Yes, it was love—unchangeable—unchanged,
Felt but for one from whom he never ranged;
Though fairest captives daily met his eye,
He shunned, nor sought, but coldly passed them by;   290
Though many a beauty drooped in prisoned bower,
None ever soothed his most unguarded hour.
Yes—it was Love—if thoughts of tenderness,
Tried in temptation, strengthened by distress,
Unmoved by absence, firm in every clime,   295
And yet—Oh more than all!—untired by time;
Which nor defeated hope, nor baffled wile,
Could render sullen were she ne'er to smile,
Nor rage could fire, nor sickness fret to vent
On her one murmur of his discontent;   300
Which still would meet with joy, with calmness part,
Lest that his look of grief should reach her heart;
Which nought removed, nor menaced to remove—
If there be love in mortals—this was love!
He was a villain—ay—reproaches shower   305
On him—but not the passion, nor its power,
Which only proved, all other virtues gone,
Not guilt itself could quench this loveliest one!

281 quickening round] clinging to *ML*; clinging round *M*, *all proofs*, *Corsair1–Corsair7*
283 Oft] Yet *ML*, *cor. in M*; others ⟨as the slaves⟩ *ML*   288 ⟨And⟩ Felt *ML*
289 fairest] ⟨lovely⟩ *ML*   291 beauty . . . bower] ⟨victim sighed to share his power⟩
beauty droops in prisoned bower *ML*; droops *M*   293 thoughts] ⟨years⟩ *ML*
294 in . . . by] ⟨by all times and proved by all⟩ / in Temptation—⟨deepened⟩ by *ML*
297 ⟨Which neither baffled hope nor useful toil⟩ / ⟨neither useless toils / plans⟩ *ML*
298 sullen] ⟨fretful⟩ *ML*   ne'er] near *Proof 8–C*, *More*   300 one murmur] the
⟨accents⟩ *ML*   301 Which ⟨ever such with smiles / joy—with smiles could⟩ part *ML*
302 look . . . reach] ⟨sigh . . . seek⟩ *ML*   304 ⟨He was a villain—true—but this
was Love!⟩ / If there be ⟨any Love on earth—oh⟩ love in *ML*   305 villain—ay]
villain ⟨true—but from⟩ ay *ML*   306 its] ⟨his⟩ *ML*   307 only] ⟨even⟩ *ML*
308 quench . . . one] quell this ⟨mightier⟩ one *ML*   loveliest] ⟨earliest⟩ *M*

13.

He paused a moment—till his hastening men
Passed the first winding downward to the glen.   310
'Strange tidings!—many a peril have I past,
Nor know I why this next appears the last!
Yet so my heart forebodes, but must not fear,
Nor shall my followers find me falter here.
'Tis rash to meet, but surer death to wait   315
'Till here they hunt us to undoubted fate;
And, if my plan but hold, and Fortune smile,
We'll furnish mourners for our funeral-pile.
Ay—let them slumber—peaceful be their dreams!
Morn ne'er awoke them with such brilliant beams   320
As kindle high to-night (but blow, thou breeze!)
To warm these slow avengers of the seas.
Now to Medora—Oh! my sinking heart,
Long may her own be lighter than thou art!
Yet was I brave—mean boast where all are brave!   325
Ev'n insects sting for aught they seek to save.
This common courage which with brutes we share,
That owes its deadliest efforts to despair,
Small merit claims—but 'twas my nobler hope
To teach my few with numbers still to cope;   330
Long have I led them—not to vainly bleed:
No medium now—we perish or succeed!
So let it be—it irks not me to die;
But thus to urge them whence they cannot fly.
My lot hath long had little of my care,   335
But chafes my pride thus baffled in the snare:
Is this my skill? my craft? to set at last
Hope, power, and life upon a single cast?

---

309 till] ⟨watched⟩ ML   312 appears] should seem ML   313 but must] ⟨yet doth⟩ ML   314 shall] ⟨must⟩ ML   315 surer] ⟨certain⟩ ML   317 And if my ⟨steel⟩ / ⟨purposed⟩ plan ⟨but hold tonight⟩ / hold firm and Fortune smile ML   318 We'll . . . for] ⟨Nor many gaze upon⟩ / ⟨Shall / Will find some⟩ mourners for ML   320 ne'er awoke] ⟨never waked⟩ ML   321 ⟨As (hold / blow thou breeze!) tonight shall flash⟩ ML   323 Medora] Francesca ML, M; ⟨Francesca⟩ Genevra Proof 1; Genevra Proof 2; ⟨Genevra⟩ Medora Proof 3 [The name is thus uniformly corrected in the proofs throughout the text.]   sinking] ⟨heavy⟩ ML   326 Why ⟨all defend / fight⟩ ML Ev'n] Why ML, M   seek] wish ML   327 brutes] ⟨slaves⟩ ML   328 ⟨And / Which⟩ That ML   deadliest] strongest ML, cor. in M   329 claims] ⟨this⟩ ML   332 No . . . now] ⟨But now too late⟩ ML   333 not me] me not ML, cor. in M   336 thus . . . the] that could not in this ML   338 Hope—⟨Life—sway⟩ ML

8127553   G

Oh, Fate!—accuse thy folly, not thy fate—
She may redeem thee still—nor yet too late.'   340

14.

Thus with himself communion held he, till
He reached the summit of his tower-crowned hill:
There at the portal paused—for wild and soft
He heard those accents never heard too oft;
Through the high lattice far yet sweet they rung,   345
And these the notes his bird of beauty sung:

1.

'Deep in my soul that tender secret dwells,
    Lonely and lost to light for evermore,
Save when to thine my heart responsive swells,
    Then trembles into silence as before.   350

2.

'There, in its centre, a sepulchral lamp
    Burns the slow flame, eternal—but unseen;
Which not the darkness of despair can damp,
    Though vain its ray as it had never been.

3.

'Remember me—Oh! pass not thou my grave   355
    Without one thought whose relics there recline:
The only pang my bosom dare not brave,
    Must be to find forgetfulness in thine.

4.

'My fondest—faintest—latest—accents hear:
    Grief for the dead not Virtue can reprove;   360
Then give me all I ever asked—a tear,
    The first—last—sole reward of so much love!'

340 may] would *ML*   343 the . . . wild] its . . . ⟨sweet⟩ *ML*   345 sweet they]
⟨sweetly⟩ *ML*   346 notes] ⟨words⟩ *ML*   347 soul] ⟨heart⟩ *ML*   354 it had
never] if it neer had *ML, alternate reading in M*   355 pass not thou] never pass *ML,*
M, cor. in Proof 6   356 one] ⟨the⟩ *ML*   359 Take my last look—my latest
accents hear *ML*   My . . . latest] ⟨Take my / This gaze forgive / return these⟩ Yet heed
my prayer my *M*   360 not . . . reprove] ⟨even Virtue may approve⟩ *ML*

He passed the portal—crossed the corridore,
And reached the chamber as the strain gave o'er:
  'My own Medora! sure thy song is sad—'   365

'In Conrad's absence wouldst thou have it glad?
Without thine ear to listen to my lay,
Still must my song my thoughts, my soul betray:
Still must each accent to my bosom suit,
My heart unhushed—although my lips were mute!   370
Oh! many a night on this lone couch reclined,
My dreaming fear with storms hath winged the wind,
And deemed the breath that faintly fanned thy sail
The murmuring prelude of the ruder gale;
Though soft, it seemed the low prophetic dirge,   375
That mourned thee floating on the savage surge.
Still would I rise to rouse the beacon fire,
Lest spies less true should let the blaze expire;
And many a restless hour outwatched each star,
And morning came—and still thou wert afar.   380
Oh! how the chill blast on my bosom blew,
And day broke dreary on my troubled view,
And still I gazed and gazed—and not a prow
Was granted to my tears—my truth—my vow!
At length—'twas noon—I hailed and blest the mast   385
That met my sight—it neared—Alas! it past!
Another came—Oh God! 'twas thine at last!
Would that those days were over! wilt thou ne'er,
My Conrad! learn the joys of peace to share?
Sure thou hast more than wealth; and many a home   390
As bright as this invites us not to roam:
Thou know'st it is not peril that I fear,
I only tremble when thou art not here;
Then not for mine, but that far dearer life,
Which flies from love and languishes for strife—   395

363 portal—⟨strode⟩ crossed ML   366 wouldst . . . it] ⟨how should it be⟩ ML
370 Unhushed my heart ML   373 breath that faintly fanned] ⟨blast that gently
swelled⟩ ML   374 murmuring . . . ruder] ⟨fluttering . . . tempest⟩ ML   375 it
. . . prophetic] ⟨and low it seemed the rising⟩ ML   376 mourned] ⟨swept⟩ ML
⟨crowned⟩ Proof 1   379 outwatched] ⟨have watched⟩ ML   382 broke] ⟨seemed⟩
ML   384 ⟨Repaid my prayings⟩—tears—my ⟨hope⟩—my vow ML   386 Alas]
⟨Oh God⟩ ML   390 more than wealth] wealth enough ML   395 Which] That
ML, M, cor. in Proof 1

How strange that heart, to me so tender still,
Should war with nature and its better will!'

'Yea, strange indeed—that heart hath long been changed;
Worm-like 'twas trampled—adder-like avenged,
Without one hope on earth beyond thy love,   400
And scarce a glimpse of mercy from above.
Yet the same feeling which thou dost condemn,
My very love to thee is hate to them,
So closely mingling here, that disentwined,
I cease to love thee when I love mankind: 405
Yet dread not this—the proof of all the past
Assures the future that my love will last;
But—Oh, Medora! nerve thy gentler heart,
This hour again—but not for long—we part.'

'This hour we part!—my heart foreboded this: 410
Thus ever fade my fairy dreams of bliss.
This hour—it cannot be—this hour away!
Yon bark hath hardly anchored in the bay:
Her consort still is absent, and her crew
Have need of rest before they toil anew;   415
My love! thou mock'st my weakness; and would'st steel
My breast before the time when it must feel;
But trifle now no more with my distress,
Such mirth hath less of play than bitterness.
Be silent, Conrad!—dearest! come and share   420
The feast these hands delighted to prepare;
Light toil! to cull and dress thy frugal fare!
See, I have plucked the fruit that promised best,
And where not sure, perplexed, but pleased, I guessed
At such as seemed the fairest: thrice the hill   425
My steps have wound to try the coolest rill;

397 Should ⟨steel? its strings to work all others ill⟩ *ML*   398 Aye strange indeed
⟨Francesca⟩ *ML*   Yea] ⟨Ay⟩ *M*   399 ⟨Wronged / Trod like the worm⟩ *ML*
402 which] that *ML*   404 ⟨If not the same—so closely these entwined⟩ *ML*
406 proof ⟨has in⟩ the *ML*   408 thy gentler] ⟨I pray⟩ *ML*   409 ⟨Tonight this
hour⟩ *ML*   411 Thus] So *ML*   413 hardly] scarcely *ML*   415 before] ere
yet *ML*   416 my] ⟨the⟩ *ML*   417 breast] ⟨heart⟩ *ML*   419 mirth . . . play]
⟨jest⟩ play . . . mirth *ML*   421 feast ⟨though⟩ these *ML*   422 ⟨Light . . . fare!⟩
ML   423 plucked . . . promised] ⟨chosen all that⟩ / ⟨saved⟩ plucked the fruit that
likes thee *ML*; plucked the fruit allures thee *M*   426 ⟨I've / Hath seen me⟩ *ML*
try] find *ML*

Yes! thy Sherbet to-night will sweetly flow,
See how it sparkles in its vase of snow!
The grapes' gay juice thy bosom never cheers;
Thou more than Moslem when the cup appears: 430
Think not I mean to chide—for I rejoice
What others deem a penance is thy choice.
But come, the board is spread; our silver lamp
Is trimmed, and heeds not the Sirocco's damp:
Then shall my handmaids while the time along,   435
And join with me the dance, or wake the song;
Or my guitar, which still thou lov'st to hear,
Shall soothe or lull—or, should it vex thine ear,
We'll turn the tale, by Ariosto told,
Of fair Olympia loved and left of old.   440
Why—thou wert worse than he who broke his vow
To that lost damsel, shouldst thou leave me now;
Or even that traitor chief—I've seen thee smile,
When the clear sky showed Ariadne's Isle,
Which I have pointed from these cliffs the while   445
And thus, half sportive half in fear, I said,
Lest Time should raise that doubt to more than dread,
Thus Conrad, too, will quit me for the main:
And he deceived me—for—he came again!'

'Again—again—and oft again—my love!   450
If there be life below, and hope above,
He will return—but now, the moments bring
The time of parting with redoubled wing:
The why—the where—what boots it now to tell?
Since all must end in that wild word—farewell!   455
Yet would I fain—did time allow—disclose—
Fear not—these are no formidable foes;
And here shall watch a more than wonted guard,
For sudden siege and long defence prepared:

428 ⟨And⟩ See *ML*   428a-b ⟨Wine thou wilt never taste—and I rejoice | What
others deem a penance is thy choice⟩ *ML*   429 gay] red *ML*   437 Or] ⟨Then⟩
ML   438 Will lull to sleep—⟨at least—or sound to cheer⟩ *ML*   443 even that]
⟨he⟩ the *ML*   445 ⟨And⟩ I have pointed ⟨to the spot⟩ the while *ML*   446–7 ⟨And
thus I've sensed? thou'dst quit me for the main | And thou deceivedst me—for thou camst
again.⟩ *ML*   449 And he] ⟨He more⟩ *ML*; ⟨But⟩ he *M*   450 oft] yet *ML*
451 hope] ⟨truth⟩ tears *ML*   452 ⟨But now—alas each⟩ *ML*   the . . . bring] ⟨alas
the hour⟩ *ML*   455 end in] close with *ML*   456 ⟨My / It needs must be⟩ *ML*
457 ⟨Since thou⟩ Fear not—⟨these⟩ they are ⟨not⟩ no *ML*

Nor be thou lonely—though thy lord's away,   460
Our matrons and thy handmaids with thee stay;
And this thy comfort—that, when next we meet,
Security shall make repose more sweet:
List!—'tis the bugle—Juan shrilly blew—
One kiss—one more—another—Oh! Adieu!'   465

She rose—she sprung—she clung to his embrace,
Till his heart heaved beneath her hidden face.
He dared not raise to his that deep-blue eye,
Which downcast drooped in tearless agony.
Her long fair hair lay floating o'er his arms,   470
In all the wildness of dishevelled charms;
Scarce beat that bosom where his image dwelt
So full—*that* feeling seemed almost unfelt!
Hark—peals the thunder of the signal-gun!
It told 'twas sunset—and he cursed that sun.   475
Again—again—that form he madly pressed,
Which mutely clasped, imploringly caressed!
And tottering to the couch his bride he bore,
One moment gazed—as if to gaze no more;
Felt—that for him earth held but her alone,   480
Kissed her cold forehead—turned—is Conrad gone?

15.

'And is he gone?'—on sudden solitude
How oft that fearful question will intrude?
' 'Twas but an instant past—and here he stood!
And now'—without the portal's porch she rushed,   485
And then at length her tears in freedom gushed;

460 Nor be ⟨thy loneliness⟩ thou lonely though ⟨without thy mate⟩ *ML*   461 ⟨Since all our ?⟩ with thee stay *ML*   463 repose more] ⟨our greeting⟩ *ML*   464 List!— 'tis] ⟨Hark / Ah twas⟩ *ML*   466 sprung] ⟨flew⟩ *ML*   467 ⟨And hid the sorrows⟩ *ML*   468 raise to his] ⟨gaze upon⟩ *ML*   469 Which] ⟨Thou tearless⟩ That ⟨scarcely / barely raised⟩ *ML*; That *M, all proofs, Corsair 1–Corsair 9*   472 Scarce beat that] ⟨And that chilled⟩ *ML*   473 ⟨Scarce beat with all the fullness which it felt⟩ *ML*   seemed almost] ⟨which seems most⟩ *ML*   474 peals] ⟨to⟩ *ML*   475 ⟨He curst the sound too late—the⟩ *ML*   476–7 Oh he could bear no more—but madly ⟨clasped⟩ grasped | Her ⟨hand⟩ form and trembling then his own unclasped *ML, cor. in M*   478 And . . . bride] ⟨With⟩ tottering ⟨steps to her couch her form⟩ *ML*   his bride] ⟨her form⟩ *M*   480 that . . . held] as if earth contained *ML, M, cor. in Proof 1*   482 ⟨Yes he is gone / Is Conrad gone—from ?⟩ *ML*   483 How . . . will intrude] ⟨Too . . . still intrudes⟩ *ML*   484 here] there *ML*   485 without] into *ML, cor. in M*   486 at length . . . in] indeed . . . ⟨to⟩ *ML*

Big—bright—and fast, unknown to her they fell;
But still her lips refused to send—'Farewell!'
For in that word—that fatal word—howe'er
We promise—hope—believe—there breathes despair.   490
O'er every feature of that still, pale face,
Had sorrow fixed what time can ne'er erase:
The tender blue of that large loving eye
Grew frozen with its gaze on vacancy,
Till—Oh, how far!—it caught a glimpse of him,   495
And then it flowed—and phrenzied seemed to swim
Through those long, dark, and glistening lashes dewed
With drops of sadness oft to be renewed.
'He's gone!'—against her heart that hand is driven,
Convulsed and quick—then gently raised to heaven;   500
She looked and saw the heaving of the main;
The white sail set—she dared not look again;
But turned with sickening soul within the gate—
'It is no dream—and I am desolate!'

16.

From crag to crag descending—swiftly sped   505
Stern Conrad down, nor once he turned his head;
But shrunk whene'er the windings of his way
Forced on his eye what he would not survey,
His lone, but lovely dwelling on the steep,
That hailed him first when homeward from the deep: 510
And she—the dim and melancholy star,
Whose ray of beauty reached him from afar,
On her he must not gaze, he must not think,
There he might rest—but on Destruction's brink:
Yet once almost he stopped—and nearly gave   515
His fate to chance, his projects to the wave;
But no—it must not be—a worthy chief
May melt, but not betray to woman's grief.

---

487 Big] ⟨And⟩ Big *ML*; ⟨Pure⟩ *M*   488 send] ⟨say⟩ *ML, M*   490 breathes]
⟨speaks⟩ *ML*   492 ne'er] not *ML*   493 loving] ⟨ranging / lightening⟩ *ML*
494 ⟨Loved⟩ *ML*   495 Till ⟨in her swound?⟩ *ML*   496 it . . . seemed] ⟨again—
again sight⟩ seemed *ML*   497 glistening] ⟨deepening⟩ *ML*   499 ⟨Too lone⟩ *ML*
500 ⟨With hurried stroke⟩—then *ML*   503 ⟨With sickening⟩ *ML*   506 Stern
Conrad ⟨nor delayed his hurrying tread⟩ *M L*   507 ⟨To look although⟩ the *ML*
509 on the steep] ⟨place so high⟩ *ML*

He sees his bark, he notes how fair the wind,
And sternly gathers all his might of mind: 520
Again he hurries on—and as he hears
The clang of tumult vibrate on his ears,
The busy sounds, the bustle of the shore,
The shout, the signal, and the dashing oar;
As marks his eye the seaboy on the mast,   525
The anchor's rise, the sails unfurling fast,
The waving kerchiefs of the crowd that urge
That mute adieu to those who stem the surge;
And more than all, his blood-red flag aloft,
He marvelled how his heart could seem so soft.   530
Fire in his glance, and wildness in his breast,
He feels of all his former self possest;
He bounds—he flies—until his footsteps reach
The verge where ends the cliff, begins the beach,
There checks his speed; but pauses less to breathe   535
The breezy freshness of the deep beneath,
Than there his wonted statelier step renew;
Nor rush, disturbed by haste, to vulgar view:
For well had Conrad learned to curb the crowd,
By arts that veil, and oft preserve the proud;   540
His was the lofty port, the distant mien,
That seems to shun the sight—and awes if seen:
The solemn aspect, and the high-born eye,
That checks low mirth, but lacks not courtesy;
All these he wielded to command assent: 545
But where he wished to win, so well unbent,
That kindness cancelled fear in those who heard,
And others' gifts shewed mean beside his word,

---

519 notes] ⟨marks⟩ *ML*   520 And ⟨gathers sternly⟩ *ML*   521 and as]
⟨again⟩ *M*   525 As] ⟨And⟩ *ML*   526 anchor's] anchors *Corsair10, 1831,
1832, C, More*   528 That . . . stem] ⟨The mute farewell . . . seek⟩ *ML*   who] that
M, cor. in Proof 2   530 marvelled] marvels *ML*   531 glance . . . breast]
looks . . . ⟨soul⟩ *ML*   532 He feels ⟨for him doth⟩ *ML*   534 The . . . cliff]
The ⟨sandy⟩ verge . . . hill *ML*   535 but . . . breathe] ⟨and / but less to pause for
breath⟩ / but pauses ⟨not to breathe⟩ less ⟨to gain⟩ *ML*; but pauses less ⟨from⟩ to
breathe *M*   536 ⟨Now / From / His / A short ? from breathless haste⟩ *ML*
breezy] dewy *ML, cor. in M*   537 wonted . . . step] ⟨statelier wonted march⟩ *ML*
538 Nor ⟨seem in him⟩ *ML*   539 For well ⟨knew⟩ *ML*   curb] awe *ML, M, all
proofs, Corsair1–Corsair9*   540 veil] ⟨mark⟩ *ML*   542 That ⟨shuns⟩ *ML*
544 but] yet *ML*   545 to . . . assent] to ⟨his own intent⟩ / ⟨demand⟩ command assent
ML   548 ⟨And / Another's gift less solaced than his word⟩ *ML*   others'] other's
all early edns.—1829

When echoed to the heart as from his own
His deep yet tender melody of tone: 550
But such was foreign to his wonted mood,
He cared not what he softened, but subdued;
The evil passions of his youth had made
Him value less who loved—than what obeyed.

                              17.

Around him mustering ranged his ready guard.   555
Before him Juan stands—'Are all prepared?'

'They are—nay more—embarked: the latest boat
Waits but my chief——'
                          'My sword, and my capote.'
Soon firmly girded on, and lightly slung,
His belt and cloak were o'er his shoulders flung;   560
'Call Pedro here!' He comes—and Conrad bends,
With all the courtesy he deigned his friends;
'Receive these tablets, and peruse with care,
Words of high trust and truth are graven there;
Double the guard, and when Anselmo's bark   565
Arrives, let him alike these orders mark:
In three days (serve the breeze) the sun shall shine
On our return—till then all peace be thine!'
This said, his brother Pirate's hand he wrung,
Then to his boat with haughty gesture sprung.   570
Flashed the dipt oars, and sparkling with the stroke,
Around the waves' phosphoric brightness broke;
They gain the vessel—on the deck he stands,
Shrieks the shrill whistle—ply the busy hands—
He marks how well the ship her helm obeys,   575
How gallant all her crew—and deigns to praise.

---

549 ⟨There was a softness in his gentler tone⟩ *ML*   550 ⟨That / Made / That when
he sought / Was ? to the hearts / excused all hearts his own⟩ *ML*   552 ⟨Nor recked
what⟩ *ML*   554 Him . . . than] Him ⟨seek not / value not what⟩ loved—⟨but⟩ *ML*
556 Before . . . Are] ⟨And Juan waits—is⟩ *ML*   557 ⟨It is⟩ *ML*   559 slung]
⟨flung⟩ *ML*   560 belt] ⟨blade⟩ *ML*   563 peruse ⟨them all⟩ *ML*   564 high]
deep *ML*   565 guard] ⟨watch⟩ *M*   566 Arrives] ⟨Returns⟩ *M*   567 In ⟨two⟩
days—speed the breeze— ⟨we must again⟩ *ML*   serve] ⟨speed⟩ *M*   568 all] ⟨may⟩
ML   570 haughty gesture] ⟨air of triumph⟩ *ML*   571 with the] with each *ML*,
cor. in M   572 ⟨The⟩ Around the ⟨brightness of the billows⟩ broke *ML*   573 gain]
⟨seek?⟩ *ML*   574 Shrieks . . . ply] ⟨Rings the shrill pipe and ply⟩ *ML*   whistle] pipe
ML, *cor. in M*

His eyes of pride to young Gonsalvo turn—
Why doth he start, and inly seem to mourn?
Alas! those eyes beheld his rocky tower,
And live a moment o'er the parting hour;   580
She—his Medora—did she mark the prow?
Ah! never loved he half so much as now!
But much must yet be done ere dawn of day—
Again he mans himself and turns away;
Down to the cabin with Gonsalvo bends,   585
And there unfolds his plan—his means—and ends;
Before them burns the lamp, and spreads the chart,
And all that speaks and aids the naval art;
They to the midnight watch protract debate;
To anxious eyes what hour is ever late?   590
Mean time, the steady breeze serenely blew,
And fast and Falcon-like the vessel flew;
Passed the high headlands of each clustering isle,
To gain their port—long—long ere morning smile:
And soon the night-glass through the narrow bay   595
Discovers where the Pacha's galleys lay.
Count they each sail—and mark how there supine
The lights in vain o'er heedless Moslem shine.
Secure, unnoted, Conrad's prow passed by,
And anchored where his ambush meant to lie;   600
Screened from espial by the jutting cape,
That rears on high its rude fantastic shape.
Then rose his band to duty—not from sleep—
Equipped for deeds alike on land or deep;
While leaned their leader o'er the fretting flood,   605
And calmly talked—and yet he talked of blood!

577 His . . . young] ⟨With . . . old⟩ ML   578 doth he] ⟨do they⟩ M   580 a] ⟨one⟩ M
583–4 transposed in ML   583 But] Since ML   587 spreads the] here the ML;
lies the / spreads the M; lies the Proofs 1–5, cor. in Proof 6a   589 watch] ⟨hour⟩ ML
591 breeze] gale ML   593 high] bold ML   594 To . . . ere] To ⟨reach her
destined port⟩ ere ML   596 galleys] squadron ML   597 Count . . . mark]
Counts every sail and marks ML   598 heedless] ⟨drowsy⟩ ML   599 ⟨Securely
Conrad's bark⟩ ML   unnoted . . . by] unmarked ⟨passed Conrad's vessel by⟩ / fierce Conrad's
prow passed by ML   unnoted] ⟨unseen—fierce⟩ M   600 where . . . to] where he
meant ⟨to⟩ concealed to ML   601 Screened] ⟨Secured⟩ Proof 1   602 That . . . rude]
⟨And / That from ? / rises there⟩ / rears on high its ⟨wild⟩ ML   603 to . . . from] from
duty or from ML ⟨from⟩ duty—not ⟨to⟩ M   604 Equipped] ⟨Prepared⟩ ML   for
deeds alike] ⟨alike for deeds⟩ M   605 ⟨And there amidst them all their leader stood⟩
ML   leaned] leant M

CANTO II

'Conosceste i dubiosi desiri?'
DANTE.

I.

In Coron's bay floats many a Galley light,
Through Coron's lattices the lamps are bright,
For Seyd, the Pacha, makes a feast to-night:
A feast for promised triumph yet to come,
When he shall drag the fettered Rovers home;   5
This hath he sworn by Alla and his sword,
And faithful to his firman and his word,
His summoned prows collect along the coast,
And great the gathering crews, and loud the boast;
Already shared the captives and the prize,   10
Though far the distant foe they thus despise;
'Tis but to sail—no doubt to-morrow's Sun
Will see the Pirates bound—their haven won!
Mean time the watch may slumber, if they will,
Nor only wake to war, but dreaming kill.   15
Though all, who can, disperse on shore and seek
To flesh their glowing valour on the Greek;
How well such deed becomes the turbaned brave—
To bare the sabre's edge before a slave!
Infest his dwelling—but forbear to slay,   20
Their arms are strong, yet merciful to-day,
And do not deign to smite because they may!
Unless some gay caprice suggests the blow,
To keep in practice for the coming foe.
Revel and rout the evening hours beguile,   25
And they who wish to wear a head must smile;
For Moslem mouths produce their choicest cheer,
And hoard their curses, till the coast is clear.

Canto II
    1 floats] ⟨lies⟩ *ML*   2 lattices] ⟨batteries⟩ *Proof 1* ⟨In Coron's towers there stream
the torches bright⟩ *ML* ⟨From Coron's walls torches high⟩ *ML*   are] ⟨burn⟩ *M*   3 For]
⟨And / There⟩ *ML*   makes] gives *ML*, *M*, *all proofs*, *Corsair1–Corsair8*   4 triumph]
triumphs *ML*   8 summoned] ⟨gathering⟩ *ML*   15 ⟨And dream / Nor wake⟩ *ML*
16 Though] But *ML*   18 such . . . turbaned] that . . . Moslem *ML*   19 the . . .
a] his . . . his *ML*   21 Their . . . yet] ⟨Because his arm is⟩ *ML*   22 do . . .
they] ⟨it⟩ doth . . . it *ML*   25 ⟨A feast tonight the Pacha's⟩ *ML*   evening] midnight
ML   28 And] To *ML*

2.

High in his hall reclines the turbaned Seyd;
Around—the bearded chiefs he came to lead. 30
Removed the banquet, and the last pilaff—
Forbidden draughts, 'tis said, he dared to quaff,
Though to the rest the sober berry's juice,
The slaves bear round for rigid Moslem's use;
The long Chibouque's dissolving cloud supply, 35
While dance the Almahs to wild minstrelsy.
The rising morn will view the chiefs embark;
But waves are somewhat treacherous in the dark:
And revellers may more securely sleep
On silken couch than o'er the rugged deep; 40
Feast there who can—nor combat till they must,
And less to conquest than to Korans trust;
And yet the numbers crowded in his host
Might warrant more than even the Pacha's boast.

3.

With cautious reverence from the outer gate, 45
Slow stalks the slave, whose office there to wait,
Bows his bent head—his hand salutes the floor,
Ere yet his tongue the trusted tidings bore:
'A captive Dervise, from the pirate's nest
Escaped, is here—himself would tell the rest.' 50
He took the sign from Seyd's assenting eye,
And led the holy man in silence nigh.
His arms were folded on his dark-green vest,
His step was feeble, and his look deprest;
Yet worn he seemed of hardship more than years, 55
And pale his cheek with penance, not from fears.

30 bearded chiefs] men of might *ML*   31 banquet] supper *ML, M, cor. in Proofs*
3, 4   32 dared] deigned *ML*   33 to ... the] oft between the *ML*   34 bear ...
rigid] ⟨bore⟩ ... wiser *ML*   35 The ⟨frequent⟩ *ML*   dissolving cloud] expiring
smoke *ML*; ⟨expiring⟩ cloud *M*   36 dance] danced *ML*   Almahs *cor. by B in Text*
JJ Almas *all other texts*   37 morn] sun *ML*   40 On ... couch] ⟨In⟩ ... couches
ML   41 there ... they] ⟨when we can and combat when we⟩ *ML*; ⟨while they⟩ ...
they *ML*   42 And more to Korans than to conquest trust *ML, cor. in M*   43 ⟨Yet
all that numbers may achieve⟩ *ML*   crowded] ⟨wounded⟩ *Proof 1*   his] ⟨one's⟩ *ML*
45 ⟨A⟩ Tumult is heard and from *ML*   46 ⟨Approach the slaves whose duty there to
wait⟩ Slow stalks the slave who here may penetrate *ML*   48 Ere ... the] Thrice oer
his tongue its *ML*   50 is ... would] ⟨would kiss your feet and⟩ / awaits—himself
would *ML*   51 ⟨Admit him⟩ *ML*   52 nigh] ⟨by⟩ *ML*   56 with]⟨from⟩ *ML*

Vowed to his God—his sable locks he wore,
And these his lofty cap rose proudly o'er:
Around his form his loose long robe was thrown,
And wrapt a breast bestowed on heaven alone;   60
Submissive, yet with self-possession manned,
He calmly met the curious eyes that scanned;
And question of his coming fain would seek,
Before the Pacha's will allowed to speak.

4.

'Whence com'st thou, Dervise?'
                                    'From the outlaw's den,   65
A fugitive—'
                    'Thy capture where and when?'
'From Scalanova's port to Scio's isle,
The Saick was bound; but Alla did not smile
Upon our course—the Moslem merchant's gains
The Rovers won: our limbs have worn their chains.   70
I had no death to fear, nor wealth to boast,
Beyond the wandering freedom which I lost;
At length a fisher's humble boat by night
Afforded hope, and offered chance of flight:
I seized the hour, and find my safety here—   75
With thee—most mighty Pacha! who can fear?'

'How speed the outlaws? stand they well prepared,
Their plundered wealth, and robber's rock, to guard?
Dream they of this our preparation, doomed
To view with fire their scorpion nest consumed?'   80

'Pacha! the fettered captive's mourning eye
That weeps for flight, but ill can play the spy;
I only heard the reckless waters roar,
Those waves that would not bear me from the shore;

57 sable] ⟨long⟩ ML   58 his ⟨spirits⟩ lofty ML   60 breast] ⟨form⟩ ML
62 He ⟨holily⟩ ML   63 fain would] seemed to ML   68 The] Our M   69 Upon
our course] On this our voyage ML   70 the ⟨Pirates ?⟩ ML   71-2 not in ML
72 the] ⟨my⟩ M   73 ⟨Last night⟩ ML   74 Afforded] ⟨Presented⟩ ML   77 speed]
⟨stand⟩ M   stand] ⟨are⟩ ML   79 this] ⟨aught⟩ M   doomed] ⟨soon⟩ ML
80 scorpion] scorpion's ML   81 the ⟨captive⟩ fettered ML   82 ⟨hath⟩ but
ill ML   83 ⟨I heard their ?—and beheld their sport⟩ ML

I only marked the glorious sun and sky,　　85
Too bright—too blue—for my captivity;
And felt—that all which Freedom's bosom cheers
Must break my chain before it dried my tears.
This may'st thou judge, at least, from my escape,
They little deem of aught in peril's shape;　　90
Else vainly had I prayed or sought the chance
That leads me here—if eyed with vigilance:
The careless guard that did not see me fly,
May watch as idly when thy power is nigh:
Pacha!—my limbs are faint—and nature craves　　95
Food for my hunger, rest from tossing waves;
Permit my absence—peace be with thee! Peace
With all around!—now grant repose—release.'

'Stay, Dervise! I have more to question—stay,
I do command thee—sit—dost hear?—obey!　　100
More I must ask, and food the slaves shall bring;
Thou shalt not pine where all are banqueting:
The supper done—prepare thee to reply,
Clearly and full—I love not mystery.'

'Twere vain to guess what shook the pious man,　　105
Who looked not lovingly on that Divan;
Nor showed high relish for the banquet prest,
And less respect for every fellow guest.
'Twas but a moment's peevish hectic past
Along his cheek, and tranquillized as fast:　　110
He sate him down in silence, and his look
Resumed the calmness which before forsook:
The feast was ushered in—but sumptuous fare
He shunned as if some poison mingled there.
For one so long condemned to toil and fast,　　115
Methinks he strangely spares the rich repast.

87–8 ⟨This thou will judge at least from my escape | They little deem of aught in Danger's shape⟩ *ML*　　88 ⟨? my crag—but could not quell my tears⟩ *ML*　　90 peril's] Danger's *ML*　　92 eyed] ⟨watched⟩ *ML*　　93 guard] ⟨watch⟩ *ML*　　94 idly] ⟨vainly⟩ *ML*　　96 my . . . rest] ⟨her fast—repose⟩ *ML*　　98 repose] relief *ML*, *cor. in M*　　99 to . . . stay] ⟨to⟩ of question— ⟨yet⟩ *ML*　　100 obey] ⟨stay⟩ *ML*　　101 I . . . food] ⟨can I ask—but first⟩ *ML*　　102 pine] starve *ML*　　107 for the ⟨coming f⟩ banquet *M*　　108 every] ⟨each his⟩ *ML*　　114 He ⟨seemed to shun as if a⟩ poison there *ML*　　115 ⟨The feast he⟩ *ML*　　116 rich] long *ML*

'What ails thee, Dervise? eat—dost thou suppose
This feast a Christian's? or my friends thy foes?
Why dost thou shun the salt? that sacred pledge,
Which, once partaken, blunts the sabre's edge,   120
Makes even contending tribes in peace unite,
And hated hosts seem brethren to the sight!'

'Salt seasons dainties—and my food is still
The humblest root, my drink the simplest rill;
And my stern vow and order's laws oppose   125
To break or mingle bread with friends or foes;
It may seem strange—if there be aught to dread,
That peril rests upon my single head;
But for thy sway—nay more—thy Sultan's throne,
I taste nor bread nor banquet—save alone;   130
Infringed our order's rule, the Prophet's rage
To Mecca's dome might bar my pilgrimage.'

'Well—as thou wilt—ascetic as thou art—
One question answer; then in peace depart.
How many?—Ha! it cannot sure be day?   135
What star—what sun is bursting on the bay?
It shines a lake of fire!—away—away!
Ho! treachery! my guards! my scimitar!
The galleys feed the flames—and I afar!
Accursed Dervise!—these thy tidings—thou   140
Some villain spy—seize—cleave him—slay him now!'

Up rose the Dervise with that burst of light,
Nor less his change of form appalled the sight:
Up rose that Dervise—not in saintly garb,
But like a warrior bounding on his barb,   145

118 a . . . thy] ⟨your enemy's—or these your⟩ ML   119 ⟨It may seem strange
if⟩ M   120 Which ⟨even with / blunts with⟩ ML   121 Makes . . . tribes] ⟨Bids
even the hostile⟩ guests ML   122 And ⟨makes his host / hateful⟩ hated hosts seem
⟨friendly⟩ ML   123 dainties] ⟨viands⟩ ML   126 break or mingle] ⟨mingle
breaking⟩ ML   129 thy sway] ⟨thine own⟩ ML   131 ⟨If such⟩ ML   132 To . . .
bar] ⟨Were⟩ From . . . curse ML   To] ⟨From⟩ M   133 ascetic . . . art] ⟨but now
before we part⟩ / ⟨since anchorite⟩ thou art ML   141 seize ⟨him⟩ ML   142 with
that] ⟨when⟩ the ML   143 ⟨That shocked all hearts and⟩ ML   appalled] ⟨amazed⟩
ML   144 garb] ⟨stole⟩ ML   145 on] from ML, M, all proofs, Corsair1–
Corsair7

Dashed his high cap, and tore his robe away—
Shone his mailed breast, and flashed his sabre's ray!
His close but glittering casque, and sable plume,
More glittering eye, and black brow's sabler gloom,
Glared on the Moslems' eyes some Afrit sprite,   150
Whose demon death-blow left no hope for fight.
The wild confusion, and the swarthy glow
Of flames on high, and torches from below;
The shriek of terror, and the mingling yell—
For swords began to clash, and shouts to swell,   155
Flung o'er that spot of earth the air of hell!
Distracted, to and fro, the flying slaves
Behold but bloody shore and fiery waves;
Nought heeded they the Pacha's angry cry,
They seize that Dervise!—seize on Zatanai!   160
He saw their terror—checked the first despair
That urged him but to stand and perish there,
Since far too early and too well obeyed,
The flame was kindled ere the signal made;
He saw their terror—from his baldric drew   165
His bugle—brief the blast—but shrilly blew,
'Tis answered—'Well ye speed, my gallant crew!
Why did I doubt their quickness of career?
And deem design had left me single here?'
Sweeps his long arm—that sabre's whirling sway,   170
Sheds fast atonement for its first delay;
Completes his fury, what their fear begun,
And makes the many basely quail to one.
The cloven turbans o'er the chamber spread,
And scarce an arm dare rise to guard its head: 175
Even Seyd, convulsed, o'erwhelmed with rage, surprise,
Retreats before him, though he still defies.

146 tore . . . away] ⟨flung . . . aside⟩ *ML*   148 His ⟨closely fitting⟩ casque *ML*
149 black] ⟨dark⟩ *ML*   150 Glared on] ⟨Seemed to⟩ *ML*   151 Whose demon
⟨arm defied to ?⟩ *ML*   158 ⟨Nor know to seek / shun the land or shun the waves⟩
ML   159 ⟨Small heed had they of aught the Pacha spake⟩ *ML*   Pacha's ⟨vain⟩
angry *ML*   161 checked] and *ML*, *M, cor. in Proof 2*   163 Since] ⟨For⟩ *ML*
164 flame] fire *ML, M*   166 brief] ⟨shrill⟩ *M*   shrilly] loudly *ML*   167 ye]
you *ML, M*   169 design] their folly *ML*; ⟨neglect⟩ *M*   170 that . . . sway]
that sabre cleaves its way *ML*; his sabre cleaves its way *M, cor. in Proof 1*   171 Sheds
fast] And sheds *ML, M, cor. in Proof 1*   172 ⟨And deeds com⟩ *ML*   173 quail
to] shrink from *ML*   174 o'er] ⟨over⟩ *ML*   175 guard] save *ML*   176 Even
Seyd ⟨himself though choaked / though brave⟩ *ML*

No craven he—and yet he dreads the blow,
So much Confusion magnifies his foe!
His blazing galleys still distract his sight,   180
He tore his beard, and foaming fled the fight;
For now the pirates passed the Haram gate,
And burst within—and it were death to wait;
Where wild Amazement shrieking—kneeling—throws
The sword aside—in vain—the blood o'erflows!   185
The Corsairs pouring, haste to where within,
Invited Conrad's bugle, and the din
Of groaning victims, and wild cries for life,
Proclaimed how well he did the work of strife.
They shout to find him grim and lonely there,   190
A glutted tyger mangling in his lair!
But short their greeting—shorter his reply—
' 'Tis well—but Seyd escapes—and he must die.
Much hath been done—but more remains to do—
Their galleys blaze—why not their city too?'   195

5.

Quick at the word—they seized him each a torch,
And fire the dome from minaret to porch.
A stern delight was fixed in Conrad's eye,
But sudden sunk—for on his ear the cry
Of women struck, and like a deadly knell   200
Knocked at that heart unmoved by battle's yell.
'Oh! burst the Haram—wrong not on your lives
One female form—remember—*we* have wives.
On them such outrage Vengeance will repay;
Man is our foe, and such 'tis ours to slay: 205
But still we spared—must spare the weaker prey.
Oh! I forgot—but Heaven will not forgive
If at my word the helpless cease to live;
Follow who will—I go—we yet have time

---

178 dreads] shuns *ML, cor. in M*   181 tore his beard] cursed his birth *ML*
182 pirates] ⟨rovers⟩ *ML*   183 burst] ⟨poured⟩ *ML*   184 shrieking . . . throws]
⟨tremble / rather count the blows / rather than oppose⟩ *ML*   185 in vain] and yet *ML*
186 Corsairs] Pirates *ML, cor. in M*   189 Proclaimed ⟨he still⟩ *ML*   193 ⟨Well
have you fought⟩ *ML*   196 a] his *ML*   197 And] ⟨Some⟩ *ML*   198 Conrad's
⟨face⟩ *ML*   199 sunk] changed *ML*   201 at] on *ML*   204 ⟨Man is our
foe it is enough to slay⟩ *ML*   207 not ⟨forget⟩ *M*   208 ⟨If my rash word have
women⟩ *ML*

Our souls to lighten of at least a crime.'   210
He climbs the crackling stair—he bursts the door,
Nor feels his feet glow scorching with the floor;
His breath choked gasping with the volumed smoke,
But still from room to room his way he broke.
They search—they find—they save: with lusty arms   215
Each bears a prize of unregarded charms;
Calm their loud fears; sustain their sinking frames
With all the care defenceless beauty claims:
So well could Conrad tame their fiercest mood,
And check the very hands with gore imbrued.   220
But who is she? whom Conrad's arms convey
From reeking pile and combat's wreck—away—
Who but the love of him he dooms to bleed?
The Haram queen—but still the slave of Seyd!

6.

Brief time had Conrad now to greet Gulnare,   225
Few words to reassure the trembling fair;
For in that pause compassion snatched from war,
The foe before retiring, fast and far,
With wonder saw their footsteps unpursued,
First slowlier fled—then rallied—then withstood.   230
This Seyd perceives, then first perceives how few,
Compared with his, the Corsair's roving crew,
And blushes o'er his error, as he eyes
The ruin wrought by panic and surprize.
Alla il Alla! Vengeance swells the cry—   235
Shame mounts to rage that must atone or die!
And flame for flame and blood for blood must tell,
The tide of triumph ebbs that flowed too well—

210 of] ⟨of⟩ by ML   213 choaked gasping] waxed choaking ML   214 But] Yet
ML   215 search ⟨and save⟩ ML   218 care defenceless] ⟨reverence timid⟩ ML
219 could . . . tame] ⟨had . . . tamed⟩ ML, M   220 gore] blood ML   221 she?
⟨their⟩ ML   222 and . . . wreck] and ⟨blood-red court⟩ ML   223 love . . . dooms]
⟨spouse . . . doomed⟩ ML   224 but . . . Seyd] Gulnare—the ⟨slave⟩ love of Seyd ML,
cor. in M   225 Brief] ⟨Short⟩ M   226 ⟨And⟩ Few ML   227 snatched]
⟨stole⟩ ML   228 The ⟨slaughtered foe though⟩ ML   229 ⟨Though⟩ With wonder
⟨now⟩ saw ML   230 ⟨And⟩ First ⟨slackened—paused / fled with slowlier pace—their
panting⟩ ML   231 ⟨And⟩ This Seyd ⟨perceived—and saw⟩ ML   232 Corsair's
roving] rover's daring ML   233 And ⟨blushed for⟩ ML   235 swells] is ML
236 ⟨And burning shame⟩ ML   238 ⟨How turns / ebbs the tide of fight that flowed
so / too well / whose triumph bids farewell⟩ ⟨How those who fled before⟩ ML

The Corsair Canto II lines 215–16

(Reproduced with the permission of the British Library)

When wrath returns to renovated strife,
And those who fought for conquest strike for life.   240
Conrad beheld the danger—he beheld
His followers faint by freshening foes repelled:
'One effort—one—to break the circling host!'
They form—unite—charge—waver—all is lost!
Within a narrower ring compressed, beset,   245
Hopeless, not heartless, strive and struggle yet—
Ah! now they fight in firmest file no more,
Hemmed in—cut off—cleft down—and trampled o'er;
But each strikes singly, silently, and home,
And sinks outwearied rather than o'ercome,   250
His last faint quittance rendering with his breath,
Till the blade glimmers in the grasp of death!

7.

But first, ere came the rallying host to blows,
And rank to rank, and hand to hand oppose,
Gulnare and all her Haram handmaids freed,   255
Safe in the dome of one who held their creed,
By Conrad's mandate safely were bestowed,
And dried those tears for life and fame that flowed:
And when that dark-eyed lady, young Gulnare,
Recalled those thoughts late wandering in despair,   260
Much did she marvel o'er the courtesy
That smoothed his accents, softened in his eye:
'Twas strange—*that* robber thus with gore bedewed,
Seemed gentler then than Seyd in fondest mood.

239 When] ⟨What / How⟩ *ML*   241 ⟨The Chief⟩ beheld his peril ⟨but those fled /
and he saw⟩ *ML*   242 ⟨That led to / pursuit⟩ *ML*   243 ⟨Our charge— ? —
against them pour⟩ *ML*   one] ⟨more⟩ *M*   244 ⟨They gather—rush / Tis made⟩ *ML*
unite] ⟨rush on⟩ *ML*   245 ring ⟨and narrower still⟩ *ML*   246 ⟨They combat
hopeless—strive and strike⟩ *ML*   247 ⟨But now no more they fight in firmest file⟩
ML   248 ⟨Their ranks are stormed in / And the thinned ranks deem not now the
more⟩ All thoughts of victory with order oer *ML, cor. in M*   249 strikes . . . silently]
⟨in single / fights⟩ singly— ⟨lonely⟩ *ML*   251 ⟨Without one cry his last faint quit-
tance⟩ *ML*   252 ⟨And the blade yet glittering in / With his blade that quivers stiffened
in⟩ *ML*   253 ere ⟨when⟩ *ML*   255 and] with *M*   256 dome . . . held]
⟨mosque . . . cared?⟩ *ML*   257 safely] ⟨safely⟩ quickly *ML*   259 young]
⟨proud⟩ *ML*   260 late wandering] that wandered *ML*   261 the] ⟨that⟩ *ML*
262 That ⟨softened Conrad's actions— ? / quelled⟩ his eye *ML*   accents] ⟨voice⟩ *ML*
263 ⟨From carnage reeking⟩ ⟨Certain twas strange that robber made⟩ *ML*   gore bedewed]
⟨blood imbrued⟩ *ML*   264 then] far *ML*

The Pacha wooed as if he deemed the slave   265
Must seem delighted with the heart he gave;
The Corsair vowed protection, soothed affright,
As if his homage were a woman's right.
'The wish is wrong—nay worse for female—vain:
Yet much I long to view that chief again;   270
If but to thank for, what my fear forgot,
The life—my loving lord remembered not!'

8.

And him she saw, where thickest carnage spread,
But gathered breathing from the happier dead;
Far from his band, and battling with a host   275
That deem right dearly won the field he lost,
Felled—bleeding—baffled of the death he sought,
And snatched to expiate all the ills he wrought;
Preserved to linger and to live in vain,
While Vengeance pondered o'er new plans of pain,   280
And staunched the blood she saves to shed again—
But drop by drop, for Seyd's unglutted eye
Would doom him ever dying—ne'er to die!
Can this be he? triumphant late she saw,
When his red hand's wild gesture waved, a law!   285
'Tis he indeed—disarmed but undeprest,
His sole regret the life he still possest;
His wounds too slight, though taken with that will,
Which would have kissed the hand that then could kill.
Oh were there none, of all the many given,   290
To send his soul—he scarcely asked to heaven?
Must he alone of all retain his breath,
Who more than all had striven and struck for death?

265 The Lover ⟨smiled but looked the Master⟩ ML   as . . . slave] ⟨but neer forgot the
slave / but still would⟩ ML   Pacha] ⟨Lov⟩ M   267 ⟨The Pirate gave her freedom—
life—defense⟩ ML   268 homage] ⟨service⟩ ML   269 for female] ⟨the wish is⟩ ML;
nay ⟨more⟩ for female M   271 ⟨Twere but to thank him for the life⟩ ML   273 Yes
—him she saw—⟨as when cold fluttering spread / where Carnage thickly⟩ spread ML
275–7 ⟨Preserved to linger and to live in vain | While Vengeance pondered oer a death of
pain | And staunches the blood she longs to shed again⟩ ML   276 That] Who ML
278 expiate ⟨the havoc⟩ all ML   282–3 not in ML   284 be he ⟨who⟩ ML
285 ⟨Whose will even held / Whose ? and will were more than might⟩ ML   wild . . . waved,
a] ⟨least . . . served as⟩ ML   hand's] ⟨arm's⟩ M   286 ⟨Yet Conrad still⟩ ML   288 too]
were ML, cor. in M   289 Which] That ML   290 Oh . . . none] ⟨Was there no wound⟩
ML   291 To] Could ML   asked] cared ML, M, cor. in Proofs 6, 6a   292 of all
⟨his band⟩ ML   293 striven and struck] ⟨struck⟩ sought and strove ML, cor. in M

He deeply felt—what mortal hearts must feel,
When thus reversed on faithless fortune's wheel,   295
For crimes committed, and the victor's threat
Of lingering tortures to repay the debt
He deeply, darkly felt; but evil pride
That led to perpetrate—now serves to hide.
Still in his stern and self-collected mien   300
A conqueror's more than captive's air is seen,
Though faint with wasting toil and stiffening wound,
But few that saw—so calmly gazed around:
Though the far shouting of the distant crowd,
Their tremors o'er, rose insolently loud,   305
The better warriors who beheld him near,
Insulted not the foe who taught them fear;
And the grim guards that to his durance led,
In silence eyed him with a secret dread.

9.

The Leech was sent—but not in mercy—there   310
To note how much the life yet left could bear;
He found enough to load with heaviest chain,
And promise feeling for the wrench of pain:
To-morrow—yea—to-morrow's evening sun
Will sinking see impalement's pangs begun,   315
And rising with the wonted blush of morn
Behold how well or ill those pangs are borne.
Of torments this the longest and the worst,
Which adds all other agony to thirst,
That day by day death still forbears to slake,   320
While famished vultures flit around the stake.
'Oh! water—water!'—smiling Hate denies
The victim's prayer—for if he drinks—he dies.

294 He . . . must] ⟨Yet⟩ He . . . ⟨but⟩ ML   295 ⟨The / For crimes committed—and the coming wheel⟩ ML   faithless fortune's] fortune's faithless ML   297 ⟨His lingering tortures threatened but⟩ ML   the debt] ⟨their / them yet⟩ ML   298 He ⟨felt what none need envy—but his⟩ pride ML   300 Still] ⟨And⟩ ML   301 is] ⟨was⟩ ML   302 with ⟨toil and bleeding wound / wasted bleeding⟩ ML   304 ⟨And the grim guards that to his dungeon led⟩ ML   305 ⟨Proclaimed / In silence eyed him⟩ ML   306 beheld] ⟨surveyed⟩ ML   307 the . . . them] ⟨him who first had taught⟩ / the foe ⟨they late could⟩ ML   308 durance] ⟨dungeon / prison⟩ ML   310 sent] ⟨there⟩ ML   311 To . . . how] To ⟨watch the⟩ see how ML, cor. in M   312 load with] ⟨bear the⟩ ML   313 for the ⟨anguish⟩ taste of ML   315 see] ⟨see⟩ leave ML   319 all . . . to] ⟨to agony the Fever's⟩ ML   320 ⟨And many a day prolongs⟩ ML   323 victim's] ⟨wretch's⟩ ML

This was his doom:—the Leech, the guard were gone,
And left proud Conrad fettered and alone.   325

10.

'Twere vain to paint to what his feelings grew—
It even were doubtful if their victim knew.
There is a war, a chaos of the mind,
When all its elements convulsed—combined—
Lie dark and jarring with perturbed force,   330
And gnashing with impenitent Remorse;
That juggling fiend—who never spake before—
But cries, 'I warned thee!' when the deed is o'er.
Vain voice! the spirit burning but unbent,
May writhe—rebel—the weak alone repent!   335
Even in that lonely hour when most it feels,
And, to itself, all—all that self reveals,
No single passion, and no ruling thought
That leaves the rest as once unseen, unsought;
But the wild prospect when the soul reviews—   340
All rushing through their thousand avenues.
Ambition's dreams expiring, love's regret,
Endangered glory, life itself beset;
The joy untasted, the contempt or hate
'Gainst those who fain would triumph in our fate;   345
The hopeless past, the hasting future driven
Too quickly on to guess if hell or heaven;
Deeds, thoughts, and words, perhaps remembered not
So keenly till that hour, but ne'er forgot;
Things light or lovely in their acted time,   350
But now to stern reflection each a crime;
The withering sense of evil unrevealed,
Not cankering less because the more concealed—

---

324 This was ⟨doomed—decreed⟩ ML   326 paint] ⟨guess⟩ ML   327 It even]
⟨And⟩ it ML   328 a . . . a] ⟨that state—that⟩ ML   329 ⟨Which all who feel
have felt—but none defined⟩ ML   330 with . . . force] ⟨in . . . sleep⟩ ML
331 And . . . with] ⟨The malady of⟩ / In sternness of ML   332 spake] ⟨warned⟩ ML
333 thee] you ML   334 ⟨While⟩ Vain voice ⟨if that⟩ ML   335 May sink—
must perish—but will not repent ML   337 all—all] ⟨the all⟩ M   339 That
⟨dreads⟩ ML   once unseen] ⟨silent as⟩ ML; once unfelt ML, M   341 rushing]
⟨pouring⟩ ML   342 dreams] ⟨aims⟩ ML   344 ⟨The ? importance or /
and the baffled hate⟩ ML   345 ⟨The thought of all that meanly triumphs oer⟩ ML
347 Too . . . on] ⟨With little time⟩ ML   350 Things ⟨little recked of in their living⟩
time ML   351 to] ⟨by⟩ ML   353 cankering] ⟨punished⟩ ML

All, in a word, from which all eyes must start,
That opening sepulchre—the naked heart   355
Bares with its buried woes, till Pride awake,
To snatch the mirror from the soul—and break.
Ay—Pride can veil, and courage brave it all,
All—all—before—beyond—the deadliest fall.
Each hath some fear, and he who least betrays,   360
The only hypocrite deserving praise:
Not the loud recreant wretch who boasts and flies;
But he who looks on death—and silent dies.
So steeled by pondering o'er his far career,
He halfway meets him should he menace near!   365

II.

In the high chamber of his highest tower,
Sate Conrad, fettered in the Pacha's power.
His palace perished in the flame—this fort
Contained at once his captive and his court.
Not much could Conrad of his sentence blame,   370
His foe, if vanquished, had but shared the same:—
Alone he sate—in solitude had scanned
His guilty bosom, but that breast he manned:
One thought alone he could not—dared not meet.
'Oh, how these tidings will Medora greet?'   375
Then—only then—his clanking hands he raised,
And strained with rage the chain on which he gazed;
But soon he found—or feigned—or dreamed relief,
And smiled in self-derision of his grief,
'And now come torture when it will—or may,   380
More need of rest to nerve me for the day!'

---

355 opening] opened *ML*, *M*, *cor. in Proof 2*   356 ⟨Passes all / All these ? ere
Peril knew / till shame can make⟩ *ML*   with . . . Pride] ⟨of . . . Shame / Despair⟩ *ML*
357 ⟨Rain down the / And Shame forbid / And bids ? / And lends the destined ?⟩ / ⟨The faith-
ful mirror of the soul it breaks⟩ *ML*   358 ⟨Peace—and if time allows / give pause—
one ? fall⟩ *ML*   360 ⟨All hath that dread but⟩ he who least ⟨displays⟩ *ML*   362 Not
the ⟨craven⟩ loud *ML*   363 looks on] ⟨dreads the⟩ *ML*   364 ⟨Who marks his
distant aspect / Who hails without his own ? / Who marks with awe his ? thoughts career /
Who so considers⟩ So used to ponder oer his far career *ML*   365 He . . . meets] ⟨But . . .
meets⟩ Can . . . meet *ML*   366 his] ⟨the⟩ *ML*   370 That Moslem's sentence
little could he blame *ML*   374 ⟨And now come danger—torture when it may⟩ *ML*
375 will] would *ML*   376 ⟨Then alone he clasped his clanking⟩ *ML*   raised] ⟨clasped⟩
ML   380 torture . . . will] ⟨Danger⟩ . . . must *ML*   381 ⟨Mine eyes are heavy
with their toils today⟩ *ML*

This said, with languor to his mat he crept,
And, whatsoe'er his visions, quickly slept.

'Twas hardly midnight when that fray begun,
For Conrad's plans matured, at once were done;   385
And Havoc loathes so much the waste of time,
She scarce had left an uncommitted crime.
One hour beheld him since the tide he stemmed—
Disguised—discovered—conquering—ta'en—condemned—
A chief on land—an outlaw on the deep—   390
Destroying—saving—prisoned—and asleep!

12.

He slept in calmest seeming—for his breath
Was hushed so deep—Ah! happy if in death!
He slept—Who o'er his placid slumber bends?
His foes are gone—and here he hath no friends;   395
Is it some seraph sent to grant him grace?
No, 'tis an earthly form with heavenly face!
Its white arm raised a lamp—yet gently hid,
Lest the ray flash abruptly on the lid
Of that closed eye, which opens but to pain,   400
And once unclosed—but once may close again.
That form, with eye so dark, and cheek so fair,
And auburn waves of gemmed and braided hair;
With shape of fairy lightness—naked foot,
That shines like snow, and falls on earth as mute—   405
Through guards and dunnest night how came it there?
Ah! rather ask what will not woman dare?
Whom youth and pity lead like thee, Gulnare!

383 And ⟨strange⟩ *ML*   quickly] ⟨surely⟩ *ML*   384 ⟨Day rises and he⟩ *ML*
385 matured . . . were] ⟨conceived were quickly⟩ *ML*   386 And Havoc ⟨ever does
her work so well / borrows such / ? so well her destined time⟩ *ML*   waste] loss *ML*
387 an] one *ML*   388 since ⟨he left the deep⟩ *M*   389 ⟨A Leader / A spy—a chief—
victorious⟩ *ML*   ta'en] chained *ML*   392 for] ⟨and⟩ *ML*   393 ⟨So lightly heaved
his slumber / Was ? scarcely life⟩ *ML*   if in] ⟨were it⟩ *ML*   395 are gone] ⟨too sleep⟩
ML   398 raised . . . hid] held ⟨yet shaded from his lid⟩ a lamp yet ⟨fearful⟩ gently hid
ML   raised] ⟨waved⟩ *M*   399 ⟨Of his closed eyes⟩ *ML*   the . . . abruptly] ⟨fall /
steal the ray too fiercely⟩ *ML*   the . . . flash] ⟨fall the ray⟩ *M*   400 which] that *ML*
401 may] ⟨shall⟩ *ML*   402 That . . . cheek] ⟨Its . . . form⟩ *ML*   403 ⟨Unveiled /
And far depending black and braided⟩ *ML*   waves] ⟨braids⟩ *ML*   404 With . . .
naked] ⟨And . . . dazzling⟩ *ML*   406 dunnest night] ⟨night and dread⟩ *ML*   407 Ah!
rather] ⟨Yet wherefore⟩ *ML*   408 lead] leads *M*

She could not sleep—and while the Pacha's rest
In muttering dreams yet saw his pirate-guest,   410
She left his side—his signet ring she bore,
Which oft in sport adorned her hand before—
And with it, scarcely questioned, won her way
Through drowsy guards that must that sign obey.
Worn out with toil, and tired with changing blows,   415
Their eyes had envied Conrad his repose;
And chill and nodding at the turret door,
They stretch their listless limbs, and watch no more:
Just raised their heads to hail the signet-ring,
Nor ask or what or who the sign may bring.   420

13.

She gazed in wonder, 'Can he calmly sleep,
While other eyes his fall or ravage weep?
And mine in restlessness are wandering here—
What sudden spell hath made this man so dear?
True—'tis to him my life, and more, I owe,   425
And me and mine he spared from worse than woe:
'Tis late to think—but soft—his slumber breaks—
How heavily he sighs!—he starts—awakes!'

He raised his head—and dazzled with the light,
His eye seemed dubious if it saw aright: 430
He moved his hand—the grating of his chain
Too harshly told him that he lived again.
'What is that form? if not a shape of air,
Methinks, my jailor's face shows wond'rous fair?'

'Pirate! thou know'st me not—but I am one,   435
Grateful for deeds thou hast too rarely done;
Look on me—and remember her, thy hand
Snatched from the flames, and thy more fearful band.

409 She could not ⟨rest and while Confusion reigns⟩ ML   411 She left his side—
⟨and with the signet ring⟩ ML   412 adorned . . . before] ⟨her taper finger wore⟩ ML
414 must] still ML   415 Worn out with ⟨weary and given with mischief⟩ ML
416 ⟨They envied then⟩ ML   418 listless] stiffening ML   419 heads] ⟨eyes⟩ M
420 ask . . . who] asked or ⟨whom⟩ or ⟨what⟩ ML   423 in] ⟨for⟩ ML   wandering]
⟨lingering⟩ ML   426 spared ⟨when from⟩ ML   427 ⟨Now tis too late⟩ ML
431 grating] ⟨rattling⟩ ML   434 shows] ⟨grows⟩ M   435 Pirate] ⟨Conrad⟩ ML
438 thy] ⟨far⟩ ML

I come through darkness—and I scarce know why—
Yet not to hurt—I would not see thee die.'   440

'If so, kind lady! thine the only eye
That would not here in that gay hope delight:
Theirs is the chance—and let them use their right.
But still I thank their courtesy or thine,
That would confess me at so fair a shrine!'   445

Strange though it seem—yet with extremest grief
Is linked a mirth—it doth not bring relief—
That playfulness of Sorrow ne'er beguiles,
And smiles in bitterness—but still it smiles;
And sometimes with the wisest and the best,   450
Till even the scaffold echoes with their jest!
Yet not the joy to which it seems akin—
It may deceive all hearts, save that within.
Whate'er it was that flashed on Conrad, now
A laughing wildness half unbent his brow: 455
And these his accents had a sound of mirth,
As if the last he could enjoy on earth;
Yet 'gainst his nature—for through that short life,
Few thoughts had he to spare from gloom and strife.

14.

'Corsair! thy doom is named—but I have power   460
To soothe the Pacha in his weaker hour.
Thee would I spare—nay more—would save thee now,
But this—time—hope—nor even thy strength allow;
But all I can, I will: at least, delay
The sentence that remits thee scarce a day.   465
More now were ruin—even thyself were loth
The vain attempt should bring but doom to both.'

439 I came through ⟨peril⟩ and I ⟨scarcely⟩ ML   441 kind] ⟨fair⟩ ML   442 That would not— ⟨must not⟩ ML   444 still . . . or thine] yet . . . ⟨at least⟩ ML   445 Who would confess me ⟨with⟩ so fair a ⟨Priest⟩ ML   446 Strange . . . yet] It may seem strange but ML, M; ⟨Strange it may seem—but⟩ Proof 6a   yet . . . extremest] ⟨linked with deepest⟩ ML   447 Is linked] ⟨There is⟩ ML   448 That] ⟨An / If / Nor⟩ ML   450 with the wisest] moves the sternest ML   451 echoes with] ⟨hath beheld⟩ ML   453 save] but ML   454 that ⟨now⟩ on ML   456 these . . . had] ⟨his first accents wore⟩ ML   457 ⟨With⟩ As ML   459 thoughts ⟨of⟩ had ML   460 Corsair . . . named] ⟨Conrad . . . sealed⟩ ML   462 spare] save ML   463 But this ⟨nor⟩ time ⟨nor⟩ hope ML   even] ⟨scarce⟩ M   465 remits] ⟨permits⟩ ML   466 ⟨But more as yet were ruin—and⟩ ML

'Yes!—loth indeed:—my soul is nerved to all,
Or fall'n too low to fear a further fall:
Tempt not thyself with peril; me with hope,   470
Of flight from foes with whom I could not cope;
Unfit to vanquish—shall I meanly fly,
The one of all my band that would not die?
Yet there is one—to whom my memory clings,
'Till to these eyes her own wild softness springs.   475
My sole resources in the path I trod
Were these—my bark—my sword—my love—my God!
The last I left in youth—he leaves me now—
And Man but works his will to lay me low.
I have no thought to mock his throne with prayer   480
Wrung from the coward crouching of despair;
It is enough—I breathe—and I can bear.
My sword is shaken from the worthless hand
That might have better kept so true a brand;
My bark is sunk or captive—but my love—   485
For her in sooth my voice would mount above:
Oh! she is all that still to earth can bind—
And this will break a heart so more than kind,
And blight a form—till thine appeared, Gulnare!
Mine eye ne'er asked if others were as fair.'   490

'Thou lov'st another then?—but what to me
Is this—'tis nothing—nothing e'er can be:
But yet—thou lov'st—and—Oh! I envy those
Whose hearts on hearts as faithful can repose,
Who never feel the void—the wandering thought   495
That sighs o'er visions—such as mine hath wrought.'
'Lady—methought thy love was his, for whom
This arm redeemed thee from a fiery tomb.'

468 nerved] manned *ML*   469 ⟨The fear short⟩ *ML*   470 with . . . with]
⟨to . . . to⟩ *ML*   471 Of] ⟨A⟩ *ML*   472 vanquish— ⟨wherefore should⟩ shall
ML   475 her . . . softness] ⟨my⟩ another's weakness *ML*   482 enough—
⟨he⟩ I *ML*   483 is shaken] ⟨is shivered⟩ ⟨was⟩ shaken *ML*   484 That ⟨ill deserved
to wield too bright a⟩ brand *ML*   486 her ⟨above⟩ in *ML*   487 is] ⟨was⟩ *M*
can] could *ML*   489 And ⟨made⟩ a form ⟨that until now⟩ *ML*   490 ⟨I never
thought / asked my breast—are others⟩ fair *ML*   492 Is this ⟨why ask I—what⟩
—'tis nothing—nothing ⟨could it be / had it been⟩ *ML*   493 lovest ⟨another—well⟩
and *ML*   494 as] ⟨so⟩ *ML*   495 void] ⟨voice⟩ *ML*   497 love . . . for]
⟨heart . . . to⟩ *ML*

'My love stern Seyd's! Oh—No—No—not my love—
Yet much this heart, that strives no more, once strove   500
To meet his passion—but it would not be.
I felt—I feel—love dwells with—with the free.
I am a slave, a favoured slave at best,
To share his splendour, and seem very blest!
Oft must my soul the question undergo,   505
Of—"Dost thou love?" and burn to answer "No!"
Oh! hard it is that fondness to sustain,
And struggle not to feel averse in vain;
But harder still the heart's recoil to bear,
And hide from one—perhaps another there.   510
He takes the hand I give not—nor withhold—
Its pulse nor checked—nor quickened—calmly cold:
And when resigned, it drops a lifeless weight
From one I never loved enough to hate.
No warmth these lips return by his imprest,   515
And chilled remembrance shudders o'er the rest.
Yes—had I ever proved that passion's zeal,
The change to hatred were at least to feel:
But still—he goes unmourned—returns unsought—
And oft when present—absent from my thought.   520
Or when reflection comes, and come it must—
I fear that henceforth 'twill but bring disgust;
I am his slave—but, in despite of pride,
'Twere worse than bondage to become his bride.
Oh! that this dotage of his breast would cease!   525
Or seek another and give mine release,
But yesterday—I could have said, to peace!
Yes—if unwonted fondness now I feign,
Remember—captive! 'tis to break thy chain.

499 love . . . love] ⟨heart . . . heart⟩ ML   501 passion] ⟨fondness⟩ ML   502 I felt
⟨that love belongs but to the⟩ free ML   505 ⟨The question "dost thou love"⟩ ML
soul] ⟨heart⟩ ML   506 and . . . No!"] and ⟨sinking / burn to / long to⟩ pant to answer
"no." ML   507 it is ⟨to⟩ that ML   508 struggle . . . averse] ⟨labour . . . disgust /
dislike⟩ ML   509 But . . . still] ⟨Oh hard it is⟩ ML   513 resigned] he quits
ML, M, all proofs, Corsair1–Corsair5   514 one] him ML   517 ⟨No—how⟩
Yes . . . ever ⟨met⟩ proved ML   519 still] no ML   520 ⟨My mind to him a
smooth dull waste of thought⟩ ML   521 And when ⟨it ponders⟩ ML   523 I am his
⟨purchased⟩ slave— ⟨my faith⟩ ML   524 become] ⟨have been⟩ ML   525–6 I breathe
but in the hope his altered breast | May seek another and leave mine at rest ML, M
526 Or] ⟨And⟩ Ma   527 not in ML, M   528 Yes] Or ML, M   529 captive
Conrad ML

Repay the life that to thy hand I owe;   530
To give thee back to all endeared below,
Who share such love as I can never know.
Farewell—morn breaks—and I must now away:
'Twill cost me dear—but dread no death to-day!'

15.

She pressed his fettered fingers to her heart,   535
And bowed her head, and turned her to depart,
And noiseless as a lovely dream is gone.
And was she here? and is he now alone?
What gem hath dropped and sparkles o'er his chain?
The tear most sacred, shed for other's pain,   540
That starts at once—bright—pure—from Pity's mine,
Already polished by the hand divine!

Oh! too convincing—dangerously dear—
In woman's eye the unanswerable tear!
That weapon of her weakness she can wield,   545
To save, subdue—at once her spear and shield:
Avoid it—Virtue ebbs and Wisdom errs,
Too fondly gazing on that grief of hers!
What lost a world, and made a hero fly?
The timid tear in Cleopatra's eye.   550
Yet be the soft triumvir's fault forgiven,
By this—how many lose not earth—but heaven!
Consign their souls to man's eternal foe,
And seal their own to spare some wanton's woe!

16.

'Tis morn—and o'er his altered features play   555
The beams—without the hope of yesterday.

530 Repay . . . hand] ⟨And / Return . . . hands⟩ *ML*   532 Who . . . as] And share
the love which *ML*   533 Farewell ⟨the morning now will roll⟩ *ML*   534 ⟨And /
But if I live—thou shalt not die today⟩ *ML*   dread no death] ⟨thou art safe / live at least⟩
ML   535 fingers to her] ⟨hand to that warm / her wild⟩ *ML*   538 ⟨The tear
that dropped and sparkled on his chain⟩ *ML*   540 ⟨It is her tear that⟩ *ML*   sacred]
blessed *M, cor. in Proof 6*   541 That ⟨tokens⟩ starts ⟨already of⟩ *ML*   543–54 *late
addition to ML*   543 Oh ⟨ever touching / tender—more than⟩ too convincing—⟨oft ?⟩
dear *MLa*   544 eye ⟨the magic of her⟩ tear *MLa*   545–6 ⟨And yet / So powerful—
well the manly eye prefers | To hide its deepest grief than gaze on hers⟩ *MLa*   547 ebbs]
⟨flies⟩ *MLa*   549 made] ⟨bade⟩ *MLa*   550 in] of *M*   551 Yet] But *MLa*
552 By] ⟨For⟩ *M*   553 Consign] ⟨And yield⟩ *MLa*   556 without] ⟨but not⟩ *ML*

What shall he be ere night? perchance a thing
O'er which the raven flaps her funeral wing:
By his closed eye unheeded and unfelt,
While sets that sun, and dews of evening melt,   560
Chill—wet—and misty round each stiffened limb,
Refreshing earth—reviving all but him!—

CANTO III

'Come vedi—ancor non m'abbandona.'
DANTE.

I.

Slow sinks, more lovely ere his race be run,
Along Morea's hills the setting sun;
Not, as in Northern climes, obscurely bright,
But one unclouded blaze of living light!
O'er the hushed deep the yellow beam he throws,   5
Gilds the green wave, that trembles as it glows.
On old Aegina's rock, and Idra's isle,
The god of gladness sheds his parting smile;
O'er his own regions lingering, loves to shine,
Though there his altars are no more divine.   10
Descending fast the mountain shadows kiss
Thy glorious gulph, unconquered Salamis!
Their azure arches through the long expanse
More deeply purpled meet his mellowing glance,
And tenderest tints, along their summits driven,   15
Mark his gay course and own the hues of heaven;
Till, darkly shaded from the land and deep,
Behind his Delphian cliff he sinks to sleep.

On such an eve, his palest beam he cast,
When—Athens! here thy Wisest looked his last.   20
How watched thy better sons his farewell ray,
That closed their murdered sage's latest day!

558 her] his *ML*   560 ⟨And / The Sun⟩ While . . . of twilight melt *ML*
561 ⟨Descending⟩ *ML*

Canto III
  1–54 *text from a corrected copy of Curse of Minerva*   17 from] ⟨by⟩ *M*   18 cliff]
⟨rock⟩ *M*

Not yet—not yet—Sol pauses on the hill—
The precious hour of parting lingers still;
But sad his light to agonizing eyes,   25
And dark the mountain's once delightful dyes:
Gloom o'er the lovely land he seemed to pour,
The land where Phoebus never frowned before,
But ere he sunk below Cithaeron's head,
The cup of woe was quaffed—the spirit fled;   30
The soul of him who scorned to fear or fly—
Who lived and died, as none can live or die!

But lo! from high Hymettus to the plain,
The queen of night asserts her silent reign.
No murky vapour, herald of the storm,   35
Hides her fair face, nor girds her glowing form;
With cornice glimmering as the moon-beams play,
There the white column greets her grateful ray,
And, bright around with quivering beams beset,
Her emblem sparkles o'er the minaret: 40
The groves of olive scattered dark and wide
Where meek Cephisus pours his scanty tide,
The cypress saddening by the sacred mosque,
The gleaming turret of the gay Kiosk,
And, dun and sombre 'mid the holy calm,   45
Near Theseus' fane yon solitary palm,
All tinged with varied hues arrest the eye—
And dull were his that passed them heedless by.

Again the Aegean, heard no more afar,
Lulls his chafed breast from elemental war;   50
Again his waves in milder tints unfold
Their long array of sapphire and of gold,
Mixt with the shades of many a distant isle,
That frown—where gentler ocean seems to smile.

2.

Not now my theme—why turn my thoughts to thee?   55
Oh! who can look along thy native sea,

42 pours] sheds *M, Curse, cor. in Proof* 6a   45 dun] ⟨sad / bleak⟩ *M*   55 why
⟨turns⟩ *ML*   56 thy native] ⟨the glorious⟩ *ML*

Nor dwell upon thy name, whate'er the tale,
So much its magic must o'er all prevail?
Who that beheld that Sun upon thee set,
Fair Athens! could thine evening face forget?   60
Not he—whose heart nor time nor distance frees,
Spell-bound within the clustering Cyclades!
Nor seems this homage foreign to his strain,
His Corsair's isle was once thine own domain—
Would that with freedom it were thine again!   65

3.

The Sun hath sunk—and, darker than the night,
Sinks with its beam upon the beacon height—
Medora's heart—the third day's come and gone—
With it he comes not—sends not—faithless one!
The wind was fair though light; and storms were none.   70
Last eve Anselmo's bark returned, and yet
His only tidings that they had not met!
Though wild, as now, far different were the tale
Had Conrad waited for that single sail.

The night-breeze freshens—she that day had past   75
In watching all that Hope proclaimed a mast;
Sadly she sate—on high—Impatience bore
At last her footsteps to the midnight shore,
And there she wandered heedless of the spray
That dashed her garments oft, and warned away: 80
She saw not—felt not this—nor dared depart,
Nor deemed it cold—her chill was at her heart;
Till grew such certainty from that suspense—
His very Sight had shocked from life or sense!

It came at last—a sad and shattered boat,   85
Whose inmates first beheld whom first they sought;

59 that] ⟨eer⟩ ML   60 evening] ⟨twilight⟩ ML   62 the clustering] thy circling
ML   within] beyond M   63 seems . . . his] ⟨seemed thy mention⟩ foreign to ⟨my⟩
ML   64 His] ⟨My⟩ ML   65 not in ML   66 and dark as coming night ML
69 With it] ⟨And yet⟩ ML   70 was . . . though] ⟨as . . . as⟩ ML   73 Though . . .
far] ⟨Had they united⟩ ML   74 ⟨But Conrad / That / And Conrad saved his / From
that which ? his / The ? risked his solitary sail⟩ ML   75 ⟨and⟩ she ML   76 pro-
claimed] ⟨could deem / proclaimed⟩ misdeemed ML   77 on high] ⟨at length⟩ M
78 midnight] ⟨silent / rippling⟩ ML   79 of the ⟨foam⟩ ML   80 dashed . . .
away] reached . . . ⟨her home⟩ ML   81 She . . . this] She saw but felt ⟨these⟩ it not
ML   82 ⟨the⟩ chill ML   86 ⟨And her⟩ Whose ML

Some bleeding—all most wretched—these the few—
Scarce knew they how escaped—*this* all they knew.
In silence, darkling, each appeared to wait
His fellow's mournful guess at Conrad's fate: 90
Something they would have said; but seemed to fear
To trust their accents to Medora's ear.
She saw at once, yet sunk not—trembled not—
Beneath that grief, that loneliness of lot,
Within that meek fair form, were feelings high,   95
That deemed not till they found their energy.
While yet was Hope—they softened—fluttered—wept—
All lost—that softness died not—but it slept;
And o'er its slumber rose that Strength which said,
'With nothing left to love—there's nought to dread.'   100
'Tis more than nature's; like the burning might
Delirium gathers from the fever's height.

'Silent you stand—nor would I hear you tell
What—speak not—breathe not—for I know it well—
Yet would I ask—almost my lip denies   105
The—quick your answer—tell me where he lies?'

'Lady! we know not—scarce with life we fled;
But here is one denies that he is dead:
He saw him bound; and bleeding—but alive.'

She heard no further—'twas in vain to strive—   110
So throbbed each vein—each thought—till then withstood;
Her own dark soul—these words at once subdued:
She totters—falls—and senseless had the wave
Perchance but snatched her from another grave;
But that with hands though rude, yet weeping eyes,   115
They yield such aid as Pity's haste supplies:

88 ⟨That⟩ Scarce *ML*   90 mournful] ⟨fearful⟩ *ML*   92 ⟨Their⟩ To *ML*
95 meek] still *ML, cor. in M*   97 fluttered—⟨still⟩ *M*   98 ⟨When⟩ All *ML*
99 ⟨And oer its slumbers was that strength instead⟩ *ML*   rose] ⟨felt⟩ woke *ML*
100 ⟨That feels / springs when nothing's left to⟩ / ⟨That felt her heart had nothing now to
dread⟩ / ⟨That felt at least / from danger more delight than might / dread⟩ *ML*   101 'Tis]
⟨And⟩ *ML*   102 ⟨That⟩ Delirium *ML*   103 ⟨You do not⟩ *ML*   nor . . . tell]
⟨I would not hear you speak⟩ *ML*   105 lip] ⟨tongue⟩ *ML*   108 here . . . denies]
he is here ⟨who⟩ denies *ML*   109 and bleeding] in fetters *ML*   111 So ⟨rushed
the⟩ *ML*   112 Her . . . words] All other tidings—these *ML*   soul] ⟨though⟩ *M*
114 but . . . another] ⟨preserved her from a guiltless⟩ *ML*   115 with ⟨? / rough hands⟩
ML   eyes] ⟨eyes⟩ eye *Proof 1*; ⟨eye⟩ eyes *Proofs 3, 4*   116 They gather round and
each his aid supplies *ML, M*; They gather round and ⟨each his aid supplies⟩ willing aid supply
Proof 1; and ⟨willing aid supply⟩ each his aid supplies *Proofs 3, 4*

Dash o'er her deathlike cheek the ocean dew,
Raise—fan—sustain—till life returns anew;
Awake her handmaids, with the matrons leave
That fainting form o'er which they gaze and grieve;   120
Then seek Anselmo's cavern, to report
The tale too tedious—when the triumph short.

4.

In that wild council words waxed warm and strange,
With thoughts of ransom, rescue, and revenge;
All, save repose or flight: still lingering there   125
Breathed Conrad's spirit, and forbade despair;
Whate'er his fate—the breasts he formed and led
Will save him living, or appease him dead.
Woe to his foes! there yet survive a few,
Whose deeds are daring, as their hearts are true.   130

5.

Within the Haram's secret chamber sate
Stern Seyd, still pondering o'er his Captive's fate;
His thoughts on love and hate alternate dwell,
Now with Gulnare, and now in Conrad's cell;
Here at his feet the lovely slave reclined   135
Surveys his brow—would soothe his gloom of mind,
While many an anxious glance her large dark eye
Sends in its idle search for sympathy,
His only bends in seeming o'er his beads,
But inly views his victim as he bleeds.   140

'Pacha! the day is thine; and on thy crest
Sits Triumph—Conrad taken—fall'n the rest!

117 deathlike . . . ocean] ⟨lifeless . . . water / sea / watery⟩ *ML*   118 ⟨Till / Sustain / Watch⟩ Raise *ML*   120 o'er . . . grieve] ⟨to breathe again and grieve / that ? again to grieve⟩ ⟨for⟩ oer whom they watch and grieve *ML*   gaze] ⟨view⟩ *M*   122 ⟨To him and ? tidings⟩ / ⟨Their baffled / A tale as mournful as their⟩ *ML*   triumph] triumph's *ML*   123 Within that ⟨isle is⟩ / cave ⟨debates grew high⟩ and strange *ML*   In . . . words] Within that cave Debate *M*; ⟨Within⟩ Loud in *Proof 2*; ⟨Loud in that cave⟩ In that dark cave *Proofs 3, 4*   124 ransom] ⟨ransoms⟩ *ML*   129 foes—⟨while yet / many a restless hand⟩ *ML*   131–207 *not in ML, M; marked for insertion by B in Proof 1 margin*   131 secret ⟨soft recess⟩ *MLa*   132 Stern] ⟨Sate⟩ *MLa*   133 ⟨Despair his heart / From love to hate his wandering thoughts withdrew⟩ *MLa*   134 ⟨And / Gulnare⟩ Now with Gulnare ⟨or Conrad's lonely⟩ cell *MLa*   135 Here] There *MLa, cor. in Ma*   136 ⟨And watched his eyes and guessed his gloom of mind⟩ *MLa*   brow] ⟨eye⟩ *Ma*   137 While . . . glance] And . . . ⟨gaze⟩ *MLa, cor. in Ma*   138 Sends] ⟨Casts⟩ *MLa*   139 his] ⟨the⟩ *MLa*   140 But] ⟨And⟩ *MLa*   141 is] ⟨is⟩ was *MLa*   142 fall'n] ⟨slain⟩ *MLa*

His doom is fixed—he dies: and well his fate
Was earned—yet much too worthless for thy hate:
Methinks, a short release, for ransom told   145
With all his treasure, not unwisely sold;
Report speaks largely of his pirate-hoard—
Would that of this my Pacha were the Lord!
While baffled, weakened by this fatal fray—
Watched—followed—he were then an easier prey;   150
But once cut off—the remnant of his band
Embark their wealth, and seek a safer strand.'

'Gulnare!—if for each drop of blood a gem
Were offered rich as Stamboul's diadem;
If for each hair of his a massy mine   155
Of virgin ore should supplicating shine;
If all our Arab tales divulge or dream
Of wealth were here—that gold should not redeem!
It had not now redeemed a single hour;
But that I know him fettered, in my power;   160
And, thirsting for revenge, I ponder still
On pangs that longest rack, and latest kill.'

'Nay, Seyd!—I seek not to restrain thy rage,
Too justly moved for mercy to assuage;
My thoughts were only to secure for thee   165
His riches—thus released, he were not free:
Disabled, shorn of half his might and band,
His capture could but wait thy first command.'

'His capture *could!*—and shall I then resign
One day to him—the wretch already mine?   170
Release my foe!—at whose remonstrance?—thine!

143 fixed] sealed *MLa*   144 too ⟨low⟩ *MLa*   145 for . . . told] by ransom
wrought *MLa, cor. in Ma*; for ransom—gold *Ma, cor. in Proof 2*   146 Of all his
treasure not too cheaply bought *MLa, cor. in Ma*   With all] Of all *Ma, cor. in Proof 2*
147 speaks . . . pirate-] ⟨speaks⟩ prates . . . plundered *MLa*   149 fray] ⟨day⟩ *MLa*
150 ⟨He were⟩ *MLa*   he were then] ⟨he becomes⟩ *MLa*   151 once] ⟨now⟩ *Ma*
153 if for each] ⟨were every⟩ *MLa*   154 ⟨Rich / Bright as the best of Stamboul's
diadem⟩ *MLa*   Stamboul's] ⟨Selim's⟩ Othman's *MLa*   155 ⟨And every / each hair
of his a very mine⟩ *MLa*   massy] virgin *MLa*   156 ⟨A⟩ Of ⟨? / untouched⟩ ore untold
should ⟨in / midst my treasure⟩ shine *MLa*   157 divulge] disclose *MLa*   158 gold]
⟨Wealth⟩ *MLa*   162 longest rack] ⟨worst may prove⟩ *MLa*   165 My thoughts
MLa   167 might] strength *MLa*   168 could but] then could *Ma, cor. in Proof 2*
170 *not* in *MLa*   171 His life to chance?—at *MLa* ⟨Nor crush my foe / And spare
the⟩ *Ma*

Fair suitor!—to thy virtuous gratitude,
That thus repays this Giaour's relenting mood,
Which thee and thine alone of all could spare,
No doubt—regardless if the prize were fair,   175
My thanks and praise alike are due—now hear!
I have a counsel for thy gentler ear:
I do mistrust thee, woman! and each word
Of thine stamps truth on all Suspicion heard.
Borne in his arms through fire from yon Serai—   180
Say, wert thou lingering there with him to fly?
Thou need'st not answer—thy confession speaks,
Already reddening on thy guilty cheeks;
Then, lovely dame, bethink thee! and beware:
'Tis not *his* life alone may claim such care!   185
Another word and—nay—I need no more.
Accursed was the moment when he bore
Thee from the flames, which better far—but—no—
I then had mourned thee with a lover's woe—
Now 'tis thy lord that warns—deceitful thing!   190
Know'st thou that I can clip thy wanton wing?
In words alone I am not wont to chafe:
Look to thyself—nor deem thy falsehood safe!'

He rose—and slowly, sternly thence withdrew,
Rage in his eye and threats in his adieu: 195
Ah! little recked that chief of womanhood—
Which frowns ne'er quelled, nor menaces subdued;
And little deemed he what thy heart, Gulnare!
When soft could feel, and when incensed could dare.
His doubts appeared to wrong—nor yet she knew   200
How deep the root from whence compassion grew—
She was a slave—from such may captives claim
A fellow-feeling, differing but in name;

172 suitor] ⟨Pleader⟩ *MLa*   173 ⟨Thou only wishest⟩ *MLa*   175 ⟨Without regard as⟩ if *MLa*   176 due—⟨Gulnare!⟩ *MLa*   177 counsel] ⟨question⟩ *MLa* gentler] gentle *MLa, Ma*   178 mistrust] misdoubt *MLa*   179 Of thine adds certainty to all I heard *MLa, cor. in Ma*   180 ⟨Would that the⟩ *MLa*   182 thy . . . speaks] ⟨thine⟩ thy reply ⟨as now⟩ I seek *MLa*   183 Already ⟨burns⟩ reddening oer thy guilty ⟨brow⟩ cheek *MLa*   184 ⟨This I for⟩ *MLa*   Then] ⟨Then⟩ Thou *Proofs 1, 2*   185 such] thy *MLa*   186 Another word—⟨but⟩ nay *MLa*   187 the] ⟨that⟩ *MLa*   190 that . . . thing] who speaks—⟨thou falsest⟩ thing *MLa*   191 ⟨Look to thyself⟩ *MLa*   194 thence ⟨retired⟩ *MLa*   195 Rage] ⟨Wrath⟩ *Ma* 196 womanhood] woman moved *MLa*   197 frowns . . . menaces] ⟨Rules⟩ . . . words like these *MLa*   201 compassion] her Pity *MLa*   203 differing] different *MLa*

Still half unconscious—heedless of his wrath,
Again she ventured on the dangerous path,   205
Again his rage repelled—until arose
That strife of thought, the source of woman's woes!

6.

Meanwhile—long anxious—weary—still—the same
Rolled day and night—his soul could terror tame—
This fearful interval of doubt and dread,   210
When every hour might doom him worse than dead,
When every step that echoed by the gate,
Might entering lead where axe and stake await;
When every voice that grated on his ear
Might be the last that he could ever hear;   215
Could terror tame—that spirit stern and high
Had proved unwilling as unfit to die;
'Twas worn—perhaps decayed—yet silent bore
That conflict deadlier far than all before:
The heat of fight, the hurry of the gale,   220
Leave scarce one thought inert enough to quail;
But bound and fixed in fettered solitude,
To pine, the prey of every changing mood;
To gaze on thine own heart; and meditate
Irrevocable faults, and coming fate—   225
Too late the last to shun—the first to mend—
To count the hours that struggle to thine end,
With not a friend to animate, and tell
To other ears that death became thee well;
Around thee foes to forge the ready lie,   230
And blot life's latest scene with calumny;
Before thee tortures, which the soul can dare,
Yet doubts how well the shrinking flesh may bear;

204 ⟨And⟩ Still . . . ⟨fearless⟩ of *MLa*   205 ⟨And⟩ Again *MLa*   206 until] ⟨and then⟩ *MLa*   208 Meanwhile] ⟨The⟩ Meantime *ML*   209 Rolled day ⟨by day— the⟩ *ML*   211 Whose every coming hour might doom him dead *ML*; When every ⟨coming hour might view him dead⟩ *M*   212–13 gate . . . await] ⟨gates . . . awaits⟩ *Proof 7*   213 Might ⟨be to⟩ / come to lead ⟨him⟩ where ⟨torment⟩ axe ⟨and⟩ / or stake await *ML*   and] or *ML*, *M*, *cor. in Proof 5*   218 perhaps . . . silent] ⟨but wearied not—and calmly⟩ *ML*   219 conflict] ⟨tr / struggle⟩ *ML*   221 scarce] ⟨little / not⟩ *ML*   224 meditate] contemplate *ML*, *M*, *cor. in Proof 1*   225 Within thy follies—and without thy fate *ML*   226 ⟨When⟩ Too *ML*   230 Around ⟨the ready foe⟩ thee *ML*   231 And blot] ⟨That blots⟩ / And mar *ML*

But deeply feels a single cry would shame,
To valour's praise thy last and dearest claim;   235
The life thou leav'st below, denied above
By kind monopolists of heavenly love;
And more than doubtful paradise—thy heaven
Of earthly hope—thy loved one from thee riven.
Such were the thoughts that outlaw must sustain,   240
And govern pangs surpassing mortal pain:
And those sustained he—boots it well or ill?
Since not to sink beneath, is something still!

7.

The first day passed—he saw not her—Gulnare—
The second—third—and still she came not there;   245
But what her words avouched, her charms had done,
Or else he had not seen another sun.
The fourth day rolled along, and with the night
Came storm and darkness in their mingling might:
Oh! how he listened to the rushing deep,   250
That ne'er till now so broke upon his sleep;
And his wild spirit wilder wishes sent,
Rous'd by the roar of his own element!
Oft had he ridden on that winged wave,
And loved its roughness for the speed it gave;   255
And now its dashing echoed on his ear,
A long known voice—alas! too vainly near!
Loud sung the wind above; and, doubly loud,
Shook o'er his turret cell the thunder-cloud;
And flashed the lightning by the latticed bar,   260
To him more genial than the midnight star:

234 But . . . cry] And ⟨feels how much⟩ a single ⟨groan / sigh / shriek⟩ ML   235 ⟨And risk⟩ To valour's ⟨meed⟩ thy ML

236–7   ⟨Ah! / Such were the thoughts that outlaw must sustain
               And govern pangs surpassing earthly pain⟩
               ⟨The love thou leavst behind—thine only love
               Since man leaves none below⟩ ML

239 earthly hope] earth beneath ML, cor. in M   241 mortal] earthly ML, cor. in M
244 he . . . her] ⟨she came not—she—⟩ ML   245 third] ⟨rose⟩ ML ⟨passed⟩ M
246 But ⟨that her words or charms⟩ ML   247 another] that Morning ML   248 The
⟨third day rolled away and yet⟩ ML   249 darkness . . . mingling] whirlwind . . .
⟨sternest⟩ ML, cor. in M   251 broke upon his] ⟨moved his restless⟩ ML   254 ridden
on] rode upon ML   255 ⟨Nor dreaded there⟩ ML   260 ⟨And flashed with / for /
faster / high / red and redder through⟩ ML   261 midnight] Evening ML

Close to the glimmering grate he dragged his chain,
And hoped *that* peril might not prove in vain.
He raised his iron hand to Heaven, and prayed
One pitying flash to mar the form it made: 265
His steel and impious prayer attract alike—
The storm rolled onward and disdained to strike;
Its peal waxed fainter—ceased—he felt alone,
As if some faithless friend had spurned his groan!

8.

The midnight passed—and to the massy door   270
A light step came—it paused—it moved once more;
Slow turns the grating bolt and sullen key:
'Tis as his heart foreboded—that fair she!
Whate'er her sins, to him a guardian saint,
And beauteous still as hermit's hope can paint;   275
Yet changed since last within that cell she came,
More pale her cheek, more tremulous her frame:
On him she cast her dark and hurried eye,
Which spoke before her accents—'thou must die!
Yes, thou must die—there is but one resource,   280
The last—the worst—if torture were not worse.'

'Lady! I look to none—my lips proclaim
What last proclaimed they—Conrad still the same:
Why should'st thou seek an outlaw's life to spare,
And change the sentence I deserve to bear?   285
Well have I earned—nor here alone—the meed
Of Seyd's revenge, by many a lawless deed.'

'Why should I seek? because—Oh! didst thou not
Redeem my life from worse than slavery's lot?

262 the . . . grate] ⟨that . . . gate⟩ *ML*   263 ⟨To try⟩ And *ML*   264 iron] ironed *ML*   265 One] ⟨Its⟩ *ML*   form] ⟨wretch⟩ *M*   268 waxed . . . ceased] grew . . . ⟨hush⟩ ceased *ML, cor. in M*   269 As if ⟨soul⟩ some . . . had ⟨passed and gone⟩ *ML*   270 passed—and to] ⟨came⟩ and ⟨at⟩ *ML*   271 came . . . it moved] ⟨paused . . . and⟩ moved *ML*   272 and] the *ML*   273 ⟨It was⟩ *ML* 274 sins] faults *ML, M*   275 ⟨And lovely as Devotion's dream could / raptures paint⟩ *ML*   beauteous still] ⟨beautiful as⟩ *ML*   276 Yet ⟨is she⟩ changed . . . that tower she *ML*   282 Lady ⟨since last we met⟩ *ML*   283 What last ⟨they told⟩ *ML* 284 seek] ⟨urge⟩ *ML*   285 ⟨The man who⟩ *ML*   289 worse than] death and *ML*

Why should I seek?—hath misery made thee blind   290
To the fond workings of a woman's mind!
And must I say? albeit my heart rebel
With all that woman feels, but should not tell—
Because—despite thy crimes—that heart is moved:
It feared thee—thanked thee—pitied—maddened—loved. 295
Reply not, tell not now thy tale again,
Thou lov'st another—and I love in vain;
Though fond as mine her bosom, form more fair,
I rush through peril which she would not dare.
If that thy heart to hers were truly dear,   300
Were I thine own—thou wert not lonely here:
An outlaw's spouse—and leave her lord to roam!
What hath such gentle dame to do with home?
But speak not now—o'er thine and o'er my head
Hangs the keen sabre by a single thread;   305
If thou hast courage still, and would'st be free,
Receive this poignard—rise—and follow me!'

'Ay—in my chains! my steps will gently tread,
With these adornments, o'er each slumbering head!
Thou hast forgot—is this a garb for flight?   310
Or is that instrument more fit for fight?'

'Misdoubting Corsair! I have gained the guard,
Ripe for revolt, and greedy for reward.
A single word of mine removes that chain:
Without some aid how here could I remain?   315
Well, since we met, hath sped my busy time,
If in aught evil, for thy sake the crime:
The crime—'tis none to punish those of Seyd.
That hated tyrant, Conrad—he must bleed!

291 workings] strugglings *ML*   292 say? albeit] ⟨tell—although⟩ *ML*   293 should]
⟨must⟩ *ML*   294 that] ⟨my⟩ *ML*   296 thy ⟨former⟩ tale *ML*   297 ⟨I know
not / thou lost another—I in vain⟩ *ML*   298 mine her ⟨heart⟩ *ML*   299 ⟨Yet⟩
I *ML*   301 thine ... lonely] thy ... single *ML, cor. in M*   302 spouse] ⟨mate⟩
wife *ML, cor. in M*   304 speak ... o'er ... o'er] ⟨answer ... on ... on⟩ *ML*
305 Hangs ... sabre] ⟨Suspends the sabre / The sabre dangles⟩ *ML*; Oerhangs the sabre *ML,
M, cor. in Proof 1*   307 rise—and] softly *ML*   309 ⟨Nor⟩ With these ⟨light
fetters⟩ oer *ML*   311 Or is ⟨it⟩ *ML*   312 Misdoubting] ⟨Suspicious⟩ *ML*
315 how ... remain] this turret could I gain *ML, cor. in M*

I see thee shudder—but my soul is changed—   320
Wronged—spurned—reviled—and it shall be avenged—
Accused of what till now my heart disdained—
Too faithful, though to bitter bondage chained.
Yes, smile!—but he had little cause to sneer,
I was not treacherous then—nor thou too dear: 325
But he has said it—and the jealous well,
Those tyrants, teasing, tempting to rebel,
Deserve the fate their fretting lips foretell.
I never loved—he bought me—somewhat high—
Since with me came a heart he could not buy.   330
I was a slave unmurmuring; he hath said,
But for his rescue I with thee had fled.
'Twas false thou know'st—but let such augurs rue,
Their words are omens Insult renders true.
Nor was thy respite granted to my prayer;   335
This fleeting grace was only to prepare
New torments for thy life, and my despair.
Mine too he threatens; but his dotage still
Would fain reserve me for his lordly will:
When wearier of these fleeting charms and me,   340
There yawns the sack—and yonder rolls the sea!
What, am I then a toy for dotard's play,
To wear but till the gilding frets away?
I saw thee—loved thee—owe thee all—would save,
If but to shew how grateful is a slave.   345
But had he not thus menaced fame and life,
(And well he keeps his oaths pronounced in strife)
I still had saved thee—but the Pacha spared.
Now I am all thine own—for all prepared:
Thou lov'st me not—nor know'st—or but the worst.   350
Alas! this love—that hatred are the first—
Oh! could'st thou prove my truth, thou would'st not start,
Nor fear the fire that lights an Eastern heart,

321 ⟨First wronged—and then reviled—and now avenged⟩ ML   322 heart] breast ML
325 treacherous] faithless ML   329 somewhat] ⟨bought me / not too⟩ ML   330 Since
. . . came] ⟨And . . . bought⟩ ML   331 hath] has ML   332 ⟨That⟩ But ML
334 ⟨Insults are omens which their words make true⟩ ML   338 ⟨He dared not punish—
for/ He threatens⟩ ML   Mine too] ⟨And me⟩ ML   339 fain] ⟨yet⟩ M   340 wearier]
weary ML   342 for dotard's] ⟨of tyrant's⟩ ML   346 ⟨Yet not this respite granted to
my life⟩ ML   fame and] even my ML   349 all thine own] ⟨thine—my own⟩ ML
351 that . . . are the] this . . . is my ML   352 start] ⟨part⟩ ML

'Tis now the beacon of thy safety—now
It points within the port a Mainote prow: 355
But in one chamber, where our path must lead,
There sleeps—he must not wake—the oppressor Seyd!'

'Gulnare—Gulnare—I never felt till now
My abject fortune, withered fame so low:
Seyd is mine enemy: had swept my band   360
From earth with ruthless but with open hand,
And therefore came I, in my bark of war,
To smite the smiter with the scimitar;
Such is my weapon—not the secret knife—
Who spares a woman's seeks not slumber's life.   365
Thine saved I gladly, Lady, not for this—
Let me not deem that mercy shewn amiss.
Now fare thee well—more peace be with thy breast!
Night wears apace—my last of earthly rest!'

'Rest! Rest! by sunrise must thy sinews shake,   370
And thy limbs writhe around the ready stake.
I heard the order—saw—I will not see—
If thou wilt perish, I will fall with thee.
My life—my love—my hatred—all below
Are on this cast—Corsair! 'tis but a blow!   375
Without it flight were idle—how evade
His sure pursuit? my wrongs too unrepaid,
My youth disgraced—the long, long wasted years,
One blow shall cancel with our future fears;
But since the dagger suits thee less than brand,   380
I'll try the firmness of a female hand.
The guards are gained—one moment all were o'er—
Corsair! we meet in safety or no more;

354 ⟨Fierce in its fi⟩ *ML*   355 It . . . within] ⟨Awaits us in⟩ *ML*   356 But
⟨here in / through⟩ in ⟨the⟩ our chamber where our way must lead *ML*   359 withered]
⟨nor my⟩ *ML, M*   362 ⟨He never wronged me—I in the garb⟩ *ML*   367 mercy
shewn] ⟨then I did⟩ *ML*   369 ⟨The⟩ night ⟨wears down⟩ —and I have need of rest
ML, cor. in M   370 sunrise] ⟨daybreak⟩ *ML*   373 wilt . . . fall] ⟨must⟩ . . .
die *ML*   374 love—my ⟨soul—all are now⟩ *ML*   375 ⟨On this one⟩ cast
ML   376 idle—how] vain ⟨and⟩ for how *ML*   378 wasted] ⟨falling⟩ *ML*
379 with our] ⟨quell our⟩ *ML*   380 But . . . less] ⟨And . . . more⟩ *ML*   382 were]
⟨is⟩ *M*   383 ⟨Soon shall we meet again⟩ *ML*

Painted by Thos Stothard R.A.   Engraved by F. Engleheart.

CORSAIR.

BUT SINCE THE DAGGER SUITS THEE LESS THAN BRAND,
I'LL TRY THE FIRMNESS OF A FEMALE HAND.—

PUBLISHED BY JOHN MURRAY, ALBEMARLE STREET, DECR. 1.1814.

The Corsair Canto III lines 380–1

(Reproduced with the permission of the British Library)

If errs my feeble hand, the morning cloud
Will hover o'er thy scaffold, and my shroud.'   385

9.

She turned, and vanished ere he could reply,
But his glance followed far with eager eye;
And gathering, as he could, the links that bound
His form, to curl their length, and curb their sound,
Since bar and bolt no more his steps preclude,   390
He, fast as fettered limbs allow, pursued.
'Twas dark and winding, and he knew not where
That passage led; nor lamp nor guard were there:
He sees a dusky glimmering—shall he seek
Or shun that ray so indistinct and weak?   395
Chance guides his steps—a freshness seems to bear
Full on his brow, as if from morning air—
He reached an open gallery—on his eye
Gleamed the last star of night, the clearing sky:
Yet scarcely heeded these—another light   400
From a lone chamber struck upon his sight.
Towards it he moved, a scarcely closing door
Revealed the ray within, but nothing more.
With hasty step a figure outward past,
Then paused—and turned—and paused—'tis She at last!   405
No poignard in that hand—nor sign of ill—
'Thanks to that softening heart—she could not kill!'
Again he looked, the wildness of her eye
Starts from the day abrupt and fearfully.
She stopped—threw back her dark far-floating hair,   410
That nearly veiled her face and bosom fair:

384 ⟨I prosper—if I⟩ If . . . the ⟨Morn shall greet⟩ ML   385 ⟨Thee with the stake—
me with my winding sheet⟩ ML   thy ⟨stake⟩ scaffold ML   387 But . . . far] ⟨Though
. . . fast⟩ ML   388 First ⟨binding⟩ as he ML   389 ⟨His form so heavily and
sadly⟩ ML   curb] check ML   390 Since . . . bolt] The bolts unclosed ML, M
391 ⟨His fetters gathered first and then⟩ pursued ML   393 ⟨Nor lamp—nor sound—
nor guard seemed stirring⟩ there ML   394 glimmering— ⟨twas not light⟩ ML
397 morning] ⟨the open / approaching⟩ ML   399 the clearing] ⟨the⟩ and breaking ML
402 a . . . closing] ⟨unclosing / half unclosed a⟩ a scarce unclosing ML   403 the ray]
⟨that light⟩ ML   404 With ⟨that⟩ hasty ML   405 and paused] again ML
406 ⟨Nor / That poignard gone⟩ ML   nor . . . ill] ⟨but in her look⟩ ML   407 ⟨A /
She hath repented⟩ ML   409 ⟨Had fear / Bespoke today's first faint⟩ / ⟨Showed more
and more some guilty / iniquity⟩ ML   410 ⟨Her heaving breast / ghastly glance—and
long / dark far floating hair⟩ ML   411 ⟨Her heaving bosom showed / forgot / betrayed
some evil there⟩ ML

As if she late had bent her leaning head
Above some object of her doubt or dread.
They meet—upon her brow—unknown—forgot—
Her hurrying hand had left—'twas but a spot—　　　　415
Its hue was all he saw, and scarce withstood—
Oh! slight but certain pledge of crime—'tis blood!

10.

He had seen battle—he had brooded lone
O'er promised pangs to sentenced guilt foreshown;
He had been tempted—chastened—and the chain　　　　420
Yet on his arms might ever there remain:
But ne'er from strife—captivity—remorse—
From all his feelings in their inmost force—
So thrilled—so shuddered every creeping vein,
As now they froze before that purple stain.　　　　425
That spot of blood, that light but guilty streak,
Had banished all the beauty from her cheek!
Blood he had viewed—could view unmoved—but then
It flowed in combat, or was shed by men!

11.

' 'Tis done—he nearly waked—but it is done.　　　　430
Corsair! he perished—thou art dearly won.
All words would now be vain—away—away!
Our bark is tossing—'tis already day.
The few gained over, now are wholly mine,
And these thy yet surviving band shall join:　　　　435
Anon my voice shall vindicate my hand,
When once our sail forsakes this hated strand.'

412 As ⟨she had⟩ if she late ⟨leaned with downward⟩ ML   414 ⟨More near they
met—upon her lily neck⟩ ML   brow . . . forgot] ⟨cheeks⟩ unknown ⟨he saw⟩ ML
415 Her ⟨hand has passed and left—twas but a speck⟩ ML   417 pledge . . . 'tis]
⟨witness—it is⟩ ML   418 he had ⟨lived⟩ ML   lone] ⟨oer⟩ M   420 been
⟨hopeless—helpless⟩ and ML   422 But ne'er ⟨in contact—confines?⟩ ML   423 in-
most] utmost M, cor. in Proof 6   425 they . . . purple] ⟨to gaze upon⟩ that ⟨little⟩
ML   426 that . . . streak] ⟨oer all appeared imprest / that soul deforming streak⟩ ML
427 ⟨And blackened even the beauty from her breast⟩ ML   Had . . . all the] ⟨Which . . .
every⟩ ML   428–9 not in ML, M; MS. addition in Proof 1   429 It reddened on
the Scarfs and Swords of men. Proof 1; It flowed a token of the deeds of men. MS. cor. on
Proofs 3, 4 of Proof 1 text   435 thy ⟨living⟩ yet ML   436 ⟨Away—anon my
tongue shall tell thee more⟩ ML   voice] tongue ML, cor. in M   437 hated ⟨shore⟩
ML

12.

She clapped her hands—and through the gallery pour,
Equipped for flight, her vassals—Greek and Moor;
Silent but quick they stoop, his chains unbind;   440
Once more his limbs are free as mountain wind!
But on his heavy heart such sadness sate,
As if they there transferred that iron weight.
No words are uttered—at her sign, a door
Reveals the secret passage to the shore;   445
The city lies behind—they speed, they reach
The glad waves dancing on the yellow beach;
And Conrad following, at her beck, obeyed,
Nor cared he now if rescued or betrayed;
Resistance were as useless as if Seyd   450
Yet lived to view the doom his ire decreed.

13.

Embarked, the sail unfurled, the light breeze blew—
How much had Conrad's memory to review!
Sunk he in contemplation, till the cape
Where last he anchored reared its giant shape.   455
Ah!—since that fatal night, though brief the time,
Had swept an age of terror, grief, and crime.
As its far shadow frowned above the mast,
He veiled his face, and sorrowed as he past;
He thought of all—Gonsalvo and his band,   460
His fleeting triumph and his failing hand;
He thought on her afar, his lonely bride:
He turned and saw—Gulnare, the homicide!

14.

She watched his features till she could not bear
Their freezing aspect and averted air,   465

438 through the gallery] ⟨quick but silent⟩ ML; through the ⟨Corridor⟩ M   439 her
⟨minions from the door⟩ ML   440 quick] ⟨swift⟩ M they ⟨seize him⟩ stoop ML
443 they ⟨only⟩ there . . . ⟨their⟩ iron ML   444 uttered] spoken ML   448 And
Conrad ⟨reckless of his fate⟩ obeyed ML   453 His silent thoughts the ⟨past events⟩ /
present—past review ML, cor. in M   454 ⟨At last in sad⟩ ML   457 swept]
⟨passed⟩ ML   458 ⟨Beneath its shadow as the vessel passed⟩ ML   459 He
⟨turned⟩ his face and shuddered as ML   462 her . . . his] ⟨his Francesca—⟩ ML
463 ⟨He⟩ Then turned ML

And that strange fierceness foreign to her eye,
Fell quenched in tears, too late to shed or dry.
She knelt beside him and his hand she prest,
'Thou may'st forgive though Alla's self detest;
But for that deed of darkness what wert thou?   470
Reproach me—but not yet—Oh! spare me *now!*
I am not what I seem—this fearful night
My brain bewildered—do not madden quite!
If I had never loved—though less my guilt,
Thou hadst not lived to—hate me—if thou wilt.'   475

15.

She wrongs his thoughts, they more himself upbraid
Than her, though undesigned, the wretch he made;
But speechless all, deep, dark, and unexprest,
They bleed within that silent cell—his breast.
Still onward, fair the breeze, nor rough the surge,   480
The blue waves sport around the stern they urge;
Far on the horizon's verge appears a speck,
A spot—a mast—a sail—an armed deck!
Their little bark her men of watch descry,
And ampler canvas woos the wind from high;   485
She bears her down majestically near,
Speed on her prow, and terror in her tier;
A flash is seen—the ball beyond their bow
Booms harmless, hissing to the deep below.
Uprose keen Conrad from his silent trance,   490
A long, long absent gladness in his glance;
' 'Tis mine—my blood-red flag! again—again—
I am not all deserted on the main!'
They own the signal, answer to the hail,
Hoist out the boat at once, and slacken sail.   495

467 too . . . dry] of more than misery *ML, cor. in M*   469 may'st ⟨pardon⟩ though
⟨condemn / the / Heaven⟩ Allah's *ML*   470 that deed] this ⟨?⟩ *ML*   471 Reproach
me ⟨if thou wilt / if it please—yet not—not now⟩ *ML*   474 never loved] ⟨loved thee
less⟩ *ML*   476 wrongs] ⟨wronged⟩ *ML*   481 The blue waves ⟨gladden on /
seem to⟩ sporting round the prow they urge *ML*; ⟨sporting round⟩ the prow *M*   stern]
⟨prow⟩ stern *Proof 1*   482 verge] edge *ML, cor. in M*   483 sail— ⟨with⟩ an *ML*
484 ⟨Then viewed he⟩ *ML*   486 down ⟨and⟩ *ML*   487 They count the dragon
teeth ⟨that⟩ around her tier *ML, M, cor. in Proof 1*   488-9 *after line 493 in ML*
488 ⟨Her⟩ A flash is seen— ⟨her / the⟩ her ball ⟨beyond⟩ across their bow *ML, cor. in M*
489 Booms] Speeds *ML*   490 Uprose] Up rose *Corsair 10, 1831, 1832, C, More*
494 to the] to her *ML*

' 'Tis Conrad! Conrad!' shouting from the deck,
Command nor duty could their transport check!
With light alacrity and gaze of pride,
They view him mount once more his vessel's side;
A smile relaxing in each rugged face,   500
Their arms can scarce forbear a rough embrace.
He, half forgetting danger and defeat,
Returns their greeting as a chief may greet,
Wrings with a cordial grasp Anselmo's hand,
And feels he yet can conquer and command!   505

16.

These greetings o'er, the feelings that o'erflow,
Yet grieve to win him back without a blow;
They sailed prepared for vengeance—had they known
A woman's hand secured that deed her own,
She were their queen—less scrupulous are they   510
Than haughty Conrad how they win their way.
With many an asking smile, and wondering stare,
They whisper round, and gaze upon Gulnare;
And her, at once above—beneath her sex,
Whom blood appalled not, their regards perplex.   515
To Conrad turns her faint imploring eye,
She drops her veil, and stands in silence by;
Her arms are meekly folded on that breast,
Which—Conrad safe—to fate resigned the rest.
Though worse than phrenzy could that bosom fill,   520
Extreme in love or hate, in good or ill,
The worst of crimes had left her woman still!

17.

This Conrad marked, and felt—ah! could he less?
Hate of that deed—but grief for her distress;

498 With . . . gaze] With gay alacrity and ⟨looks⟩ gaze *ML*, *M*, *cor. in Proofs 3, 4*
499 his] the *ML*   500 ⟨And⟩ A *ML*   506 feelings that] ⟨joys that thus⟩ *ML*
507 Yet grieve] Half shame *ML*   508 vengeance—⟨still unknown⟩ *ML*   509 secured]
⟨had made⟩ *ML*   510 are] ⟨were⟩ *ML*   511 win] ⟨won⟩ *ML*   515 regards]
rude looks *ML* ⟨rude eyes⟩ *M*   516 To . . . turns] ⟨On⟩ Conrad ⟨fixed / glanced⟩ pleads
ML   517 drops . . . stands] ⟨dropped . . . strode⟩ *ML*   518 are . . . that] ⟨were⟩
folded meekly on her *ML*   519 Which . . . to fate resigned] And . . . resigned to fate
ML; ⟨And⟩ . . . to fate ⟨she left⟩ *M*   Which] ⟨While⟩ *Proof 1*   520 worse] ⟨more⟩
ML   523–54 *not in ML, M*   524 ⟨His honour half gave way to tenderness⟩ *Y2*
deed] ⟨guilt⟩ *Y2*

What she has done no tears can wash away,   525
And heaven must punish on its angry day:
But—it was done: he knew, whate'er her guilt,
For him that poignard smote, that blood was spilt;
And he was free!—and she for him had given
Her all on earth, and more than all in heaven!   530
And now he turned him to that dark-eyed slave
Whose brow was bowed beneath the glance he gave,
Who now seemed changed and humble:—faint and meek,
But varying oft the colour of her cheek
To deeper shades of paleness—all its red   535
That fearful spot which stained it from the dead!
He took that hand—it trembled—now too late—
So soft in love—so wildly nerved in hate;
He clasped that hand—it trembled—and his own
Had lost its firmness, and his voice its tone.   540
'Gulnare!'—but she replied not—'dear Gulnare!'
She raised her eye—her only answer there—
At once she sought and sunk in his embrace:
If he had driven her from that resting place,
His had been more or less than mortal heart,   545
But—good or ill—it bade her not depart.
Perchance, but for the bodings of his breast,
His latest virtue then had joined the rest.
Yet even Medora might forgive the kiss
That asked from form so fair no more than this,   550
The first, the last that Frailty stole from Faith—
To lips where Love had lavished all his breath,

---

525 done— ⟨though deadly was to free / alas! no words⟩ no *Y2*   526 heaven . . .
angry] ⟨Conscience . . . judging⟩ *Y2*   527 he . . . guilt] ⟨and / he felt—whateer the
past⟩ *Y2*   528 that ⟨deed was⟩ poignard *Y2*   531 dark-eyed] lady *Y2*
532 brow] eye *Y2*   534 varying] changing *Y2*   535 deeper] ⟨different⟩
varying *Y2*   536 That . . . which] Was but that streak ⟨it borrowed⟩ that *Y2*; Was
but that spot which *MLa, cor. in Proof 6*   537 trembled— ⟨and his own⟩ *Y2*
538 So soft . . . so wildly] So ⟨shook⟩ soft . . . too firmly *Y2*   539 clasped]
⟨took⟩ *Y2*   541 'Gulnare!' she answered not—again—'Gulnare!' *Y2, MLa, cor. in
Proof 6*   542 eye . . . only answer] ⟨eye⟩ glance . . . only answer *Y2*; glance . . . sole
reply *MLa, cor. in Proof 6*   543 sought] ⟨clasped⟩ *Y2*   544 driven] forced *Y2*
545 than ⟨man⟩ mortal *Y2*   547 ⟨And yet⟩ Perhaps but for the crime that stained
her breast *Y2*   548 latest] only *Y2, MLa, cor. in Proof 6*   549 Yet] And *Y2*
550 asked . . . fair] sought from lips so sweet *Y2, cor. in MLa*   551 The . . . stole]
That kiss the first ⟨the last⟩ that frailty wrung *Y2, cor. in MLa*   552 ⟨That kiss⟩
The last on lips ⟨that⟩ yet warm with ⟨living⟩ rosy breath *Y2, cor. in MLa*   where]
whose *MLa*

To lips—whose broken sighs such fragrance fling,
As he had fanned them freshly with his wing!

18.

They gain by twilight's hour their lonely isle.   555
To them the very rocks appear to smile;
The haven hums with many a cheering sound,
The beacons blaze their wonted stations round,
The boats are darting o'er the curly bay,
And sportive dolphins bend them through the spray;   560
Even the hoarse sea-bird's, shrill, discordant shriek,
Greets like the welcome of his tuneless beak!
Beneath each lamp that through its lattice gleams,
Their fancy paints the friends that trim the beams.
Oh! what can sanctify the joys of home,   565
Like Hope's gay glance from Ocean's troubled foam?

19.

The lights are high on beacon and from bower,
And midst them Conrad seeks Medora's tower:
He looks in vain—'tis strange—and all remark,
Amid so many, hers alone is dark.   570
'Tis strange—of yore its welcome never failed,
Nor now, perchance, extinguished, only veiled.
With the first boat descends he for the shore,
And looks impatient on the lingering oar.
Oh! for a wing beyond the falcon's flight,   575
To bear him like an arrow to that height!
With the first pause the resting rowers gave,
He waits not—looks not—leaps into the wave,

554 freshly with his] ⟨with his rosy⟩ MLa   555 gain] ⟨reached⟩ ML   556 ⟨Again
the haven hums⟩ ML   557 cheering] busy ML   559 curly] ⟨curling⟩ ML
560 And ⟨proudly dolphins on its⟩ ML   bend] rear ML; ⟨bend⟩ rear Proof 1; ⟨rear⟩ bend
Proof 6   561 shrill, discordant] harsh ⟨discording⟩ ML   562 Greets . . . of]
⟨Sounds⟩ like ⟨the⟩ a welcome ⟨of⟩ from ML   563 ⟨In / Round every light⟩ ML
its] ⟨the⟩ M   564 that . . . beams] ⟨around who trim⟩ that trim its beams ML
565 what can sanctify] none ⟨can ever taste / so keenly taste⟩ can prophecy ML   none so
prophecy M, cor. in Proof 1   566 ⟨As⟩ Like they who ⟨reach⟩ hail it from the Ocean-
foam ML   As they . . . foam M, cor. in Proof 1   Hope's gay] the first Proof 1, MS. cor.
in Proofs 3, 4   567 on] ⟨in⟩ M   and from] and in ML   570 Amid] Amidst ML
571 its . . . failed] ⟨its still the first beheld⟩ ML   573 descends . . . shore] he hies him
to the ⟨strand⟩ ML, cor. in M   574 looks] ⟨broods⟩ ML   577 resting rowers]
landing shallop ML   578 waits . . . leaps] ⟨waited not but leaped⟩ ML

Strives through the surge, bestrides the beach, and high
Ascends the path familiar to his eye.   580

He reached his turret door—he paused—no sound
Broke from within; and all was night around.
He knocked, and loudly—footstep nor reply
Announced that any heard or deemed him nigh;
He knocked—but faintly—for his trembling hand   585
Refused to aid his heavy heart's demand.
The portal opens—'tis a well known face—
But not the form he panted to embrace.
Its lips are silent—twice his own essayed,
And failed to frame the question they delayed;   590
He snatched the lamp—its light will answer all—
It quits his grasp, expiring in the fall.
He would not wait for that reviving ray—
As soon could he have lingered there for day;
But, glimmering through the dusky corridore,   595
Another chequers o'er the shadowed floor;
His steps the chamber gain—his eyes behold
All that his heart believed not—yet foretold!

20.

He turned not—spoke not—sunk not—fixed his look,
And set the anxious frame that lately shook: 600
He gazed—how long we gaze despite of pain,
And know, but dare not own, we gaze in vain!
In life itself she was so still and fair,
That death with gentler aspect withered there;
And the cold flowers her colder hand contained,   605
In that last grasp as tenderly were strained
As if she scarcely felt, but feigned a sleep,
And made it almost mockery yet to weep:

---

579 Strives] Wades *ML*   580 Ascends] He mounts *ML*   582 Broke]
⟨Spoke⟩ *ML*   585 his ⟨sight grew dim⟩ *ML*   586 ⟨And his heart sank⟩ *ML*
heavy] sinking *ML, M*   587 ⟨A footstep comes⟩ *ML*   589 Its] ⟨His⟩ *M*
silent] ⟨and he dare not ask⟩ *ML*   592 grasp, expiring] ⟨hand⟩ and quenched it *ML*,
M, cor. in Proof 2   593 that reviving] its returning *ML, cor. in M*   594 there
for] ⟨for the⟩ *ML, M*   596 Another . . . o'er] ⟨He⟩ Another . . . on *ML*   597 ⟨He
seeks⟩ *ML*   gain] ⟨search⟩ *ML*   599 fixed] ⟨from⟩ calm *ML, cor. in M*   600 And
⟨nerved the limbs⟩ strong the *ML*   603 ⟨There / He saw⟩ *ML*   605 her ⟨that⟩
ML   606 as] ⟨so⟩ *ML, M*

The long dark lashes fringed her lids of snow,
And veiled—thought shrinks from all that lurked below— 610
Oh! o'er the eye death most exerts his might,
And hurls the spirit from her throne of light!
Sinks those blue orbs in that long last eclipse,
But spares, as yet, the charm around her lips—
Yet, yet they seem as they forbore to smile,   615
And wished repose—but only for a while;
But the white shroud, and each extended tress,
Long—fair—but spread in utter lifelessness,
Which, late the sport of every summer wind,
Escaped the baffled wreath that strove to bind;   620
These—and the pale pure cheek, became the bier—
But she is nothing—wherefore is he here?

21.

He asked no question—all were answered now
By the first glance on that still—marble brow.
It was enough—she died—what recked it how?   625
The love of youth, the hope of better years,
The source of softest wishes, tenderest fears,
The only living thing he could not hate,
Was reft at once—and he deserved his fate,
But did not feel it less;—the good explore,   630
For peace, those realms where guilt can never soar:
The proud—the wayward—who have fixed below
Their joy—and find this earth enough for woe,
Lose in that one their all—perchance a mite—
But who in patience parts with all delight?   635
Full many a stoic eye and aspect stern
Mask hearts where grief hath little left to learn;

    609 her] their *ML*   611 eye— ⟨tis there the Spectre dwells⟩ *ML*   612 her]
its *ML*   613 ⟨Veils⟩ those blue orbs in ⟨more than⟩ that *ML*   614 spares, as
yet] ⟨longer spares / not yet leaves⟩ *ML*   615 Yet] Why *M*   618 ⟨That⟩
Long . . . but ⟨stretched⟩ in *ML*   619 Which,] So *ML*   620 ⟨Defied⟩
the idle hand that ⟨fain would⟩ bind *ML*; Escaped the idle braid that could not bind *M*
621 pale pure] ⟨dull cold⟩ *ML*   624 glance . . . marble] look on that cold soulless
ML; glance on that cold soulless *M, cor. in Proof 2*   626 better] other *ML*
627 softest wishes] ⟨purest⟩ joy and *ML*; softest joy and *M*   628 living
thing] ⟨thing on earth⟩ *ML*   632 proud] ⟨bad⟩ *ML*   635 ⟨Yet few resign⟩
ML   636 ⟨And⟩ many *ML*   637 Mask] Hide *ML, M, all proofs, Corsair1–
Corsair5*

And many a withering thought lies hid, not lost,
In smiles that least befit who wear them most.

22.

By those, who deepest feel, is ill exprest   640
The indistinctness of the suffering breast;
Where thousand thoughts begin to end in one,
Which seeks from all the refuge found in none;
No words suffice the secret soul to show,
And Truth denies all eloquence to Woe.   645

On Conrad's stricken soul exhaustion prest,
And stupor almost lulled it into rest;
So feeble now—his mother's softness crept
To those wild eyes, which like an infant's wept:
It was the very weakness of his brain,   650
Which thus confessed without relieving pain.
None saw his trickling tears—perchance, if seen,
That useless flood of grief had never been:
Nor long they flowed—he dried them to depart,
In helpless—hopeless—brokenness of heart: 655
The sun goes forth—but Conrad's day is dim;
And the night cometh—ne'er to pass from him.
There is no darkness like the cloud of mind,
On Grief's vain eye—the blindest of the blind!
Which may not—dare not see—but turns aside   660
To blackest shade—nor will endure a guide!

638 lies . . . lost] ⟨is oft represt / of anguish hid / concealed—not lost⟩ ML   640 ⟨Twere
idle / idly⟩ / ⟨By griefs painted indistinctly / Are words all thoughts⟩ ML   deepest . . . is]
⟨suffer most⟩ are ML; deepest feel are M, all proofs, Corsair1–Corsair7   who cor. by B in
Text JJ that all other texts   643 ⟨And fly to⟩ all the ML   644 ⟨There
are no words the secret soul to show⟩ No words the secret soul entirely show ML
645 denies all] ⟨will find no⟩ ML   646 ⟨If Conrad's stormy⟩ ML   647 ⟨And
even that active spirit prayed for rest⟩ ML   648 feeble] ⟨broken / shaken⟩ ML
649 To] ⟨Through⟩ ML   651 That thus confessed ⟨but not relieved from⟩ pain ML
652–61 not in M   652 ⟨That hour beheld him / In helpless hopeless brokenness of
heart⟩ ML   656 but . . . is] his day's already
ML   657 ne'er . . . from] tis the same to ML, Ma   660 Still thirsting ⟨for
what it can never see⟩ glancing where it cannot see ML; ⟨That will not / sightless / refuses
every ray⟩ / ⟨Still sightless ? from every ray⟩ / ⟨That would not—will not / Blank sightless
since its / Lost in long gloom but will⟩ / ⟨With blackest veil but will not bear a guide⟩
Which ⟨from beauty⟩ from all brightness sinking turns aside MLa; ⟨Still blackly gleaming /
Which will not dare not see and turns aside⟩ Ma   661 A sightless wanderer oer
Eternity. ML; To blackest gloom but will not bear a guide. MLa; ⟨To blackest gloom but
will not bear a guide⟩ Ma

23.

His heart was formed for softness—warped to wrong;
Betrayed too early, and beguiled too long;
Each feeling pure—as falls the dropping dew
Within the grot; like that had hardened too;   665
Less clear, perchance, its earthly trials passed,
But sunk, and chilled, and petrified at last.
Yet tempests wear, and lightning cleaves the rock;
If such his heart, so shattered it the shock.
There grew one flower beneath its rugged brow,   670
Though dark the shade—it sheltered,—saved till now.
The thunder came—that bolt hath blasted both,
The Granite's firmness, and the Lily's growth:
The gentle plant hath left no leaf to tell
Its tale, but shrunk and withered where it fell,   675
And of its cold protector, blacken round
But shivered fragments on the barren ground!

24.

'Tis morn—to venture on his lonely hour
Few dare; though now Anselmo sought his tower.
He was not there—nor seen along the shore;   680
Ere night, alarmed, their isle is traversed o'er:
Another morn—another bids them seek,
And shout his name till echo waxeth weak;
Mount—grotto—cavern—valley searched in vain,
They find on shore a sea-boat's broken chain: 685
Their hope revives—they follow o'er the main.

662–7 *not in ML, M*   662 His heart was ⟨made⟩ for softness ⟨but unmeet / early
won / time and wrong⟩ warped to wrong *MLa*   663 Betrayed . . . beguiled] ⟨Truth⟩
Betrayed . . . ⟨deceived⟩ *MLa*   664 ⟨His feelings drop by drop the trial passed /
found⟩ Each feeling pure as ⟨fountain / hidden⟩ falls *MLa*   665 Within the cave
⟨where⟩ like that ⟨were / was⟩ had *MLa, cor. in Ma*   666 Less clear ⟨but all as /
but chilled / but all at once chilled⟩ perchance—⟨each evil trial passed⟩ the freezing trial
passed *MLa, cor. in Ma*   667 But] ⟨They⟩ *MLa*   668 wear] ⟨tear⟩ *MLa*
669 ⟨And⟩ If . . . so ⟨rent it⟩ shattered *MLa*   670 ⟨Proof to the storm / Bare to the
storm but ? in the strife / Bare worn but⟩ *MLa*   671 dark]
⟨rough⟩ *MLa*   672 that] its *MLa, Ma, cor. in Proof 6*   678–81 *not in M*
679 ⟨But few dare venture⟩ *ML*   though now] yet then *ML, cor. in Ma*   680 nor
. . . along] he sought him on *ML* ⟨and vainly / nor seen upon⟩ *Ma*   681 Ere night]
Night comes *ML*   682 bids] sees *ML, cor. in M*   683 echo waxeth] ⟨Echo's self
grew / voice grew⟩ answered *ML* ⟨Echo's voice grew⟩ *M*   685 find . . . broken] ⟨find⟩
found . . . ⟨broken⟩ scattered *ML*

'Tis idle all—moons roll on moons away,
And Conrad comes not—came not since that day:
Nor trace, nor tidings of his doom declare
Where lives his grief, or perished his despair!   690
Long mourned his band whom none could mourn beside;
And fair the monument they gave his bride:
For him they raise not the recording stone—
His death yet dubious, deeds too widely known;
He left a Corsair's name to other times,   695
Linked with one virtue, and a thousand crimes.

[1814]

225   Lara. A Tale

CANTO I

1.

The Serfs are glad through Lara's wide domain,
And Slavery half forgets her fuedal chain;
He, their unhop'd, but unforgotten lord,
The long self-exiled chieftain is restored:
There be bright faces in the busy hall,   5
Bowls on the board, and banners on the wall;
Far chequering o'er the pictured window plays
The unwonted faggots' hospitable blaze;
And gay retainers gather round the hearth
With tongues all loudness, and with eyes all mirth.   10

2.

The chief of Lara is returned again:
And why had Lara cross'd the bounding main?
Left by his sire, too young such loss to know,
Lord of himself;—that heritage of woe,

687 moons . . . moons] ⟨days—weeks—months wear⟩ *ML*   688 since] ⟨from⟩ *ML*
689 of his ⟨fortune tell⟩ *ML*   690 ⟨If he by wave or⟩ *ML*; Or where he died or lingers
in despair *ML*   693 For] ⟨Of⟩ *ML*   695 Corsair's] ⟨Pirate's⟩ *ML*   696 ⟨The⟩
Linked with one ⟨passion⟩ and *ML*

225. Copy text: *L(1)*, collated with *MSS. L, LA, M, B*, and *L(2)–L(5a)*.

title   Lara *L*

Canto I

3 unhop'd] ⟨long lost⟩ *L*   9 gay] ⟨loud⟩ *L*   10 tongues all loudness] ⟨words
all ?⟩ *L*   12 And ⟨what did⟩ *L*   13 such] ⟨that⟩ *L*

That fearful empire which the human breast   15
But holds to rob the heart within of rest!—
With none to check, and few to point in time
The thousand paths that slope the way to crime;
Then, when he most required commandment, then
Had Lara's daring boyhood govern'd men.   20
It skills not, boots not step by step to trace
His youth through all the mazes of its race;
Short was the course his restlessness had run,
But long enough to leave him half undone.

3.

And Lara left in youth his father-land;   25
But from the hour he waved his parting hand
Each trace wax'd fainter of his course, till all
Had nearly ceased his memory to recall.
His sire was dust, his vassals could declare,
'Twas all they knew, that Lara was not there;   30
Nor sent, nor came he, till conjecture grew
Cold in the many, anxious in the few.
His hall scarce echoes with his wonted name,
His portrait darkens in its fading frame,
Another chief consoled his destined bride,   35
The young forgot him, and the old had died;
'Yet doth he live!' exclaims the impatient heir,
And sighs for sables which he must not wear.
A hundred scutcheons deck with gloomy grace
The Laras' last and longest dwelling place;   40
But one is absent from the mouldering file
That now were welcome in that Gothic pile.

---

15 which] ⟨of⟩ L   16 ⟨That only ℘ to rob itself⟩ of rest L   17 point ⟨the
path⟩ L   19 Then, ⟨since a child in years, in⟩ L   20 govern'd] ⟨mixed with⟩ L
21–2 ⟨First in each folly—now the last in vice— | What would it boot⟩ L   21 boots]
⟨needs⟩ L   22 ⟨The beardless⟩ L   23 his . . . had] this beardless wanderer L
24 leave] see L   26 the] that L   27 till ⟨none⟩ L   31 ⟨He came not—
sent not⟩ L   till] and L   33 ⟨His name none echoed in the castle court⟩ L   34 His
portrait ⟨darkened in its / fading in its ℘ frame⟩ L   35 consoled] ⟨had won⟩ L
36 His friends forgot him—and his dog had died! L   37 exclaims] ⟨as said⟩ L
38 ⟨Without one woman to relieve his care⟩ L   sighs for] ⟨eyes the⟩ L   39 ⟨Amidst
the scutcheons on the⟩ L   gloomy] Gothic L   41 But one is ⟨resting in the
mouldering / ℘ line⟩ L   42 ⟨To whom⟩ That ⟨most might decorate / now might best
become⟩ that gloomy pile L

4.

He comes at last in sudden loneliness,
And whence they know not, why they need not guess;
They more might marvel, when the greeting's o'er,   45
Not that he came, but came not long before:
No train is his beyond a single page,
Of foreign aspect, and of tender age.
Years had roll'd on, and fast they speed away
To those that wander as to those that stay;   50
But lack of tidings from another clime
Had lent a flagging wing to weary Time.
They see, they recognise, yet almost deem
The present dubious, or the past a dream.

He lives, nor yet is past his manhood's prime,   55
Though seared by toil, and something touch'd by time;
His faults, whate'er they were, if scarce forgot,
Might be untaught him by his varied lot;
Nor good nor ill of late were known, his name
Might yet uphold his patrimonial fame.   60
His soul in youth was haughty, but his sins
No more than pleasure from the stripling wins;
And such, if not yet harden'd in their course,
Might be redeem'd, nor ask a long remorse.

5.

And they indeed were changed—'tis quickly seen   65
Whate'er he be, 'twas not what he had been;
That brow in furrow'd lines had fix'd at last,
And spake of passions, but of passion past;
The pride, but not the fire, of early days,
Coldness of mien, and carelessness of praise;   70
A high demeanour, and a glance that took
Their thoughts from others by a single look;

47–8 *not in L*   52 Had lent] Will lend *L*   flagging] ⟨heavy / heavier⟩ *L*
53 ⟨And made his own at times to others seem⟩ *L*   55–64 *numbered paragraph 5 in L*
56 by toil] ⟨by time⟩ *L*   57 scarce] ⟨not⟩ *L*   58 ⟨Yet⟩ Might *L*   60 Might
yet ⟨be worthy of / suppo[rt]⟩ *L*   62 stripling] ⟨heedless⟩ *L*   63 such] ⟨these⟩ *L*
in their course] ⟨into / to abuse⟩ *L*   64 a] ⟨too⟩ *L*   65–6 'tis . . . be] ⟨tis⟩
and . . . was *L*   67 ⟨His years / His⟩ brow ⟨so wont to change⟩ had *L*   68 passion]
Passions *L*   72 ⟨Another's⟩ *L*

And that sarcastic levity of tongue,
The stinging of a heart the world hath stung,
That darts in seeming playfulness around,   75
And makes those feel that will not own the wound;
All these seem'd his and something more beneath
Than glance could well reveal, or accent breathe.
Ambition, glory, love, the common aim
That some can conquer, and that all would claim,   80
Within his breast appear'd no more to strive,
Yet seem'd as lately they had been alive;
And some deep feeling it were vain to trace
At moments lighten'd o'er his livid face.

6.

Not much he lov'd long question of the past,   85
Nor told of wondrous wilds, and desarts vast
In those far lands where he had wandered lone,
And—as himself would have it seem—unknown:
Yet these in vain his eye could scarcely scan
Nor glean experience from his fellow man;   90
But what he had beheld he shunn'd to show,
As hardly worth a stranger's care to know;
If still more prying such enquiry grew,
His brow fell darker, and his words more few.

7.

Not unrejoiced to see him once again,   95
Warm was his welcome to the haunts of men;
Born of high lineage, link'd in high command,
He mingled with the Magnates of his land;
Join'd the carousals of the great and gay,
And saw them smile or sigh their hours away;   100
But still he only saw, and did not share
The common pleasure or the general care;
He did not follow what they all pursued
With hope still baffled, still to be renew'd;

74 stinging] ⟨venom⟩ L   75 darts] ⟨pours⟩ L   77 seem'd] were L   78 glance]
⟨words⟩ L   79 ⟨The common aim—Ambition—Glory—Love—⟩ L   80 ⟨In
him seem⟩ That ⟨all⟩ can L   85 of the past] ⟨to be asked⟩ L   86 ⟨Of others⟩ L
wilds] ⟨men⟩ L   90 from] of L   91 had beheld] ⟨knew at last⟩ L   92 a stranger's]
⟨another's⟩ L   93 such] ⟨that⟩ L   96 to] ⟨from⟩ in L   97 of] to L
99 the carousals] ⟨in the circles⟩ L   100 smile or sigh] sigh or smile L

Nor shadowy honour, nor substantial gain,   105
Nor beauty's preference, and the rival's pain:
Around him some mysterious circle thrown
Repell'd approach, and showed him still alone;
Upon his eye sate something of reproof,
That kept at least frivolity aloof;   110
And things more timid that beheld him near,
In silence gaz'd, or whisper'd mutual fear;
And they the wiser, friendlier few confess'd
They deem'd him better than his air express'd.

8.

'Twas strange—in youth all action and all life,   115
Burning for pleasure, not averse from strife;
Woman—the field—the ocean—all that gave
Promise of gladness, peril of a grave,
In turn he tried—he ransack'd all below,
And found his recompence in joy or woe,   120
No tame, trite medium; for his feelings sought
In that intenseness an escape from thought:
The tempest of his heart in scorn had gazed
On that the feebler elements hath rais'd;
The rapture of his heart had look'd on high,   125
And ask'd if greater dwelt beyond the sky:
Chain'd to excess, the slave of each extreme,
How woke he from the wildness of that dream?
Alas! he told not—but he did awake
To curse the wither'd heart that would not break.   130

9.

Books, for his volume heretofore was Man,
With eye more curious he appear'd to scan,

105 ⟨The phantom forms of honour and of gain⟩ L   106 Nor] ⟨The⟩ L
108 Repell'd] Defied L   109 eye] ⟨brow⟩ front L   117 Woman . . . that gave]
⟨The steed . . . alike⟩ L   118 ⟨That promised⟩ L   119 In . . . tried] Twas his
to seek L   120 But ⟨then that feeling must⟩ his reward must then be joy or woe L
121 for] ⟨all⟩ L   122 Their refuge in intensity of thought L   123 ⟨Within his
heart the native ? had smiled⟩ L   in . . . gazed] ⟨had wildly / calmly⟩ gazed L   125 on
high] on Heaven L   126 Nor ⟨asked nor hoped for more⟩ prayed nor deemed of more
than then was given L   127 ⟨Wild in excess⟩ L   slave of each] ⟨victim of⟩ L
129 ⟨Too true—alas! he lived—though he awoke⟩ L   told] ⟨knew⟩ L   130 wither'd]
⟨dull, cold⟩ L   132 curious] thoughtful L

And oft in sudden mood for many a day
From all communion he would start away:
And then, his rarely call'd attendants said,   135
Through night's long hours would sound his hurried
        tread
O'er the dark gallery, where his fathers frown'd
In rude but antique portraiture around.
They heard, but whisper'd—'*that* must not be known—
The sound of words less earthly than his own.   140
Yes, they who chose might smile, but some had seen
They scarce knew what, but more than should have been.
Why gaz'd he so upon the ghastly head
Which hands profane had gather'd from the dead,
That still beside his open'd volume lay,   145
As if to startle all save him away?
Why slept he not when others were at rest?
Why heard no music, and received no guest?
All was not well they deemed—but where the wrong?
Some knew perchance—but 'twere a tale too long;   150
And such besides were too discreetly wise,
To more than hint their knowledge in surmise;
But if they would—they could—around the board
Thus Lara's vassals prattled of their lord.

10.

It was the night—and Lara's glassy stream   155
The stars are studding, each with imaged beam:
So calm, the waters scarcely seem to stray,
And yet they glide like happiness away;
Reflecting far and fairy-like from high
The immortal lights that live along the sky: 160
Its banks are fringed with many a goodly tree,
And flowers the fairest that may feast the bee;

133 And oft ⟨from / and⟩ L   for . . . day] ⟨from day by day⟩ L   134 start]
⟨shrink⟩ L   135 ⟨None saw him / saw his ? attendants—they⟩ L   rarely call'd]
⟨whispering⟩ seldom called L   136 ⟨None saw him but they heard⟩ L   would sound]
⟨was heard⟩ L   137 O'er] Through L   139 They heard—(but whispered—*that*
must not be known) L   140 The sound of other voices than his own L   141 chose]
heard L; choose L(4), L(5)   144 Which] That L   145 That] Which L   148 Why
⟨show the⟩ hear no L   151 wise] ⟨sage⟩ L   154 ⟨Of servile gossiping⟩ L
155 ⟨One night—a summer night—when all is still⟩ L   157 seem] seemed L

Such in her chaplet infant Dian wove,
And Innocence would offer to her love.
These deck the shore; the waves their channel make   165
In windings bright and mazy like the snake.
All was so still, so soft in earth and air,
You scarce would start to meet a spirit there;
Secure that nought of evil could delight
To walk in such a scene, on such a night!   170
It was a moment only for the good:
So Lara deemed, nor longer there he stood,
But turned in silence to his castle-gate;
Such scene his soul no more could contemplate:
Such scene reminded him of other days,   175
Of skies more cloudless, moons of purer blaze,
Of nights more soft and frequent, hearts that now—
No—no—the storm may beat upon his brow,
Unfelt—unsparing—but a night like this,
A night of beauty mock'd such breast as his.   180

                              II.

He turned within his solitary hall,
And his high shadow shot along the wall;
There were the painted forms of other times,
'Twas all they left of virtues or of crimes,
Save vague tradition; and the gloomy vaults   185
That hid their dust, their foibles, and their faults;
And half a column of the pompous page,
That speeds the specious tale from age to age;
Where history's pen its praise or blame supplies,
And lies like truth, and still most truly lies.   190
He wandering mused, and as the moonbeam shone
Through the dim lattice o'er the floor of stone,
And the high fretted roof, and saints, that there
O'er Gothic windows knelt in pictured prayer,

171 only for] ⟨to delight⟩ L   173 gate] ⟨hall⟩ L   174 ⟨And shunned⟩ L
176 more] ⟨as⟩ L   178 No—no—the ⟨night breeze cannot⟩ L   179 unsparing]
⟨unnoticed⟩ L   180 such breast as] ⟨a heart like⟩ L   183 painted] pictured L
185 and] ⟨which⟩ L   186 foibles] ⟨follies⟩ L   187 pompous] ⟨doubtful / lying⟩
solemn L   188 ⟨That lying History, base Flattery ?⟩ L   speeds] ⟨sends⟩ L
189 ⟨Where Fiction is the mask of History⟩ L   191 wandering mused] ⟨wandered
there⟩ L   193–4 indecipherable cancellations

Reflected in fantastic figures grew,   195
Like life, but not like mortal life, to view;
His bristling locks of sable, brow of gloom,
And the wide waving of his shaken plume
Glanced like a spectre's attributes, and gave
His aspect all that terror gives the grave.   200

12.

'Twas midnight—all was slumber; the lone light
Dimm'd in the lamp, as loth to break the night.
Hark! there be murmurs heard in Lara's hall—
A sound—a voice—a shriek—a fearful call!
A long, loud shriek—and silence—did they hear   205
That frantic echo burst the sleeping ear?
They heard and rose, and tremulously brave
Rush where the sound invoked their aid to save;
They come with half-lit tapers in their hands,
And snatch'd in startled haste unbelted brands.   210

13.

Cold as the marble where his length was laid,
Pale as the beam that o'er his features played,
Was Lara stretch'd; his half drawn sabre near,
Dropp'd it should seem in more than nature's fear;
Yet he was firm, or had been firm till now,   215
And still defiance knit his gathered brow;
Though mix'd with terror, senseless as he lay,
There lived upon his lip the wish to slay;
Some half form'd threat in utterance there had died,
Some imprecation of despairing pride;   220
His eye was almost seal'd, but not forsook,
Even in its trance the gladiator's look,

---

196 ⟨To Fancy een like⟩ L   mortal] ⟨human⟩ L   197 ⟨His waving⟩ locks of sable,
⟨pallid brow⟩ L   199 spectre's . . . gave] ⟨spectral . . . then⟩ L   200 ⟨If seen
had⟩ His aspect all ⟨we fancy fills⟩ the grave. L   201 slumber] ⟨Silence⟩ L
206 frantic . . . the] ⟨horrid . . . their⟩ L   207 and ⟨trembling⟩ tremulously L
208 invoked] ⟨invited⟩ L   209 with ⟨torch ?⟩ half-lit L   210 snatch'd in startled]
⟨pulled in hopeless⟩ L   216 knit . . . brow] ⟨filled his ghastly⟩ knitted in his brow L
217 Though . . . terror] But . . . ⟨horror⟩ madness L   219 form'd ⟨word of⟩ threat L
220 imprecation] ⟨furious accent⟩ L   221 eye . . . seal'd] ⟨eyes were almost closed⟩ L
222 ⟨That closing eye⟩ the gladiatorial look L

That oft awake his aspect could disclose,
And now was fix'd in horrible repose.
They raise him—bear him;—hush! he breathes, he speaks, 225
The swarthy blush recolours in his cheeks,
His lip resumes its red, his eye, though dim,
Rolls wide and wild, each slowly quivering limb
Recalls its function, but his words are strung
In terms that seem not of his native tongue;   230
Distinct but strange, enough they understand
To deem them accents of another land,
And such they were, and meant to meet an ear
That hears him not—alas! that cannot hear!

14.

His page approach'd, and he alone appear'd   235
To know the import of the words they heard;
And by the changes of his cheek and brow
They were not such as Lara should avow,
Nor he interpret, yet with less surprise
Than those around their chieftain's state he eyes,   240
But Lara's prostrate form he bent beside,
And in that tongue which seem'd his own replied,
And Lara heeds those tones that gently seem
To soothe away the horrors of his dream;
If dream it were, that thus could overthrow   245
A breast that needed not ideal woe.

15.

Whate'er his phrenzy dream'd or eye beheld,
If yet remember'd ne'er to be reveal'd,
Rests at his heart: the custom'd morning came,
And breath'd new vigour in his shaken frame;   250
And solace sought he none from priest nor leech,
And soon the same in movement and in speech

223 That oft ⟨in calmer words his glance disclosed⟩ L   227 resumes its] ⟨once more
is⟩ L   228 Rolls] ⟨Looks⟩ L   229 his words ⟨—what tongue⟩ L   230 terms]
⟨sounds⟩ L   231 enough they] ⟨though some could⟩ L   232 ⟨But / They deemed⟩ L
235-46 MS. LA insertion in MS. L   235 and . . . appear'd] ⟨who came with him / who
with him left the shore⟩ LA   238 should] ⟨might⟩ LA   241 ⟨He bent alone / And⟩
But LA   243 heeds] ⟨knew⟩ LA   244 soothe . . . horrors] ⟨sing⟩ . . . terrors LA
245 could ⟨shake a heart⟩ LA   246 that ⟨had not bent⟩ needed LA   247 Whate'er
⟨his eye beheld⟩ L   248 ⟨He told not⟩ L   251 And . . . none] ⟨Who . . . not⟩ L

As heretofore he fill'd the passing hours,
Nor less he smiles, nor more his forehead lours
Than these were wont; and if the coming night   255
Appear'd less welcome now to Lara's sight,
He to his marvelling vassals show'd it not,
Whose shuddering prov'd *their* fear was less forgot.
In trembling pairs (alone they dared not) crawl
The astonish'd slaves, and shun the fated hall;   260
The waving banner, and the clapping door,
The rustling tapestry, and the echoing floor;
The long dim shadows of surrounding trees,
The flapping bat, the night song of the breeze:
Aught they behold or hear their thought appals   265
As evening saddens o'er the dark grey walls.

16.

Vain thought! that hour of ne'er unravell'd gloom
Came not again, or Lara could assume
A seeming of forgetfulness that made
His vassals more amaz'd nor less afraid—   270
Had memory vanish'd then with sense restored?
Since word, nor look, nor gesture of their lord
Betrayed a feeling that recalled to these
That fevered moment of his mind's disease.
Was it a dream? was his the voice that spoke   275
Those strange wild accents; his the cry that broke
Their slumber? his the oppress'd o'er-laboured heart
That ceased to beat, the look that made them start?
Could he who thus had suffered, so forget
When such as saw that suffering shudder yet?   280
Or did that silence prove his memory fix'd
Too deep for words, indelible, unmix'd

253 fill'd] ⟨whiled⟩ L   256 less] ⟨more⟩ L   257 to his marvelling] ⟨midst
affrighted⟩ L   258 ⟨But they at shuddering proved all unforgott⟩ Whose ⟨secret⟩
shuddering L   259 In trembling pairs ⟨they creep⟩ along the galleries crawl L
261 clapping door] ⟨sighing ?⟩ L   264 the ⟨lovely⟩ night song L   265 ⟨All they
behold or hear appals⟩ L   266 saddens] ⟨closes / gathers⟩ L   267 that ⟨strange⟩
hour L   270 vassals ⟨marvelled⟩ more L   271 ⟨Nor word nor look nor question
of their Lord⟩ L   273 a ⟨trace that told to them⟩ feeling L   275 spoke] ⟨broke⟩ L
279 ⟨If such things be—yet he by / by him remembered not⟩ L   280 as ⟨merely⟩ saw L

In that corroding secrecy which gnaws
The heart to show the effect, but not the cause?
Not so in him; his breast had buried both,   285
Nor common gazers could discern the growth
Of thoughts that mortal lips must leave half told;
They choak the feeble words that would unfold.

17.

In him inexplicably mix'd appeared
Much to be loved and hated, sought and feared;   290
Opinion varying o'er his hidden lot,
In praise or railing ne'er his name forgot;
His silence formed a theme for others' prate—
They guess'd—they gazed—they fain would know his fate.
What had he been? what was he, thus unknown,   295
Who walked their world, his lineage only known?
A hater of his kind? yet some would say,
With them he could seem gay amidst the gay;
But own'd, that smile if oft observed and near,
Waned in its mirth and withered to a sneer;   300
That smile might reach his lip, but passed not by,
None e'er could trace its laughter to his eye:
Yet there was softness too in his regard,
At times, a heart as not by nature hard,
But once perceiv'd, his spirit seem'd to chide   305
Such weakness, as unworthy of its pride,
And steel'd itself, as scorning to redeem
One doubt from others' half withheld esteem;
In self-inflicted penance of a breast
Which tenderness might once have wrung from rest;   310
In vigilance of grief that would compel
The soul to hate for having lov'd too well.

283 which] that L   284 heart ⟨and⟩ to L   287 ⟨Of thoughts that told had
still ? grief⟩ ⟨Of thoughts that mortal accents should unfold⟩ L   290 Much to ⟨all⟩ L
291–2 Opinion varying as his varying eye | ⟨From⟩ In praise ⟨to⟩ or railing never passed
him by— L   294 ⟨And they that⟩ L   295 unknown] alone L
296 their] ⟨the⟩ L   298 ⟨With others he was all smooth⟩ L   301–2 Not in L
301 might ⟨pass and⟩ reach B   302 None ⟨eer beheld the⟩ ever traced that laugh-
ter ⟨of⟩ to his eye— B   303 ⟨And / Yet traces⟩ L   307 steel'd] ⟨watched⟩ L
309 In] ⟨The⟩ L   311 In] ⟨The⟩ L

18.

There was in him a vital scorn of all:
As if the worst had fall'n which could befall
He stood a stranger in this breathing world,   315
An erring spirit from another hurled;
A thing of dark imaginings, that shaped
By choice the perils he by chance escaped;
But 'scaped in vain, for in their memory yet
His mind would half exult and half regret: 320
With more capacity for love than earth
Bestows on most of mortal mould and birth,
His early dreams of good outstripp'd the truth,
And troubled manhood followed baffled youth;
With thought of years in phantom chace misspent,   325
And wasted powers for better purpose lent;
And fiery passions that had poured their wrath
In hurried desolation o'er his path,
And left the better feelings all at strife
In wild reflection o'er his stormy life;   330
But haughty still, and loth himself to blame,
He called on Nature's self to share the shame,
And charged all faults upon the fleshly form
She gave to clog the soul, and feast the worm;
'Till he at last confounded good and ill,   335
And half mistook for fate the acts of will:
Too high for common selfishness, he could
At times resign his own for others' good,
But not in pity, not because he ought,
But in some strange perversity of thought,   340
That swayed him onward with a secret pride
To do what few or none would do beside;

313–60 *Not in L*   313 There seemed in him an inward scorn of all *LA, M*
seemed] ⟨was⟩ *LA*   314 ⟨That might⟩ *LA*   had ... which] were ⟨past⟩ that *LA*
315 stood] ⟨looked⟩ *LA*   316 erring] ⟨fallen⟩ *LA*   317 dark ... that] ⟨wild⟩
... who *LA*   318 perils he by chance] dangers he ⟨had long / still⟩ by chance *LA*
320 His ⟨devil⟩ mind would triumph half—and half regret *LA*   321 than] ⟨for⟩ *LA*
322 most] ⟨those⟩ *LA*   324 troubled] ⟨sullen⟩ *LA*   325 With] ⟨No⟩
LA   329–32 And left Reflection—loth himself to blame | He called on Nature's self
to share the shame *LA, M*   He called] ⟨While⟩ But call *LA*   333 And charge
⟨his faults upon the world and man⟩ *LA*   336 the acts of] his wayward *LA, M*
337 ⟨He was thus?⟩ not shrunk up in selfishness⟩ *LA*   high for common] ⟨proud for
mortal⟩ *LA*

8127553   I

And this same impulse would in tempting time
Mislead his spirit equally to crime;
So much he soared beyond, or sunk beneath   345
The men with whom he felt condemned to breathe,
And longed by good or ill to separate
Himself from all who shared his mortal state;
His mind abhorring this had fixed her throne
Far from the world, in regions of her own;   350
Thus coldly passing all that passed below,
His blood in temperate seeming now would flow:
Ah! happier if it ne'er with guilt had glowed,
But ever in that icy smoothness flowed!
'Tis true, with other men their path he walked,   355
And like the rest in seeming did and talked,
Nor outraged Reason's rules by flaw nor start,
His madness was not of the head, but heart;
And rarely wandered in his speech, or drew
His thoughts so forth as to offend the view.   360

19.

With all that chilling mystery of mien,
And seeming gladness to remain unseen;
He had (if 'twere not nature's boon) an art
Of fixing memory on another's heart:
It was not love perchance—nor hate—nor aught   365
That words can image to express the thought;
But they who saw him did not see in vain,
And once beheld, would ask of him again:
And those to whom he spake remembered well,
And on the words, however light, would dwell: 370
None knew, nor how, nor why, but he entwined
Himself perforce around the hearer's mind;

343 would] ⟨would⟩ might *LA*   346 ⟨The fallen men he deemed unfit to breathe⟩
LA   347 longed] ⟨loathed⟩ *LA*   348 who] that *LA*   349 abhorring this
had] ⟨had maddened till it⟩ *LA*   350 Beyond this world—in ⟨planets⟩ of her own *LA*
355 'Tis true ⟨he spoke and did and mixed with men⟩ *LA*   357 ⟨Nor moved? from
Reason or by flaw or start⟩ *LA*   359 rarely . . . speech, or] never . . . ⟨brain⟩ nor
LA, cor. in M   361–82 *MS. LA insertion in MS. L*   361 that ⟨cold⟩ chilling
LA   362 gladness] ⟨gladness⟩ effort *LA*   363 ⟨There was in⟩ *LA*   if . . . boon]
⟨it might / if not from⟩ if twas not Nature's gift *LA*   367 But ⟨if you saw him⟩ *LA*
372 the hearer's] another's *LA*

There he was stamp'd, in liking, or in hate,
If greeted once; however brief the date
That friendship, pity, or aversion knew,   375
Still there within the inmost thought he grew.
You could not penetrate his soul, but found,
Despite your wonder, to your own he wound;
His presence haunted still; and from the breast
He forced an all unwilling interest;   380
Vain was the struggle in that mental net,
His spirit seemed to dare you to forget!

20.

There is a festival, where knights and dames,
And aught that wealth or lofty lineage claims
Appear—a highborn and a welcomed guest   385
To Otho's hall came Lara with the rest.
The long carousal shakes the illumin'd hall,
Well speeds alike the banquet and the ball;
And the gay dance of bounding Beauty's train
Links grace and harmony in happiest chain: 390
Blest are the early hearts and gentle hands
That mingle there in well according bands;
It is a sight the careful brow might smoothe,
And make Age smile, and dream itself to youth,
And Youth forget such hour was past on earth,   395
So springs the exulting bosom to that mirth!

21.

And Lara gaz'd on these sedately glad,
His brow belied him if his soul was sad,
And his glance followed fast each fluttering fair,
Whose steps of lightness woke no echo there: 400

373 stamp'd] fixed *LA*   375 pity] interest *LA*   376 Still . . . the] But . . .
your *LA*   377 ⟨You might abhor⟩ *LA*   soul] heart *LA*   379–80 Yes—you
might hate—abhor—but from the breast | ⟨For good or ill—he left an interest⟩ *LA*
381 ⟨You might⟩ *LA*   mental] sightless *LA*   382 spirit ⟨cast⟩ seemed *LA*
385 highborn] ⟨wellborn⟩ *L*   welcomed] welcome *1815*, *L(5a)*, *1831*, *1832*, *C*, *More*
387–8 *transposed in L*   387 illumin'd] ⟨lighted⟩ *L*   389 train] ⟨show⟩ *L*
390 happiest] ⟨that soft⟩ *L*   391 ⟨When hand to hand and heart to heart they dance⟩ *L*
393 It is a sight ⟨to smoothe the brow⟩ *L*   395 such] ⟨each⟩ *L*   396 exulting
bosom] ⟨Spirit⟩ exulting *L*   399 glance] ⟨eye⟩ *L*   400 woke] ⟨left⟩ waked *L*

He lean'd against the lofty pillar nigh
With folded arms and long attentive eye,
Nor mark'd a glance so sternly fix'd on his—
Ill brook'd high Lara scrutiny like this:
At length he caught it, 'tis a face unknown,   405
But seems as searching his, and his alone;
Prying and dark, a stranger's by his mien,
Who still till now had gaz'd on him unseen;
At length encountering meets the mutual gaze
Of keen enquiry, and of mute amaze;   410
On Lara's glance emotion gathering grew,
As if distrusting that the stranger threw;
Along the stranger's aspect fix'd and stern
Flash'd more than thence the vulgar eye could learn.

22.

'Tis he!' the stranger cried, and those that heard   415
Re-echoed fast and far the whisper'd word.
'Tis he!'—'Tis who?' they question far and near,
Till louder accents rung on Lara's ear;
So widely spread, few bosoms well could brook
The general marvel, or that single look;   420
But Lara stirr'd not, changed not, the surprise
That sprung at first to his arrested eyes
Seem'd now subsided; neither sunk nor rais'd
Glanced his eye round, though still the stranger gaz'd;
And drawing nigh, exclaim'd, with haughty sneer,   425
'Tis he!—how came he thence?—what doth he here?'

23.

It were too much for Lara to pass by
Such question, so repeated fierce and high;
With look collected, but with accent cold,
More mildly firm than petulantly bold,   430

401 ⟨He gazed⟩ L   403 glance] eye L   404 scrutiny like] such a glance as L
406 as searching] ⟨to search for⟩ L   409 ⟨Not yet / So meet their mutual glances—
now it is⟩ ⟨And Lara's / At length / And now encountered⟩ L   411 glance] ⟨cheek⟩ L
412 that ... threw] ⟨what ... knew⟩ L   415 and ... heard] ⟨to those around⟩ L
416 ⟨'Tis he' reechoed far in⟩ whispered word L   418 louder] the loud L   420 or
that single] and that ⟨Stranger's⟩ single L   421 changed] moved L   424 though
⟨and⟩ L   427 It was too much for Lara to ⟨mistake⟩ L   428 ⟨The purport of
that question⟩ L   so repeated fierce] thus repeated thrice L   429 ⟨In ? paleness—but
with accents mild / but with ? tone⟩ L   430 ⟨As might have moved a maid or ? / child⟩ L

Painted by Tho.ˢ Stothard R.A.

Engraved by R. Rhodes.

LARA.

HE LEAN'D AGAINST THE LOFTY PILLAR NIGH,
WITH FOLDED ARMS AND LONG ATTENTIVE EYE,
NOR MARK'D A GLANCE SO STERNLY FIX'D ON HIS.

PUBLISHED BY JOHN MURRAY, ALBEMARLE STREET, DECᴿ 1,1814.

Lara Canto I lines 401–3

(*Reproduced with the permission of the British Library*)

He turn'd, and met the inquisitorial tone—
'My name is Lara!—when thine own is known,
Doubt not my fitting answer to requite
The unlook'd for courtesy of such a knight.
'Tis Lara!—further wouldst thou mark or ask?   435
I shun no question, and I wear no mask.'

'Thou shun'st no question! Ponder—is there none
Thy heart must answer, though thine ear would shun?
And deem'st thou me unknown too? Gaze again!
At least thy memory was not given in vain.   440
Oh! never canst thou cancel half her debt,
Eternity forbids thee to forget.'
With slow and searching glance upon his face
Grew Lara's eyes, but nothing there could trace
They knew, or chose to know—with dubious look   445
He deign'd no answer, but his head he shook,
And half contemptuous turn'd to pass away;
But the stern stranger motioned him to stay.
'A word!—I charge thee stay, and answer here
To one, who, wert thou noble, were thy peer,   450
But as thou wast and art—nay, frown not, lord,
If false, 'tis easy to disprove the word—
But as thou wast and art, on thee looks down,
Distrusts thy smiles, but shakes not at thy frown.
Art thou not he? whose deeds——'
                                    'Whate'er I be,   455
Words wild as these, accusers like to thee
I list no further; those with whom they weigh
May hear the rest, nor venture to gainsay
The wondrous tale no doubt thy tongue can tell,
Which thus begins so courteously and well.   460
Let Otho cherish here his polish'd guest,
To him my thanks and thoughts shall be expressed.'

431 the] ⟨that⟩ L   433 fitting] ready L   434 unlook'd for] ⟨sudden⟩ L
435–6 ⟨''Tis he—' What he?—I ask not what art thou— | Though that methinks / That
Prudence should forbid thee to avow⟩ L   435 ⟨''Tis he'—'tis whom—hast thou⟩
'Tis I—what further wouldst thou ⟨view⟩ mark or ask L   437 Ponder] ⟨Pause⟩ L
438 Thy] ⟨Thine⟩ L   441 cancel half her] ⟨render all that⟩ L   443 ⟨From head
to foot—with slow and ? / searching look⟩ L   upon his face] ⟨from head to heel⟩ L
444 ⟨Gazed Lara on the Stranger⟩ L   450 who] ⟨that⟩ L   452 ⟨I speak⟩ L
the] ⟨my⟩ L   455 he . . . deeds] ⟨art thou not⟩ L   457 ⟨To me are idle
for⟩ L   461 Let Otho cherish well so kind a guest L

And here their wondering host hath interposed—
'Whate'er there be between you undisclosed,
This is no time nor fitting place to mar   465
The mirthful meeting with a wordy war.
If thou, Sir Ezzelin, hast ought to show
Which it befits Count Lara's ear to know,
To-morrow, here, or elsewhere, as may best
Beseem your mutual judgment, speak the rest;   470
I pledge myself for thee, as not unknown,
Though like Count Lara now return'd alone
From other lands, almost a stranger grown;
And if from Lara's blood and gentle birth
I augur right of courage and of worth,   475
He will not that untainted line belie,
Nor aught that knighthood may accord deny.'
'To-morrow be it,' Ezzelin replied,
'And here our several worth and truth be tried;
I gage my life, my falchion to attest   480
My words, so may I mingle with the blest!'
What answers Lara? to its centre shrunk
His soul, in deep abstraction sudden sunk;
The words of many, and the eyes of all
That there were gather'd seem'd on him to fall;   485
But his were silent, his appear'd to stray
In far forgetfulness away—away—
Alas! that heedlessness of all around
Bespoke remembrance only too profound.

24.

'To-morrow!—ay, to-morrow!' further word   490
Than those repeated none from Lara heard;
Upon his brow no outward passion spoke,
From his large eye no flashing anger broke;

466 The] ⟨This⟩ L   468 ⟨Against Count Lara's⟩ L   470 mutual judgment]
⟨several judgments⟩ L   474 blood] ⟨soul / eye⟩ L   475 ⟨I may deem⟩ L
476 ⟨He will not shrink from question⟩ L   479 several] ⟨mutual⟩ L   482 Why
speaks not Lara?— ⟨lost in seeming thought / oer his bosom crost⟩ to ⟨their⟩ its centre
shrunk L   483 His ⟨thoughts⟩ in ⟨inward / guarded secresy now⟩ sunk L   sudden]
⟨now seemed⟩ L   484 eyes] ⟨thoughts⟩ L   486 appear'd to stray] ⟨seemed far
away⟩ L   488 ⟨In far forgetfulness⟩ L   490-1 'Tomorrow—ay tomorrow'—
these were all | The words from Lara's answering lip that fall— L

Yet there was something fix'd in that low tone
Which show'd resolve, determined, though unknown.   495
He seiz'd his cloak—his head he slightly bow'd,
And passing Ezzelin he left the crowd;
And, as he pass'd him, smiling met the frown
With which that chieftain's brow would bear him down:
It was nor smile of mirth, nor struggling pride   500
That curbs to scorn the wrath it cannot hide;
But that of one in his own heart secure
Of all that he would do, or could endure.
Could this mean peace? the calmness of the good?
Or guilt grown old in desperate hardihood?   505
Alas! too like in confidence are each
For man to trust to mortal look or speech;
From deeds, and deeds alone, may he discern
Truths which it wrings the unpractised heart to learn.

25.

And Lara called his page, and went his way—   510
Well could that stripling word or sign obey:
His only follower from those climes afar
Where the soul glows beneath a brighter star;
For Lara left the shore from whence he sprung,
In duty patient, and sedate though young;   515
Silent as him he served, his faith appears
Above his station, and beyond his years.
Though not unknown the tongue of Lara's land,
In such from him he rarely heard command;
But fleet his step, and clear his tones would come,   520
When Lara's lip breath'd forth the words of home:
Those accents as his native mountains dear,
Awake their absent echoes in his ear,

496 ⟨He slightly bowed his head and passed / moved along / left the throng⟩ L   cloak]
⟨mantle⟩ L   500 mirth, nor struggling pride] ⟨scorn / rage⟩ —nor ⟨hidden rage⟩ L
501 curbs to scorn] ⟨fain would crush⟩ L   502 in] ⟨of⟩ L   504. Could this ⟨be
calmness⟩ L   505 ⟨At / And⟩ L   506 in . . . are] ⟨the . . . of⟩ L   509 the
⟨skilled⟩ unpractised L   511 stripling] boy his L   512 only follower] ⟨sole com-
panion⟩ L   514 ⟨He followed / came with Lara, oer the⟩ L   shore] ⟨land⟩ L
516 ⟨He early left⟩ L   518 ⟨To his⟩ L   519 such . . . rarely] ⟨that . . . never⟩ L
520 fleet . . . tones] ⟨fast⟩ . . . words L   521 lip . . . words] ⟨voice⟩ . . . tones L
522 native] ⟨native⟩ distant L   523 That brought their native echoes to his ear L

Friends', kindreds', parents', wonted voice recall,
Now lost, abjured, for one—his friend, his all: 525
For him earth now disclosed no other guide;
What marvel then he rarely left his side?

26.

Light was his form, and darkly delicate
That brow whereon his native sun had sate,
But had not marr'd, though in his beams he grew,   530
The cheek where oft the unbidden blush shone through;
Yet not such blush as mounts when health would show
All the heart's hue in that delighted glow;
But 'twas a hectic tint of secret care
That for a burning moment fevered there;   535
And the wild sparkle of his eye seemed caught
From high, and lightened with electric thought,
Though its black orb those long low lashes fringe,
Had tempered with a melancholy tinge;
Yet less of sorrow than of pride was there,   540
Or if 'twere grief, a grief that none should share:
And pleased not him the sports that please his age,
The tricks of youth, the frolics of the page;
For hours on Lara he would fix his glance,
As all forgotten in that watchful trance;   545
And from his chief withdrawn, he wandered lone,
Brief were his answers, and his questions none;
His walk the wood, his sport some foreign book;
His resting-place the bank that curbs the brook:
He seemed, like him he served, to live apart   550
From all that lures the eye, and fills the heart;
To know no brotherhood, and take from earth
No gift beyond that bitter boon—our birth.

524 ⟨A Love's—a mother's kindred lips recall⟩ L   525 abjured] resigned L
526 disclosed] contained L   528 darkly delicate] ⟨delicately dark⟩ L   529 ⟨That
cheek whereon the Sun had set his mark⟩ ⟨His sun-burnt / nut brown cheek / That face⟩ L
530–1 But had not marred ⟨with his intenser glow | The skin that showed the gentle blood
below⟩ L   532 Yet not ⟨that⟩ blush as ⟨Health / smiling⟩ L   533 All] ⟨With⟩ L
534 ⟨There was⟩ a hectic ⟨hue of ? thought⟩ L   535 That sometimes for a moment
⟨reddened⟩ there L   536 ⟨And the quick sparkle of his lively eye⟩ L   wild] ⟨quick⟩ L
537 From ⟨light⟩ L   538 long low lashes] ⟨and lashes darkly⟩ L   540 sorrow
than of pride] ⟨grief than of haughtiness⟩ L   547 ⟨Would answer others⟩ L   548 some]
⟨his⟩ L

27.

If aught he loved, 'twas Lara; but was shown
His faith in reverence and in deeds alone;   555
In mute attention; and his care, which guessed
Each wish, fulfilled it ere the tongue expressed.
Still there was haughtiness in all he did,
A spirit deep that brook'd not to be chid;
His zeal, though more than that of servile hands,   560
In act alone obeys, his air commands;
As if 'twas Lara's less than *his* desire
That thus he served, but surely not for hire.
Slight were the tasks enjoined him by his lord,
To hold the stirrup, or to bear the sword;   565
To tune his lute, or if he willed it more,
On tomes of other times and tongues to pore;
But ne'er to mingle with the menial train,
To whom he showed nor deference nor disdain,
But that well-worn reserve which proved he knew   570
No sympathy with that familiar crew:
His soul, whate'er his station or his stem,
Could bow to Lara, not descend to them.
Of higher birth he seemed, and better days,
Nor mark of vulgar toil that hand betrays,   575
So femininely white it might bespeak
Another sex, when matched with that smooth cheek,
But for his garb, and something in his gaze,
More wild and high than woman's eye betrays;
A latent fierceness that far more became   580
His fiery climate than his tender frame:
True, in his words it broke not from his breast,
But from his aspect might be more than guessed.

---

555 reverence] ⟨silence⟩ L   556 his] ⟨the⟩ L   557 wish] ⟨want⟩ L
560–1 ⟨As if his Will alone should sway his hands⟩ / Though no reluctance checked his
willing hand | He still obliged as others would command L   562 ⟨With no / Without
reluctance yet / but with that high air⟩ L   566–7 To tune his lute—and if none else
were there | To fill the cup in which himself might share L   569 deference] ⟨friend-
ship⟩ L   570 well . . . proved] ⟨indifferent air⟩ which showed L   572 His . . .
his] ⟨But whatsoer his⟩ L   576 So tapered and so white it might ⟨perplex⟩ bespeak L
577 smooth] soft L   578 for] ⟨that⟩ L   579 wild and high] ⟨stern and wild⟩ L
580 ⟨Dispelled the doubt⟩ L   far more] ⟨had ill⟩ L   581 ⟨Those years⟩ L   his]
that L   583 Yet still existed there though still supprest L

Kaled his name, though rumour said he bore
Another ere he left his mountain-shore;　585
For sometimes he would hear, however nigh,
That name repeated loud without reply,
As unfamiliar, or, if roused again,
Start to the sound, as but remembered then;
Unless 'twas Lara's wonted voice that spake,　590
For then, ear, eyes, and heart would all awake.

28.

He had looked down upon the festive hall,
And marked that sudden strife so marked of all;
And when the crowd around and near him told
Their wonder at the calmness of the bold,　595
Their marvel how the high-born Lara bore
Such insult from a stranger, doubly sore,
The colour of young Kaled went and came,
The lip of ashes, and the cheek of flame;
And o'er his brow the dampening heart-drops threw　600
The sickening iciness of that cold dew
That rises as the busy bosom sinks
With heavy thoughts from which reflection shrinks.
Yes—there be things that we must dream and dare,
And execute ere thought be half aware:　605
Whate'er might Kaled's be, it was enow
To seal his lip, but agonise his brow.
He gazed on Ezzelin till Lara cast
That sidelong smile upon the knight he passed;
When Kaled saw that smile his visage fell,　610
As if on something recognized right well;

---

584 ⟨Such was young Kaled / His name was Kaled—such at least he bore⟩ L
585 mountain-shore] native shore L　　586 For sometimes ⟨unto this he answered not⟩ L　　587 ⟨And if he heard⟩ L　　588 ⟨Then suddenly⟩ As unfamiliar ⟨with his name and then⟩ L　　589 ⟨Would start⟩ L　　as . . . then] ⟨as but remembering then / and memory again⟩ L　　591 would] ⟨seemed⟩ L　　592 the] that L　594 crowd . . . near] slaves and pages round L　　598 went] rose L　　599 ⟨His lip all ashes—and his cheek all flame⟩ L　　600 the . . . threw] ⟨the gathering dewdrops stood⟩ L　　604 things] ⟨thoughts⟩ L　　605 And] ⟨But⟩ L　　606 ⟨Whatever Kaled⟩ Whateer his thoughts might be—it was enow L　　607 lip] lips L　608 till Lara cast] when Lara ⟨passed⟩ L　　609 the knight] him as L　　610 When Kaled] And when he L　　611 As if ⟨he saw and⟩ on something ⟨which he knew⟩ right well L

His memory read in such a meaning more
Than Lara's aspect unto others wore,
Forward he sprung—a moment, both were gone,
And all within that hall seemed left alone;   615
Each had so fix'd his eye on Lara's mien,
All had so mix'd their feelings with that scene,
That when his long dark shadow through the porch
No more relieves the glare of yon high torch,
Each pulse beats quicker, and all bosoms seem   620
To bound as doubting from too black a dream,
Such as we know is false, yet dread in sooth,
Because the worst is ever nearest truth.
And they are gone—but Ezzelin is there,
With thoughtful visage and imperious air;   625
But long remain'd not; ere an hour expired
He waved his hand to Otho, and retired.

29.

The crowd are gone, the revellers at rest;
The courteous host, and all-approving guest,
Again to that accustomed couch must creep   630
Where joy subsides, and sorrow sighs to sleep,
And man o'er-laboured with his being's strife,
Shrinks to that sweet forgetfulness of life:
There lie love's feverish hope, and cunning's guile,
Hate's working brain, and lull'd ambition's wile,   635
O'er each vain eye oblivion's pinions wave,
And quench'd existence crouches in a grave.
What better name may slumber's bed become?
Night's sepulchre, the universal home,
Where weakness, strength, vice, virtue, sunk supine,   640
Alike in naked helplessness recline;
Glad for awhile to heave unconscious breath,
Yet wake to wrestle with the dread of death,

---

612 ⟨And his red cheek resumed a gentle hue⟩ ⟨Whose meaning ? / told to him⟩ L
615 all] ⟨each⟩ L   619 relieves . . . yon] ⟨relieved⟩ . . . that L   620 pulse]
⟨heart⟩ L   621 as . . . too black] ⟨all . . . too true⟩ L   622 dread] ⟨fear⟩ L
623 is] ⟨was⟩ L   629 courteous . . . approving] ⟨smiling . . . applauding⟩ L
635 working brain . . . wile] ⟨revenge . . . spoil⟩ L   637 And half-Existence melts
within a grave L   639 ⟨The common tomb⟩ L   640 Where ⟨strong and
weakness / helpless nakedness ?⟩ L   sunk] ⟨sink⟩ L   643 ⟨Then wake again to daily
dread of death⟩ L

And shun, though day but dawn on ills increased,
That sleep, the loveliest, since it dreams the least.   645

CANTO II

1.

Night wanes—the vapours round the mountains curl'd
Melt into morn, and Light awakes the world.
Man has another day to swell the past,
And lead him near to little, but his last;
But mighty Nature bounds as from her birth,   5
The sun is in the heavens, and life on earth;
Flowers in the valley, splendour in the beam,
Health on the gale, and freshness in the stream.
Immortal man! behold her glories shine,
And cry, exulting inly, 'they are thine!'   10
Gaze on, which yet thy gladdened eye may see,
A morrow comes when they are not for thee;
And grieve what may above thy senseless bier,
Nor earth nor sky will yield a single tear;
Nor cloud shall gather more, nor leaf shall fall,   15
Nor gale breathe forth one sigh for thee, for all;
But creeping things shall revel in their spoil,
And fit thy clay to fertilize the soil.

2.

'Tis morn—'tis noon—assembled in the hall,
The gathered chieftains come to Otho's call;   20
'Tis now the promised hour that must proclaim
The life or death of Lara's future fame;
When Ezzelin his charge may here unfold,
And whatsoe'er the tale, it must be told.

644–5 ⟨Why hugs the soul that chain of clogging flesh⟩ | ⟨Yet own? though trembling to
be thus released | That sleep is loveliest where he dreams the least⟩ L

Canto II
    1 Night wanes] ⟨This / 'Tis morn⟩ L   2 Melt into morn] ⟨Rolls darkness back⟩ L
3 ⟨Again the busy sons of toil⟩ L   4 near to little] ⟨nearer nothing⟩ L   5 mighty]
⟨glorious⟩ L   7 splendour] ⟨gladness⟩ L   9 ⟨Gaze while thou canst but while⟩ L
her] ⟨their⟩ L   14 sky will yield] ⟨heaven will send⟩ L   17 ⟨But even the worm
will ? above his spoil⟩ L   23 may] ⟨must / shall⟩ L

His faith was pledged, and Lara's promise given,   25
To meet it in the eye of man and heaven.
Why comes he not? Such truths to be divulged,
Methinks the accuser's rest is long indulged.

3.

The hour is past, and Lara too is there,
With self-confiding, coldly patient air;   30
Why comes not Ezzelin? The hour is past,
And murmurs rise, and Otho's brow's o'ercast.
'I know my friend! his faith I cannot fear,
If yet he be on earth, expect him here;
The roof that held him in the valley stands   35
Between my own and noble Lara's lands;
My halls from such a guest had honour gain'd,
Nor had Sir Ezzelin his host disdain'd,
But that some previous proof forbade his stay,
And urged him to prepare against to-day;   40
The word I pledged for his I pledge again,
Or will myself redeem his knighthood's stain.'

He ceased—and Lara answer'd, 'I am here
To lend at thy demand a listening ear;
To tales of evil from a stranger's tongue,   45
Whose words already might my heart have wrung,
But that I deem'd him scarcely less than mad,
Or, at the worst, a foe ignobly bad.
I know him not—but me it seems he knew
In lands where—but I must not trifle too: 50
Produce this babbler—or redeem the pledge;
Here in thy hold, and with thy falchion's edge.'
Proud Otho on the instant, reddening, threw
His glove on earth, and forth his sabre flew.

25 Lara's promise given] ⟨Lara would do well⟩ L   26 it] ⟨him⟩ L   27 truths
. . . divulged] ⟨secrets undivulged⟩ L   29 Lara too] noble Lara's L   30 ⟨With
self-possession—yet impatient air⟩ L   32 brow's o'ercast] ⟨looks aghast⟩ L   37 from]
⟨with⟩ L   39 some previous proof] ⟨the ? he proclaims / some urgent⟩ L   41 The]
⟨My⟩ L   44 thy . . . listening] ⟨your . . . patient⟩ L   47 But that ⟨in sooth⟩
I deemed him ⟨mischieviously⟩ scarcely L   48 a foe ignobly] ⟨ridiculously⟩ L
50 lands where] ⟨other lands⟩ L   53 on the instant] in a moment L   54 glove
on earth] cloak aside L

'The last alternative befits me best,   55
And thus I answer for mine absent guest.'
With cheek unchanging from its sallow gloom,
However near his own or other's tomb;
With hand, whose almost careless coolness spoke,
Its grasp well-used to deal the sabre-stroke;   60
With eye, though calm, determined not to spare,
Did Lara too his willing weapon bare.
In vain the circling chieftains round them closed,
For Otho's phrenzy would not be opposed;
And from his lip those words of insult fell—   65
His sword is good who can maintain them well.

4.

Short was the conflict; furious, blindly rash,
Vain Otho gave his bosom to the gash:
He bled, and fell; but not with deadly wound,
Stretched by a dextrous sleight along the ground.   70
'Demand thy life!' He answered not: and then
From that red floor he ne'er had risen again,
For Lara's brow upon the moment grew
Almost to blackness in its demon hue;
And fiercer shook his angry falchion now   75
Than when his foe's was levelled at his brow;
Then all was stern collectedness and art,
Now rose the unleavened hatred of his heart;
So little sparing to the foe he fell'd,
That when the approaching crowd his arm withheld,   80
He almost turned the thirsty point on those
Who thus for mercy dared to interpose;
But to a moment's thought that purpose bent,
Yet look'd he on him still with eye intent,

55 befits] ⟨not suits⟩ L   58 ⟨Stalked Lara / And hand that trembled not⟩ L
60 well-used to] ⟨accustomed to⟩ L   67 conflict; *1815*, L(*5a*), *1831*, *1832*, C, *More*
conflict, L(*1*)–L(*5*)   blindly] ⟨blind and⟩ L   69 deadly wound] ⟨mortal blows⟩ L
70 Stretched . . . along] ⟨Borne . . . upon⟩ L   73 upon the moment] ⟨almost to black-
ness⟩ upon the instant   75 ⟨And shot like lightning his ? on high⟩ L   angry]
vengeful L   76 Than] Then L(*1*)   78 ⟨But / Now all was hate from his un-
sparing heart⟩ L   79 ⟨And burned to smite a foe already felled⟩ L   80 That]
⟨But⟩ And L   81 thirsty . . . those] ⟨point on him around⟩ L   83 to] ⟨with⟩ L
84 him still] his foe L

As if he loathed the ineffectual strife   85
That left a foe, howe'er o'erthrown, with life;
As if to search how far the wound he gave
Had sent its victim onward to his grave.

5.

They raised the bleeding Otho, and the Leech
Forbade all present question, sign, and speech;   90
The others met within a neighbouring hall,
And he, incensed and heedless of them all,
The cause and conqueror in this sudden fray,
In haughty silence slowly strode away;
He back'd his steed, his homeward path he took,   95
Nor cast on Otho's towers a single look.

6.

But where was he? that meteor of a night,
Who menaced but to disappear with light?
Where was this Ezzelin? who came and went
To leave no other trace of his intent.   100
He left the dome of Otho long ere morn,
In darkness, yet so well the path was worn
He could not miss it; near his dwelling lay;
But there he was not, and with coming day
Came fast enquiry, which unfolded nought   105
Except the absence of the chief it sought.
A chamber tenantless, a steed at rest,
His host alarmed, his murmuring squires distressed:
Their search extends along, around the path,
In dread to meet the marks of prowlers' wrath: 110
But none are there, and not a brake hath borne
Nor gout of blood, nor shred of mantle torn;
Nor fall nor struggle hath defaced the grass,

---

85 loathed] ⟨scorned⟩ L   86 That] ⟨And⟩ L   88 victim onward] ⟨vanquished
victim⟩ L   92 ⟨And Lara⟩ And he less calm—yet calmer than them all L   93 fray]
⟨broil⟩ L   94 ⟨Now tried / Without a word⟩ L   strode] ⟨stalked⟩ L   95 back'd]
⟨mounts⟩ L   97 he] ⟨Ezzelin⟩ L   101 dome] hall L   105 ⟨Came vain
Enquiry—which discovered there⟩ L   106 ⟨His steed, his ?⟩ More than the absence L
107–8 ⟨His steed was there all ready but at rest | His squires around—but eager and distrest⟩ L
108 ⟨His squires alarmed—and anxious host distrest⟩ L   110 ⟨In dread of signs of
blood / ill and mighty wrath⟩ L   112 ⟨Nor ? blood-drops / blood—nor garments⟩ L
113 ⟨No ? / fall is on / ? of heavy / rolling⟩ L

Which still retains a mark where murder was;
Nor dabbling fingers left to tell the tale,   115
The bitter print of each convulsive nail,
When agonized hands that cease to guard,
Wound in that pang the smoothness of the sward.
Some such had been, if here a life was reft,
But these were not; and doubting hope is left;   120
And strange suspicion whispering Lara's name,
Now daily mutters o'er his blackened fame;
Then sudden silent when his form appeared,
Awaits the absence of the thing it feared
Again its wonted wondering to renew,   125
And dye conjecture with a darker hue.

7.

Days roll along, and Otho's wounds are healed,
But not his pride; and hate no more concealed:
He was a man of power, and Lara's foe,
The friend of all who sought to work him woe,   130
And from his country's justice now demands
Account of Ezzelin at Lara's hands.
Who else than Lara could have cause to fear
His presence? who had made him disappear,
If not the man on whom his menaced charge   135
Had sate too deeply were he left at large?
The general rumour ignorantly loud,
The mystery dearest to the curious crowd;
The seeming friendlessness of him who strove
To win no confidence, and wake no love;   140
The sweeping fierceness which his soul betray'd,
The skill with which he wielded his keen blade;
Where had his arm unwarlike caught that art?
Where had that fierceness grown upon his heart?
For it was not the blind capricious rage   145
A word can kindle and a word assuage;

114 still retains] ⟨ever sees⟩ L   115 Nor dabbling ⟨hands were⟩ / fingers ⟨convulsively
hath⟩ tell L   116 each] ⟨its⟩ L   117 When . . . cease to] ⟨With . . . cannot⟩ L
119 Some such] ⟨All these⟩ L   122 ⟨And daily mutters oer his darkening fame⟩ L
124 Awaits] ⟨To wait⟩ L   126 conjecture] ⟨its guessings⟩ L   130 him] ⟨all⟩ L
132 at] ⟨from⟩ L   139 seeming friendlessness] haughty ⟨kindness⟩ friendlessness L
141 ⟨The savage fierceness of his spirit⟩ L   142 ⟨And the cool art with⟩ L   145 blind
capricious] ⟨wrath⟩ / blind and headlong L

But the deep working of a soul unmix'd
With aught of pity where its wrath had fix'd;
Such as long power and overgorged success
Concentrates into all that's merciless: 150
These, link'd with that desire which ever sways
Mankind, the rather to condemn than praise,
'Gainst Lara gathering raised at length a storm,
Such as himself might fear, and foes would form,
And he must answer for the absent head   155
Of one that haunts him still, alive or dead.

                              8.

Within that land was many a malcontent,
Who cursed the tyranny to which he bent;
That soil full many a wringing despot saw,
Who worked his wantonness in form of law;   160
Long war without and frequent broil within
Had made a path for blood and giant sin,
That waited but a signal to begin
New havock, such as civil discord blends,
Which knows no neuter, owns but foes or friends;   165
Fixed in his feudal fortress each was lord,
In word and deed obeyed, in soul abhorr'd.
Thus Lara had inherited his lands,
And with them pining hearts and sluggish hands;
But that long absence from his native clime   170
Had left him stainless of oppression's crime,
And now diverted by his milder sway,
All dread by slow degrees had worn away;
The menials felt their usual awe alone,
But more for him than them that fear was grown;   175
They deem'd him now unhappy, though at first
Their evil judgment augured of the worst,

147 soul ⟨which Power⟩ L   148 aught of pity] ⟨other feelings⟩ L   151 ⟨All
these and⟩ L   152 ⟨The human spirit to condemn / crush⟩ L   158 ⟨Who
to the law⟩ L   160 Who ⟨governed⟩ L   161 Long war ⟨and frequent
tumult⟩ L   163 waited but] ⟨only waited⟩ L   164 New ⟨death or⟩ havoc L
165 knows no neuter] ⟨owns no neutral⟩ L   166 ⟨Each⟩ Fixed L   167 soul]
⟨hearts⟩ L   168 Thus] So L   172–9 added in margin in MS. L
172 The first impressions of his milder sway L   173 All] Of L   176 now]
but L

And each long restless night and silent mood
Was traced to sickness, fed by solitude;
And though his lonely habits threw of late   180
Gloom o'er his chamber, cheerful was his gate;
For thence the wretched ne'er unsoothed withdrew,
For them, at least, his soul compassion knew.
Cold to the great, contemptuous to the high,
The humble passed not his unheeding eye;   185
Much he would speak not, but beneath his roof
They found asylum oft, and ne'er reproof.
And they who watched might mark that day by day,
Some new retainers gathered to his sway;
But most of late since Ezzelin was lost   190
He played the courteous lord and bounteous host.
Perchance his strife with Otho made him dread
Some snare prepared for his obnoxious head;
Whate'er his view, his favour more obtains
With these, the people, than his fellow thanes.   195
If this were policy, so far 'twas sound,
The million judged but of him as they found;
From him by sterner chiefs to exile driven
They but required a shelter, and 'twas given.
By him no peasant mourn'd his rifled cot,   200
And scarce the Serf could murmur o'er his lot;
With him old avarice found its hoard secure,
With him contempt forbore to mock the poor;
Youth present cheer and promised recompence
Detained, till all too late to part from thence: 205
To hate he offered with the coming change
The deep reversion of delayed revenge;
To love, long baffled by the unequal match,
The well-won charms success was sure to snatch.

178 silent] ⟨guilty⟩ L   179 Was . . . to] Seemed mortal L   180 his . . . of] ⟨his
habits of seclusion⟩ L   181 Mysterious gloom around his hall and gate L   182 For
. . . unsoothed] Yet . . . ⟨unfed⟩ L   184 ⟨Stern to the mighty—careless to the high⟩ L
185 ⟨He passed not⟩ L   186 ⟨To them voice⟩ L   187 asylum] ⟨a shelter⟩ L
191 bounteous] ⟨gentle⟩ L   192–5 added in margin in MS. L   192–3 ⟨His hate /
strife / struggle left him with his fellow thanes | No hope but death or ignominious chains⟩ L
193 prepared] ⟨directed⟩ L   196 ⟨And whether this was policy⟩ L   so far] at least L
198 From him by] ⟨With him from⟩ L   199 They ⟨found⟩ but L   201 o'er] at L
202 old] ⟨his⟩ L   203 ⟨And hate its promised vengeance could allure⟩ L   204 cheer]
joy L   205 ⟨Forbade to part in⟩ L   209 The Beauty which the first success
might snatch L

All now was ripe, he waits but to proclaim   210
That slavery nothing which was still a name.
The moment came, the hour when Otho thought
Secure at last the vengeance which he sought:
His summons found the destined criminal
Begirt by thousands in his swarming hall,   215
Fresh from their feudal fetters newly riven,
Defying earth, and confident of heaven.
That morning he had freed the soil-bound slaves
Who dig no land for tyrants but their graves!
Such is their cry—some watchword for the fight   220
Must vindicate the wrong, and warp the right:
Religion—freedom—vengeance—what you will,
A word's enough to raise mankind to kill;
Some factious phrase by cunning caught and spread
That guilt may reign, and wolves and worms be fed!   225

9.

Throughout that clime the feudal chiefs had gain'd
Such sway, their infant monarch hardly reign'd;
Now was the hour for faction's rebel growth,
The Serfs contemn'd the one, and hated both:
They waited but a leader, and they found   230
One to their cause inseparably bound;
By circumstance compell'd to plunge again
In self-defence amidst the strife of men.
Cut off by some mysterious fate from those
Whom birth and nature meant not for his foes,   235
Had Lara from that night, to him accurst,
Prepared to meet, but not alone, the worst:
Some reason urged, whate'er it was, to shun
Enquiry into deeds at distance done;
By mingling with his own the cause of all,   240
E'en if he failed, he still delayed his fall.

213 Secure] Secured L   215 in] ⟨round⟩ L   216 their ⟨chains⟩ feudal L
220 some . . . fight] ⟨gives notice of the fight⟩ L   221 ⟨Religion—freedom—plunder
—all is right⟩ L   warp] ⟨blind⟩ L   222 ⟨'Tis but a watchword rightly / wisely
raised and spread⟩ L   223 ⟨And nations fled that vultures⟩ ⟨That Kings may reign and
vultures / worms and wolves be fed⟩ L   226 clime . . . gain'd] land the feudal ⟨lords all
were⟩ / chiefs ⟨all were⟩ L   228 rebel] giant L   234 mysterious] strange L
236 that ⟨fatal⟩ night L   239 Too close enquiry into deeds long done L   241 ⟨'Twas
some revenge that more / that now those ? would fall⟩ L

The sullen calm that long his bosom kept,
The storm that once had spent itself and slept,
Roused by events that seemed foredoom'd to urge
His gloomy fortunes to their utmost verge,   245
Burst forth, and made him all he once had been,
And is again; he only changed the scene.
Light care had he for life, and less for fame,
But not less fitted for the desperate game:
He deem'd himself mark'd out for other's hate,   250
And mock'd at ruin so they shared his fate.
What cared he for the freedom of the crowd?
He raised the humble but to bend the proud.
He had hoped quiet in his sullen lair,
But man and destiny beset him there: 255
Inured to hunters he was found at bay,
And they must kill, they cannot snare the prey.
Stern, unambitious, silent, he had been
Henceforth a calm spectator of life's scene;
But dragg'd again upon the arena, stood   260
A leader not unequal to the feud;
In voice—mien—gesture—savage nature spoke,
And from his eye the gladiator broke.

                            10.

What boots the oft-repeated tale of strife,
The feast of vultures, and the waste of life?   265
The varying fortune of each separate field,
The fierce that vanquish, and the faint that yield?
The smoking ruin, and the crumbled wall?
In this the struggle was the same with all;
Save that distempered passions lent their force   270
In bitterness that banished all remorse.

244–5 ⟨Roused by events that seemed to fix his fate | And mark him out an object of man's hate⟩ L   244 ⟨Burst forth⟩ L   245 fortunes to their] ⟨fortune to its⟩ L
247 And . . . he] And now must be—and L   250 himself mark'd out] ⟨him marked once more⟩ L   252–63 not in L   254 sullen lair] lonely ⟨house⟩ lair LA
255 And ⟨he was hunted thence⟩ man and ⟨fate⟩ destiny LA   258 ⟨Strife was almost / If left perchance he had been harmless⟩ LA   silent] kindly LA   259 Henceforth] Perchance LA   260 arena, stood ⟨Arena's floor⟩ LA   261 ⟨Flashed the Gladiator from his conscious eye⟩ LA; ⟨fiery⟩ leader not unskilled in fight or feud LA
262 ⟨In eye and gesture / Full from his eye⟩ In gesture—eye—the whole Gladiator spoke LA
263 ⟨A ? —a hand to stand the stroke· LA, which has no uncancelled version of 263
268 ⟨In this the struggle was the same with all L   crumbled] lonely L

None sued, for Mercy knew her cry was vain,
The captive died upon the battle-slain:
In either cause one rage alone possessed
The empire of the alternate victor's breast;   275
And they that smote for freedom or for sway
Deem'd few were slain, while more remain'd to slay.
It was too late to check the wasting brand,
And Desolation reaped the famished land;
The torch was lighted, and the flame was spread,   280
And Carnage smiled upon her daily dead.

11.

Fresh with the nerve the new-born impulse strung,
The first success to Lara's numbers clung;
But that vain victory hath ruined all,
They form no longer to their leader's call;   285
In blind confusion on the foe they press,
And think to snatch is to secure success.
The lust of booty, and the thirst of hate
Lure on the broken brigands to their fate;
In vain he doth whate'er a chief may do   290
To check the headlong fury of that crew;
In vain their stubborn ardour he would tame,
The hand that kindles cannot quench the flame;
The wary foe alone hath turn'd their mood,
And shown their rashness to that erring brood: 295
The feign'd retreat, the nightly ambuscade,
The daily harass, and the fight delayed,
The long privation of the hoped supply,
The tentless rest beneath the humid sky,
The stubborn wall that mocks the leaguer's art,   300
And palls the patience of his baffled heart,
Of these they had not deem'd: the battle-day
They could encounter as a veteran may;

272 ⟨The / No captive / The conquered wore the ? / No dungeon echoed to the clanking chain⟩ L   274 In either cause] ⟨One fiery spirit,⟩ L   276 or for ⟨power⟩ L
279 reaped] ⟨rode⟩ L   281 Carnage] ⟨Discord⟩ L   282 Fresh with] ⟨Borne by⟩ L
284 victory . . . all] ⟨triumph was the last and first⟩ L   285 form] ⟨list⟩ L
287 snatch] win L   288 lust] ⟨thirst⟩ L   289 broken ⟨ranks⟩ L   290 may]
⟨can⟩ L   291 that] the L   302 Of] ⟨To⟩ On L   303 veteran] ⟨hero⟩ L

But more preferred the fury of the strife,
And present death to hourly suffering life: 305
And famine wrings, and fever sweeps away
His numbers melting fast from their array;
Intemperate triumph fades to discontent,
And Lara's soul alone seems still unbent:
But few remain to aid his voice and hand,   310
And thousands dwindled to a scanty band:
Desperate, though few, the last and best remain'd
To mourn the discipline they late disdain'd.
One hope survives, the frontier is not far,
And thence they may escape from native war;   315
And bear within them to the neighbouring state
An exile's sorrows, or an outlaw's hate:
Hard is the task their father land to quit,
But harder still to perish or submit.

12.

It is resolved—they march—consenting Night   320
Guides with her star their dim and torchless flight;
Already they perceive its tranquil beam
Sleep on the surface of the barrier stream;
Already they descry—Is yon the bank?
Away! 'tis lined with many a hostile rank.   325
Return or fly!—What glitters in the rear?
'Tis Otho's banner—the pursuer's spear!
Are those the shepherds' fires upon the height?
Alas! they blaze too widely for the flight:
Cut off from hope, and compass'd in the toil,   330
Less blood perchance hath bought a richer spoil!

13.

A moment's pause, 'tis but to breathe their band,
Or shall they onward press, or here withstand?

304 ⟨But not endure the long post-martial strife⟩ L   fury] terror L   305 And . . .
to] ⟨But . . . than⟩ L   307 His numbers now declining day by day L   310 aid]
⟨own⟩ L   314 One] ⟨But⟩ L   316 bear within] ⟨carry with⟩ L   317 sorrows]
yearnings L, *alternate reading*   318 ⟨Another country may⟩ L   their father land]
⟨that mountain land⟩ L   320 consenting] and dusky L   321 dim] ⟨quick⟩ L
322 its] ⟨her⟩ L   323 on] ⟨in⟩ L   324 Is yon] ⟨the / its / her / is that⟩ L
326 Return] ⟨Turn⟩ L   327 the pursuer's] ⟨and the lifted⟩ L   332 pause] halt L
333 here withstand] ⟨take their stand⟩ L

It matters little—if they charge the foes
Who by the border-stream their march oppose,   335
Some few, perchance, may break and pass the line,
However link'd to baffle such design.
'The charge be ours! to wait for their assault
Were fate well worthy of a coward's halt.'
Forth flies each sabre, reined is every steed,   340
And the next word shall scarce outstrip the deed:
In the next tone of Lara's gathering breath
How many shall but hear the voice of death!

14.

His blade is bared, in him there is an air
As deep, but far too tranquil for despair;   345
A something of indifference more than then
Becomes the bravest if they feel for men—
He turned his eye on Kaled, ever near,
And still too faithful to betray one fear;
Perchance 'twas but the moon's dim twilight threw   350
Along his aspect an unwonted hue
Of mournful paleness, whose deep tint expressed
The truth, and not the terror of his breast.
This Lara mark'd, and laid his hand on his:
It trembled not in such an hour as this;   355
His lip was silent, scarcely beat his heart,
His eye alone proclaim'd, 'We will not part!
Thy band may perish, or thy friends may flee,
Farewell to life, but not adieu to thee!'

The word hath pass'd his lips, and onward driven   360
Pours the link'd band through ranks asunder riven;
Well has each steed obeyed the armed heel,
And flash the scimitars, and rings the steel;

---

335 border] barrier *L*   337 link'd] drawn out *L*   338 assault] ⟨attack⟩ *L*
339 ⟨Were neer the ? on returning back / Were fate ? and active craven's fault⟩ *L*
342 In . . . gathering breath] ⟨On . . . lip awaits⟩ *L*   343 ⟨His own—tis nothing—
but his fellows' fates⟩ *L*   344 blade is bared] sword is raised *L*   348 ⟨He
looked around and⟩ *L*   350 moon's dim twilight] ⟨moonbeam's paleness⟩ *L*   353 and]
but *L*   357 ⟨But his eye only⟩ *L*   360 The word has passed his lips— ⟨the charge
is made⟩ *L*   361 ⟨The shock⟩ *L*

Outnumber'd not outbrav'd, they still oppose
Despair to daring, and a front to foes;   365
And blood is mingled with the dashing stream,
Which runs all redly till the morning beam.

15.

Commanding, aiding, animating all,
Where foe appeared to press, or friend to fall,
Cheers Lara's voice, and waves or strikes his steel,   370
Inspiring hope, himself had ceased to feel.
None fled, for well they knew that flight were vain,
But those that waver turn to smite again
While yet they find the firmest of the foe
Recoil before their leader's look and blow;   375
Now girt with numbers, now almost alone,
He foils their ranks, or reunites his own;
Himself he spared not—once they seemed to fly—
Now was the time, he waved his hand on high,
And shook—why sudden droops that plumed crest?   380
The shaft is sped—the arrow's in his breast!
That fatal gesture left the unguarded side,
And Death hath stricken down yon arm of pride.
The word of triumph fainted from his tongue;
That hand, so raised, how droopingly it hung!   385
But yet the sword instinctively retains,
Though from its fellow shrink the falling reins;
These Kaled snatches: dizzy with the blow,
And senseless bending o'er his saddle-bow,
Perceives not Lara that his anxious page   390
Beguiles his charger from the combat's rage:
Meantime his followers charge, and charge again;
Too mix'd the slayers now to heed the slain!

364 ⟨Now wheeling⟩ L   they still oppose] ⟨? them close / they long oppose⟩ L
367 ⟨Nor ceased⟩ And raged the rivulet till the morning beam L   368–93 not in L
369 ⟨While foe ?⟩ LA   370 ⟨His voice cheers / cheered on⟩ LA   371 ⟨And yet
inspires the hope⟩ LA   373 those . . . turn] they that wavered turned LA   374 find
the firmest] found the fiercest LA   376 now] then LA   377 To break their
ranks or reunite his own LA   378 once ⟨the victory⟩ they LA   380 And shook
his plumed head ⟨and raised his voice⟩—why bends that crest LA   383 yon] ⟨that⟩ LA
384–5 not in LA   386 But yet it grasps the sword— ⟨but not remains⟩ instinctively
retains LA   387 ⟨Within the fallen hand⟩ LA   389 senseless bending] bending
senseless LA   391 combat's] ⟨battle's⟩ LA   393 ⟨And all is tumult⟩ LA

16.

Day glimmers on the dying and the dead,
The cloven cuirass, and the helmless head;   395
The war-horse masterless is on the earth,
And that last gasp hath burst his bloody girth;
And near yet quivering with what life remain'd,
The heel that urg'd him and the hand that rein'd;
And some too near that rolling torrent lie,   400
Whose waters mock the lip of those that die;
That panting thirst which scorches in the breath
Of those that die the soldier's fiery death,
In vain impels the burning mouth to crave
One drop—the last—to cool it for the grave;   405
With feeble and convulsive effort swept
Their limbs along the crimson'd turf have crept;
The faint remains of life such struggles waste,
But yet they reach the stream, and bend to taste:
They feel its freshness, and almost partake—   410
Why pause?— No further thirst have they to slake—
It is unquench'd, and yet they feel it not;
It was an agony—but now forgot!

17.

Beneath a lime, remoter from the scene,
Where but for him that strife had never been,   415
A breathing but devoted warrior lay:
'Twas Lara bleeding fast from life away.
His follower once, and now his only guide,
Kneels Kaled watchful o'er his welling side,
And with his scarf would staunch the tides that rush   420
With each convulsion in a blacker gush;

---

394 glimmers] ⟨lours⟩ *L*   396 The stiffening steed is on the dinted earth *L*
397 that] ⟨his⟩ *L*   398 ⟨Beneath his⟩ *L*   quivering] ⟨fluttering⟩ *L*   400 rolling
torrent] glassy river *L*   401 waters mock] water mocks *L*   402 which . . .
breath] ⟨that heats / fires the parting⟩ breath *L*   403 soldier's fiery] warrior's
struggling *L*   404 mouth] lip *L*   408 faint . . . such] last . . . ⟨that⟩ *L*
409 yet . . . bend to] still . . . ⟨weakly⟩ *L*   414 lime . . . the] ⟨brake that overhangs
the⟩ *L*   415 ⟨Where that tempestuous⟩ *L*   416 breathing but devoted] ⟨breath-
less but a bleeding⟩ *L*   419 watchful] watching *L*   421 blacker] ⟨deeper /
gathering⟩ *L*

And then as his faint breathing waxes low,
In feebler, not less fatal tricklings flow:
He scarce can speak, but motions him—'tis vain,
And merely adds another throb to pain.   425
He clasps the hand that pang which would assuage,
And sadly smiles his thanks to that dark page
Who nothing fears, nor feels, nor heeds, nor sees,
Save that damp brow which rests upon his knees;
Save that pale aspect, where the eye, though dim,   430
Held all the light that shone on earth for him.

18.

The foe arrives, who long had search'd the field,
Their triumph nought till Lara too should yield;
They would remove him, but they see 'twere vain,
And he regards them with a calm disdain,   435
That rose to reconcile him with his fate,
And that escape to death from living hate:
And Otho comes, and leaping from his steed,
Looks on the bleeding foe that made him bleed,
And questions of his state; he answers not,   440
Scarce glances on him as on one forgot,
And turns to Kaled:—each remaining word,
They understood not, if distinctly heard;
His dying tones are in that other tongue,
To which some strange remembrance wildly clung.   445
They spake of other scenes, but what—is known
To Kaled, whom their meaning reach'd alone;
And he replied, though faintly, to their sound,
While gaz'd the rest in dumb amazement round:
They seem'd even then—that twain—unto the last   450
To half forget the present in the past;
To share between themselves some separate fate,
Whose darkness none beside should penetrate.

---

424 him—'tis] him 'tis *all edns.*   425 And ⟨but augments⟩ *L*   427 sadly] feebly *L*
429 damp . . . which] cold . . . that *L*   431 shone on earth] ⟨earth but held⟩ *L*
432 who long had] ⟨for him they⟩ *L*   433 nought ⟨were⟩ till *L*   436 ⟨That
seemed victorious oer his⟩ *L*   441 Scarce . . . on] ⟨But gazed upon⟩ Just gazes on *L*
443 if] though *L*   444 are] were *L*   445 wildly] fondly *L*   447 reach'd]
⟨sought⟩ *L*   450 that . . . last] ⟨to stand aloof—alone⟩ *L*   451 ⟨To lose⟩ *L*
452 To share ⟨some world⟩ between *L*   453 ⟨Then none were there alive should⟩ *L*
darkness] mystery *L*

LARA.

HE SCARCE CAN SPEAK, BUT MOTIONS HIM 'TIS VAIN,

AND MERELY ADDS ANOTHER THROB TO PAIN.

PUBLISHED BY JOHN MURRAY, ALBEMARLE STREET, DEC.ᴿ 1,1814.

Lara Canto II lines 424–5

19.

Their words though faint were many—from the tone
Their import those who heard could judge alone;   455
From this, you might have deem'd young Kaled's death
More near than Lara's by his voice and breath,
So sad, so deep, and hesitating broke
The accents his scarce-moving pale lips spoke;
But Lara's voice though low, at first was clear   460
And calm, till murmuring death gasp'd hoarsely near:
But from his visage little could we guess,
So unrepentant, dark, and passionless,
Save that when struggling nearer to his last,
Upon that page his eye was kindly cast;   465
And once as Kaled's answering accents ceas'd,
Rose Lara's hand, and pointed to the East:
Whether (as then the breaking sun from high
Roll'd back the clouds) the morrow caught his eye,
Or that 'twas chance, or some remember'd scene   470
That rais'd his arm to point where such had been,
Scarce Kaled seem'd to know, but turn'd away,
As if his heart abhorred that coming day,
And shrunk his glance before that morning light
To look on Lara's brow—where all grew night.   475
Yet sense seem'd left, though better were its loss;
For when one near display'd the absolving cross,
And proffered to his touch the holy bead
Of which his parting soul might own the need,
He look'd upon it with an eye profane,   480
And smiled—Heaven pardon! if 'twere with disdain;
And Kaled though he spoke not, nor withdrew
From Lara's face his fix'd despairing view,
With brow repulsive, and with gesture swift,
Flung back the hand which held the sacred gift,   485

454–89 *not in* L   455 who] that *LA*   456–7 From it you might have deemed
⟨that Kaled's breath | And voice were weakened by the approach of death⟩ *LA*   459 pale]
white *M*   461 gasp'd] drew *LA*   462 ⟨In / On⟩ From Lara's aspect little could ⟨be
said⟩ one / we guess *LA*   463 ⟨Twas pale but passionless⟩ *LA*   dark] pale *LA, M*
464 struggling] breathing *LA*   465 that . . . was] ⟨his . . . more⟩ *LA*   466 answering]
trembling *LA*   468 ⟨Just then / as the yellow Sun began⟩ *LA*   breaking . . . high]
⟨Morn along the sky⟩ *LA*   472 ⟨We know not⟩ *LA*   473 that] this *LA*   474 And
shrunk . . . before] ⟨Nor turned . . . upon / unto⟩ *LA*   476 His sense seemed perfect—
better were its loss *LA*   484 ⟨Yet motioned with his hand / with his hand's impatient
gesture⟩ ⟨With a regardless⟩ *LA*   485 Warned thence the heaven of that sacred gift *LA*

As if such but disturbed the expiring man,
Nor seem'd to know his life but *then* began,
That life of Immortality, secure
To none, save them whose faith in Christ is sure!

20.

But gasping heav'd the breath that Lara drew,   490
And dull the film along his dim eye grew;
His limbs stretch'd fluttering and his head droop'd
   o'er
The weak yet still untiring knee that bore;
He press'd the hand he held upon his heart—
It beats no more, but Kaled will not part   495
With the cold grasp, but feels, and feels in vain,
For that faint throb which answers not again.
'It beats!'—Away, thou dreamer! he is gone—
It once was Lara which thou look'st upon.

21.

He gaz'd, as if not yet had pass'd away   500
The haughty spirit of that humble clay;
And those around have rous'd him from his trance,
But cannot tear from thence his fixed glance;
And when in raising him from where he bore
Within his arms the form that felt no more,   505
He saw the head his breast would still sustain,
Roll down like earth to earth upon the plain;
He did not dash himself thereby, nor tear
The glossy tendrils of his raven hair,
But strove to stand and gaze, but reel'd and fell,   510
Scarce breathing more than that he lov'd so well.
Than that *he* lov'd! Oh! never yet beneath
The breast of man such trusty love may breathe!

487 ⟨And⟩ Nor knew ⟨not⟩ he that his life but ⟨just⟩ there began *LA*   488–9 ⟨That⟩
life immortal ⟨glorious and secure⟩ infinite and sure | To all ⟨that⟩ whose faith the eternal
born secure. *LA*   That life immortal, infinite, secure, | To all for whom that cross hath
made it sure! *L(1)–L(4b)*   490–1 But faint the dying Lara's accents grew— | And
⟨duller every glance⟩ dull . . . eye drew *L*   492 head ⟨reclined⟩ *L*   493 The weak]
⟨With heavier⟩ The strained *L*   495 will] ⟨doth⟩ *L*   496 the cold . . . and feels]
⟨that faint . . . alas⟩ *L*   497 which] that *L*   500–1 He gazed—as doubtful—
⟨and expecting⟩ that the thing he saw | Had something more to ask from love or awe *L*
502 And] ⟨But⟩ *L*   506 breast] ⟨yet / gladly⟩ *L*   509 tendrils] honours *L*
510 reel'd] ⟨tottered⟩ *L*   511 breathing] ⟨living⟩ *L*

That trying moment hath at once reveal'd
The secret long and yet but half-conceal'd;   515
In baring to revive that lifeless breast,
Its grief seem'd ended, but the sex confest;
And life return'd, and Kaled felt no shame—
What now to her was Womanhood or Fame?

22.

And Lara sleeps not where his fathers sleep.   520
But where he died his grave was dug as deep;
Nor is his mortal slumber less profound,
Though priest nor bless'd, nor marble deck'd the
        mound;
And he was mourn'd by one whose quiet grief
Less loud, outlasts a people's for their chief.   525
Vain was all question ask'd her of the past,
And vain e'en menace—silent to the last;
She told nor whence nor why she left behind
Her all for one who seem'd but little kind.
Why did she love him? Curious fool!—be still—   530
Is human love the growth of human will?
To her he might be gentleness; the stern
Have deeper thoughts than your dull eyes discern,
And when they love, your smilers guess not how
Beats the strong heart, though less the lips avow.   535
They were not common links that form'd the chain
That bound to Lara Kaled's heart and brain;
But that wild tale she brook'd not to unfold,
And seal'd is now each lip that could have told.

23.

They laid him in the earth, and on his breast,   540
Besides the wound that sent his soul to rest,
They found the scatter'd dints of many a scar
Which were not planted there in recent war;
Where'er had pass'd his summer years of life
It seems they vanish'd in a land of strife;   545

515 half] ⟨ill⟩ L   517 Its . . . the] ⟨His⟩ . . . its L   518 and] yet L
522 ⟨And he was mourned by one whose⟩ L   523 ⟨Because of Priest nor marble⟩ L
526 was] ⟨were⟩ L   531 human love] ⟨wayward love⟩ L   534 guess] ⟨know⟩ L
536 form'd] ⟨bound⟩ L   537 and brain] in vain L   539 seal'd] ⟨cold⟩ L

But all unknown his glory or his guilt,
These only told that somewhere blood was spilt,
And Ezzelin, who might have spoke the past,
Return'd no more—that night appear'd his last.

24.

Upon that night (a peasant's is the tale)   550
A Serf that cross'd the intervening vale,
When Cynthia's light almost gave way to morn,
And nearly veil'd in mist her waning horn;
A Serf, that rose betimes to thread the wood,
And hew the bough that bought his children's food,   555
Pass'd by the river that divides the plain
Of Otho's lands and Lara's broad domain:
He heard a tramp—a horse and horseman broke
From out the wood—before him was a cloak
Wrapt round some burthen at his saddle-bow,   560
Bent was his head, and hidden was his brow.
Rous'd by the sudden sight at such a time,
And some foreboding that it might be crime,
Himself unheeded watch'd the stranger's course,
Who reach'd the river, bounded from his horse,   565
And lifting thence the burthen which he bore,
Heav'd up the bank, and dash'd it from the shore,
Then paused, and look'd, and turn'd, and seem'd to watch,
And still another hurried glance would snatch,
And follow with his step the stream that flow'd,   570
As if even yet too much its surface show'd:
At once he started, stoop'd, around him strown
The winter floods had scatter'd heaps of stone;
Of these the heaviest thence he gather'd there,
And slung them with a more than common care.   575
Meantime the Serf had crept to where unseen
Himself might safely mark what this might mean;

546–7 But all unknown the blood ⟨that he had⟩ he lost or spilt | ⟨He gained⟩ These only told his Glory or his Guilt— L   548 might . . . past] ⟨spoke but of the last⟩ L
551 crossed ⟨in moon⟩ the L   553 veil'd] ⟨hid⟩ L   554 thread] seek L
555 children's] ⟨daily⟩ L   557 broad] ⟨late⟩ L   558 He heard a tread— ⟨behold a horseman pass⟩ Wrapped oer L   559 was] seemed L   560 Wrapt round] ⟨Borne with⟩ Wrapped oer L   561 Bent . . . head] His head was bent L   564 stranger's ⟨way⟩ L   565 bounded] and bounded L   566 lifting ⟨from⟩ thence L
567 ⟨Checked the st⟩ L   569 hurried] anxious L   570–1 not in L   572 At once] ⟨Again⟩ L   573 ⟨Were many⟩ The winter floods had ⟨let fall many⟩ L   574 Of] ⟨And⟩ L

He caught a glimpse, as of a floating breast,
And something glittered starlike on the vest,
But ere he well could mark the buoyant trunk,   580
A massy fragment smote it, and it sunk:
It rose again but indistinct to view,
And left the waters of a purple hue,
Then deeply disappear'd: the horseman gaz'd
Till ebbed the latest eddy it had rais'd;   585
Then turning, vaulted on his pawing steed,
And instant spurr'd him into panting speed.
His face was mask'd—the features of the dead,
If dead it were, escaped the observer's dread;
But if in sooth a star its bosom bore,   590
Such is the badge that knighthood ever wore,
And such 'tis known Sir Ezzelin had worn
Upon the night that led to such a morn.
If thus he perish'd, Heaven receive his soul!
His undiscover'd limbs to ocean roll;   595
And charity upon the hope would dwell
It was not Lara's hand by which he fell.

25.

And Kaled—Lara—Ezzelin, are gone,
Alike without their monumental stone!
The first, all efforts vainly strove to wean   600
From lingering where her chieftain's blood had been;
Grief had so tam'd a spirit once too proud,
Her tears were few, her wailing never loud;
But furious would you tear her from the spot
Where yet she scarce believ'd that he was not,   605
Her eye shot forth with all the living fire
That haunts the tigress in her whelpless ire;
But left to waste her weary moments there,
She talk'd all idly unto shapes of air,

578 breast] ⟨vest⟩ L   580 ⟨But at the moment⟩ L   581 massy fragment]
weighty pebble L   582 but ⟨scarcely a moment⟩ indistinct L   583 purple]
redder L   584 deeply disappear'd] ⟨disappeared forever⟩ L   588 His . . . dead]
⟨His⟩ The . . . ⟨corse⟩ L   589 If ⟨corse⟩ it were escaped him in his dread L   590 ⟨But
if the heart a star⟩ L   594 If ⟨such his fate⟩ thus he perished ⟨saints pre⟩ Heaven L
597 ⟨That not ? but fair he fell⟩ L   599 Alike] ⟨The last⟩ All L   602 too ⟨high /
fond⟩ L   606 living] native L   607 haunts] ⟨lights⟩ L

Such as the busy brain of Sorrow paints,   610
And woos to listen to her fond complaints:
And she would sit beneath the very tree
Where lay his drooping head upon her knee;
And in that posture where she saw him fall,
His words, his looks, his dying grasp recall;   615
And she had shorn, but sav'd her raven hair,
And oft would snatch it from her bosom there,
And fold, and press it gently to the ground,
As if she staunch'd anew some phantom's wound.
Herself would question, and for him reply;   620
Then rising, start, and beckon him to fly
From some imagin'd spectre in pursuit;
Then seat her down upon some linden's root,
And hide her visage with her meagre hand,
Or trace strange characters along the sand—   625
This could not last—she lies by him she lov'd;
Her tale untold—her truth too dearly prov'd.

225a   Opening Lines to *Lara*

When she is gone—the loved—the lost—the one
Whose smile hath gladdened though perchance undone—
Whose name too dearly cherished to impart
Dies on the lip but trembles in the heart—
Whose sudden mention can almost convulse   5
And lightens through the ungovernable pulse—
Till the heart leaps so keenly to the word
We fear that throb can hardly beat unheard—
Then sinks at once beneath that sickly chill
That follows when we find her absent still—   10
When such is gone—too far again to bless—
Oh God—how slowly comes Forgetfulness—

613 drooping] ⟨dying⟩ L   616–19 *added in margin of* L   622 spectre] ⟨phantom⟩ L
626 by him ⟨who died⟩ L

225a. Copy text: *MS.* L, collated with *Murray's Magazine, Astarte*

1 When ⟨those are⟩ gone— ⟨when there—alas! tis none⟩ L   loved . . . lost] ⟨dear . . .
fair⟩ L   3 Whose name ⟨so dear⟩ L   5 sudden] ⟨very⟩ L   6 And ⟨speed /
fires to speed⟩ lightens L   7 so keenly] ⟨responsive⟩ L   8 that . . . hardly] ⟨its . . .
scarcely⟩ L   11 such is] ⟨thou art⟩ L

Let none complain how faithless and how brief
The brain's remembrance—or the bosom's grief—
Or e'er they thus forbid us to forget—   15
Let Mercy strip the memory of regret,—
Yet—selfish still—we would not be forgot—
What lip dare say—'My Love—remember not'—?
Oh best and dearest—Thou whose thrilling name
My heart adores too deeply to proclaim—   20
My memory almost ceasing to repine
Would mount to Hope if once secure of thine.—
Meantime the tale I weave must mournful be—
As absence to the heart that lives on thee.

                                                    [1814]

226   [The Art of Praise]

Dear are Eulogisms—when from truth they swerve;
How doubly sweet is praise we don't deserve.
Praise not Euphemia—that she's fair and chaste,
But would'st thou win attention—praise her taste.
Praise not Amelia for her gift of song   5
But tell her that she never talks too long—
But praise Contessa e'er she can begin
Or never hope to edge even flattery in.
Sit still and hear her try to talk her fill—
Impossible! what, hear her and sit still?   10
Then leave her—turn to Phyllida the tart,
And praise her innate gentleness of heart.

13 faithless] ⟨idle⟩ L   14 The ⟨mourner's memory⟩ —or the ⟨lover's⟩ grief— L
18 What lip] ⟨Oh who⟩ L   19 ⟨Azora dearest⟩ L   20 Thou ⟨to⟩ whose L
22 ⟨And⟩ Would L   24 lives on] ⟨pants for⟩ L

226. Copy text: MS. L

    1 ⟨Dear are eulogisms / ? the flattery which hath swerved from truth / Ah me how sweet
is praise when undeserved⟩ L   4 attention] ⟨her kindness⟩ L   7 ff. [B first wrote
here, then cancelled, received lines 19–20, and two further lines which are indecipherable.]
7 ⟨Praise not Contessa—listen and sit still / till she's talked her fill⟩ L   7–9 ⟨Praise not
Contessa till her tongue has done | But that's impossible— ? your own | Not even a compli-
ment⟩ L   7–8 But praise Contessa e'er ⟨her tongue's begun | Or all your opportunity
is gone⟩ L   9 ⟨Or best of all—in ? sit and hear⟩ L   10 what] ⟨to⟩ L   11 tart]
⟨smart⟩ L

8127553   K

Praise not Honoria's graces in the waltz
But modest mien, and freedom from all faults.
Praise not Armenia's eyes' most heavenly hue,   15
For know her stocking wears a deeper blue.
Swear by its colour—talk of tongues and books,
And never fear—her learning's in her looks!
Praise not Sir Bauble that his waistcoats fit—
But hear his anecdotes and laud his wit.   20
Praise not old Vates for his glorious rhymes,
Though formed to lighten through succeeding times;
But dwell upon his influence with the sex
How [many harden?] and his attentions vex;
How many wives, how many maids must lie   25
To that inhuman chin and deadly eye.—
Praise not—but all the power of praise is past
And only leaves the greatest and the last—
Praise not, he hates it, praise not mighty Guelph—
Thank and adore, and hear him praise himself.   30
The fall of France, the wondrous rise of Spain,
The speed of commerce, and the growth of grain,
To him are more—he swears, and Croker says,
And Southey sings in hymns of special praise.

[1814]

16 deeper] ⟨brighter⟩ L   20 laud] ⟨praise⟩ L   25 must lie] ⟨have been / are
froze⟩ L   26 chin and] ⟨countenance's⟩ L   33 swears] ⟨says⟩ L   34 ⟨That
wondrous man in ℓ praise⟩ L

227   Ode to Napoleon Buonaparte

Expende Annibalem:—quot libras in duce summo
Invenies?—   JUVENAL, *Sat.* X [147–8]

The Emperor Nepos was acknowledged by the *Senate*, by
the *Italians*, and by the Provincials of *Gaul*; his moral virtues,
and military talents, were loudly celebrated; and those who
derived any private benefit from his government, announced
in prophetic strains the restoration of public felicity.

   *   *   *   *   *   *   *   *   *   *
   *   *   *   *   *   *   *   *   *   *

By this shameful abdication, he protracted his life a few years,
in a very ambiguous state, between an Emperor and an Exile,
till ——————————
                         Gibbon's Decline and Fall, [chap. 36].

I.

'Tis done—but yesterday a King!
   And arm'd with Kings to strive—
And now thou art a nameless thing
   So abject—yet alive!
Is this the man of thousand thrones,   5
Who strew'd our Earth with hostile bones,
   And can he thus survive?
Since he, miscall'd the Morning Star,
Nor man nor fiend hath fall'n so far.

2.

Ill-minded man! why scourge thy kind   10
   Who bow'd so low the knee?
By gazing on thyself grown blind,
   Thou taught'st the rest to see.

---

227. Copy text: third edition for stanzas 1–16, *1832* for the 'Additional Stanzas'; collated
with *MSS. T, TA, M, L,* the Harrow Proofs, editions 1, 2, 4, 10, *1831, 1832, C, More*
title   Ode *T*
epigraphs   from Juvenal, added *Proof B*; from Gibbon, added *Proof A*

   1 done—but] done— ⟨the man / and thou⟩ but *T*   2 arm'd] ⟨fit⟩ *T*   4 abject]
⟨humbled⟩ *T*   6 our] the *T*   8 miscall'd] ⟨that shone⟩ that named *T*   10–11 ⟨Ill
minded man! with power to save | With / And satisfy thy / man-kind⟩ *TA*   10 ⟨Vain
man⟩ Ill minded man— ⟨to spare mankind⟩ / ⟨the⟩ scourge ⟨of thy⟩ thy kind *TA*
11 ⟨Who sought but peace from⟩ Who long had bowed the knee *TA*   12 ⟨Thy only
gift hath been the grave⟩ *TA*

With might unquestion'd,—power to save—
Thine only gift hath been the grave   15
  To those that worshipp'd thee;
Nor till thy fall could mortals guess
Ambition's less than littleness!

3.

Thanks for that lesson—it will teach
  To after-warriors more   20
Than high Philosophy can preach,
  And vainly preached before.
That spell upon the minds of men
Breaks never to unite again,
  That led them to adore   25
Those Pagod things of sabre-sway,
With fronts of brass, and feet of clay.

4.

The triumph, and the vanity,
  The rapture of the strife—
The earthquake voice of Victory,   30
  To thee the breath of life;
The sword, the sceptre, and that sway
Which man seem'd made but to obey,
  Wherewith renown was rife—
All quell'd!—Dark Spirit! what must be   35
The madness of thy memory!

5.

The Desolator desolate!
  The Victor overthrown!
The Arbiter of other's fate
  A Suppliant for his own!   40

14 might unquestion'd] ⟨thrones to prop⟩ might to shield—with *TA*   18 less than]
thorough *TA* ⟨thorough⟩ ⟨withering⟩ less than *Proof D*   20 after-warriors] after ages
TA   after-⟨monarchs⟩ warriors *Proof D*   21 high] ⟨high / vain⟩ *TA*   22 vainly]
idly *TA*   23 ⟨Thou God in sooth in every ?⟩ *TA*   24 Breaks . . . unite] Is
broken neer to close *TA*   25 led] taught *TA* ⟨taught⟩ led *Proof D*   26 Those
. . . of] Those ⟨things / pageant things that with the sword⟩ Pagod-things ⟨that⟩ of *TA*
28–9 ⟨The voice of flame and victory | To thee the breath of life⟩ *T*   29 rapture of]
⟨struggle and⟩ *T*   34 ⟨That name on earth⟩ *T*   35 Dark] ⟨proud⟩ *T*   37 ⟨So
pass the shadows of the great⟩ *TA*   39 other's] ⟨Europe's⟩ *TA*

Is it some yet imperial hope
That with such change can calmly cope?
　Or dread of death alone?
To die a prince—or live a slave—
Thy choice is most ignobly brave!　　　　　　45

6.

He who of old would rend the oak,
　Dreamed not of the rebound;
Chained by the trunk he vainly broke—
　Alone—how looked he round?
Thou in the sternness of thy strength　　　　50
An equal deed hast done at length,
　And darker fate hast found:
He fell, the forest-prowlers' prey;
But thou must eat thy heart away!

7.

The Roman, when his burning heart　　　　　55
　Was slaked with blood of Rome,
Threw down the dagger—dared depart,
　In savage grandeur, home.—
He dared depart in utter scorn
Of men that such a yoke had borne,　　　　　60
　Yet left him such a doom!
His only glory was that hour
Of self-upheld abandon'd power.

8.

The Spaniard, when the lust of sway
　Had lost its quickening spell,　　　　　　65

41 ⟨Or is it / With changes / Or is it from one lurking hope⟩ ⟨The ? —or brighter hope⟩ Is it some ⟨hid⟩ imperial hope *TA*　　　42 ⟨Alone / With change like this can cope⟩ That thus with change so rude can cope *TA*　　　43 ⟨Which most thy sin / soul hath shown⟩ Or Love of Life alone *TA*　　　44 ⟨Is dubious—yet the truly brave⟩ ⟨Whateer it be— the / it best becomes⟩ ⟨Perchance it more / best becomes the brave⟩ Thou mightst have died a Prince—tis brave *TA, cor. in Proof F*　　　45 ⟨To die a Prince than live a slave⟩ ⟨Perchance⟩ But not uncrowned to live a slave *TA*　　　47 ⟨Was changed by the⟩ rebound *T* 48 Chained by] ⟨Caught / Smote⟩ Chained ⟨in⟩ by *T*　　　49 ⟨He broke but to be bound⟩ *T* 51 deed . . . done] ⟨doom . . . met⟩ *T*　　　52 And] A *T*　　　55–6 The Roman when ⟨his great revenge / Had shed the⟩ blood of Rome *T*　　　55 burning] ⟨evil / angry⟩ sated *T* 56 slaked] drunk *T*　　　57 He broke the rod—he dared depart *T*　　　58 savage] ⟨fearless⟩ lonely *T, cor. in Proof D*　　　61 Yet left] And ⟨found⟩ left *T*　　　62 ⟨Great was his soul in that last⟩ hour *T*　　　63 self-upheld] ⟨sated—self-⟩ *T*　　　65 its . . . spell] ⟨the charm to home⟩ *T*

Cast crowns for rosaries away,
   An empire for a cell;
A strict accountant of his beads,
A subtle disputant on creeds,
   His dotage trifled well: 70
Yet better had he neither known
A bigot's shrine, nor despot's throne.

9.

But thou—from thy reluctant hand
   The thunderbolt is wrung—
Too late thou leav'st the high command   75
   To which thy weakness clung;
All Evil Spirit as thou art,
It is enough to grieve the heart,
   To see thine own unstrung;
To think that God's fair world hath been   80
The footstool of a thing so mean;

10.

And Earth hath spilt her blood for him,
   Who thus can hoard his own!
And Monarchs bowed the trembling limb,
   And thanked him for a throne!   85
Fair Freedom! we may hold thee dear,
When thus thy mightiest foes their fear
   In humblest guise have shown.
Oh! ne'er may tyrant leave behind
A brighter name to lure mankind!   90

11.

Thine evil deeds are writ in gore,
   Nor written thus in vain—
Thy triumphs tell of fame no more,
   Or deepen every stain—

67 An empire] ⟨A kingdom⟩ *T*   71 ⟨But⟩ better *T*   72 despot's] tyrant's *T*
73 from] ⟨too⟩ *T*   76 weakness] spirit *T*   77 Spirit] Greatness *T*   80 that God's]
that ⟨man's the⟩ God's *T*   82 spilt] ⟨shed⟩ *T*   83 thus can hoard] ⟨fears / dares to
shed⟩ *T*   87 their] ⟨can⟩ *T*   88 humblest] ⟨abject⟩ bitter *T*   89 ⟨Would that
Ambition neer⟩ *T*; Ah would no tyrant had consigned *T, cor. in Proof D*   90 lure] ⟨leave⟩
Proof A   92 ⟨Upon the minds of men⟩ *T*   94 ⟨And almost add a⟩ stain *T*

If thou hadst died as honour dies,   95
Some new Napoleon might arise,
    To shame the world again—
But who would soar the solar height,
To set in such a starless night?

12.

Weigh'd in the balance, hero dust   100
    Is vile as vulgar clay;
Thy scales, Mortality! are just
    To all that pass away;
But yet methought the living great
Some higher sparks should animate,   105
    To dazzle and dismay;
Nor deem'd Contempt could thus make mirth
Of these, the Conquerors of the earth.

13.

And she, proud Austria's mournful flower,
    Thy still imperial bride;   110
How bears her breast the torturing hour?
    Still clings she to thy side?
Must she too bend, must she too share
Thy late repentance, long despair,
    Thou throneless Homicide?   115
If still she loves thee, hoard that gem,
'Tis worth thy vanished diadem!

14.

Then haste thee to thy sullen Isle,
    And gaze upon the sea;
That element may meet thy smile,   120
    It ne'er was ruled by thee!

96 new Napoleon] ⟨other madman⟩ T   97 shame] ⟨walk⟩ T   98 But ⟨now Ambition
would disdain⟩ / ⟨Souls that might attain like / thy reign⟩ who would ⟨dream of⟩ / ⟨rise as he
arose⟩ rise ⟨to pass away⟩ in brightest day T; But who would rise in brightest day Proof A,
cor. in Proof D   99 To set without a parting ray T; To set without one parting ray
Proof A, cor. in Proof D   100 ⟨Once weighed by⟩ ⟨When Death hath⟩ ⟨Tis known how
light is⟩ hero's dust T, cor. in Proof A   101 Is light as vulgar ⟨earth⟩ T; Is vile as ⟨com-
mon⟩ clay Proof A   105 higher sparks should] brighter sparks ⟨could⟩ T   106 ⟨Un-
conquerable⟩ ⟨That⟩ To T   109 And ⟨the⟩ she TA   111 bears] ⟨bears⟩ braves TA
113 bend ... share] ⟨? ... bear⟩ TA   115 throneless] ⟨crownless⟩ TA   116 ⟨If so—in
her⟩ ⟨Oh⟩ If TA   118 sullen] lonely T   119 gaze upon] look along T, cor. in Proof B
121 For Albion kept it free T, cor. in Proof B

Or trace with thine all idle hand
In loitering mood upon the sand
   That Earth is now as free!
That Corinth's pedagogue hath now   125
Transferred his bye word to thy brow.

15.

Thou Timour! in his captive's cage
   What thoughts will there be thine,
While brooding in thy prisoned rage?
   But one—'The world *was* mine';   130
Unless, like he of Babylon,
All sense is with thy sceptre gone,
   Life will not long confine
That spirit poured so widely forth—
So long obeyed—so little worth!   135

16.

Or like the thief of fire from heaven,
   Wilt thou withstand the shock?
And share with him, the unforgiven,
   His vulture and his rock!
Foredoomed by God—by man accurst,   140
And that last act, though not thy worst,
   The very Fiend's arch mock;

122–4   But ⟨look⟩ gaze not on the land for there
             Walks crownless Power with temples bare
             And shakes her ⟨locks⟩ head at thee   *T*, *Proof A*
             ⟨But look not down upon the land
             To find it traced⟩
             Or sit thee down upon the sand
             And trace with thine all idle hand
             That Earth is ⟨also⟩ now as free *Proof B, cor. in Proof D*

125 And Corinth's ⟨exile / pedagogue / exile on / to thy brow⟩ *T*   That] And *Proof A*
cor. in Proof B   126 Transferred] ⟨Transferred / ?⟩ *T*

127–30   ⟨There brooding in thy prisoned rage
             What thoughts will there be thine
             Would then / A Timour in his captive's cage
             To say / Who said 'the world is mine'⟩ *T*

127 Thou] ⟨There⟩ *Proof A*   132 All] ⟨The⟩ *T*   134 poured] ⟨which⟩ sent *T*
137 Wilt] Will *Proof A, cor. in Proof F*   138 share . . . the] ⟨brave like him long⟩ *T*
139 His . . . his] ⟨Thy . . . thy⟩ *T*   140–1 He suffered for kind acts to men, | Who
have not seen his like again *T, cor. in Proof A*   142 The last of ⟨royal⟩ kingly stock
T; ⟨At least of kingly stock⟩ *Proof A*

He in his fall preserv'd his pride,
And if a mortal, had as proudly died!

227a   Additional Stanzas

1. [17]

There was a day—there was an hour,
    While earth was Gaul's—Gaul thine—
When that immeasurable power
    Unsated to resign
Had been an act of purer fame   5
Than gathers round Marengo's name
    And gilded thy decline,
Through the long twilight of all time,
Despite some passing clouds of crime.

2. [18]

But thou forsooth must be a king,   10
    And don the purple vest,—
As if that foolish robe could wring
    Remembrance from thy breast.
Where is that faded garment? where
The gewgaws thou wert fond to wear,   15
    The star—the string—the crest?
Vain froward child of empire! say,
Are all thy playthings snatch'd away?

143 And he was good—and thou but great *T*; Since he was good, and thou but great
Proof A; ⟨Since he at least⟩ preserved his pride *MS. correction in Proof A*   144 Thou
canst not quarrel with thy fate *T*, *Proof A*; And were he mortal would have died *MS.
correction in Proof A, cor. in Proof D*

227a. 2 While] ⟨When / Then⟩ While *TA*   Gaul] ⟨Gallia⟩ *M*
8–9   ⟨Through the long twilight of all time
                        That shows yet shadows good and crime⟩
                        ⟨Which shrouds thee / So that⟩
                        Despite ⟨the⟩ some passing dance? of crime
                        Through the long twilight of all time. *M*
10 must] would *M*   11 And don] ⟨Men⟩ And wear *M, cor. in TA*   12 wring] ⟨bring⟩ *M*
13 Remembrance] ⟨One sorrow⟩ *M*   14 ⟨Look on that tattered garment—now⟩ *M*
16 The ⟨crown commanding⟩ laurel-circled crest? *M*   17–18 ⟨What all thy playthings,
torn away— | Vain child of Empire⟩ *M*   18 snatch'd] torn *M*

3. [19]

Where may the wearied eye repose
   When gazing on the Great;   20
Where neither guilty glory glows,
   Nor despicable state?
Yes—one—the first—the last—the best—
The Cincinnatus of the West,
   Whom envy dared not hate,   25
Bequeath'd the name of Washington,
To make man blush there was but one!

                                 [1814]

228   [Translation From the Romaic.
   I Wander Near That Fount of Waters]

1.

I wander near that fount of waters
Where throng my country's virgin daughters,
And yet that haunt I might forego—
Will she, my Love, be there?—Ah! No.

2.

All—all are there save her alone;   5
Yet once along that fountain shone
Her imaged eyes within the stream
That glittered with the borrowed beam.

---

19 wearied eye] eye of man *M, L, cor. in TA*   23–4 *cancelled in L, then restored*
25 ⟨Hath / Her / Left not / Left not a fault to hate⟩ | ⟨Hath left the⟩ *L*   27 Alas!
and must there be but one! *M, cor. in L*   blush] weep *L, cor. in T*

228. Copy text: *MS. Y*, collated with *MS. Le*
title   *untitled in MSS.*

  1 ⟨I will go to the fountain of waters⟩ / ⟨I will unto the fountain of waters⟩ / I'll ⟨watch⟩
linger near that fount of waters *Le*   3 ⟨And there my / Yet vainly there my steps
may go⟩ *Le*   haunt] ⟨stream⟩ / spot *Le*   6 along] ⟨within⟩ *Le*   8 That glittered]
⟨That glittered⟩ / More lovely *Le*

3.

Yet—yet that fount is calm and clear,
Nor less to Hellas' daughters dear;   10
But there Reflection ne'er shall grace
Those waters with so fair a face.

4.

She comes not here—yet linger still
My steps around that sacred rill,
Nor know I wherefore there I stray,   15
But cannot tear myself away.

[1814]

229   Magdalen

1.

The hour is come—of darkness and of dread—
That makes Earth shudder to receive the dead,
When the first Martyr to his offered creed,
The man of heaven—the Son of God—must bleed.
The hour is come of Salem's giant Sin;   5
The doom is fixed—the bloody rites begin.

2.

There be loud cries on Sion's lofty place,
And struggling crowds of Israel's swarthy race.
Stamped on each brow an idiot hatred stood,
In every eye an eagerness of blood.   10
Each scornful lip betrayed its wayward thirst
Of ill—and cursing him became accurst.

---

9 calm] ⟨sweet⟩ *Le*   10 ⟨To Hellas' daughters still / no less dear⟩ *Le*   11 But
there ⟨no eye shall eer retrace⟩ / Reflection neer shall trace *Le*   12 Those . . . with]
The likeness of *Le*   13 comes not here] is not there *Le*   15 ⟨Twere vain to
ask why⟩ *Le*

229. Copy text: *MS. L*, collated with *Murray's Mag.*, *Ashton*
title   Calvary *Murray's Mag.*
2 makes . . . receive] ⟨gives Earth's noblest victim to⟩ *L*   makes] ⟨sees / bids⟩ *L*

Wroth without cause—revenged without a wrong—
Tribes of self-sentence! ye shall suffer long,
Through dark Milleniums of exiled grief   15
The outcast slaves of sightless unbelief.
Stung by all torture,—buffeted and sold—
Racked by an idle lust of useless gold—
Scourged—scorned—unloved—a name for every race
To spit upon—the chosen of disgrace;   20
A people nationless, whom every land
Receives to punish—and preserves to brand;
Yet still enduring all, and all in vain,
The doomed inheritors of scorn and pain,
Untaught by sufferance, unreclaimed from ill,   25
Hating and hated—stubborn Israel still!

                                        1814

230 To One Who Promised on a Lock of Hair

Vow not at all—but if thou must
O be it by some slender token!
Since pious pledge, and plighted trust,
And holiest ties too oft are broken;
Then by this dearest trifle swear,   5
And if thou lov'st as I would have thee,
This votive ringlet's tenderest hair
Will bind thy heart to that I gave thee.

                                    [1814]

14 self-sentence] ⟨long / deep suffering⟩ L   15 Through . . . of] ⟨Even now begins
the⟩ L   19 name for every] ⟨very name for⟩ L   22 preserves] ⟨protects⟩ L
25 unreclaimed from] ⟨unredeemed by⟩ L

230. Copy text: *Jesse*, collated with *MS. T*
6 lov'st] beest *T*

231   [Prometheus and Napoleon]

Unlike the offence, though like would be the fate,
His to give life, but *thine* to desolate;
He stole from Heaven the flame, for which he fell,
Whilst thine was stolen from thy native Hell.

[1814]

232   Stanzas For Music

I speak not—I trace not—I breathe not thy name,
There is grief in the sound—there were guilt in the fame;
But the tear which now burns on my cheek may impart
The deep thought that dwells in that silence of heart.

Too brief for our passion, too long for our peace,   5
Were those hours, can their joy or their bitterness cease?
We repent—we abjure—we will break from our chain;
We must part—we must fly to—unite it again.

Oh! thine be the gladness and mine be the guilt,
Forgive me adored one—forsake if thou wilt;   10
But the heart which I bear shall expire undebased,
And man shall not break it—whatever thou may'st.

231. Copy text: *Harrow MS.*, collated with *C*
title   *supplied here*
4 was] be *C*

232. Copy text: *N1827–9*, collated with *MS.*, *Life*
title   *Life, 1831, 1832, C*; I speak . . . breathe not *N1827–9*; Stanzas for Music. 'I speak
not etc.' *More; untitled in MS.*
1 ⟨I speak not—I breathe not—I write not that name⟩ *MS.*   2 grief] ⟨love⟩ *MS.*
were guilt] is guilt *MS., Life, 1831, 1832, C, More*   3 on . . . impart] ⟨on my cheek
may / to impart⟩ *MS.*   4 thought that dwells] thoughts that dwell *MS., Life, 1831,
1832, C, More*   5 ⟨We have loved—and oh still my adored one—we love⟩ *MS.*
6 ⟨Oh the moment when / is past when that Passion might cease / that forbids our release⟩
⟨Were the moments when / how could they / Remembrance can never release⟩ *MS.*   Was
that hour— ⟨ah wherefore⟩ can its hope—can its memory cease? *MS.*   7 our] ⟨the⟩
MS.   8 must . . . must] will . . . will *Life, 1831, 1832, C, More*   9 ⟨The hope /
thought may be madness the wish may be / to utter it Guilt⟩ *MS.*   10 Forgive]
⟨Forsake⟩ *MS.*   11 ⟨But I cannot repent what we neer can recall⟩ *MS.*; But the
heart which is thine ⟨would disdain to recall / is too proud of its vow / still remains undebased⟩
shall expire undebased *MS.*   I bear] is thine *MS., Life, 1831, 1832, C, More*   12 what-
ever thou may'st] ⟨whatever thou / though I feel that thou mayst⟩ *MS.*

And stern to the haughty, but humble to thee,
My soul in its bitterest blackness shall be;
And our days seem as swift—and our moments more
    sweet,   15
With thee by my side—than the world at our feet.

One sigh of thy sorrow—one look of thy love,
Shall turn me or fix, shall reward or reprove;
And the heartless may wonder at all we resign,
Thy lip shall reply not to them—but to mine.   20

                           [1814]

233   Address Intended to be Recited at
the Caledonian Meeting

Who hath not glowed above the page where Fame
Hath fixed high Caledon's unconquered name;
The mountain-land which spurned the Roman chain,
And baffled back the fiery-crested Dane,
Whose bright claymore and hardihood of hand   5
No foe could tame—no tyrant could command?
That race is gone—but still their children breathe,
And Glory crowns them with redoubled wreath:

13 ⟨Oh proud / high⟩ to the ⟨mighty⟩ *MS.*   14 My] This *MS., Life, 1831, 1832, C, More*   blackness] moment *MS.*   15 And ⟨our / the years of our⟩ *MS.*   seem] ⟨glide⟩ *MS.*   16 With thee at my side—than the world at my feet *MS.*   than the world] than with worlds *Life, 1831, 1832, C, More*
17 *three lines are cancelled before* 17 *in the MS.*:

    ⟨And thine is that love / heart / love which I will / could not
      resign / forget⟩
    ⟨Though the price that⟩ ⟨Though that love / heart may be
      bought by / the price which I pay be Eternity's woe⟩
    ⟨But if thine too must suffer—Oh take it again⟩

17 sigh] ⟨tear⟩ look] ⟨smile⟩ *MS.*   19 may . . . resign] may ⟨smile and the rig⟩ wonder at ⟨all / what⟩ all I resign *MS.*   we] I *MS., Life, 1831, 1832, C, More*

233. Copy text: *C*, collated with *MS. M, Life*
title *not in M*

O'er Gael and Saxon mingling banners shine,
And, England! add their stubborn strength to thine.   10
The blood which flowed with Wallace flows as free,
But now 'tis only shed for Fame and thee!
Oh! pass not by the northern veteran's claim,
But give support—the world hath given him fame!

The humbler ranks, the lowly brave, who bled   15
While cheerly following where the Mighty led—
Who sleep beneath the undistinguished sod
Where happier comrades in their triumph trod,
To us bequeath—'tis all their fate allows—
The sireless offspring and the lonely spouse: 20
She on high Albyn's dusky hills may raise
The tearful eye in melancholy gaze,
Or view, while shadowy auguries disclose
The Highland Seer's anticipated woes,
The bleeding phantom of each martial form   25
Dim in the cloud, or darkling in the storm;
While sad, she chaunts the solitary song,
The soft lament for him who tarries long—
For him, whose distant relics vainly crave
The Coronach's wild requiem to the brave!   30

'Tis Heaven—not man—must charm away the woe,
Which bursts when Nature's feelings newly flow;
Yet Tenderness and Time may rob the tear
Of half its bitterness for one so dear;
A Nation's gratitude perchance may spread   35
A thornless pillow for the widowed head;
May lighten well her breast's maternal care,
And wean from Penury the soldier's heir;
Or deem to living war-worn Valour just
Each wounded remnant—Albion's cherished trust—   40
Warm his decline with those endearing rays,
Whose bounteous sunshine yet may gild his days—
So shall that Country—while he sinks to rest—
His hand hath fought for—by his heart be blessed!

[1814]

37 breast's] heart's *all printed texts*   39–44 *first printed in C; not in More*

234 [Condolatory Address to Sarah, Countess of Jersey, On the Prince Regent's Returning Her Picture to Mrs. Mee]

When the vain triumph of the imperial lord,
Whom servile Rome obey'd, and yet abhorr'd,
Gave to the vulgar gaze each glorious bust,
That left a likeness of the brave, or just;
What most admired each scrutinising eye   5
Of all that deck'd that passing pageantry?
What spread from face to face that wondering air?
The thought of Brutus—for his was not there!
That absence proved his worth,—that absence fix'd
His memory on the longing mind, unmix'd;   10
And more decreed his glory to endure,
Than all a gold Colossus could secure.

If thus, fair Jersey, our desiring gaze
Search for thy form, in vain and mute amaze
Amidst those pictured charms, whose loveliness,   15
Bright though they be, thine own had render'd less;
If he, that vain old man, whom truth admits
Heir of his father's crown, and of his wits,
If his corrupted eye, and wither'd heart,
Could with thy gentle image bear depart;   20

---

234. Copy text: *1832*, collated with *MSS. L, N, M, Champion, Wilson, Paris1831*

title   *untitled in L*; Lines by Lord Byron *N*; Lines on the Removing Lady Jersey's portrait from the Gallery of Beauties *M*; Lines by Lord B *Champion*; Lines to Lady J *Wilson*; On the Prince Regent's Returning the Picture of Sarah, Countess of J——, to Mrs. Mee *1831*; To Lady Jersey on the Prince Regent's excluding her portrait from the gallery of beauties *Paris1831*

1 When] ⟨In⟩ *L*   4 ⟨Of⟩ That *L*   or] and *N, Champion, Wilson, Paris1831*
6 that] the *N, M, Champion, Wilson, Paris1831*   7 What ⟨fills / filled / scatter⟩ spread⟨s⟩ from *L*   8 thought . . . his was] ⟨brow . . . it is⟩ *L*   his] he *N, Wilson, Paris 1831*
9 That absence ⟨more attest⟩ proved *L*   11 And] Nay, *Paris1831*   decreed] ⟨commands⟩ *L*   12 Colossus] that Croesus *M*   13 Jersey] J—— *N, Champion, Wilson, 1831*   desiring] admiring *N, M, Champion, Wilson, Paris1831*   14 Search] Look *L*
15 Amidst] Amid *Paris1831*   pictured charms] ⟨portraitures⟩ *L*   16 thine] thy *Champion, N*   17–19 that vain . . . heart *omitted in 1831*   17 If ⟨that⟩ he . . . whom ⟨bull permits⟩ *L*   18 ⟨To reign / Heirship of his father's crown and wits⟩ / Heir of his father's diadem and wits *L*; Heir of his Father's —— *N, Champion, Wilson*; Heir to his Father's monarchy—and wits; *Paris1831*   19 corrupted] corroded *L*
20 depart] to part *L, M, N, Champion, Wilson, Paris1831*

That tasteless shame be *his*, and ours the grief,
To gaze on Beauty's band without its chief:
Yet comfort still one selfish thought imparts,
We lose the portrait, but preserve our hearts.
   What can his vaulted gallery now disclose?   25
A garden with all flowers—except the rose;—
A fount that only wants its living stream;
A night, with every star, save Dian's beam.
Lost to our eyes the present forms shall be,
That turn from tracing them to dream of thee;   30
And more on that recall'd resemblance pause,
Than all he *shall* not force on our applause.
   Long may thy yet meridian lustre shine,
With all that Virtue asks of Homage thine:
The symmetry of youth—the grace of mien—   35
The eye that gladdens—and the brow serene;
The glossy darkness of that clustering hair,
Which shades, yet shows that forehead more than fair!
Each glance that wins us, and the life that throws
A spell which will not let our looks repose,   40
But turn to gaze again, and find anew
Some charm that well rewards another view.
These are not lessen'd, these are still as bright,
Albeit too dazzling for a dotard's sight;
And those must wait till ev'ry charm is gone,   45
To please the paltry heart that pleases none;—
That dull cold sensualist, whose sickly eye
In envious dimness pass'd thy portrait by;
Who rack'd his little spirit to combine
Its hate of *Freedom's* loveliness, and *thine*.   50

[1814]

21 and ours] but ours *M*   22 gaze on] ⟨miss that⟩ *L*   24 the portrait] thine image *L*; that portrait *M, N, Champion, Paris1831*   25 vaulted] vaunted *L, N, Champion, Paris1831*   26 all flowers] each flower *Paris 1831*   27 its] the *Wilson* 29 to our eyes] ⟨to⟩ / on the ⟨gazers / earth / our⟩ eyes *L*   32 *shall* not] ⟨can not⟩ / fain would *L*   33 may thy ⟨charms in / former⟩ yet *L*   35 The ⟨shape⟩ of youth *L* 38 that] thy *M*   39 glance] look *L*   life that throws] ⟨all⟩ that ⟨charms⟩ *L* 40 spell which] ⟨charm⟩ spell which *L*; spell that *N, Champion, Paris1831*   41 But turn again, and find forever new *Paris1831*   42 well rewards another] well repays ⟨a second⟩ *L*; will command *Paris1831*   44 dotard's *omitted in 1831*   45–7 And those . . . sensualist *omitted in 1831*   45 those] these *Paris1831*   ev'ry charm is] ⟨all those charms are⟩ *L*   46 paltry] ⟨ignoble⟩ *L*   49 ⟨To show at once how well he could combine / how well his little souls combine⟩ *L*   50 Its] ⟨His⟩ *L*; The hate of freedom, loveliness, and thine. *Paris1831*

235 Fragment of an Epistle to Thomas Moore

'What say I?'—not a syllable further in prose;
I'm your man 'of all measures', dear Tom,—so, here
    goes!
Here goes, for a swim on the stream of old Time,
On those buoyant supporters, the bladders of rhyme.
If our weight breaks them down, and we sink in the
    flood,   5
We are smother'd, at least, in respectable mud,
Where the Divers of Bathos lie drown'd in a heap,
And Southey's last Paean has pillow'd his sleep;—
That 'Felo de se' who, half drunk with his malmsey,
Walk'd out of his depth and was lost in a calm sea,   10
Singing 'Glory to God' in a spick and span stanza,
The like (since Tom Sternhold was choked) never
    man saw.

The papers have told you, no doubt, of the fusses,
The fêtes, and the gapings to get at these Russes,—
Of his Majesty's suite, up from coachman to Hetman,— 15
And what dignity decks the flat face of the great man.
I saw him, last week, at two balls and a party,—
For a prince, his demeanour was rather too hearty.
You know, *we* are used to quite different graces,

★   ★   ★   ★   ★   ★   ★   ★   ★   ★

The Czar's look, I own, was much brighter and brisker 20
But then he is sadly deficient in whisker;
And wore but a starless blue coat, and in kersey-
-mere breeches whisk'd round, in a waltz with the
    Jersey,
Who, lovely as ever, seem'd just as delighted
With majesty's presence as those she invited.   25

★   ★   ★   ★   ★   ★   ★   ★   ★   ★
★   ★   ★   ★   ★   ★   ★   ★   ★   ★

                                    June 1814

235. Copy text: *1832*

236   Ich Dien

From this emblem what variance your motto evinces,
For the *Man* is his country's—the Arms are the Prince's!

[1814?]

237   Harmodia

'The things that were'—and what and whence were they,
Those clouds and rainbows of thy yesterday?
Their path has vanished from the eternal sky,
And now its lines are of a different dye.
Thus speeds from day to day—and Pole to Pole   5
The change of parts—the sameness of the whole,
And all we snatch amidst this breathing strife
But gives to Memory what it takes from life,
Despoils a substance to adorn a shade,
And that frail shadow lengthens but to fade.   10
Sun of the sleepless! melancholy Star!
Whose tearful beam shoots trembling from afar—
That show'st the darkness thou can'st not dispel
How like art thou to Joy remembered well;
Such is the past—the light of other days   15
That shines but warms not with its powerless rays
A moonbeam someone watches to behold
Distinct but distant—clear—but deathlike cold.

236. Copy text: *C*

237. Copy text: *MS.*

    1 what . . . they] ⟨were they?—'tis a theme⟩ *MS.*   2 clouds and] ⟨faded⟩ *MS.*
3 ⟨There is the Cloud, and the⟩ eternal sky *MS.*   4 ⟨In changing sameness / But all⟩
its lines *MS.*   6 parts] ⟨things⟩ *MS.*   7 amidst] ⟨from⟩ *MS.*   9 adorn] ⟨enrich⟩
MS.

11 ff.   What is the past? the light of other days
                            That shines but warms not with its fading / powerless rays
                            A moonbeam someone lingers to behold
                            Distinct but distant—dazzling—clear—but cold
                            Which shows the darkness it may not dispel
                            ⟨To them that she cannot⟩
                            Unto the sleepless eyes that love it well. *cancelled MS.*

13 That] ⟨Why⟩ *MS.*   17 watches] watch⟨eth⟩ *MS.*   18 clear . . . cold]
⟨dazzling⟩ —clear—but oh how cold *cancelled MS.*

Oh, as full thought comes rushing o'er the mind,
Of all we saw before—to leave behind—   20
Of all—but words—what are they? can they give
A trace of breath to thoughts while yet they live?
No—Passion, Feeling speak not—or in vain—
The tear for Grief, the groan must speak for Pain;
Joy hath its smile, and Love its blush and sigh,   25
Despair her silence, Hate her lip and eye—
These their interpreters when deeply lurk
The soul's despoilers warring as they work.
The strife once o'er, then words may find their way,
Yet how enfeebled from the forced delay.   30
But who could paint the progress of the wrecks,
Himself still clinging to the dangerous decks?
Safe on the shore the Artist first must stand—
And then the pencil trembles in his hand.

                                        8 Sept. 1814

238   On the Death of Sir Peter Parker, Bart.

There is a tear for all that die,
    A mourner o'er the humblest grave;
But nations swell the funeral cry,
    And Triumph weeps above the brave.

For them is Sorrow's purest sigh   5
    O'er Ocean's heaving bosom sent;
In vain their bones unburied lie,
    All earth becomes their monument!

A tomb is theirs on every page,
    An epitaph on every tongue: 10
The present hours, the future age,
    For them bewail, to them belong.

19 full] ⟨the⟩ MS.   21 but ⟨who⟩ words MS.   22 while yet they] ⟨that really⟩
MS.   23 Passion, Feeling] ⟨every⟩ Passion MS.   26 her silence] ⟨its⟩ her
⟨utter⟩ silence MS.   27 when] ⟨the glance⟩ when MS.   28 warring as they] ⟨at
their warring⟩ MS.   30 how enfeebled] ⟨all how feebled⟩ MS.
238. Copy text: HM1815, collated with MS. P, Morning Chronicle, CHP(10)
title   ⟨To the Memory⟩ of Sir Peter Parker MS. P
    2 o'er] ⟨for⟩ MS. P   8 ⟨The Hero makes his⟩ monument! MS. P

For them the voice of festal mirth
  Grows hushed, *their name* the only sound;
While deep Remembrance pours to Worth   15
  The goblet's tributary round.

A theme to crowds that knew them not,
  Lamented by admiring foes,
Who would not share their glorious lot?
  Who would not die the death they chose?   20

And, gallant Parker! thus enshrined
  Thy life, thy fall, thy fame shall be;
And early valour, glowing, find
  A model in thy memory.

But there are breasts that bleed with thee   25
  In woe, that glory cannot quell;
And shuddering hear of victory,
  Where one so dear, so dauntless, fell.

Where shall they turn to mourn thee less?
  When cease to hear thy cherished name?   30
Time cannot teach forgetfulness,
  While Grief's full heart is fed by Fame.

Alas! for them, though not for thee,
  They cannot choose but weep the more;
Deep for the dead the grief must be   35
  Who ne'er gave cause to mourn before.

                                    [1814]

239   They Say That Hope Is Happiness

'Felix qui potuit rerum cognoscere causas.'
                          VIRGIL.

                    I.

They say that Hope is happiness—
  But genuine Love must prize the past;
And Mem'ry wakes the thoughts that bless:
  They rose the first—they set the last.

239. Copy text: *N1827–9*, collated with *Nathan*, *Ashton*
title   Stanzas for Music *1832*, *C*, *More*

2.

And all that mem'ry loves the most   5
Was once our only hope to be:
And all that hope adored and lost
Hath melted into memory.

3.

Alas! it is delusion all—
The future cheats us from afar: 10
Nor can we be what we recall,
Nor dare we think on what we are.

[1814]

240   Julian

[A Fragment]

1.

The night came o'er the Waters—all was rest
On Earth—but rage on Ocean's troubled breast.
The waves arose and rolled beneath the blast,
The Sailors gazed upon their shivered mast.
In that dark hour a long loud gathered cry   5
From out the billows pierced the sable sky,
And borne o'er breakers reached the craggy shore—
The sea roars on—that cry is heard no more.

2.

There is no vestige, in the Dawning light
Of those that shrieked thro' shadows of the night.
The bark—the crew—the very wreck is gone,   10
Marred—mutilated—traceless—all save one.

240. Copy text: MS., collated with C
   1 o'er] on C   1–2 ⟨The Ocean rose and rolled beneath the blast— | The sailors
gazed upon their shivered mast—⟩ MS.   2 rage] ⟨storm⟩ MS.   breast] Heart C
3 waves arose] ⟨ocean rose⟩ MS.   5 a . . . gathered] ⟨was heard a fearful⟩   gathered]
⟨deadly⟩ MS.   6 pierced the sable] ⟨piercing to the / through the black⟩ MS.   7 o'er
. . . reached] ⟨through . . . to⟩ MS.   12 ⟨Mixed with the elements⟩ MS.   traceless]
formless alternate reading in MS.

In him there still is life—the wave that dashed
On shore the plank to which his form was lashed
Returned unheeding of its helpless prey,   15
The lone survivor of that yesterday,
The one of many whom that withering gale
Hath left unpunished to record their tale.
But who shall hear it? On that barren sand
None comes to stretch the hospitable hand.—   20
That shore reveals no print of human foot
Nor ev'n the pawing of the wilder brute;
And niggard Vegetation will not smile
All sunless on that solitary isle.—

3.

The naked stranger rose—and wrung his hair,   25
And that first moment passed in silent prayer;
Alas! the second sunk into despair.
He was on earth—but what was earth to him,
Houseless and homeless, bare both breast and limb?
Cut off from all but Memory, he curst   30
His fate—his folly—but himself the worst.
What was his hope? he looked upon the wave—
'Despite—of all—it still may be my grave!

4.

'Ah me'—and with a feeble effort shaped
His course unto the billows late escaped.   35
But weakness conquered—swam his dizzied glance,
And down to earth he sunk in silent trance.
How long his senses bore its chilling chain
He knew not—but, recalled to life again,
A stranger stood beside his shivering form—   40
And what was he?—had he too 'scaped the storm?

5.

He raised young Julian. 'Is thy cup so full
Of bitterness—thy hope—thy heart so dull

14 On] ⟨To⟩ MS.   15 unheeding of its helpless] ⟨all guiltless / heedless of the single⟩
MS.   16 lone] ⟨one⟩ MS.   17 withering] ⟨furious⟩ MS.   20 ⟨Appears not point
of⟩ MS.   23 will] ⟨serve⟩ will MS.   27 second] sound—he C   28 what] ⟨that⟩ MS.
31 ⟨All things above—beneath⟩ MS.   32 ⟨Why was he deemed of⟩ MS.   33 my] his C
34 'Ah me'] He rose C   36 swam] ⟨and he⟩ swam MS.   42–3 ⟨His form and
features seemed of a mortal mould | His years of middle manhood⟩ MS.

That thou shouldst from thee dash the draught of life,
So late escaped the elemental strife?   45
Rise—though these shores few aids to life supply,
Look upon me and know thou shalt not die.
Thou gazest in mute wonder—more may be
Thy marvel when thou knowest mine and me.
But come—the bark that bears us hence shall find   50
Her haven soon despite the warring wind.'

6.

He raised young Julian from the sand, and such
Strange power of healing dwelt within the touch
That his weak limbs grew light with freshened power,
As he had slept, not fainted in that hour,   55
And woke from slumber as the birds awake,
Recalled by morning from the branchéd brake
When the day's promise heralds early spring—
And Heaven unfolded woos their soaring wing:
So Julian felt—and gazed upon his guide   60
With honest wonder what might next betide.

                                              12 Dec. 1814

241   In the Valley of Waters

1.

In the valley of waters we wept o'er the day
When the host of the stranger made Salem his prey,
And our heads on our bosoms all droopingly lay,
And our hearts were so full of the land far away.

2.

The song they demanded in vain—it lay still   5
In our souls as the wind that hath died on the hill;
They called for the harp—but our blood they shall spill
Ere our right hands shall teach them one tone of their skill.

48 may] ⟨shall⟩ MS.   53 within the] ⟨upon his⟩ MS.   56 woke from] woke
⟨to Life⟩ from MS.   57 ⟨New sprung with⟩ MS.   59 ⟨And the blue/opening⟩ MS.

241. Copy text: N1827–9, collated with MSS. A, B, Nathan, Ashton
   1 o'er] ⟨on⟩ B; on C   6 that . . . the] ⟨in the cave of the⟩ A   8 Ere] ⟨Our⟩
Eer A   hands . . . their] hands . . . ⟨its⟩ A; hand . . . our N1827–9P; hand . . . their N1827–
9E, Nathan; hands . . . our More

3.

All stringlessly hung on the willow's sad tree,
As dead as her dead leaf those mute harps must be;   10
Our hands may be fettered—our tears still are free,
For our God and our glory—and, Sion!—Oh, thee.

[1815]

242   Epilogue to *The Merchant of Venice*
            Intended for a Private Theatrical

Hard is the life of those who live to please.
What Player, or Poet, ever tastes of ease—
Still doomed to suffer from the sneer or frown,
The fools who roar, the mags who write them down?
Say—to the best what bright rewards remain?   5
An hour of glory—earned by years of pain.

If such the lot of all in every age
Who pen the scene, or stalk along the stage,
And Garrick could not on his brightest day
Send all that saw in smiles or tears away,   10
What shall this more presumptuous aim excuse
Who thus untaught—unstudied—woo the Muse,
Who dare to strut an hour to Shakespeare's strain
With steps that never trod in Drury Lane?
With voices never pitched on loftier boards   15
Than those our humbler hope to please affords?

Yet if to charm away the evening hour
With all the wish to please—if not the power;
If Shakespeare seem—though this admits a doubt—
A treat, at least substantial as a *trout*;   20

9 stringlessly hung] ⟨stringless and mute⟩ *A*   on] in *C*   10 dead leaf] dead-
lea⟨ves⟩ *A*

242. Copy text: *MS.*

   1–2 ⟨There are ? with Good | And deem mankind not what they be but should.⟩ *MS.*
5 best] ⟨first⟩ *MS.*   8 stalk along] ⟨strut upon⟩ *MS.*   10 that saw] ⟨spectators⟩
MS.   13 Who . . . to] ⟨Whose boards⟩ Who dare to snatch a grace from *cancelled*
MS.   19 Shakespeare seem] ⟨Shakespeare's scenes appear⟩ *MS.*

And these his characters howe'er pourtrayed,
Less motley than our aim in Masquerade;
If (though the 'base comparison' provoke)
His wit almost eclipse a Dandy's joke,
And each 'conceit' Marlowe or Johnson shows   25
May sparkle scarce less brilliant than a Beau's;
Or should these solemn thoughts of loftier mien
Where deeper passions shudder o'er the scene
Through all our errors strike upon the heart,
And Nature force you to forget our Art;   30
Oh then confer on us the only Fame
That harmless Pleasure asks in Friendship's name:
Say you are pleased—and Shylock shall forget
His bloodless knife, and foe's uncancelled debt,
And Portia in her gentler triumph feel   35
Less proud but not less grateful than O'Neill.—

                                        26 Jan. 1815

243   [Bout-rimés from Seaham]

My wife's a vixen spoilt by her Mamma
Oh how I pity poor hen-pecked Papa.
The Lord defend us from a Honey Moon
Our cares commence our comforts end so soon.

This morn's the first of many a happy year—   5
I could not live so long with you, my dear
O ever in my heart the last and first—
And without doubt—it is the very worst.

Perplexed in the extreme to find a line
A different destiny is yours and mine.   10

27 ⟨His text shall lend a ? / through all our faults may work your hearts⟩ *MS*.   ⟨Or that
more solemn music / those more solemn tones that swell the scene⟩ *MS*.   30 ⟨And
make the actor lost within his part⟩ *MS*.   31 ⟨Do you forget the / Bestow that friendly /
cheering praise which⟩ *MS*.   34 His . . . uncancelled] ⟨Antonio's triumph / bosom
and uncancelled⟩ *MS*.

243. Copy text: *MS*. (italicized lines by Lady Byron)

If rhymes be omens what a fate is ours—
And bread and butter eagerly devours.

My husband is the greatest goose alive
I feel that I have been a fool to wive.

This weather makes our noses blue   15
Bell—that but rhymes an epithet for you.

[1815]

244   To Belshazzar

I.

Belshazzar! from the banquet turn,
    Nor in thy sensual fulness fall;
Behold! while yet before thee burn
    The graven words, the glowing wall.
Many a despot men miscall   5
    Crowned and anointed from on high,
But thou, the weakest, worst of all—
    Is it not written, thou must die?

14 ⟨I tell you Madam tis in vain to strive⟩ *MS.*

244. Copy text: *1831*, collated with *MSS.* *A* and *B*, and *Ashton*

1   ⟨Where art thou—my God!⟩
             ⟨? to / The red light glows—the wassail flows⟩
             The midnight revel loudly rings
                 Within / Around the royal hall
             And who on earth— ⟨dare / shall⟩ dare mar the mirth
                 Of that high festival
             ⟨The prophet dares—before thee glares⟩
             Belshazzar rise—nor dare despise
                 The writing on the wall! *initial stanza cancelled in A*

1 banquet] ⟨midnight / revels⟩ *A*

2   ⟨A little shame is left thee still⟩
             ⟨A head as / more high as / than thine may fall⟩
             ⟨Men pray and God decrees thy fall⟩
             ⟨Nor ? dare to fall⟩ *A*

3 Behold] ⟨And read⟩ *A*   4 The words of God— ⟨along the⟩ the graven wall *A*
graven . . . glowing] ⟨words of God—the graven⟩ *B*   5 despot] ⟨mortal de/ruler⟩ *A*
6 ⟨The/Anointed of / A thing⟩ Crowned *A*   8 ⟨The veriest slave would doom to die⟩ /
⟨Hast thou forgotten / Behold it written⟩ thou must die *A*

2.

Go! dash the roses from thy brow—
  Gray hairs but poorly wreathe with them;   10
Youth's garlands misbecome thee now,
  More than thy very diadem,
Where thou hast tarnished every gem:—
Then throw the worthless bauble by,
Which, worn by thee, ev'n slaves contemn;   15
And learn like better men to die!

3.

Oh! early in the balance weighed,
  And ever light of word and worth,
Whose soul expired ere youth decayed,
  And left thee but a mass of earth.   20
To see thee moves the scorner's mirth:
  But tears in Hope's averted eye
Lament that ever thou hadst birth—
  Unfit to govern, live, or die.

[1815]

245   Stanzas for Music

'O Lachrymarum fons, tenero sacros
Ducentium ortus ex animo: quater
Felix! in imo qui scatentem
Pectore te, pia Nympha, sensit.'
                                    Gray's Poemata.

1.

There's not a joy the world can give like that it takes away,
When the glow of early thought declines in feeling's dull decay;

9–11 ⟨Thy Vice might raise the avenging steel | Thy Meanness shield thee from the blow — | And they who loathe thee proudly feel⟩ *A*   9 Go ⟨?⟩ dash *A*   10 ⟨Thy crown scarce misbecomes thee more⟩   but poorly] ⟨ignobly/but ?⟩ *A*   12 More . . . very] ⟨More than thy sullied / Scarce less than doth thy⟩ *A*   13 hast] has *A*   18 word] wor⟨t⟩d *A*   19 soul expired] ⟨every / Virtues long⟩ *A*   22 in Hope's] in ⟨baffled⟩ Hope's *A*   23 ever] even *1831*, *1832*, *C*, *More*

245. Copy text: *Poems1816*, collated with *MSS. A*, *B*, *C*, and *D*, and the 1815 sheet music publication.
title   *untitled in MSS.*; There's Not a Joy the World Can Give *1815 sheet music*
epigraph   *not in 1815 sheet music*
  1 that] what *A*, *B*   2 declines] ⟨is gone / swift⟩ *A*

'Tis not on youth's smooth cheek the blush alone, which fades so
    fast,
But the tender bloom of heart is gone, ere youth itself be
    past.

2.

Then the few whose spirits float above the wreck of
    happiness,
Are driven o'er the shoals of guilt or ocean of excess:
The magnet of their course is gone, or only points in vain
The shore to which their shiver'd sail shall never stretch again.

3.

Then the mortal coldness of the soul like death itself comes down;
It cannot feel for others' woes, it dare not dream its own;   10
That heavy chill has frozen o'er the fountain of our tears,
And tho' the eye may sparkle still, 'tis where the ice appears.

4.

Tho' wit may flash from fluent lips, and mirth distract the
    breast,
Through midnight hours that yield no more their former hope of
    rest;
'Tis but as ivy-leaves around the ruin'd turret wreath,   15
All green and wildly fresh without but worn and grey beneath.

3 ⟨Wh⟩ Tis not ⟨the blush alone that fades from Beauty's younger cheek⟩ A   on . . .
cheek] from ⟨Beauty's⟩ cheek ⟨alone⟩ A   on] from B, 1815 sheet music   which] that 1815
sheet music   4 tender] ⟨youth⟩ A   ere youth itself] before its youth A, B, 1815 sheet
music   stanza 2 not in A, B   5 Then] And D, 1815 sheet music   And the few
⟨whose wreck of dreams / happiness is⟩ whose ⟨buoyant souls float⟩ souls still float above
the wreck of happiness C   6 Are driven o'er] ⟨Must drive along⟩ C   7 course is
gone] hope is lost D, 1815 sheet music   ⟨The magnet of their course is false—the compass⟩
The ⟨just? point⟩ / magnet of their course is ⟨sunk⟩ lost—or only ⟨yearns⟩ points in vain C
8 ⟨To where their shattered hopes no more can reach the port again⟩ C   shore] port C, D
which . . . shall] where . . . can 1815 sheet music   10 woes] woe A, B, 1815 sheet music
it . . . dream] ⟨and scarcely for⟩ A   dare] dares 1815 sheet music   11 ⟨As Ivy oer the
mouldering wall that heaviness hath crept / It wonders why it wept before⟩ A   our] their
1815 sheet music   12 'tis] ⟨till⟩ A   13 ⟨Though Gaity may⟩ Though Wit may
flash from fluent lips—and ⟨Gaity delight⟩ / Mirth beguile the breast A   distract] beguile B
14 ⟨In words to laugh away / To laugh the hours it could not⟩ / ⟨Through hours of night
which it no more can ? into rest⟩ A   their former hope of] ⟨?⟩ A   that] which A, B
their] the 1815 sheet music   15 as . . . around] like Ivy leaves that round A, B, 1815
sheet music   16 All . . . fresh] ⟨The⟩ All green and ⟨freshness⟩ A

5.

Oh could I feel as I have felt,—or be what I have been,
Or weep as I could once have wept, o'er many a vanished scene:
As springs in deserts found seem sweet, all brackish though they be,
So midst the wither'd waste of life, those tears would flow
    to me.   20

1815

246   Stanzas
[On the Death of the Duke of Dorset]

I heard thy fate without a tear,
    Thy loss with scarce a sigh;
And yet thou wert surpassing dear—
    Too loved of all to die.—
I know not what hath sear'd mine eye,   5
    The tears refuse to start;
But every drop its lids deny
    Falls dreary on my heart.

Yet—deep and heavy, one by one,
    They sink and turn to care;   10
As cavern'd waters wear the stone,
    Yet dropping harden there—
They cannot petrify more fast
    Than feelings sunk remain,
Which, coldly fix'd, regard the past,   15
    But never melt again.

[1815]

18 could . . . wept] should mourne *A, cor. in B*   19 As springs ⟨within / within
the desert found— ?* could be⟩ *A*   20 So midst] Amid *A, cor. in B*   life, those]
⟨thoughts⟩ *A*   flow to] seem to *A*; flow for *B, 1815 sheet music*

246. Copy text: *Arliss,* collated with *MSS. VA, Le,* Iowa facsimile MS., *Edinburgh
Annual Register, Paris1826*
title   *C*; Stanzas *Arliss, Edinburgh Annual Register, Paris1826, Iowa facsimile, More*
    1 fate] ⟨death⟩ *VA*   2 with scarce] ⟨without⟩ *Le*   3 yet ⟨to all⟩ thou *VA*
wert] wast *C*   5 I . . . what] ⟨But kindred thought⟩ *VA*   mine] ⟨my⟩ *Iowa facsimile*;
my *Le, C*   6 ⟨It now can weep for none⟩ *VA*   The] Its *Le, C*   7 its lids deny]
it bids me dry *C*   8 Falls dreary] ⟨Is heavy⟩ *VA*   9 deep] dull *C*   deep and
heavy] ⟨drop by drop—and⟩ *VA*   12 dropping harden] ⟨turn to marble⟩ *VA*
14 Than ⟨many a thought of mine⟩ *VA*   16 But never melt] And never will *VA*

247   Stanzas
        [In Those Young Days So Fond and Fair]

1.

In those young days, so fond and fair,
    When Childhood shone above thee,
And beating with a Brother's care
    My heart was proud to love thee—
In those young days, so fair and fond,   5
    Which saw our souls united,
I little deemed the years beyond
    Would see my hopes so blighted.

2.

But thou art gone—where all must go—
    So soon, so sadly stricken;   10
Thy heart scarce felt the sudden blow,
    But ours for-ever sicken.
The pangs that spared thee live for those
    Who mourne that now they kill not;
And many an eye like thine must close,   15
    Ere o'er thy name it fill not.

[1815]

247. Copy text: *MS. G*, collated with *MS. VA*

title   *untitled in VA*

    2 shone] ⟨smiled⟩ *VA*   4 proud] fond *VA*   7 I . . . years] ⟨I did not dream
the days⟩ *VA*   deemed] dreamed *VA*

Stanza 2 *The following stanza is cancelled in VA*

            Though ⟨years rolled on⟩ seasons rolled since that blest time
                And distance made us strangers—
            Though ⟨other suns⟩ many a sea—and many a clime
                Through Toil and ⟨Ocean's⟩ Tempest's dangers
            Had ⟨led me far⟩ lured me long—and led me far
                And ⟨we were⟩ even at home we met not
            We were among the few that are
                Whose hearts once touched forget not.—

9 ⟨The promise of thy spotless youth / Oh had the days I wished for thee / But fare thee
well—thou canst not hear⟩ *VA*   10 ⟨Demanded years / Too soon too sadly/ and ah
too sadly⟩ *VA*   11 ⟨How sudden was the stroke of woe⟩ *VA*   13 spared]
⟨passed⟩ *VA*   14 ⟨Who loved thee long and dearly / Who feel what thou hast felt
not⟩ *VA*   16 ⟨Before it close to thee / Ere at thy name it melt not⟩ *VA*

248   [On Napoleon's Escape from Elba]

Once fairly set out on his party of pleasure,
Taking towns at his liking and crowns at his leisure,
From Elba to Lyons and Paris he goes,
Making *balls for* the ladies, and *bows to* his foes.

[1815]

249–72   Hebrew Melodies

[1815]

The subsequent poems were written at the request of my friend, the
Hon. D. Kinnaird, for a Selection of Hebrew Melodies, and have been
published, with the music, arranged, by Mr. Braham and Mr. Nathan.
[Author's Note prefacing *HM1815*]

249   She Walks in Beauty

1.

She walks in beauty, like the night
    Of cloudless climes and starry skies;
And all that's best of dark and bright
    Meet in her aspect and her eyes:
Thus mellow'd to that tender light   5
    Which heaven to gaudy day denies.

2.

One shade the more, one ray the less,
    Had half impair'd the nameless grace
Which waves in every raven tress,
    Or softly lightens o'er her face;   10
Where thoughts serenely sweet express
    How pure, how dear their dwelling place.

248. Copy text: *Life*
title   *not in Life*

249. Copy text: *HM1815*, collated with *MS. W*, *MS. AL*, *N1815*
  2 Of ⟨softer climes⟩ and ⟨summer⟩ skies⟩ *W*   4 ⟨Are blended in her form and⟩ eyes
W   Meet] Meets *1815*   5 Thus] ⟨And / There⟩ So *W*   6 gaudy] ⟨gaudi⟩
garish *W*   8 impair'd . . . grace] ⟨destroyed . . . charm⟩ *W*   9 Which] That *W*
10 That ⟨lighten⟩ softly . . . face *W*   11 Where ⟨Goodness leaves no thought to guess⟩
⟨lovely thoughts⟩ ⟨Sweetness⟩ / thoughts serenely sweet express *W*   12 ⟨The pureness
of⟩ / How pure how dear the dwelling place *W*

3.

And on that cheek, and o'er that brow,
   So soft, so calm, yet eloquent,
The smiles that win, the tints that glow,   15
   But tell of days in goodness spent,
A mind at peace with all below,
   A heart whose love is innocent!

[1814]

250   The Harp the Monarch Minstrel Swept

1.

The harp the monarch minstrel swept,
   The King of men, the loved of Heaven,
Which Music hallowed while she wept
   O'er tones her heart of hearts had given,
   Redoubled be her tears, its chords are riven!   5
It softened men of iron mould,
   It gave them virtues not their own;
No ear so dull, no soul so cold,
   That felt not, fired not to the tone,
   Till David's Lyre grew mightier than his throne!   10

13 o'er that brow] ⟨in that air⟩ / on that air *W*   14 ⟨No ti / harsher tints / tints
disturb⟩ ⟨are written⟩ *W*   15 The smiles] ⟨Are written⟩ The looks *W*   16 ⟨Bespeak⟩
But tell *W*

18   Light were the sin in loving her
            For fixing there its purer thought
          The wildest heart would cease to err
            ⟨And⟩ Its evil wishes all untaught
          And ————————————————— *uncancelled*
          incomplete stanza after line 18 in W

250. Copy text: *HM1815*, collated with *MSS. A, B, AL, N1815*

1–2 ⟨Oh then farewell I could have borne | Without a murmur all the / save this— | The
false on⟩ *A*; The harp ⟨a⟩ the monarch⟨'s fingers⟩ minstrel swept *A*; Minstrel Monarch *B*
2 King] ⟨king⟩ first *A, B*   3 Which . . . hallowed] ⟨Oer which⟩ Which . . . cherished
A, B   4 O'er . . . heart of hearts] O'er . . . ⟨highest Soul⟩ *A*; On . . . Heart of Hearts
B   her] his *AL*   5 riven] risen *B*   7 It ⟨saved / made the hearts that felt its
tone / that heard its own⟩ *A*   8 no soul] ⟨nor⟩ soul *A*   10 Till . . . grew] ⟨When
Jesse's son⟩ And David's lyre was *A, B*

2.

It told the triumphs of our King,
    It wafted glory to our God;
It made our gladdened vallies ring,
    The cedars bow, the mountains nod;
        Its sound aspired to Heaven and there abode!   15
Since then, though heard on earth no more,
    Devotion and her daughter Love
Still bid the bursting spirit soar
        To sounds that seem as from above,
        In dreams that day's broad light can not remove.   20

[1815]

251   If That High World

1.

If that high world, which lies beyond
    Our own, surviving Love endears;
If there the cherish'd heart be fond,
    The eye the same, except in tears—
        How welcome those untrodden spheres!   5
        How sweet this very hour to die!
        To soar from earth and find all fears
        Lost in thy light—Eternity!

11   ⟨His Glory / Memory / Glory bids us mourne no more
            Ablest of Kings and bards the chief
            Its strain that / His name but tells of Glories / triumphs oer
            For him so hig⟩ A; ⟨An / But he is dust—and we are sunk⟩ A

12 It . . . to] ⟨The⟩ It ⟨? its⟩ wafted Glory ⟨from⟩ A   13 our] ⟨far⟩ A

16   ⟨It there abode—the / and there it rings
                            But neer on earth its sound shall be—
                            The Prophet's race hath passed away—
                            And all the hallowed Minstrelsy
                        From earth its / that sound and soul are fled
                            And shall we never near again / And shall⟩ A, B

rings] reigns B   16–20 not in A, B

251. Copy text: HM1815, collated with MS. AL, N1815, N1816

2.

It must be so: 'tis not for self
   That we so tremble on the brink;   10
And striving to o'erleap the gulph,
   Yet cling to Being's severing link.
Oh! in that future let us think
   To hold each heart the heart that shares,
With them the immortal waters drink,   15
   And soul in soul grow deathless theirs!

[1814]

252   The Wild Gazelle

1.

The wild gazelle on Judah's hills
   Exulting yet may bound,
And drink from all the living rills
   That gush on holy ground;
Its airy step and glorious eye   5
May glance in tameless transport by:—

2.

A step as fleet, an eye more bright,
   Hath Judah witness'd there;
And o'er her scenes of lost delight
   Inhabitants more fair.   10
The cedars wave on Lebanon,
But Judah's statelier maids are gone!

3.

More blest each palm that shades those plains
   Than Israel's scattered race;
For, taking root, it there remains   15
   In solitary grace:

12 severing] breaking *AL, N1816*

252. Copy text: *HM1815*, collated with *MS. A, N1815*

   1 ⟨Oer Judah's hills the wild Gazelle⟩ *A*   on] ⟨oer⟩ *A*   3 living] ⟨mountain's⟩ *A*
4 gush] ⟨spring⟩ *A*   6 in . . . transport] in ⟨untamed / unfrightened gladness⟩ *A*
7 fleet] ⟨light⟩ *A*   8 Hath Judah witness'd] ⟨Did Judah's singer's⟩ *A*   9 And
⟨round⟩ her ⟨forests a fairer sight⟩ *A*   11 wave] ⟨rest⟩ *A*   13 ⟨Ye Trees—than our
vanished / that shade our vanished plains⟩ *A*   More . . . palm . . . those] ⟨How . . . tree . . .
the⟩ *A*   14 ⟨Than Jud⟩ Than Israel's ⟨exiled⟩ race *A*   16 ⟨Eternal in its place⟩ *A*

It cannot quit its place of birth,
It will not live in other earth.

4.

But we must wander witheringly,
    In other lands to die;   20
And where our fathers' ashes be,
    Our own may never lie:
Our temple hath not left a stone,
And Mockery sits on Salem's throne.

                                    [1814]

253   Oh! Weep for Those

1.

Oh! weep for those that wept by Babel's stream,
Whose shrines are desolate, whose land a dream;
Weep for the harp of Judah's broken shell;
Mourn—where their God hath dwelt the Godless dwell!

2.

And where shall Israel lave her bleeding feet?   5
And when shall Zion's songs again seem sweet?
And Judah's melody once more rejoice
The hearts that leap'd before its heavenly voice?

3.

Tribes of the wandering foot and weary breast,
How shall ye flee away and be at rest?   10
The wild-dove hath her nest, the fox his cave,
Mankind their Country—Israel but the grave!

                                    [1814]

    19 witheringly ⟨on⟩ A   23 ⟨And where our fathers and our throne⟩ A   24 Mockery
sits] ⟨Silence / Darkness dwells⟩ A

253. Copy text: HM1815, collated with N1815
    10 rest?] rest! HM1815, 1831, 1832, C, More

254   On Jordan's Banks

I.

On Jordan's banks the Arabs' camels stray,
On Sion's hill the False One's votaries pray,
The Baal-adorer bows on Sinai's steep—
Yet there—even there—Oh God! thy thunders sleep:

2.

There—where thy finger scorch'd the tablet stone!   5
There—where thy shadow to thy people shone!
Thy glory shrouded in its garb of fire:
Thyself—none living see and not expire!

3.

Oh! in the lightning let thy glance appear!
Sweep from his shiver'd hand the oppressor's spear: 10
How long by tyrants shall thy land be trod?
How long thy temple worshipless, Oh God?

[1814]

255   Jephtha's Daughter

I.

Since our Country, our God—Oh, my Sire!
Demand that thy Daughter expire;
Since thy triumph was bought by thy vow—
Strike the bosom that's bared for thee now!

254. Copy text: *HM1815*, collated with *MS. A, N1815*

    3 ⟨God! can thy thunders sleep on dark Sinai⟩ *A*   3 Baal-adorer bows] ⟨idol⟩ Baal-
adorer ⟨walks⟩ *A*   4 thy ⟨slee⟩ thunders *A*   5 scorch'd the tablet] ⟨traced⟩ /
scorched the table⟨s of⟩ *A*   6 thy . . . to] ⟨thyself unto⟩ *A*   7 ⟨There where thy
Glory like / sate / shadowed in its⟩ / ⟨Thy Glory in its / shrouded in⟩ *A*   8 Thyself]
⟨For thee⟩ *A*   9 Oh! in the] ⟨Mask not thy⟩ *A*   10 And shiver in his grasp the
oppressor's spear *A*   11–12 trod? . . . God?] trod! . . . God! *N1815, M1815, 1815,
1831, 1832, More*   12 worshipless, Oh] ⟨Priestless—Oh my⟩ *A*

255. Copy text: *HM1815*, collated with *N1815*

2.

And the voice of my mourning is o'er,   5
And the mountains behold me no more:
If the hand that I love lay me low,
There cannot be pain in the blow!

3.

And of this, oh, my Father! be sure—
That the blood of thy child is as pure   10
As the blessing I beg ere it flow,
And the last thought that soothes me below.

4.

Though the virgins of Salem lament,
Be the judge and the hero unbent!
I have won the great battle for thee,   15
And my Father and Country are free!

5.

When this blood of thy giving hath gush'd,
When the voice that thou lovest is hush'd,
Let my memory still be thy pride,
And forget not I smiled as I died!   20

[1814]

256 Oh! Snatched Away in Beauty's Bloom

1.

Oh! snatched away in beauty's bloom,
On thee shall press no ponderous tomb;
But on thy turf shall roses rear
Their leaves, the earliest of the year;
And the wild cypress wave in tender gloom: 5

256. Copy text: *HM1815*, collated with *MSS. A, B, C, N1815, Examiner*
title   Sonnet—by Lord Byron *Examiner*

  1 ⟨Like the rays on the / yon blue gushing stream⟩ *A*   3 on] ⟨from⟩ oer *MS. C*
  4 Their leaves] ⟨The⟩ / Their ⟨tender leaf⟩ leaves *A*; Their Leaf *B*   5 tender] gentle
A, B

2.

And oft by yon blue gushing stream
   Shall Sorrow lean her drooping head,
And feed deep thought with many a dream,
   And lingering pause and lightly tread;
Fond wretch! as if her step disturb'd the dead!   10

3.

Away; we know that tears are vain,
   That death nor heeds nor hears distress:
Will this unteach us to complain?
   Or make one mourner weep the less?
And thou—who tell'st me to forget,   15
Thy looks are wan, thine eyes are wet.

[1815]

257   My Soul Is Dark

1.

My soul is dark—Oh! quickly string
   The harp I yet can brook to hear;
And let thy gentle fingers fling
   Its melting murmurs o'er mine ear.
   If in this heart a hope be dear,   5
That sound shall charm it forth again;
   If in these eyes there lurk a tear,
'Twill flow, and cease to burn my brain:

7 lean . . . head] ⟨on the waters gaze⟩ A   8 feed . . . dream] ⟨lost in deep remembrance dream⟩ A   deep] ⟨her⟩ A   9 lingering] ⟨long shall⟩ A   10 Fond . . . disturb'd] As if ⟨her steps / fearful to⟩ her footsteps could disturb A, B   step] steps Examiner   11–12 ⟨But thou for whom the land laments | Was raised / Oh neer wept⟩ A   11 that . . . vain] ⟨tis idle all⟩ A   we . . . vain] ⟨it is delusion all⟩ MS. C   12 nor heeds nor hears] ⟨is⟩ nor hears nor heeds A, B, Ashton; nor hear nor heed MS. C   13 Will] Can MS. C   15 And thou] ⟨Even⟩ thou A; And thou MS. C   16 looks are] cheek is MS. C   thine] thy Examiner

257. Copy text: HM1815, collated with N1815

2.

But bid the strain be wild and deep,
   Nor let thy notes of joy be first: 10
I tell thee, minstrel, I must weep,
   Or else this heavy heart will burst;
For it hath been by sorrow nurst,
   And ach'd in sleepless silence long;
   And now 'tis doom'd to know the worst,   15
And break at once—or yield to song.

[1814[

258   I Saw Thee Weep

1.

I saw thee weep—the big bright tear
   Came o'er that eye of blue;
And then methought it did appear
   A violet dropping dew:
I saw thee smile—the sapphire's blaze   5
   Beside thee ceased to shine;
It could not match the living rays
   That fill'd that glance of thine.

2.

As clouds from yonder sun receive
   A deep and mellow dye,   10
Which scarce the shade of coming eve
   Can banish from the sky,
Those smiles unto the moodiest mind
   Their own pure joy impart;
Their sunshine leaves a glow behind   15
   That lightens o'er the heart.

[1814]

258. Copy text: *HM1815*, collated with *MS. A*, *MS. AL*, *N1815*

    4 dew] blue *AL*   7 match] boast / match *A alternate readings*   8 that glance]
those eyes / that glance *A alternate readings*   10–12 A deep ⟨but parting glow / Ere
down the mountain⟩ coming Eve / ⟨Oershadows all below⟩ *A*   13 unto] can from *AL*
15 glow] beam / glow *A alternate readings*

259   Thy Days Are Done

1.

Thy days are done, thy fame begun;
　　Thy country's strains record
The triumphs of her chosen Son,
　　The slaughters of his sword!
The deeds he did, the fields he won, .   5
　　The freedom he restored!

2.

Though thou art fall'n, while we are free
　　Thou shalt not taste of death!
The generous blood that flowed from thee
　　Disdain'd to sink beneath: 10
Within our veins its currents be,
　　Thy spirit on our breath!

3.

Thy name, our charging hosts along,
　　Shall be the battle-word!
Thy fall, the theme of choral song   15
　　From virgin voices poured!
To weep would do thy glory wrong;
　　Thou shalt not be deplored.

　　　　　　　　　　　　　[1814]

260   It is the Hour

It is the hour when from the boughs
　　The nightingale's high note is heard;
It is the hour when lovers' vows
　　Seem sweet in every whispered word;
And gentle winds and waters near   5
Make music to the lonely ear.

259. Copy text: *HM1815*, collated with *MS. AL, N1815*

260. Copy text: *HM1815*, collated with *N1815, Parisina, MS. AL*

Each flower the dews have lightly wet,
And in the sky the stars are met;
And on the wave is deeper blue,
And on the leaf a browner hue;   10
And in the Heaven that clear obscure,
So softly dark, and darkly pure,
That follows the decline of day
As twilight melts beneath the moon away.

[1814?]

261   Song of Saul Before His Last Battle

1.

Warriors and Chiefs! should the shaft or the sword
Pierce me in leading the host of the Lord,
Heed not the corse, though a king's, in your path:
Bury your steel in the bosoms of Gath!

2.

Thou who art bearing my buckler and bow,   5
Should the soldiers of Saul look away from the foe,
Stretch me that moment in blood at thy feet!
Mine be the doom which they dared not to meet.

3.

Farewell to others, but never we part,
Heir to my royalty, son of my heart!   10
Bright is the diadem, boundless the sway,
Or kingly the death, which awaits us to-day!

[1815]

13 That] Which *Parisina*

261. Copy text *HM1815*, collated with *MSS A, B, C, D*
title   Son of Saul *A*

3 corse ... king's,] carcase that lies *A alternate reading*; ⟨carcase that lies⟩ *B*   5 buckler
and] shield and my *A alternate reading* ⟨shield and my⟩ *B*   6 soldiers of Saul] ranks of
your king *A, cor. in B*   10 to my royalty] of my Monarchy *A alternate reading*

262　　Saul

1.

Thou whose spell can raise the dead,
Bid the prophet's form appear.
'Samuel, raise thy buried head!
King, behold the phantom seer!'
Earth yawn'd; he stood the centre of a cloud:　　5
Light changed its hue, retiring from his shroud.
Death stood all glassy in his fixed eye;
His hand was withered, and his veins were dry;
His foot, in bony whiteness, glittered there,
Shrunken and sinewless, and ghastly bare:　　10
From lips that moved not and unbreathing frame,
Like cavern'd winds, the hollow accents came.
Saul saw, and fell to earth, as falls the oak,
At once, and blasted by the thunder-stroke.

2.

'Why is my sleep disquieted?　　15
Who is he that calls the dead?
Is it thou, Oh King? Behold
Bloodless are these limbs, and cold:
Such are mine: and such shall be
Thine, to-morrow, when with me:　　20
Ere the coming day is done,
Such shalt thou be, such thy son.
Fare thee well, but for a day;
Then we mix our mouldering clay.
Thou, thy race, lie pale and low,　　25
Pierced by shafts of many a bow;

262. Copy text: *HMI815*, collated with *MSS. A, B, C*

1 spell can] ⟨voice canst⟩ *A*　　4 [paragraph break after this line in *A, B, C*, and *Ashton*]　　5 ⟨He ros / stands amidst an earthly⟩ cloud *A*　　6 ⟨And the Mist mantled oer his floating⟩ shroud *A*　retiring] ⟨as shrinking⟩ *A*　　7 Death ⟨glared in⟩ stood all glassy ⟨oer⟩ in his ⟨aged⟩ fixed eye *A*　　8 was . . . were] ⟨was / is . . . are⟩ *A*　9–10 ⟨His / He stood erect and motionless | The boney whiteness of his foot was there⟩ *A*　11 From ⟨lips that / lips that moved / stir not⟩ *A*　　13 fell] ⟨bowed⟩ *A*　　14 and . . . by] and scorched beneath *A, B, C*　　15 Why is] ⟨Who is⟩ Why ⟨am⟩ is *A*　　16 he ⟨dare⟩ that *A*　　18 these limbs] ⟨my⟩ these bones *A, B, C*　　21 Ere ⟨hath sunk tomorrow's Sun⟩ / ⟨tomorrow's⟩ the coming day ⟨hath⟩ done— *A*　　23 a] ⟨the⟩ *A*　24 mix] ⟨mingle⟩ *A*　　26 by] by ⟨the⟩ *A*

And the falchion by thy side,
To thy heart, thy hand shall guide:
Crownless, breathless, headless fall,
Son and sire, the house of Saul!'

[1815]   30

263   'All is Vanity, Saith the Preacher'

1.

Fame, wisdom, love, and power were mine,
    And health and youth possess'd me;
My goblets blush'd from every vine,
    And lovely forms caress'd me;

I sunn'd my heart in beauty's eyes,   5
    And felt my soul grow tender;
All earth can give, or mortal prize,
    Was mine of regal splendour.

2.

I strive to number o'er what days
    Remembrance can discover,   10
Which all that life or earth displays
    Would lure me to live over.

There rose no day, there roll'd no hour
    Of pleasure unembittered;
And not a trapping deck'd my power   15
    That gall'd not while it glittered.

29 headless] ⟨conquered⟩ A

────────────

263. Copy text: *HM1815*, collated with *MSS. A, B. MS. A* and *Ashton* arrange the poem
in stanzas of eight continuous lines.

title   'Fame, Wisdom, Love' etc. *A*

    1 power] ⟨health / wealth⟩ *A*   2 health] ⟨wealth⟩ *A*   3 blush'd] ⟨teemed /
foamed⟩ *A*   9–10 ⟨I try to number oer the days | Which were my spring / ? begin-
ning / cured ?⟩ / ⟨? Spring of Life had such / so bright a past⟩ *A*   9 what] ⟨the⟩ *A*
10 ⟨So dear to Memory's bosom⟩ *A*   11 life or earth] ⟨Heaven and Earth / Life's last
ray⟩ / ⟨Love⟩ Life on earth *A*   12 lure] ⟨bride⟩ *A*   13 There⟨s not a⟩ day—theres
⟨not an⟩ hour *A*   roll'd] ⟨passed⟩ *A*   14 ⟨That Sun or Moon / Without ?⟩ ⟨Nor
moment ?⟩ unembittered *A*   15 ⟨And⟩ not a trapping ⟨flung⟩ decked *A*

3.

The serpent of the field, by art
　　And spells, is won from harming;
But that which coils around the heart,
　　Oh! who hath power of charming?　　　　　20

It will not list to wisdom's lore,
　　Nor music's voice can lure it;
But there it stings for evermore
　　The soul that must endure it.

[1815]

264　　When Coldness Wraps This Suffering Clay

1.

When coldness wraps this suffering clay,
　　Ah, whither strays the immortal mind?
It cannot die, it cannot stay,
　　But leaves its darken'd dust behind.
Then, unembodied, doth it trace　　　　　5
　　By steps each planet's heavenly way?
Or fill at once the realms of space,
　　A thing of eyes, that all survey?

17 ff.　　　　　　⟨And what hath been—but what shall be
　　　　　　　　The same dull scene renewing—
　　　　　　　　And all are our father's are / were / are we
　　　　　　　　　In erring and undoing—
　　　　　　　　The Growth of wisdom ? woe⟩ A
　　　　　　　　⟨My father was the Shepherds son—
　　　　　　　　　Ah were my lot as lowly—
　　　　　　　　My earthly course had slo / softly run⟩ A

17 ⟨There is no magic⟩ A　　of . . . art] ⟨of the field⟩ / of the field by ⟨spells⟩ A　　18 ⟨Is
charmed from ?⟩ And ⟨charms⟩ is ⟨lured⟩ from A　　　　21 It . . . list] ⟨Nor⟩ It will not
⟨bend⟩ A

264.　Copy text: HM1815, collated with MSS. A, B
title　'When Coldness Wraps' etc. A

1 When ⟨this corroding clay is gone⟩ A　　clay] ⟨dus?⟩ A　　　　4 But . . . dust] With
that ⟨it dearly / sadly leaves⟩ / frail flesh it leaves A cancelled　　6 By . . . heavenly] ⟨The
stars in their eternal⟩ / By steps ⟨the stars' eternal⟩ A

2.

Eternal, boundless, undecay'd,
   A thought unseen, but seeing all,   10
All, all in earth, or skies display'd,
   Shall it survey, shall it recall:
Each fainter trace that memory holds
   So darkly of departed years,
In one broad glance the soul beholds,   15
   And all, that was, at once appears.

3.

Before Creation peopled earth,
   Its eye shall roll through chaos back;
And where the furthest heaven had birth,
   The spirit trace its rising track.   20
And where the future mars or makes,
   Its glance dilate o'er all to be,
While sun is quench'd or system breaks,
   Fix'd in its own eternity.

4.

Above or Love, Hope, Hate, or Fear,   25
   It lives all passionless and pure:
An age shall fleet like earthly year;
   Its years as moments shall endure.
Away, away, without a wing,
   O'er all, through all, its thought shall fly;   30
A nameless and eternal thing,
   Forgetting what it was to die.

[1815]

10 A ⟨?⟩ thought *A*   11 ⟨Which heaven and earth can⟩ ⟨A conscious light that can
pervade / That / Mingling with aught by Nature made⟩ / ⟨Heaven—earth and ? and all—⟩
A   display'd] ⟨surveyed⟩ *A*   12 ⟨But subject to no future fall—⟩ *A*   survey] ⟨fore-
see⟩ *A*   13 Each ⟨that Memory⟩ fainter trace ⟨that⟩ that *A*   14 So darkly] ⟨And⟩
⟨Uncertain⟩ / So ⟨faintly⟩ *A*   15 In] ⟨In⟩ *A*   16 at] ⟨at⟩ *A*   17 peopled
earth] ⟨gave the Sun⟩ *A*   18 Its . . . through chaos] ⟨His . . . unbounded⟩ *A*   19 And
where . . . heaven] ⟨Before . . . stars⟩ *A*   furthest] farthest *C*   20 spirit trace its]
⟨Soul shall⟩ Spirit trace ⟨their⟩ *A*   21 mars or makes] ⟨makes or mars⟩ *A*   22 ⟨Shall
follow on its / the eternal path⟩ *A*   o'er all to] ⟨over⟩ all ⟨that⟩ *A*   23 ⟨Where
earth—or—Sun—or system breaks⟩ *A*   25 Above or] ⟨Exempt from / Ab⟩ Above oer
A, *Ashton*; Above or *B*, HM*1815*, *1831*, *1832*, *C*, *More*   26 ⟨All⟩ passionless ⟨and un-
fettered / ?⟩ / and pure *A*   27 ⟨Earth's / Shall Ages seem as⟩ / ⟨Its⟩ / An Age⟨s⟩ shall
fleet like earthly year *A*   28 ⟨Shall⟩ Its years ⟨but⟩ as *A*   29 without] ⟨beyond⟩ *A*

265   Vision of Belshazzar

1.

The King was on his throne,
  The Satraps throng'd the hall;
A thousand bright lamps shone
  O'er that high festival.
A thousand cups of gold,   5
  In Judah deem'd divine—
Jehovah's vessels hold
  The godless Heathen's wine!

2.

In that same hour and hall,
  The fingers of a hand   10
Came forth against the wall,
  And wrote as if on sand:
The fingers of a man;—
  A solitary hand
Along the letters ran,   15
  And traced them like a wand.

3.

The monarch saw, and shook,
  And bade no more rejoice;
All bloodless wax'd his look,
  And tremulous his voice.   20
'Let the men of lore appear,
  The wisest of the earth,
And expound the words of fear,
  Which mar our royal mirth.'

265. Copy text: *HM1815*, collated with *MS. A*

  2 throng'd] in *A*
5–8   A thousand cups ⟨were shown
                        Of gold along the board
                        Which till then had held alone
                        Salem's offering to the Lord⟩ *A*

6 Judah] Israel *A*   24 mar our royal] mar⟨red a Sovereign's⟩ *A*

4.

Chaldea's seers are good,
  But here they have no skill;
And the unknown letters stood
  Untold and awful still.
And Babel's men of age
  Are wise and deep in lore;
But now they were not sage,
  They saw—but knew no more.

5.

A captive in the land,
  A stranger and a youth,
He heard the king's command,
  He saw that writing's truth.
The lamps around were bright,
  The prophecy in view;
He read it on that night,—
  The morrow proved it true.

6.

'Belshazzar's grave is made,
  His kingdom pass'd away,
He in the balance weighed,
  Is light and worthless clay.
The shroud, his robe of state,
  His canopy, the stone;
The Mede is at his gate!
  The Persian on his throne!'

[1815]

25

30

35

40

45

41 Belshazzar's] ⟨Oh King thy⟩ A   42 His kingdom] ⟨Thy⟩ kingdom('s) A
43 He] ⟨Thou⟩ A   44 Is] ⟨Art⟩ A   45 his] ⟨thy⟩ A   46 His] ⟨Thy⟩ A
47 his] ⟨thy⟩ A   48 his] ⟨thy⟩ A

266 ## Sun of the Sleepless!

Sun of the sleepless! melancholy star!
Whose tearful beam glows tremulously far,
That show'st the darkness thou canst not dispel,
How like art thou to joy remembered well!
So gleams the past, the light of other days, 5
Which shines, but warms not with its powerless rays;
A night-beam Sorrow watcheth to behold,
Distinct, but distant—clear—but, oh how cold!

[1814]

267 ## Were My Bosom As False As Thou Deem'st It To Be

1.

Were my bosom as false as thou deem'st it to be,
I need not have wandered from far Galilee;
It was but abjuring my creed to efface
The curse which, thou say'st, is the crime of my race.

2.

If the bad never triumph, then God is with thee! 5
If the slave only sin, thou art spotless and free!
If the Exile on earth is an Outcast on high,
Live on in thy faith, but in mine I will die.

3.

I have lost for that faith more than thou canst bestow,
As the God who permits thee to prosper doth know; 10
In his hand is my heart and my hope—and in thine
The land and the life which for him I resign.

[1815]

266. Copy text: *HM1815*, collated with *Harmodia, MSS. B, C*

2 glows tremulously far] shoots trembling from afar *Harmodia*   3 That] ⟨Why⟩
Harmodia   5 So gleams] Such is *Harmodia*   6 Which] That *Harmodia, B*
7 night-beam] Moonbeam *Harmodia*   watcheth] watche⟨s⟩ *Harmodia*   8 clear . . .
cold] ⟨dazzling—clear⟩ clear but ⟨oh how⟩ deathlike cold *Harmodia*

267. Copy text: *HM1815*, collated with *MSS. A, B*
title   'Were my bosom as false'—etc. *A*

268   Herod's Lament for Mariamne

I.

Oh, Mariamne! now for thee
   The heart for which thou bled'st is bleeding;
Revenge is lost in agony,
   And wild remorse to rage succeeding.
Oh, Mariamne! where art thou?   5
   Thou canst not hear my bitter pleading:
Ah, could'st thou—thou would'st pardon now,
   Though heaven were to my prayer unheeding.

2.

And is she dead?—and did they dare
   Obey my phrensy's jealous raving?   10
My wrath but doom'd my own despair:
   The sword that smote her 's o'er me waving.—
But thou art cold, my murdered love!
   And this dark heart is vainly craving
For her who soars alone above,   15
   And leaves my soul unworthy saving.

3.

She's gone, who shared my diadem;
   She sunk, with her my joys entombing;
I swept that flower from Judah's stem
   Whose leaves for me alone were blooming.   20

268. Copy text: *HM1815*, collated with *MSS. A, B, C*

title   'Oh Mariamne' *A*

   3 ⟨And what was rage is⟩ agony *A*   lost in] turned to *A*   4 wild] deep *A*   6 ⟨And
what am I thy tyrant⟩ pleading *A*   7 ⟨Thou canst not ? / view / see my burning brow⟩
A   thou . . . pardon] ⟨would'st thou see me⟩ *A*   8 Though] ⟨But⟩ *A*   9 ⟨Oh
look on me if / yet / above / in / from that heaven⟩ / ⟨Thy gentle Spirit⟩ Thou art not dead
—they ⟨dared not⟩ could not dare *A*   10 ⟨? / Fulfill⟩ / Obey my jealous Fury's raving *A*
12 ⟨They might have saved me / I ?⟩ *A*   her's] thee's *A*   14 ⟨But yet in death my
soul enslaving⟩ *A*   15 For her ⟨its / I neer / shall not meet above⟩ *A*   her] he *MS. C*
soars] went *A, cor. in B*   16 leaves] left *A*   18 She's ⟨gone—who made me
blest / who made my life / blessing⟩ / low—with her my hope entombing *A*   20 ⟨While
yet the leaves⟩ *A*

And mine's the guilt, and mine the hell,
    This bosom's desolation dooming;
And I have earn'd those tortures well,
    Which unconsumed are still consuming!

[1815]

269   On the Day of the Destruction of
                Jerusalem by Titus

I.

From the last hill that looks on thy once holy dome
I beheld thee, Oh SION! when rendered to Rome:
'Twas thy last sun went down, and the flames of thy fall
Flash'd back on the last glance I gave to thy wall.

2.

I look'd for thy temple, I look'd for my home,   5
And forgot for a moment my bondage to come;
I beheld but the death-fire that fed on thy fane,
And the fast-fettered hands that made vengeance in vain.

3.

On many an eve, the high spot whence I gazed
Had reflected the last beam of day as it blazed;   10
While I stood on the height, and beheld the decline
Of the rays from the mountain that shone on thy shrine.

4.

And now on that mountain I stood on that day,
But I mark'd not the twilight beam melting away;

21 guilt] ⟨deed⟩ A   and mine] and mine⟨'s⟩ B   22 This] ⟨My⟩ A   23 And . . .
those] ⟨That / I⟩ Oh I have earned ⟨its⟩ A

269. Copy text: HM1815, collated with MSS. A, B, C
title 'From the last hill that looks' A, B

1 th⟨y⟩ last B   on] oer A, B   dome] ⟨wall⟩ A   2 when . . . Rome] ⟨the day of
thy fall⟩ A   3 sun] ⟨sun⟩ day A, B, C   and] ⟨amid?⟩ A   4 ⟨But⟩ Flashed A
6 for a moment] ⟨in their ruin⟩ B   7 death-fire] ⟨ruin⟩ death fires A, cor. in B   8 And
the ⟨chains⟩ fast A   9 the . . . gazed] ⟨on the spot where I gaze⟩ A   whence] ⟨where⟩
MS. C   11 While I ⟨looked from thy wall with that quiet⟩ A   on the] on its A, B,
cor. in MS. C   12 on] ⟨oer⟩ A; oer B   13 And] ⟨But⟩ A   14 mark'd] saw A

Oh! would that the lightning had glared in its stead, 15
And the thunderbolt burst on the conqueror's head!

5.

But the Gods of the Pagan shall never profane
The shrine where Jehovah disdain'd not to reign;
And scattered and scorn'd as thy people may be,
Our worship, oh Father! is only for thee. 20

[1815]

270 By the Rivers of Babylon We Sat Down and Wept

1.

We sate down and wept by the waters
Of Babel, and thought of the day
When our foe, in the hue of his slaughters,
Made Salem's high places his prey;
And ye, oh her desolate daughters! 5
Were scattered all weeping away.

2.

While sadly we gazed on the river
Which roll'd on in freedom below,
They demanded the song; but, oh never
That triumph the stranger shall know! 10
May this right hand be withered for ever,
Ere it string our high harp for the foe!

16 thunderbolt burst on] ⟨red bolt⟩ burst ⟨oer⟩ A; thunderbolt ⟨burst⟩ crashed on B, C
19 thy] ⟨our⟩ A

270. Copy text: HM1815, collated with MSS. A, B, C
title 'We sate down and wept' etc. B

1 We sate ⟨by⟩ down A   2 And wept ⟨oer the day / bitter tears⟩ / mourned oer
cancelled in A   3 foe] foe⟨s⟩ A   6 scattered] borne A

7–10   ⟨Our mute harps were hung on the willow
            That grew by the Conqueror's stream / Stream of our foe
            And in sadness we look / gazed on each billow
            That rolled on in freedom below— ⟩ A

7 While] ⟨And wh⟩ A   8 Which] That A, B, C   in freedom] ⟨so freely⟩ A   9 ⟨The⟩
They A   10 ⟨That sound shall⟩ ⟨Our harps shall be strung for the foe⟩ A

3.

On the willow that harp is suspended,
　Oh Salem! its sound should be free;
And the hour when thy glories were ended   15
　But left me that token of thee:
And ne'er shall its soft tones be blended
　With the voice of the spoiler by me!

[1815]

271　　The Destruction of Semnacherib

1.

The Assyrian came down like the wolf on the fold,
And his cohorts were gleaming in purple and gold;
And the sheen of their spears was like stars on the sea,
When the blue wave rolls nightly on deep Galilee.

2.

Like the leaves of the forest when Summer is green,   5
That host with their banners at sunset were seen:
Like the leaves of the forest when Autumn hath blown,
That host on the morrow lay withered and strown.

3.

For the Angel of Death spread his wings on the blast,
And breathed in the face of the foe as he pass'd;   10
And the eyes of the sleepers wax'd deadly and chill,
And their hearts but once heaved, and for ever grew still!

13 ⟨Hang mutely my harp⟩ On the willow that harp ⟨shall hang mutely⟩ A   14 should
be free] ⟨was for thee⟩ A   15 hour] day A   glories] Glor⟨y⟩ A   18 voice] song A,
cor. in B

271. Copy text: HM1815, collated with MSS. A, B
title 'The Assyrian came down' A; The Rout of Semnacherib B

3 on] ⟨in⟩ B   4 wave rolls] wave⟨s⟩ ⟨heaves⟩ A   6 ⟨Was that host at⟩ A
7 Autumn] ⟨temp? / night winds⟩ A   8 on the morrow] ⟨in⟩ on the ⟨morning⟩ A
9 on] ⟨in⟩ B   10 in] ⟨on⟩ A   11 And their ⟨eyelids grew heavy—their sentinels⟩
eyes of the sleepers ⟨grew⟩ waxed heavy and chill A, cor. in B   12 their hearts but]
⟨their slumber⟩ A   grew] ⟨were⟩ B

4.

And there lay the steed with his nostril all wide,
But through it there roll'd not the breath of his pride:
And the foam of his gasping lay white on the turf,   15
And cold as the spray of the rock-beating surf.

5.

And there lay the rider distorted and pale,
With the dew on his brow, and the rust on his mail;
And the tents were all silent, the banners alone,
The lances unlifted, the trumpet unblown.   20

6.

And the widows of Ashur are loud in their wail,
And the idols are broke in the temple of Baal;
And the might of the Gentile, unsmote by the sword,
Hath melted like snow in the glance of the Lord!

[1815]

272   # From Job

1.

A spirit pass'd before me: I beheld
The face of Immortality unveil'd—
Deep sleep came down on ev'ry eye save mine
And there it stood,—all formless—but divine:
Along my bones the creeping flesh did quake;   5
And as my damp hair stiffen'd, thus it spake:

13 all] ⟨so⟩ *A*   14 roll'd] ⟨rushed⟩ *A*   15 of . . . white] ⟨on his bit / bridle⟩
lay ⟨cold⟩ *A*   16 And] ⟨As⟩ *A*   rock-beating] cliff-beating *A, B*   18 With . . .
brow] ⟨And stiff as the ?⟩ With the crow on his breast *A, B*   20 ⟨And the trumpet
that morning was⟩ *A*   unlifted] ⟨up⟩lifted *B*   21 ⟨And God hath prevailed—and his
people⟩ *A*   Ashur are] Babel ⟨?⟩ *A, cor. in B*   23 ⟨And the voices of Israel ? / are
joyous and high⟩ *A*   unsmote by the sword] ⟨is smote by the Lord⟩ *A*   24 in] ⟨to⟩ *A*

272. Copy text: *HM1815*, collated with *MSS. A, B, C, Shepherd*
title   *untitled in MSS. A, C*
    1 ⟨In thoughts from visions in the dead of night⟩ *MS. C*   1–2 ⟨'Twas a dream—
it is nothing—except in my heart | Where it cannot deceive—yet it will not depart⟩ *A*
2 The ⟨shapeless⟩ face *A*   4 all . . . divine] ⟨strange—⟩ formless ⟨and⟩ divine *A*
but] yet *Shepherd*   5–6 Fear shook along my bones— ⟨each hair arose / stiffening hair
stood still⟩ / while earth and Heaven grew / were still | A voice went forth—and shook the
Eternal Will! *cancelled in MS. C*   Fear shook my bones and stood in every hair | A voice
went forth and cleared the silent air.— *MS. C*   5 Along . . . creeping] ⟨And on . . .
faithless⟩ *A*   6 my damp] ⟨cold⟩ my chill *A*

2.

'Is man more just than God? Is man more pure
Than he who deems even Seraphs insecure?
Creatures of clay—vain dwellers in the dust!
The moth survives you, and are ye more just?   10
Things of a day! you wither ere the night,
Heedless and blind to Wisdom's wasted light!'

[1814]

273   [Bright Be the Place of Thy Soul]

1.

Bright be the place of thy soul!
   No lovelier spirit than thine
E'er burst from its mortal control,
   In the orbs of the blessed to shine.
On earth thou wert all but divine,   5
   As thy soul shall immortally be;
And our sorrow may cease to repine,
   When we know that thy God is with thee.

2.

Light be the turf of thy tomb!
   May its verdure like emeralds be: 10
There should not be the shadow of gloom,
   In aught that reminds us of thee.

7 just] pure *Shepherd* ⟨pure⟩ *MS. C*   pure] ⟨just⟩ *MS. C*   8 ⟨Creature of Clay and
Dweller in the dust?⟩ While ⟨erring⟩ / mightier Angels are not all secure *MS. C*   9 vain]
⟨what⟩ ye *A*   11 Born with the dawn—and withered ere the Night *MS. C*; The
Morning comes— ⟨and Night you shall not see⟩ / you fall before the Night— *A*   you . . .
the] ye . . . 'tis *Shepherd*   12 Heedless] Erring *MS. C*; Impure, unwise, and helpless
in his sight! *Shepherd*

273. Copy text: *Poems1816*, collated with *MSS. A, B, C, D*, Murray proof, *Examiner,
1815 sheet music, Clarke, Nathan, Ashton*

title   Stanzas *Examiner*; Stanzas for Music *MS. C*

6 immortally] ⟨eternally⟩ *A*; immortal⟨ity⟩ *Proof*   7 sorrow] sorrows *1815 sheet music*
9 ⟨Bright / Soft be thy pillows of rest / sleep⟩ Green be the turf of thy tomb *B*   Light]
Green *MS. C, cor. in D*   of] on *1815 sheet music, Nathan*   10 ⟨Though its verdure is
nothing to thee / Though its verdure the⟩ May its verdure be ⟨b⟩ sweetest to see *B*   like
. . . be] be sweetest to see *MS. C* ⟨be sweetest / freshest to see⟩ *D*   11 be the] be *B, C,
D, Examiner, Proof, Ashton*

Young flowers and an evergreen tree
    May spring from the spot of thy rest;
But not cypress nor yew let us see;   15
    For why should we mourn for the blest?

[1815]

274   Napoleon's Farewell

(From the French)

1.

Farewell to the Land, where the gloom of my Glory
Arose and o'ershadowed the earth with her name—
She abandons me now,—but the page of her story,
The brightest or blackest, is filled with my fame.
I have warred with a world which vanquished me only   5
When the meteor of Conquest allured me too far;
I have coped with the nations which dread me thus lonely,
The last single Captive to millions in war!

2.

Farewell to thee, France!—when thy diadem crowned me,
I made thee the gem and the wonder of earth,—   10
But thy weakness decrees I should leave as I found thee,
Decayed in thy glory, and sunk in thy worth.
Oh! for the veteran hearts that were wasted
In strife with the storm, when their battles were won—

13 Fresh flowers and a far spreading tree *B, C, cor. in D*   14 spring from] wave oer
B, C, cor. in D; grow oer *D, Examiner, 1815 sheet music*; ⟨grow in / oer⟩ *Proof*   15 not]
nor *B, C, D, Proof, Examiner, 1815 sheet music, Nathan, Ashton*   us see] ⟨them⟩ it be *B*; it
be *C, cor. in D*   16 mourn] grieve *B*

274. Copy text: *Poems1816*, collated with *MS., Examiner*
title   *untitled in MS. and Examiner*

   2 her name] ⟨the / its fame⟩ my name *MS.*   4 The brightest and blackest are due
to my fame *MS.*   6 When ⟨Victory / the meteor of Victory lured me too far⟩ *MS.*
7 coped . . . dread] ⟨warred⟩ with ⟨a World⟩ —which dread⟨s⟩ *MS.*   8 in war] ⟨in war /
of foes⟩ *MS.*   10 the gem . . . wonder] ⟨queen⟩ and the ⟨monarch⟩ *MS.*   11 weak-
ness decrees] ⟨destiny wills⟩ *MS.*   12 Decayed] ⟨A / Decayed / ?⟩ *MS.*

13–16   ⟨The⟩ Oh for the ⟨thousands of those⟩ veteran hearts who have
          perished
          By ⟨winter's⟩ elements ⟨withere⟩ blasted—unvanquished by man—
          Then the hopes which till now ⟨my⟩ I have fearlessly cherished
          Had waved oer thine Eagles in Victory's van.— *cancelled in MS.*

13 were] ⟨have⟩ *MS.*

Then the Eagle, whose gaze in that moment was blasted,   15
Had still soared with eyes fixed on victory's sun!

3.

Farewell to thee, France!—but when Liberty rallies
Once more in thy regions, remember me then—
The violet still grows in the depth of thy valleys;
Though withered, thy tears will unfold it again—   20
Yet, yet, I may baffle the hosts that surround us,
And yet may thy heart leap awake to my voice—
There are links which must break in the chain that has
    bound us,
Then turn thee and call on the Chief of thy choice!

                              [1815]

275   Golice Macbane

The clouds may pour down on Culloden's red plain,
But the waters shall flow o'er its crimson in vain;
For their drops shall seem few to the tears for the slain,
But mine are for thee, my brave GOLICE MACBANE!—

Though thy cause was the cause of the injur'd and brave;   5
Though thy death was the hero's, and glorious thy grave;
With thy dead foes around thee, pil'd high on the plain,
My sad heart bleeds o'er thee, my GOLICE MACBANE!

How the horse and the horseman thy single hand slew!
But what could the mightiest single arm do?   10
A hundred like thee might the battle regain,
But cold are thy hand and heart, GOLICE MACBANE!

15 Then the Eagles whose ⟨flight by my cohorts⟩ sight / gaze in that moment was blasted
MS.   16 still soared] ⟨still⟩ soared still *MS.*   17 Farewell] ⟨Adieu⟩ *MS.*   18 me
then] ⟨then⟩ me then *MS.*   19 still . . . the] grows in ⟨thy⟩ the *MS.*   20 ⟨Though
hid from the dull eyes of ? / Tis withered—but fear not—twill flourish again⟩ *MS.*   un-
fold] ⟨revive⟩ *MS.*   21 us] ⟨me⟩ *MS.*   23 are links which] ⟨is not⟩ are links that
MS.   24 *Then* . . . and] Then ⟨think on revenge—and / think on the past⟩ turn thee
⟨in ?⟩ and *MS.*

275. Copy text: *Clarke*, collated with *MSS. L, B* (all variants below are from *MS. L*)

1 clouds . . . on] ⟨red sun looks bloody⟩   clouds] ⟨rain⟩   pour] frown   red] ⟨dark⟩
2 shall flow] ⟨may wash⟩   3 their drops] the drops   4 But mine are] ⟨And mostly⟩
9 thy single] ⟨beneath thy⟩

With thy back to the wall, and thy breast to the targe,
Full flashed thy claymore in the face of their charge;
The blood of their boldest that barren turf stain,   15
But alas!—thine is reddest there, GOLICE MACBANE!

Hewn down, but still battling, thou sunk'st on the ground,
Thy plaid was one gore, and thy breast was one wound;
Thirteen of thy foes by thy right hand lay slain;
Oh! would they were thousands for GOLICE MACBANE!   20

Oh! loud, and long heard, shall thy coronach be;
And high o'er the heather thy cairn we shall see;
And deep in all bosoms thy name shall remain,
But deepest in mine, dearest GOLICE MACBANE!

And daily the eyes of thy brave boy before   25
Shall thy plaid be unfolded; unsheath'd thy claymore,
And the white rose shall bloom on his bonnet again,
Should he prove the true son of my GOLICE MACBANE.

                                                    [1815]

276   From the French

'All wept, but particularly Savary, and a Polish officer who
had been exalted from the ranks by Bonaparte. He clung to
his master's knees: wrote a letter to Lord Keith, entreating
permission to accompany him, even in the most menial
capacity, which could not be admitted'

I.

Must thou go, my glorious Chief,
Severed from thy faithful few?
Who can tell thy warrior's grief,
Maddening o'er that long adieu?

14 ⟨Thou stoodst as their number came down in the charge⟩   15 blood . . . barren]
⟨hearts of the bravest the green⟩   that] the   16 is . . . there] ⟨is red there too⟩   is]
was   17 ⟨Thirteen lie / They hewed thee in pieces / Outworn—bruised—oerwearied⟩
on] in   18 breast] heart   19 Thirteen] But thirteen   by . . . hand] ⟨lay out-
stretched on / of thy heaping⟩   21 Oh!] But   23 bosoms] ⟨hearts⟩   25 ⟨When
babes shall appear as their Sire was before⟩   26 ⟨I will show them thy red plaid and
bloody claymore⟩   unfolded;] unfolded and

276. Copy text: Poems1816, collated with MSS. L, La, M, T, proof
title Lines—the Pole to Bonaparte Lady B's title in L
    3 can] ⟨shall⟩ L   4 o'er that long] ⟨in⟩ that mute L

Woman's love, and friendship's zeal,   5
  Dear as both have been to me—
What are they to all I feel,
  With a soldier's faith for thee?

2.

Idol of the soldier's soul!
  First in fight, but mightiest now: 10
Many could a world control;
  Thee alone no doom can bow.
By thy side for years I dared
  Death; and envied those who fell,
When their dying shout was heard,   15
  Blessing him they served so well.

3.

Would that I were cold with those,
  Since this hour I live to see,
When the doubts of coward foes
  Scarce dare trust a man with thee,   20
Dreading each should set thee free.
  Oh! although in dungeons pent,
All their chains were light to me,
  Gazing on thy soul unbent.

4.

Would the sycophants of him   25
  Now so deaf to duty's prayer,
Were his borrowed glories dim,
  In his native darkness share?

6 ⟨Dear as they to / Dear as they were⟩ Dear as they have seemed to me *L, cor. in M*
7 all] ⟨all / that⟩ *L*   8 ⟨Torn from Glory⟩ ⟨In the faith I pledged to⟩ thee *L*   10 ⟨Glory brightened from / in thine eyes⟩ ⟨Never did I grieve till now⟩ ⟨More of triumph / When the light of triumph shone⟩ *L*   but] ⟨and⟩ *L*   11 ⟨Thou who worlds / emperors didst controul⟩ *L*   12 ⟨But / Whom / Those whom Fortune can not bow⟩ *L*   doom] ⟨fate⟩ *L*
13 for . . . dared] ⟨I / through ? / in death I gaged / smiled⟩ *L*   15 was heard] ⟨appeared⟩ *L*   18 Since ⟨I breathed but survived⟩ *L*   19 ⟨When / And the ? in triumph ? foes⟩ *L*   doubts] hearts *L, cor. in M*   20 ⟨Left around thy⟩ ⟨Who dare not / Scarce dare trust a man with thee⟩ *L*   21 Dreading each should] ⟨Think they we could⟩ *L*
each] ⟨all⟩ *L*   22 ⟨Now⟩ Oh though in other dungeons pent *L, M*; Oh though in their dungeons pent *T, proof*   25 Would] ⟨Let / Will⟩ *L*   26 ⟨Who denies that best ? / Who denies thy friends to thee / their prayer⟩ *L*   duty's] Friendship's *L, cor. in M*   27 Were] ⟨Where⟩ *L*

Were that world this hour his own,
     All thou calmly dost resign,   30
Could he purchase with that throne
     Hearts like those which still are thine?

5.

My chief, my king, my friend, adieu!
     Never did I droop before;
Never to my sovereign sue,   35
     As his foes I now implore.
All I ask is to divide
     Every peril he must brave;
Sharing by the hero's side
     His fall, his exile, and his grave.   40

[1815]

29 ⟨Twice that greatness shall ? | No—the time ? not be ? | He who never knew a friend /
Kingdoms may be his⟩ *L*   30 All ⟨that⟩ thou *L*   31–2 ⟨Twould not gather
round his throne | Half the hearts that still are thine.⟩ *L*   32 ⟨One soul⟩ like those
that ⟨clung⟩ to thine. *L, cor. in M*   34 ⟨To die for thee were / Ah gladly had I⟩ *L*
35 ⟨In the front of battle / field of triumph true⟩ *L*   my] ⟨thy⟩ *L*   36 ⟨In that
hour⟩ *L*   37–8 ⟨Let me brook in him once more— | Let me share the / all the⟩ *L*

37–40   Let me still partake his doom
                    Late his soldier ⟨as⟩ now his slave
               ⟨Bid / Let⟩ Grant me but to share the gloom
                    Of his exile ⟨and⟩ or his grave. *L*

37–8   ⟨Let me still partake his doom
                    Like his soldier—Een a slave⟩
               All I ask is ⟨but to bear⟩ / to abide
                    ⟨All the perils⟩ / Every peril he must brave *M, cor. in La*

39–40   ⟨Grant me but to share the gloom
                    Of his exile or his grave⟩
               ⟨Let me but partake his doom
                    Be it exile or the grave⟩
               All my hope— ⟨my joy—to share⟩ / was to divide
                    ⟨In his exile or his grave⟩ / His fall . . . his grave. *M, cor. in La*

277   On the Star of 'The Legion of Honour'

From the French

1.

Star of the brave!—whose beam hath shed
Such glory o'er the quick and dead—
Thou radiant and adored deceit!
Which millions rushed in arms to greet,—
Wild meteor of immortal birth!   5
Why rise in Heaven to set on Earth?

2.

Souls of slain heroes formed thy rays;
Eternity flashed through thy blaze;
The music of thy martial sphere
Was fame on high and honour here;   10
And thy light broke on human eyes,
Like a Volcano of the skies.

3.

Like lava rolled thy stream of blood,
And swept down empires with its flood;
Earth rocked beneath thee to her base,   15
As thou did'st lighten through all space;
And the shorn Sun grew dim in air,
And set while thou wert dwelling there.

4.

Before thee rose, and with thee grew,
A rainbow of the loveliest hue   20
Of three bright colours, each divine,
And fit for that celestial sign;
For Freedom's hand had blended them,
Like tints in an immortal gem.

277. Copy text: *Poems1816*, collated with *Examiner*
title   On the Star of 'The Legion of Honour.' *Examiner*

5.

One tint was of the sunbeam's dyes;   25
One, the blue depth of Seraph's eyes;
One, the pure Spirit's veil of white
Had robed in radiance of its light:
The three so mingled did beseem
The texture of a heavenly dream.   30

6.

Star of the brave! thy ray is pale,
And darkness must again prevail!
But, oh thou Rainbow of the free!
Our tears and blood must flow for thee.
When thy bright promise fades away,   35
Our life is but a load of clay.

7.

And Freedom hallows with her tread
The silent cities of the dead;
For beautiful in death are they
Who proudly fall in her array;   40
And soon, oh Goddess! may we be
For evermore with them or thee!

[1815]

278   On Perceval

1.

In the dirge we sung o'er thee no censure was heard,
    Unembittered and free did the tear-drop descend:
We forgot, in that hour, how the statesman had err'd,
    And wept for the father, the husband, and friend!

2.

O proud was the meed thy integrity won,   5
    And gen'rous indeed were the tears that were shed,
When in grief we forgot all the ill thou hadst done,
    And tho' wronged by thee living, bewailed thee when dead!

278. Copy text: *MS.*

3.

Even now, if a selfish emotion intrude,
  'Tis to wish thou had'st chosen some lowlier state—   10
Had'st known what thou wert—and content to be *good*,
  Had'st ne'er for our ruin aspir'd to be *great*.

4.

So blest thro' their own little orbit to move,
  Thy years might have rolled inoffensive away;
Thy children might still have been blest with thy love,   15
  And England would ne'er have been curst with thy sway!

[1815]

279   When We Two Parted

1.

When we two parted
  In silence and tears,
Half broken-hearted
  To sever for years,
Pale grew thy cheek and cold,   5
  Colder thy kiss;
Truly that hour foretold
  Sorrow to this.

2.

The dew of the morning
  Sunk chill on my brow—   10
It felt like the warning
  Of what I feel now.
Thy vows are all broken,
  And light is thy fame;
I hear thy name spoken,   15
  And share in its shame.

279. Copy text: *Poems1816*, collated with *MS. L, MS. BM, the proof, letters to Lady Melbourne and Lady Hardy, Nathan, Clarke*
title *untitled in MSS.*; The Parting *Clarke*

  5 Pale] ⟨Cold⟩ *L*   7–8 Never may I behold | Moment like this! *L, cancelled in BM*   Never] ⟨Oh neer⟩ *L*   9 dew] ⟨drink⟩ *L*   10 Sunk . . . on] ⟨Clung . . . to⟩ *L*   13 Thy vow hath been broken *L, BM, cor. in proof*   14 ⟨But mine is the same⟩ *L*   15 ⟨When⟩ I hear *L*   16 its] ⟨thy⟩ *proof*

3.

They name thee before me,
    A knell to mine ear;
A shudder comes o'er me—
    Why wert thou so dear?   20
They know not I knew thee,
    Who knew thee too well:—
Long, long shall I rue thee,
    Too deeply to tell.

4.

In secret we met—   25
    In silence I grieve,
That thy heart could forget,
    Thy spirit deceive.
If I should meet thee
    After long years,   30
How should I greet thee!—
    With silence and tears.

                    [1815]

17–19 ⟨Our secret of sorrow/lies hidden | And deep in my soul | But deeds more forbidden⟩ L   17–18 ⟨Our secret lies hidden | But never forgot⟩ L   22 well] ⟨well/sweet⟩ L   23 Long shall I rue thee L, cor. in BM   24 a stanza was removed from the original MS. after line 24; it survives in two versions (see commentary):

            The first step of error none eer could recall
            And the woman once fallen forever must fall,
            Pursue to the last the career she begun
            And be *false* unto *many*, as *faithless* to *one*.
                        letter to Lady Melbourne
            Then fare thee well, Fanny,
                Now doubly undone,
            To prove false unto many
                As faithless to one.
            Thou art past all recalling
                Even would I recall,
            For the woman once falling
                Forever must fall.
                        letter to Lady Hardy

25 met] ⟨loved⟩ L   27 thy heart could] ⟨thou shouldst⟩ L   28 ⟨That I mus⟩ L
29 ⟨Ah should we meet more⟩ L   If we should meet then L, cor. in BM   31 How should we greet then L, cor. in BM   32 With] In L, cor. in BM

date   1808 Poems1816, 1831, 1832, More

280   [A Bridegroom]

1.

A bridegroom swore to his young wife
A passion that should last for life.
No mind—no heart—were e'er sincerer,
No wife—no woman—ever dearer
    To single or to wedded man.   5
But next door to this happy pair
There lived a certain black-eyed fair,
    Lovely Anne!

2.

Young George his young bride idolizes
And all the sex beside despises;   10
One soul—one passion—and one heart,
They never slept or dreamed apart,
    Nor shall nor may nor could nor can.
But glancing—melting—ogling—speaking,
This neighbour's eyes are sadly piquing,   15
    Naughty Anne!

3.

To Mrs. George belong such charms,
Soft eyes—sweet lips—white neck—round arms,
A bosom naught can match or hide
And such a—God knows what beside: 20
    Marks of a life of love to scan!
By heaven, I never will forsake her!
But who is there?—the Devil take her,
    I must have Anne!

                                        [1815]

280. Copy text: *MS*.

    1 wife] ⟨bride⟩ *MS*.   2 should] ⟨will⟩ *MS*.   13 ⟨Alas! they never thought apart⟩ *MS*.   15 glancing—melting] ⟨singing—sighing⟩ *MS*.   19 ⟨And such a waist as never bride⟩ *MS*.

281   The Siege of Corinth

                        A Poem

        Guns, Trumpets, Blunderbusses, Drums, and Thunder.'

                          TO

                JOHN HOBHOUSE, ESQ.

                 THIS POEM IS INSCRIBED

                        BY HIS

                       FRIEND.

                   Jan. 22, 1816.

                  ADVERTISEMENT

'The grand army of the Turks (in 1715), under the Prime Vizier,
to open to themselves a way into the heart of the Morea, and to
form the siege of Napoli di Romania, the most considerable place
in all that country, thought it best in the first place to attack
Corinth, upon which they made several storms. The garrison being
weakened, and the governor seeing it was impossible to hold out
against so mighty a force, thought fit to beat a parley: but while
they were treating about the articles, one of the magazines in the
Turkish camp, wherein they had six hundred barrels of powder,
blew up by accident, whereby six or seven hundred men were
killed: which so enraged the infidels, that they would not grant any
capitulation, but stormed the place with so much fury, that they
took it, and put most of the garrison, with Signior Minotti, the
governor, to the sword. The rest, with Antonio Bembo, proveditor
extraordinary, were made prisoners of war.'

                          History of the Turks, vol. iii. p. 151.

281. Copy text: *Siege* (1st edn.), collated with *MSS. M, T, Proof H, Siege* (edns. 2 and 3).
title   The Siege of Corinth *M; untitled in T*   A poem] ⟨A Tale⟩ *Proof H, printed text
cor. in MS.*
Dedication   *MS. addition to Proof H*
epigraph   *not in T; B's MS. addition in M;* ⟨Guns, Drums, Blunderbusses, and Thunder⟩
Proof H, printed text cor. in MS.
Advertisement   *not in M, T*

1.

Many a vanished year and age,
And tempest's breath, and battle's rage,
Have swept o'er Corinth; yet she stands
A fortress formed to Freedom's hands.
The whirlwind's wrath, the earthquake's shock,   5
Have left untouched her hoary rock,
The keystone of a land, which still,
Though fall'n, looks proudly on that hill,
The land-mark to the double tide
That purpling rolls on either side,   10
As if their waters chafed to meet,
Yet pause and crouch beneath her feet.
But could the blood before her shed
Since first Timoleon's brother bled,
Or baffled Persia's despot fled,   15
Arise from out the earth which drank
The stream of slaughter as it sank,
That sanguine ocean would o'erflow
Her isthmus idly spread below:
Or could the bones of all the slain,   20
Who perished there, be piled again,
That rival pyramid would rise
More mountain-like, through those clear skies,
Than yon tower-capt Acropolis
Which seems the very clouds to kiss.   25

2.

On dun Cithaeron's ridge appears
The gleam of twice ten thousand spears;
And downward to the Isthmian plain
From shore to shore of either main,

1 Many a year and many an age T, M, cor. in Proof H   3 ⟨Every shape that Time
and Man⟩ T   4 A ⟨marvel from her Maker's⟩ hands T   5 the] ⟨and⟩ the M
7 which] ⟨that⟩ T   8 that] that ⟨mighty⟩ T   9 to ... tide] ⟨of ... seas⟩ T
10 That] ⟨Which⟩ T   purpling] bluely T, alternate reading   11 As if ⟨they chafed⟩
their T   13 before her shed] ⟨poured oer these shores⟩ T   14 Since] ⟨Ere⟩ T
16 which] ⟨that⟩ T   20 Or could the ⟨dead be raised again⟩ T   bones of all] ⟨curses
of⟩ T   21 Who perished] That ⟨withered⟩ T   23 those] yon T, M   24 yon]
that T, M   25 Which] That T, cor. in M   26 ridge] ⟨summit⟩ T   27 gleam
of twice] ⟨glimmer of⟩ T   28 to the Isthmian] ⟨dashing toward the⟩ T   29 ⟨Stretched
on / to the edge⟩ of either plain T

The tent is pitched, the crescent shines   30
Along the Moslem's leaguering lines;
And the dusk Spahi's bands advance
Beneath each bearded pasha's glance;
And far and wide as eye can reach
The turban'd cohorts throng the beach;   35
And there the Arab's camel kneels,
And there his steed the Tartar wheels;
The Turcoman hath left his herd,
The sabre round his loins to gird;
And there the volleying thunders pour,   40
Till waves grow smoother to the roar.
The trench is dug, the cannon's breath
Wings the far hissing globe of death;
Fast whirl the fragments from the wall,
Which crumbles with the ponderous ball;   45
And from that wall the foe replies,
O'er dusty plain and smoky skies,
With fires that answer fast and well
The summons of the Infidel.

3.

But near and nearest to the wall   50
Of those who wish and work its fall,
With deeper skill in war's black art
Than Othman's sons, and high of heart
As any chief that ever stood
Triumphant in the fields of blood;   55
From post to post, and deed to deed,
Fast spurring on his reeking steed,
Where sallying ranks the trench assail,
And make the foremost Moslem quail;
Or where the battery guarded well,   60
Remains as yet impregnable,

32 And the ⟨stern Ottoman hath there⟩ T   bands advance] ⟨chargers prance⟩ T
33 ⟨Before the / And all stern⟩ T   bearded pasha's] ⟨fiery banners⟩ T   34–5 ⟨The
turbaned hordes / tribes of dusky hue | Whose march Morea's fields may rue⟩ T   36 ⟨The
trench is dug—the battery roars⟩ / And there ⟨the volleying / his steed the Tartar wheels⟩ T
40 pour] ⟨roar⟩ T   43 Wings the far] ⟨Hurls the long⟩ T   44 whirl] ⟨fall /
flash⟩ T   45 Which . . . with] That . . . ⟨to⟩ T; That . . . with M   46 foe]
⟨fire⟩ T   47 dusty] ⟨bloody⟩ T; dusky M   50 ⟨Coumourgi⟩ T   52 ⟨Of /
With deeper skill / hope and fear / more of art⟩ T   58 Where . . . trench] ⟨And⟩ . . .
trench / host T

Alighting cheerly to inspire
The soldier slackening in his fire;
The first and freshest of the host
Which Stamboul's sultan there can boast,   65
To guide the follower o'er the field,
To point the tube, the lance to wield,
Or whirl around the bickering blade;—
Was Alp, the Adrian renegade!

4.

From Venice—once a race of worth   70
His gentle sires—he drew his birth;
But late an exile from her shore,
Against his countrymen he bore
The arms they taught to bear; and now
The turban girt his shaven brow.   75
Through many a change had Corinth passed
With Greece to Venice' rule at last;
And here, before her walls, with those
To Greece and Venice equal foes,
He stood a foe, with all the zeal   80
Which young and fiery converts feel,
Within whose heated bosom throngs
The memory of a thousand wrongs.
To him had Venice ceased to be
Her ancient civic boast—'the Free';   85
And in the palace of St. Mark
Unnamed accusers in the dark
Within the 'Lion's mouth' had placed
A charge against him uneffaced:
He fled in time, and saved his life,   90
To waste his future years in strife,
That taught his land how great her loss
In him who triumphed o'er the Cross,

---

62 Alighting ⟨there to pause and cheer⟩ *T*   63 The soldier ⟨worn⟩ slackening *T*
66 guide] ⟨lead⟩ *T*   68 Or] ⟨To⟩ *T*   69 Adrian] ⟨fearless⟩ *T*   70 ⟨Venetian in
his⟩ *T*   72 But was ⟨selfexiled⟩ from ⟨the⟩ shore *T*   late] now *M, cor. in Proof H*
73 Against his ⟨son⟩ countrymen *T*   74 and] ⟨he⟩ and *T*   77 rule] ⟨sunny?⟩
rule *T*   80 foe, with] foe ⟨to both⟩ with *T*   81 Which] That *T, M*   82 ⟨Thro /
To whom ? memory belongs⟩ *T*   83 a thousand] ⟨nurtured / ?⟩ *T*   84 ⟨When
they who find their country's laws⟩ *T*   85 ⟨Too ?⟩ *T*   87 ⟨Some nameless⟩ *T*
90 ⟨He waited not to hear that charge⟩ *T*   91 his] its *T, M*

'Gainst which he reared the Crescent high,
And battled to avenge or die.   95

5.

Coumourgi—he whose closing scene
Adorned the triumph of Eugene,
When on Carlowitz' bloody plain
The last and mightiest of the slain
He sank, regretting not to die,   100
But curst the Christian's victory—
Coumourgi—can his glory cease,
That latest conqueror of Greece,
Till Christian hands to Greece restore
The freedom Venice gave of yore?   105
A hundred years have rolled away
Since he refixed the Moslem's sway;
And now he led the Mussulman,
And gave the guidance of the van
To Alp, who well repaid the trust   110
By cities levelled with the dust;
And proved, by many a deed of death,
How firm his heart in novel faith.

6.

The walls grew weak; and fast and hot
Against them poured the ceaseless shot,   115
With unabating fury sent
From battery to battlement;
And thunder-like the pealing din
Rose from each heated culverin;
And here and there some crackling dome   120
Was fired before the exploding bomb:
And as the fabric sank beneath
The shattering shell's volcanic breath,
In red and wreathing columns flashed
The flame, as loud the ruin crashed,   125

96 whose ⟨fall⟩ closing T   98 When ⟨wounding⟩ on T   100 sank ⟨and with⟩
regretting T   104 ⟨Until⟩ Till Christian hands ⟨redeem again⟩ T   106 years
⟨of⟩ have T   107 he ⟨hath⟩ refixed T   118 thunder-like] ⟨deathlike rolled⟩ T
119 ⟨Of black and⟩ T   121 before] ⟨beneath / below⟩ T   122 the . . . beneath]
⟨this roof consuming fell⟩ / the fabric sank ⟨down⟩ beneath T   123 The ⟨spreading
ruins fiery⟩ breath T   124 In red ⟨and spirey wreaths⟩ and T

Or into countless meteors driven,
Its earth-stars melted into heaven;
Whose clouds that day grew doubly dun,
Impervious to the hidden sun,
With volumed smoke that slowly grew   130
To one wide sky of sulphurous hue.

7.

But not for vengeance, long delayed,
Alone, did Alp, the renegade,
The Moslem warriors sternly teach
His skill to pierce the promised breach: 135
Within these walls a maid was pent
His hope would win, without consent
Of that inexorable sire,
Whose heart refused him in its ire,
When Alp, beneath his Christian name,   140
Her virgin hand aspired to claim.
In happier mood, and earlier time,
While unimpeached for traitorous crime,
Gayest in gondola or hall,
He glittered through the Carnival;   145
And tuned the softest serenade
That e'er on Adria's waters played
At midnight to Italian maid.

8.

And many deemed her heart was won;
For sought by numbers, given to none,   150
Had young Francesca's hand remained
Still by the church's bonds unchained:
And when the Adriatic bore
Lanciotto to the Paynim shore,

126 ⟨Till / How lost its crimson⟩ T   countless meteors] ⟨thousand sparkles⟩ T
126a Like comets in convulsion riven T, *deleted in M*   127 ⟨From fragments hurled /
One bright but indistinctly⟩ T   Its] ⟨These⟩ T   128 ⟨In blackness melted / In
smoke approaches blackening⟩ T   grew] ⟨were⟩ T   129 hidden] ⟨powerless⟩ T
130 ⟨Through sulphurous⟩ smoke ⟨whose blackness grew⟩ T   132 But not ⟨alone⟩
for T   134 sternly] ⟨fiercely⟩ T   135 skill] ⟨art⟩ T   140 Alp] ⟨he⟩ T
143 While] ⟨Ere⟩ T   144 ⟨The⟩ Gayest T   148 At midnight] ⟨Made courtship⟩ /
In midnight T, *cor. in* M   154 Lanciotto] ⟨Her lover / victor⟩ / ⟨Galvano?⟩ T

Her wonted smiles were seen to fail,   155
And pensive waxed the maid and pale;
More constant at confessional,
More rare at masque and festival;
Or seen at such, with downcast eyes,
Which conquered hearts they ceased to prize: 160
With listless look she seems to gaze;
With humbler care her form arrays;
Her voice less lively in the song;
Her step, though light, less fleet among
The pairs, on whom the Morning's glance   165
Breaks, yet unsated with the dance.

9.

Sent by the state to guard the land,
(Which, wrested from the Moslem's hand,
While Sobieski tamed his pride
By Buda's wall and Danube's side,   170
The chiefs of Venice wrung away
From Patra to Euboea's bay)
Minotti held in Corinth's towers
The Doge's delegated powers,
While yet the pitying eye of Peace   175
Smiled o'er her long forgotten Greece:
And ere that faithless truce was broke
Which freed her from the unchristian yoke,
With him his gentle daughter came;
Nor there, since Menelaus' dame   180
Forsook her lord and land, to prove
What woes await on lawless love,
Had fairer form adorned the shore
Than she, the matchless stranger, bore.

10.

The wall is rent, the ruins yawn;   185
And, with to-morrow's earliest dawn,

---

159 with] ⟨at⟩ T   161 seems] seem⟨ed⟩ T   165 Morning's glance] ⟨laughing day⟩ T   166 Breaks] ⟨Shines⟩ T   170 By] ⟨On Danube's⟩ From T, *cor. in M* 173 Minotti held] ⟨Pisani built⟩ T   178 the *added in M by B*   184 matchless] ⟨beauteous⟩ T   185 ⟨The breach was made—and with ? won⟩ T

O'er the disjointed mass shall vault
The foremost of the fierce assault.
The bands are ranked; the chosen van
Of Tartar and of Mussulman,   190
The full of hope, misnamed 'forlorn',
Who hold the thought of death in scorn,
And win their way with falchions' force,
Or pave the path with many a corse,
O'er which the following brave may rise,   195
Their stepping-stone—the last who dies!

II.

'Tis midnight: on the mountain's brown
The cold, round moon shines deeply down;
Blue roll the waters, blue the sky
Spreads like an ocean hung on high,   200
Bespangled with those isles of light,
So wildly, spiritually bright;
Who ever gazed upon them shining,
And turned to earth without repining,
Nor wished for wings to flee away,   205
And mix with their eternal ray?
The waves on either shore lay there
Calm, clear, and azure as the air;
And scarce their foam the pebbles shook,
But murmured meekly as the brook.   210
The winds were pillowed on the waves;
The banners drooped along their staves,
And, as they fell around them furling,
Above them shone the crescent curling;
And that deep silence was unbroke,   215
Save where the watch his signal spoke,

187 ⟨The Moslem ranks shall rushing⟩ T   189 ranked . . . van⟩ ⟨drawn—the leaders
named⟩ T   190 Of ⟨Adr⟩ Tartar T   192 thought] ⟨name⟩ T   193 with . . .
force] ⟨with wounds—or brave⟩ T   194 ⟨A pathway⟩ T   196 ⟨By stepping oer⟩
the last who dies T   201 those] ⟨far⟩ / her T, M   202 So ⟨blessedly—so⟩ T
206 mix] ⟨mingle⟩ T   207 lay there] ⟨remain⟩ T   208 ⟨Calm as / and⟩ T
211 ⟨The banners droop / drooped around the staff / round their staves were drooping⟩ /
⟨The banners round the staves / drooped around the staves⟩ T   212 ⟨The tents were
silent on the waves⟩ T   along] ⟨around⟩ T   213 ⟨And oer them shone the Crescent
curling⟩ T   215 And that deep ⟨still⟩ silence T

Save where the steed neighed oft and shrill,
And echo answered from the hill,
And the wide hum of that wild host
Rustled like leaves from coast to coast,   220
As rose the Muezzin's voice in air
In midnight call to wonted prayer;
It rose, that chaunted mournful strain,
Like some lone spirit's o'er the plain:
'Twas musical, but sadly sweet,   225
Such as when winds and harp-strings meet,
And take a long unmeasured tone,
To mortal minstrelsy unknown.
It seemed to those within the wall
A cry prophetic of their fall: 230
It struck even the besieger's ear
With something ominous and drear,
An undefined and sudden thrill,
Which makes the heart a moment still,
Then beat with quicker pulse, ashamed   235
Of that strange sense its silence framed;
Such as a sudden passing-bell
Wakes, though but for a stranger's knell.

                              12.

The tent of Alp was on the shore;
The sound was hushed, the prayer was o'er;
The watch was set, the night-round made,   240
All mandates issued and obeyed:
'Tis but another anxious night,
His pains the morrow may requite
With all revenge and love can pay,   245
In guerdon for their long delay.
Few hours remain, and he hath need

219 that wild host] ⟨sleepless men⟩ T   220 ⟨Where⟩ T   223 It ⟨came—all
mournfully and long⟩ T   224 lone] ⟨vexed⟩ T   225 ⟨It⟩ T   227 ⟨And
make a melancholy tone / moan⟩/ And take ⟨that melancholy⟩ tone T   long] ⟨dark⟩ T
228 minstrelsy] ⟨minstrel / voice and ear⟩ T   231 ear] ⟨heart⟩ T   232 With
something ⟨little less than fear⟩ T   233 An] ⟨That⟩ T   234 Which] ⟨That⟩ T
236 its silence] ⟨by fancy⟩ T   237 ⟨Which waking / rings a visionary knell⟩ / ⟨Which
like a distant funeral bell⟩ T   237–8 ⟨Which rings a deep internal knell | A visionary
passing bell⟩ T   242 mandates] ⟨orders⟩ T   244 the morrow] ⟨tomorrow⟩ T
245 With] ⟨And⟩ T

Of rest, to nerve for many a deed
Of slaughter; but within his soul
The thoughts like troubled waters roll.   250
He stood alone among the host;
Not his the loud fanatic boast
To plant the crescent o'er the cross,
Or risk a life with little loss,
Secure in paradise to be   255
By Houris loved immortally:
Nor his, what burning patriots feel,
The stern exaltedness of zeal,
Profuse of blood, untired in toil,
When battling on the parent soil.   260
He stood alone—a renegade
Against the country he betrayed;
He stood alone amidst his band,
Without a trusted heart or hand:
They followed him, for he was brave,   265
And great the spoil he got and gave;
They crouched to him, for he had skill
To warp and wield the vulgar will:
But still his Christian origin
With them was little less than sin.   270
They envied even the faithless fame
He earned beneath a Moslem name;
Since he, their mightiest chief, had been
In youth a bitter Nazarene.
They did not know how pride can stoop,   275
When baffled feelings withering droop;
They did not know how hate can burn
In hearts once changed from soft to stern;
Nor all the false and fatal zeal
The convert of revenge can feel.   280
He ruled them—man may rule the worst,
By ever daring to be first:

248 for many a] ⟨him for the⟩ T   250 like troubled waters] tumultuously T, M
253 plant] ⟨soar⟩ T   o'er] on M   256 loved] ⟨blest⟩ T   257 ⟨Nor his the patriot
feeling / patient / burning patriot's zeal⟩ T   260 parent] ⟨native⟩ T   266 And
⟨many⟩ great T   268 warp and wield] ⟨triumph oer⟩ T   271 ⟨And much they
marvelled⟩ T   273 Since he] ⟨And that / That he⟩ T   276 baffled . . . withering]
⟨early . . . early⟩ T   278 In hearts once] ⟨When thoughts are⟩ T

So lions o'er the jackal sway;
The jackal points, he fells the prey,
Then on the vulgar yelling press,   285
To gorge the relics of success.

13.

His head grows fevered, and his pulse
The quick successive throbs convulse;
In vain from side to side he throws
His form, in courtship of repose;   290
Or if he dozed, a sound, a start
Awoke him with a sunken heart.
The turban on his hot brow pressed,
The mail weighed lead-like on his breast,
Though oft and long beneath its weight   295
Upon his eyes had slumber sate,
Without or couch or canopy,
Except a rougher field and sky
Than now might yield a warrior's bed,
Than now along the heaven was spread.   300
He could not rest, he could not stay
Within his tent to wait for day,
But walked him forth along the sand,
Where thousand sleepers strewed the strand.
What pillowed them? and why should he   305
More wakeful than the humblest be?
Since more their peril, worse their toil,
And yet they fearless dream of spoil;
While he alone, where thousands passed
A night of sleep, perchance their last,   310
In sickly vigil wandered on,
And envied all he gazed upon.

283 So] ⟨As⟩ T   jackal] jackels C   284–6 *copied in* M *by* B   284 ⟨By springing
dauntless on the prey⟩ / ⟨They only / but provide—he fells the prey⟩ T   285 ⟨They
who follow on and⟩ / ⟨These baser⟩ T   286 relics] ⟨fragments⟩ T   289–90 ⟨He
vainly turned from side to side | And each reposing posture tried⟩ T   291 a sound, a]
⟨a sudden⟩ T   292 sunken] ⟨sinking⟩ T   294 weighed lead-like on] ⟨sank heavy
to⟩ T   295 its] their T   297 ⟨In tent or field⟩ T   298 Except] Beyond T,
M, *cor. in Proof* H   299 warrior's] ⟨soldier's⟩ T   300 the] ⟨his⟩ T   301 rest]
⟨sleep⟩ T   302 wait] sigh T, M   305 ⟨Why should they not⟩ T   306 ⟨Less⟩
More ⟨sleepless / restless⟩ than T   307 Since more . . . worse] ⟨The same . . . same⟩ T
309 While he ⟨the night in vigils⟩ passed T   310 ⟨Although⟩ A night ⟨of slumber—
though their last⟩ T

14.

He felt his soul become more light
Beneath the freshness of the night.
Cool was the silent sky, though calm,   315
And bathed his brow with airy balm:
Behind, the camp—before him lay,
In many a winding creek and bay,
Lepanto's gulf; and, on the brow
Of Delphi's hill, unshaken snow,   320
High and eternal, such as shone
Through thousand summers brightly gone,
Along the gulf, the mount, the clime;
It will not melt, like man, to time:
Tyrant and slave are swept away,   325
Less formed to wear before the ray;
But that white veil, the lightest, frailest,
Which on the mighty mount thou hailest,
While tower and tree are torn and rent,
Shines o'er its craggy battlement;   330
In form a peak, in height a cloud,
In texture like a hovering shroud,
Thus high by parting Freedom spread,
As from her fond abode she fled,
And lingered on the spot, where long   335
Her prophet spirit spake in song.
Oh, still her step at moments falters
O'er withered fields, and ruined altars,
And fain would wake, in souls too broken,
By pointing to each glorious token.   340
But vain her voice, till better days
Dawn in those yet remembered rays
Which shone upon the Persian flying,
And saw the Spartan smile in dying.

313 soul ⟨grow⟩ become *T*   316 brow with airy] ⟨heated brow with⟩ *T*   318 ⟨The /
in long / winding⟩ *T*   320 ⟨Of Liakura—his unearthly⟩ snow *T*   321 High]
⟨Bright⟩ *T*   325 are] ⟨have⟩ *T*   326 wear] ⟨yield⟩ *T*   327 white ⟨mass of⟩
veil *T*   331 In ⟨sheen a / line a ? —in height as proud⟩ *T*   332 ⟨In line a high
and hovering shroud⟩ *T*   333 ⟨Above a / A mantle oer the⟩ *T*   Thus high] ⟨The
air / On high⟩ *T*   334 fond] ⟨long⟩ *T*   336 Her ⟨spirit spoke in deathless song⟩ /
⟨deathless⟩ prophet *T*   337 Oh] ⟨And⟩ *T*   338 fields, and ruined] ⟨hopes and ?⟩ *T*
342 in those] ⟨forth in⟩ *T*   343 Which] That *T, M*

15.

Not mindless of these mighty times   345
Was Alp, despite his flight and crimes;
And through this night, as on he wandered,
And o'er the past and present pondered,
And thought upon the glorious dead
Who there in better cause had bled,   350
He felt how faint and feebly dim
The fame that could accrue to him,
Who cheered the band, and waved the sword,
A traitor in a turbaned horde;
And led them to the lawless siege,   355
Whose best success were sacrilege.
Not so had those his fancy numbered,
The chiefs whose dust around him slumbered;
Their phalanx marshalled on the plain,
Whose bulwarks were not then in vain.   360
They fell devoted, but undying;
The very gale their names seemed sighing:
The waters murmured of their name;
The woods were peopled with their fame;
The silent pillar, lone and gray,   365
Claimed kindred with their sacred clay;
Their spirits wrapt the dusky mountain,
Their memory sparkled o'er the fountain;
The meanest rill, the mightiest river
Rolled mingling with their fame for ever.   370
Despite of every yoke she bears,
That land is glory's still and theirs!
'Tis still a watch-word to the earth.
When man would do a deed of worth,
He points to Greece, and turns to tread,   375
So sanctioned, on the tyrant's head:

347 through] ⟨on⟩ in T, cor. in M   349 And thought ⟨of chiefs who⟩ upon T
351 faint and feebly] ⟨little and how⟩ T   353 Who ⟨hurled the death⟩ / led the band
T, M   357 those] ⟨all⟩ T   358 The] ⟨Of⟩ T   363 The ⟨trees—the rushes⟩
waters T   365 lone and gray] ⟨white and lone⟩ T   366 ⟨Yet sacred for their /
its⟩ T   367 wrapt the dusky] ⟨filled the shaggy⟩ T   368 Their ⟨glory hallowed
every⟩ fountain T   371 ⟨Nor in all that land is theirs⟩ T   372a–b Immortal—
boundless—undecayed—| Their souls the very soil pervade.— T, deleted in M   375 tread]
⟨trample⟩ T   376 So] ⟨Thus⟩ T

He looks to her, and rushes on
Where life is lost, or freedom won.

16.

Still by the shore Alp mutely mused,
And wooed the freshness Night diffused.   380
There shrinks no ebb in that tideless sea,
Which changeless rolls eternally;
So that wildest of waves, in their angriest mood,
Scarce break on the bounds of the land for a rood;
And the powerless moon beholds them flow,   385
Heedless if she come or go:
Calm or high, in main or bay,
On their course she hath no sway.
The rock unworn its base doth bare,
And looks o'er the surf, but it comes not there;   390
And the fringe of the foam may be seen below,
On the line that it left long ages ago:
A smooth short space of yellow sand
Between it and the greener land.

He wandered on, along the beach,   395
Till within the range of a carbine's reach
Of the leaguered wall; but they saw him not,
Or how could he 'scape from the hostile shot?
Did traitors lurk in the Christians' hold?
Were their hands grown stiff, or their hearts waxed
        cold?   400
I know not, in sooth; but from yonder wall
There flashed no fire, and there hissed no ball,
Though he stood beneath the bastion's frown,
That flanked the sea-ward gate of the town;

378 Where ⟨Freedom loveliest may be⟩ won T   379 mutely mused] ⟨wandered on⟩ T
380 ⟨Beneath⟩ the freshness ⟨Heaven⟩ diffused T   381 shrinks . . . in] ⟨comes no change
to⟩ T   383 wildest] fiercest T, cor. in M   387 ⟨Calm—or by the northwind
tost⟩ T   388 ⟨On their course her sway is⟩ T   389 doth bare] ⟨discloses⟩ T
390 ⟨Where the heaving swell reposes⟩ / ⟨Close by the surf⟩ T   looks] ⟨frowns⟩ T
393 A ⟨little⟩ space of ⟨light gray⟩ sand T   395 beach] ⟨shore⟩ T   396 ⟨Till
a carbine shot⟩ T   397 but . . . not] ⟨and the host within⟩ T   398 ⟨Or would /
spared / would not waste a single shot⟩ / ⟨Or hoarded for the Morn their shot⟩ T
399–400 ⟨And would not waste a single lead | The ball on numbers better sped⟩ T
401 sooth] faith M   402 fire] ⟨? / tube⟩ T   403 ⟨Though he above⟩ T
404 ⟨He wandered a little⟩ T

Though he heard the sound, and could almost tell   405
The sullen words of the sentinel,
As his measured step on the stone below
Clanked, as he paced it to and fro;
And he saw the lean dogs beneath the wall
Hold o'er the dead their carnival,   410
Gorging and growling o'er carcase and limb;
They were too busy to bark at him!
From a Tartar's skull they had stripped the flesh,
As ye peel the fig when its fruit is fresh;
And their white tusks crunched o'er the whiter skull,   415
As it slipped through their jaws, when their edge
    grew dull,
As they lazily mumbled the bones of the dead,
When they scarce could rise from the spot where
    they fed;
So well had they broken a lingering fast
With those who had fallen for that night's repast.   420
And Alp knew, by the turbans that rolled on the sand,
The foremost of these were the best of his band:
Crimson and green were the shawls of their wear,
And each scalp had a single long tuft of hair,
All the rest was shaven and bare.   425
The scalps were in the wild dog's maw,
The hair was tangled round his jaw.
But close by the shore, on the edge of the gulf,
There sat a vulture flapping a wolf,
Who had stolen from the hills, but kept away,   430
Scared by the dogs, from the human prey;
But he seized on his share of a steed that lay,
Picked by the birds, on the sands of the bay.

17.

Alp turned him from the sickening sight:
Never had shaken his nerves in fight;   435

407 ⟨And⟩ his ⟨very⟩ step on the ⟨bastion clanked⟩ T   409 And he ⟨heard⟩ the lean dogs ⟨whining bark⟩ / ⟨restless whine⟩ T   411 ⟨They were too busy with⟩ carcase and limb T   413 ⟨They had stripped the flesh from a Tartar skull⟩ T   414 ⟨And mauled / As ye peel the fruit⟩ T   fig] ⟨date⟩ T   417 ⟨And⟩ they lazily mumbled ⟨above the⟩ dead T   418 When] ⟨As⟩ T   419 a] ⟨their⟩ T   420 that night's] ⟨their late⟩ T   421 Alp] ⟨he⟩ T   422 best] ⟨men⟩ T   423 Crimson] ⟨Scarlet⟩ T 427 tangled] ⟨twisted⟩ T   434 Alp . . . sickening] ⟨He . . . hideous⟩ T

But he better could brook to behold the dying,
Deep in the tide of their warm blood lying,
Scorched with the death-thirst, and writhing in vain,
Than the perishing dead who are past all pain.
There is something of pride in the perilous hour,   440
Whate'er be the shape in which death may lower;
For Fame is there to say who bleeds,
And Honour's eye on daring deeds!
But when all is past, it is humbling to tread
O'er the weltering field of the tombless dead,   445
And see worms of the earth, and fowls of the air,
Beasts of the forest, all gathering there;
All regarding man as their prey,
All rejoicing in his decay.

18.

There is a temple in ruin stands,   450
Fashioned by long forgotten hands;
Two or three columns, and many a stone,
Marble and granite, with grass o'ergrown!
Out upon Time! it will leave no more
Of the things to come than the things before!   455
Out upon Time! who for ever will leave
But enough of the past for the future to grieve
O'er that which hath been, and o'er that which must
          be:
What we have seen, our sons shall see;
Remnants of things that have passed away,   460
Fragments of stone, reared by creatures of clay!

437 warm] last *T, M*   439 perishing] ⟨rotting⟩ *T*   pain] ⟨vain⟩ *T*   442-3 *added
in M by B*   444 But] And *T*   448-9 All ⟨that liveth on man will⟩ prey | ⟨Nature⟩
rejoicing in his decay *T*   449a-b ⟨All that kindles dismay and disgust | Follows his
frame from the bier to the dust⟩ *T*   450 a temple] ⟨an altar⟩ *T*   454 will leave]
⟨hath left⟩ *T*   455 Of the ⟨mightiest⟩ things ⟨that have gone⟩ before *T*   457 But]
Just *T*

461a-f   ⟨Monuments that to coming Ages⟩
          Monuments that the coming Age
          Leaves careless to the / to the spoil of the Season's rage
          Till ruin makes the relics scarce
          Then Learning acts her solemn farce
          And roaming through the marble waste
          Prates of beauty art and taste. *cancelled in T*

19.

He sate him down at a pillar's base,
And passed his hand athwart his face;
Like one in dreary musing mood,
Declining was his attitude;   465
His head was drooping on his breast,
Fevered, throbbing, and opprest;
And o'er his brow, so downward bent,
Oft his beating fingers went,
Hurriedly, as you may see   470
Your own run over the ivory key,
Ere the measured tone is taken
By the chords you would awaken.
There he sate all heavily,
As he heard the night-wind sigh.   475
Was it the wind, through some hollow stone,
Sent that soft and tender moan?
He lifted his head, and he looked on the sea,
But it was unrippled as glass may be;
He looked on the long grass—it waved not a blade;   480
How was that gentle sound conveyed?
He looked to the banners—each flag lay still,
So did the leaves on Cithaeron's hill,
And he felt not a breath come over his cheek;
What did that sudden sound bespeak?   485
He turned to the left—is he sure of sight?
There sate a lady, youthful and bright!

20.

He started up with more of fear
Than if an armed foe were near.
'God of my fathers! what is here?   490
Who art thou, and wherefore sent
So near a hostile armament?'
His trembling hands refused to sign
The cross he deemed no more divine:

462 〈That temple was more in the midst of the plain〉 T   462–3 〈What of that
shrine did yet remain | Lay to his left more in midst of the plain〉 T   466 on] 〈down〉 T
468 so downward] 〈his fingers〉 T   470 〈Impatiently like one〉 T   475 As 〈the〉
he T   476 Is it the wind? 〈that through the / oer the heavy〉 through T   479 un-
rippled as glass] 〈smooth as a mirror〉 T   482 to . . . lay] 〈on . . . droops〉 T
487 youthful] 〈young〉 T   493 to] 〈the〉 T

He had resumed it in that hour,   495
But conscience wrung away the power.
He gazed, he saw: he knew the face
Of beauty, and the form of grace;
It was Francesca by his side,
The maid who might have been his bride!   500

The rose was yet upon her cheek,
But mellowed with a tenderer streak:
Where was the play of her soft lips fled?
Gone was the smile that enlivened their red.
The ocean's calm within their view,   505
Beside her eye had less of blue;
But like that cold wave it stood still,
And its glance, though clear, was chill.
Around her form a thin robe twining,
Nought concealed her bosom shining;   510
Through the parting of her hair,
Floating darkly downward there,
Her rounded arm showed white and bare:
And ere yet she made reply,
Once she raised her hand on high;   515
It was so wan, and transparent of hue,
You might have seen the moon shine through.

21.

'I come from my rest to him I love best,
That I may be happy, and he may be blest.
I have passed the guards, the gate, the wall;   520
Sought thee in safety through foes and all.
'Tis said the lion will turn and flee
From a maid in the pride of her purity;
And the Power on high, that can shield the good
Thus from the tyrant of the wood,   525

495 had resumed] ⟨would have made⟩ T   497 gazed] ⟨looked⟩ T   498 ⟨The
form⟩ T   500 The maid] ⟨She⟩ T   might] ⟨would⟩ T   503 ⟨Her lips still /
were as red as her brow was fair⟩ T   504 ⟨Her lips had all their wonted red⟩ T
505 The ocean spread before their view M; The ocean's calm ⟨so near⟩ their view Proof H
507 But like ⟨those cold waves it lay⟩ still T   508 was] ⟨seemed⟩ T   509 twining]
⟨flung⟩ T   512 ⟨As it floated doubly⟩ T   513 ⟨Naked was her rounded arm⟩ T
519 ⟨To him in whose⟩ T   522 and flee] ⟨aside⟩ T   524 ⟨But the⟩ T   525 the
⟨mightiest / sternest⟩ tyrant T

Hath extended its mercy to guard me as well
From the hands of the leaguering infidel.
I come—and if I come in vain,
Never, oh never, we meet again!
Thou hast done a fearful deed   530
In falling away from thy father's creed:
But dash that turban to earth, and sign
The sign of the cross, and for ever be mine;
Wring the black drop from thy heart,
And to-morrow unites us no more to part.'   535

'And where should our bridal couch be spread?
In the 'midst of the dying and the dead?
For to-morrow we give to the slaughter and flame
The sons and the shrines of the Christian name.
None, save thou and thine, I've sworn   540
Shall be left upon the morn:
But thee will I bear to a lovely spot,
Where our hands shall be joined, and our sorrow forgot.
There thou yet shalt be my bride,
When once again I've quelled the pride   545
Of Venice; and her hated race
Have felt the arm they would debase
Scourge, with a whip of scorpions, those
Whom vice and envy made my foes.'

Upon his hand she laid her own—   550
Light was the touch, but it thrilled to the bone,
And shot a chillness to his heart,
Which fixed him beyond the power to start.
Though slight was that grasp so mortal cold,
He could not loose him from its hold;   555
But never did clasp of one so dear
Strike on the pulse with such feeling of fear,
As those thin fingers, long and white,
Froze through his blood by their touch that night.

528 I come ⟨to⟩ —and T   531 father's] fathers' C   540 None] ⟨All⟩ T
541 Shall] ⟨None shall⟩ T   543 Where ⟨all / even my wrongs may be⟩ forgot T
545 again] ⟨more⟩ T   546 her] ⟨the⟩ T   547 Have] ⟨Who⟩ T   549 ⟨Who
made themselves⟩ T   550 ⟨She laid her fingers on his hand⟩ T   551 ⟨Its coldness
thrilled through every bone⟩ T   553 Which] ⟨Yet⟩ That T, M, Proof H   555 loose]
⟨have loosed⟩ T   556 ⟨Through the hand⟩ T   clasp] ⟨touch⟩ T   558 As ⟨that⟩
those T   559 touch] ⟨clasp⟩ T

The feverish glow of his brow was gone,   560
And his heart sank so still that it felt like stone,
As he looked on the face, and beheld its hue
So deeply changed from what he knew:
Fair but faint—without the ray
Of mind, that made each feature play   565
Like sparkling waves on a sunny day;
And her motionless lips lay still as death,
And her words came forth without her breath,
And there rose not a heave o'er her bosom's swell,
And there seemed not a pulse in her veins to dwell.   570
Though her eye shone out, yet the lids were fixed,
And the glance that it gave was wild and unmixed
With aught of change, as the eyes may seem
Of the restless who walk in a troubled dream;
Like the figures on arras, that gloomily glare   575
Stirred by the breath of the wintry air,
So seen by the dying lamp's fitful light,
Lifeless, but life-like, and awful to sight;
As they seem, through the dimness, about to come
        down
From the shadowy wall where their images frown;   580
Fearfully flitting to and fro,
As the gusts on the tapestry come and go.

'If not for love of me be given
Thus much, then, for the love of heaven,—
Again I say—that turban tear   585
From off thy faithless brow, and swear
Thine injured country's sons to spare,

562 the] her *T*   563 So . . . what⟩ ⟨Was . . . that⟩ *T*   564 ⟨Fair but faint as if
below⟩ / ⟨Her veins the currents⟩ *T*   ray] ⟨play⟩ *T*   565 ⟨Of lineaments / Of feelings—
or the features⟩ play *T*   566 ⟨They were fixed⟩ *T*
567–8   ⟨The eye still shone—but the hideous / lids forgot
                        To move;—and unvarying shaded them not⟩
                        ⟨There was not a heave oer her bosom so fair / bosom's swell
                        And the lips through which her accents fell⟩ *T*

567 ⟨Through⟩ her motionless ⟨? breathed out the breath⟩ *T*   569 o'er] in *M*
571 ⟨And her eye through it shone with a glittering⟩ *T*   573 With ⟨varying thought
as those⟩ may seem *T*   575 ⟨Like a picture that Magic had charmed from its / come
forth from its canvas and frame⟩ *T*   Like the figures ⟨that seem from the arras to glare⟩ *T*
576 ⟨Lifeless but lifelike—and ever the same⟩ *T*   577 So] And *T, M*   585 Again
I say—⟨dash down⟩ that *T*   587 Thine] ⟨Thy⟩ *T*

Or thou art lost; and never shalt see
Not earth—that's past—but heaven or me.
If this thou dost accord, albeit   590
A heavy doom 'tis thine to meet,
That doom shall half absolve thy sin,
And mercy's gate may receive thee within:
But pause one moment more, and take
The curse of him thou didst forsake;   595
And look once more to heaven, and see
Its love for ever shut from thee.
There is a light cloud by the moon—
'Tis passing, and will pass full soon—
If, by the time its vapoury sail   600
Hath ceased her shaded orb to veil,
Thy heart within thee is not changed,
Then God and man are both avenged;
Dark will thy doom be, darker still
Thine immortality of ill.'   605

Alp looked to heaven, and saw on high
The sign she spake of in the sky;
But his heart was swollen, and turned aside,
By deep interminable pride.
This first false passion of his breast   610
Rolled like a torrent o'er the rest.
He sue for mercy! *He* dismayed
By wild words of a timid maid!
He, wronged by Venice, vow to save
Her sons, devoted to the grave!   615
No—though that cloud were thunder's worst,
And charged to crush him—let it burst!

He looked upon it earnestly,
Without an accent of reply;

589 ⟨That country more—or⟩ *T*   590 accord ⟨though⟩ albeit *T*   591 ⟨On
earth / The selfsame⟩ *T*   592 That doom ⟨at ? shall be deemed⟩ *T*   600 vapoury
sail] ⟨flimsy veil⟩ *T*   604 ⟨And / Sad⟩ Dark *T*   606 saw on high] ⟨saw that
cloud⟩ *T*   607 in the sky] ⟨spread on high⟩ *T*   608 But ⟨though⟩ his heart
sank, nor turned aside *T*   and] ⟨nor⟩ *M*   609 By ⟨rooted and unhallowed⟩ pride *T*
612 dismayed] ⟨be scared⟩ *T*   616 were . . . worst] ⟨with thunder's tone⟩ *T*
617 And ⟨pointed sent⟩ charged *T*   618 earnestly] ⟨steadfastly⟩ *T*

He watched it passing; it is flown: 620
Full on his eye the clear moon shone,
And thus he spake—'Whate'er my fate,
I am no changeling—'tis too late:
The reed in storms may bow and quiver,
Then rise again; the tree must shiver.   625
What Venice made me, I must be,
Her foe in all, save love to thee:
But thou art safe: oh, fly with me!'
He turned, but she is gone!
Nothing is there but the column stone.   630
Hath she sunk in the earth, or melted in air?
He saw not, he knew not; but nothing is there.

22.

The night is past, and shines the sun
As if that morn were a jocund one.
Lightly and brightly breaks away   635
The Morning from her mantle grey,
And the Noon will look on a sultry day.
Hark to the trump, and the drum,
And the mournful sound of the barbarous horn,
And the flap of the banners, that flit as they're
　　　borne,   640
And the neigh of the steed, and the multitude's hum,
And the clash, and the shout, 'they come, they come!'
The horsetails are plucked from the ground, and the
　　　sword
From its sheath; and they form, and but wait for the
　　　word.
Tartar, and Spahi, and Turcoman,   645
Strike your tents, and throng to the van;
Mount ye, spur ye, skirr the plain,
That the fugitive may flee in vain,
When he breaks from the town; and none escape,
Aged or young, in the Christian shape;   650

620 flown] ⟨gone⟩ T   634 morn] ⟨hour⟩ T   635 brightly breaks] ⟨gaily
wreathes⟩ T   636 The ⟨mantle⟩ morning T   637 Noon . . . sultry] ⟨Morn . . .
lovely⟩ T   640 flit] ⟨flap⟩ T   643 horsetails] ⟨banners⟩ T   644 but wait
for] ⟨they wait but⟩ T

While your fellows on foot, in a fiery mass,
Bloodstain the breach through which they pass.
The steeds are all bridled, and snort to the rein;
Curved is each neck, and flowing each mane;
White is the foam of their champ on the bit: 655
The spears are uplifted; the matches are lit;
The cannon are pointed, and ready to roar,
And crush the wall they have crumbled before:
Forms in his phalanx each Janizar;
Alp at their head; his right arm is bare,   660
So is the blade of his scimitar;
The khan and the pachas are all at their post;
The vizier himself at the head of the host.
When the culverin's signal is fired, then on;
Leave not in Corinth a living one—   665
A priest at her altars, a chief in her halls,
A hearth in her mansions, a stone on her walls.
God and the prophet—Alla Hu!
Up to the skies with that wild halloo!
'There the breach lies for passage, the ladder to scale;   670
And your hands on your sabres, and how should ye fail?
He who first downs with the red cross may crave
His heart's dearest wish; let him ask it, and have!'
Thus uttered Coumourgi, the dauntless vizier;
The reply was the brandish of sabre and spear,   675
And the shout of fierce thousands in joyous ire:—
Silence—hark to the signal—fire!

23.

As the wolves, that headlong go
On the stately buffalo,
Though with fiery eyes, and angry roar,   680
And hoofs that stamp, and horns that gore,

653 are all] are *M*   bridled . . . to the rein] ⟨saddled . . . with disdain⟩ *T*   655 their
. . . on] ⟨the *?*⟩ oer *T*   658 ⟨To crush the breach⟩ they have ⟨*?*⟩ before *T*   659 ⟨Each
Janizar's right / The Janizaries arms are heard⟩ *T*   660 his . . . is] with his right arm
M   661 his] ⟨their⟩ *T*   662 ⟨Alp / The Chief⟩ The *T*   665 Leave not ⟨of⟩ Corinth
⟨a life⟩ —a ⟨single⟩ one *T*   666 at her altars] ⟨in her chambers⟩ *T*   667 hearth]
⟨life⟩ *T*   669 ⟨The Mountains are *?* by the wild Halloo⟩ / ⟨All sounds are lost in⟩ *T*
the skies] ⟨heaven⟩ *T*   670 lies] ⟨is⟩ *T*   673 His ⟨dearest⟩ heart's *T*
676 thousands— ⟨fierce⟩ in ⟨joyful⟩ joyous *T*   677 ⟨The signal is ready —fire!⟩ *T*
hark] ⟨Look⟩ *T*   678 As] ⟨Like⟩ *T*   680 ⟨Despite his eye and angry⟩ *T*
681 And] ⟨His⟩ *T*

He tramples on earth, or tosses on high
The foremost, who rush on his strength but to die:
Thus against the wall they went,
Thus the first were backward bent;   685
Many a bosom, sheathed in brass,
Strewed the earth like broken glass,
Shivered by the shot, that tore
The ground whereon they moved no more:
Even as they fell, in files that lay,   690
Like the mower's grass at the close of day,
When his work is done on the levelled plain;
Such was the fall of the foremost slain.

24.

As the spring-tides, with heavy plash,
From the cliffs invading dash   695
Huge fragments, sapped by the ceaseless flow,
Till white and thundering down they go,
Like the avalanche's snow
On the Alpine vales below;
Thus at length, outbreathed and worn,   700
Corinth's sons were downward borne
By the long and oft renewed
Charge of the Moslem multitude.
In firmness they stood, and in masses they fell,
Heaped, by the host of the infidel,   705
Hand to hand, and foot to foot:
Nothing there, save death, was mute;
Stroke, and thrust, and flash, and cry
For quarter, or for victory,
Mingle there with the volleying thunder,   710
Which makes the distant cities wonder
How the sounding battle goes,
If with them, or for their foes;

682 tramples] ⟨dashes⟩ T   earth] ⟨ground⟩ T   on high] ⟨in air⟩ T   687 ⟨With such volley yields like glass⟩ T   688 ⟨Strewed and shivered by⟩ T   689 they ⟨lay in the thick of / stood⟩ moved T   690 ⟨They fell—they lay even where they fell⟩ T   691 grass] ⟨ridge⟩ T   692 on the levelled] ⟨and smooth the⟩ T   693 fall] ⟨view⟩ T   694 with heavy] heavy T   695 From the ⟨invaded⟩ cliff's T   696 sapped ⟨and shaken⟩ by T   698 ⟨As on the Alps⟩ T   704 firmness] ⟨masses⟩ T   711 Which] That T, M   712 ⟨How the battle's⟩ T

If they must mourn, or may rejoice
In that annihilating voice,   715
Which pierces the deep hills through and through
With an echo dread and new:
You might have heard it, on that day,
O'er Salamis and Megara;
(We have heard the hearers say)   720
Even unto Piraeus' bay.

25.

From the point of encountering blades to the hilt,
Sabres and swords with blood were gilt:
But the rampart is won, and the spoil begun,
And all but the after carnage done.   725
Shriller shrieks now mingling come
From within the plundered dome:
Hark to the haste of flying feet,
That splash in the blood of the slippery street;
But here and there, where 'vantage ground   730
Against the foe may still be found,
Desperate groups, of twelve or ten,
Make a pause, and turn again—
With banded backs against the wall,
Fiercely stand, or fighting fall.   735

There stood an old man—his hairs were white,
But his veteran arm was full of might:
So gallantly bore he the brunt of the fray,
The dead before him, on that day,
In a semicircle lay;   740
Still he combated unwounded,
Though retreating, unsurrounded.

714 ⟨If they / Whether they yet may⟩ T   may *added in* M *by* B   716 through
and through] ⟨and sounds on high⟩ T   717 ⟨Far beyond the reach of eye⟩ T
718 ⟨You might have⟩ T   719 ⟨For beyond⟩ T   720 We] ⟨Some / And / I⟩ I
T, M   721 Piraeus'] Piraeus T–*1829*   723 swords ⟨to⟩ with T   724 rampart]
⟨breach⟩ T   726 now . . . come] ⟨are mingled by now⟩ T   728 ⟨And the hurry-
ing tramp⟩ of flying feet T   729 ⟨Went walki⟩ T   That] ⟨They⟩ M   733 pause]
⟨stand⟩ T   734 banded] bandied *edns.* 2, 3   735 or] ⟨and⟩ T   736 *no verse
paragraph here in* C   737 But his ⟨arm / heart and⟩ arm T   might:] might *1st edn.*
738 ⟨So firm he stood—so⟩ So gallantly ⟨he stood⟩ bore T

Many a scar of former fight
Lurked beneath his corslet bright;
But of every wound his body bore,   745
Each and all had been ta'en before:
Though aged he was, so iron of limb,
Few of our youth could cope with him;
And the foes, whom he singly kept at bay,
Outnumbered his thin hairs of silver gray.   750
From right to left his sabre swept:
Many an Othman mother wept
Sons that were unborn, when dipped
His weapon first in Moslem gore,
Ere his years could count a score.   755
Of all he might have been the sire
Who fell that day beneath his ire:
For, sonless left long years ago,
His wrath made many a childless foe;
And since the day, when in the strait   760
His only boy had met his fate,
His parent's iron hand did doom
More than a human hecatomb.
If shades by carnage be appeased,
Patroclus' spirit less was pleased   765
Than his, Minotti's son, who died
Where Asia's bounds and ours divide.
Buried he lay, where thousands before
For thousands of years were inhumed on the shore:
What of them is left, to tell   770
Where they lie, and how they fell?
Not a stone on their turf, nor a bone in their graves;
But they live in the verse that immortally saves.

26.

Hark to the Allah shout! a band
Of the Mussulman bravest and best is at hand: 775

743 fight] ⟨fields⟩ *T*   744 Lurked] ⟨Lay⟩ *T*   747 Though . . . so] ⟨And / Yet
. . . and⟩ *T*   749 And ⟨I wot that⟩ *T*   754 His] This *M*   755 a] ⟨in⟩ *T*
756 ⟨Sire of all—Grandsire of some⟩ *T*   758 For] But *T, M*   761 His] That
T, cor. in M   762 His] ⟨With⟩ *T*   765 ⟨No Spirit⟩ *T*   767 bounds] ⟨land⟩ *T*
770 ⟨Dardan and Greek⟩ / ⟨Nameless and glorious—of Dardan and Greek⟩ *T*

Their leader's nervous arm is bare,
Swifter to smite, and never to spare—
Unclothed to the shoulder it waves them on;
Thus in the fight is he ever known:
Others a gaudier garb may show,   780
To tempt the spoil of the greedy foe;
Many a hand's on a richer hilt,
But none on a steel more ruddily gilt;
Many a loftier turban may wear,—
Alp is but known by the white arm bare;   785
Look through the thick of the fight, 'tis there!
There is not a standard on that shore
So well advanced the ranks before;
There is not a banner in Moslem war
Will lure the Delhis half so far;   790
It glances like a falling star!
Where'er that mighty arm is seen,
The bravest be, or late have been;
There the craven cries for quarter
Vainly to the vengeful Tartar;   795
Or the hero, silent lying,
Scorns to yield a groan in dying;
Mustering his last feeble blow
'Gainst the nearest levelled foe,
Though faint beneath the mutual wound,   800
Grappling on the gory ground.

27.

Still the old man stood erect,
And Alp's career a moment checked.
'Yield thee, Minotti; quarter take,
For thine own, thy daughter's sake.'   805

'Never, renegado, never!
Though the life of thy gift would last for ever.'

777 Swifter] ⟨The⟩ Swifter *T*   778 shoulder⟨s⟩ *T*   782 ⟨Many a richer / loftier turban may wear⟩ *T*   783 ⟨But Alp is⟩ *T*   785 arm bare] arm ⟨and⟩ bare *M*   786 ⟨When you gaze⟩ *T*   789 Moslem] ⟨all the⟩ *T*   790 lure] ⟨lead⟩ *T*   791 falling] ⟨bending?⟩ *T*   795 ⟨Silent dies the sterner / mighty⟩ *T*   796 hero] ⟨bolder⟩ *T*   801 Grappling ⟨side by side⟩ on *T*   807 gift] giving *T*, *M*

'Francesca!—Oh my promised bride!
Must she too perish by thy pride?'

'She is safe.'—'Where? where?'—'In heaven;   810
From whence thy traitor soul is driven—
Far from thee, and undefiled.'
Grimly then Minotti smiled,
As he saw Alp staggering bow
Before his words, as with a blow.   815
'Oh God! when died she?'—'Yesternight—
Nor weep I for her spirit's flight:
None of my pure race shall be
Slaves to Mahomet and thee—
Come on!'—That challenge is in vain—   820
Alp's already with the slain!

While Minotti's words were wreaking
More revenge in bitter speaking
Than his falchion's point had found,
Had the time allowed to wound,   825
From within the neighbouring porch
Of a long defended church,
Where the last and desperate few
Would the failing fight renew,
The sharp shot dashed Alp to the ground;   830
Ere an eye could view the wound
That crashed through the brain of the infidel,
Round he spun, and down he fell;
A flash like fire within his eyes
Blazed, as he bent no more to rise,   835
And then eternal darkness sunk
Through all the palpitating trunk;
Nought of life left, save a quivering
Where his limbs were slightly shivering:

808 Where's Francesca?—my promised bride, *T, M*; ⟨Where is Francesca?⟩ my promised bride⟨,⟩ *Proof H*   811 soul] ⟨hope⟩ *T*   812 ⟨Grimly smiled Minotti⟩ *T*
814 bow] ⟨back⟩ *T*   815 with] ⟨at⟩ *T*   816 *new verse paragraph here in 1831, 1832, C, More*   817 ⟨An hour before the morn's⟩ *T*   822 *no verse paragraph here in any earlier text; marked for paragraph by Byron in MS. M*   826–7 ⟨From a small but desperate band | Who still held a⟩ *T*   827 long] ⟨still⟩ *T*   829 the ⟨lost⟩ failing *T*   830 ⟨A shot⟩ A sharp shot ⟨came—Alp's on the⟩ ground *T*   835 bent] ⟨sank⟩ *T*   839 were] are *T*

They turned him on his back; his breast   840
And brow were stained with gore and dust,
And through his lips the life-blood oozed,
From its deep veins lately loosed;
But in his pulse there was no throb,
Nor on his lips one dying sob;   845
Sigh, nor word, nor struggling breath
Heralded his way to death:
Ere his very thought could pray,
Unanealed he passed away,
Without a hope from mercy's aid,—   850
To the last a renegade.

28.

Fearfully the yell arose
Of his followers, and his foes;
These in joy, in fury those:
Then again in conflict mixing,   855
Clashing swords, and spears transfixing,
Interchanged the blow and thrust,
Hurling warriors in the dust.
Street by street, and foot by foot,
Still Minotti dares dispute   860
The latest portion of the land
Left beneath his high command;
With him, aiding heart and hand,
The remnant of his gallant band.
Still the church is tenable,   865
    Whence issued late the fated ball
    That half avenged the city's fall,
When Alp, her fierce assailant, fell:
Thither bending sternly back,
They leave before a bloody track;   870
And, with their faces to the foe,
Dealing wounds with every blow,

840 ⟨Not a⟩ T   841 gore] ⟨blood⟩ T   842 through] from T, M, cor. in Proof H
843 lately] ⟨slowly⟩ T   846 Sigh nor ⟨sign nor parting word⟩ T   848 ⟨From / With-
out a prayer⟩ T   849 Unanealed] Unaneled 1831, 1832, C, More   854 These in
rage—in triumph those T, cor. in M   855 conflict] fury T, M   858 ⟨Strew-
ing / Laying helms⟩ T   860 dares] ⟨will⟩ T   861 the land] ⟨his hold⟩ T   864 his]
a T   869 Thither ⟨slowly / sternly⟩ bending T   872 Dealing] ⟨Leaving⟩ T

The chief, and his retreating train,
Join to those within the fane:
There they yet may breathe awhile,   875
Sheltered by the massy pile.

29.

Brief breathing-time! the turbaned host,
With added ranks and raging boast,
Press onwards with such strength and heat,
Their numbers balk their own retreat;   880
For narrow the way that led to the spot
Where still the Christians yielded not;
And the foremost, if fearful, may vainly try
Through the massy column to turn and fly;
They perforce must do or die.   885
They die; but ere their eyes could close
Avengers o'er their bodies rose;
Fresh and furious, fast they fill
The ranks unthinned, though slaughtered still;
And faint the weary Christians wax   890
Before the still renewed attacks:
And now the Othmans gain the gate;
Still resists its iron weight,
And still, all deadly aimed and hot,
From every crevice comes the shot;   895
From every shattered window pour
The volleys of the sulphurous shower:
But the portal wavering grows and weak—
The iron yields, the hinges creak—
It bends—it falls—and all is o'er;   900
Lost Corinth may resist no more!

30.

Darkly, sternly, and all alone,
Minotti stood o'er the altar stone:

873 ⟨They rejoin the banded foe⟩ / ⟨Minotti and his banded ?⟩ T   874 ⟨Join with⟩ T
877 host] ⟨crowd⟩ T   878 raging boast] ⟨clamour loud⟩ T   879 such ⟨numbers⟩
strength T   880 balk] ⟨foiled⟩ T   881 way] ⟨straits⟩ T   883 And the
foremost ⟨too vainly turned to fly⟩ T   886 They ⟨died—but ere their bodies rose⟩ T
894 And still ⟨from every crevice⟩ all T   895 comes] ⟨pours⟩ M   896 every]
⟨out the⟩ M   897 sulphurous] ⟨fiery⟩ T   898 and] ⟨too⟩ T   901 ⟨Corinth's
last hold⟩ T   903 o'er] ⟨by⟩ T

Madonna's face upon him shone,
Painted in heavenly hues above,   905
With eyes of light and looks of love;
And placed upon that holy shrine
To fix our thoughts on things divine,
When pictured there, we kneeling see
Her, and the boy-God on her knee,   910
Smiling sweetly on each prayer
To heaven, as if to waft it there.
Still she smiled; even now she smiles,
Though slaughter streams along her aisles:
Minotti lifted his aged eye,   915
And made the sign of a cross with a sigh,
Then seized a torch which blazed thereby;
And still he stood, while, with steel and flame,
Inward and onward the Mussulman came.

                         31.

The vaults beneath the mosaic stone   920
Contained the dead of ages gone;
Their names were on the graven floor,
But now illegible with gore;
The carved crests, and curious hues
The varied marble's veins diffuse,   925
Were smeared, and slippery—stained, and strown
With broken swords, and helms o'erthrown:
There were dead above, and the dead below
Lay cold in many a coffined row;
You might see them piled in sable state,   930
By a pale light through a gloomy grate;
But War had entered their dark caves,
And stored along the vaulted graves

904 ⟨The face of the Mado⟩ T   upon] ⟨above⟩ T   905 heavenly]
⟨lambent?⟩ T   907 placed upon] ⟨fixed above⟩ T   908 ⟨To awake her votaries⟩ T
909 pictured ⟨oer the⟩ there T   911 Smiling ⟨oer our prayers⟩ sweetly T
914 streams] ⟨streamed⟩ T   915 ⟨One look on that⟩ T   916 of a] of ⟨the⟩ T
917 which blazed thereby] ⟨he raised it on high⟩ T   920 mosaic stone] ⟨marble floor /
inlaid / checquered⟩ T   923 illegible with] ⟨half blotted with the⟩ T   926 ⟨Were
all of a colour ?⟩ T   strown] ⟨strewed⟩ T   927 swords . . . o'erthrown] ⟨weapons—
and blood inlaid⟩ T   928 ⟨And the steps ? fleet and fast⟩ T   929 cold] ⟨calm⟩ T
932 But War ⟨must ? most of her beams⟩ T

Her sulphurous treasures, thickly spread
In masses by the fleshless dead: 935
Here, throughout the siege, had been
The Christians' chiefest magazine;
To these a late formed train now led,
Minotti's last and stern resource
Against the foe's o'erwhelming force.   940

32.

The foe came on, and few remain
To strive, and those must strive in vain:
For lack of further lives, to slake
The thirst of vengeance now awake,
With barbarous blows they gash the dead,   945
And lop the already lifeless head,
And fell the statues from their niche,
And spoil the shrines of offerings rich,
And from each other's rude hands wrest
The silver vessels saints had blessed.   950
To the high altar on they go;
Oh, but it made a glorious show!
On its table still behold
The cup of consecrated gold;
Massy and deep, a glittering prize,   955
Brightly it sparkles to plunderers' eyes:
That morn it held the holy wine,
Converted by Christ to his blood so divine,
Which his worshippers drank at the break of day,
To shrive their souls ere they joined in the fray.   960
Still a few drops within it lay;
And round the sacred table glow
Twelve lofty lamps, in splendid row,
From the purest metal cast;
A spoil—the richest, and the last.   965

934 treasures ⟨by the / in gloomy ?⟩ T   941 and few remain] ⟨but few were there⟩ T
942 ⟨And the⟩ T   943 further lives] ⟨victims more⟩ T   944 now] ⟨all⟩ T
945 gash] ⟨maim⟩ T   946 lop] ⟨gash⟩ T   948 And ⟨plun⟩ spoil the shrine ⟨in
plunder⟩ rich T   of] with T, M   950 silver] ⟨richer⟩ M   954 The] ⟨A⟩ M
cup] ⟨vessels⟩ T   955 glittering prize] ⟨goodly spoil⟩ T   956 plunderers'] ⟨Mus-
sulman⟩ T   957 the holy wine] ⟨the Sacrament⟩ T   959 ⟨And⟩ Which the
Christians partook at the break of day T, M   960 ⟨Ere / The last⟩ T   962 glow]
⟨rose⟩ T   964 From] ⟨Of⟩ T

33.

So near they came, the nearest stretched
To grasp the spoil he almost reached,
    When old Minotti's hand
Touched with the torch the train—
        'Tis fired!   970
Spire, vaults, the shrine, the spoil, the slain,
    The turbaned victors, the Christian band,
All that of living or dead remain,
Hurled on high with the shivered fane,
        In one wild roar expired!   975
The shattered town—the walls thrown down—
The waves a moment backward bent—
The hills that shake, although unrent,
        As if an earthquake passed—
The thousand shapeless things all driven   980
In cloud and flame athwart the heaven,
        By that tremendous blast—
Proclaimed the desperate conflict o'er
On that too long afflicted shore:
Up to the sky like rockets go   985
All that mingled there below:
Many a tall and goodly man,
Scorched and shrivelled to a span,
When he fell to earth again
Like a cinder strewed the plain: 990
Down the ashes shower like rain;
Some fell in the gulf, which received the sprinkles
With a thousand circling wrinkles;
Some fell on the shore, but, far away,
Scattered o'er the isthmus lay;   995
Christian or Moslem, which be they?
Let their mothers see and say!
When in cradled rest they lay,

---

968 When ⟨trusted dark⟩ old T   971 spoil] ⟨tombs⟩ T   974 ⟨Mixed with the
ruins of their⟩ fane T   976 ⟨The town⟩ T   977–8 ⟨The hills as by an earthquake
rent | The waves a moment backward bent⟩ T   983 ⟨Proclaimed whateer the deed?
before / Proclaim a / Weapons and⟩ T   985–97 *written across the page in* T   985 the
sky] ⟨the heavens / the skies⟩ T   989 ⟨Fell to earth again through⟩ T   997 ⟨Who
can see or who can say⟩   998–1002 *not in* T, M

And each nursing mother smiled
On the sweet sleep of her child,   1000
Little deemed she such a day
Would rend those tender limbs away.
Not the matrons that them bore
Could discern their offspring more;
That one moment left no trace   1005
More of human form or face
Save a scattered scalp or bone:
And down came blazing rafters, strown
Around, and many a falling stone,
Deeply dinted in the clay,   1010
All blackened there and reeking lay.
All the living things that heard
That deadly earth-shock disappeared:
The wild birds flew; the wild dogs fled,
And howling left the unburied dead;   1015
The camels from their keepers broke;
The distant steer forsook the yoke—
The nearer steed plunged o'er the plain,
And burst his girth, and tore his rein;
The bull-frog's note, from out the marsh,   1020
Deep-mouthed arose, and doubly harsh;
The wolves yelled on the caverned hill,
Where echo rolled in thunder still;
The jackal's troop, in gathered cry,
Bayed from afar complainingly,   1025
With a mixed and mournful sound,
Like crying babe, and beaten hound:
With sudden wing, and ruffled breast,
The eagle left his rocky nest,

1003 matrons] ⟨mothers⟩ T   1007 ⟨And with that / what late was blood and
bone⟩ / ⟨The mass of bl⟩ T   1008 came ⟨bla / rafters bla⟩ blazing rafters ⟨down⟩ T
1009 Around and ⟨crushed each mass of⟩ stone T   1010 ⟨And⟩ Deeply . . . in the
⟨ground⟩ T   1011 ⟨And / Along / All was torn and blackened ?⟩ T   1012 All
⟨that heard / that hear⟩ the T   1013 deadly earth-shock] ⟨fearful thunder⟩ T   earth-
shock] earth shock T–1829   1014 flew] ⟨yelled / shrieked⟩ T   1015 And
⟨howling⟩ left their food—the untasted dead T, M   1016 broke] ⟨burst⟩ T
1022 yelled] ⟨howled⟩ T   1023 in thunder] ⟨the / in horror⟩ T   1024 ⟨Even /
The Eagle / The frighted jackall's shrill short cry⟩ T   troop] ⟨whelp⟩ T   1025 ⟨Bayed
in the distance / from the ruins⟩ / ⟨Bayed from afar complainingly⟩ T   from afar] ⟨like a
hound⟩ T   1026-7 not in T   1026 Mixed and mournful is the sound M
1028 sudden . . . ruffled] ⟨ruffled . . . startled⟩ T

And mounted nearer to the sun,   1030
The clouds beneath him seemed so dun;
Their smoke assailed his startled beak,
And made him higher soar and shriek—
   Thus was Corinth lost and won!

281a   Lines Associated With *The Siege of Corinth*

In the year since Jesus died for men,
Eighteen hundred years and ten,
We were a gallant company,
Riding o'er land, and sailing o'er sea.
Oh! but we went merrily!   5
We forded the river, and clomb the high hill,
Never our steeds for a day stood still;
Whether we lay in the cave or the shed,
Our sleep fell soft on the hardest bed;
Whether we couch'd in our rough capote,   10
On the rougher plank of our gliding boat,
Or stretch'd on the beach, or our saddles spread
As a pillow beneath the resting head,
Fresh we woke upon the morrow:
   All our thoughts and words had scope,   15
   We had health, and we had hope,
Toil and travel, but no sorrow.
We were of all tongues and creeds;—
Some were those who counted beads,
Some of mosque, and some of church,   20
   And some, or I mis-say, of neither;
Yet through the wide world might ye search
Nor find a motlier crew nor blither.

1030 mounted] ⟨soared him / bore him⟩ *T*   1031 beneath] ⟨below⟩ *T*   1032 ⟨And /
Their sulphurous fumes scorched his far-scenting⟩ beak *T*

281a. Copy text: *Life*, collated with *MS. L*

title   ⟨The Stranger—a tale.—Oct. 23rd⟩ *L*

7 Never] ⟨Seldom⟩ *L*   8 Whether we] ⟨We⟩ *L*   9 fell] ⟨came⟩ *L*   10 ⟨With
the⟩ *L*   couch'd in] ⟨?⟩ *L*   11 On the ⟨plank that checked⟩ / ⟨hollow⟩ rougher plank
⟨of the / in⟩ of our gliding boat *L*   12 Or ⟨couched⟩ stretched *L*   13 resting]
⟨member's⟩ *L*   15–16 *transposed in L, then corrected*   16 We had health ⟨and
hope⟩ and *L*   18 ⟨Of all tongues and hues were we⟩ *L*   23 Nor . . . nor] ⟨Ere . . .
or⟩ *L*

But some are dead, and some are gone,
And some are scatter'd and alone,   25
And some are rebels on the hills
   That look along Epirus' valleys
   Where Freedom still at moments rallies,
And pays in blood Oppression's ills;
   And some are in a far countree,   30
And some all restlessly at home;
   But never more, oh! never, we
Shall meet to revel and to roam.

But those hardy days flew cheerily,
And when they now fall drearily,   35
My thoughts, like swallows, skim the main,
And bear my spirit back again
Over the earth, and through the air,
A wild bird, and a wanderer.
'Tis this that ever wakes my strain,   40
And oft, too oft, implores again
The few who may endure my lay,
To follow me so far away.

Stranger—wilt thou follow now,
And sit with me on Acro-Corinth's brow?   45

[1813]

27 ⟨And some are in their own / Aetolia's valleys⟩ L   30 a far countree] the holy city⟩ L
33 Shall ⟨we that⟩ meet to revel ⟨or⟩ to roam L   34 hardy] winged L   36 ⟨I think upon
those⟩ L   swallows] ⟨birds⟩ L   38 through] ⟨over the⟩ L   41 implores] ⟨attempts /
?⟩ L   42 The kindly few who love my lay L   45 And sit with me ⟨upon Mount
Athos'⟩ brow. L

282   Parisina

TO

SCROPE BEARDMORE DAVIES, Esq.

THE FOLLOWING POEM

IS INSCRIBED

BY ONE WHO HAS LONG ADMIRED HIS TALENTS

AND VALUED HIS FRIENDSHIP.

Jan. 22, 1816

The following poem is grounded on a circumstance mentioned in Gibbon's 'Antiquities of the House of Brunswick'.—I am aware, that in modern times the delicacy or fastidiousness of the reader may deem such subjects unfit for the purposes of poetry. The Greek dramatists, and some of the best of our old English writers, were of a different opinion: as Alfieri and Schiller have also been, more recently, upon the continent. The following extract will explain the facts on which the story is founded. The name of *Azo* is substituted for Nicholas, as more metrical.

'Under the reign of Nicholas III. Ferrara was polluted with a domestic tragedy. By the testimony of an attendant, and his own observation, the Marquis of Este discovered the incestuous loves of his wife Parisina, and Hugo his bastard son, a beautiful and valiant youth. They were beheaded in the castle by the sentence of a father and husband, who published his shame, and survived their execution. He was unfortunate, if they were guilty; if they were innocent, he was still more unfortunate: nor is there any possible situation in which I can sincerely approve the last act of the justice of a parent.'—*Gibbon's Miscellaneous Works*, vol. 3d. p. 470, new edition [1814].

282. Copy text: *Parisina*(*1*), collated with *MS. M, Proofs M, H, Ha, Hb, Parisina*(*2*) and (*3*)

Advertisement   may deem] ⟨will⟩ deem *M*

1.

It is the hour when from the boughs
The nightingale's high note is heard;
It is the hour when lovers' vows
Seem sweet in every whisper'd word;
And gentle winds, and waters near,   5
Make music to the lonely ear.
Each flower the dews have lightly wet,
And in the sky the stars are met,
And on the wave is deeper blue,
And on the leaf a browner hue,   10
And in the heaven that clear obscure,
So softly dark, and darkly pure,
Which follows the decline of day,
As twilight melts beneath the moon away.

2.

But it is not to list to the waterfall   15
That Parisina leaves her hall,
And it is not to gaze on the heavenly light
That the lady walks in the shadow of night;
And if she sits in Este's bower,
'Tis not for the sake of its full-blown flower—   20
She listens—but not for the nightingale—
Though her ear expects as soft a tale.
There glides a step through the foliage thick,
And her cheek grows pale—and her heart beats quick.
There whispers a voice through the rustling leaves,   25
And her blush returns, and her bosom heaves:
A moment more—and they shall meet—
'Tis past—her lover's at her feet.

3.

And what unto them is the world beside
With all its change of time and tide?   30
Its living things—its earth and sky—
Are nothing to their mind and eye.

1 ff. [Stanzas 1 and 2 were originally printed with *HM* in slightly variant form;
for collation see 'It Is the Hour' and 'Francisca' in *HM*.]   3 lovers'] lover('s) *M*

And heedless as the dead are they
Of aught around, above, beneath;
As if all else had passed away,   35
They only for each other breathe;
Their very sighs are full of joy
So deep, that did it not decay,
That happy madness would destroy
The hearts which feel its fiery sway: 40
Of guilt, of peril, do they deem
In that tumultuous tender dream?
Who that have felt that passion's power,
Or paused, or feared in such an hour?
Or thought how brief such moments last: 45
But yet—they are already past!
Alas! we must awake before
We know such vision comes no more.

4.

With many a lingering look they leave
The spot of guilty gladness past;   50
And though they hope, and vow, they grieve,
As if that parting were the last.
The frequent sigh—the long embrace—
The lip that there would cling for ever,
While gleams on Parisina's face   55
The Heaven she fears will not forgive her,
As if each calmly conscious star
Beheld her frailty from afar—
The frequent sigh, the long embrace,
Yet binds them to their trysting-place.   60
But it must come, and they must part
In fearful heaviness of heart,
With all the deep and shuddering chill
Which follows fast the deeds of ill.

5.

And Hugo is gone to his lonely bed,   65
To covet there another's bride;
But she must lay her conscious head
A husband's trusting heart beside.

39 That] ⟨A⟩ M   40 which] ⟨that⟩ M

But fevered in her sleep she seems,
And red her cheek with troubled dreams,   70
And mutters she in her unrest
A name she dare not breathe by day,
And clasps her Lord unto the breast
Which pants for one away:
And he to that embrace awakes,   75
And, happy in the thought, mistakes
That dreaming sigh, and warm caress,
For such as he was wont to bless;
And could in very fondness weep
O'er her who loves him even in sleep.   80

6.

He clasped her sleeping to his heart,
And listened to each broken word:
He hears—Why doth Prince Azo start,
As if the Archangel's voice he heard?
And well he may—a deeper doom   85
Could scarcely thunder o'er his tomb,
When he shall wake to sleep no more,
And stand the eternal throne before.
And well he may—his earthly peace
Upon that sound is doomed to cease.   90
That sleeping whisper of a name
Bespeaks her guilt and Azo's shame.
And whose that name? that o'er his pillow
Sounds fearful as the breaking billow,
Which rolls the plank upon the shore,   95
And dashes on the pointed rock
The wretch who sinks to rise no more,—
So came upon his soul the shock.
And whose that name? 'tis Hugo's,—his—
In sooth he had not deemed of this!—   100
'Tis Hugo's,—he, the child of one
He loved—his own all-evil son—
The offspring of his wayward youth,
When he betrayed Bianca's truth,

70 troubled] ⟨evil⟩ *M*   74 Which] ⟨That⟩ *M*   83 Prince] ⟨Lord⟩ *M*   84 voice]
⟨trump⟩ *M*   95 Which] ⟨And⟩ *M*   97 who] that *M, cor. in Proof M*
100 deemed] ⟨dreamed⟩ *M*   104 Bianca's] ⟨Medora's⟩ *M*

The maid whose folly could confide   105
In him who made her not his bride.

7.

He plucked his poignard in its sheath,
But sheathed it ere the point was bare—
Howe'er unworthy now to breathe,
He could not slay a thing so fair—   110
At least, not smiling—sleeping—there—
Nay, more:—he did not wake her then,
But gazed upon her with a glance
Which, had she roused her from her trance,
Had frozen her sense to sleep again—   115
And o'er his brow the burning lamp
Gleamed on the dew-drops big and damp.
She spake no more—but still she slumbered—
While, in his thought, her days are numbered.

8.

And with the morn he sought, and found,   120
In many a tale from those around,
The proof of all he feared to know,
Their present guilt, his future woe;
The long-conniving damsels seek
    To save themselves, and would transfer   125
    The guilt—the shame—the doom—to her:
Concealment is no more—they speak
All circumstance which may compel
Full credence to the tale they tell:
And Azo's tortured heart and ear   130
Have nothing more to feel or hear.

9.

He was not one who brooked delay:
    Within the chamber of his state,
The chief of Este's ancient sway
    Upon his throne of judgment sate;   135

---

109 now] more *M, cor. in Proof M*   114 Which] ⟨That⟩ *M*   115 frozen]
⟨froze⟩ *Proof M*   126 the doom] ⟨entire⟩ *M*   128 which] that *M, cor. in Proof M*

His nobles and his guards are there,—
Before him is the sinful pair;
Both young,—and *one* how passing fair!
With swordless belt, and fettered hand,
Oh, Christ! that thus a son should stand   140
    Before a father's face!
Yet thus must Hugo meet his sire,
And hear the sentence of his ire,
    The tale of his disgrace!
And yet he seems not overcome,   145
Although, as yet, his voice be dumb.

                    10.

And still, and pale, and silently
    Did Parisina wait her doom;
How changed since last her speaking eye
    Glanced gladness round the glittering room,   150
Where high-born men were proud to wait—
Where Beauty watched to imitate
    Her gentle voice—her lovely mien—
And gather from her air and gait
    The graces of its queen: 155
Then,—had her eye in sorrow wept,
A thousand warriors forth had leapt,
A thousand swords had sheathless shone,
And made her quarrel all their own.
Now,—what is she? and what are they?   160
Can she command, or these obey?
All silent and unheeding now,
With downcast eyes and knitting brow,
And folded arms, and freezing air,
And lips that scarce their scorn forbear,   165
Her knights and dames, her court—is there:
And he, the chosen one, whose lance
Had yet been couched before her glance,
Who—were his arm a moment free—
Had died or gained her liberty;   170
The minion of his father's bride,—
He, too, is fettered by her side;

137 sinful] ⟨guilty⟩ *M*

Nor sees her swoln and full eye swim
Less for her own despair than him:
Those lids o'er which the violet vein—   175
Wandering, leaves a tender stain,
Shining through the smoothest white
That e'er did softest kiss invite—
Now seemed with hot and livid glow
To press, not shade, the orbs below;   180
Which glance so heavily, and fill,
As tear on tear grows gathering still.

11.

And he for her had also wept,
 But for the eyes that on him gazed:
His sorrow, if he felt it, slept;   185
 Stern and erect his brow was raised.
Whate'er the grief his soul avowed,
He would not shrink before the crowd;
But yet he dared not look on her:
Remembrance of the hours that were—   190
His guilt—his love—his present state—
His father's wrath—all good men's hate—
His earthly, his eternal fate—
And hers,—oh, hers!—he dared not throw
One look upon that deathlike brow!   195
Else had his rising heart betrayed
Remorse for all the wreck it made.

12.

And Azo spake:—'But yesterday
 I gloried in a wife and son;
That dream this morning passed away;   200
 Ere day declines, I shall have none.
My life must linger on alone;
Well,—let that pass,—there breathes not one
Who would not do as I have done:
Those ties are broken—not by me;   205

Let that too pass;—the doom's prepared!
Hugo, the priest awaits on thee,
    And then—thy crime's reward!
Away! address thy prayers to Heaven,
    Before its evening stars are met—   210
Learn if thou there canst be forgiven;
    Its mercy may absolve thee yet.
But here, upon the earth beneath,
    There is no spot where thou and I
Together, for an hour, could breathe: 215
    Farewell! I will not see thee die—
But thou, frail thing! shalt view his head—
    Away! I cannot speak the rest:
    Go! woman of the wanton breast;
Not I, but thou his blood dost shed: 220
Go! if that sight thou canst outlive,
And joy thee in the life I give.'

                    13.

And here stern Azo hid his face—
    For on his brow the swelling vein
    Throbbed as if back upon his brain   225
    The hot blood ebbed and flowed again;
And therefore bowed he for a space,
And passed his shaking hand along
His eye, to veil it from the throng;
While Hugo raised his chained hands,   230
And for a brief delay demands
His father's ear: the silent sire
Forbids not what his words require.

'It is not that I dread the death—
    For thou hast seen me by thy side   235
    All redly through the battle ride;
And that not once a useless brand
Thy slaves have wrested from my hand,
Hath shed more blood in cause of thine,
Than e'er can stain the axe of mine: 240

236 ride;] ride, *Parisina*(*1*), (*2*), (*3*) [see also commentary]

Thou gav'st, and may'st resume my breath,
A gift for which I thank thee not;
Nor are my mother's wrongs forgot,
Her slighted love and ruined name,
Her offspring's heritage of shame;   245
But she is in the grave, where he,
Her son, thy rival, soon shall be.
Her broken heart—my severed head—
Shall witness for thee from the dead
How trusty and how tender were   250
Thy youthful love—paternal care.
'Tis true, that I have done thee wrong—
But wrong for wrong—this deemed thy bride,
The other victim of thy pride,
Thou know'st for me was destined long.   255
Thou saw'st, and coveted'st her charms—
And with thy very crime—my birth,
Thou taunted'st me—as little worth;
A match ignoble for her arms,
Because, forsooth, I could not claim   260
The lawful heirship of thy name,
Nor sit on Este's lineal throne:
Yet, were a few short summers mine,
My name should more than Este's shine
With honours all my own.   265
I had a sword—and have a breast
That should have won as haught a crest
As ever waved along the line
Of all these sovereign sires of thine.
Not always knightly spurs are worn   270
The brightest by the better born;
And mine have lanced my courser's flank
Before proud chiefs of princely rank,
When charging to the cheering cry
Of "Este and of Victory!"   275

'I will not plead the cause of crime,
Nor sue thee to redeem from time

262 lineal] ⟨ducal⟩ ⟨princely⟩ *M*   267 haught] ⟨bright⟩ *M*

A few brief hours or days that must
At length roll o'er my reckless dust;—
Such maddening moments as my past,   280
They could not, and they did not, last—
Albeit, my birth and name be base,
And thy nobility of race
Disdained to deck a thing like me—
Yet in my lineaments they trace   285
Some features of my father's face,
And in my spirit—all of thee.
From thee—this tamelessness of heart—
From thee—nay, wherefore dost thou start?—
From thee in all their vigour came   290
My arm of strength, my soul of flame—
Thou didst not give me life alone,
But all that made me more thine own.
See what thy guilty love hath done!
Repaid thee with too like a son!   295
I am no bastard in my soul,
For that, like thine, abhorred controul:
And for my breath, that hasty boon
Thou gav'st and wilt resume so soon,
I valued it no more than thou,   300
When rose thy casque above thy brow,
And we, all side by side, have striven,
And o'er the dead our coursers driven:
The past is nothing—and at last
The future can but be the past;   305
Yet would I that I then had died:
For though thou work'dst my mother's ill,
And made thy own my destined bride,
I feel thou art my father still;
And, harsh as sounds thy hard decree,   310
'Tis not unjust, although from thee.
Begot in sin, to die in shame,
My life begun and ends the same:
As erred the sire, so erred the son—
And thou must punish both in one.   315

297 abhorred] knew no *M, Proof M*   304–5 *not in M or Proof M*   310–17 *not*
in M; MS. addition in Proof M

My crime seems worst to human view,
But God must judge between us too!'

14.

He ceased—and stood with folded arms,
On which the circling fetters sounded;
And not an ear but felt as wounded,   320
Of all the chiefs that there were ranked,
When those dull chains in meeting clanked:
Till Parisina's fatal charms
Again attracted every eye—
Would she thus hear him doomed to die!   325
She stood, I said, all pale and still,
The living cause of Hugo's ill:
Her eyes unmoved, but full and wide,
Not once had turned to either side—
Nor once did those sweet eyelids close,   330
Or shade the glance o'er which they rose,
But round their orbs of deepest blue
The circling white dilated grew—
And there with glassy gaze she stood
As ice were in her curdled blood;   335
But every now and then a tear
So large and slowly gathered slid
From the long dark fringe of that fair lid,
It was a thing to see, not hear!
And those who saw, it did surprise,   340
Such drops could fall from human eyes.
To speak she thought—the imperfect note
Was choked within her swelling throat,
Yet seemed in that low hollow groan
Her whole heart gushing in the tone.   345
It ceased—again she thought to speak,
Then burst her voice in one long shriek,
And to the earth she fell like stone
Or statue from its base o'erthrown,
More like a thing that ne'er had life,—   350
A monument of Azo's wife,—

317 too] ⟨two⟩ *Proof M*   323 Till] But *M, cor. in Proof M*   328 full] ⟨wild⟩ *M*
329 turned] ⟨glanced⟩ *M*   332 their] th⟨ose⟩ *M*   338 dark . . . fair] ⟨long fringe
of that dark⟩ *M*

Than her, that living guilty thing,
Whose every passion was a sting,
Which urged to guilt, but could not bear
That guilt's detection and despair. 355
But yet she lived—and all too soon
Recovered from that death-like swoon—
But scarce to reason—every sense
Had been o'erstrung by pangs intense;
And each frail fibre of her brain 360
(As bow-strings, when relaxed by rain,
The erring arrow launch aside)
Sent forth her thoughts all wild and wide—
The past a blank, the future black,
With glimpses of a dreary track, 365
Like lightning on the desart path,
When midnight storms are mustering wrath.
She feared—she felt that something ill
Lay on her soul, so deep and chill—
That there was sin and shame she knew; 370
That some one was to die—but who?
She had forgotten:—did she breathe?
Could this be still the earth beneath?
The sky above, and men around;
Or were they fiends who now so frowned 375
On one, before whose eyes each eye
Till then had smiled in sympathy?
All was confused and undefined,
To her all-jarred and wandering mind;
A chaos of wild hopes and fears: 380
And now in laughter, now in tears,
But madly still in each extreme,
She strove with that convulsive dream;
For so it seemed on her to break:
Oh! vainly must she strive to wake! 385

15.

The Convent bells are ringing,
    But mournfully and slow;
In the grey square turret swinging,
    With a deep sound, to and fro.

Heavily to the heart they go!
  Hark! the hymn is singing—
The song for the dead below,
  Or the living who shortly shall be so!
For a departing being's soul
The death-hymn peals and the hollow bells knoll: 395
He is near his mortal goal;
Kneeling at the Friar's knee;
Sad to hear—and piteous to see—
Kneeling on the bare cold ground,
With the block before and the guards around—   400
And the headsman with his bare arm ready,
That the blow may be both swift and steady,
Feels if the axe be sharp and true—
Since he set its edge anew:
While the crowd in a speechless circle gather   405
To see the Son fall by the doom of the Father.

16.

It is a lovely hour as yet
Before the summer sun shall set,
Which rose upon that heavy day,
And mocked it with his steadiest ray;   410
And his evening beams are shed
Full on Hugo's fated head,
As his last confession pouring
To the monk, his doom deploring
In penitential holiness,   415
He bends to hear his accents bless
With absolution such as may
Wipe our mortal stains away.
That high sun on his head did glisten
As he there did bow and listen—   420
And the rings of chestnut hair
Curled half down his neck so bare;
But brighter still the beam was thrown
Upon the axe which near him shone
With a clear and ghastly glitter——   425

---

394 departing] departed *C*   395 The death-hymn ⟨swells⟩ and the ⟨dark⟩ bells ⟨toll⟩ *M*
401–4 *marginal addition in* M

Oh! that parting hour was bitter!
Even the stern stood chilled with awe:
Dark the crime, and just the law—
Yet they shuddered as they saw.

17.

The parting prayers are said and over   430
Of that false son—and daring lover!
His beads and sins are all recounted,
His hours to their last minute mounted—
His mantling cloak before was stripped,
His bright brown locks must now be clipped,   435
'Tis done—all closely are they shorn—
The vest which till this moment worn—
The scarf which Parisina gave—
Must not adorn him to the grave.
Even that must now be thrown aside,   440
And o'er his eyes the kerchief tied;
But no—that last indignity
Shall ne'er approach his haughty eye.
All feelings seemingly subdued,
In deep disdain were half renewed,   445
When headman's hands prepared to bind
Those eyes which would not brook such blind:
As if they dared not look on death.
'No—yours my forfeit blood and breath—
These hands are chained—but let me die   450
At least with an unshackled eye—
Strike':—and as the word he said,
Upon the block he bowed his head;
These the last accents Hugo spoke:
'Strike'—and flashing fell the stroke—   455
Rolled the head—and, gushing, sunk
Back the stained and heaving trunk,
In the dust, which each deep vein
Slaked with its ensanguined rain;
His eyes and lips a moment quiver,   460
Convulsed and quick—then fix for ever.

432 His latest beads and sins are counted *M, Proof M, cor. in Proof H*

He died, as erring man should die,
Without display, without parade;
Meekly had he bowed and prayed,
As not disdaining priestly aid,   465
Nor desperate of all hope on high.
And while before the Prior kneeling,
His heart was weaned from earthly feeling;
His wrathful sire—his paramour—
What were they in such an hour?   470
No more reproach—no more despair;
No thought but heaven—no word but prayer—
Save the few which from him broke,
When, bared to meet the headman's stroke,
He claimed to die with eyes unbound,   475
His sole adieu to those around.

18.

Still as the lips that closed in death,
Each gazer's bosom held his breath:
But yet, afar, from man to man,
A cold electric shiver ran,   480
As down the deadly blow descended
On him whose life and love thus ended;
And with a hushing sound comprest,
A sigh shrunk back on every breast;
But no more thrilling noise rose there,   485
Beyond the blow that to the block
Pierced through with forced and sullen shock,
Save one:—what cleaves the silent air
So madly shrill—so passing wild?
That, as a mother's o'er her child,   490
Done to death by sudden blow,
To the sky these accents go,
Like a soul's in endless woe.
Through Azo's palace-lattice driven,
That horrid voice ascends to heaven,   495
And every eye is turned thereon;
But sound and sight alike are gone!

462 as erring] ⟨and as a⟩ M   480 shiver] ⟨shudder⟩ M   481 As] ⟨And⟩ M
485 noise] voice M, cor. in Proof M

It was a woman's shriek—and ne'er
In madlier accents rose despair;
And those who heard it, as it past,   500
In mercy wished it were the last.

19.

Hugo is fallen; and, from that hour,
No more in palace, hall, or bower,
Was Parisina heard or seen:
Her name—as if she ne'er had been—   505
Was banished from each lip and ear,
Like words of wantonness or fear;
And from Prince Azo's voice, by none
Was mention heard of wife or son;
No tomb—no memory had they;   510
Theirs was unconsecrated clay;
At least the knight's who died that day.
But Parisina's fate lies hid
Like dust beneath the coffin lid:
Whether in convent she abode,   515
And won to heaven her dreary road,
By blighted and remorseful years
Of scourge, and fast, and sleepless tears;
Or if she fell by bowl or steel,
For that dark love she dared to feel;   520
Or if, upon the moment smote,
She died by tortures less remote;
Like him she saw upon the block,
With heart that shared the headman's shock,
In quickened brokenness that came,   525
In pity, o'er her shattered frame,
None knew—and none can ever know
But whatsoe'er its end below,
Her life began and closed in woe!

20.

And Azo found another bride,   530
And goodly sons grew by his side;

502 fallen] ⟨gone⟩ *M*

But none so lovely and so brave
As him who withered in the grave;
Or if they were—on his cold eye
Their growth but glanced unheeded by,   535
Or noticed with a smothered sigh.
But never tear his cheek descended,
And never smile his brow unbended;
And o'er that fair broad brow were wrought
The intersected lines of thought;   540
Those furrows which the burning share
Of Sorrow ploughs untimely there;
Scars of the lacerating mind
Which the Soul's war doth leave behind.
He was past all mirth or woe: 545
Nothing more remained below,
But sleepless nights and heavy days,
A mind all dead to scorn or praise,
A heart which shunned itself—and yet
That would not yield—nor could forget,   550
Which when it least appeared to melt,
Intently thought—intensely felt:
The deepest ice which ever froze
Can only o'er the surface close—
The living stream lies quick below,   555
And flows—and cannot cease to flow.
Still was his sealed-up bosom haunted
By thoughts which Nature hath implanted;
Too deeply rooted thence to vanish,
Howe'er our stifled tears we banish;   560
When, struggling as they rise to start,
We check those waters of the heart,
They are not dried—those tears unshed
But flow back to the fountain head,
And resting in their spring more pure,   565
For ever in its depth endure,
Unseen, unwept, but uncongealed,

   537–8 But never smile his brow unbended | And never tear his cheek descended *M, cor.*
in Proof M   539–44 *not in M*; *MS. addition in Proof M*   539 that ⟨love⟩ fair
Proof M   540 The ⟨lines of inters⟩ *Proof M*   551–6 *not in M*; *MS. addition in*
Proof M   552 Intently thought] Intensely thought *1831, 1832, C, More*   557 Oh!
still unwelcomely 'twas haunted *M, Proof M*   560 stifled] ⟨smothered⟩ *M*

And cherished most where least revealed.
With inward starts of feeling left,
To throb o'er those of life bereft;   570
Without the power to fill again
The desart gap which made his pain;
Without the hope to meet them where
United souls shall gladness share,
With all the consciousness that he   575
Had only passed a just decree;
That they had wrought their doom of ill,
Yet Azo's age was wretched still.
The tainted branches of the tree,
If lopped with care, a strength may give,   580
By which the rest shall bloom and live
All greenly fresh and wildly free.
But if the lightning, in its wrath,
The waving boughs with fury scathe,
The massy trunk the ruin feels,   585
And never more a leaf reveals.

                                        [1815 ?–16]

283   Ode

                   (From the French)

                        [1.]

We do not curse thee, Waterloo!
Though Freedom's blood thy plain bedew;
There 'twas shed, but is not sunk—
Rising from each gory trunk.

572 made his] ⟨gave him⟩ M   576 passed] sealed M, cor. in Proof Ha

283. Copy text: Poems1816, collated with MS., the proofs, Morning Chronicle, Berg Collec-
tion corrected text of Morning Chronicle
title   untitled in MS.; French Ode. Said to be done into English verse by R. S. —— P. L.
P. R. Master of the Royal Spanish Inqn. &c. &c. &c. Morning Chronicle, cor. in first proof
[1] [The poem is divided into stanzas in all versions except the Morning Chronicle, C, and
More. B inserted the proper stanza numberings by hand into the Berg copy of the Morning
Chronicle text.]
    1 We] ⟨I⟩ MS.   4 Rising] ⟨Learning⟩ MS.

Like the Water-spout from ocean,   5
With a strong and growing motion—
It soars and mingles in the air,
With that of lost LABEDOYERE—
With that of him whose honoured grave
Contains the 'bravest of the brave'.   10
A crimson cloud it spreads and glows,
But shall return to whence it rose;
When 'tis full 'twill burst asunder—
Never yet was heard such thunder
As then shall shake the world with wonder—   15
Never yet was seen such lightning,
As o'er heaven shall then be bright'ning!
Like the Wormwood Star foretold
By the sainted Seer of old,
Show'ring down a fiery flood,   20
Turning rivers into blood.

2.

The Chief has fallen, but not by you,
Vanquishers of Waterloo!
When the soldier citizen
Swayed not o'er his fellow men—   25
Save in deeds that led them on
Where Glory smiled on Freedom's son—
Who, of all the despots banded,
     With that youthful chief competed?
     Who could boast o'er France defeated,   30
Till lone tyranny commanded?
Till, goaded by ambition's sting,
The Hero sunk into the King?
Then he fell;—So perish all,
Who would men by man enthral!   35

8 With that of Labedoyere *MS*.   9 ⟨Murdered brother chief of Ney / With that
of Ney—with that of all / With that of him who Glory gave⟩ *MS*.   10 ⟨The⟩ Con-
tains *MS*.   18–21 *not in MS., Morning Chronicle*; *MS. addition to first proof*
18 ⟨Which⟩ like *first proof*   19 By ⟨Patmos'⟩ sainted *first proof*   20 ⟨Shall
rain down fire in showery flood⟩ *first proof*   21 Turning] ⟨And turn the⟩ *first proof*
22 ⟨Think ye slain of / bended / that ? the Hero⟩ *MS*.   has fallen] ⟨is gone⟩ hath fallen
MS.   23 ⟨His weakness made you⟩ *MS*.   24 When ⟨himself a⟩ citizen *MS*.
24 When ⟨himself ⟩ citizen *MS*.   25 Swayed] ⟨He towered⟩ *MS*.   27 Where
⟨life was lost or Freedom won⟩ *MS*.   28 Which of all the ⟨banded Kings⟩ ⟨Tyrants⟩
Despots banded *MS*.   32 Till ⟨the hero⟩ *MS*.

3.

And thou too of the snow-white plume!
Whose realm refused thee ev'n a tomb,
Better hadst thou still been leading
France o'er hosts of hirelings bleeding,
Than sold thyself to death and shame   40
For a meanly royal name;
Such as he of Naples wears,
Who thy blood-bought title bears.
Little did'st thou deem, when dashing
    On thy war horse through the ranks,   45
    Like a stream which burst its banks,
While helmets cleft, and sabres clashing,
Shone and shivered fast around thee—
Of the fate at last which found thee:
Was that haughty plume laid low   50
By a slave's dishonest blow?
Once—as the Moon sways o'er the tide,
It rolled in air, the warrior's guide;
Through the smoke-created night
Of the black and sulphurous fight,   55
The soldier rais'd his seeking eye
To catch that crest's ascendancy,—
And as it onward rolling rose,
So moved his heart upon our foes.
There, where death's brief pang was quickest,   60
And the battle's wreck lay thickest,
Strew'd beneath the advancing banner
    Of the eagle's burning crest—
(There with thunder-clouds to fan her,

---

36 And thou too] ⟨Chieftain⟩ *MS.*   37 ⟨Great thy fame—horrible thy tomb⟩ /
⟨Could⟩ Whose realms ⟨but gave a bloody⟩ tomb *MS.*   39 hosts of] ⟨desperate⟩ *MS.*
40 Than ⟨thyself⟩ sold *MS.*   41 Fear an unavailing name *MS.*   43 blood-
bought] late-worn *MS.*   44 dashing] ⟨charging⟩ *MS.*   45 the] ⟨each⟩ *MS.*
46 burst] bursts *MS., Morning Chronicle*   48 Shone] ⟨Sunk⟩ *MS.*   52–3 Once
it onward bore the brave | Like Foam upon the highest wave *MS., Morning Chronicle, cor.
in first proof*   ⟨Seen through all the ? / flying⟩ *cancelled line after MS. version of lines
52–3*   52 Once as the Moon impels the tide *MS. addition in first proof, cor. in second
proof*   54–9 *not in MS., Morning Chronicle; MS. addition in first proof*   58 rolling]
⟨rolled⟩ *first proof*   61 battle's wreck lay thickest] battle's ⟨harvest thickest / streamed/
broken⟩ *MS.*   62 ⟨There that plume was like a banner⟩ / ⟨And now⟩ Strewed beneath
the shivering banner *MS.*   63 ⟨Where the Eagles waved ?⟩   64 There] Where
MS.

Who could then her wing arrest—   65
Victory beaming from her breast?)
While the broken line enlarging
Fell, or fled along the plain;
There be sure was MURAT charging!
There he ne'er shall charge again!   70

4.

O'er glories gone the invaders march,
Weeps Triumph o'er each levelled arch—
But let Freedom rejoice,
With her heart in her voice;
But, her hand on her sword,   75
Doubly shall she be adored;
France hath twice too well been taught
The 'moral lesson' dearly bought—
Her Safety sits not on a throne,
With CAPET or NAPOLEON!   80
But in equal rights and laws,
Hearts and hands in one great cause—
Freedom, such as God hath given
Unto all beneath his heaven,
With their breath, and from their birth,   85
Though Guilt would sweep it from the earth;
With a fierce and lavish hand
Scattering nations' wealth like sand;
Pouring nations' blood like water,
In imperial seas of slaughter!   90

5.

But the heart and the mind,
And the voice of mankind,
Shall arise in communion—
And who shall resist that proud union?

---

65 ⟨And Victory's bright/glowing ?⟩   could . . . wing] her wing could then *MS*.
66 from] on *MS*.   67 the broken] the ⟨foes the line⟩ broken *MS*.   71 ⟨The
chiefs are gone—the victims⟩ march *MS*.   72 ⟨Oer each / Did Triumph mourne⟩ *MS*.
73 let Freedom] Freedom ⟨may⟩ *MS*.   75–6 ⟨Which ? but the ?⟩ / ⟨To leap forth—as
it leapt from its sheath / And renew/reclaim each lost wreathe⟩ *MS*.   79 ⟨That⟩ Safety
MS.   80 With] ⟨Fear⟩ *MS*.   82 ⟨And⟩ Hearts *MS*.   84 his] the *MS*.
86 Though] ⟨Till⟩ *MS*.   90 seas] ⟨streams⟩ *MS*.   93 communion] ⟨proud union⟩ *MS*.

The time is passed when swords subdu'd—   95
Man may die—the soul's renew'd:
Even in this low world of care
Freedom ne'er shall want an heir;
Millions breathe but to inherit
Her for ever bounding spirit—   100
When once more her hosts assemble,
Tyrants shall believe and tremble—
Smile they at this idle threat?
Crimson tears will follow yet.

[1816]

284   Stanzas for Music

There be none of Beauty's daughters
    With a magic like thee;
And like music on the waters
    Is thy sweet voice to me:
When, as if its sound were causing   5
The charmed ocean's pausing,
The waves lie still and gleaming,
And the lulled winds seem dreaming.

And the midnight moon is weaving
    Her bright chain o'er the deep;   10
Whose breast is gently heaving,
    As an infant's asleep.
So the spirit bows before thee,
To listen and adore thee;
With a full but soft emotion,   15
Like the swell of Summer's ocean.

[1816]

---

96 die] ⟨sin⟩ *MS.*   98 shall] should *More*   99 ⟨While thanks to⟩ Millions
⟨lightened by / and the⟩ *MS.*   100 Her unconquerable spirit *MS., Morning Chronicle,*
cor. in first proof   102 Let the tyrants only tremble *MS., Morning Chronicle*
103 ⟨Smilst thou at this menace—ye!⟩ / ⟨Who⟩ Smile *MS.*

284. Copy text: *Poems1816*, collated with *MS.*
    11 gently] ⟨softly⟩ *MS.*

285   Fare Thee Well!

Alas! they had been friends in Youth;
But whispering tongues can poison truth;
And constancy lives in realms above:
And Life is thorny; and youth is vain:
And to be wroth with one we love,
Doth work like madness in the brain:

* * * * * * * * * * *

But never either found another
To free the hollow heart from paining—
They stood aloof, the scars remaining,
Like cliffs, which had been rent asunder;
A dreary sea now flows between,
But neither heat, nor frost, nor thunder
Shall wholly do away, I ween,
The marks of that which once hath been.

Coleridge's Christabel [408–13, 419–26].

Fare thee well! and if for ever—
  Still for ever, fare *thee well*—
Even though unforgiving, never
  'Gainst thee shall my heart rebel.—
Would that breast were bared before thee   5
  Where thy head so oft hath lain,
While that placid sleep came o'er thee
  Which thou ne'er can'st know again:
Would that breast by thee glanc'd over,
  Every inmost thought could show!   10
Then, thou would'st at last discover
  'Twas not well to spurn it so—
Though the world for this commend thee—
  Though it smile upon the blow,
Even its praises must offend thee,   15
  Founded on another's woe—

---

285. Copy text: *Poems1816*, collated with *MSS. P, M, MC, Proofs BM, M, MA,* and
the private printing
title   *untitled in all MSS.*
epigraph   *added in Poems1816*

2 ⟨Fare thee / Still⟩ *P*   4 Gainst thee ⟨not can⟩ my heart rebel *P*   5 ⟨Were
my⟩ breast ⟨laid⟩ bare before thee *P*   breast] ⟨heart⟩ *MC*   6 head] ⟨own⟩ *Proofs BM,
MA*; own *Proof M*   7 ⟨Not a thought is pondering oer thee⟩ *P*   8 can'st ⟨thus⟩
know *P*   9 by . . . over] ⟨before⟩ thee ⟨read⟩ *P*   13–20 *MS. addition in Proofs
BM, M*   14 Can it sanctify the blow? *Proof BM*   16 Founded on] ⟨Built
upon⟩ *Proof BM*

Though my many faults defaced me,
　　Could no other arm be found
Than the one which once embraced me,
　　To inflict a cureless wound!　　　　　　　　　　20
Yet—oh, yet—thyself deceive not—
　　Love may sink by slow decay,
But by sudden wrench, believe not,
　　Hearts can thus be torn away;
Still thine own its life retaineth—　　　　　　　　25
　　Still must mine—though bleeding—beat,
And the undying thought which paineth
　　Is—that we no more may meet.—
These are words of deeper sorrow
　　Than the wail above the dead,　　　　　　　　30
Both shall live—but every morrow
　　Wake us from a widowed bed.—
And when thou wouldst solace gather—
　　When our child's first accents flow—
Wilt thou teach her to say—'Father!'　　　　　　35
　　Though his care she must forego?
When her little hands shall press thee—
　　When her lip to thine is prest—
Think of him whose prayer shall bless thee—
　　Think of him thy love had bless'd.　　　　　　40
Should her lineaments resemble
　　Those thou never more may'st see—
Then thy heart will softly tremble
　　With a pulse yet true to me.—
All my faults—perchance thou knowest—　　　　45
　　All my madness—none can know;

17 ⟨Though my faults from love ？ | so far defaced me | might pass all pardon⟩ *Proof BM*　　my many] ⟨to thee my⟩ *Proof M*　　　　19 ⟨Could no other heart so hasten？⟩ Than the soft one which embraced me *Proof BM*　　20 To inflict] Thus to plant *Proof BM, cor. on Proof M*　　22 sink by slow] ⟨wither to⟩ *P*　　23 wrench] ⟨blow⟩ *P*　　24 thus] ⟨eer⟩ *P*　　25 ⟨If thine own a spark⟩ retaineth *P* 26 Still ⟨in⟩ must mine *P*　　27 undying thought which] ⟨moment most that | lasting | eternal⟩ *P*　　29 deeper] ⟨deadlier⟩ *P*　　30 the wail] ⟨the wail⟩ bewail *P* ⟨bewail⟩ *MC*　　31 ⟨Every future Night and⟩ Morrow *P* ⟨Still⟩ will live ⟨but⟩ | yet every morrow *P*　　but] ⟨yet⟩ *MC*　　34 ⟨From thy⟩ *P*　　36 ⟨With unaltered eye and brow⟩ *P*　　37–44 *added in margin of P*　　40 Think of ⟨one⟩ th⟨e⟩y ⟨once oft | heaven⟩ blessed　　had] ⟨hath⟩ *M*　　bless'd] bless⟨e⟩d *M, Proof MA*; blessed *P, MC, Proofs BM, M, Poems1816*　　41 her ⟨features⟩ lineaments *P*　　46 madness] ⟨follies⟩ *P*

All my hopes—where'er thou goest—
Wither—yet with *thee* they go.—
Every feeling hath been shaken,
   Pride—which not a world could bow—   50
Bows to thee—by thee forsaken
   Even my soul forsakes me now.—
But 'tis done—all words are idle—
   Words from me are vainer still;
But the thoughts we cannot bridle   55
   Force their way without the will.—
Fare thee well!—thus disunited—
   Torn from every nearer tie—
Seared in heart—and lone—and blighted—
   More than this, I scarce can die.   60

[1816]

286   A Sketch from Private Life

'Honest—Honest Iago!
If that thou be'st a devil, I cannot kill thee.'
                Shakespeare

Born in the garret, in the kitchen bred,
Promoted thence to deck her mistress' head;
Next—for some gracious service unexprest,
And from its wages only to be guess'd—
Rais'd from the toilet to the table,—where   5
Her wondering betters wait behind her chair,
With eye unmoved, and forehead unabash'd,
She dines from off the plate she lately wash'd.

48 Wither] ⟨Blighted⟩ *P*   50 a] the *all MSS. and Proofs*   51 ⟨Fades / Faints /
Falls at once⟩ —by thee forsaken *P*   52 ⟨Humbled to the soul / Exiled loveless wretch
am I⟩ / ⟨Few have humbler thoughts than I⟩ *P*   53 all] ⟨and⟩ *P*   54 ⟨Tears and
sighs⟩ are ⟨idler⟩ still *P*   57 disunited] ⟨lone and blighted⟩ *P*   59 and lone]
⟨alone⟩ *M*; and lo⟨v⟩e *Proofs BM, M*   60 this I ⟨can⟩ scarce *M*

286. Copy text: Murray's copy of the privately printed first edition, collated with *MSS. M,
MA, MB, Proofs A, A1, BM, K, 1819*
title   A Sketch from Life *M*
epigraph   *in Proof BM the line* I have a weapon *appears between the two extant lines, and it
is cancelled in MS.*
     2 deck] ⟨comb⟩ *M*   6 betters] ⟨fellows / equals⟩ *M*   7 eye unmoved] cheek
⟨severe⟩ unmov'd *M*   eye] cheek *MA, cor. on Proof A*

Quick with the tale, and ready with the lie—
The genial confidante, and general spy—   10
Who could, ye gods! her next employment guess—
An only infant's earliest governess!
She taught the child to read, and taught so well,
That she herself, by teaching, learn'd to spell.
An adept next in penmanship she grows,   15
As many a nameless slander deftly shows:
What she had made the pupil of her art,
None know—but that high Soul secur'd the heart,
And panted for the truth it could not hear,
With longing breast and undeluded ear.   20

  Foil'd was perversion by that youthful mind,
Which Flattery fooled not—Baseness could not blind,
Deceit infect not—near Contagion soil—
Indulgence weaken—nor Example spoil—
Nor master'd Science tempt her to look down   25
On humbler talents with a pitying frown—
Nor Genius swell—nor Beauty render vain—
Nor Envy ruffle to retaliate pain—
Nor Fortune change—Pride raise—nor Passion bow,
Nor Virtue teach austerity—till now.   30
Serenely purest of her sex that live,
But wanting one sweet weakness—to forgive,
Too shock'd at faults her soul can never know,
She deems that all could be like her below:
Foe to all Vice, yet hardly Virtue's friend,   35
For Virtue pardons those she would amend.

  But to the theme:—now laid aside too long
The baleful burthen of this honest song—

12 earliest] early M   16 slander] ⟨libel⟩ M   17 What] ⟨Till⟩ M   18 high . . .
the] ⟨pure Spirit saved her⟩ M   19–20 *inserted in MA*   21 Foil'd . . . by] Vain
was each effort on M, MA, cor. on Proof A   23 near] ⟨nor⟩ M   25–6 Much
Learning madden—when with scarce a fear | She soared through Science with a bright career.
M, cor. in MA   25 tempt] teach MA, cor. on Proof A   27 Genius] talents
M, cor. in MA, Proof A   28 Envy ruffle] ⟨bigotry provoke⟩ M   31 ⟨Perfect
and⟩ Serenely purest ⟨above all⟩ of the things that live M   32 sweet] ⟨bright⟩ M
35–6 *inserted in MA*   36 For Virtue pardons] For she would pardon MA, Proofs
A, A1   37 too] ⟨so⟩ M   38 The ⟨heavy⟩ trusty burthen of my ⟨this slander |
my slight⟩ honest song M   baleful] ⟨trusty⟩ hateful MA ; ⟨hateful⟩ baleful Proof A

Though all her former functions are no more,
She rules the circle which she served before.   40
If mothers—none know why—before her quake;
If daughters dread her for the mother's sake;
If early habits—those false links, which bind
At times the loftiest to the meanest mind—
Have given her power too deeply to instil   45
The angry essence of her deadly will;
If like a snake she steal within your walls,
Till the black slime betray her as she crawls;
If like a viper to the heart she wind,
And leave the venom there she did not find;—   50
What marvel that this hag of hatred works
Eternal evil latent as she lurks
To make a Pandemonium where she dwells,
And reign the Hecate of domestic hells?
Skill'd by a touch to deepen scandal's tints   55
With all the kind mendacity of hints
While mingling truth with falsehood—sneers with smiles—
A thread of candour with a web of wiles;
A plain blunt show of briefly-spoken seeming,
To hide her bloodless heart's soul-harden'd scheming;   60
A lip of lies—a face formed to conceal;
And, without feeling, mock at all who feel:
With a vile mask the Gorgon would disown;
A cheek of parchment—and an eye of stone.
Mark, how the channels of her yellow blood   65
Ooze to her skin, and stagnate there to mud,
Cased like the centipede in saffron mail,
Or darker greenness of the scorpion's scale—
(For drawn from reptiles only may we trace
Congenial colours in that soul or face)—   70

40 which] where *M*   43–6 *late addition in M*   43 those false links] ⟨and
those links⟩ those ⟨deceits⟩ false links *M*   44 loftiest] highest *M*   46 deadly] evil
M, cor. in MA   48 betray her as] betray ⟨the track⟩ her ⟨where⟩ as *M*   51 hag . . .
works] ⟨misbred-demon worked⟩ *M*   52 latent as she lurks] where⟨soeer she lurked⟩
she latest lurks *M*; where she latent lurks *cor. reading on MA*; where she latest lurks *cor.
in Proof A. Proof BM calls for removal of comma after lurks*   53–4 ⟨The very Hecate
of domestic hells | She makes a Pandemonium where she dwells⟩ *M*   55–6 *inserted
in MA*   57 with smiles] and smiles *M, cor. in MA*   58 A . . . with] A glass
of candour or *M, cor. in MA*   62 mock] ⟨scoff⟩ *M*   63 With] ⟨Like⟩ *M*
65 Mark, how] Mark ⟨how⟩ where *MB*; Mark ⟨where⟩ how *Proof BM*   70 colours
in] colours ⟨for⟩ in *MB*

Look on her features! and behold her mind
As in a mirror of itself defined:
Look on the picture! deem it not o'ercharged—
There is no trait which might not be enlarged:
Yet true to 'Nature's journeymen', who made   75
This monster when their mistress left off trade,—
This female dog-star of her little sky,
Where all beneath her influence droop or die.

Oh! wretch without a tear—without a thought,
Save joy above the ruin thou hast wrought—   80
The time shall come, nor long remote, when thou
Shalt feel far more than thou inflictest now;
Feel for thy vile self-loving self in vain,
And turn thee howling in unpitied pain.
May the strong curse of crush'd affections light   85
Back on thy bosom with reflected blight!
And make thee in thy leprosy of mind
As loathsome to thyself as to mankind!
Till all thy self-thoughts curdle into hate,
Black—as thy will for others would create: 90
Till thy hard heart be calcined into dust,
And thy soul welter in its hideous crust.
Oh, may thy grave be sleepless as thy bed,—
The widow'd couch of fire, that thou hast spread!
Then, when thou fain would'st weary Heaven with prayer, 95
Look on thine eathly victims—and despair!
Down to the dust!— and, as thou rott'st away,
Even worms shall perish on thy poisonous clay.
But for the love I bore, and still must bear,
To her thy malice from all ties would tear—   100
Thy name—thy human name—to every eye
The climax of all scorn should hang on high,

71 features] body M   75 to . . . made] to Nature who thus woman made M
76 monster] woman M ⟨woman⟩ ⟨being⟩ /monster Proof A   78 beneath her influence]
that gaze upon her MA, cor. in MB   79 thought] ⟨feeling⟩ M   81 nor . . . thou]
⟨nor far remote the day⟩ M   83 for thy vile] for ⟨thyself—self loving⟩ thy vile M
84 And turn ⟨unpitied on the rack of⟩ pain M   86 on . . . blight] cor. in Proof BM
from to . . . light   89 Till . . . curdle] Till ⟨every⟩ all thy thoughts be curdled MB;
received reading written as correction on Proof BM   91 ⟨And⟩ Till MB   92 welter]
⟨sicken⟩ MB   94 fire] thorns M   97 and, as] ⟨and / yet⟩ and ⟨as thou shalt decay⟩
as M   98 Even . . . poisonous] ⟨The⟩ Even . . . ⟨poisoned⟩ poisonous M

Exalted o'er thy less abhorred compeers—
And festering in the infamy of years.

30 Mar. 1816

287　　　An Extract from a Parish Register

'Give me a child!' exclaimed the Baronet.
Through nineteen wedded springs—it came not yet;
At length the tedious miracle appears,
An Advent! after *twenty* barren years!
But not hereditary this delay: 5
His honoured mother had a brisker way—
A vigourous dame of such prolific powers,
She married:— he was born in *twenty hours*!

[1816]

288　　　　To [Augusta]

1.

When all around grew drear and dark,
　　And reason half withheld her ray—
And hope but shed a dying spark
　　Which more misled my lonely way;

2.

In that deep midnight of the mind,   5
　　And that internal strife of heart,
When dreading to be deemed too kind,
　　The weak despair—the cold depart;

---

103 ⟨And⟩ Exalted *M*　　　　104 festering] weltering *M, MA, cor. on Proof A*

287. Copy text: *MS.*

288. Copy text: *Poems1816*, collated with *MSS. M, MA, MB, MC*
title To Augusta *M, MB, MC*; To ⟨Augusta⟩ *MA*; Stanzas to Augusta *1832, C, More*;
To —— *Poems1816–1831*
　　1 drear] ⟨dark / cold / bleak⟩ waste *M*　　　　3 shed] shot *M*

3.

When fortune changed—and love fled far,
   And hatred's shafts flew thick and fast,   10
Thou wert the solitary star
   Which rose and set not to the last.

4.

Oh! blest be thine unbroken light!
   That watched me as a seraph's eye,
And stood between me and the night,   15
   For ever shining sweetly nigh.

5.

And when the cloud upon us came,
   Which strove to blacken o'er thy ray—
Then purer spread its gentle flame,
   And dashed the darkness all away.   20

6.

Still may thy spirit dwell on mine,
   And teach it what to brave or brook—
There's more in one soft word of thine,
   Than in the world's defied rebuke.

7.

Thou stood'st, as stands a lovely tree,   25
   That still unbroke, but gently bent,
Still waves with fond fidelity
   Its boughs above a monument.

9 When fortune changed] When Friendship ⟨paused⟩ shook *M*, *MA*, *MB*, *MC*
11 Thou wert the] ⟨Thou wert my⟩ Thine was the *M*; ⟨Thine was⟩ the *MA*, *MB*, *MC*
12 Which rose] ⟨That shone⟩ *M*   13 thine] ⟨thy⟩ *MA*   14 seraph's] ⟨Spirit's⟩ *M*
17 upon] ⟨between⟩ *M*   18 Which would have ⟨swept the last away / blackened thy /
his ?⟩ / closed ⟨around⟩ / oer thy ray *M*   strove to blacken] ⟨would have closed⟩ *MA*;
Which would have closed on that last ray *MB*; Which would have closed ⟨me in its⟩ / on
that last ray *MC*   19 purer spread] ⟨steadier⟩ / stiller stood *M*, *MB*, *MC*; purer ⟨stood /
broke⟩ *MA*   20 all] ⟨far⟩ *M*   21 dwell on] dwell in *MA*; sit on *MB*
22 ⟨And temper all that's sterner there⟩ *M*   it] ⟨me⟩ *M*   24 Than in the waves]
World's ⟨contemned⟩ rebuke *M*   25 And thou ⟨art⟩ wert as a lovely tree *M*, *MB*, *MC*
26 That still] Whose ⟨branches⟩ branch *M*, *MA*, *MB*, *MC*, *Poems1816*   27 Still waves]
⟨Stands⟩ Still ⟨waves⟩ waved *M*, *MC*   waves] wave⟨d⟩ *MA*, *MB*   28 boughs] ⟨bou /
grass⟩ *M* [*MSS*. *M*, *MB*, *MC* end with this line]

8.

The winds might rend—the skies might pour,
  But there thou wert—and still wouldst be   30
Devoted in the stormiest hour
  To shed thy weeping leaves o'er me.

9.

But thou and thine shall know no blight,
  Whatever fate on me may fall;
For heaven in sunshine will requite   35
  The kind—and thee the most of all.

10.

Then let the ties of baffled love
  Be broken—thine will never break;
Thy heart can feel—but will not move,
  Thy soul, though soft, will never shake.   40

11.

And these, when all was lost beside—
  Were found and still are fixed in thee—
And bearing still a breast so tried,
  Earth is no desart—ev'n to me.

[1816]

33 thou and thine] they and thou *MA*   35 in] ⟨with⟩ *MA*   39 can feel]
⟨that feels⟩ *MA*   40 will never] ⟨which will not⟩ *MA*   41–4 *not in MA*

COMMENTARY

175. *MS. and Publishing History.* B's rough draft, undated (*MS. L*, location: Bodleian–Lovelace). First published *C* from a Murray *MS.*, presumably a holograph copy made from *MS. L.* This MS. is not now at Murray's.

Another poem dealing with Susan Vaughan (see no. 176).

176. *MS. and Publishing History.* B's draft MS., undated (*MS. M*, location: Murray); his fair copy, dated Jan. 1812 (*MS. L*, location: Bodleian–Lovelace), on the same sheet with no. 177 below. First published *C*, but not from *MS. M*, as *C* indicated. Copy text for *C* was either another MS., or *MS. L.*

The poem concerns Susan Vaughan, and the quotation referred to in the title is from a poem she sent to B in a letter of 12 Jan. 1812 (see *Paston and Quennell*, 26–7). She was a Welsh servant girl at Newstead with whom B was much enamoured, until he discovered her infidelity to him when he was away from the abbey. See Doris Langley Moore, *Lord Byron. Accounts Rendered* (1974), 164–74 for the fullest account of this episode.

25. B wrote his letter of farewell on 28 Jan. (see Moore, *op. cit.* 173). The girl was sent back to her home in Wales.

177. *MS. and Publishing History.* B's first fair copy (*MS. L*, location: Bodleian–Lovelace); B's revised fair copy (*MS. Y*, location: Yale). Both dated 1812. *MS. L* version published in D. L. Moore, *The Great Byron Adventure* (1959), 13.

Another poem about Susan Vaughan: see above.

epigraph *Macbeth*, V. v. 13.

15–16. See 'L'Amitié Est L'Amour Sans Ailes', no. 26.

178. *MS. and Publishing History.* B's first draft, undated, untitled, and lacking stanzas 6, 7, 8, is in the Huntington Library. This was one of the Bixby MSS. reproduced in facsimile by the Society of Dofobs (see commentary for no. 166). The Huntington also has a proof copy for *CHP*(7) with two accidental corrections in ll. 58–9. The William Andrew Clark Library has what appears to be a separate printing of the poem, published privately for B in 1812, though there is some controversy over the precise nature of this printing: see commentary for 'Euthanasia', no. 172. Collating of the Clark and Huntington copies shows that in the Huntington proof the unaccented 'e's in the past participles are elided, but they are not elided in the Clark printing. Also, the Clark copy has 'shew' in line 62 whereas the Huntington proof has 'show'. First published, *CHP*(2); collected thereafter.

The poem is one of the Thyrza poems. It was first dated Feb. 1812 in *1832*. The authority for this dating has never been given, but it has been generally accepted as an accurate dating. B in fact discusses his grief at Edleston's death in a letter to Hodgson of 16 Feb. 1812 (*BLJ* II. 163–4), and the end of the letter distinctly echoes ll. 23 ff. of the lyric.

epigraph   quoted from Shenstone's Inscription 'On an Ornamented Urn'. The inscription was for a 'Miss Dolman, a beatiful and amiable relation of Mr. Shenstone's, who died . . . about twenty-one years of age'.

24. Echoes *Antony and Cleopatra*, II. ii. 240.

39. Echoes *Macbeth*, v. viii. 16.

45. Echoes *Macbeth*, I. i. 11.

179. *MS. and Publishing History*. B's fair copy, undated, on same sheet as 'Lines to a Lady Weeping' (no. 182). From this MS. (*MS. M*) was printed a proof dated 15 Jan. 1814 by B's publisher Murray. *MS. M* and *Proof M* are both at Murray, along with a second uncorrected proof bound up with various proofs from *CHP*(5) and *CHP*(7). A third proof (*Proof H*), with a few typographical corrections by B, is in Huntington, part of a 24-page proof of various parts of *CHP*(7) and *Corsair*(2). First published, *Corsair*(2), removed in *Corsair*(3), restored in *Corsair*(4); collected thereafter.

The date of composition is problematic; it could have been written at any time from 1809 to 1813. It is placed here with the poems of Feb.–Mar. 1812 because of (*a*) its MS. association with no. 182, and (*b*) its thematic parallels with the poems of the Susan Vaughan cycle. If there was a Turkish original for the poem, it has not been found, though the sentiment is common in Turkish love poetry. B sent *MS. M* to Murray in Jan. 1814 (see *BLJ* IV. 32–3, 37).

180. *MS. and Publishing History*. B's fair copy, corrected, undated, is in the Murray archives. The Murray collection also has an uncorrected proof bound up in a volume of proofs of various poems from *CHP*(5) and *CHP*(7). First published, *CHP*(7), collected thereafter. Though the poem is not printed in the Huntington proof for *CHP*(7), B has a MS. note on those proofs calling for its insertion. The poem belongs to 1812 or 1813, but more probably 1812 since the poem seems to generalize the melancholy sentiments of poems of that period, for example, the Thyrza poems. The poem has a recurrent echo of *Macbeth*, v. v. 19 ff.

181. *MS. and Publishing History*. No MS.; the poem is known to be B's from a letter first printed in 1880 in a small pamphlet by John Pearson. The letter is dated 1 Mar. 1812, and addressed to James Perry, editor of the *Morning Chronicle*, where the poem was first printed (see *BLJ* II. 166–7). The letter calls for a revision of lines 15–16 to their present state, and directs that the poem be printed anonymously on the next day, which it was. First published *Morning Chronicle*, 2 Mar. 1812, anonymously; printed again, as B's, in *Political Ode by Lord Byron, hitherto unknown as his production*, by John Pearson (London, 1880). First collected, *C*.

The immediate context of the poem dates to Nov. 1811, when economically impoverished workers in the Midlands began destroying some new weaving frames which had been recently introduced into the mills. The military was called out and there were a number of violent encounters with crowds of workers. Early in February Lord Liverpool (Robert Banks Jenkinson, created Baron Hawkesbury) introduced a bill into the House of Lords which carried the death penalty for frame breaking. The Tory measure was opposed by the Whigs, and B delivered his first speech in the House, opposing the bill, on 27 Feb. The measure was subsequently passed, but the offence was reduced to a misdemeanour, less serious than a felony. See B's speech in *LJ* II. 424–30 and the general discussion in D. N. Raymond, *The Political Career of Lord Byron* (New York, 1924), 37–47.

1. *E*[*ldo*]*n and R*[*yde*]*r.* John Scott, first Lord Eldon (1751–1839), was Lord Chancellor in 1812; Richard Ryder (1766–1832), second son of the first Baron Harrowby, was Home Secretary, but not a 'Lord'.

8. Lord E[ldon] on Thursday night, said the riots at Nottingham arose from a '*mistake*'. [Note in *Morning Chronicle*, presumably by B]

20. *Quorum*: i.e. the 'Justices of the Quorum', without whom the Justices of the Bench were not permitted to act. In the eighteenth century the term was applied to Justices in general.

29–32. Cf. '[Song for the Luddites]' (no. 306).

182. *MS. and Publishing History.* B's fair copy, titled 'Stanzas', undated, is in the Murray archives on the same sheet as a fair copy of 'From the Turkish'. The Murray collection also has two uncorrected proofs of the poem bound up with a proof of *Corsair* dated by Murray 15 Jan. 1814. On the second of these proofs B has written, at the end of the lyric, 'March, 1812'. A third, corrected proof is in the Huntington Library. This is a proof of 24 pages pulled primarily for *CHP*(*7*), but it includes a few poems which were eventually published in the *Corsair*(*2*) volume instead. Augusta Leigh made a MS. copy (*MS. AL*, location: *BM*; see no. 249) with a correction, evidently made at a later time. *MS. AL* seems to have been made from a previous MS. First published anonymously in the *Morning Chronicle* (7 Mar. 1812); published next in *Corsair*(*2*), omitted from *Corsair*(*3*), republished in *Corsair*(*4*): collected thereafter.

The lines were written after a famous incident at Carleton House, where the Prince Regent gave a banquet on 22 Feb. 1812 and caused his young daughter, the Princess Charlotte, to weep when he openly abused his former Whig supporters. A furore arose when it became known, with the publication of *Corsair(2)*, that B was the author of the lines. See *Marchand*, I. 318–19, 322–3, and *LJ* II. 463–92. B was not present at the banquet, but he heard about it afterwards and wrote these verses early in March. For B's commentary on his poem see *BLJ* IV. 41–3.

183. *MS. and Publishing History.* A draft holograph, untitled, undated (location: Princeton–Taylor). Huntington has an uncorrected proof for *CHP(7)*. First published, *CHP(2)*; collected thereafter.

The poem is dated 14 Mar. 1812 in *CHP(2)*. It is part of the Thyrza cycle.

36. Cf. Childe Harold's 'Good Night', st. 9 (*CHP I.* 185).

184. *MS. and Publishing History.* No MS.; Huntington has an uncorrected proof for *CHP(7)*. First published, *CHP(2)*; collected thereafter.

The poem deals with the cornelian heart which B received as a gift from Edleston. See commentaries for nos. 87 and 166. B wrote to retrieve the cornelian on 28 Oct. 1811. The poem was dated 16 Mar. 1812 in *1832*, though no authority for this date was given. Subsequent editors have accepted it, however. The placement of the poem in *CHP(2)*, immediately after no. 183, suggests that the poem was written after 14 Mar.

185. *MS. and Publishing History.* Unpublished; sent in a letter of 12 Apr. 1812 to Samuel Rogers (*MS. W*, location: Watson Library, University College, London).

The great chemist had just married Jane Apreece, a rich and socially ambitious widow. B in his letter introduces the epigram as being 'on the late nuptials between Conceit and Chemistry' (see also *BLJ* III. 44 and n.).

186. *MS. and Publishing History.* No MS.; first published *Poems1816*, collected thereafter.

B's first poem on Rogers, whom he later came to distrust (see 'Question and Answer', no. 323).

187. *MS. and Publishing History.* Caroline Lamb's MS. copy (*MS. B*, location: Berg), with her head-note: 'These are the first lines Ld Byron wrote to me— I had made him a present of a gold neck chain and these lines were written at the moment.' Published only in *The Mirror of Literature*, 7 (6 May 1826), apparently from this MS.

The verses were probably written in Apr. or May 1812.

188. *MS. and Publishing History.* B's rough draft fragment, dated 31 Aug. 1812 (*MS. L*, location: Bodleian–Lovelace). Published with commentary by J. J. McGann, 'Byron's First Tale: An Unpublished Fragment', *KSMB* 19 (1968). B plundered the fragment of stanza 10 for an addition in *CHP(7)*: see *CHP II*, st. 27.

The fragment seems related to B's earlier fragmentary poem 'The Monk of Athos'. B's note on *MS. L* reads: 'the thought from Cazotte's Diable amoureux and the Armenian', i.e. from Jacques Cazotte's *Le Diable Amoureux*, and the Revd. William Render's *The Armenian* (1800), a bad translation of Schiller's *Der Geisterseher*. See also B's letter to Moore of 28 Aug. 1813.

epigraph   *Hamlet* II. ii. 600.

39. i.e., the Austrians.

189. *MS. and Publishing History*. B's holograph fair copy is in Texas (*MS. T*) immediately after his fair copy of 'Hear My Prayer'; untitled, undated, though 'Hear My Prayer' is dated 10 Oct. 1812. This MS. version has never been published, and the poem has never been collected in any form. It was first published in Captain Jesse's *Life of Beau Brummell* (1886), I. 288 from an album in which Brummell had copied it. It was published again by H. M. Combe Martin N *&* Q, Jan. 1967, 26) from a MS. owned by him in the hand of Lady Anne Hardy (*MS. H*), who copied it from a MS. found by Lady Langdale at Eywood, the seat of the Harleys.

The supposition made in *MS. H* that the poem was addressed to Lady Frances Wedderburn Webster is not correct, though it was a plausible one to make because lines 13–16 are a variant version of the lines B said he dropped from 'When We Two Parted', which he told Lady Hardy he had written about Lady Frances (see commentary for no. 279). The present poem was actually written in Sept. 1812 and its subject is Lady Caroline Lamb, with whom B was at that time breaking off relations. The best commentary on the poem is in B's letters to Lady Melbourne of 10, 13, and 18 Sept. 1812 (*BLJ* II. 192–201). B in fact sent a copy of lines 13–16 in his letter of 18 Sept.

7–8. Cf. no. 177, lines 1–2.

190. *MS. and Publishing History*. All of B's MSS. of this poem, as well as his numerous separate additions and corrections, are in his letters to Lord Holland in the British Library *MS. BM*, (Add. 51639). B's corrected proof for *CHP(7)* is in the Huntington Library, which also has, in its Larpent Collection, a MS. copy of the poem (*MS. H*) not in B's hand. The latter was probably the copy used by Robert Elliston when he delivered the address orally. B destroyed a first draft of the address (*BLJ* II .191). Murray has an amanuensis copy (*MS. M*).

Besides the copy which he destroyed, B wrote five other drafts of the poem:

1. The first (extant) draft sent to Lord Holland on 23 Sept. 1812 (*MS. BMa*). This is a draft of 91 lines and lacks lines 13–16, 25–6, 44–9, 56–7 of the received text.

2. Second draft sent to Lord Holland on 25 Sept. and headed by B: 'Corrected Copy—with some omissions (and one addition) but I fear still too long.' This draft also has 91 lines, and lacks lines 25–6, 47–8, 56–7 of the received text. (*MS. BMb*).

3. The third draft sent to Lord Holland on 29 Sept. (*MS. BMc*). This contains 69 lines and only lacks lines 25–6, 47–8.

4. The fourth draft sent to Lord Holland on 30 Sept. and headed by B: 'Copy Penultimate' (*MS. BMd*). It contains 71 lines and lacks lines 23–4, 47–8.

5. The fifth draft sent to Lord Holland on 2 Oct. (*MS. BMe*). It contains 73 lines, lacking only 47–8.

B also sent a number of corrections by letter to Lord Holland. These are designated in the apparatus in the following way: (1) letter of 24 Sept. with corrections for lines 66–9 (*MS. R*); (2) letter of 24 Sept. again, with corrections for lines 16, 52–3, and the cancelled passage after 24 (*MS. Ra*); (3) letter of 25 Sept. with two corrections for lines 13–14 (*MS. Rb*); (4) letter of 26 Sept. with corrections for lines 5–6 (*MS. Rc*); (5) letter of 27 Sept. with corrections for line 13 (*MS. Rd*); (6) letter of 28 Sept. with corrections for lines 13–14 and 21–2 (MS. *Re*); (7) second letter of 28 Sept. which sends a revision for lines 58–65 (*MS. Rf*); (8) letter of 30 Sept. with a version of the cancelled couplet after line 41 (*MS. Rg*); (9) letter of 9 Oct. with revision for lines 45–8 (*MS. Rh*).

First published *Morning Chronicle*, 12 Oct. 1812, from a copy made from B's corrected *MS. BMe*, perhaps *MS. H*; reprinted without permission in *The Genuine Rejected Addresses* . . . (1812): see *BLJ* II. 249; printed again in *CHP*(7), from *MS. M*, collected thereafter.

The Drury Lane Theatre was destroyed by fire in 1809. On the occasion of its reopening, the theatre committee offered a competition, with a prize of 20 guineas, for an address to be delivered on the opening night. B declined Lord Holland's first invitation to enter the competition, but when all the addresses had been rejected, Lord Holland asked B to write one, and he accepted. The incident was cleverly parodied by James and Horace Smith in *Rejected Addresses* . . . (1812), which included a parody of B in the style of *Childe Harold*. (See also no. 193.) B's address was delivered by Robert William Elliston, one of Drury Lane's leading actors. For B's letters to Lord Holland see *BLJ* II. 191–226 *passim*.

8. 'The word "fiery pillar" was suggested by the "pillar of fire" in the book of Exodus.' [B to Lord Holland, *BLJ* II. 213]

10. 'I hope no unlucky wag will say I have set [the Thames] on fire, though Dryden in his Annus Mirabilis [st. 231] and Churchill in his "Times" [ll. 701–2] did it *before* me.' [B to Lord Holland, *BLJ* II. 207] 'By the bye the best view of the said fire, (which I myself saw from a house-top in C[ovent] Garden) was at W[estminster] Bridge from the reflection on the Thames.' [ibid.] As B was revising the whole passage from 5–20, he observed to Lord Holland, in rhyme:

> This is a place where if a poet
> Shined in description he might show it. [*BLJ* II. 213]

22. Echoes Shakespeare, Sonnet XII. 13.
31. *Siddons*: Sarah Kemble Siddons (1755–1831), the actress.
33. *Garrick*: David Garrick (1717–79), actor, and manager of Drury Lane from 1747.
34. *Roscius*: the boy actor William Betty (see above no. 108, 'Reply', 29).
40. *Menander*: (342–291? B.C.), Greek poet of the New Comedy.
41. The cancelled passage refers to Sheridan's *Monody on Garrick* (1779).
43. *Brinsley*: i.e. the dramatist Richard Brinsley Sheridan (1751–1816); see no. 295.
46. See *Macbeth*, IV. i.
52. 'Churchill has *Player* as a monosyllable frequently.' [B to Lord Holland, *BLJ* II. 206]
55–63. Samuel Whitbread, Whig politician and the manager of Drury Lane Theatre, objected to B's attack upon the public taste for bringing animals on stage (see *BLJ* II. 212–14).
71. Sovereign of the willing Soul.—Gray. [B's note to the cancelled couplet, in *MS. BMe*] The allusion is to 'The Progress of Poesy', 13.

191. *MS. and Proofs.* B's undated fair copy (*MS. B*, location: Bodmer) was printer's copy for the first edition (*W1813*), the only authorized printing of *Waltz* in B's lifetime in England. *B* contains the prose 'To the Publisher' and the following text: 1–14, 29–174, 178–203, 204–9 (only two lines in *B*), 210–57. Many of the notes were expanded on, and added, in the proofs.
There are eight separate proofs which survive (location: Murray). They all carry corrections and all are dated 1813 (see *C* I. 478).

1. A composite proof with pp. [1]–16 being from an early (probably the first) proof. The MS. addition at 15–28 appears here on page 9ʳ. These pages carry lines 1–172. Pages 17–23 are from a later proof made to accommodate the MS. addition; they carry lines 163–257.
2. Complete proof, pp. [1]–22.
3. Complete proof, pp. [1]–24.
3a. Partial proof, pp. 17–24 only. A revise of the conclusion of Proof 3.
4. Complete proof, pp. [1]–25.
5. Complete proof, pp. [1]–26.
6. Complete proof, pp. [1]–26. Dated by B, Feb. 1813.
7. Complete proof, pp. [1]–27.

Publishing History. B wrote *Waltz* in Oct. 1812 when he was at Cheltenham (see *BLJ* II. 228). At that time he sent it to Murray for anonymous publication, but the poem was not set up in type until Feb. 1813. Both B and Murray evidently feared to publish the work openly under their own names (see *Wise*, I. 72) because of possible legal and political repercussions, so *Waltz* was issued anonymously under the imprint of Sherwood, Neely, and Jones, Paternoster Row. When precisely *W1813* was published is not clear, but it was out by 21 Apr. 1813 (see *BLJ* III. 41). The printing run was small, but the precise number printed is not known.

The poem was next published in a pirated edition in 1821 (see *Wise*, I. 73) and this text has served as the basis for all later printings. Strangely enough, not even *1831* or *1832* used *W1813*. The result is that a series of small substantive errors introduced in 1821 have always been perpetuated, and in later editions (like *1856* and *C*) further errors crept in. The present edition is based upon *W1813*.

Literary and Historical Background. The poem depends upon the traditional idea that the character of a nation's dancing habits is an index of the cultural climate. B takes waltzing as a symbol of a wider phenomenon which he also deplored: the cultural and political influence which Germany increasingly exerted upon England during the reigns of the first four Georges. The worst aspect of this influence, for B, was the political affiliations which they helped England to make and maintain. The Prince Regent is specifically attacked in the poem. He greatly loved waltzing and was influential in making it popular.

The craze for waltzing was at its peak in London in 1812. B's attitude to the dance is very conservative (see also *BLJ* II. 218 and *LJ* II. 453), and echoes the widely held opinion that the dance was a sign of indecorum, even depravity. In this respect *Waltz* is, as B suggested, a continuation of the ideas treated in all his early satires, but especially in *EBSR*.

B wrote *Waltz* when he was at Cheltenham and the immediate impetus may have been from parties he attended there rather than in London. In the poem B specifically addresses Lord Moira, whose family was one with which B was particularly intimate while he was staying at Cheltenham (see *BLJ* II. 215). For further comment see William Childers, 'Byron's *Waltz*: The Germans and their Georges', *K-SJ* 18 (1969), 81–95. B's poem follows the general argument laid out in Sheridan's 'The Walse'.

epigraph   not Ovid but Virgil, *Aeneid*, I. 498–9.

To the Publisher
4. General T . . . election: State of the poll—last day—5. [B; added in MS. in *Proof 1*] Sir Banastre Tarleton (1754–1833), a general, unsuccessfully contested Liverpool in Oct. 1812. The poll stood at five for three days, but was eleven on the last day.

30. *Black Joke*: an old tune (sometimes called 'The Sprig of Shillelagh') which Thomas Moore adapted in his song 'Sublime was the warning which Liberty spoke.'

affettuoso: expressive [B's n. in *MS. B*, removed in *Proof 1*]

34. *quam familiariter.* My Latin is all forgotten, if a man can be said to have forgot what he never remembered—but I bought my title-page motto of a Catholic priest for a three shilling Bank token, after much haggling for the *even* sixpence. I grudged the money to a Papist, being all for the memory

of Perceval and 'No Popery', and quite regret the downfall of the Pope, because we can't burn him any more. [B, n. added in *Proof 5*]

to have forgot] to have forgotten *all other edns.* three shilling] *added Proof 6*

The Latin expression is proverbial.

three shilling Bank token. See below, 166 and n.

Perceval . . . any more: i.e. Sir Spencer Perceval, the Prime Minister, who was assassinated 11 May 1812 (see poem no. 278). He opposed Catholic Emancipation. See B's speech on behalf of the Catholics (*LJ* II. 431–43). Hornem regrets that he 'can't burn' the Pope in effigy any more, because the Catholics' Claims bill was defeated.

38. *Wilhelmina . . . Wakefield*: Miss Carolina Wilhelmina Amelia Skeggs, in *Vicar of Wakefield*, chap. XI.

51–4. W. F. is William Fitzgerald (see *EBSR* 1 ff.); Dr. B and Master B are Dr. William Busby and his son (see no. 193 and commentary).

text

1. 'Glance their many-twinkling feet.' GRAY. [B, n. added in *Proof 2*] See the 'Progress of Poesy', 35.

21. To rival Lord W.'s, or his nephew's, as the Reader pleases:—the one gained a pretty woman, whom he deserved by fighting for her—and the other has been fighting in the Peninsula many a long day, 'by Shrewsbury clock', without gaining anything in *that* country but the title of 'the Great Lord', and 'the Lord', which savours of profanation, having been hitherto applied only to that Being to whom '*Te Deums*' for carnage are the rankest blasphemy.—It is to be presumed the General will one day return to his Sabine farm, there

> 'To tame the genius of the stubborn plain
> '*Almost as quickly* as he conquered Spain!'

The Lord Peterborough conquered continents in a summer—we do more —we contrive to conquer and lose them in a shorter season.—If the 'Great Lord's' *Cincinnatian* progress in agriculture be no speedier than the proportional average of time in Pope's couplet, it will, according to the farmer's proverb, be 'ploughing with dogs'.

By the by—one of this illustrious person's new titles is forgotten—it is however worth remembering—'*Salvador del Mundo!*'—*credite posteri!* If this be the appellation annexed by the inhabitants of the Peninsula to the name of a *man* who has not yet saved them—query—are they worth saving even in this world?—for, according to the mildest modifications of any Christian

rival Lord W.'s] rival Lord Wellington *Proof 4, 5, 6*; rival Lord Wellesley *1832, C, More*
he deserved] he at least deserved *Proof 4*   fighting for her—] fighting for; *all other*
edns.   savours] smacks *Proof 4*   applied. . .Being] the property of 'the Lord Jehovah'
Proof 4   the General] he *Proof 4*   The Lord Peterborough . . . dogs'. *added in Proof 5*
shorter season] ⟨life time⟩ *Proof 5*   By the by . . . his country. *added in Proof 6*   any]
⟨the⟩ *Proof 6*

creed, those three words make the odds much against them in the next.—
'Saviour of the World', quotha!—it were to be wished that he, or any one
else, could save a corner of it—his country. Yet this stupid misnomer,
although it shows the near connexion between Superstition and Impiety—
so far has its use—that it proves there can be little to dread from those
Catholics (inquisitorial Catholics too) who can confer such an appellation
on a *Protestant.*—I suppose next year he will be entitled the 'Virgin Mary'—
if so, Lord George Gordon himself would have nothing to object to such
liberal bastards of our Lady of Babylon. [B. The n. was gradually built up
through *Proofs* 4–7; see apparatus below.]

> *Lord W.'s, or his nephew's*: i.e. the Duke of Wellington and his nephew,
William Pole-Wellesley, later fourth Lord Mornington (1785?–1857). B
alludes to the duel between 'Long Pole Wellesley' and Lord Kilworth:
see *Hints*, the long note to the poem which B rejected. Kilworth miscon-
ceived something Pole said at Lady Hawarden's party on 6 Aug. 1811.
They met on Hounslow Heath on 15 Aug., but the affair was settled by
the seconds without shots being fired. Most of the note, however, deals
with the Duke of Wellington's exploits in the Peninsular War: see above,
CHP I, sts. 24–6, 85–7, and the rejected stanzas and notes. B makes an
invidious comparison between Wellington and Charles Mordaunt, third
Earl of Peterborough (1658–1735), who commanded England's expedi-
tionary force to Spain in 1705.

> *by Shrewsbury clock*': *I Henry IV*, v. iv. 151.

> '*Te Deums*' *for carnage*: Cf. *DJ* VIII, st. 9.

> *Sabine farm*: Cicero's country retreat.

> *To tame . . . Spain!*': Pope, *Imitations of Horace*, Satire II, i. 131–2.

> *Cincinnatian*: Cincinnatus, semi-legendary Roman hero who left his farm
in 458 to defeat the Acqui and Volsci, and immediately returned to his
farm.

> '*Virgin Mary*': a reference to Wellington's amours.

> *Lord George Gordon*: (1751–93), led the Gordon riots of 1780.

> *Lady of Babylon*: Protestant tag for the Church of Rome.

25. See above, 'To the Publisher', final note.

26. See no. 193, commentary.

39–44. The union of Hanover and Great Britain was broken by the
Confederation of the Rhine (1803–13). In 1807 Napoleon assigned part of
Hanover to Westphalia, and in 1810 the remainder was divided between
France and Westphalia.

50. e.g. Queen Caroline of Brunswick (see no. 357 below).

54. Queen Caroline's sons were—besides the Prince Regent (1762–1830)
—Frederick, Duke of York (1763–1827); William, Duke of Clarence, later

Yet this stupid . . . Babylon. *added in Proo* 7   stupid ⟨piece of⟩ misnomer *Proof* 7   our
Lady] ⟨the Whore⟩ *Proof* 7

William IV (1765–1837); Edward, Duke of Kent (1767–1820); Ernest, Duke of Cumberland and King of Hanover (1771–1851); Adolphus, Duke of Cambridge (1774–1850).

60–2. When Hamburg fell to Napoleon in 1810, the mail from the north of Europe came through Gothenberg, or Heligoland, or Anholt. *C* (i. 488 n.) suggests that B is punning on '*Mails*': 'In 1811 an attempt to enforce the conscription resulted in the emigration of numbers of young men of suitable age for military service. The unfortunate city was deprived of mails and males at the same time.'

65. The patriotic arson of our amiable allies cannot be sufficiently commended nor subscribed for. Amongst other details omitted in the various dispatches of our eloquent Ambassador, he did not state (being too much occupied with the exploits of Col. ——, in swimming rivers frozen, and galloping over roads impassable) that one entire province perished by famine in the most melancholy manner, as follows:—In General Rostopschin's consummate conflagration, the consumption of tallow and train-oil was so great, that the market was inadequate to the demand; and thus one hundred and thirty-three thousand persons were starved to death by being reduced to wholesome diet! The lamplighters of London have since subscribed a pint (of oil) apiece, and the tallow-chandlers have unanimously voted a quantity of best moulds (four to the pound), to the relief of the surviving Scythians—the scarcity will soon, by such exertions, and a proper attention to the *quality* rather than quantity of provision, be totally alleviated. It is said, in return, that the untouched Ukraine has subscribed 60,000 beeves for a day's meal to our suffering manufacturers. [B, n. added in *Proof 1*]

B's reference is to the burning of Moscow in Sept. 1812 the day after the Russians evacuated the city and the French occupied it. The military governor of the city at the time was Count Feodor Vassilievich Rostoptschin (1763–1826). The burning of Moscow was said to have been carried out under his instigation. Much of the humour in B's note springs from the dispatch of 23 Nov. from 'our eloquent ambassador' to the court of Russia, Sir William Schaw Cathcart, Viscount and Earl of Cathcart (1755–1843). The dispatch was printed in the *London Gazette* (16 Dec.). Cathcart discussed 'the exploits of' Colonel Alexander Chernychev, a young officer of the Guards who had insinuated himself into Napoleon's favour in Paris in 1811. He was a spy for Czar Alexander.

69. Austerlitz was fought 2 Dec. 1805. The news of Napoleon's victory was believed to have hastened Pitt's death.

72. August Frederick Ferdinand von Kotzebue (1761–1819), German dramatist whose influence in England in the 1790's and early 1800s was widespread.

Col.——] Col. C—— *all other edns.*   surviving Scythians] ⟨triumphant⟩ Scythians
Proof 1 than quantity] than the quantity *1831, 1832, C, More*   untouched Ukraine
Ukraine *Proofs 1–6, cor. in Proof 7*   60,000] sixty thousand *all other edns.*

75. Christopher Meiner, *A History of the Female Sex* (1808). It is Lapland wizards, not witches, who are said to raise storms.

77–8. The scholars Richard Brunck (1729–1803) and Christian Heyne (1729–1812).

83–8. *David*: see 2 Samuel 6: 14, and *Hints*, 318; *Quixote*: see Cervantes, *Don Quixote*, chaps. 25 and 26; *Herodias*: see Matthew 14: 3–12.

94. i.e. horns.

107. A reference to Kotzebue's play, *Menschenhass und Reue* (1789), adapted in England in 1798 as *The Stranger*.

116. *Othello*, v. ii. 7.

127. *Almas*: Dancing girls—who do for hire what Waltz doth gratis. [B, added in *Proof 4*]

131. *Morier*. See 211 n.; John Galt, *Voyages and Travels* (1812), 190.

142. It cannot be complained now, as in the Lady Baussiere's time, of the 'Sieur de la Croix', that there be 'no whiskers'; but how far these are indications of valour in the field, or elsewhere, may *still* be questionable. Much may be and hath been avouched on both sides. In the olden time philosophers had whiskers, and soldiers none—Scipio himself was shaven—Hannibal thought his one eye handsome enough without a beard; but Adrian, the Emperor, wore a beard (having warts on his chin, which neither the Empress Sabina, nor even the Courtiers, could abide)—Turenne had whiskers, Marlborough none—Buonaparte is unwhiskered, the R[egent] whiskered; '*argal*' greatness of mind and whiskers may or may not go together; but certainly the different occurences, since the growth of the last-mentioned, go further in behalf of whiskers than the anathema of Anselm did *against* long hair in the reign of Henry I.

Formerly *red* was a favourite colour. See Lodowick Barrey's comedy of Ram Alley, 1611, Act I. Sc. 1.

'*Taffeta*.—Now for a wager—What coloured beard comes next by the window?

Adriana.—A black man's, I think.

Taffeta.—I think not so: I think a *red*, for that is most in fashion.'

There is 'nothing new under the sun'; but *red*, then a *favourite*, subsided into a *favourite's* colour. [B, n. added in *Proofs 2* and *3*, see apparatus below.]

> It cannot . . . Henry I. *added in Proof 2; remainder added in Proof 3*
> '*argal*'] therefore *Proof 2, 3a*
> Ram Alley, 1611] Ram Alley, 1661 *all other edns.*
> *Lady Baussiere*: unidentified
> *Scipio*: Scipio Africanus Major (234?–183 B.C.), who defeated Hannibal at the decisive battle of Zama (202 B.C.).
> *Turenne . . . Marlborough*: Henri de la Tour d'Auvergne, Vicompte de Turenne (1611–75); John Churchill, first Duke of Marlborough (1650–1722): both perhaps the greatest military geniuses of their age.

argal: perversion of *ergo*; hence, indicative of a clumsy piece of reasoning.
Anselm: St. Anselm of Canterbury (1033–1109), Doctor of the Church.
Barrey: Lodowick Barry (or Barrey), a seventeenth-century actor and dramatist. His play *Ram Alley, or Merry Tricks*, printed in 1611, was performed in 1720.
'*nothing new under the sun*': Ecclesiastes 1: 9.
favourite's colour: a reference to Francis Charles Seymour-Conway, third Marquis of Hertford and Lord Yarmouth (1777–1842). He was the original of Thackeray's Marquis of Steyne, in *Vanity Fair*.

148–52. Stéphanie Ducrest de Saint-Aubin, Comtesse de Genlis, Marquise de Sillery (1746–1830): B is referring to the passage in the *Selections from the Works of Madame de Genlis* (1806), 65, where she cites *Werter*, Letter 9. For Madame de Staël see *CHP IV*, st. 54, B's n., and no. 218, 193 n.

162. An anachronism—Waltz, and the battle of Austerlitz, are before said to have opened the ball together—the Bard means (if he means any thing), Waltz was not so much in vogue till the R——t attained the acme of his popularity. Waltz, the Comet, Whiskers, and the new Government, illuminated heaven and earth, in all their glory, much about the same time: of these the Comet only has disappeared; the other three continue to astonish us still. PRINTER'S DEVIL.
[B, n. added in *Proof 1*]
The comet appeared in 1811, the new (Lord Liverpool) government was formed in June 1812, the year of the Prince Regent's social ascendancy.

164. In 1812 the Regent changed the uniforms of the Life Guards (see *Historical Record of the Life Guards* (1835), 177).

165. The so-called Frame-work Bill, which B denounced in his first speech in the Lords (*LJ* II. 424–30). When the bill was passed in Mar. 1812, sixteen of the 'frame-breakers' were sentenced to death; five were hanged.

166. Amongst others a new Ninepence—a creditable coin now forthcoming, worth a pound, in paper, at the fairest calculation. [B, added in *Proof 1*] By the Circulating Medium Bill of 1811 the Bank of England was empowered to issue new bank tokens of various denominations. The ninepence token was never actually issued. B is punning on 'creditable': see *Curse*, 245 ff. and n.

167. The victories of Ciudad Rodrigo (17 Jan.), Badajoz (7 Apr.), and Salamanca (12 July 1812).

168. Robert Banks Jenkinson, second Earl of Liverpool, the new Prime Minister (1812).

169. The War of 1812, with the United States.

171–2. Presumably a reference to the Prince Regent and Mrs. Fitzherbert.

173. 'Oh that *right* should thus overcome *might*!'

Waltz was not . . . popularity] till the Regent attained the acme of his popularity Waltz was not so much in vogue *Proof 1*   R——t] Regent *Proofs 1–3a, 1832, C, More*   Oh that *right* . . . *might!*'] *not in Proof 7*

Who does not remember the 'delicate Investigation' in the 'Merry Wives of Windsor'?—

'*Ford*.—"Pray you come near: if I suspect without cause, why then make sport at me; then let me be your jest; I deserve it.—How now? whither bear you this?"

'*Mrs. Ford*.—"What have you to do whither they bear it?—you were best meddle with buckwashing." '

[B, n. added in *Proof 7*]

See *The Merry Wives of Windsor*, III. iii.

174. *white-sticks, gold-sticks*: the staffs of various offices, e.g. the colonel of the Life Guards and the captain of the Gentlemen-at-arms (gold-sticks) or the Steward of the king's household and the Lord High Treasurer (white-sticks). For the new promotions of 1812 see *Annual Register* for 1812, 'Chronicle', 162–7. B's 'broom-sticks' refer to all the sweeping changes of 1812. The 'new sticks' is a resort to slang, where 'stick' signifies a stupid or incompetent person.

177. The gentle, or ferocious Reader, may fill up the blank as he pleases—there are several dissyllabic names at *his* service (being already in the R——t's): it would not be fair to back any peculiar initial against the alphabet, as every month will add to the list now entered for the sweepstakes—a distinguished consonant is said to be the favourite, much against the wishes of the *knowing ones*. [B, n. added in *Proof 3*]

B's original note, and the MS. (see apparatus), show that he intended here Lord Moira, Francis Rawdon, first Marquis of Hastings (1754–1826): see *LJ* v. 430–1.

187. Kent: see above, line 54 n.; 'sapient Gloucester' is William Frederick, second Duke of Gloucester (1776–1834), the great-grandson of George II. In contrast to the 'gay' and worldly Duke of Kent, the Duke of Gloucester was noted for his philanthropy, and his blameless life. He is 'sapient' also because he stood with the Opposition.

191. 'We have changed all that,' says the Mock Doctor—'tis all gone—Asmodeus knows where. After all, it is of no great importance how women's hearts are disposed of; they have Nature's privilege to distribute them as absurdly as possible. But there are also some men with hearts so thoroughly bad, as to remind us of those phenomena often mentioned in natural history;—viz. a mass of solid stone—only to be opened by force—and when divided you discover a *toad* in the centre, lively, and with the reputation of being venemous. [B, added in *Proofs 1* and *3*]

R——t's] Regent's *Proof 3, 3a, 1832, C, More*   We have changed . . . knows where.]
Proof 1, remainder added in Proof 3   distribute] ⟨dispose of⟩ *Proof 3*   But there are . . .
mentioned] In this country there is ⟨perhaps/but⟩ one man with ⟨a thoroughly bad one/ heart⟩
heart so thoroughly bad ⟨and his⟩ that it reminds us of those unaccountable petrifactions
⟨rather⟩ often ⟨remarked⟩ mentioned *Proof 3*   a toad] a ⟨living⟩ toad *Proof 3*   venemous.]
venemous. 'Such things we know are neither rich nor rare, But wonder how the devil they
got there.' *Proof 3*

Asmodeus; the demon of vanity and dress; *those phenomena*: see Oliver Goldsmith, *A History of the Earth and Animated Nature* (1852) II. 354–61 ('Of the Toad and its Varieties'). In the apparatus, the couplet is from Pope's 'Epistle to Dr. Arbuthnot', 171–2.

196–7. Echoes Sheridan, 'The Walse', 7–8.

211. In Turkey a pertinent—here an impertinent and superfluous question —literally put, as in the text, by a Persian to Morier, on seeing a Waltz in Pera.—*Vide Morier's Travels*. [B] James Morier, *A Journey Through Persia . . .* (1812), 365.

217. B sees Sheridan and Richard Fitzpatrick (1747–1813) as representative gallants of the past generation. Fitzpatrick dabbled in literature and was a member of the Ministry of All the Talents. For B's comments on the 'Great Worlds' of Sheridan and the Regency see his 'Detached Thoughts', *LJ* v. 411–31 *passim*.

220. William Douglas, third Earl of March and fourth Duke of Queensberry (1724–1810), a fast liver known as 'Old Q.'

224. Echoes Thomson's *Seasons*, 'Spring', 1149.

192. *MS. and Publishing History.* B's holograph fair copy MS. is in Texas (*MS. T*), titled, signed, dated, without stanza breaks. First published in Vere Foster's *The Two Duchesses* (1898), 374 from the MS. (in unknown hand) now in Library of Congress (*MS. LC*) in the Augustus John Foster papers. First collected, *C*.

The Hon. Mrs. George Lamb, sister-in-law of Lady Caroline Lamb, was born Caroline Rosalie Adelaide St. Jules (1786–1862). B wrote the poem while at Cheltenham shortly after the end of his affair with Lady Caroline (to whom he refers in line 6).

193. *MS. and Publishing History.* B's holograph fair copy, dated 19 Oct. 1812, is in the bound volume of Miscellaneous Poems in Murray (*MS. M*). First published (anonymously) in the *Morning Chronicle*, 23 Oct. 1812; four lines were published in the *Life* (I. 381) which were then picked up in *Paris1831*; first collected, *1832*, and collected thereafter. B's poem is a parody, using quotations from the original, of the poem sent to the Drury Lane theatre committee's competition by Dr. Thomas Busby (1755–1838), who was a composer and journalist (see *LJ* II. 176n. and above, no. 190). For Busby's poem see the *Genuine Rejected Addresses*; it was reprinted in *C* III. 55–7. B sent the poem to the *Chronicle* through Murray (see *BLJ* II. 227–8; this letter is conjecturally dated 17 Oct. by Marchand, but it should be 19 Oct.).

11. Busby's translation of Lucretius, *The Nature of Things*, was published in 1813 (see II. 880–1).

16. Busby's son tried unsuccessfully to deliver his father's address at the theatre on 14 Oct. On 15 Oct. Busby himself introduced his son from one

of the boxes, but the young man could not be heard, a fact alluded to by B in the stage direction for his parody.

35. *in petto*: literally 'in the breast'; hence, 'undisclosed'.

56. B was one of the subscribers for Busby's translation of Lucretius. He felt more favourably towards Busby after the latter published an explanation of his conduct, along with an apology to B, in the same issue of the *Morning Chronicle* that published the 'Parenthetical Address'.

194. *MS. and Publishing History*. B's fair copy of version one—signed but not dated—is in the Murray archives (*MS. M*). The MS. of the fourth version is in the Bodleian, Lovelace papers (*MS. L*), a holograph fair copy corrected, undated. Texas has a fair copy MS. of version three (*MS. T*) on the verso of the MS. of 'Hear My Prayer'. The fourth version is first published here; the third version was published by Richard Edgecumbe (N *& Q*, sixth series, VII. 46) from a copy he saw written by B in Lady Lansdowne's album at Bowood in 1815. First version published in *CHP*(7), collected thereafter; second version published in *Life*, I. 521, collected *1831*, *1832*, and thereafter.

The lines translate the Portuguese song 'Tu mi chamas'. The existence of *MS. T* indicates that B first wrote the poem not in 1814, as previously believed, but in late 1812.

The several versions of this translation indicate that B was not entirely satisfied with his first effort. He said as much in a letter to Murray of 22 Jan. 1814: 'Lady West[morlan]d thought [the translation] so bad—that after making me translate it she gave me her *own version*—which is for aught I know the best of the two' (*BLJ* IV. 37). The second version here, which Thomas Moore first printed as B's, may very well be Lady Westmorland's translation.

195–203. A complete single set of MS. versions of these nine poems is in the Lovelace papers (*MS. L*, location: Bodleian), under the general heading by B: 'Imitations of Martial'. The collection has both draft and fair copies for nos. 199, 200, and 201. Other MSS. for three of the poems exist elsewhere: for no. 195, a fair copy holograph (*MS. M*, location: Murray), written in the margin by the Latin original in Byron's copy of *M. Valerii Martialis Epigrammatica* (1670); for no. 201, a fair copy holograph (*MS. Mo*, location: Morgan); for no. 203, a fair copy holograph (*MS. TP*, location: Princeton–Taylor). The latter is a copy evidently made later than *MS. L*, for it is dated Brussels, 6 May 1816. None of the poems has been collected, and only two have been previously published in any form: nos. 195 and 201. The watermarks on a few of the poems in *MS. L*, plus the relation of no. 195 to no. 193 above, indicate the series was originally composed in 1812. See individual commentaries below.

195. First published in *The Examiner* 24 (7 Nov. 1824), whence it was reprinted in *Iley*, II. 317 and *Paris1831*, *Paris1835*. The corrected fair copy holograph of the poem in the Lovelace papers carries an 1811 watermark. The poem must belong to 1812 for it is a companion piece to the 'Parenthetical Address by Doctor Plagiary' (no. 193). The poem is directed at W. J. Fitzgerald: see *EBSR* 1–2 and no. 204 below.

1. The variant reads 'The Laureate's' because Fitzgerald was the acknowledged 'laureate' of the Literary Fund, of which he was a founding member. His 'house' is Drury Lane Theatre, which burned down 24 Feb. 1809. See the note to *EBSR*, 1–2.

196. B's fair copy MS. of this couplet is on the same leaf as his '[Imitation from Martial XI. 93]' (no. 195).

197. In *MS. L*, a draft on the same leaf as no. 198. Harry B. Smith's *Sentimental Library* (privately printed, 1914) prints a version of the epigram under the heading: 'Autograph quotation from Horace [*sic*], with English adaptation of it, in Byron's hand.' Smith adds that the correction in line 2 was made 'at the time of Byron's controversy with Southey'. The present location of the Smith MS is not known.

When B made this translation, he probably had W. J. Fitzgerald in mind.

198. In *MS. L*, a draft MS. If B had anyone specifically in mind for the poem, the person is not known.

199. The draft and fair copy are on a single sheet in *MS. L*. B may have had himself in mind in this imitation.

200. B's draft and fair copies are on the same MS. leaf as no. 199. The subject of the imitation is not known.

201. The fair and rough copies in *MS. L* are watermarked 1811. *MS. Mo* is a fair copy later than *MS. L*. The echoes of Catullus, V and VII are originally Martial's. The poem has been published once, in Doris Langley Moore's *The Great Byron Adventure* (1959).

202. *MS. L*, a draft MS. on the same leaf with no. 203. The subject is Samuel Rogers.

203. Unpublished; B's draft MS. is on the same leaf as the previous poem (*MS. L*, location: Bodleian–Lovelace). But the text here is printed from B's fair copy (*MS. TP*, location: Princeton–Taylor), which B apparently made in 1816. *MS. TP* is signed by B: 'Brussels.—Byron May 6th 1816.'

204. *MS. and Publishing History.* R. C. Dallas's transcript in a front blank leaf of a copy of *EBSR5* (*MS. M*, location: Murray). Another MS. copy by Dallas (*MS. PM*, location: Morgan) is inserted loose into a copy of Dallas's *Private Correspondence of Lord Byron.* The transcripts were made from B's MS. in another copy of *EBSR* at the Alfred Club. Published first in *Paris1822* (I. 234), but not again until it was included in a footnote in *C* (I. 298 n.).

MS. M explains the lines as an 'Answer Written on the same page by Lord Byron' to the following lines 'Written in a copy of English Bards at the Alfred by W. J. Fitzgerald Esqe.'.

> 'I find Lord Byron scorns my Muse
> Our fates are ill agreed
> His verse is safe I can't abuse
> Those lines I never read. W. J. F.'

B was elected to the Alfred Club late in 1811. He had ridiculed Fitzgerald at the opening of *EBSR*. The date for the lines is approximate.

205. *MS. and Publishing History.* The revisions and accretions for *The Giaour* are among the most extensive and complex in B's works. Equally remarkable is the body of MSS. and Proofs which has survived. To simplify the analysis of so large a mass of data, four tables have been prepared. The first two list and briefly describe the different MSS., Proofs, and Revises. The third table describes the content of the poem from its first MS. state to its ultimate form in the seventh edition. The final table outlines the order of composition of the various parts of the poem.

TABLE A: Manuscripts

MS. L (Bodleian–Lovelace)
   The original rough draft, undated, containing: lines 1–6, 168–99, 277–87, 352–87, 422–4, 426–72, 519–602, 604–19, 655–88, 723–32, 735–8, 787–831, 1319–34.

MS. M (Murray archives)
   A fair copy dated at beginning 1813, containing the epigraph, the dedication, and a brief version of the 'Advertisement', as well as the following additional lines: 425, 473–89, 491–503.

MS. LA (Bodleian–Lovelace; these are additions to *MS. L*)
   1. Lines 729–34, 739–86, rough draft.
   2. Lines 473–503, rough draft.
   3. Lines 971–99, 1029–74, rough draft.
   4. Lines 1099–126, rough draft.
   5. Lines 1257–316, rough draft with B's note: 'Fragment of The Giaour toward the conclusion.'

6. Seven brief rough draft alterations for the poem headed with B's note: 'Alterations etc in The Giaour.' (*a*) Lines 922–3. (*b*) Line 918. (*c*) Lines 1103–9. (*d*) Lines 1275–80. (*e*) Lines 1308–9. (*f*) Lines 1317–18. (*g*) Lines 1315–18.

7. Lines 916–17, 920–35, rough draft.

MS. MA (Murray archives; these are additions to *MS. M.*)

1. Lines 21–2, 25–45, fair copy, with B's note: 'Insert this in paragraph 2nd after the line "That wakes and wafts the fragrance there".' Dated by Murray: '1813 July 27, 3rd ed. first copy.'

2. Lines 7–20, 46–67, fair copy, with his note: 'I have not yet fixed the place of insertion for the following lines but will when I see you—as I have no copy.' Dated by B: 19 June 1813.

3. Corrected fair copy of *MA2* above with B's note: 'These lines may form the second paragraph of the fragment.'

4. Lines 68–97, rough draft, with B's note: 'Third paragraph of The Giaour continue with a separation—but *no asterisks.*'

5. Lines 68–102, fair copy, corrected version of *MA4* above.

6. Lines 103–67, first draft, undated.

7. Lines 200–45, 247–50, 253–72. Corrected fair copy with note by Murray: 'Giaour inserted in second revise of Third Edition July 30, 1813.'

8. Lines 264–6 and 273–6, revisions for *MA7* above, with B's note: 'Add these to the passage sent this morning.' Dated by Murray: 31 July 1813.

9. Lines 504–18, fair copy, with Murray's note: '1813 July 31 Giaour inserted in second revise of the third edition.'

10. Lines 288–325, 330–51. (*a*) Rough draft, undated. (*b*) Fair copy with Murray's note: 'Aug. 5, 1813—in the last of third and first of fourth editions.'

11. Lines 620–54, fair copy, and a revised version of lines 1000–1. Lines 620–54 preceded by B's note: 'Lost Leila's love—accursed Giaour (continue in a second paragraph but without asterisks here.)'

12. Lines 689–722. (*a*) Rough draft, undated. (*b*) Fair copy with B's note: 'Continue from p. 34 line 611—and now I go but go alone—leave in the asterisks but make this the next paragraph.' Dated by Murray: 11 Aug. 1813.

13. Lines 739–86. Fair copy, undated.

14. (*a*) Lines 832–915, corrected fair copy with B's note: 'Oct. 2, 1813. Separate paragraph insert after line 831 "And lures to leap into the wave".' (*b*) On a separate sheet, a revision for lines 893–8 with B's note: 'Alteration in some of the lines sent today—to be sent to the printer directly —by reading the M.S. he will see where.'

15. Lines 937–64, 966–8. Corrected fair copy, undated.

16. Lines 971–99, 1029–61. Undated fair copy.

17. Lines 997–1023, fair copy corrected with B's note at top: 'P. 31 XXX.'

18. Lines 1075–9, fair copy with B's note: 'Continue from [quotes line 1074].' Undated.

19. Lines 1062–74, 1099–126, 1257–316. Fair copy, undated.

20. Lines 1080–98, fair copy with B's note: 'Continue after [quotes line 1079].' Murray's note reads: '1813 July 28 third edition.'

21. Lines 1131–91. Three versions of these lines: (*a*) The rough draft containing lines 1131–4, 1137–8, 1135–6, 1149–77. (*b*) Intermediate rough draft containing lines 1131–4, 1137–40, 1135–6, 1141–91. (*c*) Corrected fair copy containing, in correct order, lines 1131–91 and headed with B's note: 'Continue from [quotes line 1126].' The MS. is dated by Murray 23 Aug. 1813.

22. Lines 1192–217. There are two versions: (*a*) an early corrected fair copy; (*b*) a later corrected fair copy headed with B's note: 'Separate paragraph. Insert after line 1098 [quotes line 1191].' Murray dates the MS. 28 Sept. 1813, and B has a note at the end: 'Let this copy go to the printer—there are some lines added.'

23. Lines 1218–56, in two versions: (*a*) a first draft containing lines 1218–45, 1247–56; (*b*) a fair copy of the full passage with B's note: 'Continue from the M.S. sent today [that is, *MA21* above]—in a separate paragraph. August 23, 1813.'

24. Lines 872–5, rough draft, undated.

25. Lines 859–71, rough draft, undated.

26. Lines 893–910, rough draft, undated.

27. Lines 912–15, rough draft, undated.

28. Lines 1192–213, rough draft, undated.

29. Lines 1214–17, rough draft, undated.

30. Corrections for the poem's final prose note.

Other Additions (*OA*)

1. On the same leaf, a revised version of lines 98–9 and a fair copy of lines 1127–30. Undated; location: Yale.

2. Lines 832–58, 883–90, undated rough draft; location: Texas.

3. Lines 963–70, a fair copy with B's head-note: 'Continue from [quotes line 962].' From the private collection of L. McCormick-Goodheart.

4. Three fragments on a MS. scrap headed 'Alterations': (*a*) Lines 1196–7; (*b*) Lines 1127–30; (*c*) Lines 893–8 (location: Princeton–Taylor).

5. Lines 937–8, 963–8, draft (location: Bodleian–Lovelace; these lines are bound up with the MS. additions to *Lara*).

6. Revised version of the prose note to line 1328 (location: Mitchell Library, Univ. of New South Wales, Sydney).

7. B's corrections for lines 335 and 343 (location: Murray; see *BLJ* III. 132).

8. Draft of lines 1075–9, with note (location: Pforzheimer).

TABLE B: Proofs and Revises (Murray archives)

1. An uncorrected copy of the privately circulated proof edition of 28 pages (460 lines).

2. Another copy of (1) above, with B's corrections, and used in preparing the text of the first published edition.

3. A portion of an early proof for the first edition, the concluding passages of the poem (numbered pp. 27–37). Heavily corrected by B.

4. A revise for the first edition (pp. 1–32) headed in MS.: 'The last revise May 22, 1813.' With numerous corrections.

5. Another revise for the first edition (pp. 1–16) dated at beginning: Monday, 24 May 1813. No corrections.

6. Uncorrected revise for the first edition (pp. 1–24).

7. A proof text of the first edition marked up and corrected by B in preparing the second edition (41 pages).

8. A 47-page proof of the second edition, with no substantive corrections.

9. A 47-page proof of the second edition containing 795 lines and dated 24 June 1813. With numerous corrections.

10. Another 47-page proof of the second edition with a few corrections and a new title-page.

11. A 48-page proof for the third edition, marked as the first revise and dated 30 July 1813. With B's corrections.

12. A 53-page proof for the third edition (950 lines).

13. A 53-page proof for the third edition (954 lines), with numerous corrections.

14. Uncorrected proof of the third edition (53 pages). The latest extant proof of the text of the third edition, first state.

15. A revise of pp. 1–16 to incorporate the addition of lines 288–351: for fourth edition. Many MS. revisions.

16. The earliest proof for the third edition, second state (56 pages, 1002 lines): with B's additions and corrections in MS.

17. A 56-page proof of third edition, second state (1004 lines), with no corrections.

18. A revise (pp. 1–16) of the third edition, second state. No corrections. Dated 6 Aug. 1813.

19. A 56-page proof of the third edition, second state, marked up as copy for the fourth edition. Dated 10 Aug. 1813 with note at end by printer: 'Addition at page 34 [lines 689–722, sent separately by B] and addition to note at end [in the proof in B's MS.]'

20. Two sets of revises for the fourth edition (pp. 1–32 and pp. 49–58), with minor revisions.

21. A 58-page proof of the fourth edition marked up as copy for the fifth edition, with numerous insertions and corrections. Dated 19 Aug. 1813.

22. A 63-page proof of the fifth edition (1148 lines), with many corrections, and dated 25 Aug. 1813.

23. Another 63-page proof of the fifth edition, also dated 25 Aug. but with 1149 lines. No MS. corrections.

24. Final proof for the fifth edition (65 pages, 1215 lines), with a few minor MS. corrections.

25. Partial proof dated by Murray 10 Nov. 1813, with B's corrections; proof for seventh edition (ends at p. 48, line 991). With a note at top of p. 42 in unknown hand: 'Please to look to pointing this and the following pages.'

26. A 75-page proof of the seventh edition (1334 lines), dated 27 Nov. 1813.

27. Three fragments of proofs for the seventh edition: (*a*) A revise showing that lines 893 ff. originally followed line 882. (*b*) A revise of lines 893–5. (*c*) A revise of lines 1127–30 with B's note: 'Insert these four after line 1037 [quotes line 1126] and conclude with them the paragraph.'

28. A copy of the eleventh edition with B's note on the inside front cover: 'Why did not the printer attend to the solitary correction so repeatedly made [in lines 236–7]? I have no copy of this and desire to have none till my request is complied with.'

29. *Text JJ*. A copy of the ninth edition with B's MS. correction of 'reddening' to 'hasty' in line 236. The correction was carried into the twelfth edition, but was removed thereafter by the correction called for in *Proof 28* above. *Text JJ* is in the collection of J. Geoffrey Jones, of Cambridge, N.Y.

In addition to the above proofs, the Murray archive has two duplicates of *Proof 9* (uncorrected, but one dated by B 24 June 1813); and uncorrected duplicates of *Proofs 19* and *21*. Finally, the Huntington Library has a single leaf of uncorrected proof for lines 783–823.

MS. L 344 lines	MS. M 375 lines	Proof edn. 453 lines	1st edn. 684 lines	2nd edn. 816 lines	3rd edn. (first state) 950 lines	3rd edn. (second state) 1014 lines	4th edn. 1048 lines	5th edn. 1215 lines	7th edn. 1334 lines	12th edn.
1–6										
				7–20, 46–102	21–45					
								103–67		
168–99										
					200–50					
								251–2		(236–7)
					253–76					
277–87										
						288–351				
352–87										
		388–421								
422–4	425									
426–72	473–89, 491–503	490								
					504–18					
519–602, 604–19				603						
				620–54						
655–88										
							689–722			
723–32, 735–8		733–4	739–45							
		746–86								
787–831										
			916–98						832–915	
			1029–79	999–1023					1024–8	
			1099–126		1080–98					
								1131–91	1127–30	
			1257–318					1218–56	1192–217	
1319–34										

TABLE D: Additions: Order of Composition

Additions to MS. L and MS. M

(These were made before 24 Mar. for inclusion in the Proof edition of 28 pages.)

    1. Lines 473–503 (*LA2*).

    2. Lines 729–34, 739–86 (*LA1*), (*MA13*). But lines 739-45 did not appear until the first edition.

    3. Lines 388–421 (inserted on a separate sheet into *MSS. L* and *M*).

Additions for the First Edition

    1. Lines 916–35 (*LA7*).

    2. Lines 918, 922–3 (*LA6ab*).

    3. Lines 937–68 (*MA15*); 937–8, 963–8 (*OA5*).

    4. Lines 963–70 (*OA3*).

    5. Lines 971–99, 1029–74 (*LA3*), (*MA16*).

    6. Lines 1099–126 (*LA4*).

    7. Lines 1103–9 (*LA6c*).

    8. Lines 1257–316 (*LA5*).

    9. Lines 1275–80 and 1308–9 (*LA6de*).

    10. Lines 1062–74, 1099–126, 1257–316 (*MA19*).

    11. Lines 1075–9 (*MA18*).

    12. Lines 1315–18 (*LA6fg*), (*Proof 3*).

Additions to the Second Edition

(The earliest of these is dated 19 June, the latest 24 June.)

    1. Lines 7–20, 46–67 (*MA2*), (*MA3*).

    2. Lines 68–102 (*MA4*), (*MA5*).

    3. Lines 997–1023 (*MA17*).

    4. Lines 620–54 and a revised version of lines 1000–1 (*MA11*).

    5. Line 603 (*Proof 9*).

Additions for the Third Edition (First State)

(The earliest of these is dated 27 July, the latest 31 July.)

    1. Lines 21–2, 25–45 (*MA1*).

    2. Lines 1080–98 (*MA20*).

    3. Lines 200–50, 253–72 (*MA7*).

    4. Lines 23–4 (*Proof 11*).

    5. Lines 264–6 and 273–6 (*MA8*).

    6. Lines 504–18 (*MA9*).

Addition for the Third Edition (Second State)

(This is dated 5 Aug.)

    1. Lines 288–351 (*MA10ab*).

Addition for the Fourth Edition

(This is dated 11 Aug.)

    1. Lines 689–722 (*MA12ab*).

Additions for the Fifth Edition

(The earliest of these is dated 23 Aug., the latest is undated, but was probably written before the end of Aug.)

1. Lines 1131–91 (*MA21abc*).
2. Lines 1218–56 (*MA23ab*).
3. Lines 251–2 (*Proof 21*).
4. Lines 103–67 (*MA6*).

Additions for the Seventh Edition

(The earliest of these belongs to 27 or 28 Sept., the latest to 2 Oct.)

1. Lines 1192–217 (*MA22ab*), (*MA28*), (*MA29*), (*OA4a*).
2. Lines 1127–30 (*OA4b*), (*OA1*), (*Proof 26*).
3. Lines 832–915 (*OA2*), (*MA25*), (*MA24*), (*MA26*), (*OA4c*), (*MA27*), (*MA14*).

The exact date of the composition of *Giaour* is not known, but it must have been written between Sept. 1812 and Mar. 1813, and it probably belongs to late 1812 (see *BLJ* III. 40 and *Marchand*, I. 386–7). The first version of the poem (*MS. L*) was 344 lines long. When B wrote the first corrected text (*MS. M*, 375 lines) he initiated the famous sequence of accretions which would not end until the poem reached its seventh edition in Dec. 1813.

Fifteen copies of the poem were struck off for private circulation in late Mar. 1813 (*BLJ* III. 28). This version of *Giaour*, of which two copies survive in the Murray archives, contains 453 lines in twenty-eight pages. By May B had decided to issue the work to the public and he continued to augment and revise throughout that month. When the first edition appeared on 5 June the work had grown to 684 lines. B's 'snake of a poem' continued 'lengthening its rattles every month' (*BLJ* III. 100) until December, when the seventh edition appeared. The poem was extremely popular and passed through fourteen editions by 1815, when it was issued by Murray in his first collected edition of B's poems.

The dating of the other earliest editions is as follows: edn. 2 (early July); edn. 3, first state (1–5 Aug.); edn. 3, second state (mid-Aug.); edn. 4 (late Aug.); edn. 5 (early Sept.); edn. 6 (end of Sept.); edns. 9–12 (1814); edns. 13–14 (1815). It is clear from B's letters that he did not expect the poem to take well with the public (cf. *BLJ* III. 59 and 63). Consequently, Murray's printing runs for the earliest editions were small (8,743 copies of edns. 1–11 were printed). But the poem was popular and the early editions sold out quickly. Of the first thirteen editions, 12,050 copies were printed.

The text that descends to us through *1831*, *1832*, *C*, and *More*—indeed, all editions of the poem except edn. 7—has incorrect readings in lines 403 and 407. B revised these lines in *Proof 25* for edn. 7, but subsequent editions reverted to the readings in edns. 1–6. Copy text here is edn. 7, the last edition which we know B corrected in proof.

For further bibliographical data see *Wise*, I. 74–85 and *C* III. 78–80, VII. 234–40.

Literary and Historical Background. The *Giaour* was born, phoenix-like, from 'The Monk of Athos' and 'Il Diavolo Inamorato', the ashes of 'a poem of 6 Cantos . . . as like the last 2 [i.e. *CHP I–II*] as I can make them' (*BLJ* II. 191: to Murray, 5 Sept. 1812). B's poem came to fragments, however, in two senses. When he found himself unable to continue with the two Spenserian pieces just mentioned, he abandoned the projected 'poem of 6 Cantos' and used some of that material in his revisions for the seventh edition of *CHP I–II* (see commentaries above). The general plan for the aborted project can be guessed from B's letter to Moore (*BLJ* III. 101–2: 28 Aug. 1813), from the two surviving fragments, and from the final prose note to the *Giaour*, where B says that 'the story . . . is one told of a young Venetian'.

B's initial plan resulted in the 'Fragment of a Turkish Tale', which is the *Giaour* itself (cf. *BLJ* III. 62, 105). Unlike the story B initially planned to write, the central incident in the *Giaour* is based upon B's personal experience, though some important details connected with the adventure remain obscure. B thought that the incident 'had been *unknown*, and [I] wish it were' (*BLJ* III. 230, and see also 102, 155, 200); but a report of it reached Lord Sligo when he was in Athens on 12 Sept. 1810, a few days after the incident had occurred. Sligo later wrote out for B the account as he originally heard it of 'the affair of that girl who was so near being put an end to while you were . . . at Athens' (*LJ* II. 257–8):

> The new governor, unaccustomed to have the same intercourse with the Christians as his predecessor, had, of course, the barbarous Turkish ideas with regard to women. In consequence, and in compliance with the strict letter of the Mohammedan law, he ordered this girl to be sewed up in a sack, and thrown into the sea—as is, indeed, quite customary at Constantinople. As you were returning from bathing in the Piraeus, you met the procession going down to execute the sentence of the Waywode on this unhappy girl. Report continues to say, that on finding out what the object of their journey was, and who was the miserable sufferer, you immediately interfered; and on some delay in obeying your orders, you were obliged to inform the leader of the escort that force should make him comply; that, on further hesitation, you drew a pistol, and told him, that if he did not immediately obey your orders, and come back with you to the Aga's house, you would shoot him dead. On this the man turned about and went with you to the governor's house; here you succeeded, partly by personal threats, and partly by bribery and entreaty, in procuring her pardon, on condition of her leaving Athens. I was told that you then conveyed her in safety to the convent, and despatched her off at night to Thebes, where she found a safe asylum. Such is the story I heard, as nearly as I can recollect it.

Byron acknowledged that 'our adventure (a personal one) . . . first suggested to me the story of *The Giaour*,' and that Lord Sligo's account was 'not very far from the truth' (*BLJ* III. 200). There is every reason to believe, though unfortunately little data to substantiate, that B's involvement in the adventure had other 'personal' aspects to it unknown to Lord Sligo (see *Marchand*, I. 257–8 and below, B's unpublished n. for line 1334).

The literary influences on the poem are many. For the 'fragment' form B was indebted to Samuel Rogers' *Voyage of Columbus* (1812). As B suggested in his poem's final note, the incidents follow the general form of the modern Greek ballads about Euphrosyne which B had heard when he was in the Near East. (For an example of these songs see M. de Marcellus, *Chants du Peuple en Grèce* (Paris, 1851), II. 30.) As for the ancestry of the famous Byronic Hero, the skein of influence is complex (see Peter Thorslev, *The Byronic Hero* (Minneapolis, 1962)), but the near and specific debt to Scott's *Rokeby* (1813) and *Marmion* (1808) has been well argued (K. Hoffmann, *Über Lord Byrons 'The Giaour'* (Halle, 1898)). A hitherto unnoticed influence is Thomas Campbell's 'Love and Madness' (1795). There is a general resemblance of thought between the two works, but a specific influence is evident between lines 61–72 of Campbell's poem and lines 822–31 of *The Giaour*, where the Giaour is distracted with visions summoning him to death and raves 'as to some bloody hand . . . Invisible to all but him'.

B was well acquainted with large areas of the Near East and was widely read in the classical and modern literature on its geography, its peoples, and their cultures. (See especially Martha Pike Conant, *The Oriental Tale in England in the Eighteenth Century* (New York, 1908), S. C. Chew, *The Crescent and the Rose* (Oxford, 1938), W. C. Brown, 'Byron and English Interest in the Near East', *SP* 34 (1937)). Specific debts to the works of Sir William Jones, d'Herbelot's *Bibliothèque Orientale*, and George Sale's edition of *The Koran* (1734) are traceable. In addition, *The Giaour* owes a special debt to Beckford's *Vathek*, and in particular to Henley's Notes for the novel. (See H. S. C. Wiener, 'Byron and the East: Literary Sources of the "Turkish Tales" ', *Nineteenth-Century Studies*, ed. Herbert Davis *et al.* (Ithaca, 1940)).

epigraph Thomas Moore, 'As a beam o'er the face', *Irish Melodies*.

Advertisement B establishes the date of his story as shortly after 1779, when Hassan Ghazi broke the forces of the Albanians (i.e. the Arnauts) in the Morea. The Russians invaded the Morea in 1770 and took Misithra that same year. Their fleet left the Levant in 1774, when the Peace of Kainardji was signed between the Turks and the Russians. See George Finlay, *A History of Greece . . .* (Oxford, 1877), v. 252–69.

1–167. Introductory lines which do not belong to the 'Turkish Tale' proper; their point of view is, like B's, contemporary and English.

3. The tomb above the rocks on the promontory, by some supposed the sepulchre of Themistocles. [B]

> on the promontory] between Munychium and the Piraeus *MS*. *M*.

Cf. Plutarch's *Life of Themistocles*, XXXII. The legendary tomb is on the westernmost promontory of the Piraeus, less than a mile from the harbour entrance.

8. Alluding to the legendary Isles of the Blessed (see *CHP IV* 243).

9. *Colonna*: Cape Sunium.

22. The attachment of the nightingale to the rose is a well-known Persian fable—if I mistake not, the 'Bulbul of a thousand tales' is one of his appellations. [B]

> Reads only Persian Fable in *MA1*.

B's n. depends upon *Vathek* (1786), 286–7 (n. to p. 104).

40. The guitar is the constant amusement of the Greek sailor by night; with a steady fair wind, and during a calm, it is accompanied always by the voice, and often by dancing. [B]

52–3. Matthew 6: 28.

68. This 'trailing anacoluthon' typifies B's recurrent lapses from ordinary grammar. Ethel C. Mayne showed a keen insight when she saw in the construction 'that strange, slipshod loveliness, where He never fulfils his destiny as the subject of the opening phrase. Bent o'er the dead he remains immovable to the end of time' (*Byron* (1924), 177).

68–90. Though not an epic simile as such, the passage is a self-conscious, 'modern' imitation of the device. It anticipates the heroic similes which appear recurrently in the body of B's 'Turkish Tale' proper (see below, 388–95 e.g.)

81.   'Aye, but to die and go we know not where,
                        To lie in cold obstruction.'

Measure foe Measure, III. i. 118–19. [B]

89. I trust that few of my readers have ever had an opportunity of witnessing what is here attempted in description, but those who have will probably retain a painful remembrance of that singular beauty which pervades, with few exceptions, the features of the dead, a few hours, and but for a few hours after 'the spirit is not there'. It is to be remarked in cases of violent death by gun-shot wounds, the expression is always that of languor, whatever the natural energy of the sufferer's character; but in death from a stab the countenance preserves its traits of feeling or ferocity, and the mind its bias, to the last. [B]

> It is to be . . . to the last *added Proof 9*
> '*the spirit is not there*': unidentified.

103. Cf. *CHP II*, st. 3.

138–9. Miltonic. For B's fascination with this (and associated) ideas, cf. *McGann(2)*, 26 ff.

151. Athens is the property of the Kislar Aga (the slave of the seraglio

and guardian of the women), who appoints the Waywode. A pandar and eunuch—these are not polite yet true appellations—now *governs* the *governor* of Athens. [B] Cf. Hobhouse, *Travels in Albania*, I. 246. The Waiwode, or Turkish governor of Athens, was subject to the Kislar Aga, who lived in Constantinople and was responsible for the protection of the city.

171. *Mainote.* The people of Maina were celebrated alike as fiercely independent spirits, and as outlaws.

177. *Port Leone*: the ancient Piraeus.

182–4. Cf. Scott's *Lady of the Lake*, I. 3. 2.

190. Infidel. [B]

218–19. Cf. Scott's *Lay of the Last Minstrel*, I. 17. 1–3.

225. 'Tophaike', musket.—The Bairam is announced by the cannon at sunset; the illumination of the Mosques, and the firing of all kinds of small arms, loaded with *ball*, proclaim it during the night. [B] At the end of the period of the Ramadhan (the ninth month of the Arabic calendar), a three-day festival takes place, the Bairam. See *CHP II*, st. 55, and d'Herbelot, article 'Ramadhan'.

237. See commentary above, *Proof 28.*

251. Jerreed, or Djerrid, a blunted Turkish javelin, which is darted from horseback with great force and precision. It is a favourite exercise of the Mussulmans; but I know not if it can be called a *manly* one, since the most expert in the art are the Black Eunuchs of Constantinople.—I think, next to these, a Mamlouk at Smyrna was the most skilful that came within my own observation. [B]
Mamlouk: a slave warrior, originally designating those from Circassia. Cf. d'Herbelot, article 'Mamlouk'.

272. B told his publisher that the idea came from the Arabian story (recounted by Addison in *Spectator*, 94) of the Sultan who immersed his head in water for a brief period but who imagined, in that time, that he lived for many years (*Smiles*, I. 219 n.).

282. The blast of the desart, fatal to every thing living, and often alluded to in eastern poetry. [B]
The ⟨deadly⟩ blast of the desart, ⟨a like⟩ fatal *MS. M*

290–4. Cf. the Persian couplet cited by Sir William Jones, *Grammar of the Persian Language* (Works (1807), V. 289); also Demetrius Cantimir, *A History of the Growth and Decay of the Ottoman Empire* (1756), 102.

335, 343. Cf. *BLJ* III. 132.

339. *Fakir*: Arabic for a beggar. 'Dervish' is the Turkish word. Cf. d'Herbelot, article 'Fakir', and *Vathek*, 107 (n. on 288, 289).

343. To partake of food—to break bread and salt with your host—insures the safety of the guest, even though an enemy; his person from that moment is sacred. [B] The pledge of hospitality with all Mussulmans, particularly the Arabs *4th–6th edns.*

351. I need hardly observe, that Charity and Hospitality are the first

duties enjoined by Mahomet; and to say truth, very generally practised by his disciples. The first praise that can be bestowed on a chief, is a panegyric on his bounty; the next, on his valour. [B] Cf. *The Koran*, chap. 4.

355. The ataghan, a long dagger worn with pistols in the belt, in a metal scabbard, generally of silver; and, among the wealthier, gilt, or of gold. [B]

357. Green is the privileged colour of the prophet's numerous pretended descendants; with them, as here, faith (the family inheritance) is supposed to supersede the necessity of good works; they are the worst of a very indifferent brood. [B]

358. Salam aleikoum! aleikoum salam! peace be with you; be with you peace—the salutation reserved for the faithful;—to a Christian, 'Urlarula', a good journey; or saban hiresem, saban serula; good morn, good even; and sometimes, 'may your end be happy'; are the usual salutes. [B]

389. The blue-winged butterfly of Kashmeer, the most rare and beautiful of the species. [B] Cf. *Vathek*, 113 (n. on 293).

391–421. Cf. *CHP I*, sts. 82–4 and 'To Inez'; and Canto II, sts. 32–5.

434. Alluding to the dubious suicide of the scorpion, so placed for experiment by gentle philosophers. Some maintain that the position of the sting, when turned towards the head, is merely a convulsive movement; but others have actually brought in the verdict 'Felo de se'. The scorpions are surely interested in a speedy decision of the question; as, if once established as insect Catos, they will probably be allowed to live as long as they think proper, without being martyred for the sake of an hypothesis. [B] In actual fact, the scorpion is immune to its own venom. The old legend to which B alludes has been long since disproved. B said that the famous scorpion simile came to him in a dream (Dallas, *Recollections*, 264).

449. The cannon at sunset close the Rhamazan; see note [above, l. 225]. [B]

468. Phingari, the moon. [B]

479. The celebrated fabulous ruby of Sultan Giamschid, the embellisher of Istakhar; from its splendour, named Schebgerag, 'the torch of night'; also, the 'cup of the sun', &c.—In the first editions 'Giamschid' was written as a word of three syllables; so D'Herbelot has it; but I am told Richardson reduces it to a dissyllable, and writes 'Jamshid'. I have left in the text the orthography of the one with the pronunciation of the other. [B]

In the first . . . of the other *added in 5th edn.*

See d'Herbelot, article 'Giamschid', and *Vathek*, 230–1 (n. to p. 64), 305–7 (n. to p. 127). *Richardson*: John Richardson, *Dictionary of Persian, Arabic, and English* (1777); cf. *LJ* II. 254.

483. Al-Sirat, the bridge of breadth less than the thread of a famished spider, over which the Mussulmans must *skate* into Paradise, to which it is

brood] ⟨people⟩ *M*   the Rhamazan; see note] the Rhamazan; and the illumination of the mosques, and firing of guns through the night, announce the Bairam; it lasts three days; and after a month's fast is pleasant enough *M, 1st–3rd edns.; cor. Proof 16*

the only entrance; but this is not the worst, the river beneath being hell itself, into which, as may be expected, the unskilful and tender of foot contrive to tumble with a 'facilis descensus Averni', not very pleasing in prospect to the next passenger. There is a shorter cut downwards for the Jews and Christians. [B] Cf. *Vathek*, 313–14 (n. to p. 141).

facilis . . . Averni: Virgil, *Aeneid*, VI. 26.

488. A vulgar error; the Koran allots at least a third of Paradise to well-behaved women; but by far the greater number of Mussulmans interpret the text their own way, and exclude their moieties from heaven. Being enemies to Platonics, they cannot discern 'any fitness of things' in the souls of the other sex, conceiving them to be superseded by the Houris. [B] *Added in 2nd edn. (Proof 7)*

Cf. George Sale, 'Preliminary Discourse', *The Koran*, 59, and compare 'To Miss E[lizabeth] P[igot]'. 'any fitness of things': cf. *Tom Jones*, IV, chap. 4.

494. An oriental simile, which may, perhaps, though fairly stolen, be deemed 'plus Arabe qu'en Arabie'. [B] Cf. *Vathek*, 309–10 (n. for p. 129).

496. Hyacinthine, in Arabic, 'Sunbul', as common a thought in the eastern poets as it was among the Greeks. [B] Cf. *Vathek*, 275–7 (n. for p. 98).

506. 'Franguestan', Circassia. [B]

528. *Parne*: Parnassus.

566. *Liakura*: Parnassus.

568. Bismallah—'In the name of God'; the commencement of all the chapters in the Koran but one, and of prayer and thanksgiving. [B] Cf. *Vathek*, 268 (n. for p. 95).

571. *Chiaus*: a Turkish messenger or, as here, a sergeant.

593. A phenomenon not uncommon with an angry Mussulman. In 1809, the Capitan Pacha's whiskers at a diplomatic audience were no less lively with indignation than a tiger cat's, to the horror of all the dragomans; the portentous mustachios twisted, they stood erect of their own accord, and were expected every moment to change their colour, but at last condescended to subside, which, probably, saved more heads than they contained hairs. [B]

603. 'Amaun', quarter, pardon. [B]
Added in 2nd edn. (Proof 9)

612. The 'evil eye', a common superstition in the Levant, and of which the imaginary effects are yet very singular on those who conceive themselves affected. [B] Cf. *Vathek*, 213 (n. to p. 1).

619. Echoes *Vathek*, 25.

620 ff. Ossianic: cf. 'Fingal', Book I or 'Temora', Book I.

666. The flowered shawls generally worn by persons of rank. [B]
Cf. *Vathek*, 259 (n. to p. 88).

690. Cf. Judges 5: 28.

shawls generally] shawls of Kashmeer, generally *M* and *1st–2nd edns*.

717. The 'Calpac' is the solid cap or centre part of the head-dress; the shawl is wound round it, and forms the turban. [B]

723. The turban—pillar—and inscriptive verse, decorate the tombs of the Osmanlies, whether in the cemetery or the wilderness. In the mountains you frequently pass similar mementos; and on enquiry you are informed that they record some victim of rebellion, plunder, or revenge. [B]

734. 'Alla Hu!' the concluding words of the Muezzin's call to prayer from the highest gallery on the exterior of the Minaret. On a still evening, when the Muezzin has a fine voice (which they frequently have) the effect is solemn and beautiful beyond all the bells in Christendom. [B] Cf. d'Herbelot, article 'Valid', and *CHP II*, st. 59.

735-6. Cf. Exodus 2: 22.

743. The following is part of a battle song of the Turks:—'I see—I see a dark-eyed girl of Paradise, and she waves a handkerchief, a kerchief of green; and cries aloud, Come, kiss me, for I love thee', &c. [B]

748. Monkir and Nekir are the inquisitors of the dead, before whom the corpse undergoes a slight noviciate and preparatory training for damnation. If the answers are none of the clearest, he is hauled up with a scythe and thumped down with a red hot mace till properly seasoned, with a variety of subsidiary probations. The office of these angels is no sinecure; there are but two; and the number of orthodox deceased being in a small proportion to the remainder, their hands are always full. [B] Cf. Sale's 'Preliminary Discourse', *op. cit.* 101, and *Vathek*, 313 (n. to p. 141).

750. Eblis, the Oriental Prince of Darkness. [B] Cf. *Vathek*, 323-4, 326-8 (nn. to pp. 183, 193). Lines 750-2 also recall the conclusion of *Vathek*, where the hearts of those doomed to the Halls of Eblis are shown to be consumed with fire.

753. Perhaps recalling 1 Corinthians 2: 9.

755. The Vampire superstition is still general in the Levant. Honest Tournefort tells a long story, which Mr. Southey, in the notes on *Thalaba*, quotes about these 'Vroucolochas', as he calls them. The Romaic term is 'Vardoulacha'. I recollect a whole family being terrified by the scream of a child, which they imagined must proceed from such a visitation. The Greeks never mention the word without horror. I find that 'Broucolokas' is an old legitimate Hellenic appellation—at least is so applied to Arsenius, who, according to the Greeks, was after his death animated by the Devil.—The moderns, however, use the word I mention. [B]
Cf. Joseph Pitton de Tournefort, *Relation d'un Voyage du Levant* (1717) I. 131, quoted in Southey's *Thalaba the Destroyer*, Book VIII, n. See also Bayle's *Dictionnaire*, 'Arsenius'. *Arsenius*: (*c.* 1530), Bishop of Monembasia.

781. The freshness of the face, and the wetness of the lip with blood, are the never-failing signs of a Vampire. The stories told in Hungary and Greece

term is 'Vardoulacha'. I recollect] term is 'Vardoulacha', which the worthy old traveller has thus transposed. I recollect *M and 1st–6th edns*.

of these foul feeders are singular, and some of them most *incredibly* attested. [B] Cf. Bayle, *op. cit.* and Augustine Calmet, *Dissertations sur les Apparitions* (1746), 395.

784. Cf. *Vathek*, 259, 304–5 (nn. for pp. 90, 124).

787. Cf. *CHP II*, st. 49. The narrative here is picked up by the fisherman, in converse with a monk of the community in which the Giaour has been staying for six years.

826–31. Cf. above, 655–8.

922–7. Cf. *BLJ* III. 141.

942. Cf. *Cain* I. 461–78.

951. The pelican is, I believe, the bird so libelled, by the imputation of feeding her chickens with her blood. [B] *Reads only* The Pelican *in MA15*

990–1. Cf. *Othello*, III. iii. 270 ff.

1011. Cf. 'To the Po', 48 (no. 333).

1048–9. Pope, *Essay on Criticism*, 625.

1057–8. Cf. Genesis 4: 15.

1077. This superstition of a second-hearing (for I never met with downright second-sight in the East) fell once under my own observation.—On my third journey to Cape Colonna early in 1811, as we passed through the defile that leads from the hamlet between Keratia and Colonna, I observed Dervish Tahiri riding rather out of the path, and leaning his head upon his hand, as if in pain.—I rode up and enquired. 'We are in peril,' he answered. 'What peril? we are not now in Albania, nor in the passes to Ephesus, Messalunghi, or Lepanto; there are plenty of us, well armed, and the Choriates have not courage to be thieves'—'True, Affendi, but nevertheless the shot is ringing in my ears.'—'The shot!—not a tophaike has been fired this morning.'—'I hear it notwithstanding—Bom—Bom—as plainly as I hear your voice.'—'Psha.'—'As you please, Affendi; if it is written, so will it be.' —I left this quickeared predestinarian, and rode up to Basili, his Christian compatriot; whose ears, though not at all prophetic, by no means relished the intelligence.—We all arrived at Colonna, remained some hours, and returned leisurely, saying a variety of brilliant things, in more languages than spoiled the building of Babel, upon the mistaken seer. Romaic, Arnaout, Turkish, Italian, and English were all exercised, in various conceits, upon the unfortunate Mussulman. While we were contemplating the beautiful prospect, Dervish was occupied about the columns.—I thought he was deranged into an antiquarian, and asked him if he had become a '*Palao-castro*' man: 'No.' said he, 'but these pillars will be useful in making a stand'; and added other remarks, which at least evinced his own belief in his troublesome faculty of *fore-hearing*.—On our return to Athens, we heard from Leoné (a prisoner set ashore some days after) of the intended attack of the Mainotes, mentioned, with the cause of its not taking place, in the notes to *Childe Harolde*, Canto 2d.—I was at some pains to question the man, and he described

the dresses, arms, and marks of the horses of our party so accurately, that
with other circumstances, we could not doubt of *his* having been in 'villainous
company', and ourselves in a bad neighbourhood.—Dervish became a sooth-
sayer for life, and I dare say is now hearing more musquetry than ever will
be fired, to the great refreshment of the Arnaouts of Berat, and his native
mountains.—I shall mention one trait more of this singular race.—In March
1811, a remarkably stout and active Arnaout came (I believe the 50th on
the same errand) to offer himself as an attendant, which was declined:
'Well, Affendi,' quoth he, 'may you live!—you would have found me useful.
I shall leave the town for the hills to-morrow; in the winter I return, perhaps
you will then receive me.'—Dervish, who was present, remarked as a thing
of course, and of no consequence, 'in the mean time he will join the Klephtes'
(robbers), which was true to the letter.—If not cut off, they come down in
the winter, and pass it unmolested in some town, where they are often as well
known as their exploits. [B]

> . . . not at all ⟨augurous⟩ prophetic . . . these pillars will ⟨serve to⟩ be
> useful in . . . where they are ⟨generally⟩ often as well known as their
> exploits *MA18*

> *Dervish Tahiri . . . Basili*: B's Albanian servants (see *BLJ* II. 262 and
> *Marchand*, I. 206, 210–11, 215, 270).
> *Canto 2d*: Cf. *CHP II*, st. 12 n.
> *villainous company*: *I Henry IV*, III. iii. 10.
> *Palao-castro*: modern Greek for 'old fortress'.

1127–30. Cf. the epigraph for 'Epitaph on a Friend' (no. 32), and Revela-
tion 2: 28.

1131–256. Cf. *BLJ* III. 100.

1131–3. Cf. Scott's *Lay of the Last Minstrel*, III. 2. 7 and v. 13. 4 and 15.

1207. The monk's sermon is omitted. It seems to have had so little effect
upon the patient, that it could have no hopes from the reader. It may be
sufficient to say, that it was of a customary length (as may be perceived
from the interruptions and uneasiness of the penitent), and was delivered in
the nasal tone of all orthodox preachers. [B]. Compare 1202–7 with *Manfred*
III. i. 52–159 *passim*.

1273. 'Symar'—Shroud. [B] Cymar is a loose robe worn by women. B's
note thus emphasizes the special funereal suggestions which his image was
meant to evoke.

1285–6. Echoes 432 above.

1298 ff. Cf. above, 826–31.

1318. Echoes Pope, 'Epistle to Mr. Murray', 70.

1334. The circumstance to which the above story relates was not very
uncommon in Turkey. A few years ago the wife of Muchtar Pacha complained
to his father of his son's supposed infidelity; he asked with whom, and she

had the barbarity to give in a list of the twelve handsomest women in Yanina. They were seized, fastened up in sacks, and drowned in the lake the same night! One of the guards who was present informed me, that not one of the victims uttered a cry, or shewed a symptom of terror at so sudden a 'wrench from all we know, from all we love'. The fate of Phrosine, the fairest of this sacrifice, is the subject of many a Romaic and Arnaut ditty. The story in the text is one told of a young Venetian many years ago, and now nearly forgotten.—I heard it by accident recited by one of the coffee-house story-tellers who abound in the Levant, and sing or recite their narratives.— The additions and interpolations by the translator will be easily distinguished from the rest by the want of Eastern imagery; and I regret that my memory has retained so few fragments of the original.

For the contents of some of the notes I am indebted partly to D'Herbelot, and partly to that most eastern, and, as Mr. Weber justly entitles it, 'sublime tale', the 'Caliph Vathek'. I do not know from what source the author of that singular volume may have drawn his materials; some of his incidents are to be found in the 'Bibliothèque Orientale'; but for correctness of costume, beauty of description, and power of imagination, it far surpasses all European imitations; and bears such marks of originality, that those who have visited the East will find some difficulty in believing it to be more than a translation. As an Eastern tale, even *Rasselas* must bow before it; his 'Happy Valley' will not bear a comparison with the 'Hall of Eblis'. [B]

   For the contents . . . the 'Caliph Vathek' *added in 2nd edn. The remainder of the note was added in the 4th edn.*
   wrench . . . love: unidentified.
   Weber: Henry Weber, *Tales of the East* (Edinburgh, 1812).
   Rasselas. Dr. Johnson's tale was published in 1759.
   B's revised (but never published) version of this note was more candid about the actual circumstances on which the poem was based: 'The circumstance related in the following letter I have kept back for reasons which will be sufficiently obvious—and ⟨had no other testimony than a⟩ indeed till no very long time ago I was not aware that the occurrence to which it alludes was obvious to the writer [i.e. Lord Sligo]—and when once aware of it—it will not perhaps appear unnatural that I should feel desirous to be informed of "the tale as it was told to him" on the spot and in a country where oral tradition is the only record—and where in a ⟨few years⟩ short time facts are either forgotten or distorted from the truth.—
   'Here print the letter [see commentary above]. As a picture of Turkish ethics and having in some degree a reference to the fiction of the foregoing poem—the perusal may not perhaps displease the reader—the writer of the letter was the only countryman of mine who arrived on the spot—for sometime after the event to [which] he alludes—he relates what he heard— it is not requisite for me to subjoin either assent or contradiction.' [*OA6*] B received Lord Sligo's letter in the summer of 1813. The revised note must

have been intended for one of the later editions, perhaps the fifth or seventh. See *Marchand*, I. 409–10 and n., and *Travels in Albania*, I. III n.

206. *MS.* B's draft, untitled, undated, watermark 1809 (location: *BM*). This is the MS. which C said was at Murray's, and from which C first printed the poem.

The date of the poem probably lies between the autumn of 1812 and the summer of 1813. C conjectures that it is addressed to B's future wife, Annabella Milbanke. This is possible, but Lady Adelaide Forbes (1789–1858) and Miss Mercer Elphinstone (1790–1867) are also possible candidates. See *Blessington*, 70, and *Paston and Quennell*, 188–201.

207. *MS. and Publishing History.* MS. not forthcoming. But C saw the MS., not in B's hand, of the variant version of this poem. First published, *Medwin* (1824), 214–15; first collected, *Paris 1828*; first collected in England, *1837*. The poem has to do with an incident involving Lady Caroline Lamb in late Jan. or Feb. 1813. B was refusing to see her after the breakup of their affair, but she was importunate. One day she visited his apartments when he was out, and 'finding "Vathek" on the table, she wrote in the first page, "Remember me!" Yes! I had cause to remember her; and, in the irritability of the moment, wrote under the two words these two stanzas' (*Medwin, loc. cit.*). Marchand (I. 458–9) dates the lines June 1814, but this is probably not correct, as the dating on the alternate version of the poem shows. An uncorrected proof of the Medwin text is at Leeds. *alternate version:* 'From a MS. (in the possession of Mr. Hallam Murray) not in Byron's handwriting' (*C*, III. 60).

title Echoes *Hamlet*, I. v. 91–7, III.

208. Unpublished. Draft MS., untitled, undated, watermark 1812 (location: Bodleian–Lovelace). The poem's subject is probably Lady Oxford, with whom B had a brief affair in 1812–13. The likely date of the lines is early 1813, when the liaison was drawing to an end. See *Medwin*, 70, where B refers to their relationship and his awareness of her inconsistency. But the poem could be another in the Susan Vaughan cycle. Lady Oxford was born Jane Elizabeth Scott. In 1794 she married Edward Harley, fifth Earl of Oxford and Mortimer. She was 40 when B met her in 1812. She had an independent mind, with strong (Whiggish) political views. See also *Blessington*, 149.

209. B wrote several versions of the poem which, by tradition, goes under this title. Three versions of the poem are printed here.

Version A. This version represents the first printed appearance of the poem. It was printed initially in *English Bards and Scotch Reviewers . . . etc. Suppressed*

Poems (Paris: Galignani, 1818), p. 79, where it was dated '1813' (see for bibliography *C* VII. 230). This version was subsequently printed in all Galignani editions of B, and Murray's first printing of the poem, in *1831*, followed this text, as do all subsequent printings of the poem under the heading 'Windsor Poetics'. No MS. for this version has appeared, though a copy by James Northcote in the Bodleian Library (MSS. Eng. Misc. e 143) approximates some of its special features.

Version B. This is the MS. poem which B sent in a letter to Lady Melbourne on 7 Apr. 1813. The MS. is in the Murray archives, a fair copy with one correction. This version is close to that of the copy made by Maj. Thomas Wildman, in his Commonplace Book now in the William Andrews Clark Library (Los Angeles) under the title 'Impromptu'.

Version C. This version was first printed in *C* (VII. 36) as 'Another Version' of 'Windsor Poetics' from a MS. then in the possession of the Hon. Mrs. Norbury. The MS. is now in the Berg Collection of the New York Public Library. It is essentially a variant of *Version B*. The MS. is B's fair copy, with one correction.

The discovery that Charles I was buried in the same vault with Henry VIII was made early in 1813. The Prince Regent superintended the opening of the coffin of Charles I on 1 Apr. (see *An Account of what appeared on opening the Coffin of King Charles the First*, by Sir Henry Halford (1813), pp. 6–7). In a letter to Moore of 12 Mar. 1814, B professed himself unable to 'conceive how the *Vault* [i.e. his poem] has got about; but so it is' (*LJ* III. 57–8 and n.). The fact is, however, that B encouraged the dissemination of the verses, as his letter to Lady Melbourne makes clear (see *BLJ* III. 38). Copies of the poem(s) exist in a number of places (an unrecorded one in an unknown hand is in the National Library of Scotland, MS. 683 f. 119). See for general comment Molly Tatchell, 'Byron's *Windsor Poetics*', *KSMB* XXV (1974), 1–5. Copies unnoticed by Tatchell (and not mentioned above) are at the Huntington (a second copy); Murray's (R.C. Dallas's copy in *EBSR5*); National Library of Scotland; Texas; University of Aberdeen Library; University Library, Cambridge.

8. (Versions B, C). Echoing *King Lear*, IV. vi. 109.

10. (Version C). πηλὸν αἵματι πεφυραμένον. [B's note at the end of the poem in the MS.] The phrase means 'mud kneaded with blood' and was used to characterize the emperor Tiberius by his teacher of rhetoric. See Suetonius, *The Lives of the Caesars*, Book III, 'Tiberius', LVII.

210. *MS.* Two fair copies by B (the earlier, *MS. B*, location: Berg; the later, *MS. M*, location: Murray). Two uncorrected proofs are also extant (locations: Murray and Huntington). First published *CHP(7)*, collected thereafter.

The poem is addressed to the Lady Charlotte Harley, daughter of Lady

Oxford (see 'To Ianthe' in *CHP I–II*). Probably written in Apr. 1813 (see *BLJ III.* 36, 42).

211. *MS. and Publishing History.* The verses are part of an epistle which B sent to Moore on 19 May 1813, but none of the MSS. of B's letters to Moore have appeared. First published, in present fragmentary form, *Life*, I. 401; collected *1831*, *1832*, and thereafter. Hunt was at the time serving a two-year prison sentence in Surrey Gaol for libelling the Prince Regent.

2. B refers to Moore's early volumes of poetry, which were published under several names.

4. *Intercepted Letters, or The Twopenny Post-Bag*, by Thomas Brown, the Younger (1813).

12. *Sotheby*. Compare *EBSR* 818, *Beppo*, st. 72, and *The Blues*, I. 149–50.

14. Lady Heathcote, born Catherine Sophia Manners. B sometimes went to her parties (see *BLJ III.* 252).

16. See Catullus, XXIX. 1–4.

212. *MS. and Publishing History. No MS.* The poem was sent in a letter to Moore dated conjecturally June 1813 (see *BLJ III.* 54–5). First published, in present expurgated form, in *Life*, I. 397; collected *1831*, *1832*, and thereafter. When B and Moore were dining with Rogers, the latter brought out a copy of Lord Thurlow's *Poems on Several Occasions* (1813). B opened it at 'On the Poem of Mr. Rogers, "An Epistle to a Friend" ', but when he tried to recite it, he could not get beyond the first line ('When Rogers o'er this labour bent') without bursting into laughter, which infected the company. A few days later he sent these verses in a letter to Moore.

title Edward Hovell (1781–1829), second Lord Thurlow (1806), published several volumes of poetry.

8. *Hermilda in Palestine* (1812), was reprinted by Lord Thurlow in *Poems on Several Occasions*.

213. *MS.* Not forthcoming. B sent these verses to Moore on the same day, and perhaps in the same letter, as '[On Lord Thurlow's Poems]'. First published, *Life*, I. 397, collected *1831*, *1832*, and thereafter. For commentary see '[On Lord Thurlow's Poems]'. This piece is another parodic thrust at Thurlow's poem on Rogers, this time taking off from the last three lines.

6. *Donne*. Thurlow was an advocate for Elizabethan verse (see his Preface to the second edition of *Poems on Various Occasions* (1813)).

15. Proverbial for labour in vain.

16. The owl was sacred to Athena, patroness of Athens (see Aristophanes, *The Birds*, 301.

17. Caroline of Brunswick (1768–1821), Princess of Wales, was separated from her husband in 1796. See below, '[George IV on Queen Caroline]' (no. 357).

18. Lord Liverpool (see no. 214, line 20).

20. B's first thrust at Lord Castlereagh, whom he despised (see no. 218, line 170). This line anticipates the point of the famous line in *DJ*, 'Dedication', st. 11: 'the intellectual eunuch Castlereagh'.

214. *MS.* B's draft (location: Bodleian-Lovelace) of these unpublished verses was written in the latter part of 1813, when Southey was given the laureateship after the death of Henry James Pye on 11 Aug. 1813. The MS. is torn at the end of lines 5–7, and the emendation in the rhyme word in line 7 is a pure guess. Lines 11–20 are not thus separated in the MS., but as it is plain that they represent four alternate endings for the poem (none cancelled), it seemed best to print them in this way. The piece is particularly interesting not so much because its subject anticipates *Don Juan* as because its form is so close to *ottava rima*. Indeed, the stanza only seems to lengthen the measure of *ottava rima* to ten (or twelve) lines.

1. *annual Malmsey barrel.* The laureate traditionally receives a butt of wine every year.

2. *Busby.* See 'Parenthetical Address' (no. 193).

4–6. One of Southey's early Jacobin poems was 'Inscription for the Apartment in Chepstow Castle, where Henry Marten, the Regicide, Was Imprisoned Thirty Years'. Southey's poem was parodied in the *Anti-Jacobin.*

7. *sapphic*: alluding to Southey's notorious poem, 'The Widow. Sapphics', which was also parodied in the *Anti-Jacobin*, and for which B expressed a particular distaste (*BLJ* III. 122)

20. *Jenky's*: Robert Banks Jenkinson, Lord Liverpool (1770–1828), Prime Minister from 1812 to 1828.

215. *MS.* From a letter to Lady Melbourne, 21 Sept. 1813 (location: Murray). Uncollected; first published *LBC* I. 182, again in *BLJ* III. 117.

216. *MS. and Publishing History.* B's corrected fair copy, dated 23 Sept. 1813, is in the Murray archives (*MS. M*), along with another fair copy, not in B's hand, which was used as copy text for the proof (*MS. Ma*). This proof is also in the Murray collection. Both MSS. and the proof carry the same date. First published, *CHP(7)*, collected thereafter. The poem was written to Lady Frances Wedderburn Webster while B was staying at the Websters' country house, but before his brief affair with her had begun (see no. 217). B sent the poem in a letter to Moore on 27 Sept. (see *BLJ* III. 123).

217. *MS. and Publishing History.* The Murray collection has two MSS.: B's rough draft, untitled, undated (*MS. Ma*); and his fair copy, titled 'Remember him etc' (*MS. Mb*). *MS. Ma* shows that B first wrote the poem as a unit that included the following lines, in this order: 1–20, 41–52, 21–8. B then added the poem's remaining lines, but he did not rearrange the material in *MS. Ma* (lines 29–40 were placed at the end of the poem in this version). *MS. Mb* added the numbered stanzas to the poem and arranged the lines in their received order. This MS. was printer's copy for the first proof. Three proofs of the poem are extant, all in the Murray collection: *Proof a*, pulled in Dec. 1813, containing six poems which would eventually appear in *Corsair*(*2*) or *CHP*(*7*); *Proof b*, pulled on 15 Jan. 1814, with poems originally intended for *Corsair*(*2*), though some appeared in *CHP*(*7*); and *Proof c*, pulled for *CHP*(*7*), in a bound volume of different proofs for *CHP*(*5*) and *CHP*(*7*). First published, *CHP*(*7*), collected thereafter.

The poem belongs to late Oct. 1813; it treats B's liaison with Lady Frances Wedderburn Webster, and is addressed to that lady. For B's own running commentary on the affair see *BLJ* III. 144–57 *passim*.

218. *MS. and Publishing History.* B's draft (*MS. L*, location: Bodleian–Lovelace), dated by B 8 Dec. 1813. *MS. L* contains: a cover leaf with the heading 'The Devil's Drive—Dec.ʳ 1813. B.'; a foolscap leaf, folded into four sides, with eight stanzas numbered consecutively, and an unnumbered stanza (lines 1–30, stanzas numbered 1–4; 91–114, stanzas numbered 5–8; 83–90, the unnumbered stanza); on a single leaf, four stanzas numbered 5–8 and an unnumbered stanza written across stanza numbered 6 (lines 31–43, stanza numbered 5; 64–76, stanza numbered 6; 77–82, unnumbered stanza; 44–63, stanzas numbered 7–8); on four sheets, stanzas numbered 15–26, with an extra stanza at end numbered 21 (this comprises lines 115–248, with the extra stanza numbered 21 containing 175–84). B's corrected copy from *MS. L*, dated 9 Dec. 1813 (*MS. H*, from the papers of Lord Holland, written at the beginning of a notebook; location, *BM*). *MS. H* has pencil excisions of certain stanzas made by Thomas Moore, who first printed portions of the unfinished poem in *Life*, I. 471–4 (stanzas 1–5, 8, 10–12, 17–18). *MS. H* ends with the number 28 heading for a new stanza. First printed complete in *C*, which generally follows *Life* for the stanzas first printed there, and *MS. H* for the omitted stanzas. Collected editions from *1831* until *C* print the *Life* text, which makes certain alterations in its copy text, *MS. H*; and *C* mistranscribes a few readings in the new stanzas first published in *C*.

MS. H shows that B never in fact completed this poem, which he called 'a wild, unfinished rhapsody. . .the notion of which I took from [Richard] Porson's "Devil's Walk" ' (*BLJ* III. 240). B's model was actually the joint composition of Southey and Coleridge and was published in *Morning Post*, 6 Sept. 1799 as 'The Devil's Thoughts'. Southey later expanded the poem and published it as *The Devil's Walk*, and it was widely supposed to be the work of Professor Porson.

The reader should consult the subsequent commentaries for *Siege* and *Manfred* since portions of both of those poems are nearly related to 'The Devil's Drive'. All three show the influence of certain parts of Goethes'

Faust which Mme de Staël made available to B in her *De L'Allemagne* (published by Murray in 1813).

20. According to C, Lord Yarmouth, 'the eldest son of the Regent's elderly favourite, the Marchioness of Hertford . . . lived at No. 7, Seamore Place'. See also Thomas Moore's 'Epigram' ('I want the Court-Guide'), and *Waltz*, 142 and n.

30. C suggests a reference to the Bishop of Winchester, who owned property at the entrance to Portsmouth Harbour, and who was involved in litigation about the property with the Attorney-General (see C VII. 22 n.)

33, 48. The battle of Leipzig (16 Oct. 1813), where the Russian and Austrian troops were largely composed of veterans while the Prussians brought a large body of 'Landwehr', i.e. militia.

47. i.e. W. J. Fitzgerald (see *EBSR* 1).

55–63. See *Morning Chronicle*, 8 Nov. 1813, where the incident is reported in 'Paris Papers, October 30'. A bridge was blown up prematurely so that a contingent of Russian troops were trapped as they were trying to retreat. Prince Poniatowsky was among them, and was drowned when he attempted to cross the river on horseback. The Prince was reported as mounted 'on a spirited horse'.

82. See *DJ* VIII, st. 132.

96. *barouche*: a four-wheeled carriage with a seat for a driver and space for two couples, facing each other.

115–22. Sir Thomas Tyrwhitt (*c.* 1762–1833), Private Secretary to the Prince of Wales. In 1813 he was sent by the Regent to the Czar in charge of the Garter mission. See also Moore's *Twopenny Post-Bag* (1813), 'From G. R. to the E. of Y——th' (p. 12).

125. *Vetus*. Edward Sterling's letters to *The Times* of 1812, 1813 were published separately in 1813 and reviewed (unfavourably) in the *Morning Chronicle* in Dec. 1813. The letters were aggressively patriotic and urged a policy of 'defensive' conquest.

141–9. *Lord Liverpool*: the Prime Minister, Robert Banks Jenkinson (see no. 214, line 20); *Lord Westmoreland*: the Lord Privy Seal, John Fane, tenth Earl of Westmoreland (1759–1841); *Norfolk*: Charles Howard (1746–1815), eleventh Duke of Norfolk, known as 'Jockey of Norfolk'; *Chatham*: John Pitt (1756–1835), second Earl of Chatham and the son of William Pitt, whom he was said to resemble; *Eldon*: John Scott, Earl of Eldon (see no. 182); *Chief Justice*: Edward Law (1750–1818), first Baron Ellenborough, Lord Chief Justice of the King's Bench, who was known for his strong language.

163, 166. George Canning (1770–1827), Samuel Whitbread (1758–1815), Sir Philip Francis (1740–1818).

170. *Lord Castlereagh*: Robert Stewart, second Marquis of Londonderry, Viscount Castlereagh (1769–1822). See no. 213, line 20.

175–6. George Rose (1744–1818), Treasurer of the Navy, who had a reputation for duplicity.

185–92. Ernest Augustus (1771–1851), Duke of Cumberland and King of Hanover, gazetted as Field-Marshall 27 Nov. 1813. His 'wounds' were those received in his encounter with his valet Joseph Sellis, who tried to assassinate the Prince on 1 June 1810. When Sellis was found dead with his throat cut and a jury brought in a verdict of suicide, there was a great scandal, but the Duke was later exonerated.

193. A dress ball was held at Carlton House on 8 Dec. 1813 at which Mme de Staël was present (see the report in the *Morning Chronicle*, 10 Dec. 1813). Anne Louise Germaine Necker (1766–1817), married (1786) the Baron de Staël Holstein, who died in 1802. Her opposition to Napoleon caused her exile from France. Her chief work, *De l'Allemagne* (1811), was (and is) a signal document in the history of Romanticism. She came to England in June 1813, when Murray brought out an English edition of *De l'Allemagne*. For further details see *BLJ* III. 272–3.

202–4. Sir James Mackintosh reviewed Mme de Stael's *De l'Allemagne* in the *Edinburgh Review* (Oct. 1813, pp. 198–238) and praised Kant effusively.

218. See *Waltz*, and comment.

226. See the 'Address, Spoken at the Opening of Drury-lane Theatre' (no. 190).

229. *Illusion, or the Trances of Nourjahad*, by Mrs. Frances Sheridan (1724–66), opened at Drury Lane on 25 Nov. 1813. B saw it on the 27th (see *BLJ* III. 226).

231–2. Mrs. Sheridan's play was attributed to B, much to his annoyance (see *BLJ* III. 175).

235–6. Job 31: 35.

219. *MS. and Publishing History.* B's rough draft, undated, is in Bodleian–Lovelace (*MS. L*); his corrected fair copy (*MS. M*) is in the Murray archives, which also has two proofs: one pulled late in Dec. 1813 which contained five other poems to be published either in *Corsair*(2) or *CHP*(7); another among the proofs for *Corsair*(2) dated 15 Jan. 1814 (for December proof see *BLJ* III. 201). First published *Corsair*(2), removed from *Corsair*(3), restored in *Corsair*(4), and collected thereafter.

The subject of the poem is Lady Frances Wedderburn Webster. For B's strongly negative comments on the sonnet form, and the pain of his effort to write in it, see *BLJ* III. 240, where the date of his two sonnets to Genevra is also established: 17–18 Dec. 1813. The title is a sly allusion to B's relationship with Lady Frances: Genevra is the Italian form of Guenevere. The name is taken from Ariosto's *Orlando Furioso*, and B seems to be recalling specifically the incidents narrated in Cantos V–VII.

12. Guido Reni (1575–1642); the painting is in the National Gallery.

220. *MS. and Publishing History.* See previous 'Sonnet. To Genevra': the information is identical for both sonnets.

6–7. The Lovelace MS. is a mass of largely irrecoverable corrections in which it is apparent that B was having trouble changing the original rhymes of *thine–mine* to the final *gush–rush*.

221. *MS. and Publishing History.* B's draft, untitled, undated (*MS. BM*, location: *BM*); B's corrected fair copy (*MS. M*, location: Murray), undated. *MS. M* was printer's copy for *CHP(7)*; the correction at line 9 must have been made later. Proofs: Huntington Library, with corrections of accidentals, for *CHP(7)*; Murray, uncorrected, for *CHP(10)* and *1815*. First published: *CHP(7)*, collected thereafter. The subject of the poem is Lady Frances Wedderburn Webster (see esp. B's letters to Lady Melbourne, 22 and 25 Nov. 1813 (*BLJ* III. 170–5). B sent the poem to Murray in December (*BLJ* III. 186–7).

222. *MS. and Publishing History.* B's first fair copy (*MS. M*, location: Murray), undated, which was printer's copy for the two corrected proofs (also at Murray). The first proof (*Proof a*) is on two separate sheets containing the six poems published in *Corsair(2)*. They are arranged differently than the ordering in *Corsair(2)*. The second, later proof (*Proof b*) is part of the proofs for the poem's original publication in *Corsair(2)*. This proof is headed by Murray 15 Jan. 1814. A second fair copy of the poem in B's hand is in the Morgan Library (*MS. ML*). Augusta Leigh has placed the following date on the back of the MS.: Newark, 19 July 1814. This MS. also carries the following note in another hand: 'Written from memory by Lord Byron given to his sister on their road to Newstead Abbey.' First published *Corsair(2)*, removed from *Corsair(3)*, replaced in *Corsair(4)*; collected thereafter.

The subject of this poem is not easy to decide upon, for at the time he wrote it B was acutely conscious of, and troubled by, his relations with both Lady Frances Wedderburn Webster and his sister Augusta (see *Marchand*, I. 410–30). The principal focus of the poem is probably Lady Frances. The date on the back of the Morgan MS., and the attached note, refer to the trip B and Augusta took to Newstead on 20 July 1814 (see *Marchand*, I. 469). The poem was written very late in 1813, probably in December.

223. *MS. and Proofs.* With three exceptions, noted below, all the extant MSS. and proofs of the *Bride* are in the Murray archive. The MSS. are bound together in a single volume, but they make up three distinct MS. groups: (*a*) B's first draft (*MS. A*), dated at the beginning 1 Nov. 1813; the dates 4 Nov. and 8 Nov. are placed by B at the end of the first and second cantos respectively. *MS. A* contains: Canto I. 20–43, 47–141, 144–69, 182–232, 234–331, 340–3, 343a–b, 344–66, 369–417, 439–82 (total: 415 lines); Canto II. 1–11, 14–42, 57–66, 72–111, 114–25, 127–267, 270–314, 321–40, 343–97, 468–528, 533–63, 565, 569–82, 621–5, 628–40, 651–8 (total: 496 lines).

(*b*) B's fair copy (*MS. B*), from which the poem was printed, dated at the beginning by Murray 11 Nov. 1813 and at the end by B 8 Nov. 1813. The following lines were added in *MS. B*: Canto I. 1–8, 11–17, 142–3, 367–8, 418–38 (40 additional lines: total, 455 lines); Canto II. 12–13, 43–56, 126, 268–9, 315–20, 529–30, 626–7 (29 additional lines: total, 525). (*c*) A large group of separate MS. leaves containing various corrections and additions made while the poem was passing through proof (*MSS. X*). Group *X* includes: *1.* Rough draft, I. 1–17. *2.* Corrected fair copy, I. 170–81, dated by Murray 13 Nov. and headed by *B*: 'Lines to be inserted page 9—stanza 6th after "but not of grief"—a separate paragraph but not a new stanza.' *3.* Rough draft, I. 425–8. *4.* Rough draft, II. 44–53. *5.* Rough draft, II. 67–71. *5a.* Corrected fair copy, II. 67–71, headed by B: 'Continue from fourth line of paragraph 5th (I think) in Canto II from these lines [B quotes II. 65–6].' *6.* Rough draft, II. 317–20. *7.* Corrected fair copy, II. 398–401, 408–11, headed by B: 'Insert page 45—an additional insertion in the passage Canto 2nd after the line [B quotes II. 397].' *8.* Fair copy, II. 404–7, dated by Murray 3 Dec. 1813 and headed by B: 'Bride of Abydos page 45 line 400 after [B quotes II. 401].' Another note by Murray at the bottom shows the MS. was received while *Bride1* was in course of printing. *8a.* Fair copy, II. 402–7, with note by Murray: '12 of each Dec. 3 1813'; headed by B 'Correction Bride of Abydos page 45 Canto II line 400. After [B quotes II. 401] read [B gives correction]' and with his note: 'If this (as doubtless it is) be too late for cancel at any rate it can be printed in your E[rrat]a column.' *8b.* Corrected fair copy, II. 402–7, headed by B: 'Last alteration of the lines on p. 45 C[ant]o 2nd after [B quotes II. 401]', and with his note: 'Let this go early—and be done as soon as possible.' *9.* Rough draft, II. 408–11, 450, on verso of *X3* above. *9a.* Rough draft, II. 408–29, 444–6, 448. *10.* Corrected fair copy, II. 408–29, 444–53, 464–7, headed by B: 'The Dove of peace and promise to mine ark—continue from.' *10a.* Corrected fair copy, II. 408–29, 434–7, 444– 53, 464–7, headed by B: 'Continue from [B quotes II. 397] in Canto 2nd by these lines.' *11.* Rough draft, II. 438–43, 454–5, 458–63. *12.* Three cancelled and one uncancelled rough draft of II. 563–8. *12a.* Fair copy, II. 563–8, headed by B: 'Insert the following lines after [B quotes II. 562]'; and a correction for II. 732. *13.* Rough draft, II. 583–620. *13a.* Corrected fair copy, II. 583–620, headed by B: 'Last paragraph but one of Canto 2nd'. *14.* Rough draft, II. 641–4. *14a.* Rough draft, II. 641–50. *14b.* Corrected fair copy, II. 641–50, headed by B: 'Continue after line 558th p. 55.' *15.* Fair copy, II. 651–61, on verso of *X 14a* above. *16.* Rough draft, II. 664–6, 669–86, 688–718, 729–32. *16a.* Corrected fair copy, II. 664–86, 688–718, 729–32 headed by B: 'Conclusion—Last Paragraph Canto 2nd'. *17.* Fair copy, II. 719–24, headed by B: 'Near the Conclusion insert these lines after [B quotes II. 718]', and with his note: 'By casting his eye over the MSS. the printer will see where these lines come in. To be sent immediately.'

Other MSS. include the following fragments (*MSS. D*): *1.* Correction for

1. 180, 398, and II. 66 n. (in letters to Murray: see *BLJ* III. 169, 192). *2.* Correction for II. 400–1, 402–3 (in letters to Murray: see *BLJ* III. 163–4, 190–1). *3.* II. 404–7 (written by B into a copy of *Bride1a* at Murray's). *3a.* II. 402–7 (written by B into John Galt's copy of *Bride1a*: location, Albe Library, on deposit in the University of Pennsylvania Library). *4.* Correction for II. 406–7 (in a letter to Murray, *BLJ* III. 177: location, Pforzheimer). *5.* II. 431 (in a letter to Murray, *BLJ* III. 173). *6.* II. 456–7 (two versions sent in separate letters to Murray: *BLJ* III. 183). *7.* II. 591–2 (in a letter to Murray: *BLJ* III. 156).

An extensive set of proof material is also extant. In the description below, the numbers to the left of the solidus are those provided in the proof itself; MS. numeration changes on the proof are given in parentheses. To the right of the solidus are the actual number of lines in the proof text; the actual number of printed lines is given first, and the actual number of lines including MS. additions made on the proof is placed next in parentheses.

1. Uncorrected incomplete proof dated by Murray 12 Nov. 1813 and marked as 'First Proof'. Canto I, 454/455. Canto II, 599/641. The proof breaks off at received line II. 695. pp. [1]–56.

1a. Corrected incomplete proof, undated. This is a portion of another copy of *Proof 1* and contains Canto II, 149–630 (i.e. the first proof version of received lines II. 151–732). pp. 33–58. Proofs *1* and *1a* together show the make-up of the first proof, which contained: Canto I, 454/455; Canto II, 630/674. The first proof augmented *MS. B* with the following additions: II. 67–71, 341–2, 408–29, 434–7, 444–53, 464–7, 583–620, 664–86, 688–724, 729–32 (total: 149 additional lines). In addition, *Proof 1a* adds the following lines in MS.: II. 398–401, 659–61, 725–8.

2. Uncorrected proof. Canto I, 454/456; Canto II, 630/687. pp. [1]–59 text, [60]–70 notes. Adds II. 641–50, 659–61.

3. Corrected proof dated by Murray 13 Nov. and marked as 'First Revise'. With title-page, epigraph, and Dedication. Canto I, 462/460 (463); Canto II, 706/696. pp. [1]–59 text, [58]–61 notes. Added in print: I. 18–19, 44–6; II. 398–401, 641–50, 659–61, 687, 725–8. Added in MS.: I. 9–10, 233.

4. Corrected proof dated by Murray 15 Nov. Canto I, 462/463; Canto II, 706/696(698). pp.[1]–59 text, [58]–61 notes. Added in MS.: II. 112–13. There is also an uncorrected copy of this proof marked by Murray as 'Second Revise' and dated 15 Nov.

5. Corrected proof dated by Murray 16 Nov. Canto I, 462/463; Canto II, 708(710)/698(700). pp. [1]–59 text, [60]–71 notes. Added in MS.: II. 566–7. There is also an uncorrected copy of this proof.

6. Corrected proof dated by Murray 18 Nov. Canto I, 462(472)/463(472); Canto II, 700(705)/702(704). Pagination as *Proof 4*. Added in print: II. 564, 568. Added in MS.: I. 332–9; II. 531–2.

7. Corrected proof dated by Murray 19 Nov. Canto I, 473(483)/472(482); Canto II, 705/704. Pagination as *Proof 4*. Added in MS.: I. 170–81; and I. 343a-b are cancelled in MS.

7a. Two uncorrected proofs, one dated by Murray 24 Nov. Canto I, 483/482; Canto II, 705/704. pp. [1]–59 text, [60]–64 notes. These proofs incorporate the corrections from *Proof 7*. Another copy of this proof, with identical pagination, has slightly altered line numbering (Canto II, 706/704).

8. Corrected proof fragment of pp. 45–6 containing early version of II. 396–465 (here numbered 397–439), with the following MS. additions: 430–3, 438–43, 454–5, 458–61. Location: Bodleian–Lovelace.

9. Uncorrected proof. Canto I, 483/482; Canto II, 720/720. Incomplete, with only pp. 17–60 text, 61–72 notes. Incorporating additions from *Proof 8*.

10. Corrected proof. Canto I, 483/482; Canto II, 722/722. pp. [1]–60 text, 61–72 notes. Added in print: II. 462–3. Dated by B 23 Nov.

10a. Corrected proof. Canto I, 483/482; Canto II, 722/722. Pagination as *Proof 10* and incorporating *Proof 10* corrections. Dated by B 21 Nov.

11. Corrected proof dated by Murray 25 Nov. Contents and pagination as *Proof 10*.

11a. Uncorrected proof incorporating *Proof 11* corrections. Contents and pagination as *Proof 11*.

Some of the proofs are bound up together. These are: *3*, *5*, *6*, *7*, *1a*, *7a* (dated copy), *10*, *10a*; *7a* (third copy), *9*; *11a*, *5* (uncorrected copy), *2*; *7a* (undated copy), *1*.

Composition and Publication. The dates on *MSS. A* and *B* indicate that B began the poem on 1 Nov. 1813 and finished the first draft on 8 Nov., and the fair copy on 11 Nov. He must have sent it to Murray immediately (see *BLJ* III. 161). After a favourable reading by Gifford, *Bride* was quickly set up in type, on 12 Nov., when B began correcting the first of an extensive set of proofs (see *BLJ* III. 162). Between 12 and 27 Nov. B corrected and augmented the poem. Murray began printing the first edition (*Bride1*) on 28 or 29 Nov., but B had a number of last-minute corrections and additions. An errata slip was inserted in *Bride1* with some of these alterations (see *N & Q* (1909), 405, 518 and *Wise*, I. 86). Two new lines (II. 456–7) first appeared in the second issue of the first edition (*Bride1a*). B wrote these two lines in manuscript in a copy of *Bride1* (location: Berg), and another autograph MS. of the lines is found on a scrap of paper inserted in Vol. I of an *1856* edition of B's *Poetical Works* (location: Meyer Davis Collection, Univ of Pennsylvania Library). Six other lines were added in the third edition (*Bride3*: II. 402–7), and two more were added in the fourth edition (*Bride4*: II. 662–3). Several corrections were also made in these editions. The poem was announced as published on 29 Nov., but B said it appeared on 2 Dec. (see *C* III. 151 and

BLJ III. 230). B is probably correct; Murray must have held up distribution while the late corrections were being made. The first five editions carry an 1813 date; editions six to ten were published in 1814, and an eleventh edition appeared in 1815. The poem was reset in the tenth edition. Editions 1–6 made up a total of 12,500 copies.

The most complex set of additions and corrections (II. 398–467) requires some explanation. B began this addition with *X9* (where line 450 was intended originally to follow 411). *X9a* then continued the *X9* addition, at which point B composed the first fair copy of the addition, *X10*, where *X9* and *X9a* were significantly revised. B then made the corrected fair copy *X10a* and sent this to Murray for printing (*X10a* was copy text for *Proof 1*). When B received *Proof 1a* he added 398–401 to the passage, and in *Proof 3* he made a number of further revisions. He then composed *X11*, and when he received *Proof 8* he added the *X11* material (438–43, 454–5, 458–63) to the proof, along with the final addition to the passage (430–3). Lines 402–7 were one of the late November additions and first appeared in *Bride3*.

For further bibliographical details see: *C* III. 149–53, 211–13, VII. 172–6; *Wise*, I. 85–92.

Literary and Historical Background. The impetus that set B writing *Bride* was his recollections of his love for Augusta, on the one hand, and of his more recent 'platonic' affair with Lady Frances Wedderburn Webster on the other (see *BLJ* III. 157, 205 and *Marchand*, I. 418–24). The poem was written 'to dispel reflection during *inaction*', and B emphasized on several occasions that he had some personal acquaintance with the incidents of the poem (see *BLJ*, *loc. cit.* and 195–6, 199). This has led to the idea that B actually witnessed certain events in the Levant which more or less correspond to the narrative of *Bride* (*C* III. 150). The supposition may be true, but B never said precisely this, nor has any other evidence shown it to be so. But B did say (in a discreet Latin quotation) that the poem dealt with matters 'quaeque ipse . . . vidi et quorum pars magna fui' (*BLJ* III. 205).

What B knew from personal experience was the Eastern culture which lent verisimilitude to the plot of *Bride*, a number of specific incidents and scenes, and much local colouring. All this he had at first hand. In addition, he himself 'saw and was a part of' two personal liaisons which strongly affected *Bride*. His relations with Lady Frances entered *Bride* in the poem's specific allusion (insisted upon in the notes) to the story of Potiphar's wife, which in Turkish literature formed the story of the love of Zuleika and Mejnoun. Secondly, B 'wrung [his] thoughts from reality to imagination' (*BLJ* III. 230) by treating his own love for Augusta under the guise of his tale. When he began the poem he intended to represent Selim and Zuleika as brother and sister, but 'the times and the *North* . . . induced me to alter their consanguinity and confine them to cousinship' (*BLJ* III. 199). B said he made this change while composing the poem.

Of possible literary influences B himself said that 'the finest works of the Greeks, one of Schiller's [*The Bride of Messina*] and Alfieri's [*Mirra*] in modern times, besides several of our *old* (and best) dramatists [like Ford], have been grounded on incidents of a similar cast' (*ibid.* 196). But none of these provided an actual model for his own treatment; B cited them merely as authorities for justifying the incest-theme. For specific local influences see the notes below. *Gleckner* (134–8) sees parallels with *Hamlet*. Beckford's *Vathek*, so important for *Giaour*, seems an influence on *Bride* as well: the general relations between Caliph Vathek, Nouronihar, and Gulchenrouz resemble those in the *Bride* in certain respects. For further details of local colour see also *Giaour*, comment and notes; in *Bride* B resorted to many of the same authorities.

epigraph   'Song. Ae Fond Kiss', 13–16.

Canto I

1 ff. Echoing Goethe's 'Kennst du das Land wo die citronen blühn', which B knew through Mme de Staël's French redaction in *Corinne* (1807), Book 1, chap. 4.

8. 'Gúl', the rose. [B, added in *MS. B*]

17.   'Souls made of fire, and children of the Sun,
                  With whom Revenge is Virtue.'
Young's *Revenge*. [B, added in *MS. B*] See *The Revenge*, v. ii.

72. Mejnoun and Leila, the Romeo and Juliet of the East. Sadi, the moral poet of Persia. [B, added in *MS. B*] See tale XIX in Sadi's *Gulistan*, an ethical miscellany in rhymed prose.

73. Tambour, Turkish drum, which sounds at sunrise, noon, and twilight. [B, added in *MS. B*]

144. The Turks abhor the Arabs (who return the compliment a hundred fold) even more than they hate the Christians. [B]

179. This expression has met with objections. I will not refer to 'Him who hath not Music in his soul', but merely request the reader to recollect, for ten seconds, the features of the woman whom he believes to be the most beautiful; and if he then does not comprehend fully what is feebly expressed in the above line, I shall be sorry for us both. For an eloquent passage in the latest work of the first female writer of this, perhaps, of any age, on the analogy (and the immediate comparison excited by that analogy) between 'painting and music', see vol. iii. cap. 10. DE L'ALLEMAGNE [1813]. And is not this connexion still stronger with the original than the copy? With the colouring of Nature than of Art? After all, this is rather to be felt than described; still I think there are some who will understand it, at least they would have done had they beheld the countenance whose speaking harmony suggested the idea; for this passage is not drawn from imagination but

for this passage . . . multiplied] ⟨In this line I have not drawn from fiction but memory—that mirror of regret memory—the too faithful mirror of affliction the long vista through which memory, that mirror which Affliction dashes to the earth, and looking down upon the fragments, only beholds the reflection multiplied! [B, note not in MS.]

For the broken mirror simile see *CHP II*, st. 33; for the compliment to Mme de Staël see *BLJ III*. 235, B's Journal entry for 7 Dec.

    frozen music. The phrase is Goethe's, 'eine estarrte musik' (see *BLJ III*. 211.)

    201. Carasman Oglou, or Kara Osman Oglou, is the principal land-holder in Turkey, he governs Magnesia; those, who by a kind of feudal tenure, possess land on condition of service, are called Timariots: they serve as Spahis, according to the extent of territory, and bring a certain number into the field, generally cavalry. [B, added in *MS. B*] The 'line of Carasman' was founded in the late fourteenth century. In line 206, Bey Oglou means 'noble-man' or 'chief'.

    213. When a Pacha is sufficiently strong to resist, the single messenger, who is always the first bearer of the order for his death, is strangled instead, and sometimes five or six, one after the other, on the same errand, by command of the refractory patient; if, on the contrary, he is weak or loyal, he bows, kisses the Sultan's respectable signature, and is bowstrung with great complacency. In 1810, several of these presents were exhibited in the niche of the Seraglio gate; among others, the head of the Pacha of Bagdat, a brave young man, cut off by treachery, after a desperate resistance. [B, added in *MS. B*]

    ... order for his death ⟨returns with his head⟩ is strangled ... *MS. B*

    232. Clapping of the hands calls the servants. The Turks hate a super-fluous expenditure of voice, and they have no bells. [B, added in *MS. B*]

    233. Chibouque, the Turkish pipe, of which the amber mouthpiece, and sometimes the ball which contains the leaf, is adorned with precious stones, if in possession of the wealthier orders. [B]

    235. Maugrabee, Moorish mercenaries. [B, added in *MS. B*]

    236. Deli, bravos who form the forlorn hope of the cavalry, and always begin the action. [B, added in *MS. B*] See *CHP II*, 'Suliote Song', st. 10.

    forlorn hope: cf. *Siege*, 236.

    237–8. See Jonathan Scott, *The Arabian Nights Entertainments* ... (1811), I, 'Introduction', xviii–xix.

    239. *Kislar*. The Kizlar aghasi was the head of the harem eunuchs.

    248. A twisted fold of *felt* is used for scimitar practice by the Turks, and few but Mussulman arms can cut through it at a single stroke: sometimes a tough turban is used for the same purpose. The jerreed is a game of blunt javelins, animated and graceful. [B]

---

we gaze. Someone has said that the perfection of Architecture is frozen music—the perfection of Beauty to my mind always presented the idea of living Music.⟩ *var. recorded in C, but not in extant MSS.*   sometimes ... graceful.] *added in MS. B*   sometimes ... graceful —⟨in the notes to the Giaour it is attempted to be described.⟩ *MS. B*

251. 'Ollahs', Alla il Allah, the 'Leilies', as the Spanish poets call them, the sound is Ollah; a cry of which the Turks, for a silent people, are somewhat profuse, particularly during the jerreed, or in the chase, but mostly in battle. Their animation in the field, and gravity in the chamber, with their pipes and comboloios, form an amusing contrast. [B, added in *MS. B*]

270. 'Atar-gul', ottar of roses. The persian is the finest. [B, added in *MS. B*]

272. The ceiling and wainscots, or rather walls, of the Mussulman apartments are generally Painted, in great houses, with one eternal and highly coloured view of Constantinople, wherein the principal feature is a noble contempt of perspective; below, arms, scimitars, &c. are in general fancifully and not inelegantly disposed. [B, added in *MS. B*]

288. It has been much doubted whether the notes of this 'Lover of the rose' are sad or merry; and Mr. Fox's remarks on the subject have provoked some learned controversy as to the opinions of the ancients on the subject. I dare not venture a conjecture on the point, though a little inclined to the 'errare mallem', &c. *if* Mr. Fox *was* mistaken. [B. In *MS. A* the note is simply: 'The Nightingale'.] *Fox*: see no. 36. For the 'controversy' see Martin Davy, *Observations upon Mr. Fox's Letter to Mr. Grey* (1809).

317 ff. Cf. Horace, *Odes* 2. 17. 5–12.

323. 'Azrael'—the angel of death. [B]

358. The treasures of the Preadamite Sultans. See D'HERBELOT, article *Istakar*. [B, added in *MS. B*] In d'Herbelot the article is 'Estekhar *ou* Istekhar'.

374. Musselim, a governor, the next in rank after a Pacha; a Waywode is the third; and then come the Agas. [B]

the next . . . Agas.] *added in MS. B*

375. Egripo—the Negropont. According to the proverb, the Turks of Egripo, the Jews of Salonica, and the Greeks of Athens, are the worst of their respective races. [B]

Egripo—the Negropont.] *added in MS. B*

See Gibbon's *Decline and Fall*, chap. 62. Negropont is the modern Euboea.

381. Echoes Schiller's *Die Braut von Messina*, line 1817 (Act III, scene iii).

449. 'Tchocadar'—one of the attendants who precedes a man of authority. [B, added in *MS. B*]

Canto II

17. See Ovid, *Heroides*, XIX.

30. See 'Written After Swimming from Sestos to Abydos', no. 142.

36. The wrangling about this epithet, 'the broad Hellespont' or the 'boundless Hellespont', whether it means one or the other, or what it means at all, has been beyond all possibility of detail. I have even heard it disputed on the spot; and not foreseeing a speedy conclusion to the controversy, amused myself with swimming across it in the mean time, and probably may again, before the point is settled. Indeed, the question as to the truth of

generally] ⟨always⟩ *MS. B*   feature] ⟨thing⟩ *MS. B*

'the tale of Troy divine' still continues, much of it resting upon the talismanic word '*ακειρος*': probably Homer had the same notion of distance that a coquette has of time, and when he talks of boundless, means half a mile; as the latter, by a like figure, when she says *eternal* attachment, simply specifies three weeks. [B]

 it . . . spot] the dispute carried on oer the spot *MS. B*

 Hobhouse describes the issues in detail: see his *Travels in Albania*, II. 179–85. In *MS. A* the note is: 'The wrangling about this epithet—and whether it means broad or what it means is beyond my time to detail and ?.'

 44–5. Achilles, slain by the arrow of Paris; his tomb was supposed to be on Mount Ida.

 47. Before his Persian invasion, and crowned the altar with laurel, &c. He was afterwards imitated by Caracalla in his race. It is believed that the last also poisoned a friend, named Festus, for the sake of new Patroclan games. I have seen the sheep feeding on the tombs of Aesietes and Antilochus; the first is in the centre of the plain. [B] Alexander was pronounced the son of the god Ammon in 331 B.C. For the ceremony alluded to in the text see Plutarch's *Lives*, 'Alexander', chap. 25. Caracalla (188–217), Emperor of Rome (211–17): for B's details here see Gibbon, *Decline and Fall*, chap. 6, and esp. Herodian, III. iv *passim*.

 Aesietes and Antilochus: the tombs are discussed in Hobhouse's *Travels in Albania*, II. 149–51.

 66. When rubbed, the amber is susceptible of a perfume, which is slight but not disagreeable. [B, added in *MS. B*]

 69. The belief in amulets engraved on gems, or enclosed in gold boxes, containing scraps from the Koran, worn round the neck, wrist, or arm, is still universal in the East. The Koorsee (throne) verse in the second cap. of the Koran describes the attributes of the Most High, and is engraved in this manner, and worn by the pious, as the most esteemed and sublime of all sentences. [B]

 The Koorsee . . . sentences. *added in MS. X5a*

 72. 'Comboloio'—a Turkish rosary. The MSS. particularly those of the Persians, are richly adorned and illuminated. The Greek females are kept in utter ignorance; but many of the Turkish girls are highly accomplished, though not actually qualified for a Christian coterie; perhaps some of our own '*blues*' might not be the worse for *bleaching*. [B. In *MS. A* the note reads: 'Comboloio—a Turkish rosary—⟨but whether for prayer or ? or religion I cannot be certain.']

 75. Cf. Ephesians 5: 16.

 81. Shiraz' attar of roses, for which it is famous.

 106–7. See *Giaour*, 490 and n.

 142. *Candiote*: i.e. a native of Candia, the capital of Crete. B probably means a Cretan.

150. 'Galiongée'—or Galiongi, a sailor, that is, a *Turkish* sailor; the Greeks navigate, the Turks work the guns. Their dress is picturesque; and I have seen the Capitan Pacha more than once wearing it as a kind of *incog*. Their legs, however, are generally naked. The buskins described in the text as sheathed behind with silver, are those of an Arnaut robber, who was my host (he had quitted the profession) at his Pyrgo, near Gastouni in the Morea; they were plated in scales one over the other, like the back of an armadillo. [B]

The buskins . . . armadillo. *not in MS. A*

his Pyrgo, near Gastouni: Gastuni lies about eight miles SW. of Palaeopolis. The 'Pyrgo' is the fort at Chelmutzi (Castel Tornese, built in 1218).

189. The characters on all Turkish scimitars contain sometimes the name of the place of their manufacture, but more generally a text from the Koran, in letters of gold. Amongst those in my possession is one with a blade of singular construction; it is very broad, and the edge notched into serpentine curves like the ripple of water, or the wavering of flame. I asked the Armenian who sold it, what possible use such a figure could add: he said, in Italian, that he did not know; but the Mussulmans had an idea that those of this form gave a severer wound; and liked it because it was 'piu feroce'. I did not much admire the reason, but bought it for its peculiarity. [B, added in *MS. B*]

204. It is to be observed, that every allusion to any thing or personage in the Old Testament, such as the Ark, or Cain, is equally the privilege of Mussulman and Jew: indeed the former profess to be much better acquainted with the lives, true and fabulous, of the patriarchs, than is warranted by our own Sacred writ, and not content with Adam, they have a biography of Pre-Adamites. Solomon is the monarch of all necromancy, and Moses a prophet inferior only to Christ and Mahomet. Zuleika is the Persian name of Potiphar's wife, and her amour with Joseph constitutes one of the finest poems in their language. It is therefore no violation of costume to put the names of Cain, or Noah, into the mouth of a Moslem. [B, note not in the MSS.] See *BLJ* III. 164.

219. Bosnia, the north-westernmost part of the Ottoman Empire in the eighteenth century.

220. Paswan Oglou, the rebel of Widin, who for the last years of his life set the whole power of the Porte at defiance. [B, added in *MS. B*] For a history of the rebel Passwan Oglou (1758–1807) see G. A. Olivier, *Voyage dans l'Empire Othoman* (1801), I. 108–25.

232. Horsetail, the standard of a Pacha. [B]

245. Giaffir, Pacha of Argyro Castro, or Scutari, I am not sure which, was actually taken off by the Albanian Ali, in the manner described in the text. Ali Pacha, while I was in the country, married the daughter of his victim, some years after the event had taken place at a bath in Sophia, or

Armenian] ⟨merchant⟩ *MS. B*

Adrianople. The poison was mixed in the cup of coffee, which is presented before the sherbet by the bath-keeper, after dressing. [B]

Giaffir Pacha was literally taken off at Sophia in this manner by Ali of Albania—who has married the daughter of his victim. *MS. A*

B is conflating two stories involving Ali Pacha; see R. A. Davenport, *The Life of Ali Pacha* (1837), chaps. 4 and 9.

293. *Roumelie*: across from Lepanto on the Gulf of Corinth, where there were important fortifications.

335. *Brusa*: i.e. Bursa, the Asian capital of the Ottoman Empire before the capture of Constantinople.

344. I must here shelter myself with the Psalmist—is it not David that makes the 'Earth reel to and fro like a Drunkard'? If the Globe can be thus lively on seeing its Creator, a liberated captive can hardly feel less on a first view of His work. [B, *MS. B, cancelled*] See Isaiah 24: 20.

357. The Turkish notions of almost all islands are confined to the Archipelago, the sea alluded to. [B, added in *MS. B*]

380. Lambro Canzani, a Greek, famous for his efforts in 1789–90 for the independence of his country; abandoned by the Russians he became a pirate, and the Archipelago was the scene of his enterprizes. He is said to be still alive at Petersburg. He and Riga are the two most celebrated of the Greek revolutionists. [B. In *MS. A* the note reads: 'Lambro Canzani a Greek famous for his efforts for his country and piratical enterprizes in the Archipelago.'] For details of Lambros Katzones see Hobhouse's *Travels in Albania*, II. 5 and *Finlay* V. 330, 333; see also *DJ* III, st. 26.

384. 'Rayahs', all who pay the capitation tax, called the 'Haratch'. [B, added in *MS. B*] See the Koran, chap. IX.

388. This first of voyages is one of the few with which the Mussulmans profess much acquaintance. [B, added in MS. B]

389. The wandering life of the Arabs, Tartars, and Turkomans, will be found well detailed in any book of Eastern travels. That it possesses a charm peculiar to itself cannot be denied. A young French renegado confessed to Chateaubriand, that he never found himself alone, galloping in the desart, without a sensation approaching to rapture, which was indescribable. [B. The note is not in the MSS.]

391. *Serais*: i.e. caravanserais.

409. 'Jannat al Aden', the perpetual abode, the Mussulman Paradise. [B, added in *MS. X10a*]

Paradise.] Paradise Lost of Adam. *MS. X10a*

See Sale's *Koran*, 'Preliminary Discourse', sec. I and *BLJ* III. 211.

431. Translating Tacitus, *Agricola*, 30: 'Solitudinem faciunt—pacem appellant.'

454–7. Paraphrasing Ovid, *Metamorphoses*, VII. 66–9. See *BLJ* III. 181.

This first of] ⟨Patriarch Noah—whose⟩ *MS. B*

492–6. *Niobe*: see *CHP IV*, line 703 and n.

501. Echoing Young's *The Revenge*, IV (1811 edn., p. 43).

606–10. A scene from the life, when B was on the *Salsette* frigate off the Dardanelles (see John Galt, *Life of Lord Byron* (1830), 144).

618. A turban is carved in stone above the graves of *men* only. [B]

626. The death-song of the Turkish women. The 'silent slaves' are the men whose notions of decorum forbid complaint in *public*. [B] See also *BLJ* III. 165, and Scott's *Arabian Nights*, *op. cit*. I. lxxxiii–lxxxiv.

646. Cf. Isaiah 66: 25.

652–3. Cf. Lamentations 2: 10.

663. 'I came to the place of my birth and cried, "The friends of my youth, where are they?" and an Echo answered, "Where are they?"' *From an Arabic MS.*

The above quotation (from which the idea in the text is taken) must be already familiar to every reader—it is given in the first annotation, page 67, of 'The Pleasures of Memory': a poem so well known as to render a reference almost superfluous; but to whose pages all will be delighted to recur. [B, note not in the MSS.] See Samuel Rogers, *The Pleasures of Memory*, I. 103 n.

712. 'And airy tongues that *syllable* men's names.' MILTON. [*Comus*, 208.]

For a belief that the souls of the dead inhabit the form of birds, we need not travel to the East. Lord Lyttleton's ghost story, the belief of the Duchess of Kendal, that George I. flew into her window in the shape of a raven (see Orford's *Reminiscences*), and many other instances, bring this superstition nearer home. The most singular was the whim of a Worcester lady, who believing her daughter to exist in the shape of a singing bird, literally furnished her pew in the Cathedral with cages-full of the kind; and as she was rich, and a benefactress in beautifying the church, no objection was made to her harmless folly.—For this anecdote, see Orford's *Letters*. [B, added in *MS. X16a* See *Works of Horatio Walpole* (1798), IV. 283 and V. 279.

726–8. See J. B. Le Chevalier, *Voyage de la Propontide . . .* (1800), 17.

224. *MS. and Proofs.* B's first draft (*MS. ML*, location: Morgan) is dated at the beginning 18 Dec. 1813. Canto II is headed 22 Dec., but there is no date before Canto III, or at the end of the MS. *ML* contains: Canto I. 1–226, 249–68, 281–606; Canto II. 1–70, 73–281, 284–526, 529–42, 555–62; Canto III. 1–64, 66–130, 208–427, 430–522, 555–651, 682–96 (total: 1,671 lines). *ML* also contains II. 543–54 as a MS. insertion dated 26 Dec., and I. 227–48, III. 131–207 (dated by B 3–4 Jan. 1814), and III. 523–54 are also fair copy MS. insertions in *ML*. B's rough draft of III. 660–1 is written on the final leaf of *ML*, and a rough draft MS. insertion of III. 662–81 is also part of *ML*. These additional MSS. are designated *MLa* in the apparatus.

B's fair copy (*MS. M*, location: Murray) is dated at the beginning 27 Dec. and at the end 31 Dec. 1813, 1 Jan. 1814. *M* augments *ML* with the following lines: I. 269–76, II. 71–2, 282–3, 543–54, III. 65 (25 additional lines, total: 1,696 lines). Bound up with *M* is a two-page proof (see below) and the following MS. insertions (*Ma*): a separate sheet with the poem's various epigraphs; the Dedication and the suppressed alternative Dedication (dated 7 Jan.); II. 525–8 (fair copy), III. 131–207 (fair copy dated by Murray as received on 5 Jan.); III. 652–61, 678–81 (rough draft), and 662–77 (fair copy).

Other fragmentary MSS.: I. 277–80 (two fair copies, one written by B into his presentation copy of the first edition of the poem given to Lady Harrington; *MS. L*, location: Leeds; the other on a proof page for the seventh edition; *MS. Y*, location: Yale); III. 523–52 (*MS. Y2*, rough draft, location: Yale).

As with *Giaour* and *Bride*, an extensive series of proofs, corrected and uncorrected, survive for *Corsair*. With one exception (Proof 3), all these proofs are in the Murray archive. The line numbering in all the proofs is slightly wrong. The poem has five broken lines, and some or all of these are counted in all the proofs. In addition, Proof 6 wrongly adds one extra line to its numbering.

Proof 1. Corrected proof dated and headed by Murray as the first proof, 4 Jan. 1814. No Dedication, an 88-page proof of 1,696 printed lines later numbered by B in MS. to 1,780; no end-notes. The proof is imperfect, lacking pages 49–64 (i.e. received text II. 355–562, III. 1–72). The numbering of 1,780 takes account of MS. additions at II. 527, III. 131–207, 428–9. Actual total number of lines with the MS. additions: 1,776.

Proof 2. Corrected proof dated and headed by Murray as second revise, 6 Jan. No Dedication, a 93-page proof with 3 pages of end-notes; a total of 1,790 lines numbered in proof as 1,795. This proof first prints III. 652–61, 678–80.

Proof 3. Corrected proof dated and headed by Murray as second revise, 8 Jan. No Dedication, a 93-page proof of 1,795 numbered lines (actual total, 1,790); no end-notes. Location: Huntington.

Proof 4. Corrected proof dated by Murray 15 Jan. Both Dedications, no end-notes, a 93-page proof with additional proofs of several short poems that were printed in *CHP*(7) and *Corsair 1a*. Line total same as *Proof 3*.

Proof 5. Corrected proof dated by Murray 12 Jan. No Dedication, a 93-page proof with 3 pages of notes. This proof first prints III. 662–77 and has 1,811 numbered lines (actual total: 1,806). Despite the discrepancy in dates written on *Proofs 4* and *5*, *Proof 5* is definitely 'subsequent' to Proof 4 in terms of the poem's process of revision.

Proof 6. Corrected proof, undated, with suppressed Dedication, 95 pages of text, 3 pages of notes, a total of 1,844 numbered lines (actual total: 1,838). This proof first prints III. 523–54.

Proof 6a. A printer's proof incorporating B's corrections made on *Proofs 5* and 6, with the corrections here in an unknown hand. No Dedication, 93 pages of text, no end-notes, with 1,811 numbered lines (actual total: 1,806) renumbered in MS. to 1,843 to accommodate the addition of III. 523–54.

Proof 6b. Uncorrected proof, undated, with Dedication, no end-notes. 1,844 numbered lines (actual total: 1,838).

Proof 7. Corrected proof, undated, with Dedication, 95 pages of text, no end-notes; 1,863 numbered lines (actual total: 1,860). This proof first prints I. 227–48.

Proof 7a. A printer's proof incorporating B's corrections made in *Proof 7*, with corrections here in unknown hand. With suppressed Dedication, 95 pages of text, 3 pages of end-notes; 1,863 numbered lines (actual total: 1,860).

Proof 8. This is the 2-page proof fragment bound up with *MS. M.*; leaves numbered 15, 16, containing received lines I. 271–314 (here numbered 273–316). This is a proof made for *Corsair 7* where I. 277–80 were added to the poem. This proof prints 'near' for 'ne'er' in I. 298, a misprint that has been preserved in all later editions to the present.

The collation shows that at least one of B's corrected proofs is not extant. In a few cases, the texts of *Corsair 1* and of the printer's copy MS. (usually *MS. M*) differ substantively, and the differences are not accounted for in the corrections we see on the extant proofs (see e.g. II. 164, 167, III. 615, 620). Moreover, the *MS. M* reading in these cases appears as part of the poem until *Proof 7*, when the *Corsair 1* reading finally appears. Evidently B received and corrected at least one more proof between *Proofs 6* and *7*.

Text EM. This is a copy of the fifth edition (*Corsair 5*) marked on the front cover by B: 'See pages 13 and 92 for the alterations marked theron.' On p. 13 B corrects I. 235 (putting 'tread' for 'step') and on p. 92 he changes III. 627 (putting 'wishes,' for 'joy and'). *Text EM* is in the collection of Mrs. Earle Miller of Philadelphia.

Text JJ. A copy of the sixth edition (*Corsair 6*) with the following MS. additions and corrections by B: a version of I. 277–80, and two corrections at II. 36 and III. 640. This book is owned by J. Geoffrey Jones, of Cambridge, N.Y.

Publishing History. For the process of composition and revision between 18 Dec. 1813, when B began the poem, and 16 or 17 Jan. 1814, when B finished his proof corrections, see above. The first edition appeared on 1 Feb. 1814, when 10,000 copies were sold. The first issue (*Corsair 1*) did not contain the six supplementary poems at the end, but they were added in most copies of the second issue (*Corsair 1a*) and kept in the first issue of the second edition (*Corsair 2*). Murray removed them once again from the second issue of the second edition (*Corsair 2a*) and did not replace them until *Corsair 4*, after which they remained in all subsequent early editions of the poem. Murray's 'shuffling' with these poems occurred because of his fear of the political repercussions which might, and in the end did, take place because of B's verses on the Princess Charlotte ('To a Lady Weeping') which were among the supplementary poems. B insisted they be kept, however. The first four editions appeared in the first two weeks of February. He received a copy of *Corsair5*, the fifth edition, on 18 Feb.

B complained about certain errors that still persisted in the book throughout *Corsair5*. Between Mar. and Dec. 1814 *Corsair6* and *Corsair7* appeared carrying the changes B wanted, as well as the addition of I. 277–80 and the prose note at II. 50 in *Corsair7*. B added the first part of the note (MS. location: Texas) to the poem's concluding line in *Corsair8*, which appeared in 1815, and the second part of that note was sent to Murray on 6 Jan. 1815, but it did not appear in print until *Corsair9*, also issued in 1815. During the process of correction, one new error appeared in the text at I. 298 in *Corsair6*. This error has never been corrected in later editions. A tenth edition appeared in 1818, when the poem was reset and given a new punctuation system.

Copy text here is *Corsair9*. Early issues of the collected edition *1815* conform to *Corsair8*, later issues to *Corsair9*.

For further information see *Wise*, I. 92–8; *C* III. 217–21 and VII. 201–6; *BLJ* IV. 11–36 *passim*, 48, 52, 65, 83, 95, 167, 250–1.

Literary and Historical Background. The most important document for understanding *Corsair* is B's Journal of Nov. 1813–Apr. 1814 (*BLJ* III. 204–58), where the political and personal contexts of the poem are clearly revealed.

It was at this time that B's disillusion and weariness with Regency society and politics reached a critical level. *Corsair* is partly a symbolic formulation of the political situation of the day, as B saw it, with its contest between equivocal forces of revolt and the established powers of an old and corrupt order. The figure of Conrad focuses the rebellious careers of a whole series of similar historical characters referred to in the poem's notes. In fact, the name of Conrad (like that of Ezzelin, in *Lara*, *Corsair*'s acknowledged sequel) was lifted from B's reading in Sismondi. The latter's narrative of the history of the defeats of the Ghibelline Party at the end of the thirteenth century is presented as the turning-point in Italian history, when the citizenry began to abandon their adherence to republicanism and to accept the rule of despots. 'Guelph' was, for B, a contemptuous code-phrase which he liked to apply to the political world of George III and the Prince Regent: the House of Hanover descended from the Guelphs.

B's Journal focuses the personal aspect of the poem as well, which he said was written '*con amore*, and much from *existence*' (*BLJ* III. 243). As in the *Bride*, the crucial figures here are Lady Frances Wedderburn Webster and B's sister Augusta. At the end of Nov. 1813, as B daydreamed about going to Holland, where the European political struggle was currently focused, he wrote in his Journal: 'And why not? [Lady Frances] is distant [i.e. at Aston, which her husband was renting], and will be at [Edinburgh], still more distant, till spring. No one else, except Augusta, cares for me' (*BLJ* III. 218). In the end he stayed home to write a poem about a failed criminal revolutionary whose 'one virtue' among his 'thousand crimes' was love. Most of the poem was written while he stayed with his sister at Newmarket.

Besides the general traditions which fed the development of the Byronic hero, *Corsair* is particularly indebted to Schiller. B was aware of the political implications of *Die Raüber*, which he admired, but *Fiesco* seems even closer to *Corsair*, and B in fact preferred it to *The Robbers*. The political tragedies of Alfieri and Monti—especially the latter's *Aristodemo* and *Manfredi*, both of which B knew—also had an influence on *Corsair*.

Dedication B wrote a second dedicatory letter after some objections had been made to the political allusions in the first. B asked Moore to choose between them. The suppressed (second) Dedication follows:

My dear Moore—

I had written to you a long letter of dedication which I suppress because though it contained ⟨more⟩ something relating to you which everyone had been glad to hear—yet there was too much about ⟨myself and⟩ politics—and poesy—and all things whatsoever—ending with that topic on which ⟨all⟩ most men are fluent and none very amusing—one's self.—It might have been rewritten—but to what purpose? ⟨The⟩ My praise could add nothing to your well-earned and firmly established fame—and with my most hearty admiration of your talents—and delight in your conversation you are already acquainted. In availing myself of your friendly permission to inscribe this poem to you I can only wish the offering were as worthy your acceptance as your regard is dear to

yours most affectionately
and faithfully

January 7, 1814   Byron

Ded. 16 i.e. Moore's *Lalla Rookh* (1817).

Ded. 20–1 See William Collins, 'Preface', *Oriental Eclogues* (1757).

23–6. B refers to the romantic tradition which believed that Ireland was settled by ancient Scythians. Among the antiquarians B has in mind are Giraldus Cambrensis, Edward Ledwich, Thomas Leland, John Milner, and Sylvester O'Halloran.

Ded. 31 Horace, *Ars Poetica*, 373.

Ded. 46 i.e. *EBSR* and *Curse*.

Canto I

epigraph *Inferno*, v. 121–3.

1. The time in this poem may seem too short for the occurences, but the whole of the Aegean isles are within a few hours sail of the continent, and the reader must be kind enough to take the *wind* as I have often found it. [B]

4. Cf. Pope's *Windsor Forest*, 256.

226. *C* incorrectly places part of the note for II. 50 at this line. There was no note placed here by B.

361. Echoes 'The Epitaph' of Gray's 'Elegy . . . '.

420–30. Cf. *Paradise Lost*, v. 321–48.

440. Orlando, Canto X. [B, note not in MSS.] See Ariosto's *Orlando Furioso*.

572. By night, particularly in a warm latitude, every stroke of the oar, every motion of the boat or ship, is followed by a slight flash like sheet lightning from the water. [B, note not in MSS.]

601. Cape Gallo, a few miles south of Corone.

Canto II

epigraph   *Inferno*, v. 120.

1. *Coron*. Corone, 'the ancient Colonides, is situated a little to the north of a promontory, Point Lividia, on the western shore of the Gulf of Kalamata, or Coron, or Messenia' (*C* III. 249 n.).

33. Coffee. [B, note in *MS. M*]

35. Pipe. [B, note not in MSS.]

36. Dancing-girls. [B, note not in MSS.]

50. It has been objected that Conrad's entering disguised as a spy is out of nature.—Perhaps so. I find something not unlike it in history.

'Anxious to explore with his own eyes the state of the Vandals, Majorian ventured, after disguising the colour of his hair, to visit Carthage in the character of his own ambassador; and Genseric was afterwards mortified by the discovery, that he had entertained and dismissed the Emperor of the Romans. Such an anecdote may be rejected as an improbable fiction; but it is a fiction which would not have been imagined unless in the life of a hero.' *Gibbon, D. and F. Vol.* VI. *p.* 180.

That Conrad is a character not altogether out of nature I shall attempt to prove by some historical coincidences which I have met with since writing 'The Corsair'.

'Eccelin prisonnier' dit Rolandini, 's'enfermoit dans un silence menaçant, il fixoit sur la terre son visage féroce, et ne donnoit point d'essor à sa profonde indignation.—De toutes partes cependant les soldats & les peuples accouroient; ils vouloient voir cet homme, jadis si puissant, et la joie universelle eclatoit de toutes partes.

*   *   *   *   *   *

'Eccelin étoit d'une petite taille; mais tout l'aspect de sa personne, tous ses mouvemens indiquoient un soldat.—Son langage étoit amer, son déportment superbe—et par son seul egard, il faisoit trembler les plus hardis.' Sismondi, tome III. page 219, 220.

'Gizericus (Genseric, king of the Vandals, the conqueror of both Carthage and Rome,) statura mediocris, et equi casu claudicans, animo profundus, sermone rarus, luxuriae contemptor, ira turbidus, habendi cupidus, ad solicitandas gentes providentissimus', &c. &c. *Jornandes de Rebus Getius, c.* 33.

I beg leave to quote these gloomy realities to keep in countenance my Giaour and Corsair. [B, note added in 7th edn.]

B quotes from chap. 36 of Gibbon, and from Sismondi's *Histoire des Républiques Italiennes du Moyen Âge* (1809), which is also his source for the Jornandes quotation.

67–8. *Scalanova*: twenty miles south of Smyrna on the coast of Asia Minor.
Saick: a small boat, a ketch.

119. Cf. *Giaour*, 343 n.

125. The Dervises are in colleges, and of different orders, as the monks.
[B, note added in *MS. M*]

160. *Zatanai*: Satan. [B, note not in MSS.]

181. A common and not very novel effect of Mussulman anger. See Prince Eugene's Memoirs, page 24. 'The Seraskier received a wound in the thigh; he plucked up his beard by the roots, because he was obliged to quit the field.' [B, note not in MSS.] See *Memoirs of Prince Eugene of Savoy* (1811).

225. Gulnare, a female name; it means, literally, the flower of the Pomegranate. [B]

328. Cf. Richard Savage, *The Wanderer*, V. 464.

335. Cf. Edward Young, *Night Thoughts*, III. 225.

451. In Sir Thomas More, for instance, on the scaffold, and Anne Boleyn in the Tower, when grasping her neck, she remarked, that it 'was too slender to trouble the headsman much'. During one part of the French Revolution, it became a fashion to leave some 'mot' as a legacy; and the quantity of facetious last words spoken during that period would form a melancholy jest-book of a considerable size. [B]

Canto III
   epigraph   *Inferno*, V. 105.

22. Socrates drank the hemlock a short time before sunset (the hour of execution), notwithstanding the entreaties of his disciples to wait till the sun went down. [B]

34. The twilight in Greece is much shorter than in our own country; the days in winter are longer, but in summer of shorter duration. [B, note not in MSS.]

44. The Kiosk is a Turkish summer-house: the palm is without the present walls of Athens, not far from the temple of Theseus, between which and the tree the wall intervenes.—Cephisus' stream is indeed scanty, and Ilissus has no stream at all. [B, note not in MSS.]

   Cephissus, a river irrigating the plain of Athens; Ilissus, a small river rising on Mt. Hymettus and joining the Cephissus south of Athens.

54. The opening lines as far as section II have, perhaps, little business here, and were annexed to an unpublished (though printed) poem [*Curse of Minerva*]; but they were written on the spot in the Spring of 1811, and—I scarce know why—the reader must excuse their appearance here if he can. [B, note not in MSS.]

colleges] ⟨convents⟩ *MS. M*

64. Paros came under the dominion of Athens after the battle of Salamis (480 B.C.).

139. The Comboloio, or Mahometan rosary; the beads are in number ninety-nine. [B]

530. Echoes Scott's *Marmion*, III. xvii. 9–10.

605. In the Levant it is the custom to strew flowers on the bodies of the dead, and in the hands of young persons to place a nosegay. [B]

657. Cf. John 9: 4.

664–5. Cf. no. 246, lines 11–12.

667. 'B had, perhaps, explored the famous stalactite cavern in the island of Anti-Paros, which is described by Tournefort, Clarke, Choiseul-Gouffier, and other travellers' (*C* III. 295 n.).

695–6. This famous couplet perhaps echoes the conclusion of *Vathek*, where the Caliph is said to have 'sullied himself with a thousand crimes'.

696. That the point of honour which is represented in one instance of Conrad's character has not been carried beyond the bounds of probability may perhaps be in some degree confirmed by the following ANECDOTE of a BROTHER BUCCANEER in the present year 1814.

Our readers have all seen the account of the enterprise against the pirates of Barrataria; but few, we believe, were informed of the situation, history, or nature of that establishment. For the information of such as were unacquainted with it, we have procured from a friend the following interesting narrative of the main facts, of which he has some personal knowledge, and which cannot fail to interest some of our readers.

Barrataria is a bay, or a narrow arm of the gulf of Mexico: it runs through a rich but very flat country, until it reaches within a mile of the Mississippi river, fifteen miles below the city of New Orleans. The bay has branches almost innumerable, in which persons can lie concealed from the severest scrutiny. It communicates with three lakes which lie on the southwest side, and these, with the lake of the same name, and which lies contiguous to the sea, where there is an island formed by the two arms of this lake and the sea. The east and west points of this island were fortified in the year 1811, by a band of pirates, under the command of one Monsieur La Fitte. A large majority of these outlaws are of that class of the population of the state of Louisiana who fled from the island of St. Domingo during the troubles there, and took refuge in the island of Cuba: and when the last war between France and Spain commenced, they were compelled to leave that island with the short notice of a few days. Without ceremony, they entered the United States, the most of them the State of Louisiana, with all the negroes they had possessed in Cuba. They were notified by the Governor of that State of the clause in the constitution which forbad the importation of slaves; but,

beads . . . number] ⟨number of beads is⟩ *MS. Ma*

at the same time, received the assurance of the Governor that he would obtain, if possible, the approbation of the general Government for their retaining this property.

The island of Barrataria is situated about lat. 29 deg. 15 min. lon. 92 30. and is as remarkable for its health as for the superior scale and shell fish with which its waters abound. The chief of this horde, like Charles de Moor, had mixed with his many vices some virtues. In the year 1813, this party had, from its turpitude and boldness, claimed the attention of the Governor of Louisiana; and to break up the establishment, he thought proper to strike at the head. He therefore offered a reward of 500 dollars for the head of Monsieur La Fitte, who was well known to the inhabitants of the city of New Orleans, from his immediate connection, and his once having been a fencing-master in that city of great reputation, which art he learnt in Buonaparte's army, where he was a Captain. The reward which was offered by the Governor for the head of La Fitte was answered by the offer of a reward from the latter of 15,000 for the head of the Governor. The Governor ordered out a company to march from the city to La Fitte's island, and to burn and destroy all the property, and to bring to the city of New Orleans all his banditti. This company, under the command of a man who had been the intimate associate of this bold Captain, approached very near to the fortified island, before he saw a man, or heard a sound, until he heard a whistle, not unlike a boatswain's call. Then it was he found himself surrounded by armed men who had emerged from the secret avenues which led into Bayou. Here it was that the modern Charles de Moor developed his few noble traits; for to this man, who had come to destroy his life and all that was dear to him, he not only spared his life, but offered him that which would have made the honest soldier easy for the remainder of his days, which was indignantly refused. He then, with the approbation of his captor, returned to the city. This circumstance, and some concomitant events, proved that this band of pirates was not to be taken by land. Our naval force having always been small in that quarter, exertions for the destruction of this illicit establishment could not be expected from them until augmented; for an officer of the navy, with most of the gunboats on that station, had to retreat from an overwhelm-ing force of La Fitte's. So soon as the augmentation of the navy authorised an attack, one was made; the overthrow of this banditti has been the result; and now this almost invulnerable point and key to New Orleans is clear of an enemy, it is to be hoped the government will hold it by a strong military force.—*From an American Newspaper.*

In Noble's continuation of Granger's Biographical Dictionary, vol. iii. p. 68, there is a singular passage in his account of archbishop Blackbourne; and as in some measure connected with the profession of the hero of the foregoing poem, I cannot resist the temptation of extracting it.

There is something mysterious in the history and character of Dr. Blackbourne. The former is but imperfectly known: and report has even asserted he was a BUCCANEER: and that one of his brethren in that profession having asked, on his arrival in England, what had become of his old chum, Blackbourne, was answered, he is archbishop of York. We are informed, that Blackbourne was installed sub-dean of Exeter, in 1694, which office he resigned in 1702: but after his successor, Lewis Barnet's death, in 1704, he regained it. In the following year he became dean; and, in 1714, held with it the archdeanery of Cornwall. He was consecrated bishop of Exeter, February 24, 1716; and translated to York, November 28, 1724, as a reward, according to court scandal, for uniting George I. to the Duchess of Munster. This, however, appears to have been an unfounded calumny. As archbishop he behaved with great prudence, and was equally respectable as the guardian of the revenues of the see. Rumour whispered he retained the vices of his youth, and that a passion for the fair sex formed an item in the list of his weaknesses; but so far from being convicted by seventy witnesses, he does not appear to have been directly criminated by one. In short, I look upon these aspersions as the effects of mere malice. How is it possible a buccaneer should have been so good a scholar as Blackbourne certainly was? He who had so perfect a knowledge of the classics, (particularly of the Greek trage-dians) as to be able to read them with the same ease as he could Shakespeare, must have taken great pains to acquire the learned languages; and have had both leisure and good masters. But he was undoubtedly educated at Christ-church College, Oxford. He is allowed to have been a pleasant man: this, however, was turned against him, by its being said, 'he gained more hearts than souls'. [B, note added in *Corsair8*; see commentary above.]

The *American Newspaper* to which B refers was probably the Boston *Weekly Intelligencer* (4 Nov. 1814).

Noble: the Revd. Mark Noble, *Biographical History of England* (1806).

'The only voice that could soothe the passions of the savage (Alphonso 3d) was that of an amiable and virtuous wife, the sole object of his love; the voice of Donna Isabella, the daughter of the Duke of Savoy, and the grand-daughter of Philip 2d, King of Spain.—Her dying words sunk deep into his memory; his fierce spirit melted into tears; and after the last embrace, Alphonso retired into his chamber to bewail his irreparable loss, and to meditate on the vanity of human life.' *Miscellaneous Works of Gibbon, New Edition* [1814], 8vo, vol. 3, page 473. [B, note added in *Corsair9*; see com-mentary above.]

225. *MS.* B's draft MS. (*MS. L*) is dated at the beginning 15 May 1814, at the beginning of Canto II 5 June, and at the end of the poem 12 June 1814 (location: Bodleian–Lovelace). *MS. L* contains: Canto I. 1–46, 49–234, 247–300, 303–12, 383–645; Canto II. 1–251, 264–367, 394–453, 490–569, 572–627 (total: 1,110 lines). Collected together with *MS. L* is a group of MS. leaves (*MS. LA*) containing the following corrections and insertions: Canto I. 235–46 (corrected fair copy), 313–60 (corrected draft), 361–82 (corrected draft); Canto II. 254–62 (draft), 368–93 (draft), 454–89 (corrected draft), 458–65 and 468–75 (drafts). Other extant MSS. include: I. 301–2 (*MS. B*, location: Boston Public Library); and the following fair copy MSS. at Murray's (*MS. M*): the 'Advertisement' as it was printed in the first edition; I. 313–60 (dated on verso by Murray 14 July 1814 and headed by B: 'Canto 1st page 22 insert XVIII'); II. 454–89 (dated on verso by Murray 15 July 1814 and headed by B: 'Page (I forget which) Canto 2nd. After the line [B quotes II. 453] insert this new paragraph').

B made a fair copy of *Lara* (*BLJ* IV. 126, 129) between 14 and 23 June, and this was copy text for the first edition. B also corrected several sets of proofs between 24 June and the middle of July (*BLJ* IV. 134, 140). None of this material has been found, nor has it been used by earlier editors.

Also with *MS. L* is the draft MS. of the 'Opening Lines to Lara' (thus titled in the MS., and undated). B did not publish the lines with *Lara*, however.

Composition and Publication. As *MS. L* shows, Canto I was written relatively slowly, but B finished Canto II in a week. The datable additions are the lines in *MS. M*, II. 368–93 (sent on 27 June: see *BLJ* IV. 134), and the 'Advertisement', which must have been written between 31 July and 3 Aug., when B finally decided to publish the poem (anonymously) with Samuel Rogers's *Jacqueline* (*BLJ* IV. 147–50).

Lara appeared shortly after 5 Aug. (*BLJ* IV. 154). Three editions of the poem were printed with *Jacqueline* (*L(1)*, *L(2)*, *L(3)*) in 1814 (almost 7,000 copies). *Lara* was first printed separately, and under B's name, in the fourth edition, of which there were two separate issues (*L(4a)*, *L(4b)*) totalling 3,000 copies. *L(4b)* first printed the long prose note on the Duke of Gandia. An unrecorded fifth edition—*L(5)*—was issued in which the correction of II. 488–9 was made. Another edition marked the fifth, *L(5a)*, appeared in 1817.

The minor substantive variant at I. 385 is important because it first appeared in Murray's collected edition of *1815*. It is not in *L(5)* or any earlier editions, but it reappears in *L(5a)* and was kept in subsequent printings. B did not read *1815* in proof, however, and the variant is almost certainly a misprint.

The 'Opening Lines to Lara' have never been collected, but the MS. was published (in print and facsimile) in *Astarte* (1905). The lines were first printed in *Murray's Magazine* (Jan. 1887).

Literary and Historical Background. B said the poem was 'a sequel to' *Corsair*, and *Lara* makes the political dimension of the earlier poem even more explicit. The two pieces together form an objective narrative that parallels the subjective history represented in *CHP I–II*. For further details see commentary for *Corsair* and especially *McGann(2)*, chap. 2. As in *Corsair*, Sismondi's history of the Italian Republics was an important influence (and see *BLJ* IV. 161 for some other historians who may have been important to the poem). The Spanish name of Lara B probably first encountered in Southey's *Chronicle of the Cid* (1808), 4n. Whether B knew at first hand any of the Chronicles of the Infantes de Lara is not clear. For the name of Ezzelin see *BLJ* III. 253-4.

The 'Opening lines to Lara' may have been written before he began the narrative proper, but they were almost certainly written early on, in May or June 1814. Their subject is B's sister (see B's letters to Lady Melbourne of 16 May and especially 10 June about his love for Augusta: *BLJ* IV. 116, 123-4), and they further highlight the connections which *Lara* has with *Corsair*.

title The following 'Advertisement' was prefixed to *L(1)*, *L(2)*, *L(3)*:

THE reader of LARA may probably regard it as a sequel to a poem that recently appeared [*Corsair*]: whether the cast of the hero's character, the turn of his adventures, and the general outline and colouring of the story, may not encourage such a supposition, shall be left to his determination. To his conjecture is also referred the name of the writer, the knowledge of which would be of no service in assisting his decision on the failure or success of the attempt.

THE Poem of JACQUELINE is the production of a different author, and is added at the request of the writer of the former tale, whose wish and entreaty it was that it should occupy the first pages of the following volume; and he regrets that the tenacious courtesy of his friend would not permit him to place it where the judgment of the reader, concurring with his own, will suggest its more appropriate station.

Canto I

1. 'The reader is advertised that the name only of Lara being Spanish, and no circumstance of local or national description fixing the scene or hero of the poem to any country or age, the word "*Serf*", which could not be correctly applied to the lower classes in Spain, who were never vassals of the soil, has nevertheless been employed to designate the followers of our fictitious chieftain.' [Note in *L(1)*, *L(2)*, *L(3)*. The note was probably written by Hobhouse: see *BLJ* IV. 145-6.]

86. Echoing *Othello*, I. iii. 140-1.

158. Perhaps echoing John Dyer, 'The Country Walk' (*Poetical Works of Armstrong, Dyer, and Green* (1858), p. 221).

289-382. B's portrait here is heavily in debt to Scott's portrait of Bertram in *Rokeby* (1813), Canto I.

604-5. Perhaps recalling *Macbeth*, III. iv. 139-40.

Canto II

1-2. Perhaps recalling William Sotheby, *Constance de Castile* (1810), III. v. 17-18.

73-4. Cf. Mrs. Ann Radcliffe, *The Mysteries of Udolpho* (1794), II. 279.

368-71. Recalling Voltaire's *Henriade*, VIII. 127-8.

396. *C* compares Fairfax's translation of Tasso's *Jerusalem Delivered*, VII. cvi. 3–4.

402–5. Cf. Luke 16: 22–4.

550. The event in section 24, Canto 2d, was suggested by the description of the death or rather burial of the Duke of Gandia. 'The most interesting and particular account of this mysterious event is given by Burchard; and is in substance as follows:—"On the eighth day of June, the Cardinal of Valenza, and the Duke of Gandia, sons of the pope, supped with their mother, Vanozza, near the church of *S. Pietro ad vincula*; several other persons being present at the entertainment. A late hour approaching, and the cardinal having reminded his brother, that it was time to return to the apostolic palace, they mounted their horses or mules, with only a few attendants, and proceeded together as far as the palace of Cardinal Ascanio Sforza, when the duke informed the cardinal, that before he returned home, he had to pay a visit of pleasure. Dismissing therefore all his attendants, excepting his *staffiero*, or footmen, and a person in a mask, who had paid him a visit whilst at supper, and who, during the space of a month or thereabouts, previous to this time, had called upon him almost daily, at the apostolic palace, he took this person behind him on his mule, and proceeded to the street of the Jews, where he quitted his servant, directing him to remain there until a certain hour; when, if he did not return, he might repair to the palace. The duke then seated the person in the mask behind him, and rode, I know not whither; but in that night he was assassinated, and thrown into the river. The servant, after having been dismissed, was also assaulted and mortally wounded; and although he was attended with great care, yet such was his situation, that he could give no intelligible account of what had befallen his master. In the morning, the duke not having returned to the palace, his servants began to be alarmed; and one of them informed the pontiff of the evening excursion of his sons, and that the duke had not yet made his appearance. This gave the pope no small anxiety; but he conjectured that the duke had been attracted by some courtesan to pass the night with her, and, not choosing to quit the house in open day, had waited till the following evening to return home. When, however, the evening arrived, and he found himself disappointed in his expectations, he became deeply afflicted, and began to make inquiries from different persons, whom he ordered to attend him for that purpose. Amongst these was a man named Giorgio Schiavoni, who, having discharged some timber from a bark in the river, had remained on board the vessel to watch it; and being interrogated whether he had seen any one thrown into the river, on the night preceding, he replied, that he saw two men on foot, who came down to the street, and looked diligently about, to observe, whether any person was passing. That seeing no one, they returned, and in a short time afterwards two others came, and looked around in the same manner as the former; no person still appearing, they gave a sign to their companions, when a man came, mounted on a white horse,

having behind him a dead body, the head and arms of which hung on one side, and the feet on the other side of the horse; the two persons on foot supporting the body, to prevent its falling. They thus proceeded towards that part where the filth of the city is usually discharged into the river, and turning the horse, with his tail towards the water, the two persons took the dead body by the arms and feet, and with all their strength flung it into the river. The person on horseback then asked if they had thrown it in; to which they replied, *Signor, sì* (yes, Sir). He then looked towards the river, and seeing a mantle floating on the stream, he enquired what it was that appeared black, to which they answered, it was a mantle; and one of them threw stones upon it, in consequence of which it sunk. The attendants of the pontiff then enquired from Giorgio, why he had not revealed this to the governor of the city; to which he replied, that he had seen in his time a hundred dead bodies thrown into the river at the same place, without any inquiry being made respecting them; and that he had not, therefore, considered it as a matter of any importance. The fishermen and seamen were then collected, and ordered to search the river, where, on the following evening, they found the body of the duke, with his habit entire, and thirty ducats in his purse. He was pierced with nine wounds, one of which was in his throat, the others in his head, body, and limbs. No sooner was the pontiff informed of the death of his son, and that he had been thrown, like filth, into the river, than, giving way to his grief, he shut himself up in a chamber, and wept bitterly. The Cardinal of Segovia, and other attendants on the pope, went to the door, and after many hours spent in persuasions and exhortations, prevailed upon him to admit them. From the evening of Wednesday till the following Saturday, the pope took no food; nor did he sleep from Thursday morning till the same hour on the ensuing day. At length, however, giving way to the entreaties of his attendants, he began to restrain his sorrow, and to consider the injury which his own health might sustain by the further indulgence of his grief."' *Roscoe's Leo Tenth*, vol. I, page 265. [B, note added in *L*(4*b*). See *The Life and Pontificate of Leo Tenth* (1805)].

226. *MS.* Unpublished, B's draft MS. (location: Bodleian–Lovelace). The work satirizes the social world of the Prince Regent, whose politics were as distasteful to B as the vanity, hypocrisy, and toadyism which the poet observed in the Regent's circle of acquaintances and court hangers-on. The contemporary references in the last four lines set the probable date of the poem in 1814. The reverses of France in 1813 on the Continent were celebrated by the new Laureate Southey in Jan. 1814 with his *Carmen Triumphale for the Commencement of the Year 1814*. The subject of this ode, which B sketches in lines 31–2, was suggested to Southey by the critic John Wilson Croker (1780–1857). Byron may have composed these verses around 12 Mar. 1814, when he wrote to Moore of his plan for a satirical epistle 'at and to' the Prince Regent (*BLJ* IV. 80).

19. *Sir Bauble*: perhaps Beau Brummell.

21. *old Vates*: William T. Fitzgerald (see letter to Moore of 8 Jan. 1814, *BLJ* IV. 19).

227. *MS.* The first draft of B's Ode has not survived. It contained ten stanzas and was composed on 10 Apr. 1814. The same day B copied the Ode and increased its length to twelve stanzas. This heavily corrected draft is in Texas (*MS. T*), undated, headed 'Ode', and contains lines 1–9, 28–36, 46–108, 118–44 in numbered stanzas. Also in Texas are MSS. (*MS. TA*) of lines 10–27, 37–45, 109–17, and 145–71 (present stanzas 2, 3, 5, 13, [17–19]). Stanzas [17–19] are a corrected fair copy headed by B: 'These may be the last—17—18—19.' The other stanzas of *MS. TA* are working drafts. The working draft of [17–19] is in Murray (*MS. M*). Six sets of proofs, as well as a few separate sheets of MS. additions, are preserved in the library of Harrow School. A draft copy of stanza [19] also survives (*MS. L*, location: Leeds).

B sent *MS. T* to Murray on 10 Apr. On 11 Apr. he received and sent back two corrected copies of the first proof (*Proofs A* and *B*). *Proof A* is dated by Murray 11 Apr. 1814, *Proof B* is undated. *Proof C* (dated by Murray 12 Apr.) incorporated the corrections from *Proofs A* and *B* and added one minor punctuation correction. A second copy of this proof (*Proof D*), undated, carries further corrections, as well as a separate MS. sheet containing stanzas 2 and 3. *Proof E* (dated by Murray 13 Apr.) incorporates the corrections and additions from *Proofs C* and *D*, as well as a few minor corrections. *Proof F* (dated by Murray 15 Apr.) shows further corrections and includes the MS. of stanzas 13 (dated by Murray 14 Apr.) and 5 (dated by Murray 17 Apr.). Murray subsequently asked B for some further stanzas, which B sent on 25 Apr. (stanzas [17–19]). For further details see *BLJ* III. 257 and IV. 94–6.

Publishing History. The first edition of 15 stanzas (lacking 5, [17–19]) was published anonymously on 16 Apr. In the third edition, published around 20 Apr., Murray added stanza 5. His request for further stanzas was made to avoid paying a stamp tax (levied on pamphlets of less than a single sheet). The addition of stanza 5, which increased the printed pages from fourteen to fifteen, seems to have served the purpose, and Murray never added stanzas [17–19] to the numerous early editions of the poem. In this action he was following B's explicit instructions (see *BLJ* IV. 103–4, 107). The poem was first issued in his name in the tenth edition (1814). Stanzas [17–19] were first printed in *Life*, I. 546; they were first collected in *1831* as 'Additional Stanzas', and first incorporated into the poem in *1832*. These three stanzas have been printed as part of the poem ever since. I have relegated them to the position of 'Additional Stanzas'. Though this manoeuvre contradicts a long tradition, it conforms to B's own expressed intentions. As poetry, the three stanzas are more than acceptable; but as a new conclusion to the Ode, they injure the poem's accomplished pace. B's decision to exclude them was a good one. But however one feels about this aesthetic question, the editorial question is clear, and admits of only one answer, given B's explicit instructions to his publisher.

Two other stanzas were printed in the *Morning Chronicle* (27 Apr. 1814) and attributed to B, but they are certainly spurious (*C* prints them as variants at III. 314–15). See also *Wise*, I. 98–100.

Along with *CHP III*, sts. 17–45, *IV*, sts. 89–92, and *Age of Bronze*, III–VI, this is B's major poetical statement on a man in whom he had made an intense personal investment. The Ode should also be compared with the series of short pieces B wrote in 1815–16 in the aftermath of Waterloo. Critical commentary on the poem has been curiously scant: see Gerhard Eggert, *Lord Byron und Napoleon* (Leipzig, 1933). Most of the ideas and allusions in the poem are anticipated in B's journal entries for 8 and 9 Apr. 1814 (*BLJ* III. 256–7).

8–9. Isaiah 14: 12.

26–7. Cf. Daniel 2: 31–45.

29. Certaminis *gaudia*, the expression of Attila in his harangue to his army, previous to the battle of Chalons, given in Cassiodorus. [B's note, 1st edn., sent with *Proof A* to Murray on 12 Apr.] See Cassiodorus (*c*. A.D. 480–575), in his *Historia Gothica*, which survives only in the abridgement by Jordanus of Ravenna, *De Getarum origine* (written *c*. 551). Cf. August Mommsen's edn., 1882: chap. 39.

47. Milo. [B's note *MS. T*, removed in *Proof D*] Milo of Crotona, a celebrated Athenian athlete. The story of his death as a result of the oak's 'rebound' is told in Aulus Gellius, *Noctes Atticae*, XV. 16. B chooses this peculiar allusion in order to make a reference (via the 'Oak's' rebound) to England's defeat of Napoleon. See below ll. 120–1 for a similar oblique reference to England.

55. Sylla. [B's note *MS. T*, removed in *Proof D*] Lucius Sulla, the great Roman dictator who resigned his office in 79 B.C.: cf. *CHP IV*, st. 83.

64. Charles Vth. [B's note *MS. T*, removed in *Proof D*] Charles V, the Roman Emperor and, as King of Spain, Charles I (1500–58). He abdicated in 1556, an action popularly understood in the terms B has set forth.

80–1. Cf. Isaiah 66: 1.

100–1. Cf. the Juvenal epigraph.

109. Marie Louise of Austria (1791–1847), Napoleon's second wife.

125–6. Dionysius the Younger (*fl.* 368–44 B.C.), a byword for a person who has suffered an extreme reversal of fortunes. He was tyrant of Syracuse, but was banished (for the second time) in 344 B.C. He later died at Corinth, where he was said to have started a school for boys.

127. In allusion to the well known fable of the Cage of Bajazet by order of Tamerlane. [B's note *MS. T*, removed in *Proof D*] The legend has it that when Tamerlane conquered Bajazet I, Sultan of Turkey, in 1402, he then confined him in a cage to prevent his escape.

131. Nebuchadnezzar, King of Babylon (see Daniel 4: 5).

136. Prometheus. [B's note *MS. T*, removed in *Proof D*]

141–2. 'The fiend's arch mock./ To lip a wanton, and suppose her chaste.' —Shakespeare. [B's note, 1st edn., sent with *Proof A* to Murray on 12 Apr.] See *Othello*, IV. i. 69–70. The 'last act' was a false and malicious story that Napoleon had a casual affair just before he left for Elba.

227a. 10–16. According to *C* (III. 314 n.), the details are from a print of Napoleon owned by B.

228. *MS.* B's draft (*MS. Le*, location: Leeds), undated; B's fair copy (*MS. Υ*, location: Yale). Unpublished. B made the translation at the request of Lady Sitwell (see his letter to her of 15 Apr. 1814, *BLJ* IV. 97) and told her at the time that the song 'had escaped my observation or my memory when in Greece'. For the original see P. Arabantinos, Συλλογὴ δημωδῶν ᾀσμάτων τῆς Ἠπείρου (Athens, 1880), p. 235, no. 396. B echoed his own translation later in writing his stanzas 'To the Po'.

The poem's 'fount of waters' is the Castalian spring on Mt. Parnassus (see also *CHP I*, st. 1). The speaker's 'love', therefore, is the poetic Muse, or (in the political context) the ancient spirit of Greek freedom, or (more literally, and according to the myth) the daughter of Achelous, who threw herself into the spring to escape the pursuit of Apollo.

229. *MS.* B's draft (*MS. L*, location: Bodleian–Lovelace), dated 18 Apr. 1814. Published first in *Murray's Magazine*, 1 (May 1887) from *L* under title 'Calvary', and again in *Ashton*, 20 n.; facsimile of *L* in *Astarte* (1905). Uncollected. The poem distinctly anticipates B's series of *Hebrew Melodies*, though on a rather severe note. Ashton rightly suggests the political overtones of the poem, for B is making an unexpressed connection between Jesus and the Jewish people, and Napoleon and the people of Europe (especially England). Napoleon abdicated on 11 Apr.

230. *MS.* A copy in unknown hand, undated, with 'Byron' written at end (*MS. T*, location: Texas). Uncollected, first published in Capt. Jesse's *Life of George Brummell* (1844), I. 288, from a copy in Brummell's (now lost) album book of verses; *MS. T* printed in *Pratt*, 128, where a date of 1806 is conjectured. Jesse's *Life* prints the poem with the verses '[To Lady Caroline Lamb]' (no. 189), and in fact the poems are companion pieces. B sent the present poem to Lady Melbourne in a letter of 25 Apr. 1814, with the remark: 'I don't often bore you with rhyme—but as a wrapper to this note—I send you some upon a *brunette*—which I have shewn to no one else—if you think them not much beneath the common places—you may give them to any of your "Album" acquaintances' (*BLJ* IV. 105). In 1812 B had sent at least one stanza of '[To Lady Caroline Lamb]' to Lady Melbourne, and it is probable that Brummell had both poems from her, though B could have given them to Brummell himself (B's close acquaintance with Brummell in fact began only a few weeks after his 25 Apr. letter to Lady Melbourne: see *BLJ* IV. 117). After their bitter falling-out, B was seeing Lady Caroline again on friendly terms in Apr. 1814 (see *BLJ* IV. 103–5 and *Marchand*, I. 457–8), much to the alarm of Lady Melbourne. The lock of hair B had from Lady Caroline was on display at the Victoria and Albert Museum Byron Exhibition (1974).

231. *MS. and Publishing History.* B's MS. of these couplets is on a single sheet (dated by Murray 25 Apr. 1814) among the proofs of the *Ode to Napoleon* at Harrow. They were first published in a textual note in *C* III. 313. Hitherto uncollected. The couplets are a pendant to stanza 16 of the *Ode*.

232. B's draft MS. (Bodleian–Lovelace), untitled, undated, unsigned. At the top of the MS., in another hand, is written: 'Stanzas for Music May 10–14.' Facsimile reproduction: *Astarte* (1905). First published in *A Selection of Hebrew Melodies*, Revised Edition, by Isaac Nathan (1827–9). A slightly different version was published in *Life*, I. 554–5 from a letter B sent to Moore of 4 May 1814. All subsequent collected editions have reproduced the Moore text. *Ashton*, however, follows the N*1827–9* text, which was published from a MS. (not forthcoming) which B gave Nathan to publish, specifying only that, when he published the verses, he indicate that they 'were written two years previously to his marriage' (Nathan, *Fugitive Pieces*, 66). The subject of the poem is B's sister, Augusta, as indicated in *Astarte*, 162: 'Lady Byron wrote (in 1817) of these meetings with Augusta: "She acknowledged that the verses ('I speak not, I trace not, I breathe not thy name') of which I have the original, were addressed to her." ' (See also *Marchand*, I. 448–9 and *Ashton*, 93–4, 129–31.)

1. Cf. Pope's *Eloisa to Abelard*, 9 and Thomas Moore's 'Oh! breathe not his name', 1 (*Irish Melodies*).

17. *Astarte* (329) compares the cancelled lines to *Manfred*, II. iv. 124–6.

233. MS. Charles Hanson's copy (*MS. M*, location: Murray). First printed in *Life*, I. 559–60 (without the final six lines), collected thereafter, with the last six lines added from *M* in *C*.

Moore (*Life*, I. 254) says the meeting for which these lines were intended was in May 1814. It was the annual gathering of the Royal Caledonian Asylum, whose subscribers helped in the education and support of the children of Scottish soldiers, sailors, and marines who fought for Britain.

234. B's draft (*MS. L*, location: Bodleian–Lovelace); copy by R. C. Dallas (*MS. M*, location: Murray, written in a copy of *EBSR5*); copy in another hand (*MS. N*, location: Marlay Papers, Univ. of Nottingham Library). One and probably two fair copies by B existed at one time (see *LJ* III. 85 n.), and a copy from one of these may have been printer's copy for the unauthorized printings (see below). First published in the *Champion*, 31 July 1814, and reprinted from there in *Morning Chronicle* on 1 Aug., both without B's knowledge or permission (*BLJ* IV. 152). Reprinted in Effingham Wilson's piracy *Three Poems* . . . (1818); a new text appeared in *Paris1831* (first printing in a collected edition). First collected in England in *1831* (imperfect), reprinted (complete) in *1832*, and this text has been reprinted since. Collation shows that *1831* and *1832* were almost certainly based on one of B's lost fair copies. *MS. M* is also derived from a non-extant text, perhaps from one of B's MSS. as well. B said the unauthorized printings were made from an imperfect copy (*BLJ* IV. 149).

B sent a copy of the poem to Lady Jersey on 29 May 1814 (*BLJ* IV. 120), when it was written. The portrait which the Prince Regent removed from his gallery of pictures of Regency beauties was by Mrs. Anne Mee, a miniaturist employed by the Prince Regent. That the Regent's act, and B's poem, were politically motivated, see *Blessington*, 36–8, and line 50 here.

8. See *CHP IV*, st. 54, line 3 and note.

25–7. Cf. Revelation 7: 17.

235. *MS.* Not extant. First published *Life*, I. 561–2, from B's verse letter to Moore sent in June 1814. Reprinted *1831*, *1832*, and thereafter.

4–8. Recalling Pope, *Dunciad*, II. 269–351.

9. See '[On Southey's Laureateship]', no. 214.

11. B quotes the final line of Southey's *Carmen Triumphale* . . . (1814).

12. Thomas Sternhold (d. 1549), the versifier of the Psalms.

14. The Czar of Russia and the King of Prussia visited England in June 1814, amidst great festivities (see B's letter to Moore of 14 June (*BLJ* IV. 125–6 and *LJ* III. 93 n.).

15. *Hetman*: a Cossack chief.

23. *C* quotes the *Journal of Mary Frampton*: 'The Emperor is fond of dancing. . . . He waltzed with Lady Jersey, whom he admires, to the great discomposure of the Regent, who has quarrelled with her' (*C* VII. 40 n.).

236. *MS. and Publishing History.* The couplet was first printed in *C* 'from an autograph MS. in the possession of Mr. A. H. Hallam Murray' (VII. 36). The MS. has not reappeared. The title of the epigram is the motto of the Prince of Wales. The date, suggested in *C*, is conjectural.

237. B's draft, titled, dated (location: Bodleian–Lovelace). B plundered the fragment for the Hebrew Melody 'Sun of the Sleepless!' (no. 266). Uncollected; published only in facsimile, in *Astarte* (1905). The lyric seems to have been extracted from the fragment between 8 and 19 Sept. (see *Ashton*, 22).

6–8. Echoes no. 162, lines 3–4.

34. Echoes Dante, *Paradiso*, XIII. 78.

238. *MS. and Publishing History. MS. P* (B's fair copy, corrected: lines 1–12 reproduced in facsimile in J. Pearson & Co. Catalogue, n.d., item 22; seen in a clipping from the 'Byron Personal File', New York Public Library MSS. Dept.). The original stanza numbers are crossed out; and *MS. P* was copy text for the poem's first publication. First published anonymously in the *Morning Chronicle*, 7 Oct. 1814; reprinted in Murray's first edition of *Hebrew Melodies* (1815) and in *CHP(10)*, collected *1815* and thereafter. Sir Peter Parker was B's first cousin (1785–1814) and the brother of Margaret Parker, one of B's boyhood loves. He died in August while storming the American camp at Baltimore. B wrote the memorial stanzas at the request of his relations (see *BLJ* IV. 197–8).

1. *C* compares Tasso's sonnet 'Questa tomba non è, che non è morto'.

239. *MS.* Not extant. First published in *N1827–9*, again in *Nathan*; first collected *1832*, and thereafter. *Ashton* prints a critical text. In *N1827–9* the lines are apparently wrongly arranged into two stanzas of eight and four lines respectively. Probably written in late 1814 (see *Ashton*, 25).

B destroyed his first copy of the poem when Kinnaird spoke slightingly of it, but B gave Nathan another copy, which Nathan kept (see *Nathan*, 71). For B's attitude towards hope see also his Diary for 1821 (*LJ* V. 190).

epigraph *Georgics* II. 490.

240. *MS.* B's draft, titled and dated, is in the Murray archives. *Publishing History*: first published, *C*. The fragment is an unfinished Byronic tale of guilt and suffering. Its chief interest lies in the clarity of its method, and consequently in the light it throws on all of B's gloomy narratives. The lack of picturesque detail in this poem, evident in poems like *Giaour*, emphasizes the fantasy element present in all such stories. The poem is largely a psychological projection, a dream narrative. This fact is emphasized in lines 33–4, where B's neglect in furnishing inverted commas in the MS. produces a confusion between the voice of Julian and the narrator's voice. (Inverted commas are provided for the stranger's words at lines 42 ff. in the MS.) *C* eliminated this quality in the poem by printing 'his' for 'my' in line 33, and by writing 'He rose' for 'Ah me' in line 34.

241. *MS.* B's draft (*MS. A*, location: Bodleian–Lovelace) dated 'Halnaby 1815'; Lady B's fair copy (*MS. B*, location: Harvard) with a note from B to Kinnaird: 'Vide note on Number 2 [i.e. 'By The Rivers of Babylon We Sat Down and Wept']—I think this the *best* of the two.' (See *Ashton*, 164, 167 nn.) Written in Jan. 1815. First published in *N1827–9* (see no. 232), again in *Nathan*; first collected in *C*, *More*. For further comment see 'By The Rivers of Babylon . . . ' (no. 270), and *Nathan*, 69.

8var. *N1827–9P* and *E* distinguish the letterpress and the engraved printings in Nathan's edition.

242. *MS.* B's draft, dated 26 Jan. 1815, with the title in Lady B's hand supplied afterwards (location: Bodleian–Lovelace); unpublished. The play was apparently never performed (see *LBW* 273–89).

13. *Macbeth*, v. v. 25.

23. *I Henry IV*, II. iv. 277.

25. B means Ben Jonson, not Samuel Johnson.

36. Elizabeth O'Neill (1791–1872), actress; afterwards Lady Becher.

243. Except for the first lines, which Malcolm Elwin printed (*LBW* 276, n. 1), these verses are unpublished. They are preserved in MS. in the Lovelace Papers, and endorsed by Annabella: 'Bout-rimés Nonsense at Seaham 1815.' The italicized lines are by Lady Byron. In 1816, during the Separation proceedings, she recalled 'making bout-rimés together in the drawing room with that sort of mirth which seeks to jest away bitter truths' (*LBW* 275–6). The verses were probably written in late January or early February.

244. *MS.* Two MSS. survive, B's rough draft (*MS. A*), untitled, but dated at the top by Lady B 12 Feb. 1815. In this MS., the cancelled initial stanza was numbered '1', and the present stanza 1 was numbered '2'. This shows that B changed his mind about the metrical form of the poem while writing the present stanza 1. The second MS. is a fair copy in Lady B's hand, untitled, undated, with B's corrections (*MS. B*). *MS. A* is in the Lovelace papers, and *MS. B* is in the Murray collection. *Publishing History.* First published, *1831* (and collected thereafter), probably from *MS. B*, though with a probable copyist's error in line 23. *Ashton* has a critical text. B probably wrote the poem with the 'Vision of Belshazzar' (no. 265) and then chose the latter for inclusion in his *Hebrew Melodies*, apparently on the advice of William Gifford. An undated letter from Gifford to B in the Murray archives discusses the subject of B's two poems and concludes: 'If one of the two melodies . . . must be omitted let it be the former [i.e. no. 244], the latter [i.e. no. 265] is beyond all praise.' The poem's general allusion is to Daniel 5. It is a (not very darkly) veiled political allegory on the Prince Regent. For commentary see *Ashton*, 89–90.

245. All the MSS. of this poem are in Bodleian–Lovelace. *MS. A* is B's draft and *MS. B* is Lady B's fair copy. Both are untitled and undated, and both lack stanza 2. Two autograph copies of this stanza survive: *MS. C*, a draft headed 'Addition', and *MS. D*, a fair copy headed '2'. *Publishing History.* The poem was first published by Power in 1815 with a musical setting, in five pages, as *There's not a Joy this World Can Give. Written by Lord Byron.—Composed* *by Sir John Stevenson*. It was published again, in a revised form, in *Poems1816*, and collected thereafter in the revised form. The poem was written in the middle of Feb. 1815, shortly after B learnt of the death of his youthful friend the Duke of Dorset (see nos. 47, 246, 247), who was killed by a fall from his horse on 14 Feb. 1815. Lady B has dated *MS. D* above 'Feb. 24. 1814. Seaham' (but '1814' should be 1815). B sent the poem (probably *MS. B*) to Moore in a letter of 2 Mar. 1815 (see *BLJ* IV. 277, 279–80). A year later, in another letter to Moore (*BLJ* V. 45), B spontaneously mentioned the poem again 'as being the truest, though the most melancholy, I ever wrote'. Though written a year before, stanza 2 was not included in the poem's first printing. It was probably at the time of his Mar. 1816 letter to Moore, or shortly afterwards, that he decided to include the stanza, and to permit the poem to acquire a suggestive application to the melancholy events of his marriage separation. That B was aware of this application is plain from his comments to Moore in his Mar. 1816 letter, where he rhetorically asked of his verses: 'Were they not a little prophetic?'

title   These Verses were given by Lord Byron to Mr. Power, Strand, who has published them, with very beautiful music by Sir John Stevenson. [Note to the poem in *Poems1816*]

epigraph   Gray, 'Alcaic Fragment'.

stanza 2   The lines recall numbers of passages in B's poems from Switzerland in 1816. See esp. *CHP III* and 'Stanzas to [Augusta]' (no. 299), 17 ff.

19. Cf. 'Stanzas to [Augusta]', 45 ff.

246. *MS. and Publishing History*. B's first draft, untitled, undated (*MS. VA*, location: *V* and *A*, Forster Collection); his fair copy, untitled, undated, with the heading in another hand: 'Lines Written on the Death of the Duke of Dorset a College Friend of Lord Byron's who was killed by a fall from his horse while Hunting' (*MS. Le*, location: Leeds); facsimile of a copy in another hand, undated and titled 'Stanzas' (location: Univ. of Iowa Library). The two corrections written in here are not in B's hand.

First published in *Arliss's Pocket Magazine* in 1824, then edited by R. A. Davenport (1777?–1852), to whom B sent *MS. VA*, as well as a MS. of the next poem (see commentary below; and see also R. R. Madden, *The Literary Life and Correspondence of the Countess of Blessington* (1855), II. 215, and Thomas Lombardi, *BNYPL* 71 (1967), 39–46). The *Arliss* text prints the Iowa facsimile MS., and this text was reprinted in the *Edinburgh Annual Register* (1824), by Madden, in *More*, and by W. T. Bandy (*MLR*, Jan. 1949). *Paris 1826* also reprints this text. First collected in England in *C*, which states that its text is taken from a Murray *MS*. The latter is no longer at Murray's, and has not appeared, but it must have been a late fair copy, intermediate between *MS. Le* and the Iowa facsimile.

Copy text here is *Arliss*, which requires some explanation. Though the Murray MS. has not been seen, it—or a copy made from it—must have been copy text for the Iowa facsimile MS., and thence for *Arliss*. *C*'s transcription of the Murray MS. has clearly gone astray somehow in line 7, probably by a misreading of B's original MS. Another problematical variant ('my' or 'mine') in line 5 probably arises from either an alternative reading in the Murray MS., or from *C*'s reading of a correction by B as an alternative reading. *C*'s reading of 'wast' for 'wert' in line 3 is probably also a mistake, as the collation indicates. In general, when *C* prints from B's MSS., one finds numerous errors of these sorts.

B sent *MS. VA* to Davenport in Mar. 1816 (*BLJ* v. 43), after Davenport had requested, in 1815, a poem or two from B for Davenport's *Poetical Register*. This is shown by Davenport's covering note to *MS. VA*, which corroborates B's letter to him: 'These lines are in Lord Byron's own handwriting. I received them from him, along with another poem, in 1815. I add the seal and postmark, in confirmation of my statement.' The date is, however, 1816. But B's letter of Mar. 1816 shows that he had placed certain MSS., then at Murray's, at Davenport's disposal. Thus, the Iowa facsimile, from which Davenport printed the poem in *Arliss*, was probably an exact transcription of the Murray MS., the last corrected fair copy. Murray either had it copied for Davenport, or the latter himself had the copy made. Whichever was the case, the Iowa facsimile and *Arliss* text must be the preferred one. Indeed, the corrections in the facsimile almost certainly represent an attempt to copy B's original MS. exactly. The text of the facsimile is signed 'Byron' just as B normally signed his MSS.

For further discussion see commentaries for nos. 47, 245, 247.

10–16. Cf. *Corsair*, III. 664–8.

247. Unpublished. B's draft MS. is on the same leaf as the previous poem (*MS. VA*, location: *V and A*, Forster Collection); untitled, undated. A fair copy (*MS. G*, location: in collection of W. F. Godden, Quinns Rock, W. A.) in Augusta's hand, headed by her 'Stanzas'. Beneath this title R. A. Davenport has added 'By Lord Byron', and at the bottom of the MS. is his note: 'I received this poem from Lord Byron and can vouch that it is in his own handwriting. R. A. D.' The autograph MSS. which Davenport had are in fact now in *V* and *A*, but his note here shows that he was somehow provided with multiple copies of the two poems which B gave him. For a discussion of these matters, and the circumstances of the poem (which is on the death of the Duke of Dorset), see the commentary for the previous poem.

248. *MS. and Publishing History.* The lines were sent as part of a letter to Thomas Moore, 27 Mar. 1815. Collected, *1831*, *1832*, and thereafter. The MS. is not extant. *C* (VII. 41n.) notes that the verses were occasioned by 'a paragraph in the *Morning Chronicle* of 27 March 1815: "In the *Moniteur* of Thursday we find the Emperor's own account of his *jaunt* from the Island of

Elba to the palace of the Thuilleries. It seems certainly more like a jaunt of pleasure than the progress of an invader through a country to be gained." '

249–72. HEBREW MELODIES. This book (*HM*) is a group of the songs which B wrote for Isaac Nathan, who wanted to set to music a series of sacred songs on Jewish subjects written by B. The project came about through the intervention of B's friend Douglas Kinnaird, who wrote to B on 15 Sept. 1814 to propose the project (three months after Nathan had also written to B, but unsuccessfully). The songs were written in 1814 and 1815, some in fact before the project was specifically begun (and one possibly as early as 1813), and a few of the pieces are not on sacred subjects. B began specifically writing poems for Nathan in late Sept. or early Oct. 1814, and the last poem he gave to him was 'Bright Be the Place of Thy Soul', written in June 1815.

The poems printed here as a unit comprise the series issued by Murray as *Hebrew Melodies* (*HM1815*) around 23 May 1815. It includes one piece ('It Is the Hour') whose better-known appearance is as the opening lines of *Parisina* (1816). I have kept it in order to preserve the integrity of *HM1815*. But the complete corpus of poems that can properly be called 'Hebrew Melodies' (i.e. poems written by B to be set to music by Nathan) is larger than *HM1815*, and has been collected in Thomas Ashton's critical edition. The additional poems printed by Ashton include: 'Francisca' (a version of lines 15–28 of *Parisina*), 'Stanzas for Music' ('I speak not—I trace not— I breathe not thy name'), 'They Say That Hope Is Happiness', 'In the Valley of Waters', 'To Belshazzar', and 'Bright Be the Place of Thy Soul'. Of this larger corpus Nathan printed, in 1815, 1827, and 1829, different editions of various songs with his own musical settings; only 'To Belshazzar' was not set to music by Nathan.

The history of Nathan's publications is complex but has been admirably detailed by Ashton. Suffice it to say that Nathan and Kinnaird had a falling-out late in 1814, that Murray became interested in publishing the lyrics, and that Nathan determined to continue with his project independently. He was the first to publish twelve of the pieces with music in Apr. 1815 as *A Selection of Hebrew Melodies* (*N1815*). *HM1815* was published next, containing twenty-five poems, including the pieces in *N1815* as well as twelve more songs and (not a Hebrew Melody) 'On the Death of Sir Peter Parker, Bart.' A second issue of *HM1815* appeared in June when *HM* was incorporated into Murray's first collected edition, *1815*. Nathan's second part of *N1815* appeared in November and included the rest of *HM1815*, except 'From Job', as well as 'Francisca'. Various other editions, none of them textually relevant, appeared between 1815 and 1827, when Nathan began the issue of his second, augmented *Selection of Hebrew Melodies* (*N1827–9*). This later selection included the poems from *N1815*, 'From Job', 'Stanzas for Music', 'They Say That Hope Is Happiness', and 'In the Valley of Waters'. Nathan added yet another Hebrew Melody to his corpus when he published 'Bright Be the Place of Thy Soul' in his *Fugitive Pieces* . . . (1829, cited herein as *Nathan*). He had not previously collected this poem, but had issued it only as a separate song-sheet in 1815. 'To Belshazzar' was not published until *1831*.

Printer's copy for *HM1815* were copies made by Lady B. These B had himself supervised and, where necessary, corrected. Though no proofs survive for *HM1815*, collation shows that B intervened with corrections between the printer's copy and the final printed text. Printer's copy for the first part of *N1815* must have been the MSS. which Nathan had in his possession, fair copies by B; for the second part it was *HM1815* (excluding 'Francisca'). In *N1827-9* Nathan printed his new poems from the MSS. he had in his possession from B. These facts explain the choice of copy texts here: *HM1815* (for all poems which are printed there); *N1827-9* (for the poems first printed there); *1831* (for 'To Belshazzar'). *Poems1816* is copy text for 'Bright Be the Place of Thy Soul' because this was the only printing for which B corrected proof. B did not correct any of Nathan's editions in proof.

In the present edition, the poems which Ashton includes in his work, but which are not part of *HM1815*, are placed in the general chronological sequence of B's poetry. *Ashton* has been automatically included in all collations. I have retained, for the most part, *Ashton*'s notations and sigla for the different editions and MSS., mainly to allow the reader easier reference if he should wish to consult that edition.

The reader may note that B began, but left unfinished, the poem 'Magdalen' in Apr. 1814, before this project was suggested to him. It is on a Jewish theme but is not a song, and—what is noteworthy—its attitude towards its subject is rather different from that which we find in the later Melodies.

Finally, B began, but quickly cancelled, one further Melody which would have versified the text of Psalms 107: 23 ff.

> They that go down upon the Deep
>   Behold the Almighty's wonders
> When oer the ⟨deep⟩ deck the surges sweep
>   And Oceans echo thunders—

The fragment is on the verso of *MS. A* of 'Saul' but was evidently written before 'Saul'—at Halnaby in Jan. 1815. It is printed in *Ashton*, 174 n.

For more detailed comment the reader can consult Ashton's edition, which has full historical, bibliographical, and critical commentaries and descriptions, as well as notes and apparatus. The individual commentaries below contain information relevant to the specific poems. Mention should be made of Teresa Guiccioli's MS. copy of *Hebrew Melodies* (location: Newstead). Her copies of the poems were made from *HM1815*, however, not from MSS., and they are not textually relevant.

headnote: John Braham (born Abraham, 1774–1856), composer and singer.

249. *MS. and Publishing History.* B's draft, dated June 1814 (*MS. W*: see the facsimile in Peter Croft, *Autograph Poetry in the English Language* (1973), II. 103-4; location, unknown, in private hands); Augusta Leigh's MS. copy headed 'Lines Written by Lord Byron after seeing Mrs. Wilmot at Lansdowne House' (*MS. AL*, location: *BM*, in her Commonplace Book, Add. MS. 58802). The title, along with the text of some of her other MS. copies in this Commonplace Book, suggests that she may have copied the poem from MS., rather than from the early publications. First published *N1815*, again in *HM1815*, collected thereafter.

Composed, according to James Wedderburn Webster, on 12 June, the day after B had been to 'Lady Sitwell's party in Seymour Place. He there for the first time saw his cousin, the beautiful Mrs. Wilmot. When we returned to his rooms in Albany, he said little, but desired Fletcher to give him a *tumbler* of *Brandy*, which he drank at once to Mrs. Wilmot's health, then retired to rest, and was, I heard afterwards, in a sad state all night' (see *BLJ* IV. 124 and n.).

There is a recurrent confusion in the Byronic literature about the identity of this Mrs. Wilmot (see e.g. *LJ* II. 332 and n., or *BLJ* IV. 290 and n., and compare *C* III. 381 and *Ashton*, 132 n.). She is not the authoress Barbarina Ogle (1768–1854), afterwards Lady Dacre (1819), but Anne Wilmot (1784–1871), daughter of Eusebius Horton of Derbyshire. She married B's first cousin Robert John Wilmot (1784–1841). The confusion occurs because Lady Dacre's first husband was Valentine Wilmot (see *LBW* 301, 426, 524).

When B saw Mrs. Wilmot at Lady Sitwell's party, she 'appeared in mourning, with dark spangles on her dress' (*1832* X. 75). Earlier, when B observed her in the 'Coteries' of Regency life, he remarked: 'Mrs. Wilmot . . . is a swan, and might frequent a purer stream' (see his Journal for 22 Nov. 1813, *BLJ* III. 214). Both *LJ* (II. 332 n.) and *BLJ* identify this as Barbarina Ogle, but the description suggests Mrs. Robert Wilmot. In this case the confusion seems to arise from Webster's remark (above) that B 'first' saw his cousin at Lady Sitwell's party. But Webster is wrong (see *LBW* 193 n.).

250. *MS.* B's draft, undated (*MS. A*, location: *BM*); Charles Hanson's copy of *MS. A* (*MS. B*, location: Murray) with Hanson's note: 'Ch. H. 8 Feb [18] 15 N.B. The last stanza crossed out in original [i.e. in *MS. A*].' Augusta Leigh's MS. copy in her Commonplace Book (*MS. AL*, location: *BM*; see no. 249 above) has an interesting variant at line 4. First printed *N1815*, again in *HM1815*, collected thereafter. *N1815* divides the poem into numbered quatrains. The format of lines 2, 16, 20 is wrong in *HM1815*. Probably composed early in 1815, but the final stanza was added some time later when B gave the first version of the poem to Nathan (*Nathan*, 33). Ashton (p. 23) thinks it may have been written late in 1814.

1. Recalling Moore's Irish Melody, 'The Harp that once, thro' Tara's halls'.

12–13. Cf. Psalms 65: 13.

17–20. Cf. *Giaour*, 1135–8.

251. *MS.* The only MS. is Augusta's copy (*MS. AL*, location: *BM*; see no. 249 above), which must have been made from a MS. First published *N1815*, then in *HM1815*, collected thereafter. Ashton (p. 23) points out that it must have been written late in 1814.

1–4. Cf. Revelation 7: 17.

252. *MS.* B's draft, undated (*MS. A*, location: Murray); first published *N1815*, again in *HM1815*, collected thereafter. Ashton (p. 25) dates it Nov.–Dec. 1814.

5. Cf. 'To Ianthe', st. 4 and *Giaour*, 473–4.

253. *MS.* Not extant; first published *N1815*, again in *HM1815*, collected thereafter. Written in early Sept. 1814 (*Ashton*, 23), and probably the first of the series which B specifically wrote as a 'Hebrew Melody'.

6–8. Echoes Lamentations 5: 15.

10. Echoes Psalms 55: 6.

11. Echoes Matthew 8: 20.

254. *MS.* B's draft, undated (*MS. A*, location: *BM*); first published *N1815*, again in *HM1815*, collected thereafter. Composed probably in Sept. 1814 (*Ashton*, 23).

3. Cf. I Kings 19: 18.

5. Cf. Exodus 32: 15–16.

6–7. Cf. Exodus 34: 29–35.

8. Cf. Exodus 33: 20.

255. *MS.* Not extant; first published *N1815*, again in *HM1815*, collected thereafter. Composed probably Nov.–Dec. 1814 (*Ashton*, 25). The poem is based on Judges 11: 29–40.

256. *MS.* B's draft, undated (*MS. A*) and Charles Hanson's copy of *MS. A* (*MS. B*, dated 8 Feb. 1815): location, Murray; B's later corrected fair copy (*MS. C*, location: Bodleian–Lovelace) with a note by Lady B: 'Given me at Seaham before my Marriage.' Written in late 1814, in Sept.–Oct. according to Ashton (p. 23). First published *N1815*; this text reprinted in *Examiner*, 23 Apr. 1815; in *HM1815*, and collected thereafter.

Of the subject of the poem B said to Nathan: 'She is no more, and perhaps the only vestige of her existence is the feeling I sometimes fondly indulge' (*Nathan*, 30). *C* suggests that the poem is part of the Thyrza cycle.

4. See B's Journal entry for 27 Feb. 1821 (*LJ* v. 210).

257. No extant MS.; first published *N1815*, again in *HM1815*, collected thereafter. Probably written in Nov.–Dec. 1814 (*Ashton*, 25).

According to Nathan, B wrote this poem to 'try how a *Madman* could write; seizing the pen with eagerness, he for a moment fixed his eyes in majestic wildness on vacancy; when like a flash of inspiration, without erasing a single word, the above verses were the result, which he put into my possession with the remark: "if I am mad who write, be certain that you are so who compose!" ' (*Nathan*, 37). B's text is 1 Samuel 16: 14–23.

1. Cf. Ossian, 'Oina-Morul' (*The Poems of Ossian* (1803), I. 285).

1–6. Cf. Ossian, 'The War of Caros' (*ibid.* II. 9–10).

258. *MS.* B's corrected fair copy (*MS. A*, location: Texas), undated, watermark 1814. Augusta made a MS. copy (*MS. AL*, location: BM; see no. 249 above) from a MS. not now extant. First published *N1815*, again in *HM1815*, collected thereafter. Ashton (pp. 22–3) conjectures an early date of composition: early 1814, or even late 1813. Both *Ashton* and *C* associate the poem with Lady Frances Wedderburn Webster, largely because of the 'eye of blue' in line 2: compare B's sonnets to Genevra (nos. 219, 220).

1–4. Echoing Sir William Jones's 'Essay on the Poetry of the Eastern Nations', *Works*, X. 335.

259. *MS.* The only MS. is Augusta's copy (*MS. AL*, location: BM; see no. 249), headed 'Thy Days are done'. First published *N1815*, again in *HM1815*, collected thereafter. Ashton (p. 23) conjectures plausibly that the subject of the poem is B's cousin Sir Peter Parker, and that it was written early in Oct. 1814. See 'On the Death of Sir Peter Parker, Bart.' (no. 238).

8. Cf. Matthew 16: 28 and John 8: 52.

260. *MS.* The only extant MS. is by Augusta Leigh (*MS. AL*, location: BM; see no. 249 above), headed 'It is the Hour'. But the lines were published as the opening of *Parisina*, of which we have Lady B's copy (see commentary for *Parisina*); first published *N1815*, again in *HM1815*, collected in Murray's editions until 1819. The lyric may have been written as part of *Parisina* as early as 1813, but it is probably later, 1814 (see *Ashton*, 28–9 and nn. and commentary for *Parisina*).

261. *MS.* B's first fair copy dated 'Seaham 1815' (*MS. A*, location: Bodleian–Lovelace); Lady B's copy of *A* with B's corrections (*MS. B*); Lady B's fair copy (*MS. C*); clerk's copy (*MS. D*). MSS. *B*, *C*, *D* are at Murray's. First published *HM1815*, collected thereafter. Written in early Feb. 1815 (and perhaps begun in late Jan.).

B's text is 1 Samuel 28–31, but especially the final chapter (which B quotes from in *MS. C* as a general note to the poem):

Samuel—Chapter the last

('Then said Saul unto his armour bearer, Draw out thy sword and thrust me thorow therewith, lest the uncircumcised come and thrust me thorow and marke me: but his armour bearer would not, for he was sore afraid. Therefore Saul tooke a sword and fell upon it.')

'And when the battle went sore against Saul, the archers and bowmen hit him, and he was sore wounded of the archers. Then said Saul unto his armour bearer, Draw out thy sword and thrust me thorow therewith, lest the uncircumcised come and thrust me thorow and marke me: but his armour bearer would not, for he was sore afraid. Therefore Saul tooke a sword and fell upon it.'

Translation of the scriptures—Edition 1608

For B's remarks on the tragic character of Saul see *Nathan*, 42–3.

7–8. Perhaps recalling Lucan, *Pharsalia*, VII. 310–11.

10. Jonathan. [note in *MS. C*]

262. *MS.* B's draft, dated 'Seaham Feb. 1815' (*MS. A*, location: Bodleian–Lovelace); Lady B's fair copy from *A* (*MS. B*); clerk's copy (*MS. C*). MSS. *B*, *C* are at Murray. Written in early Feb. 1815. First published *HM1815*, collected thereafter.

B's text is 1 Samuel 28: 7–20. Saul's encounter with the witch of Endor was one of B's favourite stories.

27–8. Cf. 1 Samuel 31: 4.

263. *MS.* B's draft (*MS. A*, location: Bodleian–Lovelace), dated 'Seaham 1815'; Lady B's fair copy of *A* (*MS. B*, location: Murray). First published *HM1815*, collected thereafter. Written in Feb. 1815, 'probably the last of the poems to be composed at Seaham' (*Ashton*, 27). B's text is of course the opening chapter of Ecclesiastes, another favourite passage of his.

5. Perhaps recalling Scott, *The Lady of the Lake* XXIV. 19.

264. *MS.* B's draft dated 'Seaham Feb. 1815' (*MS. A*, location: Bodleian–Lovelace); Lady B's copy of *A* (*MS. B*, location: Murray). First published *HM1815*, collected thereafter. Written in Feb. 1815.

E. Sarmiento's 'A Parallel Between Lord Byron and Fray Luis De León' (*RES* IV (1953), 267–73) discusses a curious and remarkable similarity which may in fact be a borrowing.

1–4. Cf. Ecclesiastes 12: 7.

9. Cf. *Siege*, 417var.

19. Cf. *Prophecy*, III. 9.

20. Cf. 'On This Day I Complete My Thirty Sixth Year' (no. 402).

26. Cf. *Heaven and Earth*, 715.

265. *MS.* Lady B's fair copy with B's corrections (*MS. A*, location: Murray). First published *HM1815*, collected thereafter. Written at Seaham in Feb. 1815 (*Ashton*, 26–7).

B's text is Daniel 5.

5–8. Cf. 2 Kings 16.

16. Cf. *DJ* III, st. 65 and VII, st. 134.

34. Daniel was not 'a youth' when he interpreted the 'writing on the wall' for Belshazzar.

42–3. Cf. *Ode to Napoleon*, 109–12.

266. *MS.* B first wrote the lines as part of the unfinished poem 'Harmodia' (see commentary for no. 237) on 8 Sept. 1814; B's first fair copy (*MS. B*, location: Bodleian–Lovelace); another fair copy by B (*MS. C*, location: Murray). B extracted the poem for a Hebrew Melody before 19 Sept. First published *HM1815*, collected thereafter.

When asked whether the poem addressed the moon or the evening star, B made a facetious reply (*Nathan*, 81). But the MSS. show he was thinking of the moon. For further comment and notes see no. 237.

6. Cf. no. 162, lines 3–4 and *Giaour*, 101–2.

267. *MS.* B's fair copy (*MS. A*, location: Bodleian–Lovelace); Lady B's fair copy (*MS. B*, location: Murray). *MS. A* dated 'Seaham 1815'; the poem was written in Feb. First published *HM1815*, collected thereafter.

As Ashton points out (p. 93), the poem is a sort of companion piece to 'On the Day of the Destruction of Jerusalem by Titus'. The speaker is a Jew of the Diaspora.

268. *MS.* B's draft dated 'Halnaby Jan. 1815' (*MS. A*), and his fair copy dated 13 Jan. 1815 (*MS. B*): both in Bodleian–Lovelace; Lady B's fair copy (*MS. C*, location: Murray). First published *HM1815*, collected thereafter.

The poem is a 'mad song', spoken by Herod to his dead wife Mariamne, whom Herod had executed (*c.* 30 B.C.) for infidelity. His later remorse for her murder brought on his temporary madness. B probably knew the story best from Voltaire's play *Mariamne*, though she is famous in literature and history for her noble character, beauty, and tragic fate. In B's poem, Herod should also be recognized as a veiled *figura* of the Prince Regent. For the circumstances of the poem's composition see *Nathan*, 51; and for B on Herod see *BLJ* II. 84.

269. *MS.* B's draft dated 1815 (*MS. A*) and B's fair copy dated 'Halnaby Jan. 18 1815' (*MS. B*): location, Bodleian–Lovelace. Lady B's fair copy with B's corrections (*MS. C*, location: Murray). First published *HM1815*, collected thereafter.

Jerusalem was destroyed in A.D. 70.

1–4. Ashton sees an echo of Moore's 'Tho' the Last Glimpse of Erin with Sorrow I See' (*Irish Melodies*, II).

270. *MS.* B's draft (*MS. A*) and his fair copy (*MS. B*): location, Bodleian–Lovelace. *MS. B* is dated 'Jan. 15 1815 Halnaby'. Lady B's fair copy (*MS. C*, location: Murray) with a pencil note from B to Kinnaird (see *Ashton*, 164 n.) asking him to choose either this poem or the other 'version', 'In the Valley of Waters' (see also *BLJ* IV. 249). First published *HM1815*, collected thereafter.

B's text is Psalm 137.

271. *MS.* B's draft dated 'Seaham Feb. 19 1815' (*MS. A*, location: Bodleian–Lovelace); Lady B's fair copy with B's corrections (*MS. B*, location: Murray). First published *HM1815*, collected thereafter.

B's text is 2 Kings 19 and Isaiah 37. B probably means to draw a comparison with Buonaparte in his poem (see *Ashton*, 80 n.).

See also B's letter to Murray of 7 Sept. 1820 (*LJ* v. 72).

272. *MS.* A draft by B on verso of 'On Jordan's Banks' (*MS. A*, location: BM); Lady B's fair copy (*MS. B*, location: Murray); another draft by B, perhaps the first (*MS. C*, location: Institute of Russian Literature, Academy of Sciences, Leningrad; printed with a facsimile in *Literaturnoe Nasledstvo*, 58 (1952), 982–4). First printed in *HM1815*, collected thereafter; a slightly different text printed in the *Poetical Remains of the Late Henry Savile Shepherd* (1835), 53. Written probably in Oct. 1814 (see *BLJ* IV. 220). See also *Nathan*, 73.

B's text is Job 4: 13–21.

273. *MS.* B's fair copy (*MS. A*) of lines 1–8, dated 9 June 1815 (written on the calling card of Lady Louisa Katherine Forester); B's draft of lines 9–16 (*MS. B*) and his fair copy of 9–16 (*MS. C*): location of *MSS. A, B, C*, Bodleian–Lovelace. Lady B's copy, with B's corrections (*MS. D*, location: Texas); and B's corrected proof for *Poems1816* (location: Murray, on proof sheet with nos. 276 and 279). *Publishing History.* First published in the *Examiner*, 11 June 1815, next as a separate song sheet by Isaac Nathan (1815), then in *Poems1816*; collected thereafter. Hitherto unnoticed publication by John Clarke, set to music, in *Twelve Vocal Pieces* (1817), I. 11. According to Clarke's note, B originally gave it to him 'expressly for this publication; but (owing, possibly, to the delay which has taken place in preparing it) the same poem has appeared in the later editions of his Lordship's Works'. *1832* dates the poem 1808 in a second four-stanza version (VII. 211), but the date and format are both incorrect; *More* prints the incorrect version. For details see *Ashton*, 29–30 and nn. According to *Nathan*, 114, B wrote the poem on a morning when Nathan was visiting B, and recited it the same evening at Drury Lane for the comedian William Dowton.

9. Ossian, 'The War of Inis-Thona': 'Green be the place of my rest' (*The Poems of Ossian* (1803), II. 37). But the substance of the allusion is to the Latin commonplace 'sit tibi terra levis' (may the earth lie lightly on thee).

10. Ashton cites Moore's 'Oh! Breathe Not His Name' (*Irish Melodies*, I).

274. *MS.* B's draft (location: Bodleian–Lovelace). The cover sheet has on it, in Lady B's hand: 'Farewell to the Land—First Copy 1815'. At the bottom of the verso of the actual MS. the poem is dated by Lady B: 'July 25. 1815 London'. The received readings of 'Conquest allured' (6), 'the nations' (7), 'weakness decrees' (11), 'gaze' (15), and 'unfold' (20) are inserted into the MS. in Lady B's hand. *Publishing History*. First published anonymously in the *Examiner*, 30 July 1815 (see *BLJ* IV. 305–6); published again in *Poems 1816*, collected thereafter. B heard with dismay of Napoleon's defeat at Waterloo on 20 June (see *HVSV* 126). Napoleon announced his abdication on 22 June, and he was taken at sea by the British man-of-war *Bellerophon* on 15 July. B wrote his poem while Napoleon was being held aboard the *Bellerophon* at Torbay and awaiting his exile to St. Helena, where he was sent on 8 Aug. As usual in B's poetry, Napoleon is here at least in part a figural self-projection of B himself. The poem is not, of course, a translation.

title We scarcely need remind our readers, that there are points in the following spirited Lines, with which our opinions do not accord; and indeed the Author himself has told us, that he rather adapted them to what may be considered as the speaker's feelings, than his own. [Editorial note preceding the poem in the *Examiner*]

275. B's draft, dated by Lady B 18 Aug. 1815 (*MS. L*, location: Bodleian–Lovelace); uncollected and, though hitherto unknown, it was published and set to music by John Clarke in *Twelve Vocal Pieces* (1817), I. 6–7. According to Clarke, it was 'written expressly for this work by Lord Byron'.

An interesting MS. copy of the poem also survives (*MS. B*) in the hand of James Bain, a descendant of the Macbanes who settled in South America in this century. I have not seen the MS., which does not appear to descend directly from either B's draft or the Clarke text, but a typescript was sent to me by Tessa Bridal, of Minneapolis, Minn. It agrees substantively with the Clarke text, except that Golice Macbane is spelt throughout Gillies MacBean. A letter from James Bain accompanying the MS. reads in part: 'Here is the poem I told you of. It is reputed to be one of the earliest poems of Lord Byron. Gillies MacBean stood 6 ft. 4 and a quarter inch. in his bare feet and the poem was about his death at the Battle of Culloden where he was a major in the MacIntosh battalion of Clan Chattan. . . . The MacBeans were an independant clan—their tartan predominantly red, the great Clan Chattan was a kind of tribal alliance of the MacPhersons, the MacIntoshes, the MacBeans, the Shaws of which alliance MacPherson of Cluny was recognised as chief and the MacBeans were regarded as the military chiefs of the allied clans, i.e., captains of Clan Chattan.'

The following note (not in the MSS.) was appended to the poem in Clarke's text, presumably by B:

The determined fierceness of the Highland Character urges to acts of desperate resolution and heroism. One of a clan, at the battle of Culloden, being singled out and wounded, set his back against a park wall, and with his targe and claymore bore singly the onset of a party of dragoons.—Pushed to desperation, he made resistless strokes at his enemies, who crowded and encumbered themselves to have each the glory of slaying him.—'Save that brave fellow,' was the unregarded cry of some Officers. GOLICE MACBANE was cut to pieces, and thirteen of his enemies lay dead around him. Cromek's Remains, page 200. [Cf. R. H. Cromek, ed., *Remains of Nithsdale and Galloway Song . . .* (1810).]

276. B's draft, untitled, but with a cover sheet in Lady B's hand: 'Lines—the Pole to Bonaparte. First copy. 1815' (*MS. L*, location: Bodleian–Lovelace, with *MS. La*, Lady B's fair copy of stanza 5, with B's corrections); Augusta Leigh's fair copy made from *MS.* L, with B's corrections (*MS. M*, location: Murray, where there is also an uncorrected proof for *Poems 1816*); Lady B's fair copy (*MS. T*, location: Texas). *MS. T* was printer's copy for the proof. First published *Poems 1816*, collected thereafter.

The prefatory note and the note to line 16 are both from letters sent to B from Hobhouse when the latter was in Paris (see *BLJ* IV. 287, 294, 306). The poem was written between May and Sept. 1814, and is not 'From the French'.

Prefatory note   *Savary . . . Lord Keith*: Jean Marie Savary, Duc de Rovigo (1774–1833), general, politician; George Keith Elphinstone, Viscount Keith (1746–1823), the English government's intermediary with Napoleon in the correspondence concerning his removal to St. Helena.

16. At Waterloo, one man was seen, whose left arm was shattered by a cannon ball, to wrench it off with the other, and throwing it up in the air, exclaimed to his comrades, 'Vive l'Empereur, jusqu'à la mort.' There were many other instances of the like: this you may, however, depend on as true. *A private Letter from Brussels*. [B's note in *MS. T, proof*]

277. *MS*: not forthcoming. First published, anonymously, in *Examiner*, 7 Apr. 1816; published again *Poems 1816*, collected thereafter. Leigh Hunt came to dine with B, Scrope Davies, and Hobhouse on 3 Apr. (see *Marchand*, II. 596–7). B either gave Hunt these lines that evening, for publication in the *Examiner*, or he promised Hunt a poem for the paper, and sent it shortly after. But the poem was probably written much earlier, in Sept. 1815 and the period when he was writing a series of Napoleonic poems. On 17 Sept.

1815 he received 'a cross of the "Legion of Honour" ' from Lady Caroline Lamb, who sent it to him from Paris (*BLJ* IV. 312).

title   The friend who favoured us with the following lines, the poetical spirit of which wants no trumpet of ours, is aware that they imply more than an impartial observer of the late period might feel, and are written rather as by Frenchman than Englishman:—but certainly neither he, nor any other lover of liberty, can help feeling and regretting, that in the latter time, at any rate, the symbol he speaks of was once more comparatively identified with the cause of freedom. [Editorial note in the *Examiner*]
   21. The tri colour. [B's note in *Examiner* and *Poems1816*]

278. *MS.* Lady B's fair copy, undated. Not published. The poem almost certainly dates from 1815, when Lady B was copying out the poems B was then writing. The paper is the same as several other poems she copied out at the time. It is a retrospective comment on the political legacy left by Sir Spencer Perceval (1762–1812), the Tory Prime Minister, who was assassinated on 11 May 1812.

279. *MS.* B's draft, undated (*MS. L*, location: Bodleian–Lovelace; the final received stanza is numbered 5 in the MS., then corrected to 4, and the original stanza 4 has been removed); Lady B's fair copy, with B's corrections, undated (*MS. BM*, location: *BM*, the stanzas numbered 1 to 4); B's corrected proof for *Poems1816* (location: Murray). First published as a song-sheet in 1815 by Isaac Nathan (see G. Pollard, *TLS*, 16 Oct. 1937, p. 764); next in *Poems1816*, and collected thereafter. It was also published by John Clarke in *Twelve Vocal Pieces* (1817), II. 3 with a note by Clarke saying that B gave it to Clarke expressly for him to publish.
   The subject of the poem, and date, was a mystery until John Gore printed a letter from B to Lady Hardy of 10 June 1823 (see *Cornhill Magazine*, 64 (1928), 39–53) in which B sent to her what he called 'the concluding stanza [of 'When We Two Parted'] which was never printed with the others'. It was actually the penultimate stanza removed from *MS. L*. B's letter to Lady Hardy shows that the true date of the poem was 1815, and that its subject was Lady Frances Wedderburn Webster, with whom he had a brief, 'platonic' affair late in 1813. He wrote the poem in 1815 when he heard the London gossip about her affair with the Duke of Wellington in Paris (see *LJ* II. 2 n., III. 262; *Marchand*, II. 537 n., 580–1, 1045, 1055). But the deleted stanza was in fact originally written even earlier, in 1812, as a four-stress quatrain in '[To Lady Caroline Lamb]' (no. 189). B quoted this stanza in a letter to Lady Melbourne of 18 Sept. 1812 (*BLJ* II. 200).
   When B dated the poem 1808 in *Poems1816* he was being deliberately—and in a sense doubly—misleading. Marchand (II. 580–1) suggests that the poem was written some time in early 1816, but the existence of *MS. BM*

shows this to be impossible. The poem was certainly written in 1815, and almost as certainly in August or September, when B was corresponding with Webster about the scandal involving his wife (see *BLJ* IV. 310–13). Furthermore, the poem seems to involve a double reference to Lady Caroline as well, for her behaviour in Paris with Wellington and his troops was equally the subject of London scandal at the time. In fact, B wrote her a note in mid-September, sent through Webster, in which he hoped she 'was as happy with the regiment as he was with his "Wife Bell" ' (see *BLJ*, *loc. cit.* and *Marchand*, II. 537).

280. *MS.* B's draft, untitled, undated (location: Bodleian–Lovelace); an unpublished fragment. Though the lines undoubtedly date from 1815, the historical existence of 'Lovely Anne' remains problematical. The verses may represent a slightly transformed narrative of Byron's feelings for Susan Boyce (see *Paston and Quennell*, pp. 177–87, and *Marchand*, II. 548–50).

281. B's remarks on the composition of *Siege*, and later commentators' speculations about the MSS., have created some confusion. In fact, a real problem exists here, and although some questions remain to be answered, the situation can be clarified.

MSS. and Proofs. We begin with the MSS. E. H. Coleridge worked with two MSS. when he edited the poem. The earliest of these is the holograph, which he calls *MS. G*, and which was then in the possession of Lord Glenesk. Coleridge called this the 'original' MS. and, after giving a brief description (*C* III. 448), he concluded: 'To judge from the occasional and disconnected pagination, this MS. consists of portions of two or more fair copies of a number of detached scraps written at different times, together with two or three of the original scraps which had not been transcribed.'

Coleridge did not discuss the other MS., which he calls the 'copy'. This is Lady B's transcription, made from the Glenesk MS., with B's corrections and additions. Lady B's copy is here designated *MS. M* (location: Murray). It is dated by her at the beginning 'Novr 2nd 1815', which must represent the date when she finished making her copy (see dates below). B has corrected the MS. throughout, though lightly, and he has inserted most of the prose notes, as well as the epigraph. Neither the Advertisement nor the Dedication are in *MS. M*. The MS. lacks the note for line 598, and lines 998–1002. It was printer's copy for the first edition.

All the problems with the date of composition hinge on the problems connected with the so-called Glenesk MS. After Coleridge, the only scholar to have addressed himself to these matters is Robert Gleckner (164–76 *passim*), whose commentary is acute in many ways. (Also noteworthy are the brief remarks in *Ashton*, 28 n.) Gleckner's discussion is largely dependent upon his examination of the MS. here designated *MS. T.* (location: Texas).

Gleckner compared *C*'s MS. descriptions and variant readings with *MS. T* and he concluded that the Glenesk MS. 'is a fair copy of the University of Texas' *MS. T* (165). But the fact is that the Glenesk MS. and *MS. T* are the same.

Gleckner's error is the result of three factors. (*a*) He did not know of the existence of *MS. M*, or that Coleridge had used this MS. and had called it the copy in his notes. In truth, Coleridge's notes and commentaries do not make the distinction entirely clear between *MS. T* and *MS. M* (i.e. between his *MS. G* and his 'copy'). (*b*) Gleckner too readily accepted the accuracy and completeness of Coleridge's record of MS. variants. Throughout his edition, Coleridge's record of MS. variants is selective, and also, in many cases, inaccurate. (*c*) Gleckner accepted, again too readily, Coleridge's sketchy and misleading description of *MS. G/MS. T*.

Neither Coleridge nor Gleckner has described *MS. G/MS. T* sufficiently. This physical data is necessary if one is to understand *Siege*'s probable dates of composition. The MS. consists of 50 pages comprising 16 folio and 8 quarto sheets, plus a final, slightly smaller leaf. All 16 folio sheets originally stood as 8 large sheets folded into 2 folio leaves with 4 pages each. The same is true of all the quarto sheets. (We can tell this by the manner in which B numerated the pages.) The final two pages of *MS. T* are on one smaller MS. leaf. The leaves, with the lines they contain and their watermark dates, are as follows:

Pages 1–4: folio, watermarked 1813. Lines 1–95. p. 1 (numbered 1 at upper left), 1–21; p. 2 (verso of p. 1), 22–49; p. 3, 50–69; p. 4 (verso of p. 3), 70–95.

Pages 5–8: folio, watermarked 1813. Lines 96–190. p. 5 (numbered 2 at upper left), 96–119; p. 6 (verso of 5), 120–41; p. 7, 142–66; p. 8 (verso of 7), 167–90.

Pages 9–12: quarto, watermarked 1812. Lines 191–252. p. 9 (numbered [4]3 at upper left, and there is an additional number 4 at centre top, cancelled), 191–206; p. 10 (verso of 9), 207–20; p. 11, 221–36; p. 12 (verso of 11), 237–52.

Pages 13–16: quarto, watermarked 1812. Lines 253–322. p. 13 (numbered [5]4 at upper left), 253–68; p. 14 (verso of 13), 269–86; p. 15, 287–306; p. 16 (verso of 15), 307–22.

Pages 17–20: quarto, watermarked 1812. Lines 323–88. p. 17 (numbered 5 at upper left), 323–38; p. 18 (verso of 17), 339–56; p. 19, 357–72a–b; p. 20 (verso of 19), 373–88.

Pages 21–4: folio, watermarked 1815. Lines 389–473. p. 21 (numbered 6 at upper left), 389–412; p. 22 (verso of 21), 413–39; p. 23, 440–61; p. 24 (verso of 23), 462–73.

Pages 25–8: folio, watermarked 1813. Lines 474–563. p. 25 (numbered 7 at upper left), 474–500; p. 26 (verso of 25), 501–23; p. 27, 524–43; p. 28 (verso of 27), 544–63.

Pages 29–32: folio, watermarked 1815. Lines 564–658. p. 29 (numbered 8 at upper left), 564–82; p. 30 (verso of 29), 583–605; p. 31, 606–27; p. 32 (verso of 31), 628–58.

Pages 33–6: folio, watermarked 1815. Lines 659–755. p. 33 (numbered 9 at upper left), 659–77; p. 34 (verso of 33), 678–701; p. 35, 702–27; p. 36 (verso of 35), 728–55.

Pages 37–40: folio, watermarked 1815. Lines 756–849. p. 37 (numbered 10 at upper left), 756–79; p. 38 (verso of 37), 780–800; p. 39, 801–21; p. 40 (verso of 39), 822–49.

Pages 41–4: folio, watermarked 1815. Lines 850–940. p. 41 (numbered 11 at upper left), 850–76; p. 42 (verso of 41), 877–97; p. 43, 898–916; p. 44 (verso of 43), 917–40.

Pages 45–8: quarto, watermarked 1814. Lines 941–97. p. 45 (numbered 12 at upper left), 941–54; p. 46 (verso of 45), 955–69; p. 47, 970–82; p. 48 (verso of 47), 983–97.

Pages 49–50: smaller single leaf, not watermarked. Lines 998–1034. p. 49, 998–1015; p. 50 (verso of 49), 1016–34.

Pages 1–8 and 25–8 are the same paper; pages 9–20 are the same paper and represent a continuous unit; pages 21–4, 29–44 are the same paper and represent a unit into which 25–8 has been inserted; on p. 48 lines 985–97 are written across the page and were clearly written at a later time than the other lines on pp. 45–8. The lines (concluding) on pp. 49–50 are a direct continuation of 985–97.

MS. T is untitled and dated by B at the beginning 'J[anuar]y 30th 1815'. This date applies only to the leaf on which it was written and represents the time when B began his final process of revision. *MS. T* lacks the epigraph, Dedication, Advertisement, and most of the notes, as well as lines 442–3, 998–1002, and 1026–7, and there is an extra line after 126 and an extra couplet after 372.

One other MS. relevant to *Siege* is B's draft (*MS. L*, location: Bodleian–Lovelace) of the 'Lines Associated With *The Siege of Corinth*' (here printed following *Siege*). *MS. L* is a single sheet, watermarked 1813, folded into four quarto pages, with the lines written only on the first three pages. It is headed by B: 'The Stranger—a tale.—Oct. 23rd', but B later cancelled the heading. The date of this fragment is almost certainly 1813, and it has been incorporated into *Siege* as lines 1–45 in all editions from *1832* onwards. For further discussions, see below.

One proof survives. *Proof H* (location: Huntington), with B's corrections, is headed on the title-page in the hand of B's publisher: 'Overrun and put 24 lines in a page. Revise on Monday without fail. Jan[uar]y 19th 1816.' Murray has corrected the title-page and added B's name to it. B added the Dedication in MS. and corrected the epigraph. The Advertisement is here in print, and so is the complete text, including lines 998–1002, and all the notes. The collation of *Proof H* with the MSS. and the first edition indicates clearly that B received and corrected at least two other proofs, one preceding *Proof H* and one following it. These proofs are not extant.

Also relevant here is *Text G* (location: Murray), which at first appears to be a corrected proof but is in fact a copy of the first edition. It is headed by Murray: 'With Mr. Gifford's corrections with Lord Byron's permission.' B has not corrected *Text G* at all, and Gifford's corrections were made well after the initial publication—in fact, in Jan. 1817 (see *BLJ* v. 157–8). B never authorized these corrections.

Composition History. Gleckner's analysis of *MS. T*, while inadequate in certain ways, makes some shrewd guesses about the probable history of composition. 'My guess is that he almost entirely scrapped his earlier beginning as a false start, wrote the 190 lines of the first two folio sheets to replace it, dovetailed this new beginning with the already completed lines 191–322 (of the first two quarto sheets), and then continued the poem to the end through the spring and summer of 1815.' (166) This is not precisely the case, but the conjecture is on the right track. Gleckner's analysis is an attempt to explain two comments which B made about the poem. On 27 Oct. 1815 he wrote to S. T. Coleridge about *Siege* in order to assure Coleridge that *Siege* had not been plagiarized from *Christabel*: 'the enclosed extract from an unpublished poem . . . I assure you was written before (not seeing your "Christabelle" for that you know I never did till this day) but before I heard Mr. S[cott] *repeat* it—which he did in June last—and this thing was begun in January & more than half written before the Summer' (*BLJ* IV. 321). This confirms the evidence of the MSS. and their dates: that B began putting *MS. T* together in late Jan. 1815, and that the poem was finally completed by November.

B wrote an even more interesting remark to Leigh Hunt on 26 Feb. 1816: 'I desired Murray to forward to you a pamphlet with two things of mine in it—the most part of both of them—& of one in particular—written before *others* of my composing—which have preceded them in *publication*. . . .you will perhaps wonder at my dwelling so much & so frequently on former subjects & *scenes*—but the fact is that I found them fading fast from my memory—and I was at the same time so partial to their *place* (& events connected with it) that I have stamped them while I could—in such colours as I could trust to *now*—but might have confused & misapplied hereafter— had I longer delayed the attempted delineation' (*BLJ* v. 32). The 'pamphlet' was the 1816 volume containing *Siege* and *Parisina*, and the suggestion is that these poems—and in particular *Siege* (see *Parisina* commentary below)— had their beginnings prior to other poems of 1812–14.

The draft MS. of *Parisina* does not seem to survive. Nevertheless, certain peculiar publication circumstances connected with that poem (see *Parisina* commentary below), along with the evidence of present *MSS. T* and *L*, strongly suggest that both *Siege* and *Parisina* developed out of an original

MS. tale, begun in 1812 and continued in 1813, in which Alp and Francesca were the main characters. *MS. T* in particular is a composite of material begun in late 1812, possibly even before *Giaour*. The watermark dates on *MSS. T* and *L*, the physical condition of both MSS., and B's letters all suggest the following dates of composition: 1–190 (autumn 1813), 191–388 (autumn–winter 1812), 389–473 (Jan.–June 1815), 474–563 (autumn 1813), 564–90 (June–Oct. 1815), 941–84 (some time in late 1814, but possibly early in 1815), 985–1034 (Oct. 1815). In certain cases, these dates apply only to approximations of the corresponding passages from the text. *MS. T* shows that *Siege* was pieced together at various times between 1813 and 1815. Consequently, some of the material towards the end of 1–190 may have been written in 1812; the leaves containing 1–190 belong to the autumn, 1813, but at that point B was attempting to join already written material (191–388) to a new beginning. Some of lines 1–190 may have been part of the original poem, and B may have simply recopied them in order to make a neat join with the pages containing 191–388. As *C* noted (see above), much of *MS. T* seems to be corrected fair copy material. The lines in *MS. T* which are clearly draft MS. material are 191–388 (from 1812), and the lines written in 1815. The lines from 1813 and 1814 are corrected fair copy, and may contain some lines which were written earlier.

B probably began the original poem in the autumn of 1812. He must have left it incomplete at the time, along with his other aborted tales of that period, 'Il Diavolo Inamorato' and 'The Monk of Athos' (see commentaries above). But after *Giaour* was published so successfully (an event he did not expect), B seems to have returned to the story of Alp and Francesca. The 'Lines Associated With *The Siege of Corinth*' were written after 191–388 and represent either a new beginning for the original tale or the start of a new poem in Oct. 1813. Lines 1–190 and 474–563 seem to belong to this second attempt to complete the unfinished poem. But once again B must have failed to bring it into order. He probably worked at the poem at least once more in 1814, and the first two stanzas of *Parisina* were certainly lifted from the original 1812–14 MS. tale of Alp and Francesca. Lines 941–84 seem to belong to 1814 as well.

Then, in Jan. 1815, B began yet another attempt to complete his poem. But at this point he seems to have made the crucial decision to separate his existing materials into the two separate poems that would later become *Siege* and *Parisina*. Some of the original poem's material was later transferred to *Parisina* and the rest was incorporated into *Siege*. Lines 1–388 were kept and revised for *Siege*, and 474–563 were interpolated into the new material being composed in 1815. Lines 564–940 and 985–1034 were the last passages written for the poem.

Lady B finished her fair copy of *Siege* at the beginning of Nov. 1815. B sent the MS. to Murray immediately. On 4 Nov. (*BLJ* IV. 331) he sent the Advertisement and was awaiting a proof. On 25 Dec. he sent Murray a

copy of the 'Lines Associated With *The Siege of Corinth*' as a possible opening
section (*ibid.* 337–8). B continued to correct throughout January and *Siege*
finally appeared in the volume with *Parisina* on 13 Feb. 1816 (see *Marchand*,
II. 576).

Publishing History. B did not think highly of either *Siege* or *Parisina*,
probably because the composition process—particularly of *Siege*—had been
so difficult. The poem must have seemed a patchwork to B, but it is,
despite some careless passages, one of his strongest tales.

B insisted to Murray that *Siege* and *Parisina* should not be published
separately, but instead should be placed in the collected edition which
Murray was preparing at the time (*BLJ* IV. 331–2 and V. 13). When Murray
pressed for a separate publication, B was annoyed, and on 22 Jan. 1816 he
told Murray to cancel all publication plans (*BLJ* V. 17). But by 29 Jan. they
were reconciled, and Murray's wish for a separate publication won the day
(*ibid.* 19).

B sent the 'Lines Associated . . . ' with the idea that they might serve as
a new opening for the poem, but he was 'not sure that they had not better
be left out now—on that you & your Synod can determine' (*BLJ* IV. 338).
The Synod—i.e. Murray and Gifford principally—confirmed B's uncertainty,
and the lines were not published in the first edition or any of the early
editions. Nor do they appear in the proof. First added to the poem in *1832*,
they have since always been printed as the opening lines of *Siege*. But, as
with the additional stanzas associated with the *Ode to Napoleon*, B positively
decided against the inclusion of the 'Lines' in *Siege*, and there is no editorial
justification for including the lines in the poem. Though written in late
1813, they are placed here because of their long traditional association with
Siege.

A final note on *Text G*. Gifford thought *Siege* a powerful work, but marred
by passages which were 'all very easy of improvement' if B felt like making
the effort (*Smiles*, I. 356 f.). The corrections which B made in the proofs
apparently did not satisfy Gifford, who asked B's permission to go over the
poem in 1817. This is *Text G*. B never allowed these corrections into the
text, nor is it at all certain that he even saw them. The poem was severely
criticized in the reviews for its local stylistic imperfections (see *C* III. 444).
Six thousand copies of the first edition were printed, and two other editions
appeared in 1816. B presented the copyright of *Siege* and *Parisina* to Murray,
and a few months afterwards (Apr. 1816) he accepted £1,050 from Murray
for the two poems.

The most useful discussion of *Siege* is in Eugen Kölbing's critical edition
of the poem (Weimar, 1896). Some of his commentary is, of course, badly
dated, but his literary and historical notes are still quite useful.

Literary and Historical Background. As B's Advertisement indicates, *Siege* is
based on a late incident in the long struggle between Venice and the Ottoman

Empire for the control of the Peloponnesus. At the time B wrote the poem, the written historical records dealt with the event only in the briefest fashion. Finlay's *History of Greece* (1856) was the first to provide detailed particulars of the siege and sack of Corinth (see notes below).

Briefly, an Ottoman army of about 70,000 men, under the Grand Vizier Ali Coumourgi, invaded the Peloponnesus in 1715. The Porte declared war with Venice in 1714, fifteen years after the peace of Carlowitz. The attack on Corinth, crucially situated, was the opening move in the Ottoman campaign to regain control of the entire territory. At the time, the Venetian forces in the Morea were severely diminished; the small contingent of 600 soldiers who defended Corinth were under the command of the governor of the city, Giacomo Minotto (variously spelt). The attack began on 28 June and Minotto finally capitulated early in August. The massacre of the garrison took place on 3 Aug., following an explosion of the Venetian magazine in the city, which killed a number of Turkish janizaries. The cause of the explosion was not known, but the Turks attributed it to Venetian treachery. After the massacre, the surviving Greeks were sold into slavery. About 180 Venetian soldiers were taken prisoner. B follows the oral tradition of the time in having Minotto perish in the struggle, though in fact he was taken prisoner and eventually ransomed (see *Finlay*, v. 263–8).

B's tale seems to be based partly on oral histories of the siege (see line 720) which he heard when he was in Corinth in 1810, and partly on imagination. The story of the love of Alp, the Venetian renegade, and Francesca, the daughter of Minotto, seems to be purely imaginative. Their relationship —which focuses the poem's treatment of the siege—is another variation on the typical structure of the Byronic Hero's character and career.

The literary context of the poem can best be explained if we briefly outline its formal arrangement. *Siege* has four parts: General Introduction (1–196), Alp's Meditation (197–449), Alp and Francesca (450–632), and The Siege (633–1034). The last part has two separable sections (633–851 and 852–1034). These divisions are useful for indicating not only when the different parts of the poem were written, but also where the lines of influence fall. Part II, Alp's Meditation, which is closest in manner to *CHP I–II*, represents the earliest surviving part of the original poem (1812). But the passage 389–473 contains a large portion of new material added later. We can see this not only from *MS. T*, but equally well from the clear parallels that exist between this passage and 'The Devil's Drive', written in Dec. 1813 (see commentary above for that poem).

The bulk of Parts I and III contains material written in 1813. These passages have their natural parallels in B's other eastern tales, especially *Giaour*, *Bride*, and *Parisina*. Part IV, on the other hand, which was largely written in 1815, contains the freest metrical variations on the poem's basic octosyllabic couplet scheme (except for 389–473, which also belong to 1815). These divisions also help to isolate the areas of literary influence which have been noted by E. H. Coleridge and Eugen Kölbing. The influence of Southey's *Roderick, The Last of the Goths* (1814) has to be confined to the final part of *Siege*, and Coleridge's *Christabel*—which gave a model for the freer treatment of the octosyllabic couplet—also influenced directly only the later parts. The manner of the poem thus bears out B's own statements about the relation of *Siege* and *Christabel*. Finally, the bulk of the material in Parts I–III evidently falls under the same influences which stand behind poems like *Giaour* and *Bride*. The impact of the tales of Sir Walter Scott is to be especially noted.

Like *Parisina, Siege* represents B's final use of material he had abortively begun to handle in tales like 'Il Diavolo Inamorato', 'The Monk of Athos', and 'The Stranger'. This last fragment, surviving as the 'Lines Associated With *The Siege of Corinth*', was originally written in late 1813 as the beginning of another story of a Venetian renegade and expatriate. When B thought, late in 1815, that he might put these lines at the head of *Siege*, the idea was to save another passage of early poetry, the way he had saved passages from 'Il Diavolo Inamorato' and 'The Monk of Athos' in the seventh edition of *CHP I–II*. The composition of *Siege* was in fact a massive and persistent effort to salvage such early work. The result, as literary history has judged, was something of a patchwork, though the plot is unexceptionable and the style frequently more powerful than anything B had yet written.

The last part of *Siege* should also be compared with some of the *Hebrew Melodies* of 1815, especially 'On the Day of the Destruction of Jerusalem by Titus', 'The Destruction of Semnacherib', and 'Song of Saul Before His Last Battle', as well as with B's ballad, 'Golice Macbane'.

epigraph   adapting Pope, *Imitations of Horace*, Satires, II. i. 26.
Advertisement
Prime Vizier. See below, 96 n.
in all that country. Napoli di Romania is not now the most considerable place in the Morea, but Tripolitza, where the Pacha resides, and maintains his government. Napoli is near Argos. I visited all three in 1810–11; and in the course of journeying through the country from my first arrival in 1809, I crossed the Isthmus eight times in my way from Attica to the Morea, over the mountains, or in the other direction, when passing from the Gulf of Athens to that of Lepanto. Both the routes are picturesque and beautiful, though very different: that by sea has more sameness, but the voyage being always in sight of land, and often very near it, presents many attractive views of the islands of Salamis, Aegina, Poro, &c. and the coast of the continent. [B] See *CHP I–II* and nn. and *BLJ* I. 233–57 and II. 3–23.
Signior Minotti: Jacopo Minotto, the governor of Corinth. 'It was reported by the prisoners that Minoto had perished in the confusion; but it was afterwards known that a soldier of the Asiatic troops had taken him prisoner, and concealed him in order to profit by his ransom. He was secretly conveyed

to Smyrna, where he was released by the Dutch consul, who advanced his ransom money. Bembo, the second in command and about one hundred and eighty Venetian soldiers, with a few women, were saved, and . . . were conveyed to Corfu, according to the terms of the capitulation' (*Finlay*, v. 267–8). The proveditor extraordinary was in fact Alessandro Bon (1654–1715), who died at Megara, where he had been transported by the Turks after his capture.

B's Advertisement is taken from *A Compleat History of the Turks* (1719), III. 151. See also *BLJ* IV. 331.

1–3. Because of its strategic position at the isthmus between the Saronic and Corinthian gulfs, Corinth was a focus of military conflict, especially in the struggles between the eastern and western powers after the breakup of the Roman Empire.

14. Timoleon (d. 337 or 336 B.C.), Greek statesman and general born at Corinth. He was a byword for patriotism. When his brother (whom Timoleon had earlier saved in battle) tried to set himself up as tyrant in Corinth, Timoleon attempted to reason him from his purpose. When persuasion failed, however, Timoleon had his brother killed.

15. Xerxes I (519–465 B.C.), defeated by the Greeks at Salamis (480 B.C.).

26. *Cithaeron*: a mountain north of Corinth, in Boeotia.

32. *Spahi's bands*: the Turkish cavalry.

38. The life of the Turcomans is wandering and patriarchal; they dwell in tents. [B]

43. Cf. *Giaour*, 639.

69. *Alp*. The name is perhaps traceable to Mohammed (Lhaz-ed-Dyn-Abou-Choudja), surnamed Alp-Arslan (or 'Brave Lion'). He was the second of the Seljuk Dynasty (eleventh century).

Adrian: Adria, an ancient seaport in Italy between the Po and the Adige, from which the Adriatic takes its name.

76–7. The Achaean League was destroyed by Rome (146 B.C.) and the Peloponnesus became a Roman province until the division of the empire in the fourth century, when it fell under Byzantine control. At the beginning of the thirteenth century Corinth was placed under Venetian rule following the Frankish conquest of Constantinople. The Ottomans expelled the Venetians three centuries later, but Venice reconquered the Peloponnesus (1685–99). In 1715 it was regained by the Turks.

88–9. Unsigned charges against Venetians could be placed in a hole in the wall of the Doge's palace called 'The Lion's Mouth'. Such charges were then brought before the infamous Council of Ten (founded in 1310), which decided whether to pursue the matter.

96. Ali Coumourgi, the favourite of three sultans, and Grand Vizier to Achmet III. after recovering Peloponnesus from the Venetians in one campaign, was mortally wounded in the next, against the Germans, at the battle of Peterwaradin, (in the plain of Carlowitz) in Hungary, endeavouring

to rally his guards. He died of his wounds next day. His last order was the decapitation of General Breuner, and some other German prisoners; and his last words, 'Oh that I could thus serve all the Christian dogs!' a speech and act not unlike one of Caligula. He was a young man of great ambition and unbounded presumption: on being told that Prince Eugene, then opposed to him, 'was a great general', he said, 'I shall become a greater, and at his expense.' [B] Ali Coumourgi (or Ali Cumurgi, Damad Ali), was Silahdar Ali Pasha, the son-in-law and favourite of Ahmed III. Having engineered his elevation to Grand Vizier in 1713, he died of his wounds the day after the battle (6 Aug. 1716). The Austrians were under the command of Prince Eugene of Savoy (1663–1736).

General Breuner: Feldmarschall-Leutnant Graf Seyfried Breuner (d. 1716).

140. Christian name: Lanciotto (see below, line 154).

169. John Sobieski, King of Poland (1629–96), raised the siege of Vienna in 1683. Buda was regained from the Turks in 1686 by Charles VII, Duke of Lorraine.

172. i.e. between Patras, on the north coast of the Peloponnesus, and Negropont (the ancient Euboea).

177. truce: the peace of Carlowitz (1799).

180. Helen of Troy.

191. The first storming party of a besieged town was called the 'Forlorn Hope' (cf. DJ VIII, st. 73).

201. Cf. The Taming of the Shrew, III. v. 31–2.

231–2. Echoes Scott's Marmion, III. xvi. 4–5.

237–8. At the hour of death the 'passing bell' is rung, to announce the death and solicit prayers for the departed.

255–6. Cf. Giaour, 485–6, 1042–7.

320. Delphi's hill: Parnassus (cf. Giaour, 566–7).

341–4. At Thermopylae (480 B.C.). The Spartan who smiled in dying was Leonidas, king of Sparta, who was killed in the battle. Compare CHP II, sts. 73–7.

357–78. Cf. Giaour, 103 ff. and CHP II, sts. 86–90.

381. The reader need hardly be reminded that there are no perceptible tides in the Mediterranean. [B] For 381–8 compare CHP IV, sts. 179–84.

409 ff. Cf. Coleridge's 'Fire, Famine, and Slaughter', 30–5.

411–33. Crossed out by Gifford (Text G).

415. This spectacle I have seen, such as described, beneath the wall of the Seraglio at Constantinople, in the little cavities worn by the Bosphorus in the rock, a narrow terrace of which projects between the wall and the water. I think the fact is also mentioned in Hobhouse's Travels. The bodies were probably those of some refractory Janizaries. [B] See Travels in Albania, II. 215.

424. This tuft, or long lock, is left from a superstition that Mahomet will draw them into Paradise by it. [B]

437. 'Than a mangled corpse in its own blood lying': Gifford correction, *Text G*.

438–9. Cancelled by Gifford (*Text G*) with his note: 'What is a perishing dead?'

445. 'field' corrected to 'limbs', Gifford, *Text G*.

446–7. 1 Samuel 17: 44.

450–61. Cf. *CHP II*, st. 10.

454–5. Cancelled by Gifford, *Text G*.

462. 'From this all is beautiful to [line 632]': Gifford's n., *Text G*.

476. I must here acknowledge a close, though unintentional, resemblance in these twelve lines to a passage in an unpublished poem of Mr. Coleridge, called 'Christabel'. It was not till after these lines were written that I heard that wild and singularly original and beautiful poem recited; and the MS. of that production I never saw till very recently, by the kindness of Mr. Coleridge himself, who, I hope, is convinced that I have not been a wilful plagiarist. The original idea undoubtedly pertains to Mr. Coleridge, whose poem has been composed above fourteen years. Let me conclude by a hope that he will not longer delay the publication of a production, of which I can only add my mite of approbation to the applause of far more competent judges. [B] See commentary above and *BLJ* IV. 331. B's passage should be compared with *Christabel*, I. 43–8, as well as Southey's *Thalaba the Destroyer*, V. 20 and Scott's *Lay of the Last Minstrel*, I. xii. 5 ff. B was instrumental in getting Murray to publish *Christabel* and 'Kubla Khan' (see E. K. Chambers, *Samuel Taylor Coleridge* (1938), 276).

500–1. Space between. [B's n. in margin, *MS. M*]

508. Gifford inserted 'thrilling' before 'glance' in *Text G*.

518 ff. This scene between Alp and Francesca anticipates the similar encounter of Manfred with Astarte.

522. Cf. Scott's *Marmion*, II. vii. 3–7 and Spenser, *Faerie Queene*, I. iii, sts. 5–7.

548. 1 Kings 12: 11–14.

571. Cf. *Macbeth*, V. i. 30–1 and *Christabel*, I. 292–3.

575–82. Cf. *Life*, I. 27 where Moore suggests that B is here recalling his experiences in Annesley Hall in 1803, when he refused to sleep overnight in the hall because he felt haunted by the family pictures of the Chaworths. See also *Lara*, I, st. 11 and *DJ* XVI, sts. 17–19.

591–2. Cf. Southey's *Roderick*, Canto XXI (1839 one vol. edn.), p. 696.

598. I have been told that the idea expressed from lines 597 to 603 has been admired by those whose approbation is valuable. I am glad of it: but it is not original—at least not mine; it may be found much better expressed in pages 182–3–4 of the English version of 'Vathek' (I forget the precise page of the French), a work to which I have before referred; and never recur to, or read, without a renewal of gratification. [B] Cf. *Vathek* (1786), 182–5.

633–4. Cancelled by Gifford, *Text G*.

636. Cf. Milton, *Lycidas*, 187.

637. Cancelled by Gifford, *Text G*.

642. Cf. *CHP III*, st. 25.

643. The horsetail, fixed upon a lance, a Pasha's standard. [B] Cf. *CHP II*. 686 and *Bride*, II. 232.

651–2. Cancelled by Gifford, *Text G*.

658. Gifford replaces 'crumbled' with 'shaken', *Text G*.

668. Cf. *Giaour*, 734.

672. *downs*: What vulgarism is this? [Gifford's n., *Text G*, where he suggests 'Lowers' or 'Plucks down' as alternatives.]

684–5. *went . . . bent*. In *Text G* Gifford substitutes 'bent . . . sent'.

691. *Troilus and Cressida*, V. v. 24–5.

693. Gifford puts 'train' for 'slain', *Text G*.

736. *an old man*. Gifford substitutes 'a man', *Text G*.

744. *Lurked*: Bad word. [Gifford's n., *Text G*, where he replaces it with 'Was hid'.]

750. *thin*: cancelled by Gifford, *Text G*.

753. *dipped*. Gifford substitutes 'he dipp'd', *Text G*.

756. Bravo!—this is better than King Priam's fifty sons. [Gifford's n., *Text G*.]

760–1. In the naval battle at the mouth of the Dardanelles, between the Venetians and the Turks. [B] Historical records do not seem to corroborate this detail as a fact. B may have heard it from an oral source.

763. There can be no such thing; but the whole of this is poor, and spun out. [Gifford's n., *Text G*]

765. Cf. *Odyssey*, Book XI.

770–3. Cf. *DJ* IV, sts. 72–3.

774. *Allah shout*. Gifford substitutes 'Allah Hu', *Text G*.

849. *Unanealed*. Cf. *Hamlet*, I. v. 77–8.

851. *renegade*. In the first two decades of the nineteenth century this word and its cognates were so frequently used in political disputes that it almost necessarily carried political overtones. Cf. also *DJ*, 'Dedication', st. 1.

952. Cancelled by Gifford, *Text G*.

975. *expired*: meaning 'to rush forth' (*OED*), i.e. here, 'to explode'. Cf. Dryden's 'the pond'rous ball expires' (*Annus Mirabilis*, 750).

985–1011. Strike out . . . despicable stuff. [Gifford's n., *Text G*]

1012. *All the living things*. Gifford substitutes 'Every living thing', *Text G*.

1013–34. Echoes Southey's *Roderick*, Canto XVIII (1839 edn.), pp. 689–90.

1016–21. Cancelled by Gifford, *Text G*.

1020–7. Cf. B's Journal for 23 Nov. 1813 (*BLJ* III. 218).

1024. I believe I have taken a poetical license to transplant the jackal from Asia. In Greece I never saw nor heard these animals; but among the ruins of Ephesus I have heard them by hundreds. They haunt ruins, and follow armies. [B] Cf. *CHP IV*, st. 53 and *DJ* IX, st. 27.

1026–7. Leave out this couplet. [Gifford's n., *Text G*]

281a. For commentary on *MS. L* and the dating of the lines, see *Siege* commentary above. These lines were almost certainly B's first attempt at the tale that was to become *Bride*, which was written early in Nov. 1813 (see commentary above). *Bride*, it should be noted, is written in the same metrical form as this fragment.

'Lines Associated With *The Siege of Corinth*' was first published separately, untitled, in *Life*, I. 638–9; in *1831* it was included in the collection as a separate piece, and in *1832*, and thereafter, it was placed as the opening section of *Siege*.

1–2. i.e. in 1810, when B travelled around Greece and visited Corinth. Cf. *Marchand*, I. 234–40 and 250–2. B seems to be particularly referring to his trip of July–Aug. 1810, just after Hobhouse left him at Zea, to return to England (see *BLJ* II. 3–10). These opening lines invoke the ballad tradition (cf. e.g. Burns's 'John Bushby's Lamentation', 1–4).

26. The last tidings recently heard of Dervish (one of the Arnaouts who followed me) state him to be in revolt upon the mountains, at the head of some of the bands common in that country in times of trouble. [B, n. in *Life*; the n. is not in *L*.] Cf. *Giaour*, 1077 n.

31. *restlessly at home.* Cf. B's letter to Hodgson, 13 Oct. 1811, and his journal entry for 27 Nov. 1813 (*BLJ* II. 111 and III. 225).

282. *MS.* Lady B's fair copy, with B's additions and corrections, and with the first paragraph of the Advertisement in B's hand, undated (*MS. M*, location: Murray). *MS. M* contains 1–303, 306–9, 318–538, 545–50, 557–86. Also at Murray's is B's corrected (but incomplete) proof, with the Advertisement and the text of lines 1–574 (pages [3]–32), and with a note in Murray's hand: 'Given me by Lord Byron at his home Saturday January 13th 1816.' This proof (*Proof M*) was plainly set independently of *Siege*, with which *Parisina* was ultimately printed. The corrected proof of the first edition of both poems (*Proof H*, location: Huntington) is dated 19 Jan. 1816 by B's publisher, who corrects the title-page from *Parisina, A Poem* to *Parisina, A Tale*, and adds the received dedication in MS. *Proof H* is complete but the line numbering—as in the first three editions—is incorrectly put at 585 instead of 586. *Proof M* lacks lines 304–5. Included with *Proof H* are two proof scraps. (*a*) *Proof Ha*, a proof page numbered 33, with one correction by B, containing lines 575–86 (here numbered 563–74). This is the final missing page of *Proof M*. (*b*) *Proof Hb*, two leaves originally paginated 32–3 but corrected in MS. (not B's) to 103–4. They contain lines 555–86, here numbered 552–83. They are part of a proof printed to include the new material added in *Proof M*. *Proof Hb* must have lacked lines 304–5, as the line numbering shows, and hence was printed between *Proofs M* and *H*.

Finally, Augusta Leigh's fair copy of *Parisina*, 1–14, under the heading 'It is the hour', is in her Commonplace Book at the British Library. This MS.

text corresponds exactly to the lines as they were printed in *HM* and the copy seems to have been made from a MS. which B showed to her (see no. 249 above).

Composition and Publishing History. See Commentary above for *Siege*. B's note to line 14 says that *Parisina* was written 'prior to Lara', which seems to be true only in a certain sense. It is unlikely that *Parisina* was completed before *Lara* was published, but like *Siege*, the poem did emerge from B's process of revision—between 1812 and 1815—of an original poem whose materials were later dispersed, partly into *Siege* and partly into *Parisina*.

The crucial revision process that resulted in *Parisina* probably did not begin until 1815. I incline to this view because the poem is based on a passage in Gibbon's *Miscellaneous Works* (1814), which B first saw and read in Jan. 1815 (see *BLJ* IV. 248, 250–1). However, B's assertion about the composition of *Parisina* is so emphatic that one hesitates to contradict him. In fact, B could have come across the story of *Parisina* in other sources than Gibbon—e.g. in Antonio Frizzi's volumes (see below). Nevertheless, *Parisina*'s name in the earliest stages of the poem seems to have been Francesca, which also strongly suggests that B reworked his earlier materials into the story of *Parisina* only after he had read Gibbon's account.

Whatever the case, many of the passages in the poem were written before *Lara*. But B seems not to have completed *Parisina* until Dec. 1815, when he gave *MS. M* to Murray, who set *Proof M* from that MS. (see *BLJ* v. 13.)

That *Parisina* was not finished by late 1814 or early 1815 is also strongly suggested by the publishing history of its first stanza, which was issued separately in Apr. 1815 by Isaac Nathan in the first number of his *A Selection of Hebrew Melodies* as 'It Is the Hour'. B must have detached these lines from his original unfinished poem, probably late in 1814, before he knew that he would eventually complete the tale of *Parisina*. It is unlikely that B would have given the lines to Nathan as an independent 'Hebrew Melody' if he was at the same time aware that he would publish them soon as part of his verse tale. B also gave Nathan the second stanza of *Parisina* as a Hebrew Melody, which Nathan published in Apr. 1816 in the second number of his *Selection* under the title 'Francisca'. These lines were also given to Nathan either in late 1814 or early in 1815 (see *Ashton*, 19–43 *passim* and commentary for *HM* above). In short, although the absence of B's holograph MS. makes it impossible to give particular dates for the poem's composition, all the evidence, including the evidence of the MSS. of *Siege*, strongly suggests that B did not finish *Parisina* until the middle or the end of 1815, and that the materials in the poem which were composed earlier were originally part of a different but similar story of incest.

B corrected and returned *Proof M* to Murray on 13 Jan. 1816. He corrected another proof on 19 Jan., but on 22 Jan. a disagreement with Murray made B call off the publishing plans. The problem was quickly resolved, however, and on 3 Feb. B asked Murray to send him a text for some late corrections. *Parisina* appeared with *Siege* on 13 Feb. (see *BLJ* v. 13, 17, 22, 28 n.). For further discussion see *Ashton*, 27–9 and *Gleckner*, 164–6, 177, 183. Murray published three editions in 1816.

Literary and Historical Background. B's treatment of the story of Azo, Parisina, and Hugo (i.e. of Niccolò III d'Este, his second wife Parisina de Malatesta, and his bastard son Ugo) does not follow the historical facts in a strict sense (see notes below), but instead uses Gibbon's brief account as the basis for a free poetic adaptation of the actual events. The general outlines of the story were all that B needed for his purposes, for he was not trying to versify history so much as to use history as a vehicle for treating some subjects nearer to home. In the first place, *Parisina* is, both in inception and in execution, closely related to *Bride*, and the personal aspects of that poem should be compared with this (see *Bride* commentary above). In the second place, B used *Parisina* to treat current social and political affairs in a veiled way. B habitually used older historical situations—and especially people and events from the Italian Renaissance—to highlight analogous circumstances in the contemporary English and European political scene. *Parisina* exposes the moral conflict involved in the 'justice' of Niccolò III of Ferrara (1393–1441) towards his wife and son. B's generic term for such acts was 'cant'. The crux of the tale hangs on the character of Niccolò, whose personal life was notoriously profligate, according to the Ferrarese proverb: 'On both sides of the river Po, they are all Niccolò's sons.' Hugo ironically alludes to this fact several times in the poem. B probably imagined the work personally in terms of his own life, on the one hand, and the social world of the Regency on the other, which he saw as badly corrupt, though full of a canting morality. He may have even meant Azo/Niccolò as in part a figural allusion to the Prince Regent (whose relations with Mrs. Fitzherbert, for example, were accepted in society as a matter of course).

For a full account of the actual historical incidents see A. Lazzari, *Ugo e Parisina* (Florence, 1949), and see *Diario Ferrarese dall' anno 1409 sino al 1502 di autori incerti*, ed. G. Pardi (Bologna, 1928), 17. B probably did not read Antonio Frizzi's account of the story, in *Memorie per la Storia di Ferrara* (1793), III. 408–10, until 1818 (see *BLJ* VI. 59).

Advertisement

I am aware . . . upon the Continent. Cf. letter to Edward Daniel Clarke, 15 Dec. 1813 (*BLJ* III. 199).

The name . . . metrical. B takes the name not *simply* for metrical reasons. The first of the Este family to rule in Ferrara was Azo V, in the twelfth century.

their execution: in 1425. See also B's Advertisement to the *Lament*. C quotes from the extended treatment by Antonio Frizzi (III. 505–7). Niccolò married Parisina in 1418.

14. The lines contained in Section I were printed as set to music some

time since: but belonged to the poem where they now appear, the greater part of which was composed prior to 'Lara' and other compositions since published. [B]

70 ff. According to Leigh Hunt (*Autobiography* (1860), 252), he gave B the idea for 'the incident of the heroine talking in her sleep'. *C* cites Henry Mackenzie's *Julia de Roubigné* (1777), II. 101.

83–7. Cf. 1 Thessalonians 4: 16.

91–2. Niccolò in fact discovered the liaison when he secretly observed one of the lovers' trysts.

102–4. Ugo was Niccolò's son by his favourite mistress, the Sienese noblewoman Stella dei Tolomei (d. 1419). B's lines seem to mean that Azo/Niccolò 'betrayed' the true love of his mistress Bianca/Stella by not marrying her. Historically, however, there was never any question of marriage. Hugo/Ugo was born when Niccolò was married to his first wife, Gigliola de Carrara (d. 1416), who died childless.

103–4. Perhaps recalling *Christabel*, II. 408–9.

134–5. Cf. Proverbs 20: 8.

156–9. Cf. Burke's eulogy of Marie Antoinette in his *Reflections on the Revolution in France* (1790), 112–13.

234–40. The construction is difficult, and the punctuation in the early editions is not helpful. Later editors have proposed solutions (see e.g. *C* III. 516 and n.), and I have followed *More's* emendation.

253–62. None of this is historically accurate. Furthermore, Niccolò recognized the legitimacy of all his sons by Stella dei Tolomei.

267. Haught—haughty—'Away *haught* man, thou art insulting me.' Shakespeare, *Richard II*. [B] The note misquotes B's authority, at IV. i. 254.

323. Perhaps recalling *Marmion*, II. xxi; see also B's letter to Murray of 3 Feb. 1816 (*BLJ* v. 22).

339. Cf. *Christabel*, I. 253.

395. *Knoll*. As a verb the form is uncommon, but not extremely so (see *OED*, and *CHP III*, st. 96).

480. Cf. Coleridge's 'Song of the Pixies', v. 59–60.

514. In fact, Parisina was beheaded with Ugo.

530. Niccolò married, for the third and last time, in 1431. His last bride was Ricciarda da Saluzzo.

530–3. The construction is a bit difficult, but *C*'s interpretation ('The comparison is between Hugo and "goodly sons," not between Hugo and "bride",' III. 526 n.) does not seem right. The comparison is to both: Hugo's 'loveliness' to the female bride, and his 'bravery' to the male sons.

283. *MS*. B's first draft (location: Bodleian). It is untitled and undated and lacks lines 18–21, 54–9, and 87–8. There are also two corrected proofs for *Poems1816* (location: Murray). *Publishing History*. First published, anonymously, in *Morning Chronicle*, 15 Mar.1816; published again in *Poems1816*, and collected thereafter. The Berg Collection in the New York Public Library has a clipping of the *Morning Chronicle* version of lines 1–53 with B's corrections. The *Morning Chronicle* text lacks lines 18–21 and 54–9. B's poem was probably written on or shortly after 8 Mar. 1816. On that day B had written to Moore and mentioned, scornfully, 'Mr. Fitzgerald in the *Morning Post*' claiming the 'character of *Vates*'. The reference is to 'The White Cockade, being an Address to the French Nation, by William Thomas Fitzgerald', which appeared in the *Morning Post* 13 Jan. 1814 and in which Fitzgerald claimed to have prophesied the fall of Napoleon. B disliked Fitzgerald's verse (see *EBSR* 1), and was particularly incensed with him for his anti-Napoleonic rhymes (published as a collection in 1814). This poem, then, is as it were a counter-prophecy. B explicitly called attention to this fact in a letter to Murray of 23, 24 Apr. 1820 (*LJ* v. 19–20), where he claims to have 'as good a right to the character of *Vates* . . . as Fitzgerald and Coleridge'. B rested his claim on 'the fact' that his Ode could be taken to have prophesied the murder of the Duc de Berri by Pierre-Louis Louvel in Feb. 1820. It is one of those curiosities of Byronic literature that B should have made so much of this minor literary affair, and remembered it so long. Needless to say, there is no French original for B's poem.

title   The French have their *Poems* and *Odes* on the famous Battle of Waterloo as well as ourselves.—Nay, they seem to glory in the battle as the source of great events to come. We have received the following poetical version of a poem, the original of which is circulating in Paris—and which is ascribed (we know not with what justice) to the muse of M. de Chateaubriand. If so, it may be inferred that, in the Poet's eye, a new change is at hand—and he wishes to prove his secret indulgence of old principles, by reference to this effusion. [B's head-note to the poem in the *Morning Chronicle*]

6. Cf. no. 284, lines 15–16.

8. *Labedoyere*: Charles A. F. Huchet, Comte de la Bédoyère (1786–1815), a loyal and brave Bonapartist; seized in Paris after the Allied occupation, he was court-martialled and executed.

21. See Rev. chap. viii. verse 7, &c. 'The first angel sounded, and there followed fire and hail mingled with blood', &c.

Verse 8. 'And the second Angel sounded, and as it were a great mountain burning with fire was cast into the sea; and the third part of the sea became blood', &c.

Verse 10. 'And the third Angel sounded, and there fell a great star from heaven, burning as it were a lamp; and it fell upon a third part of the rivers, and upon the fountains of waters.'

Verse 11. 'And the name of the star is called *Wormwood*: and the third part of the waters became *wormwood*; and many men died of the waters, because they were made bitter. [B's note, *Poems 1816*]

37. Murat's remains are said to have been torn from the grave and burnt. [B's note, *Morning Chronicle, Poems1816*] See also B's letter to Moore, 4 Nov. 1815 (*LJ* III. 245).

52–3. To the Berg Collection copy of the *Morning Chronicle*, and the first Murray proof version of these lines, B added the following note:

'And plumed crests of chieftains brave,
Floating like foam upon the wave. *Marmion*, Canto VI.'

78. See Scott's *Field of Waterloo*, 'Conclusion', vi. 3.

101–2. Cf. James 2: 19.

284. *MS.* B's fair copy is in the Murray collection, undated by B. But Murray has written below the poem: 'Rec^d March 28, 1816.' B titled the poem in MS. 'Stanzas', but another hand has added after this, in pencil, 'for Music'. *Publishing History.* First published, *Poems1816*, collected thereafter. *Mayne* (p. 274) was the first to assert that the poem was addressed to Claire Clairmont, whose relations with B commenced in Mar. 1816 (see *Marchand*, II. 591–4). The identification was made on the basis of the presumed date of the poem's composition in Mar. 1816, and on the known beauty of Claire's voice (see Shelley's lyric to her, 'To Constantia Singing'). Marchand (I. 313 n.) has disputed this, however, and conjectured an earlier date, and an association of the poem with John Edleston, the beauty of whose voice was a constant theme of the 'Thyrza' poems. It is possible that the poem was written earlier to Edleston, but Murray's dating is unmistakable (Marchand suggests that '1816' was a conjecture). The association with Claire seems quite persuasive. The fact is that B was captivated by *any* beautiful singing voice, not just Edleston's, as his poetry frequently shows. If Claire sang for B in Mar. 1816, he would have been particularly susceptible to it since he was, at the time, entangled in the frustrations of his marital difficulties during the separation controversy.

285. *MSS. and Proofs.* B's draft, dated 18 Mar. 1816 (*MS. P*, location: Pforzheimer. This is reproduced in facsimile, with a collation of the other MSS. and Proofs—except for *Proof BM*—in *Shelley and His Circle*, IV. 638–65, by David Erdman, with an excellent accompanying essay). B's fair copy, and Augusta Leigh's fair copy, same dating, both with B's corrections (*MSS. M* and *MC*, location: Murray), both made from *MS. P*. All the MSS. contain lines 1–12, 21–60. Two copies of the first proof, both with B's corrections and the MS. addition of 13–20 (*Proof BM*, carrying MS. date in print at the end, location: *BM*; and *Proof M*, same date, at Murray's). *Proof BM* carries B's earliest corrections, *Proof M* a revised set; both printed from *MS. M*, and both arrange the poem in unnumbered quatrains. *Proof M* dated in MS. in another hand: Thursday, 4 Apr. 1816. At Murray's is another proof (*Proof MA*), with B's MS. corrections, and printing the additions and alterations from the earlier proofs; with a MS. heading by Murray, 'Correct 50 copies as early as you can tomorrow', and dated in MS. in another hand: Sunday, 7 Apr. 1816. *Proof MA* is in continuous couplets.

Composition and Publishing History. For composition see MS. and Proof dating above. First printed, for private circulation, on 8 Apr. 1816 in an edition of 50 copies. Reprinted without authorization in the *Champion*, along with 'A Sketch', on 14 Apr. under the heading: 'Lord Byron's Poems On His Own Domestic Circumstances'; reprinted frequently thereafter in newspapers and pirated editions. Only one of these other texts is textually relevant, the text printed in Leigh Hunt's *Examiner* for 21 Apr. 1816 in Hunt's article 'Distressing Circumstances in High Life'. First authorized reprinting in *Poems1816*, where the epigraph from Coleridge was first added; collected thereafter.

The preliminary Separation Agreement between B and Lady B was signed on 17 Mar. and this poem was written the day after. The final agreement was signed on 21 Apr. B sent a copy of the poem to Lady B with an accompanying letter before that date, but it did not have the intended effect—to move her to a reconciliation. Previous editors of the Letters and Journals have conjecturally dated this letter in late March, but it was probably written around 8–9 Apr. (see *BLJ* v. 51–2). The only copy of the poem in the Bodleian–Lovelace collection among Lady B's papers is the private printing.

The *Champion* spearheaded the public attack upon B at the time of the separation. It published the poem, along with 'A Sketch', through the offices of Henry Brougham. At the time, he was supposed to act as a mediator between the parties, but he in fact supported Lady B throughout. The *Champion's* was a shrewd attack on B and was probably jointly authored by Brougham and John Scott, the editor. It printed the poems along with two prose pieces. The first was a 'letter to the editor' signed A. S., attacking B (without naming him) for his politics and in particular for the 'Ode (From the French)' published in the *Morning Chronicle* of 15 Mar. 1816; the second was a critical appraisal of the two 'domestic' poems. As Erdman shows in his essay, 'Scott and Brougham lay in wait for many weeks', during which they menaced B in various ways, before the open attack of 14 Apr. For further details see comment for 'A Sketch'; *C* III. 531–5; Davidson Cook, 'Byron's "Fare Thee Well" ', *TLS* 18 Sept. 1937, 680, and Erdman's essay.

47–8. Cf. Ruth 1: 16.

286. *MS.* The Murray collection has the following items: B's draft MS. dated 30 Mar. 1816 (*MS. M*), lacking 19–20, 35–6, 55–6, 65–70, 77–8, 85–92; Augusta Leigh's fair copy with B's corrections, dated as *MS. M* and with the epigraph at the end with directions for its insertion, but lacking 65–70, 85–92; a group of MS. additions dated 2 Apr. (*MS. MB*), with lines 65–8,

69–70, 85–92; the first proof (*Proof A*) printed from *MS. MA*, with B's corrections and with the added lines 65–8, 85–92 inserted in MS. in another hand; a second copy of this proof (*Proof A1*) with Gifford's MS. corrections of accidentals; three copies of the final private printing; finally, a facsimile of the final proof (*Proof K*, owned by Lord Kinnaird), lacking only 69–70. *Proof K* picks up the corrections B added on *Proof BM* (location: *BM*, Ashley Library), which also lacks 69–70, and which is headed by Murray: 'Correct with particular care and print off 50 copies and keep standing. 1816 Apr. 2.' *Publishing History*. B sent *MS. MB* to Murray on 30 Mar., and *Proofs A, A1* were printed on 1 Apr. and sent to B, who returned *Proof A* on 2 Apr. with his corrections and additions. He quickly sent a further correction for 35–6 in another letter, and all these were incorporated into the revised *Proof BM*, which was returned to B the same day, corrected, and sent back to Murray immediately (see *BLJ* v. 58, 60–1). *Proof K* incorporated these later corrections, and on 3 Apr. (apparently) B sent the last addition, 69–70, which appears first in the final private printing. Only a few of these fifty copies have survived. The present text is from one of the copies in the Murray collection (described in *C*'s bibliography, VII. 233, item IV). According to *C1905*, the poem was first privately published on 4 Apr. (see p. 378). It was next printed on Apr. 14 in the *Champion*, a Tory newspaper edited by John Scott, and was republished in at least eight other newspapers during the next ten days, as well as in numerous piratical editions in 1816 and succeeding years. For further specific details see the commentary for 'Fare Thee Well!' (including the essays cited there by Davidson Cook and D. V. Erdman) and *C* VII. 255–9. The poem was first collected in an authorized edition in Murray's three-volume edition of 1819 (see *C* VII. 95), and was collected thereafter.

The object of this bitter satire was Mary Jane Clermont, Annabella's maid, who had also been her nurse and governess. B believed that she (along with Annabella's mother) was largely responsible for the separation. The germ of his poem's charges against her is to be found in his letter to Annabella of 26 Mar. (see *LBW* 451–2). It was the publication of this poem, rather than 'Fare Thee Well!', which brought down the general public attack upon B.

epigraph   See *Othello*, V. i. 31; III. iii. 101–3; V. ii. 287.

53. The Miltonic reference here also seems to pick up the theme of 'my self am hell' (*Paradise Lost*, IV. 75).

75. *Hamlet*, III. ii. 31.

79–104. This curse anticipates the tone and manner of Eve's famous curse of Cain in *Cain*, III. i. 419–43.

96. Compare Shelley, 'Ozymandias', 11.

104. See B's letter to Murray of 2 Apr. 1816 where he discusses the relative merits of 'weltering' and 'festering'.

287. *MS.* B's fair copy of these unpublished verses, dated 1 Apr. 1816, is in the Murray collection. The lines are directed at Byron's father-in-law, Sir Ralph Milbanke, who was born in 1747. Cokayne's *Complete Baronetage* (III. 226) gives his date of birth as 1748 and the date of his father's marriage to Elizabeth Hedworth as 'in or before 1748'. Byron has slightly altered the interval between Sir Ralph's marriage (1777) and the birth of Annabella (1792). For Sir Ralph's anxiety about having a child see: Malcolm Elwin, *The Noels and the Milbankes* (1967), chap. 15. See B's reference to the epigram in *BLJ* IV. 68.

288. *MS.* B's draft, undated, containing lines 1–28 (*MS. M*); two fair copies made from this MS. by Charles Hanson, dated 1845 (*MSS. MB, MC*); B's fair copy, containing lines 1–40, with a note by Murray: 'Given to me (and I believe composed) by Ld. B Friday April 12th 1816' (*MS. MA*). All MSS. at Murray. First published, *Poems 1816*, collected *1817* (with a change at line 26) and thereafter.

The poem was written to his sister shortly before B left England. He did not want it circulated until he was gone (see *BLJ* IV. 67–8, and *ibid.* 89, where B comments on the poem in a letter to Moore).

INDEX OF FIRST LINES